Abraham Lincoln
THE WAR YEARS
IN FOUR VOLUMES

Volume 1

BY CARL SANDBURG

ABRAHAM LINCOLN: THE PRAIRIE YEARS
MARY LINCOLN: WIFE AND WIDOW
THE AMERICAN SONGBAG
STEICHEN THE PHOTOGRAPHER

Poems

SMOKE AND STEEL
SLABS OF THE SUNBURNT WEST
CHICAGO POEMS
CORNHUSKERS
GOOD MORNING, AMERICA
SELECTED POEMS. Edited by Rebecca West
THE PEOPLE, YES

For Young Folks

ROOTABAGA STORIES
ROOTABAGA PIGEONS
ABE LINCOLN GROWS UP

MARCY   MC CLELLAN   LINCOLN   MEADE   FITZ-JOHN PORTER

President Lincoln visits Army of the Potomac Headquarters, October, 1862

Photograph in Gardner Album No. 1. From Oliver R. Barrett Collection

ABRAHAM LINCOLN

The War Years

BY CARL SANDBURG

WITH 426 HALF-TONES OF PHOTOGRAPHS, AND
244 CUTS OF CARTOONS, LETTERS, DOCUMENTS

Volume One

HARCOURT, BRACE & COMPANY
NEW YORK

Typography by Robert Josephy

PRINTED IN THE UNITED STATES OF AMERICA BY THE MURRAY PRINTING COMPANY

DEDICATED

To the constant companions on a long journey

To the attorney-at-law, collector of documents and source items in history, seeker of basic human lore, Oliver R. Barrett

To the worthy historian and able analyst, Paul M. Angle

To the fellow biographer and student, jester and solemn Friend, Lloyd Lewis

To the publisher, bookman, critic, and counselor, Alfred Harcourt

To the indefatigable scholar and keen discriminating copy-editor, Isabel Ely Lord

To the courteous helpers and kindly friends at a score of libraries from coast to coast

To three daughters, Margaret, Janet, and Helga, who "classified" thousands of items and cheerfully performed many necessary petty chores

To my wife Paula, who so often threw in with a rare mind and great heart

FOREWORD

IN the story of a great struggle we meet gaps and discrepancies.

How and why did men and women do what they did? And how can we be sure they did what the record may seem to show they did? And of what great war has the final story been written that clears all disputes as to how it moved and what came of it?

If those who are gone who had their parts and roles in it could be summoned back to tell of the gaps and discrepancies, they might give unexpected answers to questions. And many witnesses on being dug up and given speech might again be as noncommittal as ever on this or that circumstance.

This scroll presents events of wild passionate onrush side by side with cruel, grinding monotony—and second and third readings bring out things not seen at first.

The chronicles are abstracted from a record so stupendous, so changing and tumultuous, that anyone dealing with the vast actual evidence cannot use the whole of it, nor tell all of the story.

Supposing all could be told, it would take a far longer time to tell it than was taken to act it in life.

Therefore the teller does the best he can and picks what is to him plain, moving, and important—though sometimes what is important may be tough reading, tangled, involved, sometimes gradually taking on interest, even mystery, because of the gaps and discrepancies.

Many men and women, now faded and gone, lived this book before it could be written.

They do and say in these pages what they did and said in life—as seen and known to the eyes and ears, the mind and spirit, of themselves or other men and women of their own time.

Some of them spoke with action, some with words, some with both action and words.

What they say in words, within quotation marks, in these pages, is from sources deemed authentic, unless otherwise indicated.

What they say by act or deed is often beyond fathoming, because it happened in a time of great storm.

PERSONAL NOTE

Sometimes I meditate on the time factor in this book. I was born a little less than thirteen years after 1865, the year when the Second American Revolution ended. As a boy in my Illinois home town I learned about "the

late war" (having to unlearn some of it later) from veterans of hard service
under Grant and Sherman—and these veterans were still rather young men
when, as a boy, I knew them. Our Congressman was General Philip S. Post,
of recorded and stubborn valor at Murfreesboro. When I was twenty I
joined a volunteer regiment for service in the Spanish-American War, once
passing in review before an elderly visitor, General O. O. Howard, a corps
commander under General W. T. Sherman in 1864 and 1865, meeting comrades who served under the veteran Confederates, Fitzhugh Lee and Joseph
Wheeler. In our expedition to Puerto Rico—where our regiment happened
to furnish the first volunteers to set foot on that island, haul down the flag
of monarchist Spain, and run up the Stars and Stripes—our commander was
General Nelson A. Miles, who commanded the 1st Brigade of the 1st
Division of General Winfield Scott Hancock's 2d Corps of the Army of
the Potomac headed by General Ulysses S. Grant on the Rapidan, before
the Wilderness and Spotsylvania.

Taking my guitar and a program of songs and readings and traveling
from coast to coast a dozen times in the last twenty years, in a wide variety
of audiences I have met sons and daughters of many of the leading players
in the terrific drama of the 1860's. Twice I had the privilege of giving my
program before the Poetry Society of South Carolina in Charleston, and I
met audiences in the state universities of all the States that seceded except
Florida. I could have only solemn thoughts before the students of Washington and Lee University near the tomb of Robert E. Lee at Lexington,
Virginia. In San Antonio Maury Maverick gave me two one-hundred-dollar
bonds of the Confederate States of America with the signature of his grandfather, Sam Maverick, who had led in taking Texas out of the Union. In
Athens, Georgia, a niece of Alexander H. Stephens gave me a check with
the interesting signature of the Vice-President of the Confederacy. In
Colorado Springs, Colorado, I had an evening of impressive talk with a
woman whose mother was a daughter of Jefferson Davis. At the University
of Chicago I met a son of Gideon Welles. At Bennington College I sat for
charcoal sketches drawn by a great-niece of General Abner Doubleday. In
Haverhill, Massachusetts, I met a daughter of the war Governor John A.
Andrew; in Milledgeville, Georgia, I met a daughter and two granddaugh-
ters of the war Governor Joseph E. Brown; in a newspaper office in Palm
Springs, California, I met a granddaughter of a Taft boy who played with
Lincoln's boys at the White House. In Oakdale, California, I had long talks
with a niece and a grandniece of Stephen A. Douglas. In 1927 I was permitted to kiss the cheek of an eighty-two-year-old woman who as a sixteen-
year-old girl was held on Lincoln's knees in the White House. As a newspaper reporter in the Chicago "Loop" I came to feel, from men who had
known them, the almost lingering presences of attorneys who had had offices
near by, Lyman Trumbull and Leonard Swett, who constantly appear in
this book. Of the involved race question which weaves incessantly through
these pages I learned as a reporter for the *Chicago Daily News*, when I
covered the race riots of 1919 and did a series of articles on some of the

conditions which caused the riots. It was three years later that I had a week's visit at Lang Syne plantation near Fort Motte, South Carolina, under the guidance of the wise and vivid Julia Peterkin seeing conditions that, except for the slavery status, were somewhat like those of the 1850's. On the Mississippi Delta my poet friend Will Percy, who had one grandfather fighting with the North and one with the South, had light to shed on the "War of the Brothers."

As a newspaper man I have written thousands of news stories about politics, have witnessed scores of conventions and reported meetings of legislative bodies, including the Congress of the United States.

Though it was not my fate to see battle action as a soldier, I did in 1898 wear the same light-blue trousers and dark-blue jacket with brass buttons as the troops of the Army of the Potomac, and near Falls Church, Virginia, only a few miles from the Capitol dome, I lived in a tent, answered roll call six and eight times a day, cut saplings and built myself a bunk, more than once made a practice march in hot weather carrying in the first weeks a Springfield rifle, later a Krag-Jörgensen rifle, cartridge belt, canteen, and blanket roll. My first salt-water swim was in Charleston Harbor in sight of Fort Sumter. The American volunteer, including myself, is still a mystery to me, as likewise is any war, large or small.

SOURCES AND ACKNOWLEDGMENTS

A hundred and more libraries, between East and West coasts, have on their shelves and in their vaults perhaps 90 per cent of the materials consulted and used in the writing of this book. In his sketch of Lincoln in the *Dictionary of American Biography*, J. G. Randall, a trained professional historian, names the books and weighs the documents and appraises the materials on which any true Lincoln biography must rest. In the *Bulletin of the Abraham Lincoln Association*, Paul M. Angle has given the list of the books that he rates as belonging in "Basic Lincolniana." In periodical issues of *Lincoln Lore* the editor, Louis A. Warren, has listed what he considers the most worth-while books on Lincoln.

Outside of the books generally rated as basic Lincolniana may be found a mass of items scattered through scores of books and hundreds of newspapers and magazine numbers. Some Lincoln collectors have enumerated these, in part, in their files and catalogues. They are not usually listed in bibliographies, though a few of them have become standard entries. This is an area certain to have attention in the future from specialists. Besides more biographies of Lincoln and more dramas and poems around the Lincoln figure and tradition in the future, there are also to be more historical studies, explorations of fact and probability, which will serve those artists who care about the world of found and known realities in which a grand human struggler had his toils, combats, visions, and hopes.

Naturally the most essential and most formidable source is the record of Lincoln's utterance: his letters, notes, memoranda; the transmissions of his thoughts in his own handwriting which he signed, and conventional or official communications written by others to which he attached his signature; his published addresses which he wrote before delivery, as distinguished from impromptu speeches reported in the press; his arguments, declarations, meditations, remarks, or narratives noted by bystanders or participants in an interview or conference—one can go far in this field. Undoubtedly the future is to see volumes available having the strictest fidelity to the originals, in punctuation, spelling, in every detail, and possibly having informative annotations regarding the manuscript itself—on such points, for instance, as that a letter was on formal Executive Mansion stationery or that, as happened a number of times, Lincoln wrote the words "Executive Mansion" in his own hand; or whether an endorsement or a memorandum was written on the back of an envelope or on a folded sheet.

For those seeking the self-portrait of Lincoln as achieved in the mass of his unquestioned recorded utterance, all suggested improvements in the presentation of that record will add but slightly to its value. However, for the convenience of the host of Lincoln students it is hoped by many that from the present scattered repositories of this utterance it may be brought together into something that looks more like a book than a small library. Of the chief sources Paul M. Angle in the *Bulletin of the Abraham Lincoln Association* makes the following notations:

Nicolay, John G., and John Hay, editors. *Abraham Lincoln: Complete Works.* Century, New York, 1894. 2 vols.

This collection includes nearly eighty per cent of the letters and speeches printed in the enlarged edition (see next title) and is quite adequate for the general reader and for most students.

Nicolay, John G., and John Hay, editors. *Complete Works of Abraham Lincoln.* Tandy, New York, 1905. 12 vols.

Of the 2,243 items in this collection, only 486 were not printed in the original, two-volume edition. The collection, however, is larger by a third than the eight-volume *Writings of Abraham Lincoln,* edited by Arthur Brooks Lapsley (Putnam, New York, 1905). . . . .

Tracy, Gilbert A., editor. *Uncollected Letters of Abraham Lincoln.* Houghton Mifflin, Boston & New York, 1917.

Three hundred and fifty-nine letters, notes, telegrams and endorsements—many of them important—which are not to be found in the Nicolay & Hay *Complete Works* (1905 ed.). . . . .

Angle, Paul M., editor. *New Letters and Papers of Lincoln.* Houghton Mifflin, Boston & New York, 1930.

This collection contains 430 letters, speeches, legal opinions and miscellaneous writings not to be found in Nicolay & Hay or Tracy. Many important items are included, but the general level of interest is lower than Tracy's similar volume. However, it is the only compilation of Lincoln's writings in which substantial textual accuracy has been achieved. Fully annotated, but the compiler unwisely attempted to give the volume general interest—which it does not possess—by putting his notes in narrative form.

Hertz, Emanuel. *Abraham Lincoln: A New Portrait*. Liveright, New York, 1931. 2 vols.

The second volume of this work is made up of letters, documents, reports of con-versations, etc., most of which are not to be found in the collections listed above. Many interesting and valuable items are included, but almost incredibly careless editing seriously impairs the volume's usefulness. The following are spurious: letter to Mace-donio Melloni (p. 623), letter to the Secretaries of the St. Marie Brass Band & St. Cecilia Society (p. 791), promissory note to L. S. Benedict (p. 791), memorandum on corporations and corruption (p. 954), letter to E. D. Taylor (p. 957).

Louis A. Warren gives the following word totals:

The Bible, including the Apocrypha	926,877
Shakespeare, complete works	1,025,000
Lincoln's printed speeches and writings	1,078,365

There are in this book a number of hitherto unpublished or uncollected items of Lincoln's utterance, but the writer has not taken the time to com-pute their number.

For an impression of the vast, whining, snarling chaos of the Second American Revolution, the immense landscape, the variety of forces involved, no student should neglect what may be learned from a few hours of wander-ing hither and yon amid the wilderness of marching and battle orders, muni-tions and supply requisitions, transport and communications broken or re-paired, documents, diplomatic notes and proclamations—all set forth hit or miss in the *Official Record of the Rebellion* in 133 volumes—count 'em. Next to this wilderness of human motives the student may contemplate the *Con-gressional Globe* with its speeches and roll calls, with its monotony of plati-tudes, broken suddenly by flashes of abrupt genius or forthright and appeal-ing logic or plain information lighting the motives of men as to why there is a war on, an ancient desperate ordeal to test which is the stronger in will, in cunning and intelligence, in material resources. In these two wildernesses of words I have picked my way carefully, sometimes drearily and with hope and patience, or again fascinated and enthralled by the basic stuff of indis-putably great human action in play before my eyes. As reading matter I could more often find connected and understandable values in the *Congres-sional Globe*, wherein I read hundreds of speeches, scores of debates, and at times eagerly studied the roll calls. I have deep admiration for the *Century Magazine* editors who conceived and carried through the project of a series of articles by Union and Confederate officers authoritative in the events as-signed them, the whole series being later published in those superb volumes *Battles and Leaders of the Civil War* (Century, 1887-88, 4 vols.). Likewise I have salutations for the editors and writers who made *Appleton's Annual Cyclopaedia*, freighted with cold, informative, pertinent fact reporting the nation and the world for each year. For the passions underlying the action of the war, for the primitive and elemental factors of hate and love and sacrifice and greed, I found the newspapers of the hour, North and South, more indicative and explanatory and mystifying and paradoxical than any other source of utterance and revelation. It had been of no avail that Thomas Jefferson many years earlier had hoped that newspapers would label their contents under four heads: 1. Truths. 2. Probabilities. 3. Possibilities. 4. Lies.

Isaac N. Arnold's *The Life of Abraham Lincoln* (Jansen, McClurg, 1885) has importance by reason of Arnold's complete and undeviating loyalty to Lincoln at a time when such loyalty in a member of Congress was rare and exceptional in both the House and the Senate. Francis Fisher Browne's *The Everyday Life of Lincoln* (N. D. Thompson Publishing Co., 1886) was a cumulative labor of love and devotion of which Paul M. Angle writes the annotation: "In large part first-hand material skilfully woven into a narrative. The book furnishes an insight into Lincoln's personality not often provided by more formal works, and at the same time possesses considerable value as a source." Wayne Whipple's somewhat similar, though not as thoroughgoing, *The Story-Life of Lincoln* (Winston, 1908) Louis A. Warren rates "the most exhaustive collection of stories by and about Lincoln." Ida M. Tarbell's *The Life of Abraham Lincoln* (Doubleday & McClure, 1900, 2 vols.) and her various monographs pertaining to Lincoln of the war years are indispensable works for a Lincoln library, rich with reminiscences and documents not available elsewhere. William E. Barton's *The Life of Abraham Lincoln* (Bobbs-Merrill, 1925, 2 vols.) and the later *President Lincoln* (Bobbs-Merrill, 1933), unfinished at the time of his death, his monographs on Walt Whitman and Lincoln and on the letter to Mrs. Bixby, his comprehensive study of the religious phase in *The Soul of Abraham Lincoln* (Doran, 1920), his fairly exhaustive tome on *Lincoln at Gettysburg* (Bobbs-Merrill, 1930)—these represent the contribution of a Congregational minister who in the last ten years of his life poured the tireless energies of an ably analytical mind into researches and writings that have a permanent place in Lincoln libraries.

The Lincoln of myth and fact, of illusion and reality, as a shifting folk-lore creation played upon in the gossip, the wonder, and the imagination of the people, has its most comprehensive treatment in Roy P. Basler's *The Lincoln Legend* (Houghton Mifflin, 1935) and Lloyd Lewis's *Myths after Lincoln* (Harcourt, Brace, 1929). Also the subject is threshed over with dry wit and pertinent inquiry by the rigorous realist, the historically trained scholar, J. G. Randall of the University of Illinois in an essay in the *American Historical Review* of January, 1936, titled "Has the Lincoln Theme Been Exhausted?"

For Lincoln in Border State backgrounds one cannot neglect *Lincoln in His Wife's Home Town* by William H. Townsend (Bobbs-Merrill, 1929).

Books or accounts by and about men and women having personal knowledge of Lincoln, men and women who saw and heard him, form the basis of a large part of this narrative of the war years. The private secretaries John G. Nicolay and John Hay give us their impression in ten volumes titled *Abraham Lincoln: A History* (Century, 1890, 10 vols.); in various magazine articles; in a delightful memoir and study, *Personal Traits of Abraham Lincoln* by Helen Nicolay (Century, 1912), based on letters, notes, and contemporary papers of her father; in a privately printed three-volume edition of the diary and letters of John Hay; in selections from the Hay diary and letters by Tyler Dennett (*Lincoln and the Civil War*, Dodd, Mead, 1939); in a long and notable letter of John Hay to William H. Herndon in 1866. On the war years the three-volume biography by Herndon and Jesse W. Weik (*Herndon's Lincoln*, Belford, Clarke, 1889) has no such wealth of familiar detail as it has on the earlier years.

The man designated to introduce Lincoln for his Gettysburg speech, a man often entrusted with confidential errands for the President, gives his impression in a book ably written by his daughter Dorothy Lamon Teillard from her father's manuscripts and notes: *Recollections of Abraham Lincoln, 1847-1865*, by Ward Hill Lamon (McClurg, 1895). The young newspaper correspondent Noah Brooks, slated to be Lincoln's private secretary after John G. Nicolay should have taken over the Paris consulate, gives his impressions meagerly in a biography, *Abraham Lincoln, and the Downfall of American Slavery* (new ed., Putnam, 1896); richly, with intimacy and informality, in *Washington in Lincoln's Time* (Century, 1896) which omits valid items contained in the magazine articles that preceded the book and formed its basis; still further Brooks in this offhand and close-up style gives a contemporary narrative in his many news letters to the *Sacramento* (California) *Union*, of which an almost complete transcript was made for me in the San Francisco Public Library under the direction of my warbird friend Albert Barrows. Another familiar, more elderly, more sedate, more lacking in humor, having a mind often sounded by Lincoln for various ends, gives his impression, so often more definitely than he is himself aware, in *The Diary of Orville Hickman Browning* (Trustees of the Illinois State Historical Society, 1925-33, 2 vols.). It gives moments in a colossal scene where Lincoln is the central figure. An omnibus of twenty-eight witnesses from varied walks of life hold forth in the heavy volume *Reminiscences of Abraham Lincoln by Distinguished Men of His Time* (North American Publishing Co., 1886), compiled and edited with a charming and informative introduction by Allen Thorndike Rice, who first sought and published these priceless memoirs serially when editor of the *North American Review*. In the *Personal Recollections of Abraham Lincoln* by James R. Gilmore (L. C. Page, 1898) we are constantly suspicious of his quoted utterances, as we are of what we meet in *Autobiography . . . Ben Butler's Book* (Thayer, 1892) or in the published affidavit of J. Wesley Greene on what occurred when he met Lincoln for a private interview and again for an examination by Lincoln and the Cabinet. In handling these, however, we may employ the method we use often in daily life when listening to the overly garrulous or those who try to twist facts to their own ends. If Lincoln could listen to them, perhaps we can stand it.

A distinguished portrait having high merits peculiarly arrived at is achieved in *The Diary of Gideon Welles* (Houghton Mifflin, 1911, 3 vols.). On an examination of many utterances of Lincoln, put within quotation marks in the original diary in the Library of Congress, I found none had

been corrected or interlined, and in a number of passages pertaining to
Lincoln there had been no changes that might vitiate it as testimony. "The
Diary of Edward Bates 1859-1866" (American Historical Association, *Annual Report for 1930*, Vol. 4), and various passages in letters and diary
entries of Salmon Portland Chase as given in the biographies by J. W.
Schuckers (1874) and R. B. Warden (1874) and in "Diary and Correspondence of . . . Chase" (American Historical Association, *Annual Report for 1902*, Vol. 2), reveal moments of drama between Lincoln and men who saw
him through barriers of temperament. More emphatically is this so in the
letters of General George B. McClellan to his wife and his occasional
memoranda as given in *McClellan's Own Story* (Webster, 1887), where it
seemed that he attached to his almost daily letters to Mrs. McClellan the
values of a diary. This is well supplemented in *A Study in Personality:
George Brinton McClellan* by William Starr Myers (Appleton, 1934). Paragraph flashes from the brief journals of Henry J. Raymond and Irvin MacDowell render moments of high decision.

The papers and addresses of Chaplain Edward D. Neill, "Glimpses of
the Nation's Struggle," published by the Minnesota Commandery of the
Military Order of the Loyal Legion, give the impressions of a witness, at
one time a White House resident, near to being a familiar of the President.
The painter Francis Bicknell Carpenter in writing *Six Months at the White
House with Abraham Lincoln* (Hurd and Houghton, 1866) accomplished a
word portrait of Lincoln that outlasts anything from his brush. Carpenter,
like William H. Herndon, tried with sincerity and zeal to tell the truth,
and in his case, as well as that of others in this list, there are values in spite
of defects, and the notation of Paul M. Angle on the trustworthiness of
William H. Herndon also applies: "Unfortunately, Herndon lacked the
ability always to distinguish the probable from the improbable in what
others told him, and he was given to divinations which sometimes led him
far astray. But any critical reader can determine for himself, with no more
than a small percentage of error, what part of the book deserves acceptance."
Of value certainly equal to that of Carpenter's book is David Homer Bates's
Lincoln in the Telegraph Office (Century, 1907). Another White House
caller who saw Lincoln in intimate moods was Carl Schurz. His three-
volume autobiography (*Reminiscences*, McClure, 1908-09, 3 vols.) is less
revealing of Lincoln than sections of *Speeches, Correspondence and Political
Papers of Carl Schurz*, ed. by Frederic Bancroft (G. P. Putnam's Sons, 1913).
Mrs. Paul Steinbrecher of Chicago, a kinswoman of Schurz, let me have
several score of letters written by Schurz in elegant German script to his
wife and to friends and relatives; translations of many of them by Mrs.
Sandburg I have used.

Henry Villard's newspaper accounts of Lincoln's journey from Springfield to Washington for inauguration and his narrative in his autobiography
(*Memoirs*, Houghton Mifflin, 1904, 2 vols.) of his meetings with Lincoln
during the war, give his decisive estimates. Villard termed Charles A. Dana
an "informer," believed him to be playing palace politics. In Dana's im-

pressions of Lincoln as given in an address in New York City, in the Allen Thorndike Rice omnibus, and in his own *Recollections of the Civil War* (Appleton, 1898) are minor discrepancies, but in the main they seem worthy of acceptance, and a nice contribution from a man who in his day did much for the cause of good newspaper writing.

The notes of Frederick W. Seward as to moments and affairs in which he saw Lincoln are not extensive but have their importance (*Reminiscences of a War-Time Statesman and Diplomat*, 1830-1915, Putnam, 1916).

Three Sumner biographies have their niche. The two-volume *Memoir and Letters of Charles Sumner* by Edward L. Pierce (Roberts, 1877) gives many letters wherein Sumner does his thumb-nail sketches of Lincoln as applying to the hour. The Massachusetts Senator was more frank with the Duke and Duchess of Argyll regarding Lincoln than he was in letters to his American friends. *Charles Sumner* by Anna Laurens Dawes (Dodd, Mead, 1892) has the advantage that her father was an active participant in angry sessions of Congress, and understood Lincoln better than most of his colleagues. *The Life and Public Services of Charles Sumner* by C. Edwards Lester (U. S. Publishing Co., 1874) profits by the fact that Lester mingled in the Washington scene and more than once personally interviewed Lincoln. In *The Life and Times of Frederick Douglass by Himself* (rev. ed., Fiske, 1895), in stenographic reports of the American Anti-Slavery Society, and in the Allen Thorndike Rice omnibus, the foremost Negro freedman of the time gives three accounts, with slight discrepancies, of his meetings with Lincoln. Reserved, but not lacking some basic bond of affection and friendship, are the impressions Alexander H. Stephens wrote of Lincoln in his *A Constitutional View of the War between the States* (National Publishing Co., 1868-70, 2 vols.) and *Recollections* (Doubleday, Page, 1910). *The Life of Thurlow Weed, Including His Autobiography* (Houghton Mifflin, 1883-84, 2 vols.) is remarkable for how little he tells, considering how many times he met Lincoln and how long their sessions were and what we know from other sources was transacted. The book lives up to the characterization of Weed as one who could take you to one side with a confidential manner and persuade you there was importance in the nothings he whispered in your ear.

In their memoirs and here and there in letters Grant and Sherman give their impressions of Lincoln. In letters to his wife Meade (*The Life and Letters of George Gordon Meade* by George Meade, Scribner, 1913, 2 vols.) gives the atmosphere of several tense moments when he met Lincoln or heard from the Commander in Chief. Nor can we pass over the Yankee incisiveness of *The Life and Public Services of William Pitt Fessenden* by Francis Fessenden (Houghton Mifflin, 1907, 2 vols.). Brief but having portent are the references to Lincoln in the two-volume *Life of John Ericsson* by William Conant Church (Scribner, 1890). With plenty of detail Henry Greenleaf Pearson in *The Life of John A. Andrew* (Houghton Mifflin, 1904) gives the involved difficulties of the Massachusetts governor with Lincoln regarding Negro troops, emancipation delayed instead of immediate, and other matters. The Adams boys, Henry and Charles Francis, Jr., in their several books and in their streaming flow of letters have not failed to record the impacts of the Lincoln personality on the Adams family. With U.S. Navy gusto, spitting over the deck rail and splitting his sides with old-salt laughter, not too particular about the facts or how many knots an hour the flagship is making, the fast and careless-writing David D. Porter delivers his carte de visite of the President who moved him up from lieutenant to admiral (*Incidents and Anecdotes of the Civil War*, Appleton, 1885). Amid the solid and unadorned biographies *The Life and Times of Hannibal Hamlin* by Charles Eugene Hamlin (Riverside Press, 1899), *James Louis Petigru* by William J. Grayson (Harper, 1866), and *Biographical Memoir of Clement L. Vallandigham* by James L. Vallandigham (J. Walter, 1864) are accounts of Lincoln incidents or methods not found elsewhere.

When the wife of General John C. Frémont tells us of the President's inhospitable remark to her, "You are quite a female politician!" we are inclined to believe that under all the peculiar and crying circumstances, it could hardly have been invented. It seems to belong, along with all else she relates. In his *Frémont, the West's Greatest Adventurer* (Harper, 1928) and *Frémont, Pathmarker of the West* (Appleton-Century, 1939) Allan Nevins gives us clues to one of the strangest wanderers on the American continent—one of the candidates for place and identification whom Lincoln meant when he told John Eaton of some character that Eaton wouldn't name: "He's a thistle. I don't see why God lets him live." Eaton's paragraphs about Lincoln are not many nor long in his book (with E. O. Mason) *Grant, Lincoln and the Freedmen* (Longmans, Green, 1907) but they seem valid and are illuminating. In one short letter that Colonel Theodore Lyman wrote to his wife from Meade's headquarters he sketched Lincoln as though burning a face on copper with acid. Many Lincoln faces and voices as seen and heard by a varied array of persons stand forth from the later biographies *Thaddeus Stevens* by Thomas Frederick Woodley (The Telegraph Press, Harrisburg, Pa., 1934) and *Thaddeus Stevens: The Sinister Patriot* by Alphonso B. Miller (Harper, 1939); that of *Alexander H. Stephens, Little Aleck* by Eudora Ramsay Richardson (Bobbs-Merrill, 1932); the quick but deep and subtly drawn Lincoln in Douglas Southall Freeman's skilled and massive *R. E. Lee* (Scribner, 1934, 4 vols.). The hard-riding and straight-shooting Lloyd Lewis of Chicago, author of *Sherman: Fighting Prophet* (Harcourt, Brace, 1932), swift and imaginative, deeply sensitive to the epic flow of human forces, with a fidelity to fact and affirmation in the brightest of Quaker traditions, has during the years this work proceeded been a friend and a resource.

Among solid American biographies is *Henry Ward Beecher* by Paxton Hibben (Doran, 1927). Besides this volume I have used a number of newspapers and periodicals for gathering Beecher's series of changing impressions of Lincoln. Horace White in *The Life of Lyman Trumbull* (Houghton Mifflin, 1913) renders a Lincoln as seen close up by an Illinois Senator who slowly veered from his alignment with radicals to a position as a manager on the Senate floor of Lincoln's most favored project. In the latter phase I found that White had not used the *Congressional Globe* as effectively as he might have to show how what a fine partnership had grown up between Lincoln and Trumbull. But he does give a keen account of Lincoln's quiet sabotage of the Confiscation Act from which the radicals had expected much in the way of seizures of Southern property.

Not until, in company with Clifton J. Furness, I ransacked the Sumner Papers in the Widener Library at Harvard University did I realize the extent of the fierce suspicions and fevers of rage held by extremist abolitionists toward Lincoln. Louis Ellsworth Laflin, Jr., of Lake Forest, Illinois, preeminent authority on Elmer E. Ellsworth, showed me his collection of letters, gave me copies, and pointed to shameless and useless interpolations of mushy romantic clichés in some of them as published in the only biography of Ellsworth that might be termed official. In Council Bluffs, Iowa, J. R. Perkins, who wrote a biography of Grenville M. Dodge under the title *Trails, Rails and War* (Bobbs-Merrill, 1929), gave me help with unused material, particularly with reference to the relations of Lincoln and the "Pacific railway crowd." In Albany, New York, Louis C. Jones gave me the results of his researches in newspaper files as to Lincoln in Albany and the Erie Canal zone. In Chicago Ralph Newman, bookman and book-dealer, helped me with many suggestions and inquiries. The elaborate researches of Otto Eisenschiml on the closing scenes of Lincoln's life are a distinct contribution; his failure to prove the main implied thesis of his book *Why Was Lincoln Murdered?* (Little, Brown, 1937) does not invalidate his other work in revealing the melancholy role of the muddled John F. Parker and of other figures in drab. So great was the need I felt for an adequate biography of Robert Barnwell Rhett, titanic revolutionary who inaugurated secession, that I was grateful to find that Laura White of the University of Wyoming, at the instigation of the American Historical Association, had written just such a book (*Robert Barnwell Rhett*, Century, 1931). The factor of desertion was at times so peculiar and controlling during the war that I was thankful to Ella Lonn of Goucher College for having done a masterly piece of work in her *Desertion during the Civil War* (Century, 1928).

The transactions of Lincoln and Swett in the affair of the New Almaden mine were not made clear until Milton H. Shutes gave us his monograph on that subject. Likewise this physician of Oakland, California, has given us the best biographical sketch thus far written of Edward Dickinson Baker, with interesting phases of Lincoln's relations with this old friend. Also there are solid merits in Dr. Shutes's volume *Lincoln and the Doctors: A Medical Narrative of the Life of Abraham Lincoln* (Pioneer Press, 1933).

To Dr. Tomizo Katsunuma must go acknowledgment. On a hot afternoon in Honolulu this physician gave me a translation of a passage from the autobiography of Joseph Heco which is persuasive of the presence of Lincoln. Nels M. Hokanson, an Evanston, Illinois, real-estate man, loaned me the unpublished manuscript of his solidly factual book *Swedish Immigrants in Lincoln's Time*. Harmony Twichell Ives, wife of Charles E. Ives the American composer, and daughter of the Reverend Joseph H. Twichell, gave me the use of letters written by her father when he was a chaplain in a New York regiment with the Army of the Potomac on the Peninsula in Virginia, when he saw Lincoln and told vividly of the Commander in Chief and his troops. In Santa Fe, New Mexico, Alice Corbin Henderson sought out materials bearing on the charming Federal Judge Kirby Benedict; Lincoln appointed Benedict and retained him in spite of complaints. To my old Lombard College friend and dancing partner Elizabeth Philbrook Pollock go thanks for the use of a large bundle of letters written by her kinsman William F. Goodhue, one of the finest types of the American volunteer soldier, who marched and fought through the whole war. To John Richie Schultz, of Allegheny College, I express appreciation for the use of advance sheets of his book on the letters of Bayard Taylor. W. Freeman Galpin of Syracuse University was considerate in letting me have portions of letters to be used in his forthcoming biography of Samuel J. May, Jr. Appreciation is due Mrs. Etta J. Camp of New Paltz, New York, for the strange narrative of the adventure of her kinsman Joseph H. Johnston, wounded at the Wilderness.

During last years of his life Clark Prescott Bissett, dean of the Law Department of the University of Washington, gave me his suggestions and granted me many hours in the large Lincoln library which he housed in a fireproof room in his Seattle residence. Governor Henry Horner of Illinois, then judge of the probate court of Cook County, several times through the night till near daybreak discussed problems of the evidence and of the imponderables in the career and the personality of Lincoln. Judge Horner gave me free range in his extensive Lincoln library, containing nearly everything listed in the Fish and Oakleaf Lincoln bibliographies, and going farther, let me carry away for my own use any scarce items I needed.

From time to time in the progression of this work Oliver R. Barrett brought out letters, manuscripts, notes, cards, memoranda, and documents written or signed or endorsed by Lincoln, besides hundreds of letters and original data associated with Lincoln, the conduct of the war, and the political course of the nation. Once we spread on his large office table a group of letters bearing on the inauguration of the war, written by leaders North and South. Years later we spread out an exhibit that held among other items the farewell address to the Army of Northern Virginia signed by R. E. Lee and the telegram that Lincoln sent to U. S. Grant tendering him "the nation's grateful thanks." Often I was interested and instructed in points my friend would develop in regard to rules of legal evidence as applied to a historical narrative. Scarce books and pamphlets, political broadsides and satires, cartoons, handbills, joke books, caricatures, hymns of hate, military orders, rosters and regulations, almanacs—all contemporary—were made available. There were something like three hundred stereoscopic photographs of army and war scenes and well-made prints from original negatives of the best photographs of Lincoln. One of the latter is used as a frontispiece.

The collector's flair leading Barrett since he was a boy has resulted in a mass of source materials wherein are many items that would have probably been lost for historical purposes but for the sagacity and method by which they were sought out. This is a story by itself, a man-sized narrative of many findings related to a passion for the genuine, and to the personal attachment that may go with tokens, belongings, keepsakes, records touching great occasions of the past. To repeat from the preface to *The Prairie Years:* "Oliver R. Barrett requires further portraiture. [And in far wider scope than thirteen years ago.] As a collaborator and commentator he has given honest values to some [many] of these pages."

From one odd corner Barrett brought out the text of the love letter written by young Jefferson Davis to the daughter of Zachary Taylor with whom he later eloped. In my portrait of Jefferson Davis I tried to use this naïve, charming letter entire, but found that it overweighted the chronicle. The Copperhead weekly voicing southern Illinois, the *Salem Advocate*, and the extremist revolutionary proslavery *Charleston* (South Carolina) *Mercury*, in almost complete files were loaned by Barrett without hesitation. When I overloaded three or four chapters about the middle of the book with quotations from original source documents, Barrett protested it was not necessary, saying that the reader would be equally convinced by my own report on the gist of those documents, and I followed his suggestion. He protested my inclusion of several roll calls on a bill in Congress endorsed by Lincoln, favoring universal selective service in conscription, Barrett urging that most readers would skip reading of the roll calls, because he did. However, I have left the roll calls in, believing that in a work of this scope there can be no harm in having a few roll calls in the third volume. Anyone who has read that far will stay with me through Volume Three into Volume Four.

For one piece of research and statement, unique in its field, students of Lincoln are grateful. The unintermitted labors of Frederick H. Meserve, a business executive with a literary avocation, for more than forty years, his unflagging pursuit and meticulously careful collection of data, have had the result that his published work is the central authority on the life of Lincoln as told in photographs of the man. Among his privately printed monographs illustrating his collection of historical portraits *The Photographs of Abraham Lincoln* stands as an American classic. In very limited edition, with supplements as additional portraits have been discovered, it has been accepted by collectors and students as definitive. The photographs of Lincoln are known and discussed by the chronological numbers Meserve has assigned to them. In one sense it is a camera biography of Lincoln with "others in the cast." It is a priceless service in rendition of an external man and a changing apparition.

Mainly to the Barrett and Meserve collections are we under obligation for the progression of photographs in half-tone engravings marching through these seventy-six chapters of printed text. From my own little array of cartes de visite came a few. Several hitherto unpublished photographs are from an album that came into my hands in 1929 through a generous deal proposed by Barrett because he knew I wanted to live with the book and its many faces. The album's leaves have no mounted prints, each leaf being itself a photographic print from an original negative, the whole bound in boards.

Several collectors and men widely versed in photographic lore, including Steichen, tell me they have never seen another book made by this plan. Whether other copies than this one were issued I have not been able to learn. Its title page reads: *McClees' Gallery of Photographic Portraits of the Senators, Representatives & Delegates of the Thirty-Fifth Congress, Photographed and Published by McClees & Beck*—their address No. 308 Pennsylvania Avenue, Washington, D.C. Each Senator and Representative autographs his own photograph. All but three members of the Congress of the United States for the year 1859 are camera-recorded, apparently by a photographer named McClees whose publishing partner was named Beck. For these photographs McClees is credited as they appear herein.

For other contributions to the camera record we are indebted to the Library of Congress, the Lincoln Library of the University of Chicago, the Chicago Historical Society, the United States Signal Corps, the John Hay Library of Brown University, and the L. C. Handy studio in Washington, D.C. It was my privilege once in 1933 to have a long afternoon of talk with L. C. Handy, nephew of Matthew B. Brady, and to hear this veteran photographer comment and discourse on the Lincoln negatives in his possession made by his famous uncle.

Among illustrations in this book are a few drawings by Charles W. Reed from *Hardtack and Coffee* by John D. Billings (G. M. Smith, 1888) and several drawings, including tailpieces, from *A Pictorial History of the Civil War by Benson J. Lossing* (1866-68; Vol. 1, Childs; Vol. 2, Belknap).

Parts of this manuscript were read by Louis Gottschalk, by William E. Dodd, by Ferdinand Schevill of the University of Chicago, department of history, and they were kindly with counsel and stimulating with comment.

Once came a letter from my old friend John L. Hervey, translator of Spanish poets, a unique man of learning, thirty years editor of the *Horse Review*, intensely American, his father an Ohio acquaintance of Ben Wade. And Hervey was saying, "While you are writing the life of the greatest American I am writing the life of the greatest American *horse*." As he went on with his complete narrative of Man o' War, I sent him copies of chapters of my book. At his suggestion I obeyed my inclinations to lengthen the portraits of Jefferson Davis and Charles Sumner. After an argument with him I hunted out Longfellow's journals, saw Sumner as his best friend wrote about him, and shaded some judgments that were too decisive. For his many courteous hints, and because he never hesitated to argue for any point of belief deep in him, for his sometimes upholding me when I was doubtful of myself, I am thankful to Hervey.

To President Franklin Delano Roosevelt for personally conducting me in 1937 to Lincoln corners of special interest in the White House I am deeply grateful. To Herbert Hoover, who as Chief Magistrate in 1930 extended me unusual courtesies in White House rambles and inspections, I am also deeply grateful. To my Lake Michigan shoreline neighbor John Severin, in charge of White House reconstruction during the Administration of President Calvin Coolidge, I am indebted for informative details.

One afternoon in the early fall of 1927 there came to my dusty third-floor corner of the *Chicago Daily News* building a woman of humility and inner grace, crowned with eighty-seven years of life and hair snow-white—Julia Taft Bayne, who as a child with her brothers "Bud" and "Holly" was a playmate of Tad and Willie Lincoln in the White House. Magazines were then publishing parts of her book *Tad Lincoln's Father* (Little, Brown, 1931). It is, as William E. Barton wrote in a foreword, "a most readable tale," having "its fitting place with the permanently valuable documents of the Lincoln home." Photographs of the winsome Taft boys and their demure sister are used herein by the permission of Little, Brown and Company.

M. L. Raney, custodian of the Lincoln Library of the University of Chicago, was freehanded in giving access to the treasures of the Barton collection and other materials. Louis Warren gave me photostats of the John P. Usher papers and ready use of the library and collection of the National Lincoln Life Insurance Company of Fort Wayne, Indiana. Eugene Meyer of the *Washington Post* and Crosby Noyes Boyd of the *Washington Star* made available morgues, files, and accumulated data. Robert W. Gordon of Washington, D.C., resolved into certainties several doubts concerning war songs and literature. The Tennesseans Allen Tate and Caroline Gordon in their books, and in long conversations, were luminous on lights and loyalties that moved the Confederacy.

In major and minor matters, favors, errands, loans, services, I am indebted to my brother Martin G. Sandburg of Galesburg, Illinois; to Charles H. Dennis of the *Chicago Daily News;* to James O'Donnell Bennett of the *Chicago Tribune;* to Jacob and Hazel Buchbinder of Chicago; to President Stewart McClelland of Lincoln Memorial University; to President Ewald Lawson of Upsala College; to George E. Q. Johnson of Chicago; to Frederick Dickinson and Mitchell Dawson of Winnetka, Illinois; to Harold C. Holmes of Oakland, California; to Helen Hope Page of Oakdale, California; to Jesse J. Ricks of Plandome, Long Island, New York; to Joseph Schaffner of New York City; to Helene Champlain of the Union News Company; to Vivian Johnson and Martha Moorman of Harbert, Michigan; to Ken Holden of the Lafayette Escadrille; to the World War artilleryman Archibald MacLeish of Conway, Massachusetts; to members of the Benton Harbor, Michigan, Twin City Post No. 1459 of the Veterans of Foreign Wars.

. . . Sometimes I regret that I have generally used the . . . "three dots of elision" . . . for unimportant matter omitted in quotations. However, I have never been able to stifle suspicions that any "tearing of text from context" in a letter or document . . . any act of the selection of what is deemed "essential" or "significant" in distinction from what is not . . . has always a touch of the hazardous and very often of the arrogant. . . .

CARL SANDBURG

Chikaming Goat Farm
Harbert, Michigan
July, 1939

CONTENTS

FOREWORD   vii

1. AMERICA—WHITHER?   3
   Doubt – Fog – Delicate decisions – Portraits of James Buchanan,
   Harriet Lane, Winfield Scott

2. FROM SPRINGFIELD TO WASHINGTON   35
   The President-elect meets immense crowds in key cities – Secret
   night journey from Harrisburg to Washington

3. PEACE EFFORTS FAIL   85
   A convention babbles – Emissaries of many stripes – Portrait of
   Charles Sumner

4. LINCOLN TAKES THE OATH AS PRESIDENT   120
   Tense atmosphere in the national capital – Structure of the inaugural address – Its delivery – Repercussions

5. CABINET PORTRAITS   140
   Seward – Chase – Cameron – Welles – Bates – Smith – Montgomery Blair – Vice-President Hamlin

6. OFFICE-SEEKERS   162
   An unprecedented number of place-hunters – The President
   balances favors

7. WAR CHALLENGE AT SUMTER   185
   A world drama – The majority of the Cabinet oppose the President – Responsibility for war – Sumter falls

8. THE CALL FOR TROOPS   210
   "Uprising of the North" – The South holds firm

9. JEFFERSON DAVIS—HIS GOVERNMENT   237
   The Confederate capital moved from Montgomery to Richmond
   – Portraits of Confederate leaders

10. TURMOIL–FEAR–HAZARDS   261
    Deaths of Ellsworth and Douglas – Taney and Lincoln on the
    habeas corpus – Lincoln's extra-legal acts unapproved by Con-
    gress

11. BULL RUN LOST '61–COMMANDER McCLELLAN   300
    Battle announced beforehand – Civilian spectators – Rout and
    disaster – Female spies

12. FRÉMONT IN MISSOURI–JAMES GORDON BENNETT   336
    A radical abolitionist fails as a military leader – His emancipation
    proclamation revoked by the President

13. THE TRENT AFFAIR–"ONE WAR AT A TIME"   358
    Confederate Commissioners taken from a British ship on the high
    seas – Two countries in uproar

14. THE USES OF PATRONAGE   369
    Working for your friends and your friends working for you

15. DECEMBER '61 MESSAGE–COMMITTEE ON THE CON-
    DUCT OF THE WAR   377
    Portraits of Joseph Henry, Benjamin F. Wade, Zachariah Chan-
    dler, Lyman Trumbull, Andrew Johnson, Thaddeus Stevens –
    The first slaver, Gordon, hanged – Gradual compensated eman-
    cipation first proposed by Lincoln

16. OPINION-MAKERS   400
    Portraits of Robert J. Walker, Horace Greeley, Anna Ella
    Carroll

17. EXPECTATIONS OF McCLELLAN   413
    The President studies the art of war – He offers McClellan a plan

18. CORRUPTION–STANTON REPLACES CAMERON   422
    Munitions and horse frauds – Portrait of Edwin McMasters
    Stanton

19. WHITE HOUSE CHILDREN   454
    Tad, Willie, Julie, Bud – Death of Willie

20. DONELSON–GRANT–SHILOH   459
    The first light breaks on Northern gloom – Portrait of Grant –
    McClellan constantly demands more troops – News from New
    Orleans and Shiloh cheers the North – The Davis inaugural

21. FAREWELL, WOODEN WARSHIPS!   479
The *Monitor* and the *Merrimac* – Portrait of John Ericsson

22. SEVEN DAYS OF BATTLES–SUMMER OF '62   489
"Shoveling fleas" – Spies: Timothy Webster hanged and Belle Boyd jailed

23. THE DRAFT–DECISIONS–PATHOS   504
Sketch of Halleck

24. SECOND BULL RUN AUGUST '62–CHAOS   514
Portraits of John Pope, Robert E. Lee, Stonewall Jackson – Death of Phil Kearny – McClellan's command questioned – The Cabinet and the President

25. BLOODY ANTIETAM SEPTEMBER '62   549
Lee invades the North and is turned back

26. THE INVOLVED SLAVERY ISSUE   555
The many-faceted race question – Abolitionists incessantly press Lincoln for action

27. PRELIMINARY EMANCIPATION PROCLAMATION '62   577
The long-withheld document issued after military success – Staggering effects

28. McCLELLAN'S "SLOWS" AND POLITICS   590
The tortuous relationships between a President and Commander

29. ELECTION LOSSES IN '62–INDIAN DEATHS   609
Dennis Hanks and Carl Schurz call on Lincoln – Letter to Fanny McCullough

30. DECEMBER '62 MESSAGE–"WE CANNOT ESCAPE HISTORY"   618

31. BURNSIDE–FREDERICKSBURG '62–MORALE   623
"Needless butchery" – The North despondent, the South confident

32. THUNDER OVER THE CABINET   636
Seward and Chase resign from the Cabinet and return

LIST OF ILLUSTRATIONS

President Lincoln visits Army of the Potomac Headquarters, October, 1862   *frontispiece*

Charleston Mercury broadside: "The Union Is Dissolved!"   9

An English cartoon depicts trouble in the American family of States   15

South and North   16

Two fire-eaters, a moderate, and a saint   17

Leslie's Weekly sees Lincoln on a repair job   18

Leslie's Weekly cartoons Lincoln hoisted on bayonets   19

Contemporary print of the White House or Executive Mansion   21

Vanity Fair cartoons the rising sun Lincoln melting the iceberg Buchanan   24

General Winfield Scott writes a hotel management for an extra long bed   30

An 1861 engraving of the Capitol with unfinished dome   31

Harriet Lane   32

James Buchanan of Pennsylvania   32

Stephen Arnold Douglas of Illinois   32

John Jordan Crittenden of Kentucky   32

Four companions on the trip from Springfield   33

Justice and weapons   33

Circular of instructions regarding the train of the President-elect   35

Meticulous penmanship of Colonel E. E. Ellsworth   38

Through ticket to Washington   40

The President-elect enters a carriage at the Hudson River Railroad depot, New York City   56

Lincoln in the New York City Hall received by prosecessionist Mayor Fernando Wood   59

A *Harper's Weekly* cartoonist caricatures Lincoln as convivial, droll, too easygoing   63

The President-elect raising the United States flag over Independence Hall in Philadelphia   72

Vanity Fair cartoons the MacLincoln Harrisburg highland fling   78

Vanity Fair's "Fugitive Sketch" of the new President's arrival in Washington   80

Harper's Weekly gives a four-cartoon story of the President's
    "flight"   82-83
The Concert Hall of Willard's Hotel where the Peace Convention met   85
Pen sketch of Willard's Hotel   88
Charles Sumner autographs a sentiment   104
Lincoln in early '61   112
The President-elect at a flag-raising in Philadelphia   112
Six uncompromising states' rights men   113
The crowd at the Capitol listening to Lincoln's inaugural address   124
Two sheets from which Lincoln read his inaugural address   126-27
The crowd arrives to hear inaugural address, March 4 of '61   128
Assemblage before Capitol building, March 4 of '61   128
The newly inaugurated President Lincoln, March 6, '61   129
Inauguration crowd and Capitol, March 4, '61   129
Vice-President Hannibal Hamlin   129
Speaker of the House Galusha Aaron Grow   129
Lincoln interlines and revises his first inaugural address   130
The crowd, and the platform from which the inaugural address was
    delivered   131
Seward and Lincoln revise the closing passage of the inaugural address 134
Thomas Nast cartoons in *Harper's Weekly* opposed impressions of the
    inaugural address   136
Punch sees soot in the White House   138
William Henry Seward of New York, Secretary of State, U.S.A.   144
Gideon Welles of Connecticut, Secretary of the Navy, U.S.A.   144
Montgomery Blair of Missouri, Postmaster General, U.S.A.   145
Simon Cameron of Pennsylvania, Secretary of War, U.S.A.   145
Salmon Portland Chase, Secretary of the Treasury, U.S.A.   145
Edward Bates of Missouri, Attorney General, U.S.A.   145
Thomas Nast satirizes in *Harper's Weekly* "original Lincoln men"
    seeking office   164
German script of Carl Schurz telling White House news to his wife   167
A sarcastic Congressman receives a sweet memorandum   175
Vanity Fair cartoons Seward and Weed bringing pressure to bear on the
    President   178
Harper's Weekly cartoons the tangled skein passed to Lincoln by
    Buchanan   186
Vanity Fair cartoons "Prof. Lincoln" in a circus balancing feat   187
Harper's Weekly cartoons a citizen limp from conflicting war rumors   194
Harper's Weekly cartoons a puzzled Lincoln for its puzzled readers   204

Thaddeus Stevens of Pennsylvania, Chairman of the House Ways and
Means Committee 208

Senator and Mrs. James Henry Lane of Kansas 208

Thomas Corwin, Minister to Mexico 208

John Charles Frémont 208

Kate Chase 209

The widowed Mrs. Stephen Arnold (Adèle Cutts) Douglas 209

The actress Maggie Mitchell 209

The Confederate President's wife, Varina Howell Davis 209

The inside of Fort Sumter after bombardment 209

Type of handbill during the "Uprising" 217

Volunteer-recruiting handbill 219

Jefferson Davis of Mississippi, President of the Confederate States of
America 224

Alexander Hamilton Stephens of Georgia, Vice-President of the Confederate States of America 224

Robert Toombs of Georgia, Secretary of State, C.S.A. 225

Judah Philip Benjamin of Louisiana, Attorney General and later
Secretary of State, C.S.A. 225

Muster-out paper of the White House "Frontier Guard" 236

Punch cartoons Lincoln and Jeff Davis in bonds 252

Harper's Weekly cartoons officer Lincoln arresting outlaw Jeff Davis 254

Harper's Weekly cartoons robbery in the national apple orchard 262

Elmer Ephraim Ellsworth 264

The Marshall House, Alexandria, Virginia, where Ellsworth was killed 264

Francis E. Brownell, who killed Ellsworth's killer 264

Sam Houston of Texas 265

Zebulon Baird Vance, Governor of North Carolina 265

Lincoln writes sorrow and affection to Mr. and Mrs. Ellsworth 267

Lincoln gravely revises a diplomatic note of Seward's 282

Roger Brooke Taney, Chief Justice of the Supreme Court 296

Abner Doubleday 296

Robert Anderson, "Bob Anderson, my beau" 296

Winfield Scott, "Head of the Army" 296

John Henninger Reagan of Texas, Postmaster General, C.S.A. 297

Christopher Gustavus Memminger of South Carolina, Secretary of the
Treasury, C.S.A. 297

Leroy Pope Walker, Secretary of War, C.S.A. 297

Stephen Russell Mallory, Secretary of the Navy, C.S.A. 297

Harper's Weekly cartoons Greeley kicking out the Cabinet 306

Map of the fort-encircled national capital   315
Section of a printed address of McClellan to his soldiers   316
Mrs. John Jordan Crittenden   328
Jefferson and Varina Howell Davis   328
Mrs. John Slidell   328
Mrs. William McKendree Gwin   328
The McClellans at home   329
George Brinton McClellan, commanding the Army of the Potomac   329
General and Mrs. George Brinton McClellan   329
Lincoln writes memoranda on a letter to Frémont   346
James Murray Mason of Virginia   360
Charles Ferguson Smith   360
John Slidell of Louisiana   360
Samuel Ryan Curtis   360
Nathaniel Lyon   360
Edward Dickinson Baker   360
David Dixon Porter   361
David Glasgow Farragut   361
Gideon Welles   361
John Adolph Dahlgren   361
An English cartoon of mixed motives   361
A *Punch* cartoon interprets the Trent Affair   367
William H. Herndon writes an explanation of himself as an office-
    holder   370
Andrew Johnson autographs his definition of a traitor   391
Horace Greeley "makes a few scratches"   405
Fitting out gunboats at Cincinnati   460
Some called it "David and Goliath"   482
John Ericsson   488
John Lorimer Worden, battle commander of the *Monitor*   489
Crew of the *Monitor* in its fight with the *Merrimac*   489
Gustavus Vasa Fox, a sponsor of the *Monitor*   489
John Ericsson, inventor of the *Monitor*   489
Stanton writes "By order of the President"   505
Drawing names of drafted men   506
An order directed by the President relating to the treatment of enemy
    prisoners   508
Robert Edward Lee, 1852   520
The wartime Robert Edward Lee   520

George Washington Custis Lee, son of R. E. Lee   520

The Lee family residence in Richmond, Virginia   520

John Pope   521

Fitz-John Porter   521

The younger and older Thomas Jonathan ("Stonewall") Jackson   521

Reduced facsimile of two pages from the diary of Gideon Welles   536-37

Three Cabinet members sign a demand on the President   540-41

Pro-Confederate *Punch* of London cartoons a scared Lincoln   546

Wendell Phillips's autographed prewar sentiment   557

Lincoln writes his only long private letter to Horace Greeley   565

Handbill of '62 offering a reward for a runaway Negro   576

Punch cartoons Lincoln as desperate and Jeff Davis as pleased   589

Allan Pinkerton, President Lincoln, and General John Alexander
    McClernand   592

Another Brady photograph of Allan Pinkerton, President Lincoln, and
    General John Alexander McClernand   593

The published order for the final removal of McClellan from command   602

Ambrose Everett Burnside, afoot and horseback   608

Philip Kearny   608

Hermann Haupt   608

The Chief Magistrate confers with the Army of the Potomac commander
    in October of '62   609

Harper's Weekly cartoons Lincoln "dropping" Stanton and Halleck   628

Harper's Weekly cartoons Barnum presenting his midgets to the
    President   631

Leslie's Weekly cartoons Lincoln deep in mud   633

Greenback signature of Francis E. Spinner   653

Seward writes briefly and familiarly to the President   654

Abraham Lincoln
THE WAR YEARS

ABRAHAM LINCOLN: The War Years

CHAPTER I

AMERICA—WHITHER?

THE famous lawyer, Rufus Choate, listening to foreign-language grand opera in New York, had told his daughter to be sure to let him know when to laugh or cry or just sit still and keep cool. From the shifting stage scenes he could hear words, but he didn't know what they were saying. He needed help. "Interpret for me the libretto lest I dilate with the wrong emotion," he told the daughter.

Men and women in this mood in early 1861 looked on the American scene and listened and wished they could tell what the noise and pain meant today and was going to mean next week.

The sweet-tempered Reverend Samuel J. May had long ago tried to slow down his fellow abolitionist William Lloyd Garrison with saying at one of their meetings, "Mr. Garrison, you are too excited—you are on fire!" The reply of the veteran agitator: "I have need to be on fire, for I have icebergs around me to melt!"

Now in '61 it was hardly seven years since that yearly meeting of the Anti-Slavery Society in Framingham Grove near Boston, on a Fourth of July, when Garrison had read the Fugitive Slave Act, had then read the court order of a Federal judge handing a fugitive slave back to its owner, and had then lighted matches to both documents, crying as they burned, "And let all the people say Amen!"

The Amens were shouted—and then Garrison raised high a copy of the Constitution of the United States, read its clauses that sanctioned slave property, declared it the source of all other atrocities, termed it the original "covenant with death and agreement with hell," set a lighted match to it, and held it up burning till the last ashes of it must have singed his fingers. "So perish all compromises with tyranny!" cried Garrison, "and let all the people say Amen!" Then with the shouted Amens were mingled hisses and some voices of protest.

As a piece of drama it was tense. As a testament and a reality it had a flicker of great storm. Lincoln had given his interpretation of its impetus and drift in his House Divided speech.

The red-haired man at the head of the Military Academy of Louisiana was saying as South Carolina seceded, "The country will be drenched in

3

blood," and was writing to his daughter in Ohio, "Dear little Minnie, man proposes and God disposes," adding further, "Men are blind and crazy." And still further, "Mamma will explain it to you," though on later thought he knew very well Mamma could not explain it to little Minnie—though Minnie did understand that where the letter was signed "Your loving papa," it meant a big tight hug. This same papa, this William Tecumseh Sherman, wept in his sandy beard on Christmas Eve. And to a Southern friend he said: "The North can make a steam-engine, locomotive or railway car; hardly a yard of cloth or a pair of shoes can you make. You are rushing into war with one of the most powerful, ingeniously mechanical and determined people on earth—right at your doors. You are bound to fail."

The Texas Senator, Louis Wigfall, a finished orator, cool, melodious, elegant, witty, "having the eye of a sea rover," credited with winging his man in eight duels (chiefly in his native State of South Carolina), enjoyed facing the Northern Senators with packed galleries watching, waving a hand toward them and delivering a remark shaded as delicately as one of his death-dealing revolver shots. "The difficulty between you and us, gentlemen," he would say with measured intonation, "is, that you will not send the right sort of people here. Why will you not send either Christians or gentlemen?" The Michigan Senator, Zachariah Chandler, millionaire dry-goods merchant and real-estate operator of Detroit, having said that if the Union were merely a rope of sand he would go live among the Comanches, Wigfall flashed: "God forbid! The Comanches have already suffered much —too much—from contact with the white man!"

The little pale genius of Georgia, Aleck Stephens, explained why he had been keeping out of politics: "When I am on one of two trains coming in opposite directions on a single track, both engines at high speed—and both engineers drunk—I get off at the first station."

That remarkably picturesque and vehement Boston merchant, scholar, wit, and abolitionist, John Murray Forbes, who tended to the American investments of the widow of Alexis de Tocqueville, had a letter from her in the Old World cheerfully closing: "Tell me the probable result of this conflict. . . . You are a most volcanic people, and when one fancies you are in a dead calm, out bursts a tremendous storm."

Whether Abraham Lincoln would be certified as President-elect through a canvass of the November electoral results by Congress in regular, orderly session on February 13, as scheduled, was not yet sure. In the hair-trigger suspense at the national capital, with nerves of men on edge, General Winfield Scott was saying to an aide, "A dog fight now might cause the gutters to run with blood."

In Meriden, Connecticut, a circumstantial story arose that when Lincoln spoke there a year before he was interrupted in a crowded hall by a man on a window sill piping, "Do you believe, Mr. Lincoln, that if the Republicans should elect a President they would be able to inaugurate him?" Lincoln had pointed a long finger and closed a reply: "I reckon, friend, that if there are votes enough to elect a Republican President, there'll be men enough to put him in." Among those who had risen to shout and cheer was President Theodore Dwight Woolsey of Yale College.

"Resistance to Lincoln is Obedience to God" flared a banner at an Alabama mass meeting where an orator swore that if need be their troops would march to the doors of the national Capitol over "fathoms of mangled bodies." The sister States forming a Confederacy were satisfied with the Alabama resolution not to submit nor be party to the inauguration of Abraham Lincoln as President. Against the advice of Senator James H. Hammond and others that South Carolina should wait "till public feeling subsides" and not secede till President Buchanan's term was ended, Robert Barnwell Rhett and his forces had manipulated the precise dramatic event Rhett had sought and planned for years.

As a Congressman of six terms and a United States Senator of one term, as editor of the *Charleston Mercury*, as a lawyer and a churchman, as a manager of the Charleston Bible Society, as vice-president of the Young Men's Temperance Society, as secretary of the Charleston Port Society for promoting the Christian gospel among seamen, as the father of twelve children, the driving motive of Rhett's life was to win secession and Southern independence, build a Confederacy on the cornerstone of African slavery, and restore the African slave trade outlawed by the United States Constitution. He had reprinted Northern ridicule of South Carolina's "stale threatenings" and "windy bombast," had brought decisive action, and after years of loneliness and retirement once more heard applause, cheers, hurrahs for Rhett as "the author of disunion," "the father of secession." He had kept touch with those in agreement with Congressman W. W. Boyce telling serenaders, "The only policy is for us to arm as soon as we receive authentic intelligence of the election of Lincoln." He was aware of the feeling behind the words of A. P. Aldrich, an ordinary politician, writing how the common people didn't understand what was happening: "But who ever waited for the common people when a great movement was to be made? We must make the move and force them to follow. That is the way of all revolutions and all great achievements." Rhett formed combinations, looked to the young, and organized minutemen of the Revolution and vigilance committees, to make sure of delegates pledged to secession. He wrote the ordinance of disunion and in secret session the convention's 169 delegates in St. Andrew's Hall at Charleston on December 20, 1860, passed it without debate in forty-five minutes.

The doorkeeper told a policeman, who sent it on from mouth to mouth till it reached street crowds and set them roaring. A post-office gun belched thunder and citadel guns took up the chorus of "Thank God, it's done!" The chimes of St. Michael's rang out with "Auld Lang Syne" and other church bells joined their glee. The sun came out after three days' rain. In the evening at Institute Hall, packed with a breathless crowd, the convention delegates one by one signed the parchment sheet, 25 by 33 inches in size, engrossed with Rhett's sentence: "The union now subsisting between South Carolina and other States, under the name of 'The United States of

America,' is hereby dissolved." A great shout rocked the hall. The Reverend Dr. John Bachman, pastor of the Lutheran church in Charleston and second only to John J. Audubon as an authority on American bird life, asked Almighty God for blessing and favor on the solemn act.

A newly adopted flag was brought out with fifteen stars, one star for each Slave State. Again a great shout rocked the hall, and from lowlands to the upcountry were bells, bonfires, torchlights, parades, shotgun salutes, and cries of jubilee. The convention four days later adopted an Address to the Slaveholding States, from Rhett's pen, in which South Carolina asked "to be one of a great Slaveholding Confederacy, stretching its arms over a territory larger than any power in Europe possesses." The hypocrisy and faithlessness of thirty years of antislavery fanaticism had broken the old identity of interests: "The people of the North have not left us in doubt as to their designs and policy. United as a section in the late Presidential election, they have elected as the exponent of their policy one who has openly declared that all the States of the United States must be made Free States or Slave States." For the benefit of all who cared to read, Rhett gave his one-sentence propaganda picture, true in part, of the Northern States which had elected Lincoln: "They prefer a system of industry in which capital and labor are in perpetual conflict—and chronic starvation keeps down the natural increase of population—and a man is worked out in eight years—and the law ordains that children shall be worked only eight hours a day—and the saber and bayonet are the instruments of order—be it so."

Second only to Rhett as a torch of revolution was William Lowndes Yancey of Alabama. On the stump, when asked, "What will you do if Lincoln is elected?" he had answered, "I hope to God something will avert that awful calamity." And hearing Parson William G. Brownlow, a pro-slavery Union man of Tennessee, say that "when the Secessionists go to Washington to dethrone Lincoln" he would seize a bayonet in defense, Yancey replied, "If my State resists I shall go with her and if I meet this gentleman [pointing to Brownlow] marshalled with his bayonet to oppose us, I shall plunge mine through and through to his heart, feel no compunction for the act, but thank God my country had been freed from such a foe."

Half song thrush and half alligator, Yancey brandished a flambeau. On the evening after Lincoln's election, in a speech that fitted him as a glove, he faced a fiercely applauding audience: "Rather than live on subject to a government that breaks the compact at will and places me in a position of inequality, of inferiority to the Northern free negro, though that life be illustrated with gilded chains, by luxury and ease, I would in the cause of my State gather around me some brave spirits who, however few in number, would find a grave which the world would recognize, my countrymen, as a modern Thermopylae." In print his words lost fire, but his living voice had magnetized many a barbecue audience and led men "to clutch imaginary weapons and spring forward to meet a fancied foe." One little sentence from a widely published letter of Yancey's had set him off as a foremost Southern fire-eater: "We shall fire the Southern heart—instruct the Southern mind—give courage to each other, and at the proper moment, by one organized concerted action, we can precipitate the cotton states into a revolution."

One delegate of Union leanings at the Alabama secession convention said, "Yancey can save the Union by a wave of his hand." But Yancey was for revolution. How could he advise waiting? He had said so often that a hurricane is healthy for cleaning out scum and miasma. He took the floor on the resolution to declare the election and inauguration of Abraham Lincoln an insult and a menace, and made such a useless froth-mouthed speech for a half-hour that the convention rocked in disorder and delegates rebuked Yancey for bombast and fury in an hour requiring cool judgment.

Having led the revolution to a vortex, he was through. The time for theatricals, of his style, was over. When six States established the Confederate Government at Montgomery, Yancey introduced to the crowd its President Jefferson Davis, saying, "The man and the hour have met." But in the seats of power, in the high places, sat neither Yancey nor Rhett. Yancey would have liked Rhett to be President. So would other extremists. But a moderate element took the power, men who would rather have waited than secede, who would have held a convention and presented demands to the North, who had believed that more of their grievances would be corrected in the Union than out.

In their newly adopted constitution they struck directly at Rhett, Yancey, and the slave-traders, and bid for international goodwill by expressly forbidding the African slave trade for all time. The solemnity of probable war was in the Reverend Dr. Basil Manly's prayer at Montgomery: "Lord of all the families of the earth, we appeal to Thee to protect us in the land Thou hast given us, the institutions Thou hast established, the rights Thou hast bestowed." United States Senators and Congressmen stood up in Washington and spoke farewells, some bitter, some sad. United States postmasters, judges, district attorneys, customs collectors, by the hundreds sent their resignations to Washington. The mint for coining United States money at New Orleans, and two smaller mints, were taken over by the Confederate States. Of the 1,108 officers of the United States Regular Army, 387 were preparing resignations, many having already joined the Confederate forces. Governors of seceded States marched in troops and took over forts that had cost the United States $6,000,000: Forts Caswell, Johnston, Macon, Pinckney, Pulaski, Jackson, Clinch, Marion, Barrancas, McRae, Morgan, Gaines, Ship Island, St. Philip, Livingston, Brown, Smith; three marine hospitals; six arsenals with more than 200,000 muskets and large supplies of cannon, powder, ammunition; customhouses built at an expense of another $6,000,000; and lighthouses and light vessels at Rattlesnake Shoal, Bull's Bay, Oyster Beds, Tybee, Wolf Island, Cat Island, Dog Island, Southwest Reef, Pelican Spit, Half Moon Shoal, Swash, Aransas Pass, Red Fish Bar, and scores of other points.

The revolution hinged first on what the United States Government would do about forts, arsenals, customhouses, property gone from its possession. The country expected the President-elect, Abraham Lincoln, on that subject to speak out either on his way to Washington or in his inaugural address on arrival at the capital.

A minor affair it was that in Charleston, South Carolina, a peculiar and lovable old uncle, James Louis Petigru, lifelong friend of Rhett, whom Rhett regarded as the greatest of living lawyers, was asked if he would join the secessionists. "I should think not!" said Petigru. "South Carolina is too small for a republic and too large for a lunatic asylum." The balances that lay behind his grave face came out again one winter day when a stranger asked him which way to the lunatic asylum. Judge Petigru pointed east, "There it is"; pointed south, "and there"; pointed west, "and there"; pointed north, "and there too." The stranger was told he couldn't possibly go wrong. When he asked why, Petigru walked off, groaning: "The whole country is a lunatic asylum and the people all lunatics." Another version had it that he pointed to a church where the secession convention had assembled and said to the inquiring stranger, "It looks like a church, but it is now a lunatic asylum; go right there and you will find one-hundred and sixty-four maniacs within." When the bells rang out their announcement of secession accomplished, Petigru mistook it for a fire alarm, was corrected, and replied: "I tell you there is a fire! They have this day set a blazing torch to the temple of constitutional liberty, and please God, we shall have no more peace forever."

Over patches and areas in the South were few or no slaves, and tens of thousands of men ready to fight for the Union. They were voiced by Andy Johnson of Tennessee, crying in hoarse tone, "Secession is hell born and hell bound," also by a crossroads Unionist at a mountaineer gathering, throwing his arms wildly in the air: "For God's sake, let South Carolina nullify, revolute, secesh, and be damned!"

As speech and discussion became more useless, the paradoxes that tantalized the minds of men as to the Union of States were as inextricable as the Siamese twins, Chang and Eng, of Chinese and Chino-Siamese parents, fastened to each other for life by a living cord. They had bought a farm and slaves in North Carolina and had married sisters, one fathering five and the other six children. The *Greensboro Patriot* told of how long ago they had received letters from their mother in Siam, but now the letters no longer came and even if they should, Chang and Eng had forgotten their mother tongue. Also, "as they were passing up the road one day a gentleman inquired where they were going, whereupon Mr. Eng replied, 'I am going over the Blue Ridge in the stage'; at the same time Mr. Chang, looking over his shoulder, replied with an arch smile, 'And I am going back home to look after our wives and children.' "

Only tall stacks of documents recording the steel of fact and the fog of dream could tell the intricate tale of the shaping of a national fate, of men saying Yes when they meant No and No when they meant Perhaps; of newspapers North and South lying to their readers and pandering to the

CHARLESTON

MERCURY

EXTRA:

Passed unanimously at 1.15 o'clock, P. M., December 20th, 1860.

AN ORDINANCE

To dissolve the Union between the State of South Carolina and other States united with her under the compact entitled " The Constitution of the United States of America."

We, the People of the State of South Carolina, in Convention assembled, do declare and ordain, and it is hereby declared and ordained,

That the Ordinance adopted by us in Convention, on the twenty-third day of May, in the year of our Lord one thousand seven hundred and eighty-eight, whereby the Constitution of the United States of America was ratified, and also, all Acts and parts of Acts of the General Assembly of this State, ratifying amendments of the said Constitution, are hereby repealed; and that the union now subsisting between South Carolina and other States, under the name of " The United States of America;" is hereby dissolved.

THE

UNION

IS

DISSOLVED!

Charleston's leading newspaper spreads the news with type emphasis

cheaper passions of party, clique, and class interest; of the men and women of the ruling classes North and South being dominated more often than not by love of money, wealth, power, distinction, luxury, servants, jewels, and display beyond necessity or importance; of the Southern planters and merchants being $200,000,000 in debt to the North and chiefly to the money controllers of New York City; of the paradoxes involved in the Northern hope of the black man's freedom in the South; of the jealousy of Virginia and Kentucky slave-breeders, whose market was interfered with by the African slave-traders; of the race question that was one thing in the blizzard region of New England, where a Negro was pointed out on the streets as a rare curiosity, and something else again in the deep drowsy tropical South, where in so many areas the Negro outnumbered the white man; of the greed of Savannah and Mobile slave-traders, who mocked at the law prohibiting them from buying Negroes in Africa and selling those Negroes in Cuba for delivery in the Gulf Coast canebrakes and everglades; of how the prohibitory law as to fugitive slaves was mocked at and made a byword by abolitionists stealing slave property and running it North to freedom; of abolitionists hanged, shot, stabbed, mutilated, disfigured facially by vitriol, their home doorways painted with human offal; of the Northern manufacturer being able to throw out men or machines no longer profitable while the Southern planter could not so easily scrap his production apparatus of living black men and women; of the *New York Times* elaborately analyzing the Northern wage and money system as having "masses of disposable capital" while the assets of the South were fixed and frozen through the slavery system; of stock and bond markets becoming huge gambling enterprises in which fleeced customers learned later that the dice had been loaded; of a new mass production intricately organized in firearms and watch factories; of automatic machinery slightly guided by human hands producing shoes, fabrics, scissors, pins, and imitation jewelry sold by a chain of Dollar Stores; of a wilderness of oil derricks sprung up in western Pennsylvania, and the new gas engine of the French inventor Lenoir; of sky-climbing balloons soaring 23,000 feet and the prediction that soon there would be passenger balloons to Europe; of microscopically exact gauges to measure one ten-thousandth of an inch for you, sir; of such curious statistics as the Far Western State of Iowa having double the white population of South Carolina; of the persistent national vision of a railroad to the Pacific joining East and West coasts; of covered wagons heading west with the sign "Pike's Peak or Bust" and others returning with the sign "Busted by Gosh," of still other wagons emblazoned "Ho for California," "Oregon or Death," or "The Eleventh Commandment: Mind Your Own Business"; of five hundred westbound wagons a day passing through Fort Kearney, Nebraska; of horse stages taking passengers west across plains, desert, mountains, against thirst, heat, alkali water, sandstorms, Indians, bandits, breakdowns, in a regular twenty-three-day run from St. Louis to San Francisco; of the pony express running the United States mail from St. Joseph, Missouri, to San Francisco in eleven days, using five hundred horses and eighty riders, each taking the sacks an average of 133⅓ miles, carrying knife and revolver, riding three ponies to one stretch, sliding off one and hopping another, a living chain of human service going on day or night, in moonlight, under stars or in darkness, through rain, snow, sleet, over level prairies, hugging steep mountain trails and across desert paths laid through cactus and sage better known to the lizard and the coyote; of farming machinery that doubled and tripled the range of crop land one man could handle; of woman's household work lightened by laborsaving sewing machines, churns, egg-beaters, and like devices; of the casual and unquestioned statement that "two centuries ago not one person in a thousand wore stockings, one century ago not one person in five hundred wore them, and now not one person in a thousand is without them"; of Abraham Lincoln thumbing through his personal copy of *Blackwood's Magazine* and reading that in thirty years the population of the United States would double and in 1940 reach 303,000,000; of immense stretches of land where sod might yet be broken for unnumbered millions to come; of empires of production, trade, and profits that glimmered in the prospects of practical men who had in the past ten years spent $400,000,000 on railroads and canals between the Midwest and the Atlantic seaboard; of lands, homesteads, fortunes, and vast exploits of money and living waiting out yonder where the railroad whistle would shatter old solitudes; of backbreaking labor performed by Irish construction gangs on railroads and canals; of merciless dog-eat-dog rivalries among merchants, manufacturers, transportation interests, financiers, battling for customers and trade areas; of customers higgling and haggling over retail-store prices and the almost unbelievable announcement of A. T. Stewart's department store in New York that goods and articles had one price only, as marked, and the buyer could take it or leave it; of the animalism of the exploitation of man by man North and South; of the miscellaneous array of propertied interests in the North which would stand to lose trade and profits, land titles, mineral rights, payments of legitimate debts, through a divided Union of States; of the clean and inexplicably mystic dream that lay in many humble hearts of an indissoluble Federal Union of States; of the Mississippi River system draining 1,000,000 square miles of rich farm land, floating $60,000,000 worth of steamboats, hauling from twelve States; of the certainty that the new Republican-party power at Washington would be aimed to limit extension of slavery and put it in the course of ultimate extinction; of the 260,000 free Negroes of the South owning property valued at $25,000,000, one of them being the wealthiest landowner in Jefferson County, Virginia; of at least one in every hundred free Negroes owning one or two slaves, a few owning fifty or more; of the Southern poor white lacking slaves, land, and the decent creature comforts of the Negro house servant, lacking the guarantees of food, clothing, shelter, and employment assured the Negro field hand; of the Southern poor white often clutching as his dearest personal possession the fact that he was not born black; of Northern factory hands and garment-trade workers paid a bare subsistence wage, lacking security against accident, sickness, old age, unemployment while alive and funeral costs when finally dead; of the vague hope across the South that Northwestern States might join their Confederacy or form a confederacy of their own hostile to New England and allied to the South; of the one-crop Cotton States' heavy dependence on the Border Slave States and the North for food supplies, animal fodder, implements, and clothing; of the Cotton States' delusion that New England and Europe were economic dependents of King Cotton; of the American system having densely intricate undergrowths, old rootholds of a political past, suddenly interfered with by rank and powerful economic upshoots; of landed feudalism touched with Jeffersonian democracy, Hamiltonian individualism, medieval ecclesiasticism, shot through from the growths of oncoming modern capitalism moderated and offset by an immense domain of cheap land absorbing otherwise disturbing and antagonistic elements.

Thus might run a jagged sketch of the Divided House over which Lincoln was to be Chief Magistrate. And now before he was yet sworn in came advice from the *New York Herald*, circulating 77,000 copies daily, earning profits of $300,000 a year, mentioned by President James Buchanan as "the most powerful organ in the country for the formation of public opinion." Its owner and editor, James Gordon Bennett, publicly, so the whole country might know, told Lincoln that instead of going to Washington for inauguration he should step out of the national picture and go home. "A grand opportunity now exists for Lincoln to avert impending ruin, and invest his name with an immortality far more enduring than would attach to it by his elevation to the Presidency," read the newspaper editorial. "His withdrawal at this time from the scene of conflict, and the surrender of his claims to some national man who would be acceptable to both sections, would render him the peer of Washington in patriotism." And having instructed the President-elect, the *Herald* added a warning: "If he persists in his present position, in the teeth of such results as his election must produce, he will totter into a dishonoured grave, driven there perhaps by the hands of an assassin, leaving behind him a memory more execrable than that of Arnold —more despised than that of the traitor Catiline."

Lincoln's reply to Bennett's *Herald* and to others arranging schemes to run the country was a statement to the *New York Tribune* that he could not look on idly at the destruction of the Government itself: "I will suffer death before I will consent or advise my friends to consent to any concession or compromise which looks like buying the privilege of taking possession of the Government to which we have a constitutional right."

A New England manufacturer had come to Lincoln about trade's falling off, no orders from the South. It would pick up if Lincoln would say a few words to "reassure the men honestly alarmed." The persistence and the manner of approach, noted Nicolay, "irritated Lincoln to a warmth of retort he seldom reached." As to men honestly alarmed, said Lincoln, "There are no such men. This is the same old trick by which the South breaks down every Northern victory." He could trade away principles for immediate gains to commerce, arrive in Washington without friends. Then what? "I would be as powerless as a block of buckeye wood," Nicolay heard him say.

The man kept insisting and Lincoln looked him in the eye and went on: "The honest men (you are talking of honest men) will look at our platform and what I have said. There they will find everything I could now say, or which they would ask me to say. All I could add would be but repetition. Having told them all these things ten times already, would they believe the eleventh declaration? Let us be practical." The New England manufacturer brought out signatures, asked if they were not names of power. "Yes," retorted Lincoln, "I recognize them as a set of liars and knaves who signed that statement about Seward last year." The caller insisted there were some good names on the paper. Lincoln looked it over, cooled off a little, and laughed: "Well, after reading it, it is about as I expected to find it. It annoyed me to hear that gang of men called respectable." And the manufacturer went away with Lincoln's word that he couldn't begin yielding to threats nor begin dallying with those who threatened him. He would lose his friends: "And the South, seeing it, would deliberately kick me out."

A letter from John A. Gilmer of North Carolina hoping for "a clear and definite exposition" of Lincoln's views on several questions drew a long, courteous, and pertinent reply. Gilmer was a Congressman, a former judge, and of such caliber that Lincoln later invited him to confer on the matter of appointing him as one distinctly Southern man in his Cabinet. He wrote to Gilmer that his views were all in print and easy of access. New declarations "would make me appear as if I repented for the crime of having been elected, and was anxious to apologize and beg forgiveness." He gave numbers of pages where Gilmer could get plenty of answers to the questions asked. "I have no thought of recommending the abolition of slavery in the District of Columbia, nor the slave-trade among the slave States . . . and if I were to make such recommendation, it is quite clear Congress would not follow it." As to patronage in the Slave States, he would not inquire whether an appointee was a slaveowner. "I never have been, am not now, and probably never shall be in a mood of harassing the people either North or South." On only one point was there a substantial difference: "You think slavery is right and ought to be extended; we think it is wrong and ought to be restricted. For this neither has any just occasion to be angry with the other."

The newspaper suggestion that Lincoln should resign had partly in support of it the vague mistrust voiced in Congress by Representative Horace Maynard, speaking for Tennessee Union men. Lincoln's "honesty" was not enough to qualify him. What was known of him except that he was "born in the wilds of Kentucky, reared in the wilds of Illinois," served one term in Congress, and lost a senatorial campaign in Illinois? As a Chief Magistrate he would be "a mere wisp in the hands of those who shall succeed in getting around his person." As to complaints, Lincoln was not letting the country know what he would do. "I imagine," said Maynard, "that he keeps silence for the good and sufficient reason that he has nothing to say. But all this only serves to complicate still more the grave and difficult question that is upon us for decision." Owen Lovejoy of Illinois said he did not, could not, and never would believe the President-elect was for compromise "until I have it from his own lips or his own acts." The familiar nickname of "Honest Old Abe" still deserved regard, said Lovejoy: "All we ask is that he shall be inaugurated. Twelve months of the administration of Abraham Lincoln will do more to disabuse the public mind than all the compromises and peace measures that can be patched up in Congress. Let him have a trial, a fair trial." For himself, Lovejoy wished it known that he would not join others who reached out wrists for handcuffs and then consoled themselves by saying, "It is not as bad as it might be; we can move our fingers a little."

Senator Hale of New Hampshire expostulated December 10: "I have hoped that when the angel of Revelations stood at last with one foot upon the earth and the other upon the sea, and swore by Him that liveth forever and ever that time should be no longer, this great Republic would be the last that would be wound up." Representative Martin J. Crawford of Georgia on January 18 asked the God of his fathers to avert civil strife and, declaring the South could no longer submit to Northern terms, said, "I would rather see the broad lands from the Potomac to the Rio Grande one grand charnel-house filled with the bones of brave and gallant men, than submit to degradation." A Georgia orator wandered up into Jefferson, Missouri, to say, "The South and the North are now as widely separated as Abraham from Lazarus."

Tenderly Senator Jefferson Davis of Mississippi, pale and just risen from a sickbed, in January had spoken his words of parting from old familiar faces in the Senate: "I offer you my apology for any thing I may have done in the Senate, and I go remembering no injury I have received." His regrets coupled to a warning: "There will be peace if you so will it, and you may bring disaster on every part of the country if you thus will have it. We will invoke the God of our fathers, who delivered them from the paw of the lion, to protect us from the ravages of the bear."

Swiftly, on Jeff Davis's walking out forever, Senator Seward moved to admit Kansas, "Bleeding Kansas," as a Free State member of the Union. Twelve years she had knocked for admittance and the South said No. Now it was so ordered that Kansas be a State.

J. R. Barret of Missouri quoted for the House several Lincoln speeches as showing him to favor the proposition that "all men are born free and equal," cited the record of the Illinois Legislature in 1837, when Lincoln voted against resolutions declaring the right of property in slaves "sacred to the slaveholding States by the Federal Constitution." This related strictly to the saying of Congressman Thomas L. Anderson of Missouri: "Many of our slaves are now impressed with the idea that after the inauguration of Mr. Lincoln, they are to be free. This impression makes them restless and discontented, renders our homes, our wives, and our children, unsafe." John A. Logan of Illinois was not ready to classify Lincoln, but said Lincoln would go slow on starting a civil war, having been "so conscientious" about the Mexican War as to oppose it. In the Senate George E. Pugh of Ohio quoted Lincoln's House Divided speech as bringing fear to the South, which required reassurance from the President-elect. Senator Douglas too quoted from the House Divided speech, found it disturbing and provocative, and went on record: "I take great pleasure in saying, however, that I do not believe the rights of the South will materially suffer under the administration of Mr. Lincoln." Neither Mr. Lincoln nor his party would have the

An English cartoon depicts trouble in the American family of States

power to harm Southern interests if the Union were preserved and the Southern States retained a full delegation in both Houses of Congress. "I have some faith, too," said Douglas, "that Mr. Lincoln, after having emerged from the surroundings of a small country village . . . will sink the partisan in the patriot . . . by repudiating his extreme doctrines of a party."

Douglas wanted to know what now, with Florida seceded, became of the $5,000,000 he and other Senators had voted to buy Florida from Spain. As to President Buchanan's recommendation of the proposal to buy Cuba for $300,000,000, if it were followed, said Douglas, Cuba as one of the United States could secede, reannex herself to Spain, and "the next day the Spanish Queen would be ready to sell the island again for half price, or double price, according to the gullibility of the purchaser."

"Sir, I believe in the right of secession," said Senator Joseph Lane of Oregon, promising that Northern Democrats would not join in a war on the South: "The Republican party will have war enough at home." To the charge that Mr. Lincoln would violate the Constitution whenever without laying himself open he could damage the slavery institution, Senator Wade of Ohio replied that while the charge was of no great consequence, "I will only say that from Mr. Lincoln's character and conduct from his youth up, you have no right to draw any inference that he will trespass upon the rights of any man." Senator Robert M. T. Hunter of Virginia proposed a dual executive government with two Presidents, one each from the North and the South, one serving four years in the White House as Chief Magistrate and then being followed four years by his coequal, who had been acting as president of the Senate. Senator William Bigler of Pennsylvania said the South had been wronged and slandered; he would not shed the blood of brothers, and Pennsylvania would never draw the sword on her affectionate sister State of Virginia. Senator Cameron arose to point out that of sixty-six Senators not a dozen listened while the olive branch was offered. Having seen what he had seen, said Senator Cameron, "certainly I shall not make a speech."

But a Southern member pressed Cameron. Would he use coercion? "I will answer even that," said Cameron. "Coercion is the last remedy to which I would resort." "Is it a remedy at all?" was asked. "Yes, a bad remedy," said Cameron.

A noisy gallery often laughed, cheered, hissed, giggled, and roared, matching an equal disorder on the floor of the House, the Speaker of the House once saying it was impossible for him "to distinguish between the commotion in the House and the commotion in the galleries." Amid cries of "Order! Order!" from the Republican side, the recording clerk took down remarks of two members for the record:

—There is no occasion for excitement. We have passed that point.
—Nobody is excited.
—I did not say that anybody is excited.
—There is certainly no excitement on this side of the House.
—I have merely stated that this is no time for excitement. Men, sir, should keep cool.

In the Senate one January day Senator Lyman Trumbull of Illinois said he understood Senator James S. Green of Missouri better than Mr. Green understood himself.

MR. GREEN. Mr. President, he does not understand me. I claim the right to explain myself.

MR. TRUMBULL. If the Senator from Missouri will be a little patient, he will find that I understand him; and that I will state his position fairly.

MR. GREEN. I am misrepresented by the Senator from Illinois, and I claim the right to explain myself.

THE PRESIDING OFFICER. The Senator from Illinois is entitled to the floor unless he yields it to the Senator from Missouri.

Slaves

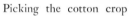
Picking the cotton crop

Chattels, fixed or removable

Broadway, New York, 1861

From stereographs in Oliver R. Barrett Collection

SOUTH AND NORTH

Robert Barnwell Rhett, Sr., of South Carolina

From Vol. I, Battles and Leaders, *Century Company*

James Louis Petigru of South Carolina

Photograph from Frederick H. Meserve Collection

William Lowndes Yancey of Alabama

Thomas Holliday Hicks, Governor of Maryland

Photographs from Frederick H. Meserve Collection

TWO FIRE-EATERS, A MODERATE, AND A SAINT

MR. GREEN. The Senator has already misrepresented me, and I claim the right to explain.

MR. TRUMBULL. If I have already misrepresented the Senator, I will hear his statement.

Without an if or a but, without a flicker of hesitation, Senator William M. Gwin of California would vote $100,000,000 for a Pacific railway. Then Crittenden of Kentucky said that, what with the Union "reeling about like a drunken man," he couldn't see a Pacific railway. "Build up the Union first; then talk about building up a railroad." In the House John Sherman of Ohio queried: "Why not let the Republican administration be inaugurated in peace and quiet? Try it, in the name of God!"

Having picked up as true a propaganda tale that Lincoln had said he wished to visit the graves of his father and mother in Kentucky and dared not because of Slave State hostility, Charles H. Van Wyck of New York told the House it was amazing that a man born in Kentucky, with no brand on his brow and no crime charged against him, "dare not travel through what he boasts to call his country, to plant flowers or shed tears upon the graves of his ancestors!"

Four Methodist preachers had been hanged the last year in one State, said Thaddeus Stevens of Pennsylvania, and now every day was bringing news of citizens mobbed, tarred and feathered, hanged without trial or hearing. A colloquy ensued:

MR. HARRIS. In behalf of Virginia I wish to say that her people never hung a northern man except John Brown and his friends; and then they hung, not by scores, but by law.

MR. STEVENS. You hung them exactly right, sir.

MR. HARRIS. Yes; they were well hung.

Violence, the smell of the kill, was in the air. If Lincoln should try to retake the seized forts, he would have to kill and kill in sickening numbers, said John Y. Brown of Kentucky: "From the blood of your victims, as from the fabled dragons' teeth, will spring up crops of armed men, whose religion it will be to hate and curse you." Concede the reasonable request of the seceded States, said Brown, or else

> A thousand years from now,
> Will sit pale ghosts upon the Stygian shore,
> And read their acts by the red light of hell.

"Very well, sir," said Thaddeus Stevens. "Rather than show repentance for the election of Mr. Lincoln, with all its consequences, I would see this Government crumble into a thousand atoms."

Stevens went over to the Senate chamber and heard a long speech by Seward, who was to sit in Lincoln's Cabinet, who was already taken as a sort of mouthpiece of the incoming Administration. What, asked Seward, was all the noise and confusion about? Was the election illegal? No. Was Lincoln personally offensive? "No; he is a man of unblemished virtue and

FRANK LESLIE'S ILLUSTRATED NEWSPAPER.

FEB. 2, 1861.

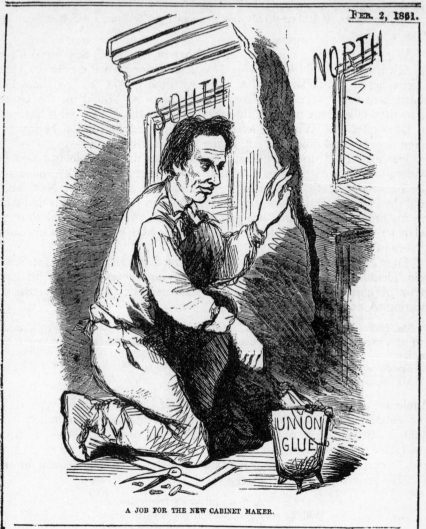

A JOB FOR THE NEW CABINET MAKER.

amiable manners. Is it apprehended the new President will usurp despotic powers? No; while he is of all men the most unambitious, he is by the partial success of those who opposed his election, subjected to such restraints that he cannot, without their consent, appoint a minister, or even a police agent, negotiate a treaty, or procure the passage of a law, and can hardly draw a musket from the public arsenals to defend his own person." And Seward went on, smooth and agreeable, as though everything was like it used to be and the little rumpus on hand would soon blow over.

Thaddeus Stevens went away saying to a colleague, "I listened to every word and by the living God I have heard nothing."

"Sir, I cannot penetrate the dismal future before us," said Representative John S. Millson of Virginia. "The fairest fabric of government ever devised

FRANK LESLIE'S ILLUSTRATED NEWSPAPER.

MARCH 2, 1861.

OLD ABE—" *Oh, it's all well enough to say, that I must support the dignity of my high office by Force—but it's darned uncomfortable sitting—I can tell yer.*"

by man is on fire," said Representative Robert Hatton of Tennessee. "Flames fierce as hell are consuming it." Representative Thomas Ruffin of North Carolina served notice that his State would go with the Deep South in secession and not join with any such central Confederacy as that proposed by Governor Hicks of Maryland. Clement L. Vallandigham of Ohio again spoke for a new form of government, with the country divided into four regions and no State permitted to secede except with the consent of all other States in the region. "I shall not stop to resurrect the bones of John Brown," said John T. Harris of Virginia. "A sheriff of my State erected a monument to his memory the day before his death." Daniel E. Somes of Maine refused to be terrorized by South Carolina's "sheet-iron thunder" and asked, "Would you compromise with a burglar?" Petitions poured in from citizens favoring the Crittenden Compromise to amend the Constitution and give legal sanction to slavery. Still other petitions poured in from citizens favoring the Union, the Constitution as it was, and the enforcement of the laws. In the matter of petitions it seemed a tie. In day sessions Congress took up revenue matters, the deficiency bill, tariff, pensions, claims, fishery bounties, mail routes, Indian hostilities in Oregon and California, river and harbor improvements, public lands, the Pacific railway. In night sessions Congress discussed "the state of the country." Several million words were spoken on slavery, abolition, secession, the Union, conciliation, force, the unspeakable horrors of war, the imperative necessity of war, Lincoln and Seward speeches which could be argued as Black Republican declarations of war, old statements of Southern leaders that secession would be folly, insanity, perfidy, stupendous madness, and texts from the slaveholders Washington, Jefferson, Jackson, favoring the earliest possible riddance of slavery. The checkered array of Republican statesmen, orators, and politicians at the end of Pennsylvania Avenue opposite to the White House, the indescribable miscellany of helpers and critics Lincoln would have in the legislative branch of the Government, was in part catalogued by Maynard of Tennessee:

I beseech you, gentlemen, to look at your own party, if you have never done so, and see of what heterogeneous elements it is composed. Old Whigs and old Democrats; followers of Thomas Jefferson, admirers of Alexander Hamilton; friends of Jackson, friends of Clay; masons, anti-masons; "barnburners," "hunkers;" "renters," "anti-renters;" "woolly-heads," "silver-grays;" Know-Nothings, Americans, foreigners, Catholics; protective-tariff men, free-trade men; bank men, bullion men; radicals, conservatives; men of strict construction, and men of no construction; men of unquestionable honesty, and men whose honesty I will not venture to call into question; men of all grades of political sentiment, all shades of political opinion, all bedded together, heads and heels, covered by a single blanket, and that woven of African wool. Such is the dapple hue of the party that has inaugurated itself to the head of public affairs, and is about to take the government into control.

But the hue was still more dappled, spotted, and crisscrossed, for the Republican-party elements throwing their hopes with Lincoln included young men who had never had any other political faith; boys of the Wide Awake marching clubs with torchlights and military formations and campaign songs and rallying calls; the Pacific-railway bloc of Eastern financiers and Western politicians who had maneuvered for Lincoln in the Chicago convention; amazingly expert propagandists trained in the agitation methods of the abolitionist movement; two-gun fighters and killers out of the Kansas border wars; ruthless political manipulators such as Thaddeus Stevens, ready for colossal violence toward one purpose; Union men such as William

Tecumseh Sherman, writing in a letter "Damn the nigger" yet ready to lose his life and "slay millions" to keep the Mississippi River within control of the Union.

In the very air of the City of Washington was coming a sense of change, of some new deal, of an impending program to be wrought out on historic anvils in smoke and mist and reckless slang, of old bonds and moorings broken beyond holding by old thongs and anchors, of a formerly confident and dominant class giving way to an element a little raw and new to government and diplomacy, young and strange in its champing and chafing.

In the White House sat James Buchanan, who had bespoken Lincoln's right to come on and see what the place might be like. "The election of any one of our citizens to the office of President," he gently urged on his friends of yesterday, "does not of itself afford just cause for dissolving the Union." When a rumor had come to Lincoln in the Midwest that Buchanan had instructed the United States commander at Fort Sumter in Charleston Harbor to surrender the fort if attacked, Lincoln, as Nicolay noted it, had burst with the exclamation regarding the President of the United States, "If that is true they ought to hang him!" It wasn't true. And Lincoln on

The White House or Executive Mansion
(Contemporary print)

second thought might have said hanging a President would do no good. But Lincoln was giving himself the same release of feeling as a country-town mass meeting of Douglas Democrats in southern Illinois demanding of President-elect Lincoln when he took office first of all to "hang the old traitor James Buchanan as high as old John Brown."

A Virginia mother calling on the President had worried lest her eight-year-old daughter should blurt out their favorite remark on secession: "Never mind! *united* will spell *untied* just as well." An Iowa Senator wrote to his wife that the President divided his time between praying and crying and "Such a perfect imbecile never held office before." Walt Whitman was writing that for twelve years the Presidents of the country, including Buchanan, had been "deformed, mediocre, sniveling, unreliable, false-hearted men." Harshly and with nerves on edge men scolded in the tone of a *Springfield* (Massachusetts) *Republican* writer who saw at Washington a pauper and idiot Government, the laughingstock of the world, "feeble-minded, non compos, worthy of guardianship by the strongest man." More softly and sadly Alexander Stephens, far down in Georgia, saw the beginning of the end of a great republic he had loved, the times distempered, the people misled: "Mr. Buchanan has ruined the country. It is past praying for." *Vanity Fair* gibbered in verse of a White Old House with a gray old rat, fidgeting ever and blind as a bat.

To a Congressman's wife Buchanan said, "Nobody knows the heart of a President." One morning that winter he had gone to a wedding breakfast and was having pleasant moments with people he liked when there came a yelling like a house afire and it turned out to be a South Carolina Congressman in the front hall shaking a telegram over his head and crying out loud: "Thank God! Oh, thank God! South Carolina has seceded." And Buchanan sat pale and stunned and came out of it to whisper, "Madam, might I beg of you to have my carriage called?"

Returned to the White House, the President did in effect nothing. His training in doing nothing, in effect, had been long. Like other fading and ineffectual figures in his circle of men grown old and out of use, he could take backward glances and meditate on what was past, on his serving as a private in the ranks in the War of 1812 nearly fifty years ago, of his horseback ride through bluegrass Kentucky, his temptation to settle in law practice there, and his going back to Lancaster, Pennsylvania, and throwing himself into politics, as they said, to forget a personal tragedy. He had met Miss Anne C. Coleman, well favored in face and form, her father one of the iron kings, and she at twenty-three was engaged to marry the twenty-eight-year-old Buchanan. And she had heard of his going to a pleasant evening party of a set not accepted by the iron kings and his name linked in Lancaster common gossip with another young woman, so Miss Coleman broke the engagement. She was found dead in a Philadelphia hotel. Talk ran that she died by her own hand, though motives were confused when a sister of Miss Coleman on the brink of marriage killed herself. The father denied James Buchanan's request to attend Anne's funeral. "Your dear, departed daughter I loved infinitely more than any other human being could love," he pleaded. "Afford me the melancholy pleasure of seeing her body before its interment." He might sustain the shock of her death, but "happiness has fled from me forever." From then on he carried "a grief not to be spoken of," said one friend who saw growing in Buchanan "a chivalrous, old-fashioned deference to women of all ages and all claims." In politics he could best forget what had happened, said associates, though he met whisperings and occasionally open accusations that he had hounded a fine young woman into her grave. Elected a Congressman, he lived on, a bachelor, always reserved as to women.

As Russian Minister thirty years back he had attended a Te Deum at the Church of St. Alexander Nevsky in St. Petersburg, had seen the Emperor cross himself and kiss the hand of the archbishop, and had written to President Andrew Jackson in 1832 of his talk with the Empress: "She observed we had troubles enough among ourselves at home and alluded to our difficulties in some of the Southern States. . . . God forbid that the Union should be in any danger."

An estate of $300,000, acquired during forty years of public officeholding, gave him little ease now, nor the degree awarded him at Oxford University when he and Alfred Tennyson were on the same day made Doctors of Civil Law, nor the comments "Buchanan has a winning way of making himself hateful" or "He doesn't know how to make people like him." Out of a dispute with an editor he had written, "It has been throughout between us a comedy of errors in which I have been the sufferer." He earned a reputation for keeping secrets better than anyone in Washington. He explained himself to himself in a winter diary of 1860-61, correct, faultless. A Congressman's wife noted anxiety on his face, though he insisted that he slept finely and enjoyed the best of health. "If one chanced to stand silently near him in a quiet corner he might be heard to mutter, 'Not in my time—not in my time.' " To John Cochrane of New York he gave his surmise that he was the last President of the United States.

He was compared to an Irish governor who had told his people that he would give up a part "and if necessary, *the whole* of the Constitution, *to preserve the remainder*." He argued that seceded States had no right to secede, yet the Federal Government had no right to use force to stop them from seceding. He urged, however, the right of the Federal Government to use force against individuals, in spite of secession, to enforce Federal laws and hold Federal property. Yet his words lacked action to give them force. His delicacy of mind, his code of a gentleman, too, stood in his way. Only violence, in the events, could speak an effective language. And how could he use that language with those who had put him in the White House? He wrote letters, negotiated, conferred, sent messengers, employed moral suasion against an organization making elaborate preparations to use guns. To Congressman Morrill of Vermont he was like an old man chuckling to his rowdy sons, "*Don't*, but if I were you I would, and I can't help it if you do."

A shattered and worn man in early February, meeting delegates to the national Peace Conference, he threw his arms around the neck of one stranger after another and with tears streaming his face begged they would save the country from "bloody, fratricidal war." A Northern delegate suggested that the November election of Lincoln had made decisions the conference couldn't reverse. Southern delegates spoke up, directly contrary. Other and more courteous delegates managed to shift the line of conversation before the argument got noisy.

The Louisiana Senator, John Slidell, the Virginia Governor, Henry A. Wise, and the New York financier August Belmont had maneuvered Buchanan's nomination for President in behalf of men South and North who knew him for what he was, an able legalist, a veteran in diplomacy and the ways of Washington, a safe man, reserved in both private manners and public issues.

One comfort to him was his niece, Harriet Lane, robust, blonde, with golden-brown hair, violet-blue eyes, a graduate of the Visitation Convent

OUR GREAT ICEBERG MELTING AWAY.

Vanity Fair believes a President of icy indifference is to be followed by one not so icy nor so indifferent

near Washington. In England at the Court of St. James they said she had the look of Victoria when the Queen was younger. The new song "Listen to the Mocking Bird" was dedicated to her, a warship had been named for her, also a race horse, a flower, a fashionable gown, and many a newborn girl child. "No American woman ever had more offers of marriage than Harriet Lane." Her uncle wrote the caution, "Never allow your affections to become interested, or engage yourself to any person, without my previous advice." He urged her to "look ahead and act wisely" as to marriage: "I have witnessed the long years of patient misery which fine women have endured from rushing precipitately into matrimonial connections without sufficient reflection." Mrs. Pryor heard at a morning reception the remark: "How does she do it? She never makes a cheese of herself." When a foreign attaché told her she had "hands that the rod of empire might have swayed," she rejoined, "Or wake to ecstasy the living liar!" She would write to a sister a report of a party, "I wore a pink silk petticoat, over-skirts of pink tulle, puffed and trimmed with wreaths of apple blossoms; train of pink silk, trimmed with blonde and apple blossoms, and so was the body." Twenty-eight years old, for ten years she had been at her uncle's side in all his large missions. They were chums; she shared as no others did his political secrets, with his warnings often not to tell others, for they "must tell it or burst."

They had dined together with Queen Victoria, with several Presidents, and had attended such functions as the Japanese Legation ball, where one Oriental inquired as to Cabinet members' wives dancing the waltz and schottische, "How much are the women paid?" The uncle as a strict Presbyterian instructed his niece, "In all calamitous events we ought to say emphatically, 'Thy will be done.'" After Dr. Gurley's Sunday sermon the President would walk down the center aisle to the door, the congregation standing. Near the door Mrs. Pryor once remarked it was "a good sermon, Mr. President." "Too long, madam, too long." His niece would write to a sister: "I have made another conquest, who comes in the true American style, *every day*. He is rich and keeps a yacht. Beaux are pleasant but dreadfully troublesome." And of another: "He will be sixty next year. He has a daughter who is a widow, and I might pass for *her* daughter. But I like him very much and know how devoted he would be." The uncle advised her as to one beau, "I consider him a rather cold lover to wait for a whole year," and as to another: "I am in favor of a considerable disparity between the ages of husband and wife. Still I do not think your husband ought to be more than double your age." Miss Harriet wrote her "Uncle Buchanan" of a woman who might be a help and he wrote back: "Our loves are mutual. I admire her very much. Return her my love with all my heart; but alas! what signifies the love of a man nearly sixty-four?"

While a hurricane was preparing, these two careful persons lived with their mild secrets in the White House. "Be quiet and discreet and say nothing"—the written advice of the old man to his niece was his own guiding motto. Once he termed himself "an old public functionary." He was old, he was public, and, in a way, functioning. "I at least meant well for my country," ran a line of his January message to Congress in farewell tone. To many he seemed half apparition, ready for the graveclothes that would swathe a past epoch.

During two years of the Buchanan regime Washington Irving, recorder of Rip Van Winkle and the Headless Horseman of Sleepy Hollow, had drifted in and out of White House parties and balls. He would nod in the middle of a conversation, a whisper passing, "Sh-h, Mr. Irving is asleep"; in a minute or two, his eyes open, he would be rubbing his hands, "Well, as we were saying," taking up the talk where it left off. Gathering material for the last of his five-volume *Life of George Washington*, he had said, "I have taken things to pieces and could not put them together again." He met "wearisome muddles" as he tried to picture the First Revolution in America on the eve of the Second.

Amid falling snow at midnight, out of a carriage bundled a mass of shawls and woolen scarfs one winter evening to ring the doorbell at the home of a Virginia Congressman. Inside the house a manservant began unwinding the bundle. Out of it came the Secretary of State, General Lewis Cass, born in 1782, seventy-nine years old, whimpering: "Mr. Pryor, I have been hearing about secession for a long time—and I would not listen. But now I am frightened, sir, I am frightened! I implore you to do what you can." For fifty-six years he had held public office, and the accomplished fact of secession shocked him to tears. He too was more apparition than living man and executive, with his midnight cry to Roger A. Pryor, an active and wrathy secessionist.

"I am a tradition," said sixty-seven-year-old Tom Corwin of Ohio, to whom words were coins of freedom and fun between man and man in good-fellowship, to whom war was betrayal, propaganda, lies, disease, gangrene, filth, famine, blood puddles, boys dying amid rain, mud, rats. An old house dear to him was falling to pieces, and in old rooms where he had for thirty years forgathered with Northern and Southern friends it seemed to him ruin would arrive, black bats' and an echoing emptiness, with spiders weaving their webs in forsaken corners and a night owl singing a watch song in lonesome moonlight. "I cannot anticipate that future," he mourned, and could wish that the House journal clerk had blotted out the record of their proceedings from day to day as conciliation failed and war crept closer.

A comedian, a laughing philosopher, what could Tom Corwin find to laugh at when the declaration he had given to Mexicans in case of American invasion—"We will welcome you with bloody hands to hospitable graves!" —was in the mouths now of Southerners who had sat with him in Congress? Now they snarled in dog-fight intonations in the halls of Congress. Now Ben Wade kept a sawed-off shotgun in his desk. Now General Scott was putting guards at doorways and vantage points to make sure of uninterrupted proceedings when the electoral vote for President would be canvassed on February 13. For thirty years the South had governed, or controlled when it did not govern. Now a House committee was investigating reports of an insurrection secretly under way to seize Washington and the

Government. Even men with young hearts felt old, and Tom Corwin said, "I am a tradition."

"Better for us that the fruitful earth be smitten and become dry dust," mourned Tom Corwin. "Better that the heavens for a time become brass and the ear of God deaf to our prayers; better that Famine with her cold and skinny fingers lay hold upon the throats of our wives and children . . . than that we should prove faithless to our trust . . . and all our bright hopes die out in that night which knows no coming dawn." This was a psalm for the people to hear. To Lincoln he sent an epistle for Lincoln's eye only: "I have been for thirty days in a Committee of Thirty-three," he wrote January 16. Members of Congress from nearly all States South and North served on this committee and it was Corwin's judgment:

If the States are no more harmonious in their feelings and opinions than these thirty-three representative men, then, appalling as the idea is, we must dissolve, and a long and bloody civil war must follow. I cannot comprehend the madness of the times. Southern men are theoretically crazy. Extreme Northern men are practical fools. The latter are really quite as mad as the former. Treason is in the air around us everywhere. It goes by the name of patriotism. Men in Congress boldly avow it, and the public offices are full of acknowledged secessionists. God alone, I fear, can help us. Four or five States are gone, others are driving before the gale. I have looked on this horrid picture till I have been able to gaze on it with perfect calmness. I think, if you live, you may take the oath.

The last two sentences were addedly profound coming from the best wit and storyteller in Washington, who felt himself a presence lingering on a threshold preparing his farewell.

Also more a tradition than a living fact was Senator John Jordan Crittenden of Kentucky, born in 1787, once Governor of Kentucky, twice a Cabinet member, six times elected United States Senator, thrice married, a White House dinner guest of Presidents for forty years, his thrice-married fashionable wife blithely telling women, "My first marriage was for love, my second was for money, my third was for position; what more could I ask?"

Like an omnibus, a raft, an umbrella, a tabernacle, the Crittenden Compromise proposals were to ride on, to save from sinking, to keep out of the rain, to gather for worship. Only the hard of hearing had not heard of the Crittenden Compromise that winter. All territory north of the southern boundary line of Missouri, running to the Pacific Ocean, would be free soil forever, and all territory south of that line would be slave soil forever, by Constitutional Amendment, said the Crittenden Compromise. And the Constitution would furthermore declare that Congress was forbidden ever to abolish slavery or interfere with it in Slave States or in the District of Columbia. Furthermore, the national Government would pay slaveowners for slave property lost through action of mobs or law courts in the North. Thus Old Man Crittenden would bargain with the seceded States and give them all they might ask for to stay in the Union.

And who could blame Old Man Crittenden for this plan from his head, this urge from his heart? Of his two strong sons, Tom was for the Union and the Constitution and George was for secession and the Confederacy. And he wept over the House Divided.

Behind his compromise rallied Douglas, Edward D. Baker, Edward Everett, Thurlow Weed, August Belmont, Cyrus McCormick, many powerful newspapers, including the *New York Herald*, and such authentic and lovable advocates of peace as Tom Corwin. Petitions came to the Senate chamber in bales and stacks. Two thousand citizens of Philadelphia who had voted for Lincoln signed themselves in favor of the Crittenden Compromise. From 182 cities and towns of Massachusetts came the signatures of 22,315 citizens. From Indiana 14,000 women subscribed themselves. Seward put in two petitions of 63,000 New York City men and women praying for some plan of adjustment. Another petition put in by Seward was signed by the New York State attorney general and others, protesting against "petitions and lamentations to Congress on the state of the country" and praying that Congress would "enact suitable and efficient laws against unmitigated scribbling."

When Seward spoke in the Senate, however, standing as the known and announced choice of Lincoln for Secretary of State, he said that in "one, two, or three years hence," when the public mind had resumed its wonted calm, a national convention might be called for amending the Constitution. On the Crittenden Compromise he had no word for or against. From Lincoln he had word that on slavery extension: "I am inflexible. I am for no compromise which assists or permits the extension of the institution on soil owned by the nation." Any trick for spreading slavery was as obnoxious as any other, and would put the country on the high road to a slave empire. "As to fugitive slaves, District of Columbia, slave trade among the slave States, and whatever springs of necessity from the fact that the institution is amongst us, I care but little, so that what is done be comely and not altogether outrageous." To an inquiring Republican-party friend, J. T. Hale, Lincoln wrote, "In my judgment but one compromise would really settle the slavery question, and that would be a prohibition against acquiring any more territory." The pretexts for extorting a compromise . . . were shallow: "We are told in advance the government shall be broken up unless we surrender to those we have beaten, before we take the offices. In this they are either attempting to play upon us or they are in dead earnest. Either way, if we surrender, it is the end of us and of the government. They will repeat the experiment upon us *ad libitum*."

John Brown was out of jail, out of his grave, stalking as a tall ghost of terror and insurrection to the South, moving as an evangel telling the antislavery cohorts of the North that taxes, war, sacrifice, rivers of blood, intimate death and personal obliteration, were better than peace and conciliation bought by saying Yes to slavery. Between extremists South and North, language was gone, words had been sucked of all meaning, and for them any compromise would only mark an intermission filled with further evasions, treacheries, and crimes.

The Crittenden Compromise marched up the hill and then marched down again. The forces against it had been long in growing and breeding, and the snarl of their release was as ancient as it was modern. Behind each event operating for peace came another to cancel it. In November the pale light of the Crittenden concessions might have brought delay and delay would have staved off secession. But the secession conventions, with curses on the Union as they declared for "perpetual separation," had wrought effects. With passing weeks the hour was reached when to Sumner, Wade, Stevens, and others in Congress and over the country the Crittenden proposals seemed an offering of bread and roses as thanks for being spit on. The bitter waters spread far.

Peace efforts were sunk for the moment whenever Senator Wigfall, whose State had not as yet completely and officially seceded, sprayed an easy bravado over his colleagues. "This Federal Government is dead," said Wigfall. "The only question is whether we will give it a decent, peaceable, Protestant burial, or whether we shall have an Irish wake at the burial. [Laughter.] Now, I am opposed to fighting, and would prefer a peaceable burial: but if the Republican Senators insist on fighting, and they can get the backbone again put into their President-elect, I do not know but we shall have to fight." And he laughed sometimes, this Wigfall, as though the Four Horsemen of the Apocalypse were a quartet of fat merry clowns and war meant neither cadavers nor ashes.

Too old and worn to sit in a saddle or work long at a desk, Winfield Scott, the head of the military establishment of the United States, with head-quarters in Winder's Building opposite the War Department, most often was to be found resting on an office sofa. Born in 1786, he would reminisce, "I was three years old when the Constitution was adopted." At Niagara Falls in Canada in the War of 1812 he was a commander of men and had horses shot under him and received two bullets he was still carrying in his body in 1861. At Chapultepec, Vera Cruz, Cerro Gordo, in the Mexican War he had held his saddle and ordered long marches and storming attacks and mapped the campaigns and run the armies of the war. And in 1852 this General Winfield Scott had been the last presidential candidate of the Whig party. A tall bulwark of a man, strict in discipline, author of books on drill regulations, infantry tactics, temperance in liquor, he was nicknamed "Old Fuss and Feathers." Six feet five inches tall, three hundred pounds of weight, in shining gold braid and buttons, in broad epaulets and a long plumed hat, when he walked he seemed almost a parade by himself. When he paused, the apparent parade halted. A Virginia Governor once exclaimed: "What a wonderful mixture of gasconade, ostentation, fuss, feathers, bluster and genuine soldierly talent and courage is this same Winfield Scott! A great smoking mass of flesh and blood!" Small boys waited of a morning to see him come out of his house and move like six regiments toward a waiting carriage. What with age, dropsy, vertigo, and old bullets to carry, he could no longer mount a horse.

He had asked President Buchanan for men and guns to garrison nine Southern forts against seizure. Buchanan refused the request, writing that to grant it would show on his part "a degree of inconsistency amounting almost to self-stultification."

And Scott wagged his head sadly, for this was not like 1832, when President Jackson had given him men and guns to control South Carolina before hotheads could get into action; that war was over before it began.

End of a letter of General Scott asking a hotel management to "please give me a bed at least 6 feet 6 inches in length or one without a foot-board." From original in the Barrett collection.

Now in 1861 the forts were gone, all but two, and any war to come would be long, costly, devastating, as he saw it. Born in Petersburg, raised a Virginian, with pride in the Old Dominion, he had set at rest Lincoln's doubts by sending word through a messenger from Lincoln that he would plant cannon and blow to hell any interference by traitors with the inauguration. In January he received thanks from Lincoln and acknowledgments from the President-elect of "copies of correspondence and notes of conversation with the President of the United States and the Secretary of War concerning various military movements suggested by yourself." Not so easy was the further matter involved when an Illinois Congressman with a letter from Lincoln presented his respects to General Scott with the word from the President-elect, "Tell him, confidentially, I shall be obliged to him to be as well prepared as he can, to either hold or retake the forts, as the case may require, at and after the inauguration."

Scott had asked the Illinois Congressman, Elihu B. Washburne, regarding Lincoln, "Is he a *firm* man?" and on Washburne's answering that Lincoln would do his whole duty "in the sight of the furnace seven times heated," the General said hopefully, "All is not lost." Few of his recommendations to the White House had been agreed with, and he once exclaimed to Washburne, "I wish to God that Mr. Lincoln was in office." Senators Cameron and Baker, after Springfield visits, carried messages of esteem and confidence from Lincoln to Scott. Cameron wrote to Lincoln: "General Scott bids me say he will be glad to act under your orders in all ways to preserve the Union. He says Mr. Buchanan at last has called on him to see that order shall be preserved at the inauguration; he has ordered here two companies of flying artillery, and will organize the militia and have himself sworn in as a constable. The old warrior is roused, and he will be equal to the occasion."

In Scott's own handwriting came a letter to Lincoln that he was "happy to reciprocate his highest respect and esteem," and the President-elect could rely on his utmost service "both before and after the approaching inauguration." He told also of stopping Federal gun shipments to the South, of reinforcing a fort, of steps to guard the count of the presidential electoral vote.

The General raised his giant creaking mass of flesh to a sitting posture on the office sofa on February 8 when L. E. Chittenden, Vermont delegate to the Peace Conference, was shown in. "I know the Vermonters," said the General. "I have commanded them in battle. What can the commander of

An 1861 engraving of the Capitol with unfinished dome

the army do for Vermont?" Chittenden said he was anxious about the count coming in Congress five days later of the electoral votes for Lincoln and Hamlin. Talk ran high of interference and trickery.

"I supposed I had suppressed that infamy," rang the General's trumpet voice. "I have said that any man who attempted by force or unparliamentary disorder to obstruct or interfere with the lawful count of the electoral vote for President and Vice-President of the United States should be lashed to the muzzle of a twelve-pounder and fired out of a window of the Capitol. I would manure the hills of Arlington with the fragments of his body, were he a senator or chief magistrate of my native State! It is my duty to suppress insurrection—my duty!" A few drunken rowdies might lose their lives, but order would be maintained: "While I command the army there will be no revolution in the City of Washington!" And though the General was impressive, Chittenden went away a little doubtful.

On the day of February 11 when Lincoln started on his trip to Washington for inauguration, Burton Craige of North Carolina brought up in the House of Representatives a resolution that the President of the United States be required to acknowledge the independence of the Confederate States and receive any ambassadors or commissioners sent by its Government. Farnsworth of Illinois moved that it be referred to the Committee on Patents, but amid laughter it went to the Committee on Foreign Affairs.

Personal estimates of Lincoln, what he could, would, or might do, went up and down like thermometer mercury. "Lincoln is all right, you can rely on that," Henry Adams wrote from Washington in December, changing his tone late in January to write of "Lincoln's utter ignorance of the right way to act" in appointments, and of how "it is said, too, here, that he is not a strong man." August Belmont in New York wrote of thousands sorry they voted for Lincoln, of his meeting every day "men who confess the error, and almost with tears in their eyes wish they could undo what they helped to do." Up in Boston "nobody knows, everybody guesses," wrote Oliver Wendell Holmes. At a light breath of compromise from Mr. Seward the whole Republican party "sways like a field of grain," while "if Mr. Lincoln says he shall execute the laws and collect the revenues though the heavens cave in, the backs of the Republicans stiffen again."

From the six States signed up for revolution now went Commissioners, agents, and committees, trying to swing the other nine Slave States into line. They pleaded, as they did to the Governor of Kentucky, that Lincoln's election was a decree of race equality, a signal to the Southern Negroes to kill their masters, burn the barns and crops, violate the wives and daughters of the South. "Property worth not less than four hundred million dollars" in African slaves, a fixed domestic institution, was to be confiscated. In religion the two sections had long ago parted company in separate churches. In politics it was time for separation. Why wait longer? "Will the South be better prepared when the North shall be strengthened by the admission of the new Territories of Kansas, Nebraska, Washington, Jefferson, Nevada, Idaho, Chippewa, and Arizona as non-slaveholding States, as we are warned from high sources will be done within the next four years under Mr. Lincoln?" The Kentucky Governor, Beriah Magoffin, replied that Lincoln seemed to be moving toward coercion, civil war, and that a united-front convention of Slave States should meet and formulate declarations that would make him realize the calamity of such a war. The Governor of Missouri, Claiborne F. Jackson, was openly for secession of his State, considered Lincoln's election "a declaration of war upon the whole slave property of the Southern States," in effect "a moral dissolution of the Union." Cool, decisive, was this man in the governor's chair at Jefferson, Missouri, and, in frontier phrase, a dangerous customer. "Let there be no threats, no bravado," he wrote his allies. "Let us take our position in the right and

Harriet Lane

Photograph from Frederick H. Meserve Collection

James Buchanan of Pennsylvania

Photograph from U. S. Army Signal Corps

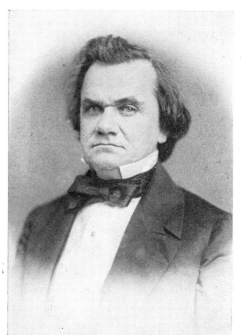

Stephen Arnold Douglas of Illinois

John Jordan Crittenden of Kentucky

Photographs by McClees in author's collection

Richard Yates, Governor of Illinois

Photograph from L. C. Handy Studios

Judge David Davis

From Oliver R. Barrett Collection

Elmer Ephraim Ellsworth

From Oliver R. Barrett Collection

Orville Hickman Browning of Illinois

Photograph from Frederick H. Meserve Collection

FOUR COMPANIONS ON THE TRIP FROM SPRINGFIELD

stand by it to the last." Equally cool, though oppositely convinced in Missouri affairs, were a little redheaded regular-army officer, Nathaniel Lyon, and his ally, Frank Blair, Jr., politician, editor, poker-player, of a family once owning slaves. These two Union men were also dangerous customers, reporting to Lincoln as though they might run the Governor out of the State.

Well-meaning persons came to Lincoln asking him for God's sake to assure the Southerners that he meant them no harm. He answered in the

tone of one of his letters: "I have bad men to deal with, both North and South; men eager for something new upon which to base new misrepresentations; men who would like to frighten me, or at least to fix upon me the character of timidity and cowardice. They would seize upon almost any letter I might write as being an 'awful coming down.' I intend keeping my eye upon these gentlemen, and to not unnecessarily put any weapons in their hands." He might or might not give out a reassuring public statement as requested by a Louisville editor: "I have not decided that I will not do substantially what you suggest. I will not forbear from doing so merely on punctilio and pluck. If I do finally abstain, it will be because of apprehension that it would do harm." To newspaper publication of a letter signed with his name, saying that instead of hanging Old John Brown he would have advised close confinement in prison, Lincoln replied that the letter was a forgery. To one interviewer Lincoln spoke of stories fabricated and spread to create fog and mist in the public mind. He was learning more keenly what Buchanan wrote about that winter to Bennett of the *New York Herald*:

The public mind throughout the interior is kept in a constant state of excitement by what are called "telegrams." They are short and spicy, and can easily be inserted in the country newspapers. In the city journals they can be contradicted the next day; but the case is different throughout the country. Many of them are sheer falsehoods, and especially those concerning myself.

The ready-tongued Donn Piatt told Lincoln war was ahead, and "I doubt whether you will be inaugurated." Lincoln had laughed a reply that Piatt was affected by the fall of pork at Cincinnati. Piatt was disgusted, and came back that in ninety days the land would be whitened with soldier tents. Lincoln's answer was: "Well, we won't jump that ditch till we come to it," and after a pause, "I must run the machine as I find it." To his old law associate and confidant Orville H. Browning, Lincoln talked more freely for an hour, and Browning wrote in his diary on February 9, "He agreed with me that far less evil & bloodshed would result from an effort to maintain the Union and the Constitution, than from disruption and the forming of two confederacies."

The mail one day had brought Lincoln, from South Carolina, a painting of himself in a coat of tar and feathers, chains around his feet, a rope dangling from his neck. It might have been sent by the Charleston man ordering flour from a New York merchant who had answered, "Eat your *cotton*, God damn ye." Rhymes were getting into the papers—

> And the bar strangled muslin, no more shall it wave
> O'er the land of the phree nor the home of the slave.

Although Senator Douglas was asking, "Are we *in our hearts* prepared for war with our brethren and kindred?" the *Indianapolis Sentinel* published a prayer by the Reverend J. W. T. McMullen at Centerville: "I pray God that I may be one of the men who will pull the rope to hang Jeff Davis; and that the spirit of Washington, Jefferson, Jackson and Adams may look over the battlements of Heaven down upon the bleaching carcass, as the flesh drops from the bones, and listen to the winds whistling Hail Columbia and Yankee Doodle through the decaying ribs which once enclosed his corrupt and traitorous heart. Amen."

The California Senator, James A. McDougall, jingling his Mexican spurs like sleigh bells, his trousers thrust in his boots and his boots lifted on his senatorial desk, could see "as many minds as men and no end of wrangling," and was only sure, "I believe in women, wine, whiskey, and war." The less lush Henry Adams of Massachusetts was writing a brother, "No man is fit to take hold now who is not as cool as death."

It was sunset and dawn, moonrise and noon, dying time and birthing hour, dry leaves of the last of autumn and springtime blossom roots. "Nobody knows, everybody guesses."

CHAPTER 2

FROM SPRINGFIELD TO WASHINGTON

THE eleven-day journey of Lincoln from Springfield to Washington for inauguration brought him face to face with the governors and legislators of five States. He set foot in key cities; spoke with important men controlling politics, money, transportation, supplies; delivered more than twenty speeches; shook the hands of thousands of people; took his own look at immense crowds who wanted their look at the pivotal figure of the American scene.

On board the Wabash Railroad train carrying the President-elect over the Indiana cornlands was a party including press correspondents, old Eighth Circuit lawyers, Ward Hill Lamon, Orville H. Browning, Jesse K. Dubois,

TO THE COMMITTEE OF ARRANGEMENTS
For the RECEPTION OF THE PRESIDENT ELECT :

GENTLEMEN:—

Being charged with the responsibility of the safe conduct of the President elect, and his suite to their destination, I deem it my duty, for special reasons which you will readily comprehend, to offer the following suggestions :

First: The President elect will under *no circumstances* attempt to pass through any crowd until such arrangements are made as will meet the approval of Col. Ellsworth, who is charged with the responsibility of all matters of this character, and to facilitate this, you will confer a favor by placing Col. Ellsworth in communication with the chief of your escort, immediately upon the arrival of the train.

SECOND: ARRANGEMENT OF CARRIAGES:

FIRST CARRIAGE,

THE PRESIDENT ELECT,
COL. LAMON, or other Members of his Suite,
One or two members of the Escort or Committee.

SECOND CARRIAGE,

COL. E. V. SUMNER, U S A.,
MAJ. D. HUNTER, U. S. A.,
HON. N. B. JUDD, of Illinois,
HON. DAVID DAVIS, of Illinois.

THIRD CARRIAGE,

COL. E. E. ELLSWORTH,
CAPT. HAZZARD,
JOHN G. NICOLAY, Esq. Private Secretary,
Member of the Escort.

FOURTH CARRIAGE,

ROBT. T. LINCOLN,
JOHN M. HAY, Assistant Secretary,
Two Members of the Escort,

The other members of the suite may be arranged at your pleasure by your committee on the cars. Two carriages will be required to convey Mrs. Lincoln and family and her escort from the cars.

ARRANGEMENT OF ROOMS:

Mr. Lincoln's Secretaries will require rooms contiguous to the President elect.
A private dining room with table for six or eight persons.
Mr. Wood will also require a room near the President elect, for the accommodation of himself and Secretary.
The other members of the suite will be placed as near as convenient.
For the convenience of the committee, a list of the names of the suite arranged in their proper order is appended.
Trusting, gentlemen, that inasmuch as we have a common purpose in this matter, the safety, comfort and convenience of the President elect, these suggestions will be received in the spirit in which they are offered, I have the honor to be your Obedient Servant,

W S. WOOD, Superintendent.

Circular of instructions

Judge David Davis, Norman B. Judd of Chicago, and the two secretaries, John George Nicolay—twenty-nine years old, sandy-haired, brought from Bavaria when he was six years old, not yet a naturalized American citizen, editor of the *Pike County Free Press*, able, systematic, loyal, responsible—and Nicolay's assistant, the somewhat aristocratic John Hay, only twenty-two, witty, suave, adroit, often writing the more formal letters for Lincoln to sign, a descendant of a Revolutionary War veteran, graduate of Brown University, verse-writer and handy with the ladies, admitted to law practice in the supreme court of Illinois. Also there was Governor Richard Yates of Illinois, a loyal Unionist, handsome, curly-haired, a hard drinker given to big talk. Their grave presence a sign, four uniformed regular-army officers and Indian-fighters were on hand, Colonel E. V. Sumner, Major David Hunter, Captain George W. Hazzard, Captain John Pope.

And not least in importance was Colonel Elmer Ephraim Ellsworth, author of a *Manual of Arms* published in 1859, twenty-four years old, welcome as the flowers that bloom in the spring. Committees ahead had been notified, "The President-elect will under no circumstances attempt to pass through any crowd until such arrangements are made as will meet the approval of Colonel Ellsworth, who is charged with the responsibility of all matters of this character." Of the personages on the train Ellsworth was second only to Lincoln in fame and national popularity. Since leaving Mechanicsville, New York, where his father was a tailor, he had been train newsboy, New York dry-goods clerk, Hell Gate construction-gang worker. While an office clerk in Chicago he took over a run-down cadet company, and the reorganized Ellsworth Zouaves had swept the country, won championship colors, performed at West Point for regular-army officers, and on the White House lawn heard President Buchanan, "If war should come I know where you will be found—in the front ranks battling against the enemy." Crowds, one of 70,000, had seen their "lightning drill" with musket, bayonet, knapsack, in scarlet baggy trousers, red caps, blue jackets with orange and yellow trimmings. At more than one Ellsworth Zouave performance branches of trees crashed with the spectators of the moving, dissolving troops forming cross, square, pyramid, human ladder, revolving circle. Banquets, swords, roses by the armful, were handed their short, well-knit leader, theatrical of stride, with "dark-brown hair that fell in careless, clinging curls about his neck, eyes of dark hazel that flashed and sparkled, a face smooth and fair as a maiden's, lips full and red, teeth of dazzling whiteness." He enforced a regime; one Zouave who forgot himself with drink and women in Detroit was given a suit of citizen's clothes and a ticket home. The often skeptical John Hay wrote, "His words were like martial music, his strength extraordinary, he seemed made of tempered steel." Of his picked men a *New York Sunday Mercury* writer burbled: "A fellow who can climb an 80-foot rope, hand over hand, with a barrel of flour hanging to his heels; who can set a 40-foot ladder on end, balance himself on top of it and shoot wild pigeons on the wing, one at a time, just behind the eye; who can take a five-shooting revolver in each hand and knock the spots out of the ten of diamonds at 80 paces, turning somersaults all the time and firing every shot in the air—that is a zouave." The Springfield Grays commander, General John Cook, had written Ellsworth, "I have seen our friend Lincoln," whose wish is "that you should make this place your home, and his office your headquarters." Further, wrote Cook, "He has taken in you a greater interest than I ever knew him to manifest in anyone before." And later Ellsworth had gone to Springfield, had made the Lincoln & Herndon office his headquarters and delivered stump speeches alongside Bill Herndon in country towns for the Lincoln ticket. Only two years back, before his name became familiar to millions, he had written in a diary of what knighthood in Chicago cost him, of how he had gone without food in the midst of plenty, slept on hard boards, received only sneers and kicks, and become "an old man of twenty-two." To a girl at Rockford, Illinois, he wrote: "Your letters are the only stars in my night of loneliness and trouble. Adieu. May God bless you," and again later, "I would give my picture to no woman without your knowledge, as that would not accord with my conception of implicit confidence." John Hay heard him recite lines from Tennyson about "a glorious company, the flower of men," who would swear with conscience as king

> To break the heathen and uphold the Christ,
> To ride abroad redressing human wrongs,
> To speak no slander, no, nor listen to it,
> To lead sweet lives in purest chastity,
> To love one maiden only, cleave to her,
> And worship her by years of noble deeds.

He was a law student in the Lincoln & Herndon office "nominally," wrote John Hay, giving his time to an elaborate bill for militia reorganization in Illinois, which the legislature rejected, and to stump speaking, wherein his deliberate and impressive manner reminded audiences of that other short-statured orator, Steve Douglas. "A relation like that of knight and squire of the age of chivalry existed between Lincoln and Ellsworth," Henry C. Whitney gathered. As a law student Ellsworth displayed no talent, according to Whitney, "and was something of a nuisance in the office, owing to his mislaying papers (one of Lincoln's most important speeches was lost to the world through Ellsworth losing the transcription of it), yet Lincoln patiently bore with him, because he recognized in the young man's one passion, which was for arms, evidence of capacity for military leadership, and he sincerely respected him for it."

Sayings of Ellsworth fitted his chosen role: "I am not better than other men." "Patriotism is not dead, even if it sleeps." Lincoln saw intellect, energy, self-control in this pet lamb of crowds, "a boy only" yet "surpassingly great" in power to command men. They had drawn closer until they were, as Lincoln put it, "as intimate as the disparity of our ages and my engrossing engagements would permit." To the photographer Hesler, Lincoln said after having seen the Zouaves drill and then meeting Ellsworth, "He is the greatest little man I ever met!" Lincoln saw in the boy a personal loyalty that belonged strictly in the adventure of the hour. "A taste altogether military," he saw also in the boy, "the best natural talent in that department I ever knew." In the purple shadows that lengthened out from Ellsworth's boyish frame lurked a million of youths North and South ready to fight for a Cause, a Flag. They might hear fifes and drums, bugles and brasses, the music of treading platoons marching into fog, black night, and red thunder—and their feet would answer before their heads could fathom why.

Armory U S "Zouave Cadets
Chicago June 5/1860

Capt R B Spelman.
Comd. Albany Burgesses Corps.
Albany New York.

My dear Sir

I have the honor to acknowledge on behalf of my Command Your kind favor of May 29th. It will Certainly afford us great pleasure to Accept Your Courtesy on the occasion of our visit to the East. I send You a pamphlet Containing an Account of our Arrangements as far as perfected; In a few days I shall be able to Communicate with You more definitely. In the meantime believe us Under many obligations

Your Obt Servants
E E Ellsworth
Commandant of Cadets.

Meticulous penmanship of the zouave cadet commander in charge of escort and parade arrangements on the journey to Washington

"I find myself far from home and surrounded by thousands I now see before me who are strangers to me," said Lincoln in an unexpected impromptu at Lafayette, Indiana. "Still we are bound together in Christianity, civilization and patriotism. . . . We all believe in the maintenance of the Union, of every star and stripe of the glorious flag." The speech seemed inoffensive, but Lincoln heard later from Jewish church representatives who wished to know since when the United States was exclusively bound to Christianity. Mr. Lincoln was carelessly using the word "Christianity" to indicate religion, said the editor of the *Israelite*: "Mr. Lincoln received the heaviest vote of infidels ever given to any man in this country. We do not believe there is a German infidel, American eccentric, spiritual rapper or atheist in the Northern States who did not vote for Mr. Lincoln. Let us see how much benefit he will derive from their Christianity. . . . He does not care for words. By and by he will learn the precise use and import of terms."

At another stop Lincoln began telling the Slow Horse story, the train pulling away and leaving the story in the air. At the next stop, however, he told it to the end and added, "If my journey goes on at this slow rate it will be resurrection day before I reach the Capitol."

The Wabash train that had left Springfield at eight o'clock in the morning drew into the Indianapolis station at five o'clock, near sundown, to a salute of thirty-four guns. Governor Oliver P. Morton took Lincoln to his carriage and a procession of members of the State legislature, the Mayor, city council, police, troops, firemen, moved to the Bates House, led by cornets and trombones, snare and bass drums, through streets of surging Hoosiers. On the balcony of the Bates House in the chill of a February evening twilight Lincoln looked out on 20,000 people and told them their magnificent reception was certainly no compliment to him personally, but only to him "as a mere instrument, an accidental instrument" of a great cause. Not until he got to Washington would he attempt any lengthy speech. Now he ventured:

I will only say that to the salvation of the Union there needs but one single thing— the hearts of a people like yours. [Applause.] When the people rise in mass in behalf of the Union and the liberties of this country, truly may it be said, "The gates of hell cannot prevail against them." [Renewed applause.] In all trying positions in which I shall be placed, and doubtless I shall be placed in many such, my reliance will be upon you and the people of the United States; and I wish you to remember, now and forever, that it is your business, and not mine; that if the union of these States and the liberties of this people shall be lost, it is but little to any one man of fifty-two years of age, but a great deal to the thirty millions of people who inhabit these United States, and to their posterity in all coming time. It is your business to rise up and preserve the Union and liberty for yourselves, and not for me. I appeal to you again to constantly bear in mind that not with politicians, not with Presidents, not with office-seekers, but with you, is the question: Shall the Union and shall the liberties of this country be preserved to the latest generations? [Cheers and applause.]

In the parlor of the Bates House that night Lincoln met the Governor and members of the legislature, agreed with Solomon there is a time to keep silence: "When men wrangle by the month with no certainty that they mean the same thing, while using the same word, it perhaps were as well if they would keep silence." He asked what the words "coercion" and "invasion" might mean: "Would the marching of an army into South Carolina without the consent of her people, and with hostile intent toward them, be 'invasion'? I certainly think it would; and it would be 'coercion' also if the South Carolinians were forced to submit. But if the United States should merely hold and retake its own forts and other property, and collect the

Special Train.

Hon. O. H. Browning

Sir: You are respectfully invited to participate in the courtesies extended to Hon. Abraham Lincoln, President elect, by the several ——— Rail Road Companys from Springfield to Washington on ——— Feby. 1861.

N. G. Wood,

Through ticket to Washington used by Orville H. Browning only as far as Indianapolis. Original in the Barrett collection.

duties on foreign importations, or even withhold the mails from places where they were habitually violated, would any or all of these things be 'invasion' or 'coercion'?" He was asking. He spoke of professed lovers of the Union "spitefully" resolved to resist coercion or invasion; their affection for the Union seemed thin and airy. "If sick, the little pills of the homeopathist would be much too large for them to swallow. In their view, the Union as a family relation would seem to be no regular marriage, but rather a sort of 'free-love' arrangement, to be maintained only on 'passional attraction.'" He asked if there was a special sacredness in the "assumed primary right of a State to rule all which is less than itself, and ruin all which is larger than itself." He closed: "I am not asserting anything; I am merely asking questions for you to consider."

In the halls and stairways of the Bates House, in the streets in front, the crowd had its way from twilight to midnight. "We did not get much sleep," wrote Browning in his diary. A through ticket to Washington had been handed him, but what he already had of noise, excitement, and social swirl was "just about as much of that sort of thing as I want." He was going back to Springfield and Quincy, taking with him an advance confidential copy of Lincoln's inaugural address. Browning, besides lawyer, was a Kentuckian, a churchman, a gentleman of the old school, an old friend, and Lincoln told him suggestions were welcome.

Yates, Dubois, and others said good-by to Lincoln, locked themselves with Ward Hill Lamon in a room for a session with the distilled spirit of corn and their friend Lamon. They were returning to Illinois. Lamon was going on with Lincoln. And their farewell to Lamon was, in the words of Dubois, "We intrust the sacred life of Mr. Lincoln to your hands; and if you don't protect it, never return to Illinois for we will murder you on sight."

In the morning a crowd straggled out to Governor Morton's house while Lincoln and two army officers took breakfast with the Governor. The breakfast over, the crowd straggled back to the Bates House, to the railroad station, to see the President-elect off to Cincinnati. Two cars filled with Cincinnatians, headed by their Mayor, R. M. Bishop, were coupled to the special train.

On Lincoln's fifty-second birthday he rode across southern Indiana near the grave of Nancy Hanks. At 4:15 in the afternoon he set foot in the largest city in Ohio, stepped into a carriage drawn by six white horses, and saw a grand marshal on horseback, with aides, with platoons of police assisting, try to clear a way for the dignified passage of a procession that included brass bands, fife-and-drum corps, La Fayette Guards, Rover Guards, German Yagers, Zouaves, Guthrie Greys, Washington Dragoons, citizens on horseback, in carriages, afoot. At the Gibson House a transparency 60 feet long and 20 feet high spread out with huge portraits of Lincoln and Hamlin, inscribed with mottoes: "A Union of Hearts, a Union of Hands." "A Union Nothing Can Sever." "The Time Has Come When Demagogues Must Go Under." At the orphan asylum, as Lincoln's carriage passed children sang "Hail Columbia." Farther along, groups of little girls in white frocks sang "The Star-spangled Banner," and as one gave Lincoln a handful of flowers he kissed her.

Mayor Bishop's carriage managed to plow through cheering thousands around the Burnet House, and the Mayor introduced the President-elect, who mentioned how at Indianapolis the day before "I said to myself I have never seen so many people assembled together in winter weather. I am no longer able to say that." He was "entirely overwhelmed by the magnificence of the reception, I will not say to me, but to the President-elect of the United States of America." He would say that all political parties were represented in the vast assemblage before him and he would hope that for centuries to come, under the free institutions of America, there would be such goodwill to the constitutionally elected President of the United States. To Kentuckians just across the Ohio River he would say, "We mean to treat you, as near as we possibly can, as Washington, Jefferson, and Madison treated you," that "under the providence of God, who has never deserted us . . . we shall again be brethren, forgetting all parties, ignoring all parties."

In the evening he held a reception in his suite at the Burnet House. A crowd roared and a band started playing outside. It was a serenade, not on the regular program, by a German workingmen's society. Their leader, Frederick Oberkleine, in behalf of 2,000 members present in person, read an address to Lincoln, who stepped out on a balcony: "We, the German free workingmen of Cincinnati, avail ourselves of this opportunity to assure you, our chosen Chief Magistrate, of our sincere and heartfelt regard. You earned our votes as the champion of Free Labor and Free Homesteads. Our vanquished opponents have, in recent times, made frequent use of the terms 'Workingmen and Workingmen's Meetings' in order to create the impression that the mass of workingmen were in favor of compromises between the interests of free labor and slave labor." Oberkleine warned against "secret treachery," as though politicians make promises and on getting power fail to keep the promises. "We firmly adhere to the principles which directed our votes in your favor." They hoped the President-elect would be true to the platform he was elected on. "If to this end you should be in need of men, the German free workingmen, with others, will rise as one man at your call, ready to risk their lives in the effort to maintain the victory already won by freedom over slavery."

Oberkleine was the voice of the radical antislavery element of Germans, as proportionately solid for Lincoln as the Irish had been for Douglas. His balcony speech to Lincoln had almost a threatening tone, as W. H. Smith, editorial writer on the *Cincinnati Gazette*, heard him. "Some abler man had put into his mouth these significant words," Smith believed.

Lincoln answered as if he knew to begin with just what it was the workingmen serenaders wanted to know. He began an unprepared speech that flowed easier and said more than some of his carefully prearranged addresses: "I thank you and those you represent for the compliment you have paid me by tendering me this address." As to views of national difficulties, "I shall have to beg pardon for not entering fully upon the questions." His duty was to wait "until the last moment for a development of the present national difficulties" before speaking with decision. "I hope, then, not to be false to anything that you have to expect of me." He continued:

I agree with you, Mr. Chairman, that the working-men are the basis of all governments, for the plain reason that they are the more numerous, and as you added that those were the sentiments of the gentlemen present, representing not only the working-class, but citizens of other callings than those of the mechanic, I am happy to concur with you in these sentiments, not only of the native-born citizens, but also of the Germans and foreigners from other countries. . . . Without entering upon the details of the question, I will simply say that I am for those means which will give the greatest good to the greatest number. In regard to the homestead law . . . I am in favor of cutting up the wild lands into parcels, so that every poor man may have a home.

As to Germans and other foreigners, "I esteem them no better than other people—nor any worse." This brought laughter. "It is not my nature, when I see a people borne down by the weight of their shackles—the oppression of tyranny—to make their life more bitter by heaping upon them greater burdens; but rather would I do all in my power to raise the yoke than to add anything that would tend to crush them." This brought cheers and was too grave for laughter. One reporter caught another version of the sentence: "They are all of the great family of men, and if there is one shackle upon any of them it would be far better to lift the load from them than to pile additional loads upon them." He gave his immigration policy in one sentence: "Inasmuch as our country is extensive and new, and the countries of Europe are densely populated, if there are any abroad who desire to make this the land of their adoption, it is not in my heart to throw aught in their way to prevent them from coming to the United States." With this, the President-elect bowed to Oberkleine and the 2,000 German free working-men: "Mr. Chairman and gentlemen, I will bid you an affectionate farewell."

The same evening fifty young men banqueted Robert T. Lincoln at the Burnet House. "Edibles and drinkables in profusion were discussed," said the *Gazette*, "particular attention being paid to Longworth's sparkling Catawba. The volley of corks that flew for a time reminded one of hostile operations." A speech was called for, but "The Prince of Rails," as the press nicknamed him, refused.

A seven-year-old boy of that day in Cincinnati kept a mental picture of what happened to him: his mother tying a wool comforter around his neck, putting on her shawl and bonnet, preparing slices of bread and butter and wrapping them in paper, then half on the run starting with him for the depot two blocks away. They were lucky to find seats on a lumber pile. Hours went by. They ate their bread and butter. Late in the afternoon the train came. The crowd began shoving and nearly heaved mother and boy off the lumber pile. The shoving went on, and at last to save her boy from being trampled she lifted him on her head. "There I sat," he told it, "there I sat, my mother looking between my legs, close where Lincoln passed. I could see him plainly."

A committee from the Ohio Legislature took the President-elect in charge for his ride the next day on the Little Miami Railroad to Columbus. A news-writer on the train found him tired, and resting himself, it seemed, by a steady flow of conversation. He touched on politics only once, then saying that the demands of the South reminded him of his two boys, Tad and Willie, when smaller. One had a toy the other wanted and clamored for. At last when told to let his brother have it in order to keep him quiet, he blurted, "No, sir, I must have it to quiet myself."

"How do you flourish?" Mrs. Lincoln asked a man passing through the rear car.

"Well, I thank you."

"Is that a Cincinnati paper you have in your hand?"

"Yes," passing the journal to her.

"Does it say anything about us?"

Thus the press reported conversation and set many people using the new greeting, "How do you flourish?" Of the travel speed after leaving Cincinnati, one reporter wrote, "The train rushed on at the rate of thirty miles an hour."

A Democratic editor saw Lincoln only at a distance, but Mrs. Lincoln nearer by he found "an unassuming and agreeable lady," and he hoped "she might find in the White House as much satisfaction as in the more modest and retired home in Illinois."

Not yet had Congress declared Lincoln elected President. This was the day excitement ran high in Washington, February 13, the date most often set for the seizure of the Capitol, White House, the governmental works. The electoral vote would come before Congress this day. Warnings had come again of a sort that Seward had written to Lincoln: "A plot is forming to seize the capital on or before the 4th of March, and has its accomplices in the public councils. You must not imagine that I am giving you suspicions and rumors. Believe me that I know what I write." Lincoln's own anxiety about this day had been in his writing to Seward: "Our adversaries have us now clearly at disadvantage. On the second Wednesday of February, when the votes should be officially counted, if the two Houses refuse to meet at all, or meet without a quorum of each, where shall we be? I do not think that this counting is constitutionally essential to the election; but how are we to proceed in absence of it?"

As early as eight o'clock in the morning of February 13 crowds began climbing up Capitol Hill for gallery seats. At every doorway they found armed guards. "Prayers, bribes, oaths, were alike unavailing," wrote L. E. Chittenden. "No one could pass except Senators and Representatives, and those who had the written ticket of admission signed by the Speaker of the House or the Vice-President, the presiding officer of the Senate. Even members of Congress could not pass in their friends." The result, according to Chittenden, was several acres of indignant citizens hurling profanity at the guards and wishing them early and languishing death. As a Peace Conference delegate Chittenden was admitted, took a gallery seat, and talked with a Washington militia colonel in civilian clothes who said his men and their rifles were within easy call. Chittenden wrote of disorder, clashes, and epithets on the House floor that day, of Pennsylvania Avenue "choked with a howling angry mob," of much street fighting and many arrests.

The *Congressional Globe*, however, recorded only mild, orderly proceedings. At twenty minutes after twelve the doorkeeper of the House announced the Senate. And headed by the Vice-President, John C. Breckinridge, the Senate entered; the Vice-President took his seat on the right of the Speaker of the House and presided over the joint convention of the two Houses. The Vice-President announced that in pursuance with the Constitution it became his duty to open the certificates of election. He then handed tellers, appointed by the two Houses, the certificates of election. The tellers read the certificates State by State. Laughter burst when the eight votes of South Carolina were called off for John C. Breckinridge. In a smooth low tone, though he was pale and a little nervous, the Vice-President, a Kentuckian whose heart lay deep with the secession cause, pronounced:

Abraham Lincoln, of Illinois, having received a majority of the whole number of electoral votes, is elected President of the United States for four years, commencing the 4th of March, 1861. Hannibal Hamlin, of Maine, having received a majority of the whole number of electoral votes, is duly elected Vice-President of the United States for four years, commencing the 4th of March, 1861.

So ended fear and rumor and muttered prophecy that the certificates of election would be lost, stolen, manipulated. Saloon and barroom talk mainly had raised up a ghost revolution and sent it around to raise a scare. "You could tell where a man had been drinking by where he located the start of the revolution." General Scott, however, had made quiet preparations to meet trickery or violence. Many guards not openly on duty watched the messengers carrying Lincoln's certificates of election. A hundred special policemen in plain clothes, brought from Philadelphia and New York, were scattered in gallery and corridor, ready with revolver and club. The quiet of Scott's methods annoyed Muscoe R. H. Garnett of Virginia, who in the House protested Scott's removal of a Maryland captain, replaced by one from Maine for Washington duty. "Have you not," asked Garnett, "troops posted at all the available avenues to this Capitol, kept, as we are told, in secret, ready to march into this Hall whenever any disorder may occur? Is there not artillery enough here for an army of ten thousand men?"

A military despotism was coming, Garnett could see: "Look at the progress of Lincoln from his home in the West; at the military escort, before unheard of; at the fawning sycophancy and adulatory praises of the thousands who have met him at every stopping place. Look at the minuteness with which every detail is paraded before the public in the newspapers; the description of the rooms in which he sleeps, the chairs in which he sits, how he has a bow for one, a smile for another, and a kiss for a third; the growth of his whiskers commented on. Sir, I challenge you to find in any English newspaper the reports of the journeys of Victoria, so filled with fawning flattery as our daily accounts of the progress of this northwestern Republican President." Garnett went on to say that Secretary of the Treasury John A. Dix, in telegraphing to New Orleans, "If anyone attempts to haul down the American flag, shoot him on the spot," was disregarding all law and "if this order ended in a murder, the Secretary would be an accessory before the fact." Garnett would have colored his point a little differently had he known that Dix's telegram was hauled down by Confederate telegraph censors at New Orleans and never reached anyone at that hour willing to shoot for the American flag. The atmosphere in which Lincoln's election was certified in Congress that week was partly reflected in the *Congressional Globe* item:

MR. GARNETT. I am in favor of the State of Virginia seceding from this northern Union at the earliest possible moment. [Great applause on the floor and in the galleries, mingled with some hisses.]

MR. BARR [Thomas J., of New York]. I hope order will be preserved here. If this occurs again, I shall ask that the galleries be cleared.

MR. HINDMAN [Thomas C., of Arkansas]. It is the first time there has been a patriotic demonstration here for two or three weeks.

THE CHAIRMAN. The Chair would say that gentlemen upon the floor ought not to set the example of applause.

When Garnett further protested "the forms of an imperial court which attend the progress of the Republican president-elect," Samuel R. Curtis of Iowa arose with the information that the standing army of United States troops menacing peace in Washington numbered exactly 900. Garnett went on record: "Recapture the forts and arsenals! March your armies to Baton Rouge and Augusta! Besiege Forts Pulaski and Morgan; and command Savannah and Mobile! Storm Barrancas and repossess yourselves of the Pensacola navy-yard! Do you dream that any or all of this can be done without rivers of blood?"

Thus the winds blew and the ship of state rocked and shook while Lincoln rode on his special train on the Little Miami Railroad to the State capital of Ohio. Making speeches with nothing to say, he told Lamon, was the hardest work he had ever done: "I wish this thing were through with, and I could find peace and quiet somewhere." Yet he must have said more than nothing at Indianapolis, for a letter had arrived to young Colonel Ellsworth from his elder acquaintance, Colonel Simon Bolivar Buckner, West Pointer, Mexican War veteran, and Kentuckian, saying it was plain that Lincoln wanted war—and war he would get.

To the State legislature at Columbus that night Lincoln made a speech peculiar from several angles. He agreed with the chairman as to the "weighty" responsibility the voters of America had placed on him:

I cannot but know what you all know, that without a name, perhaps without a reason why I should have a name, there has fallen upon me a task such as did not rest even upon the Father of his Country; and so feeling, I can turn and look for that support without which it will be impossible for me to perform that great task. I turn, then, and look to the American people, and to that God who has never forsaken them. Allusion has been made to the interest felt in relation to the policy of the new administration. In this I have received from some a degree of credit for having kept silence, and from others some deprecation. I still think I was right. . . . In the varying and repeatedly shifting scenes of the present, and without a precedent which could enable me to judge by the past, it has seemed fitting that before speaking upon the difficulties of the country I should have gained a view of the whole field, being at liberty to modify and change the course of policy as future events may make a change necessary.

Then he spoke five sentences that brought inquiry, derision, belittlement of him:

I have not maintained silence from any want of real anxiety. It is a good thing that there is no more than anxiety, for there is nothing going wrong. It is a consoling circumstance that when we look out there is nothing that really hurts anybody. We entertain different views upon political questions, but nobody is suffering anything. This is a most consoling circumstance, and from it we may conclude that all we want is time, patience, and a reliance on that God who has never forsaken this people.

Fellow-citizens, what I have said I have said altogether extemporaneously, and I will now come to a close.

The five words "there is nothing going wrong" were seized for editorials, speeches, conversations.

What could they mean?

And those seven other words "there is nothing that really hurts anybody," what could they mean?

What manner of national spokesman was this when six States were out of the Union and others hung by an eyelash? "Have not our forts and vessels been seized, our arsenals invaded, our mints robbed, by men and States in arms?" asked Edwin R. Reynolds of New York in the House at Washington. "Has not our flag been fired into, our mails rifled and intercepted, our commerce on the Mississippi obstructed? Is not the public mind today, North and South, convulsed as never before? What else crowds the bursting columns of the daily and weekly journals wherever published? What other topic now feeds the thunders of the London *Times* and attracts more undivided attention from European Governments?"

"I am doubly thankful you have appeared here to give me this greeting," said Lincoln on the west steps of the capitol at Columbus, receiving a wildly shoving crowd whose outer rim blended into black melting night. "It is not much to me, for I shall soon pass away from you; but we have a large country and a large future before us."

This too had the half-trancelike color of his saying earlier that without a name, perhaps without a reason why he should have a name, there had fallen on him an awful task. The *Ohio State Journal* noted that he "looked somewhat worn with travel and the fatigues of popularity," yet also "something in his manner, even more than in his words, told how deeply he was affected by the enthusiasm of the people."

Into the rotunda of the capitol surged waves of handshakers. Lanes were made for them. And the lanes crumbled. "A few Spartans held back the crowd," wrote W. T. Coggeshall, State librarian. "For a while he greeted with his right hand only, but as officers gave way before the irresistible crowd, he shook hands right and left with astonishing rapidity. People plunged at his arms with a frantic variety of shakes, from the wild pump-handle to the dead grip. Some glanced into his face, others gave him their last gasping assurance of devotion, others with hats crushed over their eyes, seized his hand in a convulsive grasp and passed on as if they had not the remotest idea who, what, or where they were. At last the President-elect retired to the staircase in exhaustion and contented himself with looking at the crowd as it swept before him."

Open murmurs of disapproval came from some of the crowd, in the tone of one handshaker who had brought a laugh from Lincoln by saying, "Abe, you've got to give them rebels hotter shot than that before they're licked." At his side during part of the tumult were Governor William Dennison and William G. Deshler, a leading banker, with no words of approval for either his speech or his silence.

At least, however, that night a telegram had come through from Washington: "The votes have been peaceably counted. You are elected."

In three days' speaking he had the country well baffled, at Indianapolis telling the Hoosiers "to rise in mass," at Cincinnati facing toward Kentucky and crying, "Friends! brethren!" to the Border State people, and in Columbus saying "there is nothing going wrong." Thaddeus Stevens in the House corrected a statement: "I did not say that the incoming administration would unquestionably take the forts. I said that if Mr. Lincoln was what I understood him to be when I voted for him, then, when he came in, he would retake the property of which we had been robbed." John Y. Brown of Kentucky was sure that "judging from Mr. Lincoln's Indianapolis speech, we are to be plunged into the midst of the horrors of civil war. God forbid it."

Earnestly Edward Everett in Boston wrote in his diary of "the zigzag progress" of the President-elect to Washington: "These speeches thus far have been of the most ordinary kind, destitute of everything, not merely of felicity and grace, but of common pertinence. He is evidently a person of very inferior cast of character, wholly unequal to the crisis." The *Sun* at Baltimore shone forth with comment: "We begin to wonder what manner of man he is. There is that about his speechification which, if it were not for the gravity of the occasion, would be ludicrous to the destruction of buttons. Indeed we heard his Columbus speech read yesterday amidst irresistible bursts of laughter. And it was suggested, in the language of Dr. Holmes, that Mr. Lincoln is a man who ought never to be as funny as he can. We begin to realize his qualifications as a barroom 'Phunny Phellow.' "

In "drippings from the inaugural," Mr. Lincoln was losing the high reputation he had gained as a stump speaker, was showing "no capacity to grapple manfully with the dangers of this crisis," said the *New York Herald:* "If Mr. Lincoln has nothing better to offer upon this fearful crisis than the foolish consolations of his speech in Columbus, let him say nothing at all." Publisher Bennett, however, permitted Henry Villard, his correspondent on the Lincoln train, to report in the *Herald:* "No one can see Mr. Lincoln without recognizing in him a man of immense power and force of character and natural talent. He seems so sincere, so conscientious, so earnest, so simple-hearted, that one cannot help liking him. . . . With a great self-possession and self-control, with the intimate knowledge of politics and politicians, and with the uncommon homespun common sense which his friends claim for him, Lincoln seems a man to act and decide for himself, and not be entrapped. He seems tremendously rough, and tremendously honest." The Democratic *New York World*, financially supported by August Belmont, was at moments sympathetic: "Mr. Lincoln is forced to mount the stump at every little railway station, and to remain there till the bell rings or the whistle blows. He makes his way to his lodging through people who crowd almost upon him, and pull and push him around to their heart's content, but not to his. What he has said thus far has been wise, and to the purpose; but how much better if he had been able to maintain his silence until he broke it, speaking with the power and the authority of the President of the United States."

The partisan country weekly of Democratic stripe was typified in the *Salem Advocate* of southern Illinois, aiming to enlighten its readers: "The illustrious President-elect of this great Republic having once opened his mouth cannot shut it again. Since he started from home with the White House full in view he has been troubled with a perfect diarrhoea of words. We learn that sensible leaders of the Republican party have telegraphed him to check his garrulous tongue."

Senator Wigfall of Texas told his colleagues he had expected no better enlightenment from a man elected President by the North "because he is an ex-rail splitter, an ex-grocery keeper, an ex-flatboat captain, and an ex-Abolition lecturer." Mrs. Chesnut, in Montgomery, Alabama, with her husband, wrote of a California woman describing Lincoln: "Awfully ugly, even grotesque in appearance, the kind who are always at the corner stores . . . whittling sticks, and telling stories as funny as they are vulgar." Mrs. Chesnut interposed: "But Stephen A. Douglas said one day to Mr. Chesnut, 'Lincoln is the hardest fellow to handle I have ever encountered yet.' " The California woman's husband retouched his wife's impression of Lincoln: "An utter American specimen, coarse, rough, and strong; a good-natured, kind creature; as pleasant-tempered as he is clever, and if this country can be joked and laughed out of its rights he is the kind-hearted fellow to do it."

At seven-thirty o'clock on the morning of February 14 the Lincoln special pulled out of Columbus and, what with long stops, made an all-day run to Pittsburgh. At the Steubenville stop, the President-elect murmured in modesty again: "I fear that the great confidence placed in my ability is unfounded. Indeed, I am sure it is." Amid the difficulties, "Nothing shall be wanting on my part, if sustained by God and the American people." The Constitution under which he was elected favored majority rule. If his policy proved wrong, then in four years' time "I can be turned out, and a better man with better views put in my place."

Heavy rain poured down as the train entered Pittsburgh at eight o'clock in the evening. The procession was cheerless. Cavalry horses stamped and reared their plunging hoofs dangerously close to the Lincoln carriage. At the Monongahela House after dinner a crowd called for a speech. Lincoln said he was surprised at seeing so great a crowd and such enthusiasm manifested in the nighttime to greet so unworthy an individual as himself. He would remark further that if all those whole-souled people whom he saw this evening before him were for the preservation of the Union, he did not see how it could be in much danger. "Go on!" the crowd called. He said he would—in the morning.

In the morning he thanked Mayor Wilson and the citizens for a "flat-tering reception," again said he would speak on the national difficulties when the time arrived, hoped that when he did then finally speak he would say nothing to disappoint the people generally throughout the country, and once more threw out soothing words of a bright outlook, further baffling the better-informed philosophers. Pointing southward across the Mononga-hela River "and smiling," said the press accounts, he urged:

Notwithstanding the troubles across the river, there is no crisis but an artificial one. What is there now to warrant the condition of affairs presented by our friends over the river? Take even their own view of the questions involved, and there is nothing to justify the course they are pursuing. I repeat, then, there is no crisis, excepting such a one as may be gotten up at any time by turbulent men aided by designing politicians. My advice to them, under such circumstances, is to keep cool. If the great American people only keep their temper on both sides of the line, the troubles will come to an end, and the question which now distracts the country will be settled, just as surely as all other difficulties of a like character which have originated in this government have been adjusted. Let the people on both sides keep their self-possession, and just as other clouds have cleared away in due time, so will this great nation continue to pros-per as heretofore.

He gave briefly the standard Republican arguments for a protective tariff as benefiting mechanic, farmer, manufacturer. He called Nicolay, "who has younger eyes," to read the tariff plank of the Chicago convention, said there would be shades of difference in construing the plank, and made it plain that he did not regard himself as a tariff expert: "I have by no means a thoroughly matured judgment upon this subject, especially as to details; some general ideas are about all." He would recommend each member of Congress "to post himself thoroughly" on such tariff adjustments as would be just and equal to all sections and classes of the country.

At the town of Freedom, Pennsylvania, a coal-heaver yelled from the crowd, "Abe, they say you're the tallest man in the United States, but I don't believe you're any taller than I am." Lincoln replied from the rear platform of the train, "Come up here and let's measure." The dusty shoveler in work clothes pushed through the crowd, climbed up, and stood back to back with the President-elect. The two men were so near the same height that short Colonel Ellsworth was asked to referee. He clambered up on a guard rail, ran his hand along the tops of the two heads, and called out that they were exactly the same height. The crowd cheered. The two tall men grinned and shook hands. And here and there earnest people said it was no way for a public man to act with a coal-heaver, and what was the country coming to?

Into Ohio again and up to Cleveland chugged the special train, arriving at 4:30 P.M. Artillery roared salutes. Through rain and mud two miles marched the procession of honor to the Weddell House. Again Lincoln said he knew the honor was not to him but to the Constitution. Again he said that the crisis was artificial:

In all parts of the nation there are differences of opinion on politics; there are differences of opinion even here. You did not all vote for the person who now addresses you, although quite enough of you did for all practical purposes, to be sure. What they do who seek to destroy the Union is altogether artificial. What is happening to hurt them? Have they not all their rights now as they ever have had? Do not they have their fugitive slaves returned now as ever? Have they not the same Constitution that they have lived under for seventy-odd years? Have they not a position as citizens of this common country, and have we any power to change that position? [Cries of "No!"] What then is the matter with them? Why all this excitement? Why all these complaints? As I said before, this crisis is altogether artificial. It has no foundation in fact. It can't be argued up, and it can't be argued down. Let it alone, and it will go down itself.

Thus from city to city, and no day of rest, and again six milk-white horses, or eight glossy blacks, with red plumes on their heads and flags in the harness, festoons and bunting of red, white, and blue in the roaring streets, and packed human sidewalks.

One hilarious Ohio admirer presented him with a whistle made of a pig's tail. He blew into it, found it whistled, and laughed. "I never suspected there was music in such a thing as that."

When Lincoln bowed to a crowd at the Wellsville, Ohio, station and begged to be excused from a speech, a citizen with two red apples stepped forward and handed them to the President-elect. A small boy yelled, "Say, Mr. Lincoln, that man is running for postmaster!" The crowd understood and Lincoln joined them in the laugh.

Along Lake Erie's blue and amethyst waters sped the special train. Horace Greeley showed on board, carrying, as usual on a lecture trip, a pair of red-and-blue blankets and a valise. He talked twenty minutes with Lincoln and got off at Erie.

Lincoln thought of a little girl who had written to him asking if he had daughters, and suggesting his face should have whiskers. He had answered that his family held a mother, three sons, but no daughters, and it might look like a piece of silly affectation for him to begin raising whiskers. He remembered that her town was Westfield, New York, and after he spoke greetings there from the rear platform, he told the crowd, "I have a correspondent in this place, and if she is present I would like to see her." No one came forward. "Who is it? Give us her name," came from the crowd. "Her name is Grace Bedell." And Grace was led and carried toward the platform, Lincoln saying, "She wrote me that she thought I would be better looking if I wore whiskers." He looked down at the little girl and said, "You see, I let these whiskers grow for you, Grace." Then he kissed her.

Far and wide went the press item about this. The *New York Tribune* headlined "Old Abe Kissed by Pretty Girl." The *St. Louis Republican,* under the head of "Whiskers and Kisses," jibed: "If kissing pretty girls is a Presidential privilege, Mrs. Lincoln, who knows her rights and knowing dares maintain them, ought to insist on a veto power for herself."

Trying to stem the human surges around the President-elect in Buffalo,

Major David Hunter of the regular army had his collarbone dislocated. A German Sängerbund offered songs. The crowd made merry over a man at a sawbuck sawing away to pay an election bet that Lincoln would lose. On the platform alongside Lincoln sat the pleasant, chubby-faced ex-President Millard Fillmore. The *New York Herald* man sketched Lincoln as towering in sight above all others, "with his face and forehead furrowed by a thousand wrinkles, his hair unkempt, his new whiskers looking as if not yet naturalized, his clothing illy arranged." Versifiers had begun on the whiskers, joined to piety:

> I'll put my trust in Providence,
> And let my whiskers grow.

Again Lincoln said he knew that the demonstration was not to him personally, and he would speak on national difficulties when he had all the light possible. He agreed with the Mayor of Buffalo that it was "a fortunate and agreeable journey" he had been having, and it was as it should be that he was met "not alone by those who assisted in giving the election to me—but by the whole population of the country through which we have passed." As to the Mayor's hope that he would relieve the country of its difficulties, he was sure of bringing a heart true to the work.

The next day was Sunday and Lincoln and his wife joined ex-President Fillmore in attendance at the Unitarian church, dined with the ex-President. And Lincoln at the American Hotel for a day rested his throat, so noticeably hoarse the day before. The hotel-owner's boy and Tad and Willie got up a game of leapfrog and Lincoln leaped a few times to show them he could. The trip thus far was a gay one for Tad and Willie. Their favorite sport, the press writers noticed, was to step up to someone seeking the President-elect and say, "Do you want to see Old Abe?" Then they would point out someone who wasn't Old Abe—and quietly hide to watch the stranger.

Eastward into the Erie Canal zone moved the Lincoln train in the morning, and at Rochester he confessed to being overwhelmed "with this vast number of faces at this hour of the morning." The handsome platform rigged up for him at Syracuse was too much of a platform for such a speech as he would make, he said, and "though I am unwilling to go upon this platform, you are not at liberty to draw any inferences concerning any other platform with which my name has been or is connected." At Utica he said he had no speech but appeared to see and be seen. "So far as the ladies are concerned, I have the best of the bargain." As to the men he wouldn't say the same.

Whether the crowd was large or small, he always told it, "I bid you farewell," in no case saying he might be seeing them again some time. Also invariably in the larger cities he mentioned the outpouring of people, the vastness of the assemblage before him, as though he might wish that wherever his speeches were read they would know he believed that the masses were alive and potential.

To the governors of States and to key men of importance with whom he could speak in confidence, he gave such counsel as he had written when Governor Andrew Gregg Curtin of Pennsylvania asked his advice: "I think you would do well to express without passion, threat or appearance of boasting, but, nevertheless, with firmness, the purpose of yourself and your State, to maintain the Union at all hazards. Also if you can, procure the legislature to pass resolutions to that effect."

While Lincoln crossed the Empire State from west to east that Monday of February 18, the news came over the wires that down in Montgomery, Alabama, on the Romanesque portico of the State House amid thundering cannon and cheers on cheers from an immense crowd, Jefferson Davis took his oath as President of the Confederate States of America, six today and more tomorrow. Between the agricultural people of the South and "any manufacturing or navigating community such as the Northeastern States of the American Union" there could be little rivalry, said the Davis inaugural address, and there might be mutual interest, good and kind interchanges. As a necessity and not as a choice they were taking their place among independent nations of the earth. If denied that place, they would seek "the final arbitrament of the sword"; they would with firm resolve "appeal to arms and invoke the blessings of Providence on a just cause."

An actress, Maggie Mitchell, "danced a flag dance trampling the stars and stripes beneath her nimble feet while the audience yelled itself speechless at her timely antics" in the leading theatre of Montgomery. At several places the old American flag was given burial with funeral dirges and singing of the newly published song "Farewell to the Star-spangled Banner."

On the same day, in Washington the Committee on Military Affairs reported in the House a measure to give the incoming President exceptional powers. Roger Pryor of Virginia exaggerated but slightly when screaming against it, "The bill authorizes the President to grasp all the military and naval resources of the country—the militia as well as the regular service—millions of men—and to hurl them in fatal attack upon a member of this Confederacy."

For the first time since leaving home, Lincoln on that Monday of February 18 publicly admitted weariness, ending a short speech from the steps of the capitol at Albany, "I have neither the voice nor the strength to address you at any greater length." Up a long drag of a hill from the railroad station had moved horsemen, police, troops, carriages of honor, pausing at the Delavan House, passing near the local theatre, where the tragedian John Wilkes Booth was playing in *The Apostate*, on to the capitol grounds. There Lincoln thanked the crowd for "this most hearty and magnificent welcome," and went on to remark that in any country where freedom of thought is tolerated, citizens attach themselves to political parties. "And when an election is past, it is altogether befitting a free people, as I suppose, that, until the next election, they should be one people."

He was introduced by Governor Edwin D. Morgan, millionaire merchant and philanthropist, chairman of the Republican National Committee since 1856. His evening address was before the State legislature, whose members consisted, according to *Harper's Weekly*, of a few honest men and cormorants, thieves, and "novices in corruption who do not know enough to make sale of their virtue." He thanked them for their generous manners in inviting him and receiving him.

The personal humility he had spoken in five States reached its lowest shrinking-point in the Hall of Assembly of the New York capitol: "It is with feelings of great diffidence, and, I may say, with feelings of awe, perhaps greater than I have recently experienced, that I meet you here in this place. The history of this great State, the renown of those great men who have stood here, and have spoken here, and been heard here, all crowd around my fancy, and incline me from any attempt to address you." Their gratifying reception was to him not as a person but as "the representative of the majesty of this great nation." It were fitting he should close these hasty remarks: "It is true that, while I hold myself, without mock modesty, the humblest of all individuals that have ever been elevated to the presidency, I have a more difficult task to perform than any one of them."

He would not speak of policy until he had seen and heard everything that could bring light. "When the time comes I shall speak, as well as I am able, for the good of the present and future of this country—for the good both of the North and of the South—for the good of the one and the other, and of all sections of the country. In the mean time, if we have patience, if we restrain ourselves, if we allow ourselves not to run off in a passion, I still have confidence that the Almighty, the Maker of the universe, will, through the instrumentality of this great and intelligent people, bring us through this as he has through all the other difficulties of our country."

Factional Republican leaders were bringing up the matter of Federal patronage. Press writers tried to guess the next postmasters. One wrote: "Will he favor Weed or Greeley? Either would give a small fortune to know. Lincoln acts cautiously. If he is closeted with Greeley one hour, he gives, soon, an hour to Weed. If he takes Greeley's arm, he walks upstairs by Weed's side. If he dines with Weed's governor, he sleeps at Greeley's hotel."

Weed at Albany asked about Lincoln's headquarters in Washington before moving into the White House. An army officer aboard the train had rented a house, Weed protesting: "It will never do to allow him to go to a private house. He is now public property and ought to be where he can be reached until he is inaugurated." Weed arranged for Lincoln to stay at Willard's Hotel in Washington, Lincoln agreeing: "The truth is, I suppose I am now public property; and a public inn is the place where people can have access to me."

Then down the Hudson River, past the purple Catskills, greetings at Troy, Hudson, Peekskill. Young Bob Lincoln rode the locomotive cab part way. At Poughkeepsie, the President-elect told the crowd he must rely on the people of the whole country. "With their sustaining aid, even I, humble as I am, cannot fail to carry the ship of state safely through the storm."

Then New York, the Front Door to America, where tall ships came in from the seven seas to one of the great world ports; where the 35,000 votes for Lincoln for President were a third of the total ballots; where had grown up the financial center of the country, with vast controls over trade, manufacture, transportation; where more transactions in cash and on paper took place than anywhere else in the Western Hemisphere; where commerce was a sensitive organic current responsive to fortunes and calamities a thousand miles away; where bankers, wholesalers, retailers, operated through the post office, steamships, railroads, canals, reaching the whole network of American life; where the fashions of women's gowns and men's coats and hats were decreed; where the newest popular songs came from; where drama, opera, and the merchandised amusements of the land were centralized and had their starting-points; where powerful newspapers, magazines, and publishing houses stretched out across the country with influence as opinion-makers shaping the habits, speech, and ideas of millions of people; where Beecher, Greeley, and Barnum were a famous and talked-of trio, a preacher, an editor, and a showman who studied the wants of masses of people; where Commodore Cornelius Vanderbilt, the Dutch farm boy, had become a steamboat king with millions, and had quiet plans for joining railroads into one through line from New York to Chicago; where the richest man, William B. Astor, son of John Jacob, had run his inheritance of $20,-000,000 up into $30,000,000, mostly in real estate and tenements bringing him $1,000,000 a year to add to what he already had; where A. T. Stewart, the poor Irish boy, had climbed into a fortune of $10,000,000 operating America's largest department store, with a startling innovation of selling goods at one price and one only; where A. T. Stewart was writing to Weed that week, "The refusal at Washington to concede costs us millions daily"; where poverty and disease ran gaunt and festering in miles of reeking slums; where gold and ashes, silks and rags, gathered in a gray monotonous melodrama broken with flashes of crime and heroism; where more Germans were housed than in any other city in the world except Berlin or Vienna; where Irish sway had brought a saying, "Erin e Pluribus, Unum go Bragh"; where Italian cooks, French milliners, German musicians, breeders of fast horses, and designers of coaches and carriages met the whims of those having means to be scrupulous or lavish in pleasure, while Barnum's museum, wandering German brass bands, and hand organs with monkeys catered to a working class that had the poorhouse stood off by a month or two; where gamblers, saloonkeepers, and the sporting and prize-fight element held the balance of power and swung control in politics; where Gazaway Bugg Lamar, a prosecession Georgian, was president of the Bank of the Republic, a fiscal agent of the Southern Confederacy, shipping muskets in large quantities to the South all winter, and participating in vague plans for the secession of New York City from the Union; where Mayor Fernando Wood had declared that New York should establish itself as a Free City, separate from the Union, and become sovereign in itself like the seceded States of the

South, thereby holding its trade and continuing "uninterrupted intercourse with every section" of the country; where bribe money had passed in franchise and city land deals; where the Mayor, as a party boss, had taken $5,000 apiece from two lawyers for nominations for supreme-court judgeships; where the Mayor and his aldermen awarded a street-cleaning contract for $279,000 when another bidder bid $84,000 less; where the Mayor's personal fortune had risen to at least $250,000 out of politics; where only the corruption of the courts of justice had saved the Mayor from conviction of forgery, perjury, and other crimes; where the Mayor and his brother Ben owned lotteries and were licensed as professional gamblers through charters

The President-elect enters a carriage drawn by six horses at the Hudson River Railroad depot in New York City—from *Harper's Weekly*

from Southern States; where the Mayor and his brother Ben owned the *New York Daily News*, openly advocated the rights of the Confederate States, and covertly urged secession of New York City; where the *New York Herald* in a specially spaced editorial was asking: "What will Mr. Lincoln do when he arrives? What will he say to the citizens of this great metropolis? Will he kiss our girls, and give a twirl to the whiskers which he has begun to cultivate? Will he tell our merchants groaning under the pressure of the greatest political convulsion ever experienced in America that 'nobody is hurt' or that 'marching troops into South Carolina' and bombarding its fortresses is 'no invasion'?"

Arriving in this turmoil of fables and fortunes at three o'clock in the afternoon, and leaving the Hudson River Railroad depot at Thirtieth Street and Ninth Avenue, Lincoln rode in a procession of thirty carriages led by a platoon of mounted police. His open carriage, known as a barouche, had accommodated the Prince of Wales a few months before. A small boy hooked on and rode the rear springs two blocks. Across Twenty-third Street near Eighth Avenue was a banner: "Fear Not, Abraham, I Am with Thee." At the Astor House five hundred policemen held the crowds in line.

For the first time on his journey Lincoln faced a crowd of peculiar curiosity, its silence having a touch of the sinister. The cheers and shouts were not like Buffalo, Columbus, Indianapolis. The *New York Herald* said it was plain that the masses of people were not rejoicing and clamorous as when on the same spot they welcomed La Fayette, Jackson, Webster, Kossuth, Clay, the Prince of Wales. The poet Walt Whitman agreed with the *Herald* that the crowd was lacking "that indescribable human roar and magnetism, unlike any other sound in the universe, the glad exulting thunder-shouts of countless unloos'd throats of men."

Friends of Lincoln and outspoken enemies had come armed to that Astor House reception, it was rumored, with a vague understanding that it might be better for both sides to be quiet and start nothing. From the jam of carriages Walt Whitman noted: "A tall figure step'd out, paus'd leisurely on the sidewalk, look'd up at the granite walls and looming architecture of the grand old hotel—then, after a relieving stretch of arms and legs, turn'd round for over a minute to slowly and good-humoredly scan the vast and silent crowds. . . . He look'd with curiosity upon that immense sea of faces, and the sea of faces return'd the look with similar curiosity. In both there was a dash of comedy, almost farce, such as Shakespere puts in his blackest tragedies."

Whitman noted Lincoln's "perfect composure and coolness—his unusual and uncouth height, his dress of complete black, stovepipe hat pushed back on the head, dark-brown complexion, seam'd and wrinkled yet canny-looking face, black, bushy head of hair, disproportionately long neck, and his hands held behind as he stood observing the people."

To sketch this figure properly, inside and out, Whitman believed, would require "the eyes and brains and finger-touch of Plutarch and Eschylus and Michael Angelo, assisted by Rabelais."

Those within hearing heard Lincoln on the hotel balcony say that if he did speak he would be heard by only a small fraction of those present, and "what is still worse than that, I have nothing just now to say that is worthy of your attention."

Ushered into an Astor House room where Daniel Webster and Henry Clay had made speeches, his own had to consist of saying that it was no time for a speech. He had by now, however, practiced so much at saying there was nothing to say that he had become skilled in wearing his cloak of silence and in talking about why he must wait before he really said anything when he spoke. Both the gravity and the humor of it dawned on the members of the Republican Clubs of New York, who heard him in the Astor House. Their responses were interspersed in the complete text of the address as reported in *Harper's Weekly:*

I am rather an old man to avail myself of such excuses as I am now about to do; yet the truth is so distinct, and presses so distinctly upon me, that I cannot well avoid it—that is, that I did not understand when I was brought into a room where Daniel Webster and Henry Clay had made speeches, and where I, in my position, am expected to do something like those men, or at least say something worthy of myself. I therefore beg you to make allowance for the circumstances under which I have been by surprise brought before you. I have been very much in the habit of thinking, and sometimes speaking, on the questions that have agitated the people. If I were disposed to do so, and we were to take up some of the issues, and I was called upon to make an argument, I could do it without much deliberation. But that is not what you desire to have done here tonight.

I have been occupying the position, since the election, of silence—of avoiding public speaking. I have been doing so because I thought, upon due consideration, that was the proper course for me to take. [Applause.] I am brought before you now to make a speech, while you all approve, more than anything else, that I have been keeping silence. [Great laughter and renewed cheering, the audience taking the full humor of the thing.] It seems to me the response you give to that remark ought to justify me in closing just here. [More laughter.]

I have not kept silence since the Presidential election from any party craftiness or from any indifference to the anxieties that pervade the minds of men in this country. I have kept silence for the reason that it was peculiarly proper for me to wait until the time should come when, according to the custom of the country, I would speak officially. [Applause.] I hear someone say: "According to the custom of the country?" I allude to the custom, on the President's taking the oath of office, of his declaring what course he thinks should be pursued. That is what I mean.

The political drama acting before the country at this time is rapidly shifting its scenes. It was eminently fitting that I should wait till the last minute, so that I could choose a position from which I should not be obliged to deviate. I have said several times on this journey, and now repeat to you, I shall then take the ground that I think is right—the ground that I shall then think right for the North, the South, the West, and the whole country. [Cries of "Good," "Good," and great cheering.] . . . Now, my friends, have I not said enough? [Applause, which, as the humor of the thing was fully perceived, broke forth in loud huzzas.] Now, my friends, there is a difference of opinion between you and me, and I insist on deciding the question.

Among callers of the evening were Republican committees, Electoral College delegates, and Tom Hyer, champion heavyweight pugilist. The morning *Herald* said editorially: "The masses of the people did not turn out. There was a faint cheer as Mr. Lincoln entered his carriage at the railway station, but none of those spontaneous movements for which our people are noted." A *Harper's Weekly* expert set forth that the three largest crowds ever assembled in New York came to see (1) the Prince of Wales, (2) the Japanese embassy, (3) the opening of the Atlantic undersea telegraph; and "after these the greatest crowd ever gathered in Broadway was assembled on Tuesday last to see Abraham Lincoln, President-elect." Though probably exceeding 100,000 people, the crowd was "in number far less than those who went forth to stare at the Prince of Wales and the Japanese princes, mainly from the fact that it contained few or no women . . . it would seem that the ladies did not care about seeing Mr. Lincoln." Also it was supposed that military display and some show of pageantry glittering around the central figure of the day would have brought more onlookers.

In the morning at eleven in the Governor's Room of the City Hall, surrounded by aldermen and writers for the press, Lincoln faced Mayor Wood, a table between them, two magistrates in black coats, Wood's buttoned tight across his breast and Lincoln's loose. Their eyes met, and Lincoln had his chance at fathoming the city executive who wished to secede from the United States and set up a Free City. Tall, spare, erect, clean-shaven and elegantly tailored, wearing a heavy white mustache, Wood looked very military and precise. Cool, courtly, Chesterfieldian was Wood—and somewhat poker-faced, his features telling no more emotion nor thought than those of a brass monkey. Twice in the State Assembly his own party had rejected him for Speaker when he was entitled to it by seniority: his name was bad for his party, and at many a conference of leaders the discussion was on how to get rid of him. On several occasions in the Assembly he heard himself called various kinds of a snake and toad, taking it coolly with a face smooth as marble.

"Permit me to say," said the Mayor (constantly addressing the President-elect as "Mr. Lincoln"), "that this city has never offered hospitality to a man clothed with more exalted powers or destiny, under graver responsibilities than those which circumstances have devolved upon you." New York was "sorely afflicted," with "all her material interests paralyzed," and her "commercial greatness endangered." The Mayor closed: "To you, we look for a restoration of friendly relations between the States, only to be accomplished by peaceful and conciliatory means, aided by the wisdom of Almighty God." Lincoln spoke thanks for the reception, alluded to "the large majority" in the city who did not agree with him. "In regard to the

Lincoln in the New York City Hall received by prosecessionist Mayor Fernando Wood

difficulties . . . of which you have seen fit to speak so becomingly and so justly, I can only say that I agree with the sentiments expressed."

Press writers noticed that Mayor Wood "never removed his eyes from the President-elect during the delivery of the two addresses." Also they noticed that Lincoln "did not return the steady gaze that was fixed upon him." He was talking past Wood and to the country in saying: "I understand that the ship is made for the carrying and preservation of the cargo; and so long as the ship is safe with the cargo, it shall not be abandoned. This Union shall never be abandoned, unless the possibility of its existence shall cease to exist without the necessity of throwing passengers and cargo overboard. So long, then, as it is possible that the prosperity and liberties of this people can be preserved within this Union, it shall be my purpose at all times to preserve it." For two hours in the City Hall he shook hands with citizens, and later in the afternoon again shook hands at a formal reception during which the Vice-President-elect, Hannibal Hamlin of Maine, arrived.

White kid gloves were then in style for wear at opera. And Lincoln that night sat in a box at the new and sumptuous Academy of Music on Fourteenth Street and Irving Place, wearing *black* kids on his hands in contrast with the red-velvet box front, the audience saw; the word spread, and the press commented on the one pair of black gloves in the packed house.

In a box opposite, a Southern man remarked to the ladies of his party, "I think we ought to send some flowers over the way to the Undertaker of the Union."

The opera by Giuseppe Verdi was sung in Italian by an Italian company. Its title, *Un Ballo in Maschera*, was pronounced Oon Bah-lo een Mahs-kay-rah and meant *A Masquerade Ball*. One of the songs moved to the theme *"Alla Vita Che T'Arride"* or "On the Life Thou Now Dost Cherish." As the sopranos warbled and the tenors flowed on, Lincoln's thoughts may have roamed to Rufus Choate telling a daughter, "Interpret for me the libretto lest I dilate with the wrong emotion." Or perhaps he thought of a Kentucky Congressman that afternoon in Washington accusing him of telling a Kentucky caller at Springfield that if the State of Kentucky didn't help the North retake the forts seized by the seceded States, "Let her prepare for war." Only the day before his friend Congressman Kellogg, in the National Hotel in Washington, had spat angry words at his friend Joseph Medill, editor of the *Chicago Tribune*, and Kellogg, the larger man of the two, had struck Medill and floored him. Kellogg was for compromise and Medill wasn't, and Lincoln had that to think about.

Or he might have been thinking, while a soprano climbed up and down a vocal ladder, of a man a thousand miles away, Governor Samuel J. Kirkwood of Iowa; they had talked an hour in a hotel in Springfield and Kirkwood had gone back to Iowa saying the Union would be maintained if it took "the last man and the last dollar." He might have wondered in Manhattan then, "How far this is from Iowa!" Or he might have been wondering how alike two human faces can be; at the Astor House reception the night before he had mistaken an old man who had never been West for one who had called on him in his Springfield office to sell him an illustrated copy of Shakespeare's poems.

The show half over, Lincoln stepped out and in an anteroom held an informal reception to important New Yorkers. A diary-writer noted that he looked "terribly bored, and sat on the sofa at the end of the room with his hat pushed back on his head, the most deplorable figure that can be imagined, putting his hand out to be shaken in a queer mechanical way."

Mrs. Lincoln the same evening was holding a fairly successful reception in the parlors of the Astor House. The newspapers mentioned Mrs. August Belmont as among those present, which caused Mrs. Belmont to send a note to newspapers saying she wished it known that she was not present. Of several hundred guests expected at this crinoline gathering, about one hundred came. The *Newark Daily Advertiser* saw Mrs. Lincoln as having "manner and carriage graceful and pleasing . . . a lady who would be pronounced fine looking but not beautiful." She wore a dress of "steel-colored silk, made high in the neck, with trimming of box-plaited satin ribbon, a small lace collar fastened with a diamond brooch, diamond ear-drops, and black chenille and gold headdress." At another New York party the ladies carried bouquets, and a newspaper said, "Mrs. Lincoln had a small ivory fan with which she occasionally fanned some of the gentlemen who paid their respects to her, playfully telling them 'not to get too warm in the cause.' "

Tad and Willie went with a nursemaid and saw a play at Laura Keene's Theatre. With mother and father they saw Barnum's museum and its mammoth monstrosities and concatenated curiosities.

Newspaper items had begun to appear with regularity about Mrs. Lincoln, a Kentuckian, and her blood-kin secessionists. The correct and detailed information was reprinted from the *Columbus Times* of Georgia: "Mrs. Abraham Lincoln, wife of the President of the old Union, has two married sisters now on a visit to Montgomery, Ala. One is from Kentucky, and on a visit to her sister, who resides in Selma, Ala. They are both strong secessionists, and opposed to the government of their brother-in-law, Abraham Lincoln. Of course, they attract considerable attention, and are the toast of Southerners. The husband of one has offered his services to Governor Moore, of Alabama, to further the cause of secession and State Rights and Republican Liberty."

"Abe is becoming more grave," said the partly humorous weekly *Vanity Fair*. "He don't construct as many jokes as he did. He fears he will get things mixed up if he don't look out." Metropolitan persiflage had its airy way. A *Vanity Fair* joker wrote: "As the train was slowly crossing a long bridge, Mr. Lincoln's face assumed that indescribably humorous appearance which has rendered him remarkable, and the company prepared for one of his side-splitters. Thrusting his head out of the window, he hailed some laborers in the ravine below and asked them if they wanted any rails split. This impromptu sally of wit was so infinitely superior to the ordinary sallies that the reporter of the *Boston Advertiser* immediately telegraphed the joke to that paper, but the other reporters were compelled to content themselves with laughing immoderately over it, as jokes are not allowed in the journals they represent. . . . A pleasing incident occurred at Hudson. Several young ladies came into the car and the President folded them rapturously to his throbbing bosom. They said, 'Don't' which induced the President to believe that they liked it. . . . At the Astor, where the bills of fare are printed in French, Mr. Lincoln unhesitatingly called for a sine qua non of beans, and an ipsedixit of pork. . . . Mr. Lincoln says New York and Philadelphia are larger places than Springfield, being more thickly settled. . . . Mr. Lincoln continues to measure with the tall men who present themselves."

The morning *Herald* said Lincoln was telling fewer funny stories than usual. Greeley was saying in his morning *Tribune* that the questions were plopped at Lincoln: "What is to be the issue of this Southern effervescence? Are we really to have civil war?" And Lincoln gave a Western prairie incident as a fable and a final disposition of the queries.

"Many years ago," he began, half as though it were a bedtime story for little ones, "when I was a young lawyer, and Illinois was little settled, except on her southern border, I, with other lawyers, used to ride the circuit. Once a long spell of pouring rain flooded the whole country, transforming small creeks into rivers. Ahead of us was Fox River, larger than all the rest, and we could not help saying to each other, 'If these small streams give us so much trouble, how shall we get over Fox River?' Darkness fell before we had reached that stream, and we all stopped at a log tavern, had our horses put up, and resolved to pass the night. Here we were right glad to fall in with the Methodist Presiding Elder of the circuit, who rode it in all weather, knew all its ways, and could tell us all about Fox River. So we all gathered around him, and asked him if he knew about the crossing of Fox River. 'O yes,' he replied, 'I know all about Fox River. I have crossed it often, and understand it well. But I have one fixed rule with regard to Fox River: *I never cross it till I reach it!*'"

The earnest Greeley found this "characteristic of Lincoln and his way of regarding portents of trouble."

A second little fable was offered New York political thinkers. "I once knew a good, sound churchman, whom we'll call Brown," Lincoln was quoted, "who was on a committee to erect a bridge over a dangerous and rapid river. Architect after architect failed, and at last Brown said he had a friend named Jones who had built several bridges and could build this. 'Let's have him in,' said the committee. In came Jones. 'Can you build this bridge, sir?' 'Yes,' replied Jones, 'I could build a bridge to the infernal regions, if necessary.' The sober committee were horrified, but when Jones retired Brown thought it fair to defend his friend. 'I know Jones so well,' said he, 'and he is so honest a man and so good an architect that, if he states soberly and positively that he can build a bridge to Hades—why, I believe it. But I have my doubts about the abutments on the infernal side.'"

"So," Lincoln added, "when politicians said they could harmonize the Northern and Southern wings of the democracy, I believed them. But I had my doubts about the abutments on the Southern side."

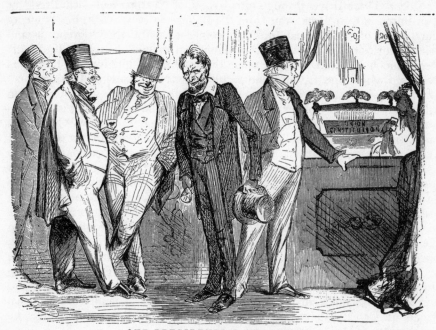

OUR PRESIDENTIAL MERRYMAN.

"The Presidential party was engaged in a lively exchange of wit and humor. The President Elect was the merriest among the merry, and kept those around him in a continual roar."—*Daily Paper*.

A *Harper's Weekly* cartoonist, not in agreement with the editorial trend of the journal, caricatures Lincoln as convivial, droll, too easygoing

Friends close to Lincoln, such as Lamon, Nicolay, Hay, Swett, Whitney, Browning, tried to follow the gyrations of events and relate them to lucid motives moving Lincoln. He was the coolest man in the United States, with a penetrating mind aware of its direction at all moments, believed the two secretaries. He was a troubled man groaning and muttering as though history had ordered him to straddle a cyclone and ride it if he could, according to the Rabelaisian Virginian who had brought along his banjo and occasionally sang "Doo-Dah" and "Nelly Bly" for Lincoln on the train and in hotels. He went through an agony of dark wrestlings with his conscience, and his mind was an arena where ideas killed ideas and resurrected themselves and came back to fight each other again to see who by survival would prove the greatest and more alive—according to Swett and Whitney. He was one more ordinary serene magistrate and there was no Gethsemane of self-searching, and his decisions were being made as smoothly as in many a law case they had tried, in the tone color of Browning's diary. His mind and temperament were still in Springfield and he did not realize as yet that he cast a far longer shadow than yesterday—so Douglas was saying.

The editor of *Harper's Weekly*, George William Curtis, had seen President Tyler drive through the streets of Boston, had seen President Van Buren pass up Broadway from the Battery in New York, but as scenes they were of "superficial interest" compared with the "significant and solemn curiosity" with which the Manhattan crowds gazed on President-elect Lincoln: "There was the same kind of hushed intensity of feeling as he passed which one may imagine in the crowds that watched Washington." One man with bare head rode quietly in a barouche, followed by a dozen other barouches, no soldiers at all, no pageantry, while thousands on sidewalks, in windows and balconies, saluted and cheered. This to Curtis was impressive, more so than "the pretty spectacle" put on for the Prince of Wales. "A simple, earnest, sincere-looking man, gazing curiously at the noble street and the vast crowd that filled it, he bowed at intervals with natural dignity, yet abstractedly, as if he were instinctively conscious, as he had so frequently said, that it was not he, but the majesty of the nation visible in his person, that aroused the profound interest of the people."

After the evening at opera Lincoln the next morning took breakfast in the Fifth Avenue mansion of Moses Hicks Grinnell, a millionaire merchant, once a Whig Congressman, once president of the Chamber of Commerce of New York, a Republican presidential elector on the Frémont ticket, contributor to the Kane Arctic expedition, commissioner of charities and corrections, member of the original Central Park Commission, personal friend of Daniel Webster, William H. Seward, and other celebrities he had breakfasted.

Over the coffee and buns Lincoln told a Public Man who kept a diary, "The Democrats must vote to hold the Union now, without bothering whether we or the Southern men got things where they are, and we must make it easy for them to do this, because we can't live through the case without them."

Aspinwall, the Panama Railroad magnate, and other men of affairs and money were at this breakfast, and the diary-writer noted: "Mr. Aspinwall says that Mr. Lincoln made a bad impression, and he seemed more provoked than I thought necessary or reasonable at a remark which Mr. Lincoln made to him on somebody's saying, not in very good taste, to Mr. Lincoln, that he would not meet so many millionaires together at any other table in New York."

Lincoln's reply was, "Oh, indeed, is that so? Well, that's quite right. I'm a millionaire myself. I got a minority of a million in the votes last November."

The diary-writer believed this to be light and frivolous of Lincoln in such a company, "but after all, it shows that he appreciates the real difficulties of the position, and is thinking of the people more than of the 'millionaires,' and I hope more than of the politicians. I tried to make Mr. Aspinwall see this as I did, but he is too much depressed by the mercantile situation and was too much annoyed by Mr. Lincoln's evident failure to show any adequate sense of the gravity of the position."

The New York reception of the President-elect was the most elaborate, pretentious, detailed, expensive—and yet the coldest—of all on the Lincoln journey toward inauguration. Greeley, Beecher, Aspinwall, Bennett, Fernando Wood—he would indeed be hearing from them again and again in the days to come.

In New York newspapers and in the nationally circulated *Leslie's Weekly* ran a small item: "We are requested to state that Mrs. August Belmont did not call on Mrs. Lincoln during her stay at the Astor House."

Ferried across to Jersey City, Lincoln met a crowd whose welcome was spoken by William L. Dayton, attorney general of New Jersey, former United States Senator, first Republican-party candidate for Vice-President, "a man with whom it is an honor to be associated anywhere, and in owning whom no State can be poor," said Lincoln. At Newark he thanked the Mayor and said he was bringing to his work "an honest desire to do right." Before the New Jersey Senate in Trenton he referred to the many American Revolutionary battlefields on New Jersey soil and how the hardships and fighting there at Trenton had been fixed in his imagination when a boy reading Weems's *Life of Washington*. "I recollect thinking then, boy even though I was, that there must have been something more than common that these men struggled for . . . something that held out a great promise to all the people of the world to all time to come." He was anxious that "the original idea for which that struggle was made" should live. "I shall be most happy indeed if I shall be a humble instrument in the hands of the Almighty, and of this, his almost chosen people, for perpetuating the object of that great struggle." A majority of the gentlemen before him did not think he was the man for Chief Magistrate. Yet they were greeting him as the constitutionally elected President of the United States. "As such, I accept this reception more gratefully than I could do did I believe it were tendered to me as an individual."

Before the New Jersey Assembly he referred to himself again as of no personal importance and thanked them for receiving him as "the representative, for the time being, of the majesty of the people of the United States." Soon he would speak officially, and he hoped in good temper and certainly with no malice toward any section, to promote a peaceful settlement of the national difficulties: "The man does not live who is more devoted to peace than I am, none who would do more to preserve it, but it may be necessary to put the foot down firmly. [Here the audience broke out in cheers so loud and long that for some moments it was impossible to hear Mr. Lincoln's voice.] And if I do my duty and do right, you will sustain me, will you not? [Loud cheers, and cries of "Yes, yes, we will."]" He closed with saying in effect that he might be the last President of the United States: "If it [the ship of state] should suffer wreck now, there will be no pilot ever needed for another voyage." After a short speech of greeting at the Trenton House, he boarded the train, arrived in Philadelphia at four o'clock, and replying to Mayor Henry's welcome, said all his political warfare had been in favor of the teachings that had come forth from the sacred walls of Independence Hall. "May my right hand forget its cunning and my tongue cleave to the roof of my mouth if ever I prove false to those teachings."

Crowds surged in the hotel office and corridors and eddied up into a parlor where Lincoln stood handshaking that night for an hour or two. His eye caught Nicolay slipping and pushing through the crowd toward him. Nicolay had word that Norman B. Judd wanted Mr. Lincoln at once on an emergency matter of unmentionable importance.

In Judd's room Lincoln met Judd and Detective Allan Pinkerton, who in 1850 single-handed constituted Chicago's first official detective force, who in the same year set up a detective agency active for years in the business of running slaves from where they were legalized property to where they were not. His reputation as a railroad detective brought him into the service of Samuel M. Felton, president of the Philadelphia, Wilmington & Baltimore Railroad, to guard trains and bridges and circumvent threatened explosions and fires.

These three, Lincoln, Judd, Pinkerton, held a long session. Judd began with saying that while with the President-elect's party at Cincinnati, Buffalo, New York, he had received word from Pinkerton as to personal danger threatening the President-elect. On Pinkerton's advice he had said nothing of this danger. "I did not care to darken your journey with any premature foreboding. Now I want him to tell you what he and Mr. Felton have been telling me."

Pinkerton opened: "We have come to know, Mr. Lincoln, and beyond the shadow of a doubt, that there exists a plot to assassinate you. The attempt will be made on your way through Baltimore, day after tomorrow. I am here to help in outwitting the assassins."

Lincoln sat with legs crossed, a good-natured curiosity on his face fading to a sober look. "I am listening, Mr. Pinkerton."

A barber named Fernandina, head of one of several treasonable secret military societies in Baltimore, was foremost among the conspirators, according to Pinkerton's spies, who, he said, had been at work for weeks and had penetrated to the innermost recesses of the traitor councils, had become "bosom friends and inseparable companions" of the plotters. A speech by Fernandina, the barber, at a secret meeting of the military company he captained was described by Pinkerton to Lincoln in somewhat the same words Pinkerton wrote it down:

He boldly advocated the doctrine of State rights; he inveighed in violent language against the policy of the so-called abolitionists, and his arraignment of Mr. Lincoln was most vile and repulsive. As these words fell from his lips, the excitement became intense. Faces were eagerly turned toward him, eyes glistened with the fires of hate, and hands were clenched as though each one present was imbued with the same feelings which animated their sanguinary leader.

As he proceeded, overcome by the violence of his emotions, he drew from his breast a long, glittering knife, and waving it aloft exclaimed:

"This hireling Lincoln shall never, never be President. My life is of no consequence in a cause like this, and I am willing to give it for his. As Orsini gave his life for Italy, I am ready to die for the rights of the South and to crush out the abolitionist."

As he stood before them, his black eyes flashing with excitement, his sallow face pale and colorless and his long hair brushed fiercely back from his low forehead, he seemed a fitting representative of so desperate a cause, and his influence over the assemblage was wonderful to behold. Loud cheers and wild clapping of hands greeted his utterances, and all seemed in perfect accord with his declared intentions.

When this was reported to Pinkerton, he went personally to Baltimore, purporting to be a Georgia secessionist, and when introduced to the leading conspirator, as Pinkerton told it, "Fernandina cordially grasped my hand, and we all retired to a private saloon, where after ordering the necessary drinks and cigars, the conversation became general."

In the course of the conversation and the drinks, Fernandina was asked if there was no other way to save the South than by killing Lincoln. He replied, in the Pinkerton report: "No, as well might you attempt to move the Washington Monument yonder with your breath, as to change our purpose. He must die—and die he shall." As to any missteps, "our plans are fully arranged, and they cannot fail; and if I alone must strike the blow, I shall not hesitate or shrink from the task." With another drink by this time, he was asked about the police. He had fixed that, too: "They are all with us. I have seen Col. Kane, the Chief Marshal of Police, and he is all right. In a week from today, the North shall want another President, for Lincoln will be a corpse."

Also it seemed that Pinkerton detected another conspirator named Hill, who also drank heavy and often, and also was ready, in his talk, to kill Lincoln. "What a pity it is that this glorious Union must be destroyed on account of that monster Lincoln!" he said, in the Pinkerton reports. "I am destined to die shrouded in glory. I shall immortalize myself by plunging a knife into Lincoln's heart. Rome had her Brutus, why should not we? I swear if it falls to me I will kill Lincoln before he reaches the Washington depot, not that I love Lincoln less, but my country more."

Lincoln interrupted the Pinkerton recital with many questions. He cross-examined the master detective as he would a witness in a momentous court case. Supporting Pinkerton's viewpoint were the practical Judd, a lawyer, and the equally practical Felton, a railroad president who considered the evidence positive of a plot to burn railroad bridges, blow up trains, "and murder Mr. Lincoln on his way to Washington." The affair hinged on Fernandina, and Lincoln asked dryly of Pinkerton, "Then do I understand, sir, my life is chiefly threatened by this half-crazed foreigner?"

"He only talks like a maniac, Mr. President. His capacity to do you harm must not be minimized. The most timely measures alone will serve to frustrate their plotting."

"But why—why do they want to kill me?"

Pinkerton replied that no conservative Northerner could grasp the fanatical sentiment then riding Baltimore.

"With all due allowance for the menacing plans of the fanatics, how do you happen to be so sure of the carrying through of the preparations against me?" Lincoln asked.

"Because, sir, at least one of my men has penetrated to the very core of the plot and learned how thoroughly the whole thing has been prepared."

"And you vouch for the integrity of this detective?"

"I do, Mr. President. He took the required oath very regretfully, perjuring himself only in the performance of a solemn duty obligation to you and to the nation."

Pinkerton gave details of a wild-eyed plot. The police chief at Baltimore was arranging to send only a small force to the railroad depot, where a gang of toughs would start a fight to draw off the policemen. Then the Fernandina assassins would close round the President-elect and deliver the fatal shot or knife thrust.

"Granting, gentlemen, that all of this is true," said Lincoln, "what do you propose to do about it?"

"We propose," said Pinkerton, "to take you on to Washington this very night, Mr. President, and steal a march on your enemies."

"Has this your approval?" Lincoln asked Judd.

Judd said it seemed for the best, though "scoffs and sneers" would follow.

Lincoln deliberated, then said: "Gentlemen, I appreciate the suggestions, and while I can stand anything essential in the way of misrepresentation, I do not feel I can go to Washington tonight. Tomorrow morning I have promised to raise the flag over Independence Hall, and after that to visit the legislature at Harrisburg. Whatever the cost, these two promises I must fulfill. Thereafter I shall be ready to consider any plan you may adopt."

On the ten o'clock train from Washington that night arrived Frederick W. Seward, son of Lincoln's announced Secretary of State. His father had told him that morning in Washington: "I want you to go by the first train. Find Mr. Lincoln wherever he is. Let no one else know your errand." Young Seward found Chestnut Street and the Continental Hotel gay with a serenade of the President-elect, music, flowers, flags, buzzing conversations, and "brilliantly lighted parlours filled with ladies and gentlemen who had come to 'pay their respects.'" At the head of a stairway Robert T. Lincoln amid young friends was pointed out. Seward introduced himself, met a warm welcome, and Robert Lincoln called to Ward Hill Lamon, just then passing, and introduced young Seward. Lamon took Seward by the arm, saying they would go back into the parlor and he would present him to Mr. Lincoln. Seward emphasized that his interview must be as private as possible. Lamon laughed. "Then I think I had better take you to his bedroom. If you don't mind waiting there, you'll be sure to meet him, for he has got to go there sometime tonight; and it is the only place I know of where he will be likely to be alone."

Young Seward waited in Lincoln's bedroom an hour or more. The quiet impressed him because of the chatter and human stirring to be heard beyond the door, where he must not show his face. "Presently Colonel Lamon called me," wrote Seward of that night, "and we met Mr. Lincoln coming down the hall. I had never before seen him; but the campaign portraits had made his face quite familiar. I could not but notice how accurately they had copied his features, and how totally they had omitted his careworn look, and his pleasant, kindly smile. After a few words of friendly greeting, with inquiries about my father and matters in Washington, he sat down by the table under the gas light to peruse the letter I had brought. Although its contents were of a somewhat startling nature he made no exclamation, and I saw no sign of surprise in his face. After reading it carefully through, he again held it to the light, and deliberately read it through a second time." The three communications his father had so secretly and hurriedly sent on to Lincoln, and which Lincoln read very deliberately twice, were as follows:

Washington, February 21, 1861

My dear Sir:

My son goes express to you. He will show you a report made by our detective to General Scott, and by him communicated to me this morning. I deem it so important as to dispatch my son to meet you wherever he may find you.

I concur with General Scott in thinking it best for you to reconsider your arrangement. No one here but General Scott, myself, and the bearer is aware of this communication.

I should have gone with it myself, but for the peculiar sensitiveness about my attendance at the Senate at this crisis.

Very truly yours,

William H. Seward

[General Scott to Seward]

February 21, 1861

My dear Sir:

Please receive my friend, Colonel Stone, chief of General Weightman's staff, and a distinguished young officer with me in Mexico. He has an important communication to make.

Yours truly,

Winfield Scott

[Colonel Stone's report]

February 21, 1861

A New York detective officer who has been on duty in Baltimore for three weeks past reports this morning that there is serious danger of violence to, and the assassination of, Mr. Lincoln in his passage through that city, should the time of that passage be known. He states that there are banded rowdies holding secret meetings, and that he has heard threats of mobbing and violence, and has himself heard men declare that if Mr. Lincoln was to be assassinated they would like to be the men. He states further that it is only within the past few days that he has considered there was any danger, but now he deems it imminent. He deems the danger one which the authorities and people in Baltimore cannot guard against. All risk might be easily avoided by a change in the traveling arrangements which would bring Mr. Lincoln and a portion of his party through Baltimore by a night train without previous notice.

After musing a moment Lincoln looked up and asked: "Did you hear anything about the way this information was obtained? Do you know anything about how they got it?"

No, young Seward knew nothing in regard to it till that morning, when called down from the Senate gallery by his father.

"Your father and General Scott do not say who they think are concerned in it. Do you think they know?"

On that point too young Seward had no additional information further than his impression that his father's knowledge was limited to what had been communicated to him by Colonel Stone, in whose statements he had implicit confidence.

"Did you hear any names mentioned?" Lincoln pressed. "Did you, for instance, ever hear anything said about such a name as Pinkerton?"

No, Seward had heard no such name as Pinkerton in connection with the matter, no name at all, in fact, except those of General Scott and Colonel Stone. Lincoln deliberated a moment, then said: "I may as well tell you why I ask. There were stories or rumours some time ago, before I left home, about people who were intending to do me a mischief. I never attached much importance to them—never wanted to believe any such thing. So I never would do any thing about them, in the way of taking precautions and the like. Some of my friends, though, thought differently—Judd and others—and without my knowledge they employed a detective to look into the matter. It seems he has occasionally reported what he found; and only today, since we arrived at this house, he brought this story, or something similar to it, about an attempt on my life in the confusion and hurly-burly of the reception at Baltimore."

"Surely, Mr. Lincoln," said Seward, "that is a strong corroboration of the news I bring you."

Lincoln smiled and shook his head. "That is exactly why I was asking you about names. If different persons, not knowing of each other's work, have been pursuing separate clues that led to the same result, why then it shows there may be something in it. But if this is only the same story, filtered through two channels, and reaching me in two ways, then that don't make it any stronger. Don't you see?"

This was unanswerable logic, Seward would say, but he must assert his strong belief that the two investigations had been conducted independently of each other, and there was enough of probability to make it prudent to adopt the suggestion and make the slight change, in hour and train, which would avoid all risk. They discussed it a little further. Lincoln rose, saying, "Well, we haven't got to decide it tonight, anyway, and I see it's getting late." Noticing that Seward looked disappointed at his slowness, his reluctance to regard the warnings brought him, Lincoln said kindly: "You need not think I will not consider it well. I shall think it over carefully and try to decide it right, and I will let you know in the morning."

In studying what to do Lincoln had to consider the silence of Baltimore and Maryland. Governor Thomas H. Hicks of that State favored the Union as against secession and was himself threatened with death by men proclaiming that their volunteer militia would shoot down Northern soldiers en route to Washington, would burn supply depots and railroad bridges, would if war came march their corps to Washington and take that city. Governor Hicks had a seething and sensitive public to handle, a people ready to show what they could do with guns, clubs, stones, bricks, in street fighting. The Marshal of Police, George P. Kane, was a straight-out secessionist. The barber Ferrandini, who thus spelled his name for the Select Committee of Five holding a congressional hearing on insurrectionary preparations, and whose name was misspelled in the Pinkerton reports, had testified on February 5 that his company of Constitutional Guards expressly aimed to stop Northern troops from reaching Washington or invading the South; that another corps named National Volunteers was drilling "to protect their State"; that he had heard of fifteen companies of minutemen in Baltimore. Thus it was natural that no governor, legislature, mayor, city council, sent greetings and invitations to Lincoln to visit their State and city, with assurances of protection and a program of pleasant welcome. Thus no Marylander had sent word that they would have a committee somewhere on the route to escort the next President to their State. A railroad official in Baltimore and a hotel-manager there had invited Lincoln and his family to share hospitality. Except for these two, Maryland and Baltimore officially stood mute, its leading newspaper saying that Lincoln's speeches were "ludicrous to the destruction of buttons."

Wild talk of what might happen to Lincoln at Baltimore had reached up into New York City, where Superintendent of Police John A. Kennedy, on his own initiative, ordered detectives to have a look at the Maryland city. One of these, David S. Bookstaver, without meeting the Pinkertons or knowing their work, had posed as an agent for a musical house, canvassed all classes, and decided that hell would break loose if Lincoln set foot in Baltimore, that in the commotions and riots staged Lincoln wouldn't come through alive. Bookstaver headed straight for Washington and told what he knew to General Scott and Colonel Stone. Their decision and Seward's that Lincoln should not go to Baltimore rested on the New York detective's certainty that Baltimore was volcanic and would erupt, and on the reports of two detectives sent to Baltimore by Colonel Stone, whose findings tallied with Bookstaver's.

Lincoln didn't sleep so well that night of February 21. He was up early. Sunrise reddened the flats of the broad Delaware River, and the venerable City of Brotherly Love. At six o'clock that morning of February 22, the anniversary of Washington's birthday, Lincoln amid cannon salutes and crowd applause pulled a rope and raised a flag over Independence Hall, where John Hancock and other American Revolutionists signed the Declaration of Independence and told the world why they were starting a long bloody war. The first flag raised had but thirteen stars, said Lincoln. Then had come more stars one by one. This morning the star added by Kansas' joining the Union was on the flag. "I think we may promise ourselves that

Harper's Weekly sketch of the President-elect raising the United States flag over Independence Hall in Philadelphia, February 22, 1861

not only the new star placed upon that flag shall be permitted to remain there to our permanent prosperity for years to come, but additional ones shall from time to time be placed there until we shall number, as it was anticipated by the great historian, five hundred millions of happy and prosperous people."

Inside Independence Hall he spoke to an audience crowding all corners and overflowing. "I am filled with deep emotion at finding myself standing in this place, where were collected together the wisdom, the patriotism, the devotion to principle, from which sprang the institutions under which we live." He had often pondered over the "dangers" incurred by the men who had assembled there and framed the Declaration, had pondered over the toils endured by officers and soldiers for national independence, had inquired what principle kept them so long together.

Not merely separation from a motherland, but liberty as a hope to all the world, for all future time, was the sentiment guiding them. "It was that which gave promise that in due time the weights would be lifted from the shoulders of all men, and that all should have an equal chance. This is the sentiment embodied in the Declaration of Independence."

He asked if the country could be saved on that basis. If so he would consider himself one of the happiest men in the world. "But if this country cannot be saved without giving up that principle, I was about to say I would rather be assassinated on this spot than surrender it."

He could see no need of bloodshed and war. "And I may say in advance that there will be no bloodshed unless it be forced upon the government. The government will not use force, unless force is used against it." His speech had been wholly unprepared. "I did not expect to be called on to say a word when I came here. . . . I may . . . have said something indiscreet. [Cries of "No, no."] But I have said nothing but what I am willing to live by, and, if it be the pleasure of Almighty God, die by."

Young Seward, sleeping late, had just had breakfast that morning, had just been a little startled to read in the morning papers of Lincoln's saying that he would rather be assassinated than give up the principles embodied in the Declaration of Independence, when he met Lamon in the hotel lobby, was taken one side, and told in a low tone that Lincoln had decided to do as advised and would change his plans so as to pass through Baltimore at a different hour. Seward hurried to telegraph his father a code word that Lincoln would arrive earlier than expected. On taking the train for Washington that day Seward also carried word from Judd that he could say to his father that "so far as human foresight could predict, Mr. Lincoln would be in Washington at six o'clock the next morning."

So it seemed on the morning of February 22 that only one thing would bring Lincoln back to his original schedule for meeting the next day the crowds expecting him at Baltimore. He said to an interviewer at a later time, "I told Mr. Judd that if I should meet at Harrisburg, as I had other places, a delegation to go with me to the next place [Baltimore] I should feel safe and go on."

Judd had been up nearly the whole night in a conference with Pinkerton ,and two other men, G. C. Franciscus, general manager of the Pennsylvania Railroad, and E. S. Sanford, president of the American Telegraph Company. They arranged for Lincoln to journey from Harrisburg on a two-car train that night under conditions they believed would deliver him safely in Washington the next morning. Judd explained the plan in detail to Lincoln as they traveled on the Pennsylvania Railroad to Harrisburg.

In greeting a crowd at Lancaster, the home town of James Buchanan and Thaddeus Stevens, Lincoln ventured: "I think the more a man speaks in these days; the less he is understood. As Solomon says, there is a time for all things, and I think the present is a time for silence."

Then came Harrisburg, and amid guns and platoons Lincoln replied to Governor Andrew G. Curtin's welcome that under the weight of his great responsibility he brought an honest heart, but "I dare not tell you that I bring a head sufficient for it."

He would lean on the people. "If my own strength should fail, I shall at least fall back upon these masses, who, I think, under any circumstances will not fail." He hoped no one of the Friends who lived in the State was a more devoted lover of peace, harmony, and concord than he.

The State troops were marshaled in impressive ranks. "While I have been proud to see to-day the finest military array, I think, that I have ever seen, allow me to say, in regard to those men, that they give hope of what may be done when war is inevitable. But, at the same time, allow me to express the hope that in the shedding of blood their services may never be needed, especially in the shedding of fraternal blood. . . . With my consent, or without my great displeasure, this country shall never witness the shedding of one drop of blood in fraternal strife."

In a speech to the legislature he referred to the flag-raising ceremony of the morning, how the flag, the cord for elevating it which his own feeble arm pulled, all the arrangements, had been made by others and he had been merely a humble instrument. By a like co-operation nationally "I think the flag of our country may yet be kept flaunting gloriously." Not with pleasure could he contemplate using the military arm of the country. The military support which Pennsylvania offered for use in a proper emergency was gratifying, yet to preclude misconstruction, he would repeat, "I do most sincerely hope that we shall never have any use for them." As to the tariff, his remarks at Pittsburgh were "rather carefully worded" and he would leave them as they stood, adding only that he was pleased that gentlemen of Pennsylvania should have expressed satisfaction with his tariff viewpoints.

A gripsack kept close to Lincoln on this journey held his copy of the inaugural address he hoped to deliver on March 4. In Harrisburg he trusted it for a while to his son Robert, who, when asked for it, said he believed he had given it to a waiter. The father spoke witheringly to his boy, in the only moment since leaving Springfield, it seemed to Lamon, that Lincoln lost his temper.

To Lamon he spoke confidentially: "I guess I have lost my certificate of moral character, written by myself. Bob has lost my gripsack containing my inaugural address. I want you to help me find it. I feel a good deal as the old member of the Methodist church did when he lost his wife at the camp meeting, and went up to an old elder of the church and asked him if he could tell him whereabouts in hell his wife was. In fact, I am in a worse fix than my Methodist friend, for if it were nothing but a wife missing, mine would be sure to pop up serenely somewhere. That address may be a loss to more than one husband in this country, but I shall be the greatest sufferer."

In the hotel baggage room they looked over a pile of bags, valises, satchels, and Lincoln's eye picked out one that looked like his gripsack. His key fitted; he opened it to find a soiled shirt, paper collars, a pack of cards, a near-filled bottle of whisky.

Farther along in the baggage tangle they found the gripsack with the missing document. Lincoln took it in charge, said it wouldn't leave his own hands again, and told of a man who saved $1,500. The bank keeping the money failed and the man got $150 as his share. This he put into another bank that failed and he got $15 as his share. As he looked at what was left of his savings he said, "Now, darn you, I've got you reduced to portable shape, so I'll put you in my pocket."

At a quarter to six o'clock on the evening of this Washington's Birthday, Lincoln was at a table in the dining-room of the Jones House in Harrisburg. He had made three speeches that day, listened to other speeches longer than his own, talked with Governor Curtin and men of power in Pennsylvania, and held a conference with members of his party. For the first time others than Judd learned of the change in plans. Judd had told Lincoln these other old friends should know what was afoot, Lincoln approving. "I reckon they will laugh at us, Judd, but you had better get them together."

Lincoln told them, "Unless there are some other reasons besides fear of ridicule, I am disposed to carry out Judd's plan." Judge Davis said, "That settles the matter, gentlemen." Colonel Sumner of the army protested: "It is against my judgment, but I have undertaken to go to Washington with Mr. Lincoln and I shall do it." In the rapid exchanges of opinion he declared the proposed move would be "a damned piece of cowardice," and once interrupted to cry out, "I'll get a squad of cavalry, sir, and *cut* our way to Washington, sir." A. K. McClure, legislative member and a founder of the Republican party, was sure he heard Lincoln say, "What would the nation think of its President stealing into its capital like a thief in the night?" while Governor Curtin declared the question not one for Lincoln to decide.

Close to six o'clock Lincoln was called from the dinner table, went upstairs to his room, changed his dinner dress for a traveling suit, and came down with a soft felt hat sticking in his pocket, and a folded shawl on his arm. A carriage was ready. Then, as Judd told it: "Mr. Lamon went first into the carriage; Col. Sumner was following close after Mr. Lincoln;

I put my hand gently on his shoulder; he turned to see what was wanted, and before I could explain the carriage was off. The situation was a little awkward." Judd had tricked Colonel Sumner into a moment of delay, and to the Colonel's furious words Judd replied, "When we get to Washington, Mr. Lincoln shall determine what apology is due you."

Lincoln and Lamon, with a lone car to themselves, drawn by a lone locomotive of the Pennsylvania Railroad, rode out of Harrisburg, no lights on, two giants, one six foot four, the other six foot two, and Lamon carrying two ordinary pistols, two derringers, and two large knives. Telegraph linemen had cut the wires; all telegrams into or out of Harrisburg were shut off till further orders.

In Philadelphia shortly after ten o'clock that night a carriage with Detective Pinkerton and Superintendent Kenney of the P.W.&B. Railroad, met Lincoln and Lamon at the Pennsylvania Railroad station and took them to the P.W.&B. station, where they were put on the last car of the New York-Washington train. A woman detective working for Pinkerton had reserved rear berths of a sleeping-car, one for her "invalid brother" to be occupied by Lincoln, who was quickly in his berth with the curtains carefully closed.

Unknown to Pinkerton, Lamon, or other passengers, on that last car a powerfully built man, armed with a revolver, slept in a berth engaged at New York. He was Superintendent John A. Kennedy of the New York police department, who did not know that his detective, Bookstaver, had rushed on to Washington and reported his Baltimore findings to Scott and Seward. Kennedy was acting on reports received from his other two men in Baltimore, and his intention, as he slept in the same car with Lincoln that night, was to warn the authorities at Washington the next morning that Lincoln would require safeguarding in his scheduled trip across Maryland the next day. Not yet did Lincoln nor the country know what valor and vitality lay in John A. Kennedy, how many scores of knife and bullet wounds he could take in an hour and yet live.

Baltimore was reached at half-past three in the morning, and of the stop there Pinkerton wrote later: "An officer of the road entered the car and whispered in my ear the welcome words 'All's well.' The city was in profound repose as we passed through. Darkness and silence reigned over all. Perhaps, at this moment, however, the restless conspirators were astir perfecting their plans for a tragedy as infamous as any which has ever disgraced a free country—perhaps even now the holders of the red ballots [those picked to do the killing] were nerving themselves for their part in the dreadful work, or were tossing restlessly upon sleepless couches. Be it as it may, our presence in Baltimore was entirely unsuspected."

An hour and more the train waited for a connecting train from the west. Pinkerton said he found Lincoln awake and sat chatting with him while the train crew outside cursed the delay. A drunken traveler on the train platform sang "Dixie," sang over and again how he would live and die in dear old Dixie. Lincoln murmured sleepily, according to Pinkerton, "No doubt there will be a great time in Dixie by and by."

Except for "a joke or two in an undertone," Lincoln was not heard from during the night, according to Lamon. At six o'clock in the morning the President-elect stepped off the train in Washington, D.C. Of the people on the station platform one man recognized Lincoln and came up close, saying, "You can't play that on me." As Lamon was hauling off a fist to hit the stranger, Lincoln called, "Don't strike him." It was the Illinois Congressman Washburne, one Lincoln was confidential with. He took Lincoln to Willard's for breakfast with Senator Seward, the smiling Irish porter at Willard's remarking to Washburne, "And by faith, it's you that has brought us a Prisidint."

In Harrisburg, Superintendent Thomas A. Scott of the Pennsylvania Railroad had the wires working again about six o'clock and got the code dispatch arranged by Pinkerton to report the safe arrival of Lincoln as planned:

PLUMS DELIVERED NUTS SAFELY

Thus ended the night ride of the vanishing and reappearing President-elect. The special train from Harrisburg drew into Baltimore in the afternoon like a clock with its hour hand gone, like the drama of *Hamlet* with Hamlet eliminated, disappointing Mayor George Brown, city officials, and an immense crowd. "At the Calvert station were not less than 10,000 people," wrote L. K. Bowen to Howell Cobb in Georgia, "and the moment the train arrived, supposing Lincoln was aboard, the most terrific cheers ever heard were sent up, three for the Southern Confederacy, three for 'gallant Jeff Davis,' and three groans for 'the Rail Splitter.' Had Lincoln been there, contrary to my preconceived opinions, he would have met with trouble. The cause of the feeling was the impudent appointment the day before of 100 Black Republicans to escort him through the city, which induced his friends wisely to anticipate trouble, and it would have occurred. The crowd retired quietly in disgust. . . . Some incidents in Baltimore the papers discreetly omit. . . . This ruse by Lincoln has produced an active feeling amongst our people and hurried their action, and we thank him for it. Ere long now we hope to see Va. and Md. move and join your noble confederacy." Bowen enclosed newspaper clippings to inform Cobb of "the extraordinary movements of the Mountebank Lincoln."

Among those cheering for Davis and groaning for Lincoln at Baltimore were men of wealth and respectability, also the gang fighter and tough known as "the Baltimore plug-ugly," also teamsters, tailors, mechanics, clerks, barbers, cooks, dishwashers. In primitive jungle feeling if not in historical grasp, a section of the Baltimore crowd agreed with the *Daily Delta* of Mississippi saying that week as to Lincoln: "His silly speeches, his ill-timed jocularity, his pusillanimous evasion of responsibility, and vulgar pettyfoggery, have no parallel in history, save in the crazy capers of Caligula, or in the effeminate buffoonery of Henry of Valois . . . in profound ignorance of the institutions of the Republic of which he has been chosen chief; in dishonest and cowardly efforts to dodge responsibility and play a double part—in disgusting levity on the most serious subjects, the speeches of Lincoln on his way to the capital have no equals in the history of any people, civilized or semi-civilized." Also the conversation and gabble of some of the waiting thousands at Baltimore paraphrased the

THE MacLINCOLN HARRISBURG HIGHLAND FLING.
Vanity Fair views the journey's beginning as hilarious

Salem Advocate editorial of February 28: "The illustrious Honest Old Abe has continued during the last week to make a fool of himself and to mortify and shame the intelligent people of this great nation. His speeches have demonstrated the fact that although originally a Herculean rail splitter and more lately a whimsical story teller and side splitter, he is no more capable of becoming a statesman, nay, even a moderate one, than the braying ass can become a noble lion. People now marvel how it came to pass that Mr. Lincoln should have been selected as the representative man of any party. His weak, wishy-washy, namby-pamby efforts, imbecile in matter, disgusting in manner, have made us the laughing stock of the whole world. The European powers will despise us because we have no better material out of which to make a President. The truth is, Lincoln is only a moderate lawyer and in the large cities of the Union could pass for no more than a facetious pettifogger."

Baltimore newspapers in the main had made it clear they would just as soon Lincoln would go around, under, over, rather than through their city. The *Exchange* in a sinisterly worded article said: "The President-elect of the United States will arrive in this city, with his suite, this afternoon, by special train from Harrisburg, and will proceed, we learn, directly to Washington. It is to be hoped that no opportunity will be afforded him—or that, if it be afforded him, he will not embrace it—to repeat in our ears the sentiments which he is reported to have expressed yesterday in Philadelphia."

The *Baltimore American* chronicled: "The prevailing feeling excited by Mr. Lincoln's quiet passage through Baltimore, was one of relief and of gratification, though expressions of disappointed curiosity were frequently heard. . . . On the arrival of the cars and the appearance on the platform of the Baltimore Republican Committee, they were received with groans and hootings. A rush was made at William E. Beale and Francis S. Corkran, but they were protected by the police, and neither of them were injured further than knocking their hats over their eyes. . . . Mrs. Lincoln and her three sons proceeded to the residence of Col. John S. Gittings, president of the Northern Central Railway, at Mount Vernon Square. . . . One fellow in the crowd at Calvert station, who was known as a violent Republican, had his hat knocked off a dozen times by the rowdies."

The *Baltimore Sun* reported an excited crowd mistaking an earlier train for the special, and "as soon as the train stopped, the crowd leaped upon the platforms, and mounted to the tops of the cars like so many monkeys, until like a hive of bees they swarmed upon them, shouting, hallooing and making all manner of noises." Then the *Sun* shone editorially: "Had we any respect for Mr. Lincoln, official or personal, as a man, or as President-elect of the United States, his career and speeches on his way to the seat of government would have cruelly impaired it; but the final escapade by which he reached the capital would have utterly demolished it, and overwhelmed us with mortification. As it is, no sentiment of respect of whatever sort with regard to the man suffers violence on our part, at any thing he may do. He might have entered Willard's Hotel with a 'head spring' and a 'summersault,' and the clown's merry greeting to Gen. Scott, 'Here we are!' and we should care nothing about it personally.

"We do not believe the Presidency can ever be more degraded by any of his successors, than it has been by him, even before his inauguration; and so, for aught we care, he may go to the full extent of his wretched comicalities. We have only too much cause to fear that such a man, and such advisers as he has, may prove capable of infinitely more mischief than folly when invested with power.

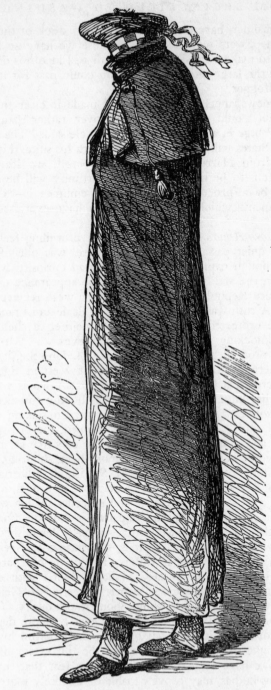

THE NEW PRESIDENT OF THE UNITED STATES
Vanity Fair's subtitle: From a Fugitive Sketch

"A lunatic is only dangerous when armed and turned loose; but only imagine a lunatic invested with authority over a sane people and armed with weapons of offense and defense. What sort of a fate can we anticipate for a people so situated? And when we reflect that fanaticism is infested with like fears, suspicions, impulses, follies, flights of daring and flights of cowardice common to lunacy itself, and to which it is akin, what sort of a future can we anticipate under the presidency of Abraham Lincoln?"

In many variations the tale went world-wide of the long-shanked Chief Magistrate in flight disguised in a Scotch plaid cap and a long military cloak. In thousands of journals it was repeated in news items, cartoons, and editorial comment; he wore a Scotch plaid cap and a long military cloak. Neither during the journey nor before nor after it did he wear a Scotch plaid cap and a long military coat. Neither Lamon nor Pinkerton en route, nor Judd, Curtin, Sumner, Davis, McClure, or any of those who wished him luck at the starting-point, nor Washburne, who first stepped up to him in Washington, saw him in a Scotch plaid cap or a long military coat or in garments resembling any such disguise. Yet millions of people believed he wore such a disguise because it was so made known in thousands of public prints.

Who started it? A lone press writer, Joseph Howard, a pathetic rascal who had a habit of getting newspapers into trouble with his frauds and hoaxes.

Howard telegraphed his newspaper, the *New York Times*, a responsible journal friendly to Lincoln, of Lincoln's arrival in Washington: "He wore a Scotch plaid cap and a very long military cloak, so that he was entirely unrecognizable." The *Times* printed it. And the world took to it as a good story.

Lincoln at a later time gave Benson J. Lossing, the historian, his version of the night ride through Baltimore, and the cap and cloak: "In New York some friend had presented me a new beaver hat, in a box, and in it had placed a soft wool hat. I never wore one in my life. I had this box in my room. Having informed a very few friends of the secret of my movements, and the cause, I put on an old overcoat that I had with me, and putting the soft hat in my pocket, I walked out of the house at a back door, without exciting any special curiosity. Then, I put on the soft hat, and joined my friends, without being recognized. I was not the same man." Lincoln at a later time told the Illinois Congressman Isaac N. Arnold, "I did not then, nor do I now, believe I should have been assassinated, had I gone through Baltimore as first contemplated, but I thought it wise to run no risk, where no risk was necessary."

Mingled with congratulations on his safe arrival in Washington, Frederick W. Seward noted "an undertone of regret that it should have been deemed necessary or wise to make the hasty night trip through Baltimore," this regret tracing to a feeling that assassination of public officials did not belong in the American system. Hostile journals used the incident. The *Crisis* of Columbus, Ohio, reprinted thirteen "Yankee Doodle" verses from

THE FLIGHT OF ABRAHAM.
(As Reported by a Modern Daily Paper.)

(1.) THE ALARM.

"On Thursday night, after he had retired, Mr. LINCOLN was aroused, and informed that a stranger desired to see him on a matter of life and death. * * * A conversation elicited the fact that an organized body of men had determined that Mr. LINCOLN should never leave the City of Baltimore alive. * * * Statesmen laid the plan, Bankers indorsed it, and Adventurers were to carry it into effect."

(2.) THE COUNCIL.

"Mr. LINCOLN did not want to yield, and his friends cried with indignation. But they insisted, and he left."

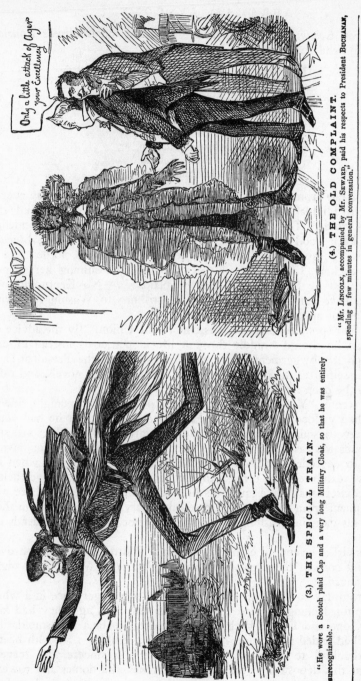

(3.) **THE SPECIAL TRAIN.**

"He wore a Scotch plaid Cap and a very long Military Cloak, so that he was entirely unrecognizable."

(4.) **THE OLD COMPLAINT.**

"Mr. LINCOLN, accompanied by Mr. SEWARD, paid his respects to President BUCHANAN, spending a few minutes in general conversation."

This series of cartoons, drawn in a current style, seem intended chiefly for fun, though they have their implications as to the "flight" of Lincoln as reported by "a modern daily paper" the *Cincinnati Commercial*, which had them from the *Louisville Courier*, one verse and the chorus reading:

> They went and got a special train
> At midnight's solemn hour,
> And in a cloak and Scotch plaid shawl,
> He dodged from the Slave-Power.
>
> Lanky Lincoln came to town,
> In night and wind and rain, sir,
> Wrapped in a military cloak,
> Upon a special train, sir.

"Lincoln ran from the first whisperings of danger as fleetly as ever a naked-legged Highlander pursued a deer upon Scotia's hills," said the *Louisville Courier*. "The men who made the Declaration of Independence did not make it good in that way. They fought for their rights; *Lincoln* runs for his . . . and leaves his wife. They ought to swap clothes. She is a true Kentuckian. Lincoln began the exchange by assuming her striped petticoat, called by his friends a 'Scotch plaid.' . . . No Kentucky-born man would have run all the way from Harrisburg to Washington, with but the ghost of an enemy in sight."

Vanity Fair spoke for Baltimore as true to the Union: "By the advice of weak men, who should straddle through life in petticoats instead of disgracing such manly garments as pantaloons and coats, the President-elect disguises himself after the manner of heroes in two-shilling novels, and rides secretly, in the deep night, from Harrisburg to Washington."

Lamon wrote: "Mr. Lincoln soon learned to regret the midnight ride to which he had yielded under protest. He was convinced that he had committed a grave mistake in listening to the solicitations of a professional spy and of friends too easily alarmed, and frequently upbraided me for having aided him to degrade himself at the very moment in all his life when he should have exhibited the utmost dignity and composure." Nevertheless Lincoln's advisers may have saved his life, said Lamon, believing there was never a moment from the time he crossed the Maryland line and from then on during his days in Washington that he was not in danger of death by violence.

In the swirl of events to come there would be little time to thresh over the pros and cons of the night ride through Baltimore. Much other night riding lay ahead.

Now from day to day Lincoln could let his eyes linger once in a while on the Capitol, lacking a dome as yet, where ten years ago they had laid the cornerstone and Daniel Webster of the craglike face and smoldering black eyes had ended his oration: "And all here assembled . . . with hearts devoutly thankful to Almighty God . . . unite in sincere and fervent prayers that this deposit, and the walls and arches, the domes and towers, the columns and entablatures, now to be erected over it, may endure forever. God save the United States of America!"

CHAPTER 3

PEACE EFFORTS FAIL

COMMENCING February 4, 1861, the Peace Convention in Washington had held its sessions behind closed doors. Though an air of secret and important deliberation was desired by many of the delegates, the main proceedings leaked out and were spread over newspaper pages from day to day. Twenty-one Border and Northern States sent delegates, California and Oregon being too far away to consider sending delegates who would reach the convention before its adjournment, while Michigan, Wisconsin, and Minnesota let it be known that they expected only useless talk or mischievous propaganda could result from the proposed confabulations.

The Concert Hall of Willard's Hotel where the Peace Convention met

Mostly the delegates were old men. One day's session was given to eulogy over an aged and almost blind delegate who died before presenting his credentials. The presiding officer was a tottering, ashen ruin, John Tyler, once a President of the United States. The record of the convention noted that nearly every speaker advised short speeches and then made a long one. Chauncey F. Cleveland of Connecticut began: "I have not got up to make a speech. We have had too much speech making here. It all does no sort of good—no opinions are changed. I shall take no such course." Then he went into a long explanation of how sensible men get together and talk things over, and finally, as to slavery, "For one, I am sick of the whole subject." He concluded, "Let us stop making long speeches."

Likewise G. C. Bronson of New York arose to say: "Why have we come here? If we are only here to make speeches, our mission is useless." Then he went ahead with a speech. Various delegates reminded each other of hoary adages: "Peace hath her victories no less than war" and "A soft answer turneth away wrath." The outcry, "For God's sake!" came at frequent intervals from the orators, Delegate Bradford of Maryland saying, "Where I reside, the universal cry is, 'For God's sake, settle these questions!'" As Delegate James A. Seddon of Virginia arose for one of several speeches, he apologized: "My voice has failed me today, and I do not know that I can speak in audible tones, but I will try." And on trying he found his vocal cords in working order.

The same conflict of wills and opinion that over the country was moving toward war was reproduced in the convention. J. Dixon Roman of Maryland pleaded: "We have never interfered with your institutions. You must now let us alone." This roused John M. Palmer of Illinois, who had changed from a Democrat to a Republican supporter of Lincoln on the slavery-extension issue, and now shouted: "You gentlemen have been talking fairly for the last twenty years, and yet this treason, black as night, has been plotted. Among you are thousands of men, guilty of treason beside which that of John Brown was paltry and insignificant." Which, of course, didn't clear the atmosphere for building a peace project to submit to Congress and the country.

Delegate Howard of Maryland rose to say that he had listened to these remarks with the deepest regret. "I agree that there is no *right* of secession. But the right of revolution always exists." Salmon Portland Chase, a practiced orator from Ohio, took the floor for one more of a number of speeches he had contributed. Enforcement of the law and the Constitution by the new President would mean war, declared Chase: "War! Civil war! Mr. President, let us not rush headlong into that unfathomable gulf." Whereupon Barringer of North Carolina interposed: "We come here to deal with facts, not theories"; and Delegate Stockton of New Jersey rose as a man of burdens and said: "I have not much to say, sir. I rise with a sadness which almost prevents my utterance," then: "In the days of Rome, Curtius threw himself into the chasm when told by the oracle that the sacrifice of his life would save his country. Alas! Is there no Curtius here?" And no Curtius arising or responding, he closed: "It is useless to attempt to dwarf this movement of the South by the name of treason. Call it by what name you will, it is a revolution, and this is a right which the people of this country have derived in common from their ancestors." It was left for Delegate Granger of New York to voice meditations derived from long study of the oratory of Daniel Webster, saying: "Mr. President, I have been deeply pained at the manner in which some of the gentlemen have here spoken of the possible dissolution of this Government. When, perchance, the rude hand of violence shall have seized upon the muniments and archives of our country's history; when all the monuments of art that time and treasure may here have gathered, shall be destroyed; when these proud domes shall totter to their fall, and the rank grass wave around their mouldering columns; when the very name of Washington, instead of stirring the blood to patriotic action, shall be a byeword and a reproach—then will this people feel what was the value of the Union!" Which was well-cadenced language, but nobody cared.

One speaker did rise who was neither lawyer nor politician. "I am here as a plain merchant, out of place, I very well know," said William E. Dodge of New York, millionaire dry-goods wholesaler, copper-dealer, iron, coal and railway capitalist, churchman, landowner in Michigan, Wisconsin, Georgia, Texas. "I came at the request of the Chamber of Commerce of New York. I speak to you as a business man, as a merchant of New York, the commercial metropolis of the nation. I am no politician. I have no interest except such as is common to the people. . . . The merchants of our great commercial cities of Baltimore, Philadelphia, New York and Boston, are not listless or unenterprising men. They are accustomed to the interests, the bustle, the excitement of business. How stands the matter in those cities today? Now, just when the spring trade should be commencing, go to the extensive and magnificent establishments for the sale of goods in any of the cities I have named. What will you see? The heavy stocks of goods imported last autumn, or laid in from our own manufactories, remain untouched upon the shelves. The customers are not there. The merchants, in despair, are poring over their ledgers; checking off the names of their insolvent debtors, a new list of whom comes by each day's mail." He spoke of clerks, mechanics; "tens of thousands belonging to these classes must have relief."

Thomas J. Turner of Illinois spoke briefly and summarized the irony of the convention: "We may call spirits from the vasty deep, but the question is, will they come?"

On the afternoon of the sixteenth day, Stephen T. Logan of Illinois, former law partner of A. Lincoln, rose to say, "I am informed that Mr. Lincoln, the President-elect, has arrived in the city." He moved that the president of the convention be instructed to call upon the President-elect of the United States and inform him that the members of the convention would be pleased to wait upon him in a body. It was so ordered. Tyler, however, sent a note to Lincoln instead of calling in person, and Lincoln replied that he would be happy to receive the delegates at nine o'clock that evening. He had been represented, Lincoln told L. E. Chittenden that day, as an evil spirit, the implacable enemy of Southern men and women; while he did not set up for a beauty, he felt that upon closer acquaintance they would not find him so ugly nor so black as painted. At nine o'clock the delegates came, some of them curious to see what they would see.

They found Lincoln in the parlor of a second-floor Willard's Hotel suite, a tall man standing alone, no secretaries, guards, formalities. Delegate Chittenden, seeing that no arrangements had been made, took a place alongside Lincoln and helped Chase of Ohio introduce the delegates. In nine cases out of ten, one noticed, on hearing the last name of a delegate, Lincoln in his greeting promptly called off the first name and middle initials, if any. As the guests were received they gathered around him in a circle which widened till it included most of the Peace Convention. Chittenden noted: "He could not have appeared more natural or unstudied in his manner if he had been entertaining a company of neighbors in his western home. His animated face towered above them, his vivacity surprised every spectator. He had some apt observation for each person the moment he heard his name." The President-elect greeted William C. Rives of Virginia: "I always had an idea you were a much taller man. It is, indeed, pleasant to meet one who has so honorably represented his country in Congress and abroad." To James B. Clay he remarked: "Your name is all the endorsement you require. From my boyhood the name of Henry Clay has been an inspiration to me." To George W. Summers of western Virginia, "You cannot be a disunionist unless your nature has changed since we were in Congress." To Reverdy Johnson, whom he had last seen in the McCormick-Hussey reaper case in Cincinnati, "I had to bid you good-bye just at the time when our intimacy had ripened to a point for me to tell you my stories." To the tall Indian-fighter, Colonel Doniphan of Missouri: "Is this the Doniphan who made that splendid march across the plains and swept

Willard's Hotel on Pennsylvania Avenue about midway between the Capitol and the White House

the swift Comanches before him? You have come up to the standard of my expectations." To F. K. Zollicoffer, "Does liberty still thrive in the mountains of Tennessee?"

In the midst of talk about the Constitution came the sepulchral voice of Seddon of Virginia telling Lincoln: "It is not of your professions we complain. It is of your sins of omission, of your failure to enforce the laws, to suppress your John Browns and your Garrisons, who preach insurrection and make war upon our property."

"I believe John Brown was hung and Mr. Garrison imprisoned," was the dry rejoinder of Lincoln. "You cannot justly charge the North with dis-obedience to statutes or with failing to enforce them. You have made some which were very offensive, but they have been enforced, notwithstanding."

The arguments of the two men were in the mouths of millions of people. Seddon led again: "You do not enforce the laws. You refuse to execute the statute for the return of fugitive slaves. Your leading men openly declare that they will not assist the marshals to capture or return slaves."

"You are wrong in your facts again," replied Lincoln. "Your slaves have been returned, yes, from the shadow of Faneuil Hall in the heart of Boston. Our people do not like the work, I know. They will do what the law commands, but they will not volunteer to act as tip-staves or bum-bailiffs. The instinct is natural to the race. Is it not true of the South? Would you join in the pursuit of a fugitive slave if you could avoid it? Is such the work of gentlemen?"

"Your press is incendiary," was the new point of attack from Seddon. "It advocates servile insurrection, and advises our slaves to cut their masters' throats. You do not suppress your newspapers. You encourage violence."

"I beg your pardon, Mr. Seddon," said the sectionally chosen President-elect. "I intend no offence, but I will not suffer such a statement to pass unchallenged, because it is not true. No northern newspaper, not the most ultra, has advocated a slave insurrection or advised the slaves to cut their masters' throats. A gentleman of your intelligence should not make such assertions."

There came exchanges of remarks with other delegates, followed at last by a curious scene. William E. Dodge, the merchant and capitalist, who had come to Washington heading a committee of twenty-five New Yorkers, stepped forward and spoke. He had met Lincoln that morning for the first time; he had on the request of the proprietor of Willard's Hotel given up his suite of rooms, the best in the house, Parlor No. 6 overlooking the main entrance, for the use of the Lincoln family; young Bob Lincoln had knocked at the door of his room and taken him to Lincoln for a greeting and thanks.

"Now," said Dodge, closing a speech, "it is for you, sir, to say whether the whole nation shall be plunged into bankruptcy, whether the grass shall grow in the streets of our commercial cities."

"Then I say it shall not," said Lincoln with a twinkling eye. "If it depends upon me, the grass shall not grow anywhere except in the fields and the meadows."

"Then you will yield to the just demands of the South. You will not go to war on account of slavery!"

"I do not know that I understand your meaning, Mr. Dodge," said Lincoln in an even tone, with all merriment gone from his face. "Nor do I know what my acts or opinions may be in the future, beyond this. If I shall ever come to the great office of President of the United States, I shall take an oath. I shall swear that I will faithfully execute the office of President of the United States, of all the United States, and that I will, to the best of my ability, preserve, protect, and defend the Constitution of the

United States. This is a great and solemn duty. With the support of the people and the assistance of the Almighty I shall undertake to perform it. I have full faith that I shall perform it. It is not the Constitution as I would like to have it, but as it *is*, that is to be defended. The Constitution will not be preserved and defended until it is enforced and obeyed in every part of every one of the United States. It must be so respected, obeyed, enforced and defended, let the grass grow where it may."

Mr. Dodge made no reply, had no further inquiry. The slow, even-toned response had the color of an oath. Chittenden noted that the faces of Republicans wore surprised satisfaction. Some of the Southerners walked out. A New Jersey delegate asked an involved question as to admitting Territories with the right to slavery, Lincoln saying: "It will be time to consider that question when it arises. Now we have other questions which we must decide. In a choice of evils, war may not always be the worst."

To a Pennsylvania delegate saying that compromise must come sooner or later and the present moment was "propitious," the reply was: "Perhaps your reasons for compromising the alleged difficulties are correct, and that now is the favorable time to do it; still, if I remember correctly, *that* is not what I was elected for!"

As the delegates drifted out, Rives of Virginia said: "He is probably not so great a statesman as Mr. Madison, he may not have the will power of General Jackson. He may combine the qualities of both. He will be the head of his administration, and he will do his own thinking."

Between the breakfast with Seward that morning and the reception in the evening, Lincoln had talked with several important people. He was turning now to his first night of sleep in Washington since he was mentioned for the job of President.

At eleven o'clock he had called with Seward at his future home, the White House, chatted with President Buchanan, shaken hands with the Cabinet. At half-past two in the afternoon he had met the Illinois Congressmen and Senators, headed by Stephen A. Douglas. At seven in the evening he had dined at Seward's home on F Street. At ten o'clock, after the Peace Convention delegates had departed, he received "reciprocal" calls from the Buchanan Cabinet members, also plenty of private citizens. Betweenwhiles he had held interviews with the army chief, General Scott, with Francis P. Blair, Sr., and Montgomery Blair, with many officials and would-be officials. He had sent a messenger to the Senate asking Senator James Harlan of Iowa to come, and Harlan saw "the room in which Lincoln stood, the corridors and halls and stairs leading to it, crowded full of people, each one, apparently, intent on obtaining an opportunity to say a few words to him *privately*." He had shut out all visitors when Senator Harlan arrived and, according to Harlan, said, "I sent for you to tell me whom to appoint as members of my cabinet." Harlan replied, "I have no names to suggest, and expect to be satisfied with your selections," which, of course, was one reason Lincoln had called him in. Those who had names to suggest were coming without being asked.

Tomorrow was Sunday. Perhaps he would sleep. Perhaps he could sleep while Cabinet-making. He had once remarked that his carpentering father, too, had been a cabinetmaker.

Mrs. Lincoln and the three Lincoln boys took their first Washington breakfast with husband and father the next morning. Of the turmoil Mrs. Lincoln cried: "Oh, will it never stop? Will Inauguration Day never come?" At Harrisburg, she had insisted that she must accompany her husband, and A. K. McClure of the group which made the final plans for the secret journey said: "The greatest difficulty we had on that occasion was to prevent Mrs. Lincoln from creating a scene that would have given publicity to the movement. I thought her a fool." Her arrival was noted by the *Evening Star:* "The peep afforded at Mrs. Lincoln in passing from the carriage to the hotel presented a comely, matronly, lady-like face, bearing an unmistakable air of goodness, strikingly the opposite of the ill-natured portraits of her by the pens of some of the sensation writers."

Lincoln went with Seward to St. John's Church (Episcopal) that Sunday morning, held a massive prayer book inscribed "The President of the United States" which had known the hands of several Presidents. The *Evening Star* reported his plain black clothes, black whiskers, and hair well trimmed, "a different man entirely from the hard-looking pictorial representations seen of him . . . some of the ladies say he is almost good looking."

Walking from church, Lincoln said to Seward, as Seward told it to his son Frederick: "Governor Seward, there is one part of my work that I shall have to leave largely to you. I shall have to depend upon you for taking care of these matters of foreign affairs, of which I know so little, and with which I reckon you are familiar."

On their walk they met persons known to Seward and he introduced them to Lincoln. These sidewalk receptions ended at Willard's, where Lincoln handed Seward a copy of the inaugural address. Seward took it home, read it closely, and prepared a letter addressed to "The Honorable Abraham Lincoln," dated "Sunday Evening, February 24th, 1861," suggesting changes.

Slated as the next Secretary of State, regarded by many as present and past leader of the Republican party, Seward wrote, "I have a common responsibility and interest with you, and I shall adhere faithfully to you in every case." His many public words and private dealings with men North and South in recent weeks led him to write for Lincoln's eye: "Only the soothing words which I have spoken have saved us and carried us along thus far. Every loyal man, and indeed every disloyal man, in the South will tell you this."

Vice-President John C. Breckinridge of Kentucky called to pay his respects to the President-elect. Francis P. Blair, Sr., came and made inquiries and suggestions which he believed befitting one who had been foremost in the Kitchen Cabinet of Andrew Jackson.

Inauguration was eight days off, days full of people and words. Republican factions wrangled over the Cabinet make-up. Chase of Ohio had antislavery views and was favored by Horace Greeley; this roused Seward, Weed, and other New Yorkers of moderate views, who for years had whetted their tomahawks for Greeley. A large anti-Chase delegation filed into Lincoln's Parlor No. 6 one day and protested.

Lincoln's answer came slow. He began only after a long pause. He pointed out that it was a time of conflicting claims and interests. His wish was to bring men together who would command the confidence of the whole country and of the party. Seward had genius, had performed eminent services, and was held in high respect. Nevertheless, Chase had claims no one could deny, claims not so great as Seward's, perhaps, but this he would not now discuss. The party and the country wanted the co-operation of all good men. . . . Again a long pause. . . . He took a paper from a desk drawer, said that he had written out his Cabinet selections with care and deliberation: "And now you are here to tell me I must break the slate and begin the thing all over again." Then he began slowly to suggest changes in the slate: "How would it do for us to agree upon a change like this?" As the changes made the slate worse than ever, the delegation, as Lamon saw it, was "shocked, disappointed, outraged." Lincoln went on, adding that Seward could go as Minister to England.

Was he playing with them? What could they do or say? They filed out, and for the moment that particular affair was settled.

However, the attacks on Simon Cameron for Secretary of War became sharper, while battalions of Republicans who hated Francis P. Blair, Sr., and all his works tried to erase from the slate the name of Montgomery Blair for Postmaster General. Hoosier committees came to say Schuyler Colfax and not Caleb B. Smith should be the choice for Secretary of the Interior.

One morning Lincoln was exercising what Congressman A. G. Riddle called "his marvelous gift of improvising illustrative stories" when "the majestic form of General Scott was seen grandly rising in the open stairway, steady and unswerving, as if lifted by noiseless machinery." The General advanced, stood at attention in full-dress uniform, a golden alphabet of gallantry, a parade halted and motionless. Colonel E. V. Sumner spoke the formal introduction to Lincoln. And the Head of the Army bowed, loosened his three-hundred-pound body in a sweeping salute of plumes. He concurred with all his heart in the dismissal from the army that week of Brigadier General David E. Twiggs of the Department of Texas "for his treachery to the flag of his country," for transferring to the use of the Confederate States supplies, clothing, harness, tools, wagons, horses, mules, to the value of $1,209,500. He believed that if war came it would take at least 300,000 troops to conquer the seceded States, and at least $250,000,-000, and then heavy garrisons couldn't keep them conquered. If the Government should say to the seceded States, "Wayward sisters, depart in peace," he would not murmur. This General Scott was writing in a letter to Seward.

The Public Man wrote of Douglas's saying: "The Blairs are moving heaven and earth to get control of Mr. Lincoln's administration. If they can get and keep their grip on Lincoln, this country will never see peace or prosperity again, in your time, or in mine, or in our children's children's time. They will be the evil genius, sir, of the republic." Douglas blamed the Blairs for Lincoln's night ride through Baltimore: "They, and nobody else, you may depend upon it."

The Public Man asked whether Lincoln was weak and pliable. "No, he is not that, sir," replied Douglas, "but he is eminently a man of the atmosphere which surrounds him. He has not yet got out of Springfield, sir. He has Springfield people with him. He has his wife with him. He does not know that he is President-elect of the United States. He does not see that the shadow he casts is any bigger now than it was last year. It will not take him long to find it out when he has got established in the White House. But he has not found it out yet. Besides, he knows he is a minority President, and that breaks him down."

Mayor James G. Berret and the Washington Board of Aldermen called to welcome Lincoln to the city. He responded, "When we shall become better acquainted—and I say it with great confidence—we shall like each other better." He spoke to a crowd of Washington serenaders as though he had come to a city of strangers. He would take the serenade as a compliment. "As such please accept my thanks for it." The people of Washington were almost all politically opposed to him. The ill feeling between them and the people from whom he came depended on "misunderstanding." He might have it in his power to remove something of this misunderstanding. They would become better acquainted and be better friends. "And expressing my desire to hear a little more of your good music, I bid you good-night."

Yet there came familiar faces, Iowa men who had gone the limit to nominate him at Chicago, Grenville M. Dodge, whom he had last talked with in Council Bluffs about the best Pacific-railway route. Dodge was writing his wife one day that week, "We are busy before the railroad committees," and later the same week: "A daily overland mail and pony express bill passed. Starting from Council Bluffs it will bring all the stock from the Butterfield route, and pay that company a million dollars to carry it overland, via Council Bluffs and Fort Kearney."

Two Congressmen, a Douglas Democrat and a Lincoln Republican, entered Lincoln's room together and urged a vigorous, firm policy. They were John A. Logan—an Irish Kentuckian from southern Illinois, with black eyes, black oily hair, and a long drooping black oily mustache, nicknamed "Black Jack"—and Owen Lovejoy of northern Illinois, with square shoulders, smooth face, sensitive mouth. Lincoln heard them and met their suggestion as cheerfully as possible: "As the country has placed me at the helm of the ship, I'll try to steer her through."

Judge David Davis of Bloomington, Illinois, had taken an expensive suite at Willard's four numbers down the hall from Lincoln's parlor. "He was located," wrote Henry C. Whitney, another Illinois man, "so that he might be in a comfortable place to respond to the invitation which never came, to advise as to early appointments." Next to Davis was a Chicago lawyer, Corydon Beckwith, seeking promotion for a brother in government service.

A delegation of Baltimore Republicans ushered themselves in, headed by a spokesman with a bristling shock of dark hair on a large head with a sour face. He began, "Mr. President," and was corrected, "Not yet." With a feeble smile he commenced over, "Mr. President-elect," and recited how he and his fellows had borne abuse, threats, obloquy, and now in justice should have offices. Lincoln thanked them for their visit, and according to Leonard Grover, a theatre-manager who had been invited to come along, likened his callers to zealous soldiers of the Crusades, marching, buffeted, suffering. He pictured an army attacking a walled city. Under fierce fire of arrows and huge catapults they dragged their scaling ladders, and with thinning ranks mounted the ramparts, turned the tide, and captured the city.

"But, gentlemen," pleasantly smiled the President-elect, "those heroic soldiers who were first on top of the walls, didn't get the offices." The delegation was answered. They walked out. They seemed pleased. They had been likened to Crusaders. Their spokesman had poured it on for Lincoln. And Lincoln in turn had poured it on.

A committee from Congress called to notify Lincoln that he was duly certified as President-elect of the United States. He replied in two sentences expressing gratitude, a distrust of his own ability, reliance on free government and the people, and above all, an unshaken faith in the Supreme Ruler of nations.

Among the earliest to see Lincoln on his Washington arrival was his first law partner, Stephen T. Logan of Springfield. Lincoln told Logan he wanted an interview that day with Charles S. Morehead, former Governor of Kentucky, a Peace Convention delegate; he and Lincoln were Whig Congressmen together in 1848. Logan went straight to Morehead, who was not yet out of bed, shocked the ex-Governor with the news of Lincoln's secret arrival, and gave him Lincoln's request for an interview. Morehead said he would prefer other gentlemen along with him at the interview. That too was Lincoln's idea, said Logan. The interview was set for that day and put off from day to day on account of the crowded Lincoln program. One night at nine o'clock, however, Morehead called in company with important and representative men from the other Border Slave States, William C. Rives of Virginia, former Minister to France, Judge George W. Summers of Virginia, Colonel A. W. Doniphan of Missouri, and James Guthrie of Kentucky, Secretary of the Treasury under President Pierce.

Morehead and Rives had been to Seward and reported to their colleagues that Seward pledged his honor that there would be no coercion or collision, and credited Seward with the graphic words: "If this whole matter is not satisfactorily settled within sixty days after I am seated in the saddle, and hold the reins firmly in my hand, I will give you my head for a football." They hoped for something like that from Lincoln.

The conversation ran several hours. Mr. Lincoln received them very kindly and began by stating (according to Morehead) that he was "accidentally elected President of the United States, that he had never aspired to a position of that kind, that it had never entered his head," that except for one abstract opinion in his House Divided speech not intended as a basis for political action, he had never in all his addresses uttered a sentence that could be tortured into enmity against the South.

Morehead replied that Mr. Lincoln was mistaken if he supposed that the deep feeling pervading the South was a personal enmity toward himself, that Mr. Lincoln's party, however, had declared antagonism to the dearest and best rights of the South, which required guarantees from him. "You hold in the hollow of your hand the destiny of thirty millions of people," said the ex-Governor of Kentucky. Any guarantees made by the next President would ensure a program of peace.

Lincoln said that he was willing to give a constitutional guarantee that slavery should not be molested in any way, directly or indirectly, in the States; that he was willing to go further and give a guarantee that it should not be molested in the District of Columbia; that he would go still further and say that it should not be disturbed in the docks, arsenals, forts, and other places within the slaveholding States; but that as for slavery in the Territories his whole life was dedicated in opposition to its extension there; that he was elected by a party which had made that a portion of its platform, and he should consider that he was betraying that party if he ever agreed, under any state of the case, to allow slavery to be extended in the Territories.

The Border State men urged that natural laws would forbid slavery in the rough lands of New Mexico and in the colder regions of the North. If Mr. Lincoln was a true and sincere Union man, why have an empty prohibition when the laws of nature were a stronger prohibition than could be passed by act of Congress? This question Lincoln waived by saying he was committed on the subject. Morehead responded: "Mr. President, when you were elected, sir, I thought—I have been taught to believe—that you were the President of the Union. I opposed you, sir, with all the zeal and energy of which I was master. I endeavored to prevent your election, not because I had any personal feelings of enmity toward you, but because I believed it would lead to the very result we now witness. I opposed you, sir, but you are my President, you have been elected according to the forms of the Constitution, and I think that some little deference is due to the opinions of those who constitute the majority."

Lincoln replied at once and rather briskly: "If I am a minority President, I am not the first. At all events, I obtained more votes than you could muster for any other man."

Morehead at once rejoined that he did not intend to recall to Lincoln that he was a minority President, but simply to announce to him that he was President of the whole people. Doniphan then interposed with an outline of the three lines of action open to Lincoln. First, he might remain perfectly idle and passive, and let the disintegration of the States go on as it had gone on; second, he might give guarantees such as were asked, and bring the whole power of his Administration to bear in obtaining those guarantees; or, third, he might resort to coercion and attempt to force the seceded States into obedience.

The conversation slackened a little among the five men, four of them in a half-circle around Lincoln's chair. Morehead then spoke with deep feeling, phrased an appeal regarding the use of force. He had trusted and prayed to God that Lincoln would not resort to coercion, knowing that if he did, the history of his Administration would be written in blood "and all the waters of the Atlantic Ocean could never wash it from his hands."

Lincoln asked Morehead: "What would you do? Do you mean by coercion the collecting of the revenue and the taking back of the forts which belong to the United States?" Morehead replied this was the only mode possible under the Constitution for a resort to coercion—by an attempt to collect revenue and take back the forts.

Lincoln had now placed himself (according to Morehead's account) in a chair with rounds to it, his heels on the highest round, his elbows on his knees, his chin and jaws resting in his hands, in an attitude of listening. When he spoke he would drop his hands and raise his head. He said he would tell Morehead a little anecdote of his first days as a lawyer.

An old man, continued Lincoln, had applied to him to bring a suit, and made out a capital case, he thought, but when the evidence was detailed before the jury it was the worst case that he had ever listened to, and while the evidence was going on the old man came listening to the evidence himself, and whispered in his ear, "Guv it up."

"Now, Governor," he asked Morehead, "wouldn't this be 'guvin' it up'?"

"Mr. President, it may be said that it would be 'guvin' it up,' but hadn't you better 'guv it up' without bloodshed than drench this land with blood, and then have to 'guv it up'?"

Lincoln said he must swear to see the law faithfully executed, and spoke directly to Morehead, "I would like to know from you what I am to do with my oath of office." Morehead said that Congress could refuse to give him the powers to collect revenue on armed vessels outside of ports, and inquired: "If Congress fails to give the necessary power, Mr. President, to you to collect the revenue by vessels outside the ports, how are you to collect it? Do you think you can send a Collector to the port of Charleston, to the port of Savannah, or of New Orleans, to collect the revenue there? Is it not an impossibility, and does your oath bind you to a thing that is impossible? As to the forts, that is a matter within your discretion. Sir, you can withdraw the troops if you please. You are Commander-in-Chief, and it belongs to you either to keep them there or to withdraw them totally and prevent a collision, and a subsequent deadly and ruinous war."

"Well," said Lincoln as he lifted his face from the chin rest formed by his hands, "I will only answer you by telling you a little anecdote which struck me—excuse me, a little anecdote which struck me as you were going on. It is from Aesop's Fables, and, doubtless, in your schoolboy days, you have read it. Aesop, you know, illustrates great principles often by making mute animals speak and act, and, according to him, there was a lion once that was desperately in love with a beautiful lady, and he courted the lady, and the lady became enamored of him and agreed to marry him, and the old people were asked for their consent. They were afraid of the lion, with his long and sharp claws and his tusks, and they said to him, 'We can have no objection to so respectable a personage as you, but our daughter is frail and delicate, and we hope that you will submit to have your claws cut off and your tusks drawn, because they might do very serious injury to her.' The lion submitted, being very much in love. His claws were cut off and his tusks drawn, and they took clubs then and knocked him on the head."

Ex-Governor Morehead replied that the anecdote was exceedingly interesting, very apropos, but not altogether a satisfactory answer. "Mr. Lincoln, this is to me, sir, the most serious and all-absorbing subject that has ever engaged my attention as a public man. I look to the injury that a fratricidal war is to do not only to my own section that is to be desolated and drenched in blood, but to the cause of humanity itself. I appeal to you, apart from these jests, to lend us your aid and countenance in averting a calamity."

Before Lincoln could reply, Rives of Virginia arose and delivered a cadenced oration in a voice sometimes trembling. He was a very old man, he said, yet there had never been a throb of his heart that was not for the perpetuation of the Union, and his every effort had been exerted to procure guarantees that would perpetuate the Union. That Mr. Lincoln might know and might not say thereafter that he was not fully warned, Rives would state that he agreed with every word spoken by Mr. Morehead, and moreover that if Mr. Lincoln did resort to coercion, Virginia would leave the Union and join the seceding States. "Nay, sir," said Rives, "old as I am, and dearly as I have loved the Union, in that event I go with all my heart."

At this, according to Morehead's account, Lincoln leaped from his chair, advanced one step toward where Rives was standing, and cried, "Mr. Rives, Mr. Rives, if Virginia will stay in, I will withdraw the troops from Fort Sumter."

Rives stepped back and said: "Mr. President, I have no authority to speak for Virginia. I am one of the humblest of her sons, but if you do that it will be one of the wisest things you have ever done. Give us guarantees and I can only promise you that whatever influence I possess shall be exerted to restore the Union to what it was."

As the others rose from their chairs and all five men were standing, Lincoln said, "Well, gentlemen, I have been wondering very much whether if Mr. Douglas or Mr. Bell had been elected President, you would have dared to talk to him as freely as you have to me."

Morehead's impression was that Guthrie answered, "Mr. President, if General Washington occupied the seat that you will soon fill, and had it been necessary to talk to him as we have to you to save such a Union as this, I, for one, should talk to him as we have to you." This, as Morehead noted, closed the conversation.

According to John P. Usher, who later received many matters in confidence from Lincoln, the President-elect during the conference with the Virginia committee said, "I understand you claim and believe yourselves to be Union men, that the Richmond Convention is opposed to a dissolution of the Union, and that you believe a majority of the people of the State want to remain in the Union." They said, "Yes," Lincoln replying, "I can't understand it at all; Virginia wants to remain in the Union, and yet wants me to let South Carolina go out and the Union be dissolved, in order that Virginia may stay in."

On the evening of March 2, Lincoln, Seward, General Scott, and others dined with Rudolf Mathias Schleiden, Minister from the Hanseatic Republic and the Free City of Bremen, Germany, whose ships in American ports outnumbered those of all other nations except Great Britain. Four days before Schleiden had written a report to his Government that "like a thief in the night, the future President arrived here on the early morning of the 23d." General Scott, sitting next to Lincoln, remarked during the dinner that he had not voted for Lincoln and in fact had not gone to the polls at all for fifty-four years. "But I have voted for you, General," was Lincoln's quick reply, "and you will have to make up for it in war." And turning to others at the table, he said that he did not hope to give the General a chance very soon.

After the dinner Schleiden sounded the President-elect on his foreign diplomatic views. About the only thing he was able to send on to his Government was Lincoln's abrupt "I don't know anything about diplomacy. I will be very apt to make blunders."

Schleiden learned that week, however, of Lincoln's domestic diplomacy, and wrote to his Government that when Border State men asked Lincoln to remove the Federal troops from Fort Sumter, the President-elect replied: "Why not? If you will guarantee to me the State of Virginia I shall remove the troops. A State for a fort is no bad business."

Without the newspapers or Congress knowing about it, Lincoln began making an offer that week, holding the offer open for weeks afterward. He spoke of it one evening at Seward's house at a later time, according to John Hay's diary, saying that a committee of Border State pseudo-Unionists came to him for guarantees: "He promised to evacuate Sumter if they would break up their [Virginia] Convention without any row or nonsense. They demurred."

Two Republican-party elements pressed Lincoln, the antislavery extremists Sumner, Chase, Wade, Stevens, and the conciliators Seward, Charles Francis Adams, Tom Corwin. "With which side would Lincoln be allied? That, north and south, was the question," wrote C. F. Adams, Jr., who saw Seward age ten years that winter. "These men had been brooding over the questions at issue and dwelling on them till their minds had lost their tone, and become morbid."

The long-standing friendship of Charles Francis Adams and his frequent house guest Sumner was at the breaking-point. The younger Adams in a

Senate cloakroom noticed Sumner excited. "But his manner and language amazed me. He talked like a crazy man, orating, gesticulating, rolling out deep periods in theatrical, whispered tones, repeating himself," blaming Seward and the compromisers. "He had thought of this matter in the day-time, and lay awake over it whole nights. Seward had been demented all the session. The whole North would have rallied to him, but now, too late! too late!" The younger Adams tried to stop the conversation. "At this, he got angry, and said that I was discussing, not he; that I began it; and then he went straight on, for evidently, he could think of nothing else. It was very painful. The man talked so without reason, and almost without connection; and yet he gave me distinctly to understand that he alone could now guide affairs; that Seward was a mere politician vainly trying to deal with great issues."

Sumner called on Lincoln to pay his respects. Their meeting and Lincoln's impression of it went into a passage of the Public Man's diary: "As I arose to go, Mr. Lincoln pulled himself together up out of the rocking chair, and scanning me good-naturedly for a moment, said, very abruptly, 'You never put backs with Sumner, did you? . . . I supposed not. When he was in here I asked him to measure with me, and do you know he made a little speech about it?' "

And Lincoln, with an indescribable glimmer all over his face, went on: "Yes, he told me he thought 'this was a time for uniting our fronts and not our backs before the enemies of the country,' or something like that. It was very fine. But I reckon the truth was, he was—afraid to measure."

Lincoln gazed at his own length of limb, then half-quizzically, half-apologetically: "He is a good piece of a man, though—Sumner—and a good man. I have never had much to do with bishops down where we live, but, do you know, Sumner is just my idea of a bishop."

This was the beginning of Sumner and Lincoln's getting acquainted. Into the White House he would stride over and again to tell Lincoln this or that must be done, must. Into the White House he would stride, the Senator from Massachusetts, the scholar in politics, the most elegantly tailored man in House or Senate, wearing maroon vests, fawn gaiters, blue-violet neckties, high silk hat, cape over shoulders, gold-headed cane, gold watch chain, born in Boston to money and leisure with all the material goods of life provided and prepared at hand for him from birth on.

He was six feet two, broad-shouldered, with a handsomely modeled head, wavy locks of hair, sideburns, like Bright and Cobden, a beau, scholar, zealot, bachelor, fifty years old. His father, Charles Pinckney Sumner, had been named for a South Carolina statesman, while his grandfather, Major Job Sumner, had marched through the Revolutionary War in hardship and danger alongside Major John Lucas of Georgia, and these two comrades from Massachusetts and Georgia were buried side by side in St. Paul's churchyard on Broadway, New York, with a bottom inscription that ran across the two gravestones:

Lucas   Sumner
Alike in arms they rang'd   the glorious field,
Alike in turn to Death   the victors yield.

Senator Sumner's father inherited an estate valued at $12,000, the bulk of it 4,600 acres of Georgia land and Georgia securities, the grandfather having lived his active years following the Revolutionary War in Georgia. Charles Pinckney Sumner had increased this small fortune by law practice, investments, and incomes from political offices, chiefly his appointment and reappointment by Governor Levi Lincoln, a distant kinsman of Abraham Lincoln, as sheriff of Suffolk County, Massachusetts. In a letter to Governor Lincoln in 1834, Senator Sumner's father wrote that he considered Governor Lincoln his "greatest earthly benefactor." The estate of $50,000 inherited by Senator Sumner in 1839 rested on Georgia land, Georgia securities, and lucrative political appointments by Governor Levi Lincoln. These odd facts had no sentimental value to Senator Sumner as related to his feeling about either the people of Georgia or the man in the White House who had a queer habit of wanting to measure with other tall men. He was the only man of whom Lincoln would remark, "Sumner thinks he runs me." Lincoln saw early what Henry Adams emphasized in letters of the hour, that Sumner had unaccountable dignity.

"He stands six feet two in his stockings—a colossus holding his burning heart in his hand to light up the sea of life," wrote the poet Longfellow to a friend in Rome, preparing for Sumner's arrival. During years in Europe attention was lavished on him, and in England he met everybody who was anybody, from titled nobility to humble authors and scholars. Returning to America, nearly thirty years old, he seemed to Longfellow "older, more manly, more European, simple and strong and most thoroughly un-American . . . his head turned a little and no wonder." A few weeks later in a letter Longfellow wrote of "a little too much Anglomania" about his friend, but it would "wear off." In the shower bath of the Longfellow home Sumner would recite poetry, and once entered without undressing, absent-mindedly pulled the cord, and drenched a new pearl-gray suit of clothes. And the young Sumner drowsed and took his ease in the fireplace chair where Longfellow had written *Evangeline*, the poet noting his belief: "He is a strong man and will see in the end that there is something better than breakfasting at ten and dining at six." Once Sumner read aloud to Longfellow the latter half of *Hiawatha*, the poet writing in his journal, "Having a cold in the head and being rather hoarse, made it sound very lugubrious." Their friendship lasted. Beyond the self-importance of Sumner, Longfellow saw a figure of heroic mold. Of the orator he noted: "Sumner stands like a cannoneer and gesticulates as if he were ramming down cartridges," and of Sumner at a threshold of decision: "From politics as a career he still shrinks back."

Though the general upper class of Boston regarded Sumner as a renegade and a menace, he won the support of a coalition of Free-Soilers and

Democrats in a legislature deadlocked three months. By the exact minimum number of votes required, he was in 1851 elected to fill the United States Senate seat vacated by Daniel Webster. No sooner was he thus chosen than he wrote to John Bigelow that he was not the man for the office. "Every heart knoweth its own secret, & mine has never been in the Senate of the United States; nor is it there yet. . . . I now embark on a career which takes from me all opportunity of study and meditation, to which I had hoped to devote myself. I do not wish to be a politician." He would rather have been a judge, and once indicated a wish to be president of Harvard College. "The true grandeur of humanity," ran a key sentence of Sumner, "is in moral elevation, sustained, enlightened and decorated by the intellect of man." His quotations from the classics and from instances in history were usually the nuggets of his discourse.

As a Phi Beta Kappa orator in 1848 Sumner took his fling at those who were satisfied with the Constitution and dead set against change: "When Sir Samuel Romilly proposed to abolish the punishment of death for stealing a pocket handkerchief, the Commons of England consulted certain officers of the law, who assured the House that such an innovation would endanger the whole criminal law of the realm. And when afterwards this illustrious lawyer (for, of all men in the history of the English law, Romilly is most truly the model lawyer) proposed to abolish the obscene punishment for high treason, requiring the offender to be drawn and quartered, and his bowels to be thrown into his face, while his body yet palpitates with life, the Attorney-General of the day, in opposing this humane amendment, asked, 'Are the safeguards, the ancient landmarks, the bulwarks of the Constitution, to be thus hastily removed?' Which gave occasion for the appropriate exclamation in reply, 'What! to throw the bowels of an offender into his face, one of the safeguards of the British Constitution! I ought to confess that until this night, I was wholly ignorant of this bulwark!'"

Sumner quoted the complaint to a Lord Chancellor, "You like not anything new unless you be yourself the author thereof," and the reply of the Lord Chancellor: "Your Grace wrongeth me. I have never been the author yet of any one new thing, for which I thank my God." Sumner put value on the art of protest. Milton was his poet and Leibnitz his "gigantic genius of knowledge" teaching "Man seems able to arrive at perfection." It charmed him that Leibnitz foresaw a universal language, confusion of tongues forgotten "and the union of hearts consummated in the union of speech." He accepted wholly the theory of the school of historians then dominant, that a law of progress underlay the march of man from age to age. As Phi Beta Kappa orator he quoted Pascal, "The whole succession of men in the course of so many ages may be regarded as one man who lives always and who learns continually," and ventured for himself, "There is but one great Human Family, in which Caucasian, Ethiopian, Chinese, and Indian are all brothers, children of *one* Father, and heirs to *one* happiness." The warriors and conquerors Nimrod and Sesostris, Alexander and Caesar, Tamerlane and Napoleon, would "in the unborn ages, illumined by a truth now, alas! too dimly perceived," become extinct types like the gigantic land reptiles and monster crocodiles imbedded in fossil crusts of rock.

Sumner's direction and portent culturally ran with the widely prevalent McGuffey's *School Readers*. Though he paid respect to law and legal forms as developed by the Anglo-Saxon system, he would refer a moral question by quoting Victor Hugo's precept that each individual must be guided by "the law of laws," his own heart, as superior to the written enactments of society and government.

In a blue dress coat with gilt buttons, white vest, and white trousers, at thirty-four years of age he delivered a two-hour Fourth of July oration against war, which he predicted the liberals of the world were to outlaw. "As those standing on the mountain tops first discern the coming beams of morning, let us, from the vantage ground of liberal institutions, first recognize the ascending sun of a new era! Lift high the gates and let the King of Glory in: the King of true glory—of Peace."

Sumner of Massachusetts had become in the United States Senate the foremost spokesman of the Negro slave of the South, repeating and constantly seeking more effective ways of saying to the Slave State Senators that slavery was a five-headed wrong: (1) in pretending that man can hold property in man; (2) in nullifying the relation of man and wife and delivering slaves into concubinage or prostitution "with each other, or it may be with their masters; they are merely 'coupled,' never married"; (3) in rejecting the relation of parent and child—"the infant legally belongs, not to the mother who bore it, but to the master who bought it"; (4) in denying instruction and making it a crime for a slave to write or read; (5) in maintaining by the lash a system of compulsory labor without wages and thereby robbing the slave of the fruits of his labor. The degradation of the slave had recoiled on the masters, according to Sumner, with the result that the Southern planters with negligible exceptions were tyrants, thieves, ruffians, adulterers, sensualists, hypocrites, vulgarians with little knowledge and less manners.

That Robert E. Lee, John A. Campbell, and other eminent Southerners agreed in effect with Virginians of an earlier generation that slavery was a curse, an institution to be somehow put in the course of ultimate extinction, did not enter into Sumner's addresses. That Mrs. James Chesnut would teach a slave to read; that some planters had never sold wife away from husband or vice versa; that often in wills slaves were given their freedom; that the institution and its folkways had become terribly complicated in the many areas where the blacks outnumbered the whites, who were determined on race supremacy; that a sublime genius of human wisdom would be necessary to bring a government of justice and equity into any area where the blacks equaled or outnumbered the whites—these points Sumner considered not worth mentioning even as history and part of the record. With men of the South he had no such fraternity as that of Lincoln with Stephens, Seward with Davis, or Tom Corwin in laughing hours of fellowship with

Virginians and Georgians who smoked, took toddy, and told stories. Not even with Yankees would Sumner smoke, drink, or tell fool stories.

"I am in morals, not politics," said Sumner. He took it as his mission and role to tell the Senate and thereby the country North and South a series of tragic and horrible facts about slavery. He knew he was telling the truth. But he believed also that any such truth as he might omit was of no importance. The categories of fact always entering into the discussions of Lincoln and Seward as to slavery were out of Sumner's range and beyond his chosen role. Such points of understanding as might have come from association with Southerners were completely absent from his arguments. He mentioned the unmentionable, said what the abolitionists wanted said, and he said it with a cold wrath and an evenly measured scorn, quoting Holy Writ to his fellow Christians, citing the classics, finding many ways of saying that the North was the guardian of Freedom and Civilization, while the South was the protector of Slavery and Barbarism, till at last there were Southern Senators and Representatives who wanted to see him suffer and die.

Could wishes kill, Sumner would have died a thousand lingering deaths. His own antislavery associates in the Senate had reservations about him, Grimes of Iowa writing to Mrs. Grimes that Sumner was "harsh, vindictive," and a friend of Benjamin Wade's noting: "For Wade there was a suspicion of arrogance, a flavor of sham, in the grand assumption of the splendid Sumner. . . . Most men at each interview with him had to tell him who and what they were."

The slave-overseer "with bloody lash"; the slave-hunter publicly advertising "I have two of the finest dogs for catching negroes in the southwest"; the slave-breeder denying any distinction between the "female slave" and the "brood mare" and converting Virginia "into one grand menagerie, where men are reared for the market like oxen for the shambles"—each had an extended presentation from Sumner. He alleged further that duelists, street fighters, brawlers, and murderers were more common in the South than the North because of slavery.

Beyond open and known misconduct of slave-masters were secret chambers of "loathsome things" resulting in "moral leprosy." Under shelter of slavery "enormities occur, stranger than fiction, too terrible for imagination, and surpassing any attested experience." The South was pictured as bawdy and lewd beyond comprehension.

"The planter will one day take a slave for his harlot, and sell her the next as a being of some lower species, a beast of labor," Sumner quoted from Southey's *History of Brazil* in a Senate speech, Douglas replying, "We have had another dish of the classics served up, classic allusions, each one only distinguished for its lasciviousness and obscenity, each one drawn from those portions of the classics which all decent professors in respectable colleges cause to be suppressed, as unfit for decent young men to read." Douglas continued, "The Senator from Massachusetts had his speech written, printed, committed to memory, practised every night before the glass, with a negro boy to hold the candle and watch the gestures, and annoying the boarders in the adjoining rooms until they were forced to quit the house." Douglas went farther: "Is it his object to provoke some of us to kick him as we would a dog in the street, that he may get sympathy upon his just chastisement?" Sumner then in his own style called Douglas a skunk.

MR. SUMNER. The Senator infused into his speech the venom sweltering for months— ay, for years; and he has alleged matters entirely without foundation, in order to heap upon me some personal obloquy. I will not descend to things which dropped so naturally from his tongue. I only brand them to his face as false. I say also to that Senator, and

Charles Sumner autographs a sentiment: "A queen on the scaffold is a less pitiful sight than a woman on the auction-block." Original in the Barrett collection.

I wish him to bear it in mind, that no person with the upright form of man can be allowed— [Hesitation.]

MR. DOUGLAS. Say it.

MR. SUMNER. I will say it—no person with the upright form of man can be allowed, without violation of all decency, to switch out from his tongue the perpetual stench of offensive personality. Sir, that is not a proper weapon of debate, at least on this floor. The noisome, squat, and nameless animal to which I now refer is not the proper model for an American Senator. Will the Senator from Illinois take notice?

MR. DOUGLAS. I will—and therefore will not imitate you, Sir.

MR. SUMNER. Mr. President, again the Senator switches his tongue, and again he fills the Senate with his offensive odor. But I drop the Senator.

By degrees Sumner had come to stand for something the South wanted exterminated from the Union; he was perhaps the most perfect impersonation of what the South wanted to secede from. No other man in the Federal Government so thrust at the sin and guilt of the South while evading the issues of sin and guilt in the North, Toombs and Wigfall accusing Sumner of hypocritical and guilty silence regarding the exploitation of white men, women, and children in the mills, factories, and slums of his own Massachusetts.

Had the Southern debaters flung at Sumner a recital of the wage scales and the twelve- and fourteen-hour workday of Massachusetts mill hands, had they pictured the square miles of slums where humanity rotted in Boston, New York, Philadelphia, had they read press items on the needle-trades workers of New York and Boston, had they quoted from Emerson and Thoreau on the status of the common laborer in the North, they would not have overwhelmed Sumner, but they would have given human color to their claim that the North was not without guilt. The Southern Senators could have openly laid bare secrets and fears of the North as Sumner boldly and at risk told the whole world of matters held private and confidential among the ruling men of the South.

From a debate in the Continental Congress Sumner quoted a South Carolinian, "Our slaves being our property, why should they be taxed more than the land, sheep, cattle, horses, &c.?" and Benjamin Franklin's reply: "Slaves rather weaken than strengthen the State, and there is therefore some difference between them and sheep. *Sheep will never make any insurrection.*"

The property status of the Negro slave was rehearsed by Sumner as though perhaps it were not fully understood: "He may be bartered, leased, mortgaged, bequeathed, invoiced, shipped as cargo, stored as goods, sold on execution, knocked off at public auction, and even staked at the gaming-table on the hazard of a card or a die,—all according to law. He may be marked like a hog, branded like a mule, yoked like an ox, hobbled like a horse, driven like an ass, sheared like a sheep, maimed like a cur, and constantly beaten like a brute,—all according to law." God had made iron but never a slave, said Sumner, quoting from the thunders of Sinai, "He that stealeth a man and selleth him, or if he be found in his hand, he shall surely be put to death."

The slave-master who justified his appropriation of the fruits of Negro toil, seriously urged Sumner, was a kindred spirit of the pious Russian described by a traveler, "devoutly crossing himself at church with his right hand, with the left deliberately picking the pocket of a fellow-sinner by his side." He quoted from a translation of Luther's Bible, "He that giveth not his wages to the laborer, he is a bloodhound." In the seats around Sumner as he delivered these sentences were slave-masters as eminent and proud as Jefferson Davis and Robert Toombs; in effect the Massachusetts Senator was saying to their faces that they were thieves, pickpockets, and bloodhounds.

Quoting Koran law and comparing the Mohammedan slave with the Negro chattel of the Christian South, Sumner wished it known that when the Mohammedan master mingled his blood with that of the bondwoman the resulting offspring was given complete freedom.

The property title to a slave in the South traced in law to an African tribal custom that captives taken in war were thereby enslaved. "Thus are barbarous prerogatives of barbarous half-naked African chiefs perpetuated in American Slave-Masters." From Boswell's *Life of Dr. Samuel Johnson*

Sumner quoted a reference: "the planters of America, a race of mortals whom, I suppose, no other man wishes to resemble."

Thus spoke the man who more than any other had given basis to the Southern epithet of *Black* Republican. Year by year as he had held to his course of defying, accusing, and taunting Southern Senators with their personal responsibility for the wrongs of slavery, the antislavery sentiment had grown in Massachusetts, and his personal popularity had increased. More than once in speeches at home he said that three things were required against the monster Slavery, first, backbone, second, *backbone,* and third, BACKBONE. That he was personally incorruptible, that neither money nor social blandishments could swerve him from a chosen course, added to his political strength. He was in his years of service, one friend noted, "never even accused of being approached by a dishonorable proposition." That he sought legislation to ensure seamen their wages in case of wreck, that he pleaded exemption of conscientious objectors from any emergency militia service in Massachusetts, that he opposed capital punishment, that he befriended the fugitive Hungarian Kossuth and Irish exiles in Australia, gave him a footing as a liberal.

He was known, however, as a one-idea man, and the idea was to abolish slavery. To the question from the Senate floor whether he would return a fugitive slave, he replied that he would not, whereupon the opposition to him had held serious conferences on measures to expel him from the Senate, but decided to endure his presence rather than risk a storm.

A Northern determination to wrest control of the Federal Government from the South, to end "the amazing disproportion of offices usurped by this Slave Oligarchy," was voiced by Sumner. The great posts of the Republic, from the beginning, seemed to him "almost perpetually" in Southern hands. His two-day speech on "The Crime against Kansas" in 1856 deepened sectional cleavage. Sir George Cornewall Lewis in England read the speech and what followed two days later as "the beginning of civil war."

In his Senate seat, after a session had closed and nearly all the members had left the chamber, Sumner had been struck on the head with a cane. The blows rained till the cane broke in pieces. Bruised and lacerated without warning or a chance to fight back, he struggled to rise and get at his unseen assailant, nearly wrenching loose his desk from the iron screws that held it to the floor, he was so powerful physically.

Several of his enemies stood by with their unspoken wishes, "Let him suffer and die—it would be a blessing to the country," while Sumner lay senseless in an aisle, the flowing blood from his head soaking his shirt collar. As the news of the assault went over the country, it set tongues raging in the North and deepened the sullen defiance of the South.

Then for Sumner had come pain, the sickbed, a wheel chair, years of grinding his teeth day by day as treatments, applications of fire, were given under the supervision of a famous European surgeon, to heal a bruised spine and a partially disordered brain area. The assailant, Congressman Preston Brooks of South Carolina, who said he had only wanted to half kill

Sumner and watch him live and suffer, had resigned his seat, had been re-elected by his constituents, had been presented with more canes and wishes that he would use them as he knew how, had died in bed of strangulation, clutching at his throat as if he would tear it open while he lay a victim of violent croup or acute inflammation of the throat. Brooks's colleagues on the House floor paid him tribute as hero and patriot and on his tomb was in-scribed: "Earth has never pillowed upon her bosom a truer son, nor Heaven opened wide her gates to a manlier spirit."

Then Sumner's party had nominated Lincoln for the Presidency, and seemed ready to capture the White House when in June of 1860 Sumner stood up in the Senate for the speech that would signalize his return to active politics. He had spent nearly four years in a wheel chair seeking restoration of a mutilated backbone, he who had said backbone, *backbone*, BACKBONE were the three things necessary to fight the monster of Slavery. What had been his meditations during his lingering struggle to escape death and lifelong invalidism? What would the sick man now well again have to say? Would he be the same as before?

The old Sumner spoke in the old accents: statistics, morals, and a finality of doom. He pronounced an excommunication titled "The Barbarism of Slavery," put the slave-masters of the South in the class with barbarous African tribal chiefs; he read the Southern people beyond the pale of civili-zation, and believed that he had overcome Edmund Burke's dictum "You cannot indict a whole people." Slavery he stigmatized as "a huge insur-rection against the eternal law of God, the denial of that divine law in which God himself is manifest, thus being practically the grossest lie and the grossest atheism." From his carefully written manuscript he read four hours. "Stripped of every defense, the chastity of a whole race is exposed to violence while the result is recorded in the telltale faces of children, glowing with their master's blood, but doomed for their mother's skin to slavery, through all descending generations."

To the Southern counsel "Put thine own house in order," to the allega-tions of Rhett of South Carolina and of Toombs of Georgia that a master class in Massachusetts had gathered fortunes out of a socially lower and economically meaner class of wage slaves, Sumner replied with a complete silence. The exposition and analysis were in character. Once when asked, "Have you never looked on the other side of slavery?" Sumner replied, "There is no other side." He finished his speech.

Senator James Chesnut of South Carolina arose to say that he and his colleagues had listened quietly and would take no other notice, leaving the abolitionists of Massachusetts to worship "at the shrine of this new idol." They had hoped, Chesnut observed, "to be relieved from the outpourings of such vulgar malice," and would not make the expected and desired re-plies. "We are not inclined again to send forth the recipient of punishment howling through the world, yelping fresh cries of slander and malice."

From antislavery men by scores came letters to Sumner rejoicing in his speech as "great," "glorious," "immortal," worth its weight in gold, a blast from a ram's horn, a morning star, a battle cry, Bill Herndon writing from Springfield, Illinois: "The speech is a withering one to Slavery. It is worthy of you, and you of it. . . . We feel well out here." The *New York Herald* printed the speech in full and commented that Sumner had the philosophical acumen of Mr. Seward without the cautious political reserve, and "the honesty of Lincoln, without the craft of a candidate in nomination." The *New York Tribune* printed the speech in full in country editions but gave it less attention for city readers, and withheld editorial comment. The *New York Times* commented: "The labor of four leisure years seems to have been devoted by Mr. Sumner to collecting every instance of cruelty, violence, passion, coarseness, and vulgarity recorded as having happened within the Slave States, or as having been committed by a slaveholder," and asked: "What general good can be hoped for from such envenomed attacks? Do they aid in the least the solution of what every sensible man acknowledges to be the most delicate and difficult problem of this age?"

The *Indianapolis Daily Journal* said that the speech showed genius, learning, hate, and "is one of the ablest, most exasperating, and most useless speeches we ever read," explaining: "Slavery is all that he charges. But slaveholders are not as barbarous as their system." The *Richmond Despatch* said it betrayed the designs of the Black Republican party and was "a godsend." The *Boston Traveler* commented, "No nobler specimen of American eloquence can be found than this logical, bold, spirited, clear, and learned exposition." Thoreau, who had compared John Brown to Jesus Christ, wrote to Sumner that it was "refreshing to hear some naked truth." Sumner himself, as E. P. Whipple wrote, "was inclined to take the compliments at more than their real worth, while he experienced another though different satisfaction in reading the calumnies."

Slave property valued at $4,000,000,000 should somehow be made nonproperty, should somehow be devalued to zero, Sumner undeniably implied. A caste society of two hundred years' development and growth should reorganize itself to conform to a new definition of its property. How this devaluation and reorganization should or could be effected Sumner did not say. Such political measures as might be necessary, in his judgment, he did not name. Whether a revolution and forcible subjugation of the South might achieve it, in his view, he would not say. And necessarily his own methods made it clear that he did not believe moral suasion or a change of conscience in the South would bring the slaveholders to free their Negroes in response to his appeals. Yet Sumner's main points had been neglected, slurred over, dropped from polite conversation, deodorized and made into conventional lies. Therefore when Sumner took up one lie after another and by ancient human tests showed it to be a lie, many of his following took it that he was telling the truth and the whole truth, whereas he was not telling the whole truth but was unmasking liars North and South. For reasons best known to himself he omitted completely his thought on the ways and means by which slave property valued at $4,000,000,000 could somehow be made nonproperty, could somehow be devalued to zero, and whether he favored forcible subjugation of Southern society toward that end.

Friends encircled him while he spoke. Against his wishes friends guarded his walk to his apartment, two of them sleeping there to protect him against expected attacks. At the Barnum Hotel in Baltimore a mob gathered outside in the hope of hanging him, but the hotel proprietor helped him to elude the mob. Lydia Maria Child, an abolitionist writer, said in a letter: "Charles Sumner called to see me and brought me his photograph. We talked together for two hours, and I never received such an impression of holiness from mortal man. . . . He says he never leaves his room to go into the Senate without thinking whether he has left everything arranged as he should wish it if he were never to return to it alive."

Once Thomas Wentworth Higginson called to find Sumner writing a speech which he said would be to his last one "what first proof brandy is to molasses-and-water," adding: "I think I shall probably be shot. I don't see what else they can do." Yet this was the same Sumner who read Horace and in younger days quoted "If you wish me to weep, you must yourself first weep." To his hard, dry eyes the Southern men answered with sullen, defiant eyes. Had he wept, they would probably not have wept. The record was that he did not weep and was lacking in the gift of tears. He seemed to insist that he could be an insolent agitator and a perfect gentleman both at once. His critics held that he was either a skunk or a white swan but not both. Horace White of Illinois rated his oratory as "sophomorical and vituperative," neither instructive nor persuasive. The poet Whittier wrote to Sumner: "*The* speech is all I could wish for. There is something really awful in its Rhadamanthine severity of justice; but it was needed."

Sumner's theory was once given in a letter of comment on an address of Senator Trumbull: "He grappled with his colleague and throttled him." A Senator's speech should if possible grapple and throttle.

Then in five campaign addresses Sumner had endorsed Abraham Lincoln, the Republican party's candidate, "whose character no breath has touched, and whose heart is large enough to embrace the broad Republic and all its people," and whose election, Sumner pledged, would put the executive department of the national Government "openly and actively on the side of Freedom." To the uniformed, officered, and drilled Wide Awakes of Concord, Massachusetts, on the evening after Lincoln was elected President, Sumner said "a new government, a new order of things is inaugurated," and the balloting had irrevocably decreed that it is "wrong to admit in the Constitution the idea that there can be property in men." He inquired as to the election, "What victory of the cartridge-box ever did so much?" and said of the crisis, "Happily, Abraham Lincoln [Prolonged cheers.] has those elements of character needed to carry us through . . . he is calm, prudent, wise, and also brave . . . the Union shall be preserved and made more precious by consecration to Human Rights."

Then came weeks that harassed Sumner, when old friends saw him as "morbid" and "crazy." The winds of doctrine roared in the caverns of his mind. Before he entered his career in politics he had been one of the fore-most antiwar advocates in America, six printings having been circulated of his oration on "The True Grandeur of Nations," saying, "War crushes with bloody heel all justice, all happiness, all that is God-like in man," saying, "In our age there can be no peace that is not honorable; there can be no war that is not dishonorable."

As he had drifted into the antislavery movement he declared that the fight must be "not with fire and sword, but with earnest words." To the American Peace Society he had said that a higher authority than the Con-stitution of the United States advised against war: "Love your enemies . . . if thine enemy hunger, feed him; if he thirst, give him drink." He mocked at the English Christian nation naming its naval vessels *Avenger, Blood-hound, Bulldog, Fury, Gladiator, Goliath, Jackal, Mastiff, Rattlesnake, Revenge, Scorpion, Scourge, Serpent, Spider, Spiteful, Spitfire, Terror, Viper, Vixen, Virago, Volcano, Vulture, Wolf.*

Sumner quoted Benjamin Franklin as saying that two nations would better throw dice than fight out a dispute: "War multiplies, instead of indemnifying, losses." Like medieval torture, dueling, cannibalism, said Sumner, war should be outlawed from civilization. He could see a Promised Land of mankind without war. "Man has waded through a Red Sea of blood, and for forty centuries wandered through a wilderness of wretched-ness and error, but he stands at last on Pisgah." Confessing the Fatherhood of God and the consequent Brotherhood of Man, how could any man win "glory" by killing a brother? Sumner asked that. In 1850 as chairman of the Peace Congress Committee of the United States he issued an address pleading for an American delegation to attend the Second General Peace Congress at Paris, where several of the leading nations of Europe would discuss plans to form a Congress of Nations, revise international law, and set up a high tribunal, a world court, for the decision of controversies among nations. For the instrument of war would be substituted stipulated arbitration. "The barbarous and incongruous War System, which now encases our Christian civilization as with a cumbrous coat of mail, will be destroyed. . . . Wise and good men will secure to themselves the inexpress-ible satisfaction of aiding the advent of that happy day when Peace shall be *organized* among nations."

The next year after this appeal Charles Sumner was hurled into a political maelstrom to find himself in the United States Senate saying that the hunter of fugitive slaves was a monster who should be vomited forth from any Northern community he entered, saying, "Nothing, Sir, can be settled which is not right," saying, "By no subtle compromise or adjustment can men suspend the commandments of God, by no trick of managers, no hocus-pocus of politicians, no 'mush of concessions' . . . are we to find peace for our country and ourselves." Thus Sumner had completely for-saken negotiation and adjudication. He stood scornfully and implacably against Massachusetts' sending any delegates to the Peace Convention at Washington in February of '61.

Paradox and terror chased through his brain as he saw that by using the barbarism of war the Federal Government might root out the barbarism of slavery, writing to Count Gurowski: "I do not doubt that any conflict will precipitate the doom of Slavery. It will probably go down in blood." To Governor John Andrew of Massachusetts he wrote late in January, "The mistake of many persons comes from this,—they do not see that we are in the midst of a revolution, where reason is dethroned, and passion rules instead."

To Andrew, Sumner wrote again, when the President-elect was in New York: "If Mr. Lincoln *stands firm*, I do not doubt that our cause will be saved. All that we hear testifies to his character. *But he is a man.*"

When the petitions of 36,000 Massachusetts voters favoring the Crittenden Compromise were brought into the Senate on February 12, the Senator from Massachusetts said he was sure they would never have signed had they understood what the papers meant. He advised against the surrender of Fort Sumter. "Bankers and merchants of New York and Boston tell us that the Government shall not have money, if we do not surrender." Very well, he believed enough in small funds would come from the people to supply the Government. "From these small sums, inspired by a generous patriotism, I am glad to believe we shall have a full treasury, even if bankers and merchants stand aloof."

After this speech he had nothing more to say. In the last three weeks of the Buchanan Administration he kept silence. Seward and Adams were afraid he might break loose with another speech so inflammatory that it would throw the Border States into secession. "The utmost that can be expected is to keep him silent," wrote young Henry Adams. "To bring him round is impossible. . . . As usual I suppose he will stand on his damned dignity. Once Governor Seward and he had a quarrel. The Governor wanted him to vote for an Atlantic steamship bill, and after exhausting all other arguments, tried to act on his feelings and urged him to vote for it as a personal favor in order to aid his re-election. Sumner replied that he wasn't sent to the Senate to get Mr. Seward's re-election. On which the Governor, losing his philosophical self-command, said, 'Sumner, you're a damned fool,' and they didn't speak for six months. I'm of Seward's opinion. Let Sumner get the idea that his dignity *is* hurt, and he is a damned fool. However, you can rely upon it, we shall do all we can to prevent his bolting, and I mean to flatter him all to pieces if I have a chance."

Thus old and tried friends were tenderly guiding the course of one possibly not fully recovered in a maimed head and spine. "Looks well in the face, but is feeble and walks with an uncertain step," Longfellow had written in his journal shortly after Sumner was assaulted, writing later to Sumner in Europe, "It will not do to go limping through the remainder of your life with a tangled brain."

Whether the Brooks assault had left its mark and shadow on his intelligence was a conjectural matter. The point was sure to be raised against a character who said, "I honor any man who in the conscious discharge of his duty dares to stand alone; the sense of duty done shall be sweeter than the applause of the world, the countenance of relatives, or the hearts of friends."

An Englishman visiting Longfellow saw the poet's little daughter nestling in Sumner's lap and wrote of Sumner, "He is a man to whom all the children come." He had a slow, lumbering, St. Bernard-dog ease that drew the little ones.

Among his adjectives in his study Sumner was not so easy, and kept six dictionaries to give him the right word. He continued to read the Latin and Greek classics in the original, regularly corresponded with eminent Englishmen, and into his conversation and letters brought little French phrases as if to add a faint fragrance of violets. Anecdotes told his aversion to humor or trifling, how he would ask what there was to laugh at. The flood tide of books that swept round the walls of his large bachelor apartment had refused to yield him a secret that would breathe music or haunting cadence into a simple unadorned statement, though he read many a night till his inflamed eyes would go no farther. "Sumner cannot bear to have anyone talk as though anything could be found in books about literature and literary men that he did not know," wrote John Bigelow. "I have seen him snap up poor Bemis, one of .his satellites, and Mr. Lyman also, in a most ferocious way, for attempting to quote a book to him, as if he did not know it already. Indeed, such are the only occasions in my long acquaintance with him when he has ever appeared unamiable. But he was then an invalid of a kind that excuses everything." The folklore of the Greeks and Italians was ready to his tongue, but he was a blank and an alien when it came to familiarity with "Cooney in the Holler," "Dinah and His Villikens," "Doo-Dah," "Susannah, Don't You Cry," or "Gentle Annie." He favored Horace, Juvenal, and Homer as against what he considered the cheap and transitory mountebanks Stephen Foster and Dan Emmett. He raised laughter in the Senate when overloading with bibliophilic knowledge his speech on lifting import duties on books. He accepted praise and adoration with little doubt or inquiry, saved all letters received, was strict about filing copies of all letters he wrote, and believed this of importance to posterity.

" 'I advise you to listen to this,' Sumner used to say when he was talking about himself (as he commonly was)," wrote James Russell Lowell to Richard Watson Gilder; " '*this* is historical.' "

His occasional caution in politics was there in his telling Lincoln that Cameron was thief, corruptionist, and hypocrite, and then in so consequential a matter refusing to give Lincoln one line of writing to that effect. In a scene where connivance and fraud were so prevalent, where men were so often controlled by personal material advancement, Sumner's charm and integrity were peculiar and extraordinary or he could not have held unwaveringly such friendships as he had with those other men of like integrity in varied walks, Longfellow the poet, John A. Andrew the politician, and

Lincoln in early '61

Photograph by C. S. German at Springfield, Illinois. From original negative owned by H. W. Fay of Springfield

The President-elect raises a flag over Independence Hall, Philadelphia, at 6 A.M., February 22, '61

Photograph by F. D. Richards. From Frederick H. Meserve Collection

Lincoln in early '61

Photograph by C. S. German at Springfield, Illinois. From Frederick H. Meserve Collection

Robert Mercer Taliaferro Hunter of Virginia

From Oliver R. Barrett Collection

Roger Atkinson Pryor of Virginia

From author's collection

Lawrence Massillon Keitt of South Carolina

Photograph by McClees in author's collection

Louis Trezevant Wigfall of Texas

From Oliver R. Barrett Collection

Howell Cobb of Georgia

Fernando Wood of New York

Photographs from Frederick H. Meserve Collection

SIX UNCOMPROMISING STATES' RIGHTS MEN

Wendell Phillips the agitator. They took him as hero and crusader, Long-fellow saying one could understand Sumner only through seeing what he *was* instead of emphasizing what he was *not*.

A Boston man noted: "Men he liked best. It was in vain for the loveliest and liveliest girl to seek his attention. He would desert the most blooming beauty to talk to the plainest of men." Yet an abolitionist woman wrote in a letter of how her adorable little bronze bust of Sumner standing in a window glowed a mystical blood-color as sunset lights fell on it and bathed it with sacred effulgence. Wrote another: "He seemed to me a new Demos-thenes or Cicero, even like a Grecian god, as he stood on the platform. I thought him the handsomest and the finest-looking man I had ever seen." Others agreed with one summary of him, "He was vain, conceited, fond of flattery, overbearing in manner, and wore a constant air of superiority." He never inspired the woman he drew as partner at a social affair "with the pleasant consciousness of possessing his regard or esteem," wrote Mrs. Jefferson Davis, noting also, "He never intruded his peculiar views in any degree, but read up on the Indian mutiny, lace, Demosthenes, jewels, Seneca's morals, intaglios, the Platonian theory, and once gave me quite an interesting résumé of the history of dancing."

The gracious Julia Ward Howe asked him to meet some friends of hers at dinner. He said he wasn't interested and, "Really, Julia, I have lost all my interest in individuals." Her quick answer: "Why, Charles! God hasn't got as far as that yet." Though a hearty eater carrying a comfortably rounded paunch, he never drank, gambled, swore, nor used slang or the vulgar idioms of American speech. "Nobody ever heard an oath slip from his lips," wrote E. P. Whipple, the author to whom Sumner showed his collection of etchings and paintings, "but he was the best swearer by proxy and quotation that I ever listened to." He would read aloud or repeat from memory the swearwords of political enemies, "roll them over his tongue in quite an innocent fashion and laugh at the profanity as something exqui-sitely comical."

Few were aware that long before Lincoln's night ride into Washington, one of Sumner's wealthy Massachusetts friends, George Luther Stearns, a Medford ship chandler and abolitionist who had supplied John Brown with money and rifles, paid a bodyguard to watch and protect Sumner constantly.

Out of long and close observation of Sumner, John Hay was to write later a judgment that tallied with that of many who liked him as a man and felt sorry for him as a political actor. "In all this ingenious and really clever and learned talk of Sumner's," wrote Hay of an evening party given by Sumner, "I could but remark the blindness of an honest, earnest man, who is so intent upon what he thinks right and necessary that he closes his eyes to the fatal consequences of such a course in different circum-stances and different times."

As a representative of Puritan New England challenging the sins and transgressions of slavery, as a voice of Northern industrialists asserting their right to take over the Government so long controlled by the Southern slaveholders, as a political leader emphasizing the British tradition of culture and scholarship in government, as a zealot beyond control, he was significant and had a loyal following.

Now with revolution and war on the horizon he strode back and forth before the Adamses, gesticulating, whispering, sputtering, till Henry Adams saw him for the time as a crazy man. Now he saw a bloody hand-print on the white cloth of his conscience and moaned about it, knowing that in war boys die amid rain, mud, rats, and certain landscapes are not worth looking at for light and healing. Now Sumner could recall his lawyer friend Jeremiah Mason's telling him in Boston after his antiwar speech of younger days, "An anti-war society is as little practicable as an anti-thunder-and-lightning society."

Lincoln too in those days immediately preceding inauguration was torn and troubled, according to the Public Man's diary: "Half an hour today with Mr. Lincoln confirms all my worst fears. I should say he is at his wits' ends, if he did not seem to me to be so thoroughly aware of the fact that some other people are in that condition."

And when the Public Man told Lincoln of stories of conspiracy and assassination going the rounds of Washington for weeks past, and that these stories came mostly from loud talkers who must be talking, Lincoln listened very attentively and "suddenly stretching out his hand, picked up and handed me a note to look at. I recognized Senator Sumner's handwriting as I took it, and was not, therefore, surprised to find it alarmish and mysterious in tone, bidding Mr. Lincoln, for particular reasons, to be very careful how he went out alone at night." Lincoln and his visitor seemed to agree that there was a sadly muddled mind and a touch of hysteria in the tone of Sumner's written warning as to assassination. It was part of Lincoln's process of getting acquainted with Sumner.

"Sumner had never seen Lincoln before he came to Washington," wrote Carl Schurz. "When he met Lincoln he was greatly amazed and puzzled by what he saw and heard. He confessed as much as this to me. He could hardly understand this western product of American democracy in the original shape. In conversations he noticed flashes of thought and bursts of illuminating expression, although, being absolutely without any sense of humor, he often lost Lincoln's keenest points. On the whole he could not get rid of his misgivings as to how this seemingly untutored child of nature would master the tremendous task before him. He had, by Mr. Lincoln's occasional utterances, been confirmed in his belief that the President was a deeply convinced and faithful anti-slavery man; and since the destruction of slavery was uppermost in Sumner's mind, he found comfort in that assurance. . . . Many thought that these two men, being so essentially different, could not possibly work together. But on the whole they did, and they were able to do so, because, however great the divergence of their views on some points, they believed in one another's sincerity."

Lincoln one day paid his respects to the Associate Justices of the Supreme Court and exchanged greetings with the Chief Justice, who on

March 4 was to administer the presidential oath of office. This was Roger B. Taney, author of the Dred Scott decision, born in Maryland in the year 1777, as old, lacking one year, as the Declaration of Independence; appointed to the supreme bench by President Andrew Jackson and now serving his twenty-fifth year; a man of books said to be "all mind and no body," of whom Mrs. Clement C. Clay of Alabama said, "He once rose tall and erect, but now was so bent that one always thought of him as small, and with a head which made me think of a withered nut." He had sworn in Presidents Van Buren, Harrison, Tyler, Polk, Taylor, Fillmore, Pierce, and Buchanan.

In the Senate on March 2 Wigfall of Texas took Lincoln as a topic. Senators had become excited, he said, "under the apprehension that, on Monday next, at the precise hour of twelve, the aforesaid Abraham is to swallow the Chicago platform and go for peace. [Laughter.] I do not know how this is. I rather suspect it is true. I do not think that a man who disguises himself in a soldier's cloak and a Scotch cap (a more thorough disguise could not be assumed by such a man) and makes his entree between day and day, into the capital of the country that he is going to govern, I hardly think that he is going to look war sternly in the face. I look for nothing else than that the commissioners from the confederated States will be received here and recognized by Abraham Lincoln. [Laughter.] We have dissolved the Union; mend it if you can; cement it with blood; try the experiment. We do not desire war; we wish to avoid it. We are not interfering with you."

Journals there were in the mood of the *Louisville Daily Courier* which saw that "never has greater responsibility devolved on any one man." And what did he have? Low ability, no education, slight information, no experience; "simply, we believe, an honest man, he will be the tool of a fanaticism which he represents, and the instrument of the able, unscrupulous, and daring men whom he will call around him." The *Courier* gave a front-page reprint of a letter "said to have been written by a prominent member of Congress," no name given, dated at Willard's Hotel, Washington, March 1, predicting that the Republican-party factions would destroy each other while Virginia seceded and took with her all the Border Slave States. "Lincoln," said this letter, "is a cross between a sand-hill crane and an Andalusian jackass. He is, by all odds, the weakest man who has ever been elected—worse than Taylor. . . . I was sent for by Lincoln. I speak what I know. He is vain, weak, puerile, hypocritical, without manners, without social grace, and as he talks to you, punches his fist under your ribs. He swears equal to Uncle Toby, and in every particular morally and mentally, I have lost all respect for him. He is surrounded by a set of toad-eaters and bottle-throwers. . . . I am completely satisfied he is an Abolitionist of the Lovejoy and Sumner type. Such is your God, Oh! Israel!"

This had the fear, though not the pointed motive, of Senator John Slidell of Louisiana telling his colleagues: "We separate because of the hostility of

Lincoln to our institutions. . . . If he were inaugurated without our consent there would be slave insurrections in the South."

A disgust verging on horror moved Sidney Lanier, the Georgia flutist and poet who was yet to write exquisitely musical verse lines. On March 1 he wrote to his father of a reception to Lincoln: "What a *disgusting* Scene was the Lincoln *hand*-Shaking affair! I think the disgrace of the United States had its fit culmination therein: the scene ought to go into History under the title of 'The Great Apotheosis of the Great Hog.'"

A petition was brought before Congress, signed by 14,000 women, led by Emma Willard, head of the Troy Female Seminary and author of the song verses "Rocked in the Cradle of the Deep." The petition recited: "History is not without examples that, when deadly strife was raging among men, women came between the hostile parties, and persuaded them to peace. So would we do now." Senator Sumner, however, brought in a petition from 37,000 Massachusetts citizens urging Congress to stand by the Constitution and ask no compromises.

On Sunday, March 3, shortly after four o'clock in the afternoon, Lincoln received in his room at Willard's the Virginia Congressman A. R. Boteler, who had just been driven from the Capitol as fast as a hack and two horses would take him. Boteler that afternoon had asked Congressman Benjamin Stanton of Ohio to withdraw his Force Bill—to fix on the President complete authority over all regular and militia troops of the nation. Boteler said the bill if passed would force Virginia out of the Union. "Well, what if she does go?" laughed the Ohioan. "The bill must pass the House this evening." Boteler asked if it was a party measure and approved by Mr. Lincoln. No, Stanton said, he had originated it himself and never spoken with Lincoln on the subject.

Boteler said he didn't know Mr. Lincoln personally, but it was no time to stand on ceremony. "Mr. Lincoln may not be so inflexible as you are in this matter, and can be induced to exert his influence to stop it in the Senate if too late to do so in the House." The Ohioan mocked, "Yes, that's likely." In the doorway of Willard's Boteler met his old County of Berkeley, Virginia, acquaintance Ward Hill Lamon, who went upstairs and came down to say Boteler could go straight up to Lincoln's room and walk in. None of the police stationed along the hall leading to Lincoln's suite said a word.

"I'm glad to see you, always glad to see an old-line Whig," said Lincoln with a handshake. "Sit down." Boteler apologized, trusted he was not trespassing too far on courtesy.

"Not a bit," said Lincoln, "not a bit. I'm really glad you have come, and wish that more of you Southern gentlemen would call and see me, as these are times when there should be a full, fair, and frank interchange of sentiment among all who have the good of the country at heart. So draw up your chair and tell me what's going on in the House today."

Boteler told his errand, as he had told it to Congressman Stanton, explained that the Force Bill was "bristling all over with war," that it was exciting painful anxiety in Virginia, frustrating patriotic efforts to prevent secession. Lincoln listened "with patient politeness." Then a compact presentation closed: "Consequently, Mr. Lincoln, I have ventured to come to you to tell you frankly what I think of the policy of this bill—to ask your opinion of it, and to invoke your influence in having it defeated." Lincoln was still listening. When it was evident that Boteler had paused for his reply, he spoke, and Boteler's transcript of their discussion read:

LINCOLN. You must allow me the Yankee privilege of answering your questions by first asking a few myself. During the late Presidential canvass, were you not Chairman of the National Executive Committee of the party that supported Bell and Everett?

BOTELER. Yes, of the Constitutional Union party.

LINCOLN. The campaign motto or platform of which was "The Union, the Constitution, and the enforcement of the laws."

BOTELER. It was, and I think that it was not only the briefest, but about the best and most comprehensive platform that could have been adopted for that canvass.

LINCOLN. And you still stand by it, of course?

BOTELER. I certainly do.

LINCOLN. Then there is no reason why we should not be of the same mind in this emergency, if I understand the meaning of your platform. How do you, yourself, interpret it?

BOTELER. Its meaning is obvious. It has nothing hidden in it—nothing more than meets the eye. We go for "The Union" as our fathers made it— to be a shield of protection over our heads, and not a sword of subjugation at our hearts; for "the Constitution" as they designed it, to be equally binding on both sections, North as well as South, in all its compromises, and in all its requirements; and for "the enforcement of the laws" by peaceable and Constitutional means, not by bayonets—Federal bayonets, especially, Mr. Lincoln.

LINCOLN. Then your idea is, that Federal bayonets should not be used for the enforcement of laws within the limits of a State?

BOTELER. As a general rule, unquestionably not. But, of course, there are exceptional cases, such as have already occurred—cases of invasion, insurrection, and so on—when the civil authorities of a State, finding themselves inadequate to the duty of protecting their people, or unable to enforce the laws within the limits of their jurisdiction, may rightfully require the Federal forces to assist them.

LINCOLN. And now, to apply your platform to the present condition of affairs in those Southern States of the Union which are assuming to be no longer part of it. How about enforcing the laws in them just now—the laws of the United States?

BOTELER. Inasmuch as the difficulties of doing so, under existing circumstances, are exceeded only by the dangers of attempting it forcibly, the practical question to be determined beforehand is whether the experiment is worth a civil war. Which consideration brings us back to the object of my visit, and I therefore again take the liberty of asking if you approve of Congress passing such a Force Bill now as this of Stanton's, and whether you will not aid us in defeating it.

LINCOLN. Of course, I am extremely anxious to see these sectional troubles settled peaceably and satisfactorily to all concerned. To accomplish that, I am willing to make almost any sacrifice, and to do anything in reason consistent with my sense of duty. There is one point, however, I can never surrender—that which was the main issue of the Presidential canvass and decided at the late election, concerning the extension of slavery in the Territories.

BOTELER. As to that matter, however important it may have seemed to some persons, we can well afford to remit it to the remote future, when there may be a practical necessity for its consideration, inasmuch as it has dwindled into utter insignificance before that issue now so unexpectedly before us.

LINCOLN. Unexpectedly indeed, and portentous enough in all conscience! But I trust that matters are not as bad as they appear.

BOTELER. Bad as they certainly are, they will be infinitely worse before long if the utmost care be not taken to allay the present excitement, and to preserve the existing status between the sections until some such plan as Mr. Crittenden's, for a general convention, can be carried into effect, which, as the Peace Conference here has failed to secure a compromise, is the ultimate reliance left us for that object. Mr. Lincoln, it may seem presumptuous in me to express my opinion to you on these subjects so decidedly. But I speak frankly because I feel deeply their vital importance to the whole country, and especially to the district I represent, a border district stretching along the Potomac from the Alleghenies to tidewater, which in the event of a sectional civil war will not only be the first to suffer from its effects, but will feel them first, last, and all the time, and in all their intensity. I speak to you as a Union man, from a Union county, of a Union district, of a Union State. . . . Her acknowledged prestige, her geographical position midway between the angry sections, can do more than any other State to preserve peace and bring a satisfactory adjustment in spite of the fanatical abolitionists and the no less fanatical secessionists—provided only that a little more time be allowed her to continue her patriotic efforts to these ends. I say to you, in all sincerity, that the passage of this Force Bill will paralyze the Unionists of Virginia, precipitate her into secession, and unquestionably involve the whole country in a civil war.

Lincoln was silent a while, absorbed, looked up with a smile. "Well, I'll see what can be done about the bill you speak of. I think it can be stopped, and that I may promise you it will be."

Boteler thanked him for this kindness and asked if he might announce from his place in the House that the incoming President did not approve of the bill to invest him with extraordinary military authority.

"By no means," said Lincoln, "for that would make trouble. The question would at once be asked, what right had I to interfere with the legislation of this Congress. Whatever is to be done in the matter, must be done quietly."

Could he tell his colleagues confidentially the substance of the conversation? Boteler asked. Lincoln said Yes. Boteler warmly thanked him and got up to leave. Lincoln insisted that he should resume his seat. And they talked some fifteen minutes longer, not about the Force Bill, but things in general, getting better acquainted.

Boteler wrote of their chat: "It served to deepen the impression already made upon me by the interview, that Mr. Lincoln was a kind-hearted man; that he was, at that time, willing to allow the moderate men of the South a fair opportunity to make further efforts for a settlement of our intestine and internecine difficulties, and that he was by no means disposed to interfere, directly or indirectly, with the institutions of slavery in any of the States, or to yield to the clamorous demand of those bloody-minded extremists, who were then so very keen to cry 'havoc!' and 'let slip the dogs of war'; and afterward so exceedingly careful, with the characteristic caution of their kind, to keep out of harm's way during the continuance of hostilities. Having concluded my visit, I was about to return to the Capitol, when, perceiving that the House flag was down (a recess having been ordered from five until seven o'clock the same evening), I went at once to my room (at Willard's, where I boarded that winter), and employed myself until dinner in making full notes of the foregoing conversation, while it was fresh in my memory."

Boteler counted it a good afternoon's work, inasmuch as the *Richmond Semi-Weekly Examiner*, favoring immediate secession of Virginia, had only two days before promised its readers that under the Force Bill Virginia would have "to bend her haughty neck beneath the paw of the Abolition orang-outang that skulked to Washington the other day from the wilds of Illinois, and who will, in three days more, be propped in the Chair of Washington by the sword of a military dictator."

The House clock indicated nearly ten that night when Stanton called up his Force Bill for consideration. The Illinois Republican Washburne moved adjournment. A question of order arose and Mr. Washburne's motion could not be entertained. Mr. Stanton moved the previous question on engrossment of his bill. A Pennsylvania Republican, Hickman, moved adjournment, which was not put to vote, the floor being obtained by a New York Republican, John Cochrane, who before taking his seat renewed the motion to adjourn. "It was well understood on both sides of the House," Boteler wrote, "that Cochrane's motion involved the fate of the Force Bill."

By a vote of 77 to 60 the House adjourned, "and the Thirty-Sixth Congress expired on the following Monday of March 4, without having given to Mr. Lincoln the power to call out the militia and to accept the services of volunteers."

In those closing hours of Congress a bill was passed to forbid the Federal Government forever from interfering with slavery in any manner whatsoever in any Slave State—requiring three-fourths of the States of the

Union to approve the measure as an Amendment to the Constitution. This was as far as Congress could go within its powers to guarantee the South that whatever it intended to do as to slavery extension in the Territories, its policy was to let slavery alone in the Slave States. The act was in line with the Republican-party platform and Lincoln's public and private declarations.

Two days before the inauguration was to take place came a pleasantly put letter from Seward, saying he couldn't take his Cabinet place as Secretary of State. He must "withdraw." That left Lincoln a Sunday to think it over. Only the Sunday before they had walked to and from church together, in tall silk hats.

CHAPTER 4

LINCOLN TAKES THE OATH AS PRESIDENT

SPRING comes gently to Washington always. In early March the green of the grass brightens, the magnolia softens. Elms and chestnuts burgeon. Redbud and lilac carry on preparations soon to bloom. The lovemaking and birthing in many sunny corners go on no matter what or who the blueprints and personages behind the discreet bureau and departmental walls.

On the slope of lawn fronting the Capitol building stood a bronze statue of Liberty shaped as a massive, fertile woman holding a sword in one hand for power and a wreath of flowers in the other hand for glory. Not yet raised to her pedestal, she looked out of place. She was to be lifted and set on top of the Capitol dome, overlooking the Potomac Valley, when the dome itself should be prepared for her.

The old dome familiar to Congressman Lincoln in 1848 had been knocked loose and hauled down. The iron-wrought material on the Capitol grounds, the hammers, jacks, screws, scaffolds, derricks, ladders, props, ropes, told that they were rebuilding, extending, embellishing the structure on March 4, 1861. Fronting the Senate wing the carpenters had set up a platform for the first man from west of the Indiana-Illinois line and north of the Ohio River to take the inaugural oath.

March 4 dawned with pleasant weather that later turned bleak and chilly for the 25,000 strangers roving the city of Washington. With hotels and rooming-houses overcrowded, hundreds had slept on the porches of public buildings and on street sidewalks. Thousands filled the streets around Willard's Hotel as the forenoon wore away, hoping the next President might leave his guarded parlors over the main entrance.

Though rumors of violence had somewhat died down, General Scott and Colonel Stone had taken precautions and arranged for riflemen in squads to be placed in hiding on the roofs of certain commanding houses along Pennsylvania Avenue. Orders were "to watch the windows on the opposite side, and to fire upon them in case any attempt should be made to fire from those windows on the Presidential carriage." Cavalry regulars were to guard side-street crossings of the avenue and "to move from one to another during the passage of the procession." From windows of the Capitol wings riflemen were to watch the inauguration platform. On the top of a slope commanding the north entrance to the Capitol, General Scott would oversee the ceremonies, ready to take personal charge of a battery of flying artillery there stationed.

President Buchanan in a room at the Capitol that morning signed bills and disposed of matters that had kept the Senate in session till six o'clock that morning. He had just managed to close up his affairs when noon came, and he drove with Senator Baker of Oregon and Senator Pearce of Maryland from the White House to Willard's in an open carriage. (An *Evening Star* reporter wrote with perhaps fantastic surmise that Buchanan had offered Lincoln a closed carriage and Lincoln answered that he would ride in the open.) Buchanan stepped out of the barouche, disappeared into the doorway of Willard's, and soon returned arm in arm with Lincoln as police kept a path for them. Then the procession, headed by Marshal in Chief Major French, with aides in blue scarfs and white rosettes, carrying blue batons with gilt ends, their saddlecloths blue and white, moved down Pennsylvania Avenue with representations from the judiciary; the clergy; foreign Ministers; the diplomatic corps; members of Congress; the Peace Convention delegates; heads of bureaus; governors of States; the army, navy, marine corps, militia; veterans of the Revolutionary War and the War of 1812 in carriages, followed by a variety of organizations and citizens afoot.

In the presidential carriage the crowds saw Buchanan and Lincoln side by side facing frontward and Senators Baker and Pearce seated opposite. Double files of a squadron of District of Columbia cavalry rode alongside the carriage. A company of West Point sappers and miners marched in front of it, and infantry and riflemen of the District of Columbia followed it. There were cheers and there were silences along the sidewalks. Washington was still a Southern city—overrun by newly arrived Northern elements.

Four milk-white horses drew the float of the Republican Association, with thirty-four pretty girls in white frocks, one pretty girl for each State in the Union. Several newspapers reported that Lincoln took occasion later in the day to kiss each pretty girl, giving one kiss for each State, which made interesting reading but was neither true nor important.

In the Senate chamber, packed with officials and civilians, Buchanan and Lincoln witnessed the swearing-in of Hannibal Hamlin of Maine as Vice-President. A new procession was formed to escort the President-elect through a corridor to the east portico and the platform outdoors, where a crowd of at least 10,000 had waited long and finally gave its applause and scattering cheers as the actors in the solemn ceremony took places on the platform. Their eyes saw the Senate Committee of Arrangements, the out-going President, the President-elect and his family, the Chief Justice in his black robes, the Clerk of the Court with the Bible, form the central group on the front of the platform. Gathered round and back were other Justices in robes, Senators, Representatives, officials, and eminent guests in tall silk hats and black swallowtail coats.

Senator Douglas took a seat, and as he looked over the crowd could have said that he and Lincoln had spoken to larger audiences on the prairies of Illinois. This, however, was a more genteel crowd, and one comment ran that rather than a sea of upturned faces it was a sea of silk hats and white shirt bosoms.

Lincoln in a new tall hat, new black suit of clothes and black boots, expansive white shirt bosom, carrying an ebony cane with a gold head the size of a hen's egg, had the crowd matched. Before taking a seat he looked around, hesitated and peered, then pushed the cane into a corner of the platform railing. His hat, too, needed a place. Young Henry Watterson, a press writer from Louisville, put out his hand for the hat, but Senator Douglas, just behind, outreached Watterson, received the hat from Lincoln's hand, and held it a half-hour.

Two riflemen lurked hidden at each window of the Capitol wings flank-ing the inaugural stand, watching for any· interference.

The Senator from Oregon stepped forward, Edward Dickinson Baker, of whom Lincoln had long ago told the story that Baker when a boy was found crying his eyes out one day because he had just learned that as an English-born child he could never be President of the United States.

Baker's silver-bell voice rang out: "Fellow-citizens, I introduce to you Abraham Lincoln, the President-elect of the United States." The applause was a slight ripple. Then came the inaugural address, which Lincoln drew from his inside coat pocket and read deliberately.

Then stepped forward Chief Justice Taney, worn, shrunken, odd, with "the face of a galvanized corpse," said Mrs. Clay of Alabama. His hands shook with age, emotion, both, as he held out an open Bible toward the ninth President to be sworn in by him.

Lincoln laid his left hand on the Bible, raised his right hand, and repeated after the Chief Justice the oath prescribed by the Constitution: "I do sol-emnly swear that I will faithfully execute the office of President of the United States, and will, to the best of my ability, preserve, protect, and defend the Constitution of the United States."

The artillery over on the slope boomed with all its guns a salute of thunder to the sixteenth President of the United States.

That was all. The inauguration was over. Men wrote their wives, former Lieutenant Governor Gustave Koerner of Illinois writing: "Dearest Sophie: Lincoln is President. In the presence of ten thousand people he took the oath and read with a firm voice his inaugural. I stood close to his chair; next to me stood Douglas. Douglas had no overcoat and I saw he was shivering. I had a thick shawl which I flung over him." Grenville M. Dodge of Council Bluffs, Iowa, dreaming as ever of a railroad to the Pacific, wrote to his wife: "Old Abe delivered the greatest speech of the age. It is backbone all over. The city bristles with bayonets." Henry Watterson wrote: "I stood just near enough to the speaker's elbow not to obstruct any gestures he might make. He delivered that inaugural as if he had been delivering inaugural addresses all his life."

The Public Man in his diary noted with more detail: "Mr. Lincoln was pale and very nervous, and did not read his address very well. His spectacles troubled him, his position was crowded and uncomfortable, and, in short, nothing had been done to render the performance of this great duty either dignified in effect or, physically speaking, easy for the President. The great crowd in the grounds behaved very well, but manifested little or no enthusiasm, and at one point in the speech Mr. Lincoln was thrown completely off his balance for a moment by a crash not far in front of him, followed by something which for an instant looked like a struggle . . . a spectator falling out of a tree. . . . Mr. Lincoln's agitation was remarked, and I have no doubt must have been caused by the impressions which the alarmists have been trying so sedulously to make on his mind, and which the exaggerated preparations of General Scott today are but too likely to have deepened."

Thurlow Weed, knowing very well what Lincoln would read as an inaugural, strolled away as Lincoln commenced reading. Near the flying artillery he met General Scott, who asked how the inauguration was going on. "It is a success," said Weed. The grizzled and timeworn warrior raised his arms, crying: "God be praised! God in His goodness be praised."

A half-hour before Lincoln read his inaugural, a little man with a bush of fiery whiskers over his face climbed a tree on the Capitol grounds, balanced himself on a large branch, pulled a manuscript, and read to the waiting crowd an oration on the vices of the day. Another performer was Senator Wigfall of Texas, who with folded arms leaned conspicuously in a Capitol doorway, listened to the inaugural, and plainly wore contempt, defiance, derision, on his face, his pantomimic posture saying what he had said in the Senate, that the old Union was a corpse and the question was how to embalm it and conduct the funeral decently.

The inaugural address itself, as a state paper from the first administration of a new party, as a definition of policy and viewpoint, as a breaking of Lincoln's long silence, was the high point of the day. Beyond the immediate hearers in silk hats and white shirt fronts was the vast unseen audience that would read the address in cold print and try to unravel its import in history.

Never before in New York had such crowds waited at newspaper offices and jammed and scrambled for the first sheets wet from the press, the lucky ones sometimes "at much cost of tumbled linen and ruffled broadcloth" getting their copies of the telegraphed report of the address and hunting at once a friendly door, post, corner, to lean and "rapidly scan the words which were even then scarcely spoken."

In its week of delivery it was the most widely read and closely scrutinized utterance that had ever come from an American President. No previous manuscript from Lincoln's hand had been so carefully written by him, rearranged, modified in various drafts, or submitted to such varied sage counselors for advice. The text from which Lincoln read and gave it final delivery had several graphic revisions. Nicolay furnished a similar copy to the press. The draft made in Springfield underwent important changes,

Old print showing the crowd at the Capitol listening to Lincoln read his long-awaited and momentous inaugural address foreshadowing war

mainly deletions, under the suggestions of Seward and Browning, with Lincoln's added light as he traveled and events shifted.

One paragraph mentioning "the Republican party" and its "avowed purpose to prevent, if they can, the extension of slavery," was omitted on Seward's suggestion. Two paragraphs following the opening one, wherein "the Chicago platform" was pointed to as pledging the Chief Magistrate— "I hold myself bound by duty . . . to follow . . . the principles therein declared"—were shortened and revised by Seward so as not to flaunt the Chicago platform. Lincoln struck out both the paragraphs. The word "submit" as applied to seceded States was shaded into "acquiesce."

A sentence "Nothing worth preserving is either breaking or burning" was dropped. Several short paragraphs were rephrased, usually from familiar conversation into the style of dignified statecraft. The Union was menaced "so far as can be on paper," in the early draft. This phrasing was dropped.

The most vital change was suggested by Browning, on whose advice

Lincoln changed the sentence reading "All the power at my disposal will be used to *reclaim* the public property and places which have fallen; to hold, occupy and possess these and all other properties and places belonging to the government" into a less threatening version: "The power confided to me will be used to hold, occupy, and possess the property and places belonging to the government."

The two closing sentences of Lincoln's original draft were too warlike, Seward believed. They read: "You can forbear the assault upon it [the Government]; I can not shrink from the defense of it. With you, and not with me, is the solemn question of 'Shall it be peace, or a sword?' " Lincoln dropped them. Seward believed "some words of affection, some of calm and cheerful confidence," should close the address and Lincoln revised a paragraph submitted by Seward.

The finished address which Lincoln gave the world that early afternoon of March 4, 1861, went to a wide realm of readers who searched and dug into every line and phrase of it. Reason and emotion wove through it—and hopes, fears, resolves. It was momentous to Lincoln and the country because it told why he would make a war if he saw a war as justified and inevitable. In the printer's proofs struck off in Springfield, Lincoln had indicated by a hand with pointed finger the paragraphs on which he would lay special stress. He read the address:

Fellow citizens of the United States: In compliance with a custom as old as the government itself, I appear before you to address you briefly, and to take, in your presence, the oath prescribed by the Constitution of the United States, to be taken by the President "before he enters on the execution of his office."

I do not consider it necessary at present for me to discuss those matters of administration about which there is no special anxiety or excitement.

Apprehension seems to exist among the people of the Southern States, that by the accession of a Republican Administration, their property, and their peace, and personal security, are to be endangered. There has never been any reasonable cause for such apprehension. Indeed, the most ample evidence to the contrary has all the while existed and been open to their inspection. It is found in nearly all the published speeches of him who now addresses you. I do but quote from one of those speeches when I declare that "I have no purpose, directly or indirectly, to interfere with the institution of slavery in the States where it exists. I believe I have no lawful right to do so, and I have no inclination to do so." Those who nominated and elected me did so with full knowledge that I had made this, and many similar declarations, and had never recanted them. And more than this, they placed in the platform, for my acceptance, and as a law to themselves, and to me, the clear and emphatic resolution which I now read:

"*Resolved*, That the maintenance inviolate of the rights of the States, and especially the right of each State to order and control its own domestic institutions according to its own judgment exclusively, is essential to that balance of power on which the perfection and endurance of our political fabric depend, and we denounce the lawless invasion by armed force of the soil of any State or Territory, no matter under what pretext, as among the gravest of crimes."

I now reiterate these sentiments; and, in doing so, I only press upon the public attention the most conclusive evidence of which the case is susceptible, that the prop-

Fellow citizens of the United States 1

In compliance with a custom as old as the government itself, I appear before you
to address you briefly, and to take, in your presence, the oath prescribed by the Constitution of the United States, to be taken by the President "before he enters on the
execution of his office."

I do not consider it necessary at present for me to discuss those matters of administration about which there is no special anxiety excitement.

Apprehension seems to exist among the people of the Southern States, that by
the accession of a Republican Administration, their property, and their peace, and personal security, are to be endangered. There has never been any reasonable cause for such
apprehension. Indeed, the most ample evidence to the contrary has all the while existed, and been open to their inspection. It is found in nearly all the published
speeches of him who now addresses you. I do but quote from one of those speeches
when I declare that "I have no purpose, directly or indirectly, to interfere with the
institution of slavery in the States where it exists. I believe I have no lawful right
to do so, and I have no inclination to do so." Those who nominated and elected me
did so with full knowledge that I had made this, and many similar declarations,
and had never recanted them. And more than this, they placed in the platform, for
my acceptance, and as a law to themselves, and to me, the clear and emphatic resolution which I now read:

"*Resolved*, That the maintenance inviolate of the rights of the States, and especially the right of each State to order and control its own domestic institutions according to its own judgment exclusively, is essential to that balance of power on which
the perfection and endurance of our political fabric depend; and we denounce the
lawless invasion by armed force of the soil of any State or Territory, no matter under
what pretext, as among the gravest of crimes."

Above is a reproduction, reduced about one-third in size, from the original page held
by Lincoln while reading his inaugural address. Engravers could not render the word
"or" preceding "excitement" and lost in a blur of dark brown ink, nor Lincoln's crossing out with his pen the hand with index finger preceding the word "apprehension."
A few minutes after he had finished reading the address Lincoln handed the complete
set of sheets to Crosby Stuart Noyes, a reporter for the *Washington Star*, later editor
of that newspaper. Noyes took them to the *Star* office. The sheets were cut into "takes"
for handsetting compositors, and the address was published in the *Star* on the day
Lincoln delivered it. The original sheets are in the possession of Mrs. James A. Vaughan
and Mr. Crosby Noyes Boyd of Washington.

" No person held to service or labor in one State, under the laws thereof, escaping into another, shall, in consequence of any law or regulation therein, be discharged from such service or labor, but shall be delivered up on claim of the party to whom such service or labor may be due."

It is scarcely questioned that this provision was intended by those who made it, for the reclaiming of what we call fugitive slaves; and the intention of the law-giver is the law. All members of Congress swear their support to the whole Constitution—to this provision as much as to any other. To the proposition, then, that slaves whose cases come within the terms of this clause, "shall be delivered up," their oaths are unanimous. Now, if they would make the effort in good temper, could they not, with nearly equal unanimity, frame and pass a law, by means of which to keep good that unanimous oath?

There is some difference of opinion whether this clause should be enforced by national or by state authority; but surely that difference is not a very material one. If the slave is to be surrendered, it can be of but little consequence to him, or to others, by which authority it is done. And should any one, in any case, be content that his oath shall go unkept, on a merely unsubstantial controversy as to *how* it shall be kept?

Again, in any law upon this subject, ought not all the safeguards of liberty known in civilized and humane jurisprudence to be introduced, so that a free man be not, in any case, surrendered as a slave? *And might it not be well at the same time to provide by law for the enforcement of that clause in the constitution which guarantees that "the citizens of each State shall be entitled to all privileges and immunities of citizens in the several States?"*

I take the official oath to-day, with no mental reservations, and with no purpose to construe the Constitution or laws, by any hypercritical rules. And while I do not *choose* now to specify particular acts of Congress as proper to be enforced, I do suggest that it will be much safer for all, both in official and private stations, to conform to, and abide by, all those acts which stand unrepealed, than to violate any of them, trusting to find impunity in having them held to be unconstitutional.

3

It is seventy-two years since the first inauguration of a President under our national Constitution. During that period fifteen different and greatly distinguished citizens, have, in succession, administered the executive branch of the government. They have conducted it through many perils; and, *generally*, with great success. Yet, with all this scope for precedent, I now enter upon the same task for the brief constitutional term of four years, under great and peculiar difficulty. A disruption of the Federal Union *heretofore only menaced, is now formidably attempted.*

Another of the sheets (reduced about one-third) held by Lincoln from which he read his inaugural address. Two of the original hands with pointing forefinger are crossed out, as also are two phrases still readable.

erty, peace, and security of no section are to be in any wise endangered by the now incoming administration. I add, too, that all the protection which, consistently with the Constitution, and the laws, can be given, will be cheerfully given to all the States when lawfully demanded, for whatever cause—as cheerfully to one section as to another.

☞ There is much controversy about the delivering up of fugitives from service or labor. The clause I now read is as plainly written in the Constitution as any other of its provisions:

"No person held to service or labor in one State, under the laws thereof, escaping into another, shall in consequence of any law or regulation therein, be discharged from such service or labor, but shall be delivered up on claim of the party to whom such service or labor may be due."

It is scarcely questioned that this provision was intended by those who made it, for the reclaiming of what we call fugitive slaves; and the intention of the law-giver is the law. All members of Congress swear their support to the whole Constitution—to this provision as much as to any other. To the proposition, then, that slaves whose cases come within the terms of this clause, "shall be delivered up," their oaths are unanimous. Now, if they would make the effort in good temper, could they not, with nearly equal unanimity, frame and pass a law, by means of which to keep good that unanimous oath?

There is some difference of opinion whether this clause should be enforced by national or by state authority; but surely that difference is not a very material one. If the slave is to be surrendered, it can be of but little consequence to him, or to others, by which authority it is done. And should any one, in any case, be content that his oath shall go unkept, on a merely unsubstantial controversy as to *how* it shall be kept?

Again, in any law upon this subject, ought not all the safeguards of liberty known in civilized and humane jurisprudence to be introduced, so that a free man be not, in any case, surrendered as a slave? And might it not be well at the same time to provide by law for the enforcement of that clause in the Constitution which guarantees that "the citizen of each State shall be entitled to all privileges and immunities of citizens in the several States"?

☞ I take the official oath to-day, with no mental reservations, and with no purpose to construe the Constitution or laws, by any hypercritical rules. And while I do not choose now to specify particular acts of Congress as proper to be enforced, I do suggest that it will be much safer for all, both in official and private stations, to conform to, and abide by, all those acts which stand unrepealed, than to violate any of them, trusting to find impunity in having them held to be unconstitutional.

☞ It is seventy-two years since the first inauguration of a President under our national Constitution. During that period fifteen different and greatly distinguished citizens have, in succession, administered the executive branch of the government. They have conducted it through many perils, and generally with great success. Yet, with all this scope of precedent, I now enter upon the same task for the brief constitutional term of four years, under great and peculiar difficulty. A disruption of the Federal Union, heretofore only menaced, is now formidably attempted.

I hold that, in contemplation of universal law and of the Constitution, the Union of these States is perpetual. Perpetuity is implied, if not expressed, in the fundamental law of all national governments. It is safe to assert that no government proper ever had a provision in its organic law for its own termination. Continue to execute all the express provisions of our National Constitution, and the Union will endure forever—it being impossible to destroy it except by some action not provided for in the instrument itself.

Again, if the United States be not a government proper, but an association of

The crowd begins to arrive to hear Lincoln deliver his inaugural
address, March 4 of '61

The assemblage before the unfinished Capitol building sees Lincoln
take the oath of office, March 4 of '61

Photographs from U. S. Army Signal Corps

The newly inaugurated President Lincoln, March 6, '61. Photograph by Brady

Inauguration crowd and Capitol, March 4, '61

Photographs from Frederick H. Meserve Collection

Vice-President Hannibal Hamlin

Photograph from Frederick H. Meserve Collection

Speaker of the House Galusha Aaron Grow

Photograph by McClees in author's collection

States in the nature of contract merely, can it, as a contract, be peaceably unmade by less than all the parties who made it? One party to a contract may violate it—break it, so to speak; but does it not require all to lawfully rescind it?

Descending from these general principles, we find the proposition that, in legal contemplation, the Union is perpetual confirmed by the history of the Union itself. The Union is much older than the Constitution. It was formed, in fact, by the Articles of Association in 1774. It was matured and continued by the Declaration of Independence in 1776. It was further matured, and the faith of all the then thirteen States expressly plighted and engaged that it should be perpetual, by the Articles of Confederation in 1778. And, finally, in 1787 one of the declared objects for ordaining and establishing the Constitution was "to form a more perfect Union."

But if the destruction of the Union by one or by a part only of the States be lawfully possible, the Union is less perfect than before the Constitution, having lost the vital element of perpetuity.

It follows from these views that no State upon its own mere motion can lawfully get out of the Union; that resolves and ordinances to that effect are legally void; and that acts of violence, within any State or States, against the authority of the United States, are insurrectionary or revolutionary, according to circumstances.

I therefore consider that, in view of the Constitution and the laws, the Union is unbroken and to the extent of my ability I shall take care, as the Constitution itself expressly enjoins upon me, that the laws of the Union be faithfully executed in all the States. Doing this I deem to be only a simple duty on my part; and I shall perform it, so far as practicable, unless my rightful masters, the American people, shall withhold the requisite means, or, in some authoritative manner direct the contrary. I trust this will not be regarded as a menace, but only as the declared purpose of the Union that it will constitutionally defend and maintain itself.

In doing this there needs to be no bloodshed or violence; and there shall be none, unless it be forced upon the national authority. The power confided to me will be used to hold, occupy and possess the property and places belonging to the Government, and to collect the duties and imposts; but beyond what may be necessary for these objects, there will be no invasion,—no using of force against or among the people anywhere. Where hostility to the United States, in any interior locality, shall be so great and universal, as to prevent competent resident citizens from holding the Federal offices, there will be no attempt to force obnoxious strangers among the people for that object. While the strict legal right may exist in the government to enforce the exercise of these offices, the attempt to do so would be so irritating, and so nearly impracticable withal, that I deem it better to forego, for the time, the uses of such offices.

The mails, unless repelled, will continue to be furnished in all parts of the Union. So far as possible, the people everywhere shall have that sense of perfect security which is most favorable to calm thought and reflection. The course here indicated will be followed unless current events and experience shall show a modification or change to be proper, and in every case and exigency my best discretion will be exercised according to circumstances actually existing, and with a view and a hope of a peaceful solution of the national troubles and the restoration of fraternal sympathies and affections.

That there are persons in one section or another who seek to destroy the Union at all events, and are glad of any pretext to do it, I will neither affirm nor deny; but if there be such, I need address no word to them. To those, however, who really love the Union may I not speak?

Before entering upon so grave a matter as the destruction of our national fabric,

4

I therefore consider that, in view of the Constitution and the laws, the Union is unbroken and to the extent of my ability I shall take care, as the constitution itself expressly enjoins upon me, that the laws of the Union be faithfully executed in all the States.

Doing this I deem to be only a simple duty on my part; and I shall perform it, so far as practicable, unless my rightful masters, the American people, shall withhold the requisite means, or, in some ~~authoritative manner~~ direct the contrary. I trust this will not be regarded as a menace, but only as the declared purpose of the Union that it will *constitutionally defend and maintain itself.*

In doing this there needs to be no bloodshed or violence; and there shall be none, unless it be forced upon the national authority.

The power confided to me will be used to hold, occupy and possess the property and places belonging to the Government, and to collect the duties and imposts; but beyond what may be necessary for these objects, there will be no invasion,—no using of force against or among the people anywhere.

Where hostility to the United States, in any interior locality, shall be so great and so universal, as to prevent competent resident citizens from holding the Federal offices, there will be no attempt to force obnoxious strangers among the people for that object. While the strict legal right may exist in the government to enforce the exercise of these offices, the attempt to do so would be so irritating, and so nearly impracticable with all, that I deem it better to forego, for the time, the uses of such offices.

Another sheet (reduced about one-third) from which the inaugural address was read. The carefully written sentence beginning "The power confided to me" became construed as the most threatening and warlike utterance in the document. The number "11" at the top indicates one of the "takes" of the handsetting compositors of the *Washington Star.*

with all its benefits, its memories, and its hopes, would it not be wise to ascertain precisely why we do it? Will you hazard so desperate a step while there is any possibility that any portion of the ills you fly from have no real existence? Will you, while the certain ills you fly to are greater than all the real ones you fly from—will you risk the commission of so fearful a mistake?

All profess to be content in the Union if all constitutional rights can be maintained. Is it true, then, that any right, plainly written in the Constitution, has been denied? I think not. Happily the human mind is so constituted that no party can reach to the audacity of doing this. Think, if you can, of a single instance in which a plainly written provision of the Constitution has ever been denied. If by the mere force of numbers a majority should deprive a minority of any clearly written constitutional right, it might, in a moral point of view, justify revolution—certainly would if such a right were a vital one. But such is not our case. All the vital rights of minorities and of individuals are so plainly assured to them by affirmations and negations, guarantees and prohibitions, in the Constitution, that controversies never arise concerning them. But no organic law can ever be framed with a provision specifically applicable to every question which may occur in practical administration. No foresight can anticipate, nor

Print giving near view of the crowd, and the platform from which the inaugural address was delivered

any document of reasonable length contain, express provisions for all possible questions. Shall fugitives from labor be surrendered by national or by State authority? The Constitution does not expressly say. *May* Congress prohibit slavery in the Territories? The Constitution does not expressly say. *Must* Congress protect slavery in the Territories? The Constitution does not expressly say.

From questions of this class spring all our constitutional controversies, and we divide upon them into majorities and minorities. If the minority will not acquiesce, the majority must, or the government must cease. There is no other alternative; for continuing the government is acquiescence on one side or the other.

If a minority in such case will secede rather than acquiesce, they make a precedent which in turn will divide and ruin them; for a minority of their own will secede from them whenever a majority refuses to be controlled by such minority. For instance, why may not any portion of a new confederacy a year or two hence arbitrarily secede again, precisely as portions of the present Union now claim to secede from it? All who cherish disunion sentiments are now being educated to the exact temper of doing this.

Is there such perfect identity of interests among the States to compose a new Union, as to produce harmony only, and prevent renewed secession?

Plainly, the central idea of secession is the essence of anarchy. A majority held in restraint by constitutional checks and limitations, and always changing easily with deliberate changes of popular opinions and sentiments, is the only true sovereign of a free people. Whoever rejects it does, of necessity, fly to anarchy or to despotism. Unanimity is impossible; the rule of a minority, as a permanent arrangement, is wholly inadmissible; so that, rejecting the majority principle, anarchy or despotism in some form is all that is left.

I do not forget the position, assumed by some, that constitutional questions are to be decided by the Supreme Court; nor do I deny that such decisions must be binding, in any case, upon the parties to a suit, as to the object of that suit, while they are also entitled to very high respect and consideration in all parallel cases by all other departments of the government. And while it is obviously possible that such decision may be erroneous in any given case, still the evil effect following it, being limited to that particular case, with the chance that it may be overruled and never become a precedent for other cases, can better be borne than could the evils of a different practice. At the same time, the candid citizen must confess that if the policy of the government, upon vital questions affecting the whole people, is to be irrevocably fixed by decisions of the Supreme Court, the instant they are made, in ordinary litigation between parties in personal actions, the people will have ceased to be their own rulers, having to that extent practically resigned their government into the hands of that eminent tribunal. Nor is there in this view any assault upon the court or the judges. It is a duty from which they may not shrink to decide cases properly brought before them, and it is no fault of theirs if others seek to turn their decisions to political purposes.

One section of our country believes slavery is right, and ought to be extended, while the other believes it is wrong, and ought not to be extended. This is the only substantial dispute. The fugitive-slave clause of the Constitution, and the law for the suppression of the foreign slave-trade, are each as well enforced, perhaps, as any law can ever be in a community where the moral sense of the people imperfectly supports the law itself. The great body of the people abide by the dry legal obligation in both cases, and a few break over in each. This, I think, cannot be perfectly cured; and it would be worse in both cases after the separation of the sections than before. The foreign slave-trade, now imperfectly suppressed, would be ultimately revived, without restriction, in one section, while fugitive slaves, now only partially surrendered, would not be surrendered at all by the other.

Physically speaking, we cannot separate. We cannot remove our respective sections from each other, nor build an impassable wall between them. A husband and wife may be divorced, and go out of the presence and beyond the reach of each other; but the different parts of our country cannot do this. They cannot but remain face to face, and intercourse, either amicable or hostile, must continue between them. Is it possible, then, to make that intercourse more advantageous or more satisfactory after separation than before? Can aliens make treaties easier than friends can make laws? Can treaties be more faithfully enforced between aliens than laws can among friends? Suppose you go to war, you cannot fight always; and when, after much loss on both sides, and no gain on either, you cease fighting, the identical old questions as to terms of intercourse are again upon you.

This country, with its institutions, belongs to the people who inhabit it. Whenever they shall grow weary of the existing government, they can exercise their constitutional right of amending it, or their revolutionary right to dismember or overthrow it. I cannot be ignorant of the fact that many worthy and patriotic citizens are desirous of having the national Constitution amended. While I make no recommendation of amendments, I fully recognize the rightful authority of the people over the whole subject, to be exercised in either of the modes prescribed in the instrument itself; and I should, under existing circumstances, favor rather than oppose a fair opportunity being afforded the people to act upon it. I will venture to add that to me the convention mode seems preferable, in that it allows amendments to originate with the people themselves, instead of only permitting them to take or reject propositions originated by others not especially chosen for the purpose, and which might not be precisely such as they would wish to either accept or refuse. I understand a proposed amendment to the Constitution—which amendment, however, I have not seen—has passed Congress, to the effect that the Federal Government shall never interfere with the domestic institutions of the States, including that of persons held to service. To avoid misconstruction of what I have said, I depart from my purpose not to speak of particular amendments so far as to say that, holding such a provision to now be implied constitutional law, I have no objection to its being made express and irrevocable.

The chief magistrate derives all his authority from the people, and they have conferred none upon him to fix terms for the separation of the States. The people themselves can do this also if they choose; but the executive, as such, has nothing to do with it. His duty is to administer the present government, as it came to his hands, and to transmit it, unimpaired by him, to his successor.

Why should there not be a patient confidence in the ultimate justice of the people? Is there any better or equal hope in the world? In our present differences is either party without faith of being in the right? If the Almighty Ruler of Nations, with his eternal truth and justice, be on your side of the North, or on yours of the South, that truth and that justice will surely prevail by the judgment of this great tribunal of the American people.

By the frame of the government under which we live, this same people have wisely given their public servants but little power for mischief; and have, with equal wisdom, provided for the return of that little to their own hands at very short intervals. While the people retain their virtue and vigilance, no administration, by any extreme of wickedness or folly, can very seriously injure the government in the short space of four years.

My countrymen, one and all, think calmly and well upon this whole subject. Nothing valuable can be lost by taking time. If there be an object to hurry any of you in hot haste to a step which you would never take deliberately, that object will be frustrated by taking time; but no good object can be frustrated by it. Such of you as are now dissatisfied, still have the old Constitution unimpaired, and, on the sensitive point, the laws of your own framing under it; while the new administration will have no immediate power, if it would, to change either. If it were admitted that you who are dissatisfied hold the right side in the dispute, there still is no single good reason for precipitate action. Intelligence, patriotism, Christianity, and a firm reliance on Him who has never yet forsaken this favored land, are still competent to adjust in the best way all our present difficulty.

[Handwritten draft by Seward:]

I close., We are not we must not be aliens or enemies but ~~countrymen~~ fellow countrymen and brethren. Although passion has strained our bonds of affection too hardly they must not be ~~broken~~ ~~they will not~~. I am sure they will not be broken. The mystic chords which proceeding from ~~every~~ so many battle fields and ~~feature~~ so many patriot graves ~~and~~ pass through all ~~the~~ hearts and ~~hearths~~ all ~~the~~ hearths in this broad continent of ours will yet. ~~reason~~ again harmonize in their ancient music when ~~touched as they~~ ~~sung~~ breathed upon ~~again~~ by the ~~better~~ ~~angel~~ guardian angel of the nation

Seward wrote the paragraph above and submitted it for the close of the inaugural address, to read: "I close. We are not we must not be aliens or enemies but fellow countrymen and brethren. Although passion has strained our bonds of affection too hardly they must not, I am sure they will not be broken. The mystic chords which proceeding from so many battle fields and so many patriot graves pass through all the hearts and all the hearths in this broad continent of ours will yet again harmonize in their ancient music when breathed upon by the guardian angel of the nation." Lincoln revised this, shortened, transmuted it into slightly different meaning and a distinctly changed verbal music, adding it to the printer's proof text brought on from Springfield, as below:

[Printer's proof text, with strikethroughs:]

You can have no conflict, without being yourselves the aggressors. You have no oath registered in Heaven to destroy the government, while I shall have the most solemn one to "preserve, protect and defend" it. ~~[struck through]~~

[Handwritten revision by Lincoln:]

I am loth to close. We are not enemies, but friends— We must not be enemies. Though passion may have strained, it must not break our bonds of affection. The mystic chords of memory, streching from every battle field, and patriot grave, to every living heart and hearthstone, all over this broad land, will yet swell the chorus of the Union, when again touched, as surely they will be, by the better angels of our nature.

In your hands, my dissatisfied fellow-countrymen, and not in mine, is the momentous issue of civil war. The government will not assail you. You can have no conflict without being yourselves the aggressors. *You* have no oath registered in heaven to destroy the government, while *I* shall have the most solemn one to "preserve, protect and defend it."

Thus flowed the reasonings, explanations, watchwords, that ended Lincoln's long silence. He finished:

"I am loth to close. We are not enemies, but friends. We must not be enemies. Though passion may have strained, it must not break our bonds of affection. The mystic chords of memory, stretching from every battle-field, and patriot grave, to every living heart and hearthstone, all over this broad land, will yet swell the chorus of the Union, when again touched, as surely they will be, by the better angels of our nature."

This closing paragraph, generally considered the noblest in tone of the entire address, had been reshaped by Lincoln from Seward's passage, which read:

"I close. We are not, we must not be, aliens or enemies, but fellow-countrymen and brethren. Although passion has strained our bonds of affection too hardly, they must not, I am sure they will not, be broken. The mystic chords which, proceeding from so many battle-fields and so many patriot graves, pass through all the hearts and all the hearths in this broad continent of ours, will yet again harmonize in their ancient music when breathed upon by the guardian angel of the nation."

One sentence lacking poetry, as such, had a rigor of logic, stood ruthless with a dilemma it flung at the human mind, and haunted many philosophers with its pertinacity: "Suppose you go to war, you cannot fight always; and when, after much loss on both sides, and no gain on either, you cease fighting, the identical old questions as to terms of intercourse are again upon you."

Far out in Iowa was a farmer who had written Lincoln not to yield: "Give the little finger and shortly the whole hand is required." Far down in Nolensville, Tennessee, W. N. Barnes had written him that the people there were "overwhelmingly loyal to the flag of their country." Barnes wanted a statement to circulate. Now he had it.

The *Montgomery Advertiser* in Alabama was sure the inaugural meant war, nothing less would satisfy "the abolition chief," and the artfully worded address was written by a pen more skillful than the Rail Splitter wielded.

"To twenty millions of people," said the *New York Tribune* of the address, "it will carry tidings, good or not, as the case may be, that the federal government of the United States is still in existence, with a Man at the head of it." Not one "fawning expression" could be found in it, observed the *Boston Transcript*. "The language is level to the popular mind, the plain, homespun language of a man accustomed to talk with the 'folks' and the 'neighbors,' whose words fit his facts and thoughts."

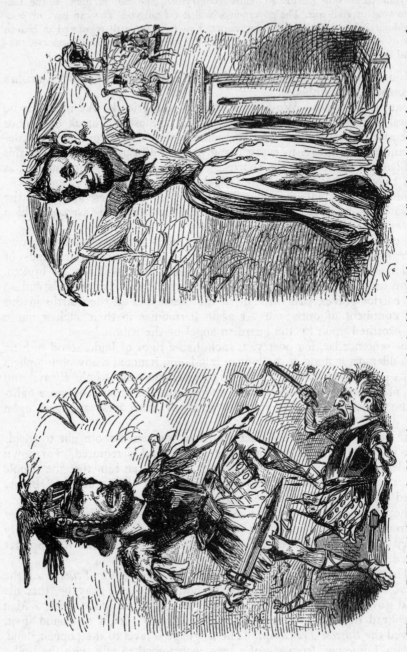

The new President's inaugural address gives some people the idea he is for war—while others think he is for peace—and still others are not sure. Thomas Nast draws for *Harper's Weekly* these conflicting impressions. At the left, wrote Nast, "As the South received it." At the right, "As the North received it."

"No one can doubt that Mr. Lincoln is the author of his own inaugural," said the *Springfield Republican*. The composition of the President's message "is generally attributed to Mr. Seward," the London *Times* correspondent wrote. Ex-President John Tyler wrote to Dr. Francis Lieber complaining of Lincoln's grammar in the inaugural. Dr. Lieber replied that secession, not grammar, was the issue.

Mayor Fernando Wood's paper in New York, the *Daily News*, suspected "the casual reader would at once be taken by the honeyed phrases in which it is couched." It was ambiguous. "We could reconcile a peaceful policy with the inaugural, but still there is a sting left." The *New York Herald* commented, "It would have been almost as instructive if President Lincoln had contented himself with telling his audience yesterday a funny story and letting them go"; however, the inaugural was "not a crude performance," for "it abounds with traits of craft and cunning." The *Baltimore Sun* read in the inaugural that "it assumes despotic authority, and intimates the design to exercise that authority to any extent of war and bloodshed. If it means what it says, it is the knell and requiem of the Union, and the death of hope." The *Baltimore Exchange* believed that "the measures of Mr. Lincoln mean war"; while Douglas said publicly, "It is a peace offering rather than a war message."

The *Richmond Enquirer* saw in it "the cool, unimpassioned, deliberate language of the fanatic. . . . Sectional war awaits only the signal gun. . . . The question, 'Where shall Virginia go?' is answered by Mr. Lincoln. She must go *to war*." The *Charleston Mercury* announced. "It is our wisest policy to accept it as a declaration of war."

A group of Southern leaders meeting in Washington the night of the inauguration sent word to their Government: "We all agreed that it was Lincoln's purpose at once to attempt the collection of the revenue, to re-enforce and hold Fort Sumter and Pickens, and to retake the other places. He is a man of will and firmness. His cabinet will yield to him with alacrity."

Following the inaugural, prices of stocks fell in Wall Street. Inquiry rose as to why Mayor Fernando Wood of New York had violated custom and refused to hoist the national flag over the City Hall.

Neither in the carriage that day nor at the White House did Lincoln have any questions to ask the outgoing President. According to a friend and biographer of Buchanan, except for their official intercourse there was no reason to suppose the two men had ever met. "All that is known is that Mr. Lincoln's demeanor, while in the carriage, produced upon Mr. Buchanan the impression that he had no fears for his personal safety or the safety of the capital. But it does not appear that at that or any other time, Mr. Lincoln sought to know what his predecessor could tell him."

The two men rode from the inauguration to the Executive Mansion, where Buchanan introduced Lincoln, according to custom, and spoke his last words to Lincoln: "If you are as happy, my dear sir, on entering this house as I am in leaving it and returning home, you are the happiest man

Punch of London cartoons Lincoln (unaware he has grown a beard) with the title "The American Difficulty" and the line: "*President Abe.* 'What a nice White House this would be if it were not for the blacks!' "

in this country." Miss Lane had seen that a good dinner was ready for the Lincolns. Tad and Willie ran over the house from top floor to basement, and in a few hours had interviewed every servant and watchman in the place.

The sixteenth President of the United States glanced over his office and the cracked oil painting of Andrew Jackson under which he was to sit. His wife entered the room where she was to hold sway as the mistress of the White House, where one of her predecessors had written on arrival there, "I look at myself like the little old woman, and exclaim, 'Can this be I?'"

On a southbound train from Memphis that day, Albert Richardson of the *New York Tribune* staff heard one passenger say, "I hope to God Lincoln will be killed before he has time to take the oath," and another passenger, "I have wagered a new hat that neither he nor Hamlin will ever live to be inaugurated." Still later Richardson, in a circle of Southern ladies, heard conversation:

"I am glad Lincoln has not been killed."

"Why so?"

"Because if he had been, Hamlin would become President, and it would be a shame to have a mulatto at the head of the government."

Inauguration night saw an attempt at gaiety, the Union Ball, in a new building on Judiciary Square, the hall light-flooded by five large gas chandeliers. Decorated with white muslin and blue trimmings, it was called The Muslin Palace. Few of the Southern men and women who for years had given Washington society its tone were present at the Union Ball. "The rooms were crowded with strangers from the north and west." A scandal arose afterward of many new hats and overcoats stolen or taken by mistake from the wardrobes.

Lincoln shook hands from 8:15 till 10:30. The estimate was twenty-five hands a minute. His gloves were now *white* kids; he had learned which color was the decree of the hour. He looked absent-minded, as young Henry Adams saw him, as though "no man living needed so much education as the new President but all the education he could get would not be enough."

Vice-President Hamlin introduced a Maine storyteller to Lincoln, Colonel James Dunning of Bangor. Hamlin vouched him one of the best raconteurs in the country. Dunning referred to coercion and the use of force and told about a soldier hauled up before a court-martial charged with pointing his gun at a man and forcing the man to eat a crow. The defendant was asked if he recognized the complainant, the fellow who on the previous day had eaten a crow while looking into the muzzle of a rifle. "Do I recognize this gentleman?" asked the soldier. "Why, yes, he's the gentleman who dined with me yesterday!" Lincoln shook with laughter and, noted Hamlin, said to Dunning, "Come up to the house some night this week and tell me some more of your stories."

The Marine Band played "Hail to the Chief" at eleven o'clock. Lincoln entered leading the grand march, arm in arm with Mayor Berret, followed by Mrs. Lincoln arm in arm with Senator Stephen A. Douglas. Lincoln avoided waltz and square dance, but Mrs. Lincoln and Douglas were partners in a quadrille. Hundreds of women in crinoline trod the waltz, schottische, polka, mazurka. Reporters wrote, "It was an animated scene." Mrs. Lincoln wore a new blue gown, a large blue feather in her hair. Many said it must be her happiest night of life, the realization of dreams long waited.

The ball over, Mr. and Mrs. Lincoln went for the first night in their new house of presences, shadows, ghosts. A passer-by in the daytime would have noticed then, said an Ohio Congressman, "the bare, worn and soiled aspect of that part of the White House devoted to the Executive, an aspect not unlike that presented by 'the breaking up of a hard winter' about a deserted farmstead."

As Lincoln slept that night, relays of ponies and men were rushing west from St. Joe, Missouri, with his inaugural address. They would be seven days and seventeen hours reaching Sacramento, California, with his plea for the East and West coasts, the Great Lakes and the Gulf, the Rio Grande and the Penobscot, to belong to one common country.

Franz Lieber, who as a fifteen-year-old boy had fought against Napoleon at Waterloo, who had served as a history professor at the University of South Carolina and in '61 held classes at Columbia College, New York, was writing that great ideas enter human history on soft feet and the Greeks had a word for it:

"The avenging gods are shod with wool."

CHAPTER 5

CABINET PORTRAITS

STEPHEN FISKE of the *New York Herald* told of meeting Lincoln at the Union Ball and asking if there were any message he could take to James Gordon Bennett, Lincoln replying, "Yes, you may tell him that Thurlow Weed has found out that Seward was not nominated at Chicago."

Whether Lincoln's remark was as brusque and abrupt as Fiske quoted, Lincoln certainly at that hour was making his own decisions as against Seward, Weed, Chase, the Blairs, trying to dictate the make-up of his Cabinet. Seward and Weed wanted an all-Seward-Weed Cabinet, which would eliminate the Chase faction, who wanted an all-Chase Cabinet.

"The President is determined he will have a compound Cabinet," Seward wrote to his wife. And not wanting to sit in a compound Cabinet, Seward had on Saturday, March 2, notified Lincoln that he must "withdraw."

Lincoln kept this note over Sunday, and on Monday while the inauguration parade horses were champing outside of Willard's and the crowds were waiting for a look at the incoming President, Lincoln sat at a desk and wrote a note to Seward.

He dated it "Executive Mansion, March 4, 1861," as though he had already moved into the White House: "I feel constrained to beg that you will countermand the withdrawal. The public interest, I think, demands that you should; and my personal feelings are deeply enlisted in the same direction."

Handing the note to John Hay to copy, he said, "I can't afford to let Seward take the first trick."

The next morning Seward with a polite note was back in the Cabinet and Lincoln was writing him, "Please give me an interview at once."

Thus far Lincoln's Cabinet slate, with two minor exceptions, stood as he had framed it when late on the November election night in the Springfield telegraph office he sat amid piles and flurries of telegrams brought in on the big wind of the day. Since then months had passed, and he was saying, "When I finally bade my friends good-night and left that room, I had substantially completed the framework of my Cabinet as it now exists."

First on the slate, in top places, were Lincoln's rivals for the presidential nomination.

He was told, "They will eat you up," and replied, "They will be just as likely to eat each other up."

One name only on the slate, that of Simon Cameron, Lincoln himself had tried to erase.

At noon on March 5 the Senate received the new President's nominations for Cabinet members, and these new heads of government departments were approved: Secretary of State, William H. Seward of New York; Secretary of the Treasury, Salmon P. Chase of Ohio; Secretary of War, Simon Cameron of Pennsylvania; Secretary of the Navy, Gideon Welles of Connecticut; Secretary of the Interior, Caleb B. Smith of Indiana; Attorney General, Edward Bates of Missouri; Postmaster General, Montgomery Blair of Maryland.

The new Cabinet had four old-line Democrats (Chase, Cameron, Welles, Blair) and three old-line Whigs (Seward, Bates, Smith), a wrong balance, Lincoln heard many times, and made clear his view: "I'm something of an old-line Whig myself and I'll be there to make the parties even."

Thaddeus Stevens, no longer quietly mentioned for Attorney General, told a Congressman the new Cabinet held "an assortment of rivals whom the President appointed from courtesy, one stump-speaker from Indiana and two representatives of the Blair family." The *Crisis* of Columbus, Ohio, remarked, "If Mr. Lincoln can get along with them, we reckon we can."

What was there notable about these seven men Lincoln chose for his close personal advisers, to head the seven main departments of the Government? Why were they logical men for their places?

Seward, eight years older than Lincoln, had been, until Lincoln's nomination and election, the leader of the Republican party. His words on "the higher law" and "the irrepressible conflict" had gone far to lose him the nomination won by Lincoln. As a New York man close to the controlling financial and commercial interests of the country, he sponsored protective tariffs, steamship subsidies, a bill for a railway to the Pacific. He analyzed canals, railroads, trade balances, tariffs, new factors in commerce, the stream of surplus capital and labor arriving from Europe, and foretold their economic role with a surer grasp than Lincoln. Although a Protestant, an Episcopalian, he had for years been close to Archbishop John Hughes of New York, the most influential Roman Catholic prelate in America; his start in politics was with the Anti-Masonic party, which elected him State senator in 1830; his recommendation as Governor of New York that public school funds be divided between Protestants and Catholics had brought the American or Know-Nothing faction clamoring against him within the Republican party. He had read history widely and often tried to meet a modern situation with an ancient solution, as if history were a series of repetitions.

During the winter since Lincoln's election Seward had been taken by many men of the North and South as the spokesman of the new Administration. As such, he had used the watchwords "moderation," "forbearance," and "conciliation." At a dinner in New York before leaders in finance and politics he had made a speech with humorous and flippant expressions, almost as though logic and laughter could restore the broken Republic. His long-awaited January 12 speech in the Senate had rambled among many topics, sounded no slogan, cleared no foggy air. "Great God! how are the mighty fallen!" Zach Chandler had cried. In that month of January, Seward was playing desperately at the role of peacemaker.

His cordial acquaintance with Senator Jefferson Davis grew into more than acquaintance as he went for one hour a day to the home at F and Fourteenth Streets where Davis lay racked with the pain of an inflamed left eye soon to go blind. He sat at the bedside and told Davis of the daily events in House and Senate, Mrs. Davis saying: "Mr. Seward inquired about every symptom, and one day when our hopes of saving the eye were small, as he went downstairs he suddenly said, with moist eyes, 'I could not bear to see him maimed or disfigured, he is a splendid embodiment of manhood, he must not lose his eye.' There was an earnest, tender interest in his manner which was unmistakably genuine." His friendship for the Davis family had begun two winters before. As Mrs. Davis told it: "Mr. Seward heard that I was at the point of death, and that a near neighbor of his, who was nursing me, could not get a carriage to bring her to our door. . . . Though he did not know us, he had his own fine horses harnessed to a sleigh, and brought her to me—but with broken harness and at some peril."

Thus in the seething of that winter Seward was receiving confidential messages from Abraham Lincoln and sitting at the bedside of Jefferson Davis. He was trying to do what Henry Clay had done in 1850, hold the Union together by negotiation and compromise. The Public Man wrote in his diary, "Much of Mr. Seward's work must necessarily be done in the dark and through agencies not appreciable by the public at all." He had traveled far since his speech as a Senator in 1848 when he told an audience in Cleveland, Ohio, as to slavery, "It must be abolished, and you and I must do it."

Once Seward had told Wendell Phillips, "You make opinion and we use it." He seemed now, to many, ready to surrender any point or principle to hold the Union together. A baffling manipulator, he was said to be "politically the uncleanest politician in the United States, but personally the cleanest." When he was joined with corrupt forces in politics, he asked of them only political advancement—not money.

His large audience over the country had been won partly through his understanding of how to use the press. In the Senate he would as soon speak to empty seats, he told Jefferson Davis. "I speak to the papers; they have a larger audience than I, and can repeat a thousand times what I want to impress on the multitude outside." Buchanan had observed this gift and said of Seward: "He understood the art of preparing in his closet and uttering before the public, antithetical sentences, well calculated both to inflame the ardor of his anti-slavery friends and to exasperate his pro-slavery opponents. He thus aroused passions, probably without so intending, which it was beyond his power to control." Of his shifts in viewpoint that winter, William Lloyd Garrison remarked, "He aims to be axiomatic and oracular, but it is evident that his moral nature is quite subordinate to his intellect."

It was long ago that Seward had been Governor of New York and brought on the statute books laws requiring jury trials for fugitive slaves, with defense-counsel fees paid by the State. Opinions of him ranged from that of E. L. Godkin, saying he was "perhaps the greatest Constitutional lawyer in America, the clearest-headed statesman, and of all public men perhaps the least of a demagogue and the most of a gentleman," to that of Horace Greeley writing in a letter to Schuyler Colfax, "Seward is a poor worthless devil and old Abe seems to have a weakness for such."

He was Welsh-Irish, slouching, slim, middle-sized, stooped, white-haired, "eyes secret but penetrating, lively with twinkling, a subtle, quick man, rejoicing in power." He had traveled in Europe, Egypt, Palestine. He had been a struggling lawyer and built a practice that paid well, though he was as careless about fees as Lincoln; he won for a convict, and again for a Negro, cases that brought them freedom and him no fees; as Governor of New York he had led in abolishing the law and custom of putting men in jail for not paying their debts.

He had quit snuff and now smoked cigars by the box. His beautiful Arabian horses were pictured in *Harper's Weekly*. His five-course dinners at his Washington apartment were a topic of smart society, and one of his loyal friends, Charles Francis Adams, Jr., noted: "When it came to drinking, Seward was, for a man of sixty, a free liver; at times his brandy-and-water would excite him, and set his tongue going with dangerous volubility; but I never saw him more affected than that—never anything approaching drunkenness. He simply liked the stimulus, and was very fond of champagne; and when he was loaded, his tongue wagged."

The historian George Bancroft wrote his wife: "I talked with Seward, who looked dirty, rusty, vulgar, and low; used such words as hell and damn, and spoke very loud. I think better of Mrs. Lincoln for her excessive dislike to him."

Walking from the Capitol with Douglas one day some years back, he had mentioned Douglas's reference that day to "nigger-worshipers," and said, "Douglas, no man will ever be President of the United States who spells 'negro' with two g's." On the one hand Seward was referred to by Mrs. Lincoln as "that dirty abolitionist sneak," while on the other hand the abolitionist Senator Benjamin Wade was saying, "If we follow such leadership, we will be in the wilderness longer than the children of Israel under Moses," and Senator Sumner now held him "demented," "a mere politician," and worse. It seemed that Seward as an antislavery man was never known to blame the Southerners personally for slavery. His door was open to Southern representatives always. The personal hatreds and guttural disgusts of so many of the abolitionists for Southern men and Southern culture were lacking in Seward. Though Southerners hated him for predicting "the irrepressible conflict," for declaring, "There is a higher law than the Constitution," he refused to lash back at them.

When a Louisiana Senator had poured out on him a series of accusations of bad faith, he had remarked, "Benjamin, give me a cigar and when your speech is printed send me a copy." Another time when an opponent had spattered him with odious epithets, he stepped over to the excited and denunciatory Senator's desk and, reaching for a little silver box, said, "Senator, will you give me a pinch of snuff?"

He had through the winter exchanged letters with Lincoln about a Southern man for a Cabinet place, Lincoln writing that they could safely take "not more than one who opposed us in the election, the danger being to lose the confidence of our own friends." Seward had sought such a Southern man, written hopes and misgivings to Lincoln, and given it up. Of his own selection for the State Department Lincoln wrote him: "I am happy to find scarcely any objection to it. I shall have trouble with every other Northern cabinet appointment, so much so that I shall have to defer them as long as possible to avoid being teased to insanity to make changes."

The same sort of ridicule Lincoln met for saying at Columbus "nothing is going wrong" had fallen on Seward for saying at a big dinner in January that the trouble would all be over and everything settled in sixty days. Seward later replied to a party critic: "When I made that speech the electoral vote was not counted, and I knew it never would be if Jeff Davis believed there would be war. We both knew that he was to be President of the Southern Confederacy, and that I was to be Secretary of State under Mr. Lincoln. I wanted the vote counted and Mr. Lincoln inaugurated. I had to deceive Davis and I did it. That's why I said it would be all settled in sixty days."

Now Seward was writing his wife that after he had withdrawn from the Cabinet and Lincoln asked him back, "I did not dare to go home, nor to England," so he had gone back into the Cabinet. To John Bigelow in Europe he wrote: "Charitable obituaries are pronounced over our remains.

Gideon Welles of Connecticut, Secretary of the Navy, U.S.A.

Photograph from Frederick H. Meserve Collection

William Henry Seward of New York, Secretary of State, U.S.A.

From Oliver R. Barrett Collection

Montgomery Blair of Missouri, Postmaster General, U.S.A.

Simon Cameron of Pennsylvania, Secretary of War, U.S.A.

Salmon Portland Chase, Secretary of the Treasury, U.S.A.

Edward Bates of Missouri, Attorney General, U.S.A.

We think we shall excite an agreeable surprise when we pronounce in the ears of the mourners the soothing assurance that we still live."

As the national crisis took higher strides, Seward told of an Irish soldier rushing into the Captain's tent, gun in hand, crying, "What shall I fire at, Captain? I don't see no one." The Captain smiled: "Fire at the crisis. Didn't you know there was a crisis in this country?"

Young Henry Adams sketched Seward as having "unorderly hair and clothes; hoarse voice; offhand manner; free talk, and perpetual cigar," a double type, political and personal, "complex because the political had become nature, and no one could tell which was the mask and which the features." Both among friends and before the public "he chose to appear as a free talker, who loathed pomposity and enjoyed a joke; but how much was nature and how much was mask, he was himself too simple a nature to know. Politicians thought it unconventionality. Bostonians thought it provincial. Henry Adams thought it charming."

Between this man and Lincoln was a friendship that might grow deeper. Seward wrote his wife of his first day in Washington with Lincoln: "We rode an hour [in the morning]. I met him again at half-past one. He is very cordial and kind toward me—simple, natural, and agreeable." To his son Fred he remarked that he had found under the Lincoln exterior "a curious vein of sentiment." He was pleased to find this, as though he and Lincoln would work better together if both had a streak of sentiment underlying their logic and solemnity. "The temper of your Administration," he advised Lincoln, "whether generous and hopeful of union or harsh and reckless, will probably determine the fate of our country."

Salmon Portland Chase, Senator from Ohio, had held off from taking the Treasury portfolio. When he had visited Springfield at Lincoln's invitation, Lincoln told Chase that he would make an excellent head of the Treasury Department. Chase knew, however, that Seward, weeks before, was definitely slated for Secretary of State, and felt that he, Chase, should have been called on earlier. His pride was hurt. Lincoln had now publicly named him for Secretary of the Treasury without his having told Lincoln he would take the place.

"I went immediately to the President and expressed my disinclination to accept," wrote Chase to J. T. Trowbridge. "After some conversation, in the course of which he referred to the embarrassment my declination would occasion him, I said I would give the matter further consideration and advise him next day of my decision. Some rumor of my hesitation got abroad, and I was immediately pressed by the most urgent remonstrances not to decline. I finally yielded to this, and surrendered a position every way more desirable to me, to take charge of the finances of the country under circumstances most unpropitious and forbidding." Having accepted, he wrote the Governor of Ohio his resignation as United States Senator, saying, "The President has thought fit to call me to another sphere of duty, fuller far of perplexing responsibilities."

Tall and portly, Chase was spoken of as "handsome," as having "a stately figure," a "classic face," a head massive as Daniel Webster's. He had been Governor of Ohio, had received 49 ballots for the presidential nomination at Chicago, had expected that Seward's nomination would bring him second place on the ticket. A restless ambition to be President lay deep, the same urge that had him writing in 1830, "I shall ever strive to be first wherever I may be, let what success will attend the effort." He knew that going into the Cabinet might shade his chances for maneuvering his way into the White House.

Though Chase filled the eye as an imposing figure, the pathos ran over his life and letters of a man trying to be hero to himself, not knowing when he was hero, marplot, or simple snob. He strove for culture, bowed low before Bostonians, wrote to Sumner: "I never feel my poverty so much as when among you affluent scholars of Boston and its environments. The humiliation is more than compensated by the pleasure and profit I derive from your learning." His letters to Sumner indicated that they felt bonds of likeness; both were solemn, handsome, portly, orators without fire or epigram; both studied the classics, spoke French, seldom laughed, and sometimes asked others, "What is there to laugh at?" And both knew grief, for Chase once wrote Sumner of the same despair Sumner had once voiced: "What a vale of misery this world is! Death has pursued me incessantly. My path has been—how terribly true it is—through the region of his shadow. Sometimes I feel as if I could give up—as if I *must* give up. And then after all I rise and press on." The facts were stark.

At twenty-four years of age Chase married Katherine Jane Garniss, three years younger than himself, and within two years she died, leaving him a girl child who lived only four years. At twenty-nine he married Eliza Ann Smith of Cincinnati, a girl of eighteen, who died six years later, having borne him three children, of whom only one had lived. A year later he married Sarah Bella Dunlop Ludlow of a well-known and propertied Cincinnati family; she died within six years, having borne him two children, of whom one lived. Thus in 1852 he had in seventeen years stood at the burial caskets of three wives and four children.

Out of these accumulated griefs he had two living daughters. One of them was a gleaming, vital creature, Katherine Garniss Chase, known as Kate and born under strange stars. On her birthnight in 1840, the father wrote in his diary: "The birth had taken place at 2 A.M. After I had seen my wife and child, I went into the library and read a few pages in Eber's book on children, a judicious treatise. At last I became tired, and, though it was now day, lay down and slept awhile. The babe is pronounced pretty. I think it quite otherwise. It is, however, well formed, and I am thankful. May God give the child a good understanding that she may know and keep his commandments."

When Kate was five he was reading the Book of Job to her and praying with her. Later she read Bible verses and recited poems for him. Still later he went over with her his involved law cases. And she had grown to be his chum and helper, playing chess with him, walking to the office, telling him what she got from a newly read book. Her glimpses into politics sometimes went farther than his. She was as much a son as a daughter, men had said. They were partners.

He had lights for leading, this man Chase, though his gnawing ambition was a chronic personal ailment beyond remedy or softening. He had no reason to fawn before such as Sumner. Somehow in few of his public acts or speeches was there a shine of the human spirit, as there was in his telling Donn Piatt when they walked away from a visit with the convicts of the Ohio State Penitentiary: "There is not much difference between convicts and the ordinary run of people. . . . These poor fellows are not wicked; they are weak; they have not sense enough to be cautious, nor strength of character to resist temptation. The law catches the small rogues; the big rascals are too wary to approach the net. I think sometimes our criminals are not in the penitentiary but in the churches." Thus Piatt recalled the words spoken by a Governor of Ohio, privately.

In his early years in Cincinnati, Chase had taken without fee so many cases of black people, claimed as fugitive slaves, that Kentuckians called him "the attorney-general for runaway negroes." When the colored people of Cincinnati presented him with a silver pitcher, his speech accepting it declared their rights to vote the same as that of whites: "I regard the exclusion of the colored people as a body from the elective franchise as incompatible with true democratic principles." He had quit the Democratic party, led in organizing the Liberty party, then the Free-Soil party, ending with the Republicans.

On a platform in Cincinnati he was hit with a brick, with rotten eggs; he carried credentials. The way had been opened to commercial and corporation law practice; a fortune in money beckoned; he chose to throw his fate with runaway Negroes; also ambition dictated politics for him.

Out of his Lincoln interview in January Chase wrote Thaddeus Stevens, extremist antislavery Congressman: "Mr. Lincoln conversed frankly and fully. *He is a man to be depended on.* He may, as all men may, make mistakes; but the cause will be want of information, not unsoundness of judgment or devotion to principle." Yet he was taking his place as Secretary of the Treasury in the mood in which he wrote Charles A. Dana, Greeley's managing editor of the *New York Tribune:* "I do not know what to say in reply to your wish that I may go into Mr. Lincoln's cabinet. I greatly prefer my position as Senator."

Against his wish, he had been drafted by Lincoln. To refuse might isolate him, with risk to his ambitions. The story was easily half true that he faced a mirror and bowed to himself, murmuring "President Chase."

Simon Cameron, the new Secretary of War, had proper claims to his portfolio. His fifty white-hatted delegates to the Chicago convention had on the first presidential nomination ballot voted for Cameron. Cameron's release of those delegates had started the stampede to Lincoln. Lincoln's managers had, without authority from Lincoln, pledged Cameron a Cabinet place.

Politics was a business, a sport, and a passion with Cameron. Born in 1799, for twenty years he had been the dominant political manager in Pennsylvania. His mother's father, a German, had fought in the Revolutionary War. His Scotch father was a country tailor, a poor provider, and nine-year-old Simon was adopted by a physician, at ten began typesetting, learned the printer's trade, and before he was twenty-one edited the *Doylestown Democrat*. He moved to Washington, set type on the *Congressional Globe*, penetrated backstage circles of Congress, developed friendships with important men, studied the mechanics of practical politics, how followings are built up and held together by doing real favors so as to have funds and influence from the rich and votes and cheers from the poor.

On borrowed money Cameron became owner and editor of the *Harrisburg Intelligencer*. With a contract for State printing his profits grew. More contracts came. He was building the Pontchartrain Canal near New Orleans when President Andrew Jackson called on him for help. His influence procured the Pennsylvania Legislature to memorialize Jackson begging him to run again for President. This rang a bell, and other legislatures followed. Cameron manipulated other matters toward electing Jackson to a second term. The Federal patronage of Pennsylvania entire came into his hands. "General" Cameron, he was usually called, having once been adjutant general of State militia.

Elected United States Senator from Pennsylvania in 1845 and in 1856, he followed in his political course such an intricate chart that it would require a heavy volume to report his expert shifts, deviations, returns, his many cheap tricks in political dickering, his several unwavering loyalties, of which one was to the iron and manufacturing interests of Pennsylvania and their demand for a high protective tariff. This "especial interest of Pennsylvania," as Lincoln had called it in his Pittsburgh speech, was to Cameron one of the cornerstones of Republican faith in the nation's future.

Ten of Cameron's earlier years had been given to bank, railroad, and canal building, getting a fortune; and later, amid the interdependent profits of business and politics, he let one hand wash the other, with varied cats and dogs of investment, saying, "You scratch my back and I'll scratch yours." His nickname as "The Czar of Pennsylvania" rested on a reputation as the most skilled political manipulator in America. The backdoor meeting, the private understanding, the weasel word, the whispered negotiation, the open agreement formulated in writing and signed by all concerned, the persistent and delicate bargaining by which differing elements were suddenly brought into effective unity, the explicit pledge or the vague expectation given to seekers of favors and benefits—Cameron with his Machiavellian technique knew how and when to use these ancient devices employed more or less by all politicians.

The abstractions so often on the tongues of Lincoln, Seward, Chase, would not fit naturally in the mouth of Cameron. Those men were, to him, actors. He was, to himself, a stage-manager. His decision had put Buchanan into the United States Senate twice. Then, suddenly seeing Buchanan's power rising to question his own in Pennsylvania, he organized the People's party, had himself elected United States Senator in 1856. In the same year he amalgamated Whigs, Know-Nothings, Republicans into the Union party of Pennsylvania, with a unique signed agreement by the national electors to give a solid vote for either Frémont, the national Republican candidate, or Fillmore, the national American or Know-Nothing candidate, if the electoral vote of the State would elect either to the Presidency. Governor Curtin's faction was hostile to him. So was Congressman Thaddeus Stevens personally. Yet it was Cameron chiefly who assembled the organization and funds that in 1860 under the name of the People's party for the first time won victory for the national Republican presidential electors of Pennsylvania.

Loose gray clothes hung from his tall, slim frame. He was smooth of face, sharp-lipped, with a delicate straight nose, a finely chiseled mask touched with fox wariness. As he pronounced dry and pretendedly forthright decisions Cameron's face was more often mask than face. He wrought effects from behind the scenes. His setup of himself as a presidential possibility at the Chicago convention was one of his effects; he did not care to be President, but he came to Chicago with something to trade and got a pledge from Davis, Swett, Medill, and others that with Lincoln elected he would be Secretary of the Treasury.

When it dawned on Lincoln that Cameron as head money-changer of the Administration would look peculiar and call for dry wit, Lincoln named him for the War Department, took it back, named him again to stay. Cameron did not care deeply about any policies or principles involved in the affair, but when Chase, Sumner, Curtin, McClure, and others started out to scalp and gut him politically, he stuck by his guns, brought as many witnesses as they to face Lincoln for him, his best ones being Seward and Weed.

When at last the opposition refused to prefer any charges against Cameron in writing, and all the accusations were exercises in oral denunciation, Lincoln said his name would stay on the original slate. Sumner urged the Public Man to go to Lincoln and represent Cameron as "reeking with the stench of a thousand political bargains," as "a political Judas from Pennsylvania, whom Providence had marked with the capillary sign of his character, and who might have sat to Leonardo da Vinci for the picture in the Milanese refectory." The Public Man asked Sumner why he did not himself go to Lincoln with these views. Sumner said he had—and the strongest language he could use would not swerve Lincoln.

The Keystone State with its iron and railroad domain was wanted by Lincoln for the national emergency, and Cameron was its leading link of business and politics. Lincoln appointed Cameron, though groaning, according to Whitney, as they talked about it, "How can I justify my title of Honest Old Abe with the appointment of a man like Cameron?"

"Mr. Lincoln asked me what I thought of Simon Cameron," wrote the Ohio Congressman Albert Gallatin Riddle, who had journeyed a short distance with the President-elect across Ohio. "I answered that to me he was a mystery, that his influence in Pennsylvania seemed out of all proportion to his ability, but that he was a wonderful manager. Mr. Lincoln replied that he had the same impression of him. I was surprised that he was appointed to the Cabinet, for I did not then know so well that intellectual ability was a small factor in selecting a Cabinet Minister."

Gideon Welles, the Connecticut Yankee named by Lincoln for Secretary of the Navy, was, like Cameron, an old Jackson Democrat. His newspaper, the *Hartford Times*, was among the earliest to cry Jackson for President, and Jackson later confidentially asked Welles to name those in Connecticut deserving of Federal jobs. Welles's sight, smell, and phrases ran to politics. Among his forefathers one was State treasurer, another governor, and he himself had been State comptroller and Hartford postmaster. His service in the Polk Administration as Chief of the Naval Bureau of Provisions and Clothing may have had a trifle to do with his new call to naval service, though he was no salt-water sailor.

Lincoln saw Welles as a more than relatively honest Democrat who had quit his party on the slavery-extension issue, who as a Republican made a losing run for the governorship in 1855 and was chairman of his State's delegation to the Chicago convention. Fifty-eight years old, his short, thickset body had a massive head surmounted by a patriarchal wig, which with his white prophet's beard gave him a Neptune savor. A smooth-shaven upper lip, and eyes kindly in repose, told those who met him not half what he could put into his diary.

Welles's name on Lincoln's first Cabinet slate got by with less criticism than any other, though some Republicans kept growling that no Democrat had a right to a Cabinet seat. Lincoln put him at the head of all of Uncle Sam's seagoing vessels, and later made jokes about Uncle Gideon's not knowing bow from stern. Uncle Gideon had a pen, a sense of history, and had decided he would write a diary from day to day of what he saw, heard, believed, suspected, conjectured. His opinions and prejudices would run free, wide, and faulty in the diary, but in recording fact as to what he saw and heard he would be a competent witness. Not all was going on that he believed or guessed, but what he put down as seeing and hearing was usually there. He lacked the humor to see that when he criticized the Secretary of the Treasury as deficient in financial training it was about as funny as a landlubber's heading the Navy Department.

Edward Bates, the new Attorney General, born in 1793, was the son of a volunteer soldier who fought under La Fayette when Washington's army and the French fleet cornered the British at Yorktown and ended the Revolutionary War. Bates was a private, corporal, and sergeant of volunteers in the War of 1812, going west and studying law in 1814 in St. Louis, then a settlement of 2,000 people. He had been attorney general of Missouri, a State senator, a Congressman. He was a Whig even after that party was dead, presiding over the Whig National Convention at Baltimore in 1856, devising ways and means of burial. Events slowly piloted him to where he had no place to go but the Republican party. As a Free-Soil Whig from a

Border State, it was argued that he was the man who as President could soften the shocks between the sections. His 48 votes on the first ballot at the Chicago convention sank to 22 on the third ballot and finally went to Lincoln. His course had been even and consistent.

Lincoln, after naming Seward for the State Department, told Bates he could have any other place in the Cabinet he chose. Most of his life Bates had been first a lawyer and secondarily a politician. President Fillmore's offer to appoint him Secretary of War he had refused. Harvard College's offer of a Doctor of Laws degree he had accepted. In Lincoln's Cabinet he chose to be Attorney General. He was quaint, old-fashioned, of a school that was passing. "An Old-Line Whig," said Bates, "is one who takes his whiskey regularly, and votes the Democratic ticket occasionally."

When Lincoln sent word he would go from Springfield to St. Louis to consult Bates about the Cabinet, Bates himself went to Springfield, explaining, "I thought I saw an unfitness in his coming to me, and that I ought to go to him."

Caleb B. Smith of Indiana, as Secretary of the Interior, also could properly have a seat at the Cabinet table of the new President. Lincoln's managers at the Chicago convention in dealing with Pennsylvania and Indiana delegates "promised them everything they asked," as was remarked by Charles H. Ray, a participant. One item promised, without Lincoln's authorization, was a Cabinet place to Indiana. Smith was Boston-born, 1808, and taken to Ohio when six years old. Lawyer, editor, orator, at Connersville, Indiana, he became a Whig Congressman, held appointive Federal office, took up the practice of law in Cincinnati in 1850, and moved to Indianapolis in 1858. Of the new Cabinet members he was nearest the class of ordinary perfunctory politician.

Pressure had come on Lincoln to appoint another Indiana man, Schuyler Colfax, Congressman, antislavery and temperance orator, and editor of South Bend. He was fifteen years younger than Caleb Smith, and Lincoln was writing to Colfax, "When you were brought forward I said, 'Colfax is a young man, is already in position, is running a brilliant career, and is sure of a bright future in any event; with Smith it is now or never.'"

Montgomery Blair, the new Postmaster General, was viewed as not merely himself having a seat in the Cabinet. He was a sign that among Lincoln's chosen advisers was the Blair family, headed by Old Man Blair, Francis Preston Blair, born in 1791 of a Scotch-Irish line, graduate of Transylvania University in Lexington, Kentucky, a volunteer in the War of 1812, a lawyer who refrained from practice because of faulty speech. He could write, however, and he plunged into politics and never came out of it alive. He was a fighting Jackson man through both of Jackson's stormy presidential terms, editing at Washington the *Globe*, which told Jackson's friends and enemies where to get on or off as to current issues. He ate many White House breakfasts, rode horses with Jackson, was one of the Kitchen Cabinet. His Silver Spring farm near Washington often had visitors seeking a wily veteran's advice.

Breaking with President Pierce over Cabinet appointments and issues he styled "true democracy," Old Man Blair joined in organizing the Republican party, presided over its first national convention at Pittsburgh, and was able to place a St. Louis man, John C. Frémont, at the head of the ticket. Many abolitionists had him under suspicion; he had once owned slaves. He welded the old Jacksonian Democrats and the liberal Germans of St. Louis into an operating unity, though the clashes were recurring more often on the slavery issue. In 1860 he sought an old-line Jacksonian to head the Republican national ticket, ending with support of the old-line Whig Bates.

His influence among Border State delegates joined to Montgomery's control of Maryland delegates, plus his son Frank's sway over Missouri delegates, was thrown to Lincoln on the third ballot at Chicago. His cordial relations with Lincoln, many feared, might grow into the same important intimacy he had held with Presidents Jackson and Van Buren. This fear was grounded partly on his tangible strength in having his first choice for President in 1860, Bates, as Attorney General, his old fellow Democrat, Welles, as Navy Department chief, his son-in-law, Gustavus Vasa Fox, slated to be Assistant Secretary of the Navy, another son-in-law, S. P. Lee, as a ranking admiral in the navy, and finally his son Montgomery as Postmaster General. Subtle, cadaverous, bald, poised he was—persistent and silken in spinning his webs, delicately sensitive to political trends.

Lincoln sought the views of this skilled professional politician. Often the views came unsought. The elder Blair was one of the few to whom Lincoln confidentially loaned a copy of the inaugural address for comment and suggestion.

"A confidential relationship as close as that maintained by Mr. Lincoln with any other man" existed with the elder Blair, according to Lamon. "To Mr. Blair he almost habitually revealed himself upon delicate and grave subjects more freely than to any other. When he had conceived an important but difficult plan, he was almost certain, before giving it practical form, to try it by the touchstone of Mr. Blair's fertile and acute mind."

In a letter to ex-President Martin Van Buren, March 7, 1861, Old Man Blair gave an estimate of Lincoln and a peculiar confession about changes that had come over American politics. "Lincoln is pure and patriotic," he wrote, "but like another confiding great man you have known [their friend and benefactor, Andrew Jackson], has suffered himself to be seduced by a grateful & unsuspicious heart into early commitments, which he has had too much pride on the point of honor involved in promises—although made by others—to revoke." This was the estimate. The peculiar confession ran: "I am now nearly 70 years old & had not learned even to suspect in advance, the tricks now laid open to me by which intriguing politicians can wind themselves into place against the wishes of him who confers it. But we must let this pass."

His two sons, the Blair boys, as they were often called, had been law partners in St. Louis. Francis Preston Blair, Jr., had graduated from Princeton—then the College of New Jersey—helped his father edit the *Globe* in

Washington, joined a company of volunteers in the Mexican War, served as attorney general of the new Territory of New Mexico. Though himself once a slaveholder, Francis P. Blair, Jr., led the Free-Soil party in Missouri and was in 1856 the only Free-Soiler elected to Congress from that State. No other man of the time, probably, spoke more urgently for deportation and colonization of Negroes as a solution of the slavery problem.

His brother Montgomery, born in 1813, was now the only member of Lincoln's Cabinet under fifty years of age; a West Point graduate, a service lieutenant in the Seminole War, he had been district attorney for Missouri, Mayor of St. Louis, judge of the court of common pleas. He had moved to Maryland to be near his large Federal Supreme Court practice. As counsel for Dred Scott, the fugitive slave, he won friends among antislavery men. He had helped get a lawyer to defend John Brown. He represented in Maryland the moderate wing of the Republican party as against the Henry Winter Davis radical faction. The Blair appointment resulted in protests to Lincoln nearly as furious as in the case of Cameron. Thurlow Weed warned the President that Blair would keep the Cabinet "constantly in hot water." Rumors spread that Blair was to be left out. Judd came one night to Lincoln asking in excitement whether there was to be a new deal, with Henry Winter Davis named instead of Blair. "Judd," said Lincoln, "when that slate breaks again, it will break at the top."

The President wanted diversity in his Cabinet, and gathered a wide variety of American viewpoints in his seven advisers. As Nicolay and Hay saw it, "He wished to combine the experience of Seward, the integrity of Chase, the popularity of Cameron; to hold the West with Bates, attract New England with Welles, please the Whigs through Smith, and convince the Democrats through Blair." In the group was not one tried and proved personal friend of the President. His closest counselors were chosen for other reasons than his personal comfort.

Only the appointments of Bates of Missouri and Blair of Maryland were protested when Lincoln submitted his Cabinet list to the Senate for confirmation. Border State Senators said no man from a slaveholding State ought to have a place in the Cabinet of a Black Republican President holding such views as Lincoln had expressed in his inaugural.

Already the Cabinet members were sharing blame with Lincoln. Caroline Howard Gilman, wife of the Unitarian minister in Charleston, South Carolina, loyal to the South, was writing on March 12 to her children: "Well may Lincoln be in tears. He with his Cabinet has made two nations weep."

The man who would inherit this Cabinet and sit at the head of it in the event of Lincoln's death, Vice-President Hamlin, had been consulted about the Cabinet several times by Lincoln. "I am anxious for a personal interview with you at as early a day as possible," Lincoln had written Hamlin in November after election, and Hamlin had come from Maine to Chicago and in the Tremont House walked into a room where Lincoln sat alone. Lincoln arose, walked toward the door, spoke abruptly though pleasantly:

"Have we ever been introduced to each other, Mr. Hamlin?"

"No, sir, I think not."

"That is also my impression, but I remember distinctly while I was in Congress to have heard you make a speech in the Senate. I was very much struck with that speech, Senator, particularly struck with it, and for the reason that it was filled chock up with the very best kind of antislavery doctrine."

"Well, now," laughed Hamlin, "that is very singular; for my one and first recollection of yourself is of having heard you make a speech in the House, a speech so full of good humor and sharp points that I, together with other of your auditors, was convulsed with laughter."

The door opened, callers poured in, and the conference of the two men was taken up the next day at the home of Judge Ebenezer Peck, where, as Hamlin heard it, Lincoln said, "Mr. Hamlin, I desire to say to you that I shall accept, and shall always be willing to accept, in the very best spirit, any advice that you, the Vice-President, may give me."

This was unusual. Hamlin said so. Except for Jackson and Van Buren, the relation between the Vice-Presidents and the Presidents had not as a rule been friendly. Hamlin pledged himself to be a friend and to render his humble advice as best he could. Lincoln then broke the news to Hamlin of his plan to weld the followers of Seward, Chase, Cameron, Bates, his presidential rivals, into a compact body by taking those leaders into his Cabinet; the crisis required that he should do this. Hamlin ordinarily would not have approved Seward for the Cabinet, but in the crisis at hand it would be discreet to appoint Seward and he complimented Lincoln on the gracious act of thus recognizing his most distinguished rival. Lincoln brought up other names, gave his theory of recognizing former Whigs and Democrats, with a motto of "Justice to all" controlling patronage, pleasing Hamlin by declaring, "You shall have the right, Mr. Hamlin, to name the New England member of the Cabinet." He gave Hamlin a list of names suggested for the Navy Department, including Charles Francis Adams, Nathaniel P. Banks, and Gideon Welles. Banks was a mill boy who had worked his way up to Speaker of the House at Washington and Governor of Massachusetts in Boston; he stood out as one of the national leaders of the Know-Nothing or American party. Lincoln remarked that Banks was able, well known, might make a capable executive, but "it is for you to decide, Mr. Hamlin, and I mean that you shall name the New England man in the cabinet."

Hamlin said he would be frank with Lincoln. He could see Banks's ability and high personal character of a sort, but Banks was a "trimmer" and in politics laid his convictions open to suspicion by a theatrical way of "coming out for a party." This for the moment erased Banks from the list.

Hamlin went from Chicago to the Senate at Washington, received letters from Lincoln referring again to Banks, who was politically then somewhat of a magnetic figure. "I need a man of Democratic antecedents from New England," wrote Lincoln, explaining he could not get "a fair share" of Democrats in his Cabinet unless Hamlin named one from New England:

"This stands in the way of Mr. Adams. I think of Governor Banks, Mr. Welles, and Mr. Tuck [a New Hampshire Congressman who had served with Lincoln in 1848]. Which of them do the New England delegation prefer?" Thus Lincoln named Banks first on his list, which indicated that Banks was his choice; in a previous letter to Hamlin, Lincoln had written, "I have had an intimation that Governor Banks would yet accept a place in the Cabinet."

Hamlin, however, named Gideon Welles, and Lincoln held to his pledge that the Vice-President should decide who from New England should enter the Cabinet. To a Massachusetts caller Lincoln said, "I like your man Banks and have tried to find a place for him in my Cabinet but I am afraid I shall not quite fetch it."

The letter notifying Seward that he would be appointed Secretary of State went from Lincoln to Hamlin for delivery to Seward. "Consult with Judge Trumbull; and if you and he see no reason to the contrary, deliver the letter to Governor Seward at once," wrote Lincoln to Hamlin. "If you see reason to the contrary, write me at once."

On his journey from Maine to Washington for inauguration, Hamlin at New Haven referred to "that great and good man whom the people have elevated to the highest office within the gift of any nation on the face of the earth—Abraham Lincoln of Illinois." Few members of the incoming Administration were so lavish in their comment on Lincoln in that hour. Though Hamlin leaned to the radical wing of the Republican party, he kept free of suspicion and jealousy of Lincoln so cleanly that Lincoln alluded more than once to the reliability of the man who would step into his shoes in case of his own assassination.

Hamlin had been elected to Congress twice as a Democrat, had then been elected United States Senator as a Democrat, and on the slavery-extension issue had resigned as United States Senator, joined in organizing the Republican party in Maine, was elected Governor of Maine, and resigned as Governor to take a seat as one of the first Republicans in the United States Senate, later resigning as United States Senator to make the run for Vice-President on the Republican ticket. He was fifty-two years of age, tall and powerfully built, saying he did not need a revolver to guard against assassination, showing two fists that he said would take care of trouble: "They are good enough to knock a man down any day." His face was swarthy, of a complexion so dark that many Southerners said and believed that he was a mulatto and that his blood accounted for his radical antislavery sentiments. His recorded ancestors were of the pure English stock that settled the colony of Massachusetts. In college when he was eighteen word came that his father was dead and he went back home to work the farm. Later he bought a country weekly paper, learned typesetting, studied law and oratory, and convinced the hardheaded, slowgoing people of Maine that he should be their leading public servant.

The Hamlins took dinner with the Lincolns in the Lincoln suite at the Astor House in New York, sat together in a box at the opera and rose to bow to applause and calls from the audience. Hamlin took note that Lincoln did not believe that the applause and large crowds on the journey from Springfield were for Lincoln personally. He took note of Lincoln's being frank and ingenuous in little things: "When, for instance, oysters on the half-shell were served, he looked at them with a half-doubting, half-smiling look, as if he had never eaten such a dish before, 'Well, I don't know that I can manage these things, but I guess I can learn.' He would not resort to a polite artifice or pretend even in the case of oysters."

And Hamlin had gone on to Washington ahead of Lincoln so as to be there for inauguration if Lincoln were not. At Baltimore rowdies had gathered under rumors that Lincoln and Hamlin were on the train. As Hamlin lay in his berth he heard oaths outside that "no damned abolitionist like Lincoln or Hamlin" would ever reach the White House. Further oaths came from drunken men rushing through Hamlin's car on a man hunt. They brushed aside the curtains of his berth, stared at him in the dim light, and said he didn't look like the one they were after, then went away leaving the breath of whisky for a memento.

Lincoln's specification that Hamlin must name a Democrat from New England for the Cabinet had eliminated Charles Francis Adams, Republican Congressman, son of President John Quincy Adams, grandson of President John Adams. Seward and Weed urged Adams for the Cabinet, but Lincoln held that New England should have one member and no more. "Mr. Lincoln certainly was not predisposed in favor of Mr. Adams for any position," wrote Charles Francis Adams, Jr., "though the evidence is clear that he entertained no particular objection to him."

Adams's good friend Seward heard from the President that John C. Frémont and William L. Dayton, Republican candidates for President and Vice-President in 1856, were to have respectively appointments as Ministers to France and England. This arrangement, proposed by Lincoln without consulting Seward, was "scarcely courteous" to his Secretary of State, and in the case of Frémont was "obnoxious" to Seward, who was no admirer of Frémont, according to C. F. Adams, Jr. "The President did not yield the point readily," and only persistent effort by Seward brought about the transfer of Dayton to Paris, and the naming of Charles Francis Adams, Sr., as Minister to the Court of St. James, London, England. "Even then Mr. Lincoln is alleged to have excused himself for yielding by the characteristic remark that the Secretary of State had begged very hard for it, and 'really, Seward had asked for so little!' "

Therefore Charles Francis Adams, son of John Quincy Adams and grandson of John Adams, journeyed to Washington and the State Department for verbal instructions, and went to the White House to meet the President. What he saw and heard was to him horrific. He made a story often told in the Adams family of this soiled occasion. A son had it from the father: "A door opened, and a tall, large-featured, shabbily dressed man, of uncouth appearance, slouched into the room. His much-kneed, ill-fitting trousers, coarse stockings, and worn slippers at once caught the eye. He seemed generally ill at ease,—in manner constrained and shy. The Secretary of State introduced the minister to the President." Adams began with conventional remarks; he appreciated the obligation; he hoped the confidence in him would not be misplaced. "They had all by this time taken chairs; and the tall man listened in silent abstraction. When Mr. Adams had finished—and he did not take long—the tall man remarked in an indifferent, careless way that the appointment in question had not been his, but was due to the Secretary of State, and that it was to 'Governor Seward' rather than to himself that Mr. Adams should express any sense of obligation he might feel; then, stretching out his legs before him, he said, with an air of great relief as he swung his long arms to his head, 'Well, governor, I've this morning decided that Chicago post-office appointment.' Mr. Adams and the nation's foreign policy were dismissed together! Mr. Adams never recovered from his astonishment, nor did the impression ever wholly fade from his mind."

That a man of the brains and experience of Seward was Prime Minister, Adams considered a piece of luck for the country, while on the other hand he held the opinion that from the birth of the United States Government no other "experiment so rash had ever been made as that of elevating to the head of affairs a man with so little previous preparation for his task" as Mr. Lincoln had.

Not least among the disgruntled was Cassius Marcellus Clay of Kentucky, a Henry Clay Whig and Mexican War veteran who had conducted an antislavery weekly paper in Lexington, escaped from mobs, advocated Negro emancipation by legal measures while having a bowie knife and two pistols handy. He had been among the original Lincoln-for-President men in Kentucky, had helped bring a delegation to the Chicago convention, had received a large vote for the vice-presidential nomination, but had been discarded because geographically the place had to go to an Eastern man, had campaigned and received letters of thanks from Lincoln. He claimed that "as soon as Lincoln was nominated he wrote me a letter offering me the post of Secretary of War."

And Clay's story, probably in the main accurate, of what happened to him and what he got at Washington ran as follows:

Without my knowledge, I was heralded as the Minister Plenipotentiary to Madrid. I at once went on to Washington and told Lincoln that I would not go to an old effete government like Spain. He seemed very reticent and grave, but asked me what office I would have. I said, since the Cabinet was full, I would go to England or France as Minister. He said Seward had promised those posts to Charles Francis Adams and Wm. L. Dayton. "Then," said I, taking my hat, "I will go home." Lincoln then said: "Clay, don't go home; I will consider the matter." The same day I dined with the leading Republicans of the nation then in Washington, at the house of the Belgian Minister, Sanford.

At an early hour I was called to the hall to see Senator Baker from Oregon, with whom I was intimate, we having been together in the Mexican War. Baker said he had conversed with Lincoln about me, and the President was anxious to satisfy my aspirations; the country was divided into personal and political factions, and it was hard to solidify the party—would I not accept the mission to Russia? I replied, that I had spent my life and fortune in the public service—canvassed for five Presidents who held power, and never asked or received an office; that now, when I could accept one—without compromise of my principles—the hungry harpies, mercenary camp-followers, swooped down upon me. No, I would go home and stay there.

Baker seemed to feel the injustice done me, but continued: "You have made great sacrifices, but does not patriotism require still more? Lincoln thinks your return home would seriously injure the party and the country; and so do I." I then said: "Well, Russia is a young and powerful nation, and must greatly figure in our affairs: I will accept." Without ceremony, Baker said: "Get your hat, and we will go to the White House at once." We went; and without sending up a card, we entered Lincoln's reception-room.

He was alone, and evidently awaiting us. He was quite sad and thoughtful. With his head bent down in silence he awaited Baker's report, who, without sitting down, said: "Mr. Lincoln, our friend Clay will accept the Russian mission." Lincoln then rose up, and, advancing rapidly toward me, firmly took my hand and said: "Clay, you have relieved me from great embarrassment."

Another expectant of Cabinet place was Norman B. Judd, general attorney of the Chicago & Rock Island Railway, chairman of the Illinois State Republican Committee, member of the Republican National Committee. As a delegate-at-large to the Chicago convention he had worked effectively to nominate Lincoln. "He was not a man of ideas," wrote Horace White, "but was fertile in expedients, sly, cat-like, mysterious, and thus considered more farseeing than he really was; but he was jovial, companionable, and popular with the boys who looked after the primaries and the nominating conventions. As a party manager his reputation was good, but his qualities were those of the politician rather than of the statesman."

Senator Trumbull favored Judd and urged that in him Lincoln would have in the Cabinet at least one old Illinois familiar. Possibly Judd would have gone in as Secretary of the Interior, but David Davis was pressing Lincoln for the pledged appointment of Caleb B. Smith as Indiana's promised portion. Lincoln deliberated, possibly consulted Seward, and sent Judd of the Rock Island Railway to Berlin as Minister to Prussia. Mrs. Lincoln, wrote Welles, had in political circles, "the credit of excluding Judd of Chicago from the Cabinet."

Without authority from Lincoln word got out that Gustave Koerner, former Lieutenant Governor of Illinois and a loyal friend of Lincoln, would have the Berlin legation. Newspapers far and wide published it as fact. Koerner received piles of congratulatory letters, and met law clients who had taken their cases elsewhere, believing Koerner was going to Berlin. When announcement was made that Judd would go to Berlin, Koerner applied for some other place that would seem a suitable award to the German Republican element, preferably Switzerland. But that post and all others had been spoken for. And the President could only wait till something turned up that could decently be offered Koerner.

With quixotic humor Lincoln signed the appointment of a Minister to

Mexico, Thomas Corwin of Ohio, easily the most illustrious and shining friend Mexico could name in the United States, the man who had lost a United States Senatorship for the sake of pleading the cause of Mexico when his own country was at war with her.

As First Assistant Postmaster General the President appointed John A. Kasson of Des Moines, Iowa, attorney for the Mississippi & Missouri Railroad, who had written much of the Chicago platform, giving special attention to the Pacific railway. "A great victory for our crowd," wrote Grenville M. Dodge to his wife at Council Bluffs, Iowa. By "our crowd" he meant the group of railroad-promoters who were in Washington near the National Hotel in a house to which came United States Senators Harlan and Grimes of Iowa, the Iowa Congressmen Curtis and Wilson, and among others Henry Farnam, president of the Chicago & Rock Island Railway. They were seeking first of all an act of Congress appropriating funds and lands for "the construction of a railroad and telegraph line from the Missouri River to the Pacific Ocean" and fixing Council Bluffs, Iowa, as the initial point of a northern route across the Platte River Valley of Nebraska. They were seeking appointment of their men as governors of the Territories through which the railroad would run.

And Lincoln named one of them, Alvin Saunders, a merchant and banker of Mount Pleasant, Iowa, a Lincoln delegate to the Chicago convention, for Governor of Nebraska. They told Lincoln they wanted too a government arsenal where the Rock Island Railway crossed the Mississippi. On these matters they were busy and bustling. "You will see a great advance in railroading in Iowa in the next twelve months," Farnam told Dodge. The Rock Island was to push its lines through to the Missouri River in the shortest possible time and be at Council Bluffs ready to connect with the first foot of track of the proposed Pacific railroad. Farnam believed Lincoln knew who had early built him up as a favorite of the Iowa delegation to the Chicago convention. Governor Kirkwood of Iowa had wavered between Chase and Seward when the Iowa delegation seemed to be two-thirds in favor of Seward. Farnam had written from Chicago that "Mrs. Farnam and myself will be most happy to see yourself and Mrs. Kirkwood at our house" during the Chicago convention, enclosing a railroad pass and giving the address of his Chicago house. And Governor Kirkwood, though not a delegate, had gone on to Chicago and joined the Lincoln rooters on the evening Greeley was writing, "Iowa is discordant and uncertain."

Lincoln's journey by rail, bus, and steamboat to Council Bluffs two years before had brought him to seventeen subdivision lots and ten acres of rolling prairie, which he looked over. He then decided to loan Norman B. Judd $3,000 and take these lots and land as security. The *Nonpareil* announced that "the distinguished 'Sucker' has yielded to the solicitations of our citizens" and would deliver a speech, which he did by candlelight in Concert Hall. The next day a young merchant and freighter was pointed out to him as knowing more about railroads than any two other men in the country, Grenville M. Dodge. They sat on benches of the Pacific House porch while

Lincoln examined Dodge on the best route for a Pacific railroad. "He shelled my woods completely," said Dodge later, "and got all the information I had collected for Henry Farnam, my employer."

Then Lincoln and Dodge walked to a tall hill and looked west into the haze of the Great Plains. As Lincoln stood gazing from that hilltop in 1859 there was between him and the West Coast not a rail for the Iron Horse to run on except a twenty-two-mile line in the Sacramento Valley of California. Three Pacific railroads had been built, on paper, imaginarily, in bills passing the Senate, the House refusing to concur. Two Pacific railroads had been built, on paper, imaginarily, in bills passing the House, the Senate refusing to concur. The reality was yet to come. A formidable group of young Westerners was determined never to let the new Republican Administration forget it. They knew their empire and would hack and hew toward it. In order to reach Washington for inauguration, Dodge had started in February and got caught in a record-breaking snowstorm. The drifts piled ten to twenty feet high, buried cattle beyond help, and blockaded and froze Colorado-bound gold-seekers, who left their dead scattered from Des Moines to the Missouri River.

On the "levee" evening of March 7 the big driveway of the Executive Mansion was blockaded with carriages; sidewalks and approaches were jammed with people. At half-past eight, when the President and Mrs. Lincoln had been handshaking a half-hour, the crowd outside the doors was so thick that for an hour the departing ladies and gentlemen stepped through windows. For two and a half hours the President "shook hands continually, a large part of the time shaking the gentleman with the right hand and the lady with the left, or vice versa." He wore plain broadcloth—and white kids. At half-past ten he "and his suite" moved from the Blue Room and passed once around for the crowd in the East Room.

"Mrs. Lincoln bore the fatigue of the two-and-a-half hour siege with great patience. She appeared remarkably well and performed her part of the honors with propriety," wrote one reporter. "Mrs. Lincoln was attired in a rich Magenta colored brocade silk, with raised figure flounces, trimmed not extravagantly with rich point lace. Her ornaments were chiefly diamonds and pearls."

Young Charles Francis Adams, Jr., was there and wrote in his diary that it was a crush the White House had never seen before. "There they were—the sovereigns; some in evening dress, others in morning suits; with gloves and without gloves; clean and dirty; all pressing in the same direction, and all behaving with perfect propriety. There was no ill temper; no vulgarity or noise; no rudeness; in spite of the crowd and discomfort, everything was respectful and decorous. The sight was one not pleasant to see, and even less pleasant to participate in; but still good of its kind. Here, as everywhere, the people governed themselves. At last I came in sight of the President—the tall, rapidly bobbing head of the good 'Abe,' as he shook hands with his guests, and quickly passed them along. The vastly greater number he hurried by him; but, when anyone he knew came along, he bent himself down to the necessary level, and seemed to whisper a few words in the ear, in pleasant, homely fashion; though not exactly becoming our President."

A trim little hundred-and-nine-pound woman author and magazine contributor known as Gail Hamilton—Mary Abigail Dodge was her real name—noted that as Lincoln entered the ballroom the band struck up "Hail to the Chief Who in Triumph Advances," the crowd parted to form a passageway, "Mr. Lincoln being conducted through it, bowing right and left, to a raised platform at the end of the room. Mrs. Lincoln followed, led by Douglas."

Miss Hamilton came up to Lincoln wearing a Paris gown of apple-green silk, green leaves and gold grapes in her forehead curls, white puffs of tulle in the bosom, and a tulle chemisette, a black velvet band around the neck, a coral bracelet on one arm and a gold bracelet on the other. As they shook hands she said, "Mr. Lincoln, I am very sorry for you, but indeed I must shake hands." He then gave her hand another shake and with a very paternal and benevolent squeeze said, "Ah! your hand doesn't hurt me." The crowd pressed and the vision in apple-green silk faded.

Hamlin, Cabinet members, Lord Lyons and other ministers and chargés d'affaires, generals and admirals in blue and gold braid, trod waltz, polka, and schottische with partners in bell-shaped balloon skirts of silk. Mrs. Lincoln danced with Senator Douglas, who held her bonnet and made it clear to the aristocracy who were staying away that socially as well as politically he now leaned to the Lincolns. Miss Hamilton took note that Kate Chase was "tall, slender, with beautiful eyes, hair, eyelashes, and feet, very graceful, great repose of manner."

Miss Hamilton was interested that Washington as a city was not yet grown up and that one morning when she took a walk with a heavyweight Senator, one of the hogs roaming the streets of the city for fodder suddenly scrambled between the legs of the Senator and upset him, threw him flat on the sidewalk.

Later in March Lincoln and his Cabinet gave a state dinner. William Howard Russell of the London *Times* was among those invited, and wrote that his eyes saw "no liveried servants, no Persic splendor of ancient plate, or chefs d'œuvre of art." Also he noted: "Vases of flowers decorated the table, combined with dishes in what may be called the 'Gallo-American' style, with wines which owed their parentage to France, and their rearing and education to the United States. The conversation was suited to the state dinner of a cabinet at which women and strangers were present. Except when there was an attentive silence caused by one of the President's stories, there was a Babel of small talk round the table, in which I was surprised to find a diversity of accent almost as great as if a number of foreigners had been speaking English."

The President was droll, almost gay, noted Russell. Attorney General Bates, for instance, was criticizing a lawyer Lincoln had appointed to the judicial bench. "Come now, Bates, he's not half as bad as you think," said Lincoln. "Besides that, I must tell you, he did me a good turn long ago. When I took to the law, I was going to court one morning, with some ten or twelve miles of bad road before me, and I had no horse. The judge overtook me in his wagon. 'Hello, Lincoln! Are you not going to the court house? Come in and I'll give you a seat.' Well, I got in, and the judge went on reading his papers. Presently the wagon struck a stump on one side of the road; then it hopped off to the other. I looked out and I saw the driver was jerking from side to side in his seat; so says I, 'Judge, I think your coachman has been taking a little drop too much this morning.' 'Well, I declare, Lincoln,' said he, 'I should not much wonder if you are right, for he has nearly upset me half a dozen of times since starting.' So, putting his head out of the window, he shouted, 'Why, you infernal scoundrel, you are drunk!' Upon which, pulling up his horses, and turning round with great gravity, the coachman said, 'By gorra! that's the first rightful decision you have given for the last twelvemonth.' " Thus Russell heard the yarn and wrote it for the London *Times*. The President was droll, almost gay.

CHAPTER 6

OFFICE-SEEKERS

BESIDES time for required social functions and for decisions regarding Fort Sumter, the Border States, Cabinet meetings, national policy, the President had to give hours daily to the Federal patronage, the distribution of offices and applicants for places—more time than to all other items on the day's program.

For thirty years, except eight Whig years, the thousands of Federal jobs had been the Democratic spoils of victory. The custom was for the new party to sweep out all officeholders and put in new postmasters, port collectors, marshals, superintendents, paymasters, doorkeepers, each having deputies or first, second, and third assistants, chief clerks and ordinary. Thousands of the applicants for these places had given time and money, influence and enthusiasm, toward the Republican victory of November, often with a clear promise of which particular jobs they would get.

"I saw Mr. Lincoln twice for a few minutes before the inauguration," wrote Villard, to whom Lincoln in Illinois in a boxcar during a rainstorm had once said, "Just think of a poor Sucker like me being President!" Now, noted Villard, "in response to an expression of sympathy with his tribulation, he groaned out, 'Yes, it was bad enough in Springfield, but it was child's play compared with this tussle here. I hardly have a chance to eat or sleep. I am fair game for everybody of that hungry lot!' "

"Half the town seem to have gone to Washington," Mrs. James Conkling wrote from Springfield, Illinois, to her son at Yale. "How many will return with office I cannot say, but certainly a vast number must be disappointed."

"A few friends so demented as to want office . . . I desire to help, and for that I may go to Washington," wrote Samuel Bowles of Springfield, Massachusetts. "I am glad I am not there [at Washington]. I can keep cool here, and calm, and am reading poetry, and pitying my friends who can't."

At Willard's one correspondent saw the main-floor corridors surging with office-seekers, overflowing up the staircases and landings into the halls, the reading-room and barbershop, the writing-room, out on the porch and steps, the hotel perhaps holding "more scheming, plotting heads, more aching and joyful hearts, than any building of the same size ever held in the world." The hotel clerk had told the correspondent: "Two thousand and five hundred patriots dined here, sir, a few days before you came. I guess you could not well equal that. Everyone wants a place and it must be found, or he'll know the reason he's not in Abraham's bosom."

From all over the Union map, except from the seceded States, "the triumphant Republicans had winged their way to the prey." Many wore the new paper collars, some had linen. They crowded the Willard bar morning and night. Target cuspidors were circled with miss shots. One excited pilgrim ordering breakfast for a crucial day called for black tea, toast, scrambled eggs, fresh spring shad, wild pigeon, pig's feet, two robins on toast, oysters, breads, and cakes. One rushed out of the Willard barbershop, his face half-lathered, a towel under his chin, calling to a Senator about the place promised him.

One stopped Lincoln in a hack at a street crossing and handed up his recommendation papers to Lincoln, who frowned. "No! no! I won't open shop in the street," and he rode on.

The atmosphere was riotous, and Lincoln understood these anxious seekers perfectly, because in the Taylor Administration twelve years before he had been one himself, had hurried to Washington for place as Commissioner of the Land Office, had written many letters, pulled wires, sought interviews, influence, recommendations, and after all his hustling saw another man get the place.

"They won't give up the offices," he was quoted in a half-jesting reference to the Southerners holding a large share of Federal jobs. "Were it believed that vacant places could be had at the North Pole, the road there would be lined with dead Virginians." The estimate of one friend and five enemies created by one appointment was familiar to him, and he alluded to hearing Daniel Webster once saying in a speech, "Politicians are not sunflowers; they don't . . . turn to their God when he sets the same look which they turned when he rose."

Herndon quoted Lincoln in one outburst: "If our American society and the United States Government are demoralized and overthrown, it will come from the voracious desire for office, this wriggle to live without toil, work, and labor, from which I am not free myself."

The trampling of anxious feet in and around the White House was told in a letter of Seward to his wife: "Solicitants for offices besiege the President and he finds his hands full for the present. My duties call me to the White House one, two, and three times a day. The grounds, halls, stairways, closets, are filled with applicants, who render ingress and egress difficult."

Senator Fessenden of Maine wrote to his wife and children: "Our poor President is having a hard time of it. He came here tall, strong and vigor-

176   HARPER'S WEEKLY.   [MARCH 16, 1861.

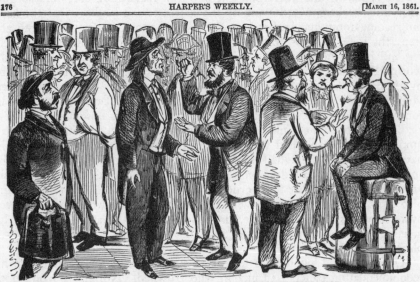

OFFICE-SEEKERS AT WASHINGTON DURING THE INAUGURATION.
These Gentlemen, who are ready, like good Patriots, to serve their Country, are all ORIGINAL LINCOLN MEN. 'Tis true, they voted for PIERCE and BUCHANAN; but this was a deep game to Insure the Election of LINCOLN in 1860.

Thomas Nast sketches for *Harper's Weekly*, writing a subtitle: "These Gentlemen, who are ready, like good Patriots, to serve their Country, are all ORIGINAL LINCOLN MEN. 'Tis true, they voted for PIERCE and BUCHANAN; but this was a deep game to insure the Election of LINCOLN in 1860."

ous, but has worked himself almost to death. The good fellow thinks it is his duty to see to everything, and to do everything himself, and consequently does many things foolishly. . . . I have been to see him two or three times, but stayed but a few moments each time, as I was pained and disgusted with the ill-bred, ravenous crowd that was around him."

Nineteen days after inauguration Senator Nesmith of Oregon came to the rescue of the President as best he could by the publicly given advice: "The Administration is very much embarrassed. A throng of countless spoilsmen desire place. I have found every avenue to the office of every Secretary and every head of a bureau of this Government crowded with hungry office-seekers—old men and young men; long, gaunt, lean young men; old, limping, bald-headed gentlemen—choking up the avenues. Here are forty thousand office-seekers fiddling around the Administration for loaves and fishes, while the Government is being destroyed. A great many have been disappointed. It would take a miracle such as that performed by our Saviour when he fed five thousand people with five loaves and two little fishes, to satisfy all these greedy camp-followers. [Laughter.] If I were in the place of Mr. Lincoln, considering that the Union is dissolving and disintegrating beneath our feet, I would turn the Federal bayonets against the office-seekers. I would drive them from this city, and I would not leave a man to tell the tale. I would determine first whether we had a Government or not."

Not so vehement, though equally pertinent, was the humorist Orpheus C. Kerr (Office Seeker) in a letter published in April. "The city is full of Western chaps, at present, who look as if they just walked out of a charity-hospital, and had not got beyond gruel diet yet," wrote Kerr. "Every soul of them knew old Abe when he was a child, and one old boy can even remember going for a doctor when his mother was born. I met one of them the other day (he is after the Moosehicmagunticook post-office), and his anecdotes of the President's boyhood brought tears to my eyes, and several tumblers to my lips. He says, that when Abe was an infant of sixteen, he split so many rails that his whole county looked like a wholesale lumber-yard for a week; and that when he took to flat-boating, he was so tall and straight, that a fellow once took him for a smoke-stack on a steamboat, and didn't find out his mistake until he tried to kindle a fire under him. . . . I tell you what, my boy, if Abe pays a post-office for every story of his childhood that's told, the mail department of this glorious nation will be so large that a letter smaller than a two-story house would get lost in it."

In his second week as private secretary to the President, Nicolay wrote that he hoped eagerly for the day when he could read and write his letters in peace without interruption from someone wanting to see the President for only five minutes. "At present this request meets me from almost every man, woman, and child I see, whether by day or night, in the house or on the street."

Two lines of callers were at the White House front each weekday, one line going, one coming. At any hour of the day ten to fifty watchers waited where Lincoln passed from his office to the other end of the building for his meals. They stepped forward and presented their claims.

From down in Alabama came news of the Confederate Government at Montgomery having its lines of office-seekers, coming and going. The *Augusta Chronicle* agreed editorially with the *Macon Chronicle*, "Let President Davis swear by the horns of the altar that no man who asks for office shall get it, and the evil would abate." The *Chronicle* cited a gentleman remarking that Montgomery was Washington "enlarged but not improved." Mary Boykin Chesnut, her husband a loyal right-hand man of Jefferson Davis, was writing in her diary at Montgomery: "Everywhere political intrigue is as rife as in Washington. Everybody who comes here wants an office, and the many who, of course, are disappointed raise a cry of corruption against the few who are successful. I thought we had left all that in Washington. Nobody is willing to be out of sight, and all will take office."

Whitney called four days after Lincoln's inauguration with a young friend needing a clerkship. And as Whitney saw it, Lincoln "almost ground his teeth with vexation" at having appointed one Illinois man to be a district judge of Kansas and another Illinois man to be Superintendent of Statistics. David Davis had pressed for the appointments, and Lincoln yielded to Davis, telling of it to Whitney: "There's Davis, with that way of making a man do a thing, whether he wants to or not, has made me appoint Archie Williams and John Jones; and I already have got a hatful of despatches asking if all appointments are to come from Illinois."

From Robert Todd Lincoln at Harvard came a letter joining others to endorse a candidate for postmaster of Cambridge, Massachusetts. The President wrote his son to attend to his studies; unless he let such matters alone he would be taken away from college. Young Bob kept his father's letter to show when someone again tried to use him.

One fellow, having learned he could not be a Federal judge, was willing to be a postmaster, but hearing that there were no vacancies, applied to the Treasury Department for a place as lighthouse-keeper; anywhere along the Atlantic Coast would suit him. Another asked to be Superintendent of the Mint and Lincoln, telling of it, laughed. "Why didn't he ask to be Secretary of the Treasury?" A port collector was instructed, "If there is any secessionist in your department I wish you would remove him." To Blair went a note favoring a Virginian who "wishes to get, for his son, a small place in your Department," the President adding, "I think Virginia should be heard, in such cases." He had to write Jesse K. Dubois that he could not do what both Dubois and he would like to have done. "I was nearly as sorry as you can be at not being able to give Mr. Luce the appointment you desired for him. Of course, I *could* have done it; but it would have been against the united, earnest, and, I add, angry protest of the Republican delegation of Minnesota in which State the office is located."

Informing Welles that the office of Engineer in Chief of the navy was vacant, the President wrote, "Please avail yourself of all the means in your power for determining, and present me the name of the best man for the service." Early he wrote Welles that no important or extensive changes should be made at the Norfolk navy yard without consulting him. He reached for friends he did not want to lose, writing to Senator Jacob Collamer of Vermont: "God help me. It is said I have offended you. I hope you will tell me how." When Collamer replied that he cherished only "kindness and confidence," Lincoln returned the letter with the notation on it, "Very glad to know that I haven't." Regarding the reappointment of a California man as consul Seward wrote, "If you say I can appoint him I will do so, and keep the matter out of the newspapers." On the back of Seward's communication Lincoln wrote, "Let it be done."

A Western editor came and Lincoln sent for Seward and said: "Here is a gentleman who had the good sense to prefer you to me for President.

He wants to go abroad and I want you to find a good place for him"—which Seward did.

Carl Schurz of Watertown, Wisconsin, scholar, politician, writer, who swayed many German voters, came to the White House to learn more about a rumor that the President was considering him for Minister to Sardinia. He had interviewed Lincoln in Springfield, was one of the few and possibly the only one for whom Lincoln had locked the door while they went over the inaugural address point by point.

Schurz wrote his wife that Lincoln had halted the conversation, said, "I will give you a mark of confidence which I have given no other man," and then read the inaugural address. Schurz wrote further to his wife: "As I was leaving him after this long conversation, in which he explained his opinions and plans with the greatest frankness, I told him I should ask his Administration for a few offices for my friends. He answered: 'You write

On March 8 of '61 Carl Schurz wrote to his wife, "My Dearest," a letter having the above passage, which translates: "This morning I went to the Whitehouse, was received at once, and Lincoln handed me a paper on which I read: I nominate Carl Schurz of Wisconsin to be Minister Plenipotentiary and Envoy Extraordinary to Spain. Abraham Lincoln. Warm handshaking and so forth. Seward's influence has therefore been overcome, and I am lord of the battlefield. Jubilation everywhere the news went. Now my nomination is up for consideration in the Senate and I hope that at this moment, while I am writing, the Senate has confirmed the nomination." He sent "a thousand, thousand warm kisses for you all" and urged, "Now, little wife, this is all. Get ready for our departure." Original letter loaned by Mrs. Paul Steinbrecher of Chicago.

to me and you may be sure that I shall attend to everything you may ask for; and as for your own case, which you have not spoken of to me, I shall never forget you.' Others tell me that he spoke of sending me to Sardinia."

Schurz came on from Watertown to attend the inauguration, had several talks with Lincoln about government policy and about appointments for Schurz's friends. Then one day came the news to Schurz: he was not going to Sardinia. Lincoln gave him the information that he was nominated to be

United States Minister to Spain. Schurz learned afterward how his case had been argued up and down in the Cabinet, Seward declaring that Schurz's record in violent, insurrectionary, red-republican movements in Germany in 1848 would be frowned on by the Spanish monarchy. Lincoln replied that Schurz would be discreet; it ought not to be held against the man that he had made efforts for liberty; and it might be well for European governments to realize this. Chase and Blair agreed with Lincoln. Seward yielded, but didn't like it.

Schurz himself later was only mildly pleased at the appointment. Suppose he should be over in Spain and the United States Government was at war. His country then would need him as a major general. He could serve his country far more effectively on horseback as a major general on the field of battle, he believed, than sitting in the quiet of a legation in old Madrid. He would go back to Watertown, Wisconsin, and think it over. He had noticed "evident satisfaction" on Lincoln's face on telling him of the appointment, but for himself he was not satisfied.

From two Wisconsin Congressmen, Schurz heard of their going to Seward and saying that a good many people would be disappointed if Schurz were not given the proposed Spanish mission. They reported that Seward jumped from his chair, paced the floor in excitement, and jerked out the words: "Disappointment! You speak to me of disappointment. To me, who was justly entitled to the Republican nomination for the Presidency, and who had to stand aside and see it given to a little Illinois lawyer! You speak to me of disappointment!" Schurz wrote the words as he recalled their being reported to him. They did not sound quite like Seward. Seward said something about disappointment, probably, and made some ironical reference to himself as the best instance of disappointment that could be singled out in the Republican party. But the reference to Lincoln as "a little Illinois lawyer" was not in character. Seward would have had another way of saying it if at the moment he wished to belittle Lincoln.

For one of his young friends Lincoln did the best he could, threw the full weight of his influence, and then dropped the matter. "I have the positive promise of both Mr. Lincoln and Cameron to create the Bureau of Militia and make me chief of it," wrote Colonel Ellsworth from his sickbed in Willard's to his fiancée's father. His letter began, "I am very sick with measles," and closed: "Both Mr. Lincoln's children have the measles. I took it from them." Ellsworth came and went as he pleased at the White House, was a favorite of the Lincoln children, of Mrs. Lincoln, of the two secretaries Nicolay and Hay.

Lincoln had written, but not signed nor sent, an order on the Secretary of War detailing Lieutenant E. E. Ellsworth of the 1st Dragoons for special duty as "Inspector General of militia affairs, for the United States," for transaction of all business pertaining to the militia, to be conducted as a separate bureau of which Lieutenant Ellsworth would be chief, to promote uniform organization, drill, equipment, and instruction systems for the militia: "You will please assign him suitable office rooms, furniture, etc., and provide him with a clerk and messenger . . . printing, stationery, access to records, etc., as he may desire. . . . Also provide, if you please, in such manner as will best answer the purpose, for a monthly payment to Lieut. Ellsworth, for this extra duty, sufficient to make his pay and emoluments equal to that of a Major of Cavalry."

The course of affairs by which Lincoln came to write this extraordinary order was sketched by Ellsworth in a letter addressed to his fiancée in a female seminary in Brooklyn, New York, and in a letter to her mother at Rockford, Illinois. His appointment by the President as a regular-army lieutenant in the 1st Dragoons was a first step: "It was necessary that I should go into the Army in order that Mr. Lincoln could appoint me Chief of a Bureau of Militia. The going into service is in name only; I don't join the regiment at all." He outlined other activities: "As soon as it was known that Cameron was to be Secretary of War, I had Thurlow Weed, Judge Davis and other persons of great influence with him go and urge my claims, and obtain from him a promise 'to do nothing' until he heard from me. I can tell you these things in a few words, but it took weeks of hard wire pulling to bring them about. I then went to Mr. Lincoln and told him I would like a note to Mr. Cameron; he immediately wrote a request to C. to appoint me Chief Clerk. As he finished it he swung round in his chair and said in a peculiarly deliberate manner, 'I've been thinking on the way, and since we have been here, a long while in fact, that by and by, when things get all straightened out and I can see how the land lies, that I'd put you in the Army, somewhere.' I thanked him, but told him that the purpose I had in view at present could be accomplished out of the Army best, etc."

Ellsworth then went to Cameron, who said that Lincoln's note and Ellsworth's reputation would be sufficient if he, Cameron, were not so "peculiarly situated." Ellsworth believed that by "peculiarly situated" Cameron meant to say gently that the office of Chief Clerk was promised elsewhere.

So Ellsworth elaborated an old plan of his for a Federal bureau to co-ordinate militia bodies of the States. He took the plan to Cameron. "He agreed to recommend it, and we arranged a meeting with Mr. Lincoln at 8 o'clock the same evening. I went up accompanied by Major Hunter of the Pay Department, and Capt. Pope of the Topographical Engineers. When we were all in the room together, I explained what brought us there, and when we had concluded Mr. Lincoln said, 'Well, gentlemen, with all proper regard for the rights of Mr. Cameron or anybody else, I want Col. Ellsworth to have a good place,' and more to the same effect. Said I, 'Mr. Lincoln, here are two old Army officers to tell you what can be done in the matter.' Major Hunter then explained that Mr. Lincoln could appoint me to the Pay Department and then make me Chief of a Bureau of Militia, etc. 'Well,' said Mr. Lincoln again, 'I am pressed to death for time and don't pretend to know anything of military matters; fix the thing up so that I shan't be treading on anybody's toes, or carrying anybody across lots, and then come to me and I'll finish it.' "

So Cameron told Ellsworth that he could depend on its all being arranged satisfactorily, and Ellsworth, to make sure Cameron would not fail, had Thurlow Weed go to Cameron again and urge the merit of Ellsworth and the proposed bureau, had Mrs. Lincoln send for Cameron and get his assurance that the Ellsworth matter would go through. Lincoln wrote with his own hand the order for the creation of the bureau with Ellsworth detailed as Chief. The next morning Lincoln was to sign this order, deliver it to the Secretary of War, and close the transaction.

On that day, however, Ellsworth met Colonel E. V. Sumner of the regular army, who had heard that Ellsworth was to be made a regular-army major on short notice, and who with emphasis made known two points: (1) that half the captains in the army were, and had been, seeking the appointment for years; (2) that the appointment would rouse the ill will of these men against Mr. Lincoln, and so on and so on. Hearing this from Colonel Sumner, Ellsworth wrote to his fiancée's mother: "I went to Mr. Cameron and asked him if he was ready to sign the papers; he said he was. Then I related the conversation which had just occurred [with Colonel Sumner], and told him that I would do nothing to cause ill feeling toward Mr. Lincoln or himself, and that I would not, therefore, take the Majority. That's the manner in which I kicked myself out of a three thousand dollar life position into the cold. Mr. Cameron said I could rely upon him; both he and Mr. Lincoln being my friends, they could take care of me. The next best thing was to take a Lieutenancy—about $1,850 a year (Cameron has positively promised to make it up to $3,000) and be ordered to duty at Washington and placed in charge of my Bureau. All the papers are drawn up. . . . The next step will be to ask Congress to create the Bureau by law."

The White House view of Ellsworth and his negotiations was phrased by John Hay: "He was a strange anomaly at the capital. He did not care for money or luxury. Though sensitive in regard to his reputation, for the honor of his work, his motto always was that of the sage Merlin, 'I follow use, not fame.'

"An office-seeker of this kind was an eccentric and suspicious personage. The hungry thousands that crowded and pushed at Willard's thought him one of them, only deeper and slier. The simplicity and directness of his character, his quick sympathy and thoughtless generosity, and his delicate sense of honor unfitted him for such a scramble. He withdrew from the contest for the position he desired, and the President, who loved him like a younger brother, made him a lieutenant in the army, intending to detail him for special service.

"The jealousy of the staff-officers of the regular army, who always discover in any effective scheme of militia reform the overthrow of their power, and who saw in the young Zouave the promise of brilliant and successful innovation, was productive of very serious annoyance and impediment to Ellsworth. In the midst of this, he fell sick at Willard's. . . .

"We were talking one night of coming probabilities, and I spoke of the doubt so widely existing as to the loyalty of the people. He rejoined, 'I can only speak for myself. You know I have a great work to do, to which my life is pledged; I am the only earthly stay of my parents; there is a young woman whose happiness I regard as dearer than my own; yet I could ask no better death than to fall next week before Sumter.'"

For Ellsworth's use in any way he saw fit toward connecting with military service Lincoln wrote a letter which phrased in a formal and precise manner his direct conversational remark to Cameron and the army officers: "I want Ellsworth to have a good place." The tone of it indicated that he had become aware that he and Ellsworth in what they had first tried to do would have been a little too abrupt for army methods of the moment. Addressing Colonel E. E. Ellsworth as "My dear Sir," he wrote: "Ever since the beginning of our acquaintance, I have valued you highly as a person[al] friend, and at the same time (without much capacity for judging) have had a very high estimate of your military talent. Accordingly I have been, and still am anxious for you to have the best position in the military which can be given you, consistently with justice and proper courtesy towards the older officers of the Army. I can not incur the risk of doing them injustice, or a discourtesy; but I do say they would personally oblige me, if they could, and would place you in some position, or in some service, satisfactory to yourself." Thus the friendship of the elderly President for the Zouave youth proceeded. Ellsworth knew it was all that could be done.

John Hay was appointed a clerk of the Pension Office at $1,600 a year, Nicolay writing of the situation, "As the existing laws do not provide an assistant for me, I have had John Hay appointed to a clerkship in the Department of the Interior and detailed to special service here at the White House, so that he gives me the benefit of his whole time." Leaning at a cigar stand in Willard's one evening, Hay was congratulated on his distinguished position and mocked, "Yes, I'm the keeper of the President's conscience."

One day in mid-March Senator John Sherman of Ohio came to the White House with his brother William Tecumseh Sherman, who had resigned as head of the Louisiana Military Academy, seeing war ahead. The Sherman brothers found Lincoln's room full of people and Lincoln at the end of a table talking with several, who soon left. John Sherman walked up, shook hands with Lincoln, took a chair near by, and handled papers referring to Ohio appointments. Lincoln took the papers, said he would be glad to refer them to the proper heads of departments and would be glad to make the appointments asked for, if not already promised. The Senator turned to his brother, saying, "Mr. President, this is my brother, Colonel Sherman, who is just up from Louisiana; he may give you some information you want."

LINCOLN. Ah! how are they getting along down there?

COLONEL SHERMAN. They think they are getting along swimmingly— they are preparing for war.

LINCOLN. Oh, well! I guess we'll manage to keep house.

And Colonel Tecumseh Sherman was silenced, said no more to Lincoln, went away sadly disappointed, breaking out on his brother with damning the politicians, saying the country was sleeping on a volcano that would burst forth any minute. He had met the President in a mood when the President chose to show no anxiety, and this worried Sherman. He left Washington to take a job as street-railway superintendent in St. Louis at $40 a week, telling his brother what he had to tell politicians in general, Lincoln included: "You have got things in a hell of a fix, and you may get them out as best you can."

He was a swift, elusive man, this Tecumseh Sherman, burning with complex motives, his thoughts outrunning his tongue. Lincoln's offhand way with him he took as a snub and he shut up like a clam. Had Lincoln known of the steeled loyalty of this Ohio man, pressed by old army comrades to stay South, held in trust and affection by men of rising power in the Confederacy such as Braxton Bragg, giving his Louisiana neighbors almost the identical opinions he was writing to his wife and his brother in the North, having no difficulty at all in his decision that he must go North, Lincoln would have met Tecumseh Sherman with a different greeting. In this month, however, Lincoln was daily hearing of army and navy officers suddenly resigning and transferring themselves South. Tecumseh Sherman's sincere admiration of the fighting fiber of the South, and his keen awareness that they were making furious preparations for war while the North was quiescent, coupled with his impulsive and almost angry way of telling Lincoln about it, threw a sort of challenge at the cornered and harassed President, whose easiest play for the moment was to drawl coolly, "Oh, well! I guess we'll manage to keep house."

Undoubtedly Sherman offered his services to the President in no ordinary office-seeker's manner; he was asking no fat job, nor an easy life. He abruptly thrust his services at Lincoln, who failed to solve the mercurial temperament he was meeting for the first time, a sorrel genius seething with the crazy contradictions of the American scene. In St. Louis while managing horsecar transit for the public, Sherman was offered high command in the Confederate Army then recruiting in Louisiana, S. A. Smith of that State being empowered to say that Louisiana would be delighted to "boast of the possession of your fine talents and high military qualities." Sherman made no reply, it seemed. However, it did appear that his brother John tried to land for him, through Chase, the St. Louis Treasury post, but failed because of Frank P. Blair, Jr., who named another man and earned Sherman's detestation of Blair, whom he called Lincoln's viceroy in Missouri.

Still later, on April 6, came a telegram to Sherman from Montgomery Blair at Washington offering the chief clerkship of the War Department and adding, "We will make you assistant Secretary of War when Congress meets." Tecumseh Sherman replied that he had a large family, had incurred obligations in St. Louis, and was not at liberty to change places. "I thank you for the compliment contained in your offer and assure you that I wish the Administration all success in its almost impossible task of governing this distracted and anarchical people." Blair read this telegram to other Cabinet members, who wagged their heads as though Sherman might not be a thoroughly safe Union man.

"When I was a member of Congress, a dozen years ago, I boarded with the lady who writes the within letter," wrote Lincoln in behalf of Mrs. Spriggs, seeking a position in the Department of the Interior. "She is a most worthy and deserving lady and, if what she desires can be consistently done, I shall be much obliged. I say this sincerely and earnestly."

Charles Francis Adams, Jr., wrote in his diary of how he called one Sunday afternoon on the old family friend, Senator Charles Sumner, of how Sumner as usual did most of the talking, and said suddenly: "By the way, I have drawn an elephant and don't know what to do with it. Yesterday I was at the Post-Office Department, and Mr. Blair informed me that the Boston Post-Office belonged to me, as a Senator living in that city; and I'm sure I don't know what to do with it." However, after thinking it over Sumner had chosen John G. Palfrey, former Whig Congressman, historian, Unitarian clergyman, professor of sacred literature at Harvard, for Boston's postmaster. And that Sunday in the evening at the Adams home for dinner, Sumner talked about what he had been hearing in his new position as chairman of the Senate Committee on Foreign Affairs: "He talked of Seward and the diplomatic corps; and told us all the secrets of the Cabinet, so far as he knew them; how Mrs. Lincoln wanted to make a Collector of the Port of Boston, on account of her son 'Bobby,' and *had* made a naval officer; how disgusted the diplomatic corps was at the possible nomination of Schurz to Turin; how Lincoln and Seward had a conversation about Schurz, in which Seward convinced Lincoln that Schurz ought not to be sent, and Lincoln sent him [Schurz] to Seward, for them to fight the matter out together; how the Western barbarians had invaded the White House, and Mrs. Lincoln was meddling with every office in the gift of the executive."

"Everything in the way of office goes west," Senator Fessenden wrote to his Maine family. "We shall hardly get the parings of a toenail in New England, and many people feel hardly about it." Leaders in other regions wrote similar complaints.

"In the White House are many mansions, and innumerable offices are in the gift of the President," chirruped *Vanity Fair*. "Lincoln is a brick, but 'no man can be happy till he is dead.'" It pictured a little fat man who routed Lincoln out at midnight, embraced his knees, and said: "Old Hoss, how are you anyhow? I voted for you, I worked for you, and now I'm here; and by the living jingo, stir I'll not, until you've promised me the Podunk Post Office."

Old Whig friends pressed for the appointment of an incompetent man to a responsible position, and according to Congressman George W. Julian, when evidence was laid before Lincoln, with a protest against the appointment, he replied, "There is much force in what you say, but, in the balancing of matters, I guess I shall have to appoint him."

Having appointed a Massachusetts Adams to London, Lincoln appointed another Bay State man, John Lothrop Motley, to Vienna, and said with what Senator Sumner regarded as a slightly annoyed air, "Now, Mr. Sumner, I hope you will give me a little time before I hear from Massachusetts again."

The appointment of John Locke Scripps to be Chicago postmaster came easy, for Scripps's campaign biography of Lincoln, though brief, was the most notable in the field, with one abrupt characterization: "He has an exquisite sense of justice."

Lincoln's own past as an office-seeker came before him when he signed a commission in the army for a young man who was the son of Justin Butterfield, victor in 1849 over Lincoln, then pulling all possible wires to become Commissioner of the General Land Office. He reminisced about it to the young man.

Among crumbs of patronage was the Springfield post office. One candidate was Dr. William Wallace, physician, brother-in-law of Lincoln, who had named one of his boys William Wallace. The other candidate was Elizabeth Todd Grimsley, cousin of Mary Todd Lincoln. Lincoln wrote to his former law partner, whose father had also married a Todd:

Washington, March 30, 1861

Dear Stuart:

Cousin Lizzie shows me your letter of the 27th. The question of giving her the Springfield post-office troubles me. You see I have already appointed William Jayne a Territorial governor and Judge Trumbull's brother to a land-office. Will it do for me to go on and justify the declaration that Trumbull and I have divided out all the offices among our relatives? Dr. Wallace, you know, is needy, and looks to me; and I personally owe him much.

I see by the papers, a vote is to be taken as to the post-office. Could you not set up Lizzie and beat them all? She, being here, need know nothing of it, so therefore there would be no indelicacy on her part.

Yours as ever,

A. Lincoln

The Public Man, with a companion, calling at the White House one day, found Lincoln's face "gloomy, care-worn." They ended an interview about Fort Sumter and were leaving when Lincoln brightened for a moment and in an abrupt kind of way laid a hand on the shoulder of the Public Man's companion, and asked, "You haven't such a thing as a postmaster in your pocket, have you?" The man thus spoken to stared at the President and for a moment seemed to be asking himself, "Has our President gone crazy?" Lincoln went on: "You see it seems to me kind of unnatural that you shouldn't have at least a postmaster in your pocket. Everybody I've seen for days past has had foreign ministers, and collectors, and all kinds, and I thought you couldn't have got in here without having at least a postmaster get into your pocket!" A minor incident was the White House call of Congressman William Kellogg of Canton, Illinois, who went away from an interview with Lincoln and in an outer room penned this paper:

Mansion of
Prest. Lincoln
Wdnsdy April 3/61

His Excellency
The Prest of the U.S.—

Sir

I desire to withdraw, the pamphlet and papers I left with you this morning relating to the appointment of Major Hinshaw. I do this that his application may not be prejudiced by the fact of its being presented by myself—and I regret to again trouble you and hope never again to feel the humiliation I did in our interview of this mrn'g— or again to solicit patronage, that I may not demand as the right—of a representative of the people and a citizen of the Republic.

Very respectfully yrs W. Kellogg

On the reverse side of this paper Lincoln wrote: "Mr. Kellogg does me great injustice to write in this strain—He has had more favors than any other Illinois member, not excepting, I think, Judge Trumbull. Is it really in his heart to add to my perplexities now?"

Above Congressman William Kellogg addresses a folded paper to the President, who wrote the sweet memorandum below. Original in Barrett collection.

More than one queer kettle of fish turned up. To please newspapers who favored James E. Harvey, Seward named him for Minister to Portugal and Lincoln made the appointment. Then suddenly it developed that Harvey had sent to a secession leader at Charleston a telegram signed "A Friend" with the information that the Government at Washington was "positively determined not to withdraw" from Fort Sumter. When the evidence of this was made clear, Senators got into action, demanding the recall of "this secessionist spy." Seward explained that Harvey's appointment was made as a recognition to "Old Whig" newspapers who favored him, that Harvey was no personal friend of his and had opposed his nomination at Chicago. Seward had given him confidential information, as he sometimes did to newspapermen. But though Harvey had come North and become a successful journalist and politician, he was born in South Carolina, favored "compromise and conciliation," and had sent his anonymous telegram to an old classmate and intimate friend, the telegram correcting previous and erroneous hearsay information. Harvey argued that his personal honor was involved.

Seward learned of Harvey's fool telegram the afternoon it was sent and wrathily advised the President to revoke Harvey's appointment. "But thinking it over coolly," said Seward, "I thought it wrong to punish a man for his stupid folly, when really he had committed no crime."

The executive problem was to fill important offices with men of ability, and at the same time to satisfy party organization leaders, who always had more applicants than there were offices. As Seward said when the President and Senate confirmed the appointment of his son Frederick for Assistant Secretary of State, "I have placed him where he must meet the whole array of friends seeking offices—a hundred taking tickets where only one can draw a prize."

Those other past masters of politics in the Cabinet, Chase, Cameron, and Blair, had their friends and allies to take care of in about the same proportion as Seward, a hundred asking an office that could only go to one. "Blair is nearly run to death with office seekers," wrote G. V. Fox to his wife. "They left him at 2 this morning and commenced at 8 this morning. The President is equally beset. I have seen Abe often."

Leslie's Weekly, under the caption "Nepotism," carried an item reading: "The son of Mr. Secretary of State Seward is Assistant Secretary of State, the son of Mr. Secretary of the Interior Smith is Assistant Secretary of the Interior, and the son of Mr. Attorney-General Bates is Assistant Attorney-General! It is wonderful that the eminent qualifications for Cabinet positions of Messrs. Seward, Smith and Bates, should be also possessed, in the second degree, by their sons!"

The most aggressive of the Cabinet members in taking care of his friends was Chase. When some of his friends wished to prod him in his efforts for them they told him that only by narrow margins had he missed being in the White House. When charged with placing friends and relatives, his own favorites, whatever their ability, Chase would explain stiffly, as in his letter to John Roberts, "In making appointments my rule always has been to give the preference to political friends, except in cases where peculiar fitness and talents made the preference of a political opponent a public duty." Chase brought arithmetic into play, computed that Ohio had one-eighth of the total population of the nation and was therefore entitled to one-eighth of the Federal offices. He notified Seward that of the 269 vacancies in the State Department, Ohio's share would be 33.

On March 20, 1861, Chase had placed only thirteen of these, and when the appointment of one of his men to the London consulate went on the rocks, he cautioned Seward, "I have not thought it respectful to go to the President about appointments in your department, except through you; others do and it seems not unsuccessfully." From the Attorney General, Chase got a place for a blood brother of his, only to have Senator Preston King of New York, a Seward ally, protest so strongly as to compel Bates to change his mind. This renewed the Chase efforts, and he hung on till his brother was placed as he wished.

Chase named a second-rate man for a responsible place in the Treasury Department at New York, which sent the New York Senators to Lincoln, who in twenty-four hours wrote Chase "to oblige" him by sending a nomination not objectionable to the New York Senators. Chase sent a note to Lincoln asking an interview. Lincoln replied that the difference between them did not lie within the range of conversation.

The New York complications got worse as Greeley and other anti-Seward Republicans worried in fear that Seward and Weed were getting control of Lincoln and would dictate all appointments. They called at the White House with a delegation including Charles A. Dana, managing editor of the *New York Tribune;* James S. Wadsworth, manager of his family estate of 15,000 acres, an early Free-Soiler, a Republican-party founder; George Opdyke, banker and millionaire mentioned as the next Mayor of New York, a Republican-party founder. These were men who, as Lincoln well knew, had for years wrestled with Seward and Weed for Republican-party control in New York. They had gone to the Chicago convention hoping to stop the nomination of Seward.

Wadsworth spoke urging that one faction should not have control of the New York offices. Opdyke followed with telling Lincoln their desires. Lincoln had been annoyed during the interview by a messenger interrupting to say he was wanted in another part of the White House. He kept his seat without answering the messenger, and said to the New Yorkers: "One side shall not gobble up everything. Make out a list of the places and men you want, and I will endeavor to apply the rule of give and take." Wadsworth said they were returning to New York, but would leave one of their men with a list of the offices desired and the names of those to fill them. Lincoln said he would meet this man the next day and "We will see what can be done."

Seward and Chase came near an open break in these factional disputes, and Lincoln one day wrote to Hiram Barney, an original Chase man whom

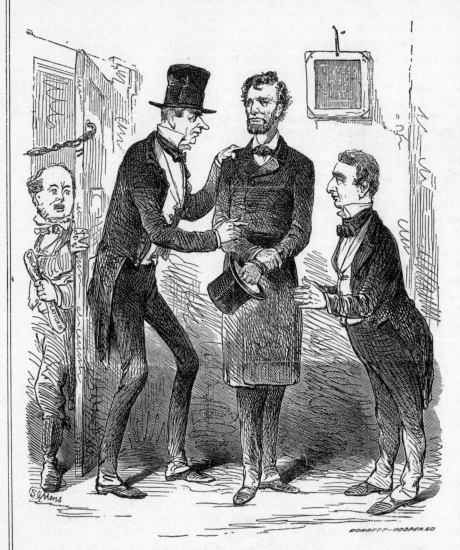

THE INSIDE TRACK.

THURLOW WEED TO PRESIDENT ELECT.—"TRUST TO MY FRIEND SEWARD—TRUST TO US. WE'LL COM-
PROMISE THIS LITTLE DIFFICULTY FOR YOU. BUT TRUST TO US. GENTLEMEN FROM THE COUNTRY ARE OFTEN EGREGIOUSLY SWIN-
DLED BY UNPRINCIPLED SHARPERS. (IMPRESSIVELY) TRUST TO US!"

Lincoln had appointed Collector of the Port of New York, to please come to Washington: "I think I can make up the New York card better after having a talk with you." Barney came, and it seemed that after his interview with Lincoln it developed that Barney and Thurlow Weed, like seconds in a duel, met and framed a code for the Chase and Weed factions. They agreed to leave Treasury appointments entirely in Chase's hands, suggesting that he confer with Seward, and that Seward on his part make an effort to be more agreeable to Chase. Weed, it was understood, would never assume to act for Seward nor attempt in any way to dictate Treasury patronage. To the President this was a welcome arrangement, as would be anything at all, he said, that would induce Secretaries Chase and Seward to work in harmony.

Seward was at this time a psychic maze. His young and affectionate friend Henry Adams could not tell when Seward wore face or mask. And Henry's brother saw Seward grow ten years older that winter. Night and day he had conferred and negotiated, become weary and rusty, vulgar and profane beyond his old habits, worn and frazzled as a castoff garment. Until Lincoln was nominated for the Presidency, Seward had been the conceded Republican-party leader, its pre-eminent mind, and he was now credited in many circles with having a disproportionate influence over the President, which Welles and Chase believed or suspected at all hours. Seward to these critics was a personal schemer, no patriot at all, and his toils and sleepless hours that winter trying to stave off war, his broken physical and mental health, were little known and seemed to have been understood only by the Adamses.

"Last night I broke down, and sent for Dr. Miller," Seward wrote his wife at Auburn, New York, on March 8. "I have kept my chamber today, except an hour, when I went on a necessary errand to the White House. . . . The Commissioners from the Southern Confederacy are here. These cares fall chiefly on me."

What to say to those Commissioners, and how to say it without recognizing their Government, he took as his own problem, and he carried on negotiations with them without consulting President Lincoln. The President he saw as lacking plan and decision, which was the view of Greeley of the *New York Tribune*, Raymond of the *New York Times*, not to mention Bennett of the *New York Herald*, or Lincoln's old Springfield crony William Butler, who in mid-March wrote to Senator Trumbull, "Is it possible Lincoln is getting scared?" Seward's incessant efforts to step in and get policies announced with a tone of decision was taken by his critics as an attempt to pull down the President and set up his own power.

His enemies brought their accusations of him as a selfish plotter directly to the President, with Seward present. In a letter to Welles, David Dudley Field, lawyer and New York Republican, noted of an interview with Lincoln: "In the presence of yourself, Mr. Chase, Mr. Seward, and Preston King, I denounced Mr. Seward's political theories, and reminded the President that Mr. Seward's friends were not only against his nomination but against his election, until they found that he would be elected without them."

Meanwhile Lincoln and Seward transacted a little affair the country heard nothing of at the time. Had the news of it leaked, the world would have jeered. The toils, ambitions, and mental turmoil of William H. Seward as Secretary of State came to a climax on April 1 in his laying before Lincoln as odd a document as ever came from a department Secretary to a Chief Magistrate. It read:

Some Thoughts for the President's
Consideration, April 1, 1861

First. We are at the end of a month's administration, and yet without a policy, either domestic or foreign.

Second. This, however, is not culpable, and it has even been unavoidable. The presence of the Senate, with the need to meet applications for patronage, have prevented attention to other and more grave matters.

Third. But further delay to adopt and prosecute our policies for both domestic and foreign affairs would not only bring scandal on the administration, but danger upon the country.

Fourth. To do this we must dismiss the applicants for office. But how? I suggest that we make the local appointments forthwith, leaving foreign or general ones for ulterior and occasional action.

Fifth. The policy at home. I am aware that my views are singular, and perhaps not sufficiently explained. My system is built upon this *idea* as a ruling one, namely, that we must

CHANGE THE QUESTION BEFORE THE PUBLIC FROM ONE UPON SLAVERY, OR ABOUT SLAVERY, for a question upon UNION OR DISUNION.

In other words, from what would be regarded as a party question, to one of patriotism or union.

The occupation or evacuation of Fort Sumter, although not in fact a slavery or a party question, is so regarded. Witness the temper manifested by the Republicans in the free States, and even by the Union men in the South.

I would therefore terminate it as a safe means for changing the issue. I deem it fortunate that the last administration created the necessity.

For the rest I would simultaneously defend and reinforce all the forts in the Gulf, and have the navy recalled from foreign stations to be prepared for a blockade. Put the island of Key West under martial law.

This will raise distinctly the question of union or disunion. I would maintain every fort and possession in the South.

For Foreign Nations

I would demand explanations from Spain and France, categorically, at once.

I would seek explanations from Great Britain and Russia, and send agents into Canada, Mexico, and Central America, to rouse a vigorous continental spirit of independence on this continent against European intervention.

And, if satisfactory explanations are not received from Spain and France,

Would convene Congress and declare war against them.

But whatever policy we adopt, there must be an energetic prosecution of it.

For this purpose it must be somebody's business to pursue and direct it incessantly.

Either the President must do it himself, and be all the while active in it, or

Devolve it on some member of his Cabinet. Once adopted, debates on it must end, and all agree and abide.

It is not in my especial province.

But I neither seek to evade nor assume responsibility.

This was saying in effect that Lincoln was a failure as a President but he, Seward, knew how to be one. It also set forth Seward's theory that by starting a war with foreign nations, the seceded Southern States would come back into the Union and fight again under the Old Flag. Lincoln, of course, knew the strain Seward had been under ever since midwinter, when many people regarded Seward as "the Administration spokesman." Also Lincoln understood what Adams and others noted of the normal minds of many men taking on "a morbid tone." Lincoln wrote this answer and Seward accepted it in the spirit in which it was written:

Executive Mansion, April 1, 1861

Hon. W. H. Seward,

My dear Sir:

Since parting with you I have been considering your paper dated this day, and entitled "Some thoughts for the President's consideration." The first proposition in it is, "*First,* We are at the end of a month's administration, and yet without a policy either domestic or foreign."

At the beginning of that month, in the inaugural, I said, "The power confided to me will be used to hold, occupy, and possess the property and places belonging to the government, and to collect the duties and imposts." This had your distinct approval at the time; and, taken in connection with the order I immediately gave General Scott, directing him to employ every means in his power to strengthen and hold the forts, comprises the exact domestic policy you now urge, with the single exception that it does not propose to abandon Fort Sumter.

Again, I do not perceive how the reinforcement of Fort Sumter would be done on a slavery or party issue, while that of Fort Pickens would be on a more national and patriotic one.

The news received yesterday in regard to St. Domingo certainly brings a new item within the range of our foreign policy; but up to that time we have been preparing circulars and instructions to ministers and the like, all in perfect harmony, without even a suggestion that we had no foreign policy.

Upon your closing proposition—that "whatever policy we adopt, there must be an energetic prosecution of it.

"For this purpose it must be somebody's business to pursue and direct it incessantly,

"Either the President must do it himself, and be all the while active in it, or

"Devolve it on some member of his cabinet. Once adopted, debates on it must end, and all agree and abide"—I remark that if this must be done, I must do it. When a general line of policy is adopted, I apprehend there is no danger of its being changed without good reason, or continuing to be a subject of unnecessary debate; still, upon points arising in its progress I wish, and suppose I am entitled to have, the advice of all the cabinet.

Your Obedient Servant,

A. Lincoln

Long editorials criticizing Lincoln for indecision and inactivity ran in the *New York Tribune* and the *New York Times* on April 3. "Come to the

Point!" demanded the *Tribune,* while the *Times* headed a two-column leader "Wanted—a Policy." The Union was weaker than a month before because the Administration had exhibited "a blindness and a stolidity without a parallel in the history of intelligent statesmanship," said the *Times.* Lincoln had "spent time and strength in feeding rapacious and selfish politicians, which should have been bestowed upon saving the Union," and "we tell him . . . that he must go up to a higher level than he has yet reached." This lent support to the *Herald's* repeated jabs: "the Lincoln Administration is cowardly, mean, and vicious," the blame resting on "the incompetent, ignorant, and desperate 'Honest Abe.' "

William Cullen Bryant in a *New York Evening Post* editorial took the *Tribune* and *Times* outbursts as nervous and peevish. To frame in thirty days a clear policy for so complex a national situation was a hard matter, as Bryant saw it, and furthermore, how could the facile critics know that Lincoln had not fixed upon his policy, with a decision to make it known to the world by action instead of a windy proclamation?

When Henry J. Raymond of the *New York Times* later went down to Washington and talked with Lincoln, he got the President's viewpoint in a brief sentence: "I am like a man so busy in letting rooms in one end of his house, that he can't stop to put out the fire that is burning in the other."

"Abraham Lincoln has no right to a soldier in Fort Sumter," said the incorruptible and spotless abolitionist Wendell Phillips at New Bedford, Massachusetts, on April 9, 1861. "A series of States, girdling the Gulf, think their peculiar institutions require that they should have separate government. They have a right to decide that question without appealing to you or me. . . . Standing with the principles of '76 behind us who can deny that right?"

The London *Times* correspondent, William Howard Russell, had made his entry and received attentions in Washington as if he were an envoy of power. "I was honoured today by visits from a great number of Members of Congress, journalists, and others," he wrote on March 28. "Judging from the expressions of most of the Washington people, they would gladly see a Southern Cabinet installed in their city. The cold shoulder is given to Mr. Lincoln, and all kinds of stories and jokes are circulated at his expense. People take particular pleasure in telling how he came towards the seat of his Government disguised in a Scotch cap and cloak, whatever that may mean."

In New York Russell had been dined and wined by the eminent in all walks, and noted: "The upper world of millionaire merchants, bankers, contractors, and great traders are glad that the vulgar republicans are suffering for their success. Not a man there but resented the influence given by universal suffrage to the mob of the city, and complained of the intolerable effects of their ascendancy—of the corruption of the municipal bodies, the venality of the electors, and the abuse, waste, and profligate outlay of the public funds."

Russell wrote as though the men with whom he dined had nothing to do with the corruption, and bribe moneys and the fortunes of New York politicians came from elsewhere than "the upper world" who gave him welcome. He heard their fears that universal suffrage must work injury on property and capital "in a city of which perhaps three-fourths of the voters were born abroad or of foreign parents, and of whom many were the scum swept off the seethings of European populations." A few hundred yards from the house and picture gallery of August Belmont, "representative of European millions," Russell saw "the hovels and lodgings of his equals in political power." The contrast made him feel that "the time is coming when the mischief can no longer be borne, and a social reform and revolution must be inevitable."

At Mrs. Belmont's reception, his eyes took in pretty statues, rich carpets, handsome furniture, "a gallery of charming Meissoniers and genre pieces, the saloons admirably lighted, a fair fine large suite filled with the prettiest women in the most delightful toilettes," a proper fringe of young men fretting against turbaned and jeweled dowagers, every accessory of wit, sense, intelligence, vivacity, to make good society. "Yet there was something wanting, conspicuous by its absence—where was it?"

Scrutinizing the faces and figures of Mrs. Belmont's party, he would judge, "Nothing could be more beautiful, easy, or natural than the womanhood or girlhood of New York." Then he would modify the compliment: "It is prettiness rather than fineness; regular, intelligent, wax-like faces, graceful little figures." As for American women in general, he was puzzled at first about something lacking and eventually concluded that they were too short—"deficient in stature," that was it. Should he find taller women, he would apprise his public.

At dinner with Seward on his first day in Washington, Russell had heard "stories of the pressure on the President for place, which very much amused the guests who knew the men," and learned that Seward wanted no extra session of Congress, had impressed the point on the President, had advised the President, "History tells us that kings who call extra parliaments lose their heads."

Russell walked with Frederick Seward next day to the White House for the President's audience to Chevalier Bertinatti, Minister of the new kingdom of Italy, who had thitherto represented only the kingdom of Sardinia. "Where is the President?" Russell heard the Secretary of State ask a servant "in attendance dressed like any ordinary citizen." Later in the spacious reception room Seward had Russell stand one side, "for you are not supposed to be here." As the President advanced through the room, amid ranks of the diplomatic corps, Russell noted that "he evidently controlled a desire to shake hands all round with everybody, and [was] smiling good-humoredly till he was suddenly brought up by the staid deportment of Mr. Seward and by the profound diplomatic bows of Chevalier Bertinatti. Then, indeed, he suddenly jerked himself back, and stood in front of the two ministers, with his body slightly drooped forward, and his hands behind his back, his knees touching, and his feet apart."

In a wrinkled suit of black clothes, the President faced the Chevalier who wore cocked hat, white gloves, diplomatic suit of blue and silver lace, sword, sash, and riband of the Cross of Savoy. After Seward had presented the new Minister, as Russell saw it, "the President made a prodigiously violent demonstration of his body in a bow which had almost the effect of a smack in its rapidity and abruptness, and, recovering himself, proceeded to give his utmost attention, whilst the Chevalier, with another bow, read from a paper a long address in presenting the royal letter accrediting him as 'minister resident.' " The King of Italy, read the Chevalier, desired frank sympathy between the two peoples who had a "common destiny as self-governing and free nations," at which phrase Russell noted that "the President gave another bow still more violent, as much as to accept the allusion." The Chevalier handed the letter to the President, who handed it to Seward for the archives. Dipping his hand in his coat pocket, the President drew out a sheet of paper from which he read a reply, Russell considering it remarkable doctrine that he should say that the United States was "bound by duty not to interfere with the differences of foreign governments and countries." After more compliments, the President shook hands with the Chevalier, who soon retired.

Seward then took Russell by the hand and said, "Mr. President, allow me to present to you Mr. Russell of the London *Times*." On which Mr. Lincoln put out his hand in a very friendly manner, and said: "Mr. Russell, I am very glad to make your acquaintance, and to see you in this country. The London *Times* is one of the greatest powers in the world—in fact, I don't know anything which has much more power—except perhaps the Mississippi. I am glad to know you as its minister."

For some minutes conversation ensued which, as Russell put it, "the President enlivened by two or three peculiar little sallies, and I left agreeably impressed with his shrewdness, humour, and natural sagacity."

It became a habit of Lincoln's to joke the State Department about the speeches they wrote for him to read off when receiving new foreign Ministers. Pompous, mellifluous, and mouth-filling statements glided forth from sections of these speeches. Secretary Seward one day presented Count Piper, duly credentialed as Envoy Extraordinary and Minister Plenipotentiary for his Majesty the King of Sweden and Norway. Then from the speech that had been handed to him, Lincoln read: "Sir, I receive with great pleasure a Minister from Sweden. That pleasure is enhanced by the information which preceded your arrival here, that his Majesty, your Sovereign, had selected you to fill the mission upon the grounds of your derivation from an ancestral stock identified with the most glorious era of your country's noble history, and your own eminent social and political standing in Sweden."

These speeches, it seemed, Lincoln would not retouch. Once however, so a story ran, Seward wanted to change a few direct and simply stated points which Lincoln had written in a note to be publicly addressed to the

British Prime Minister, Lord Palmerston. Seward urged the use of diplomatic phraseology. The Cabinet heard a dialogue:

"Mr. Secretary, do you suppose Palmerston will understand our position from my letter, just as it is?"

"Certainly, Mr. President."

"Do you suppose the London *Times* will?"

"Certainly."

"Do you suppose the average Englishman of affairs will?"

"Certainly. It cannot be mistaken in England."

"Do you suppose that a hackman on his box will understand it?"

"Very readily, Mr. President."

"Very well, Mr. Secretary, I guess we'll let her slide just as she is."

CHAPTER 7

WAR CHALLENGE AT SUMTER

ON the second day he was President, Lincoln made a cool, dry little speech to a visiting Pennsylvania delegation, saying he would like to spread the idea "that we may not, like Pharisees, set ourselves up to be better than other people." The delegation chairman had faintly implied that with a President and a Government at Washington there would be action. Lincoln replied, "I hope we have a government and a President," yet he also hoped, and wished it understood, that there would be "no allusion to unpleasant differences," and that citizens would "act in such a way as to say nothing insulting or irritating."

As a President he would prefer them to feel "while we exercise our opinion, that others have also rights to their exercises of opinions, and that we should endeavor to allow these rights, and act in such a manner as to create no bad feeling." He alluded to "the hope you entertain that you have a President and a government" and in respect to that "I wish to say to you that in the position I have assumed I wish to do more than I have ever given reason to believe I would do." Nevertheless "I do not wish you to believe that I assume to be any better than others who have gone before me."

His second speech that day included thanks to a Massachusetts delegation for its sanctioning his inaugural address and assuring him of support. He would hold *national views* as President: "I hope to be man enough not to know one citizen of the United States from another, nor one section from another."

Both of these speeches had the equilibrist air of a man refusing to lose self-possession—refusing to be swept off his feet by hotheads—refusing to be

WINDING OFF THE TANGLED SKEIN.

Harper's Weekly tries to depict the tangle passed from President Buchanan to President
Lincoln

PROF. LINCOLN IN HIS GREAT FEAT OF BALANCING.

Vanity Fair sees a national circus centered in Lincoln balancing "Peace" and "Sumpter,"
with Seward as master of ceremonies

put in a hole by shrewd schemers trying to outguess him. In his place at this hour he had to be, as young Adams had written, "cool as death."

Except for a few remarks at a flag-raising, he would for the next five weeks deliver no more speeches, short or long.

The morning after inauguration Lincoln studied dispatches from Major Robert Anderson, commanding the Fort Sumter garrison in Charleston Harbor, reporting that his food supplies would last four weeks or by careful saving perhaps forty days. The armed forces of South Carolina had him penned in and would no longer let him receive anything to eat. The Confederates, whose now encircling fortifications and batteries held the United States garrison at their mercy, stood ready to batter Fort Sumter to pieces and run down its flag whenever the word came from their Government at Montgomery. In the Senate at Washington, Douglas was saying that a few weeks ago Sumter could have been relieved and reinforced by a single sloop of war, but "now it could not be done by your Navy, unless you had ten thousand land troops." To this Douglas added that General Scott estimated 20,000 co-operating land troops necessary to hold Sumter.

To Douglas, Lincoln said that week he meant the fort should be evacuated "as soon as possible," according to what Douglas told the Public Man, whose diary read: "Mr. Douglas says that the President sent for him after his speech of Wednesday [March 6] to assure him that he entirely agreed with all its views, and sympathized with its spirit. All the President desired was to get the points of present irritation removed, so that the people might grow cool, and reflect on the general position all over the country, when he felt confident there would be a general demand for a National Convention at which all the existing differences could be radically treated. . . . He said to Mr. Douglas, 'What I want is to get done what the people desire to have done, and the question for me is how to find that out exactly.'"

The Senate on March 25 requested from the President the dispatches of Major Anderson to the War Department. The President replied that he had examined this correspondence, and "I have, with the highest respect for the Senate, come to the conclusion that at the present moment the publication of it would be inexpedient."

The Senators from Virginia, North Carolina, Tennessee, Arkansas, Texas, were in their seats answering roll call from day to day, their States not having officially and formally seceded. Wigfall of Texas told the Senate it was no longer an important deliberative body but "merely a respectable public meeting." When he roused a gallery of secessionists to laughter and cheers and Vice-President Hamlin threatened to clear the galleries, Wigfall retorted that the galleries might yet come down and clear out the Senate. Senator Breckinridge predicted that if war came Kentucky would not "lay her bright and beaming forehead in the dust" but would rally to "the noble Republic of the Confederacy" with a ringing cry "from peak to peak of her mountain tops, and along all her smiling plains."

Senator Thomas L. Clingman of North Carolina would vote for the printing of the President's inaugural, though he could not endorse its war-like tone. Senator Nesmith of Oregon said a third of his constituents were from the slaveholding States, that he was starting home soon and would like to tell his folks whether peace or war was ahead. "If I tell them I do not know, they will at once institute an inquiry as to what they sent me here for." They would want explanations of how a Union of States bound in fraternal friendship and brotherly love could be held together by bayonets. "I do not believe I can make a man love me any better by thrusting a bayonet into his stomach." Some of the warmakers, he hoped to say, were "people who are invincible in peace and invisible in war."

Lincoln called his Cabinet for its first meeting on March 9 and put a written question, "Assuming it to be possible to now provision Fort Sumter, under all the circumstances, is it wise to attempt it?" The new Cabinet Ministers went away, considered this written question, returned March 16 on Lincoln's request with lengthy written answers. Seward advised No: it was not a time for the use of force. Chase advised Yes and No; Yes if it meant peace, No if the attempt was to bring on civil war, armies, million-dollar budgets, "I cannot advise it." Cameron advised No, seeing that "No practical benefit will result to the country." Welles advised No: "I entertain doubts." Smith advised No: giving up Fort Sumter would cause "surprise and complaint" but it could be "explained and understood." Bates advised No: "I am willing to evacuate Fort Sumter." Blair was the only one with a straight, unmodified Yes: Buchanan had hesitated and failed; Jackson had acted and won; provisioning the fort would "vindicate the hardy courage of the North, and the determination of the people and their President to maintain the authority of the Government."

Thus the seven new counselors stood five against sending food to Anderson, one for it, and one neither for nor against it.

On the same day Confederate Commissioners in Washington sent messages to their Government at Montgomery, Alabama: "Things look better here than was believed" and "The impression prevails in Administration circles that Fort Sumter will be evacuated in ten days."

On March 10 it was widely published that the Administration intended to withdraw the garrison from Fort Sumter. "About this time," wrote Major Abner Doubleday of the Fort Sumter garrison, "my wife, who was in Washington, was very much surprised at receiving a call from the President. He came quietly to request her to show him my letters from Fort Sumter, so that he might form a better opinion as to the condition of affairs there, more particularly in regard to our resources."

The President was about ready to say the word and give up Sumter, according to Welles, when Montgomery Blair in disgust wrote his resignation, but before handing it to the President let his father go to the White House, where, Welles believed, the elder Blair had "aroused and electrified the President" so that "the President decided from that moment that an attempt should be made to convey supplies to Major Anderson, and reinforce Sumter." From then on this determination of the President he "communicated to the Members of his Cabinet as he saw them, without a general announcement in Cabinet meeting."

The days had been hurrying along and in the heady crosscurrents of events Lincoln may have retreated from his first position that the forts must be held, and then returned to that position on being "electrified" by Old Man Blair. The two secretaries of the President, however, wrote their observation, "The idea of the evacuation and abandonment of the fort was so repugnant, that Mr. Lincoln could hardly bring himself to entertain it." Whether he did seriously entertain it for a time or not, the moment came when he gave his mind completely to somehow staging a combat in the Charleston Harbor in which his Government would be making the best fight possible for its authority. He later wrote that the Administration in that hour, from a purely military point of view, was reduced to the mere matter of getting the garrison safely out of the fort. He believed: "That to so abandon that position, under the circumstances, would be utterly ruinous; that the necessity under which it was to be done would not be fully understood; that by many it would be construed as a part of a voluntary policy; that at home it would discourage the friends of the Union, embolden its adversaries, and go far to insure the latter a recognition abroad; that in fact it would be our national destruction consummated. This could not be allowed."

This final decision that the North in the main would interpret a decent, necessary withdrawal from Sumter as a shameful slinking away from plain challenge meant immediate action, the end of deliberation over what to do, with every effort concentrated on how to do what was to be done. The President called in Gustavus Vasa Fox, a Swedish-blooded Yankee born in Saugus, Massachusetts, thirty-nine years of age, a Naval Academy graduate of eighteen years' service in coast survey, of Mexican War experience, commander of United States mail steamers, resigned in 1856 to become agent of woolen mills in Lawrence, Massachusetts. Sentimental about the Union, the navy, and possible war, backed by prominent New York merchants and shippers, Fox had on request of General Scott prepared plans for the holding of Sumter, which plans President Buchanan in February had refused to consider, but which now, further elaborated, were personally urged by Captain Fox before the President, the Cabinet, and military officers. Troops on steamers, tugboats from New York Harbor, naval convoys and armed vessels, would co-operate toward crossing sand bars at high water and moving reinforcements into Sumter.

Fox had calculated as to moving and stationary targets, the Confederate land batteries, and other factors, had convinced the President and a majority of the Cabinet, against General Scott and subordinate officers, that the plans were worth trying.

Then on March 21, acting as Lincoln's messenger and observer, Fox had arrived in Fort Sumter under escort of a Confederate captain formerly of the United States Navy and a former friend of Fox. This escort stood within earshot while Major Anderson and Fox held a conversation.

Fox journeyed back to Washington, reported to Lincoln that from what he had seen of Charleston Harbor he still considered his plans good, but no time was to be lost, for Anderson's final scraping of flour and last slab of bacon would be used up at noon of April 15.

On March 28 Lincoln instructed Fox to prepare a short order detailing the ships, men, supplies, required for his plans. Fox wrote five sentences: "Steamers *Pocahontas* at Norfolk, *Pawnee* at Washington, *Harriet Lane* at New York, to be under sailing orders for sea, with stores, etc., for one month. Three hundred men to be kept ready for departure from on board the receiving ships at New York. Two hundred men to be ready to leave Governor's Island in New York. Supplies for twelve months for one hundred men to be put in portable shape, ready for instant shipping. A large steamer and three tugs conditionally engaged."

Lincoln kept this memorandum for use in a day or two. Lamon had now arrived from his trip to Charleston, where in one day he had seen all he cared to see. His instructions from Lincoln required him to interview the postmaster of Charleston, from whom he learned in few words that the postmaster was no longer affiliated with the United States Government. A Confederate officer escorted Lamon to Major Anderson at Fort Sumter, where Lamon learned that the food supply would give out at noon of April 15, that Anderson was "deeply despondent" and the garrison "spoiling for a fight."

From the Governor of South Carolina Lamon brought the message to Lincoln: "Nothing can prevent war except the acquiescence of the President of the United States in secession. . . . Let your President attempt to reinforce Sumter, and the tocsin of war will be sounded from every hilltop and valley in the South."

At the Charleston hotel Lamon had found an excited crowd, and he was the man they were looking for. Their leader, as Lamon told it to Lincoln, wore a fork-tailed coat with brass buttons, a rusty bell-crowned hat, a red bandanna cravat under a wide-winged collar, and gave the impression he would as soon hang Lamon as look at him. Kicking a rope from a corner to the middle of the reading-room, the leader squared himself before Lamon, and nodding toward the rope: "Do you think *that* is strong enough to hang a damned Lincoln abolition hireling?"

Lamon replied: "Sir, I am a Virginian by birth, and a gentleman, I hope, by education and instinct. I was sent here by the President of the United States to see your Governor—" when the crowd spokesman interrupted, "Damn your President!"

Lamon was saying that such insults to an unoffending stranger in a city noted for its hospitality and chivalry were cowardly. Just then former Congressman Lawrence Keitt came along and said he was glad to see Lamon. The brass buttons cried, "Keitt, do you speak to that Lincoln hireling?"

"Stop," roared Keitt, "you insult Lamon, and you insult me! He is a gentleman and *my* friend. Come, Lamon, let us take a drink."

On the night train leaving Charleston Lamon met Stephen A. Hurlbut, born in Charleston, once an adjutant in a South Carolina regiment, who at thirty years of age had moved to Illinois and practiced law in Belvidere, where Lincoln had known him. Now Hurlbut reported to Lincoln that he had visited his sister in Charleston, and had a long talk with James L. Petigru, under whom he had once studied law four years. Petigru, seventy-one years old, "is now the only man in Charleston who avowedly adheres to the Union," Hurlbut wrote. The South would in the end be overwhelmed, Petigru had told his people; the resources of the North and the feeling for the Union would be too strong against them. And the people of South Carolina loved and trusted Petigru, out of his long peculiar record as an honest lawyer, a kindly neighbor, and a man of humor and philosophy; they respected his sincerity while they laughed at his judgment. He was pointed out in the streets as the only Union man left in the State.

Out of talk with Petigru and relatives, former neighbors, and friends, Hurlbut reported to Lincoln: "Unquestionably separate nationality is a fixed fact. . . . There is no attachment to the Union. . . . Political economy taught for years has now become an axiom, and merchants and business men believe, and act upon the belief, that great growth of trade and expansion of material prosperity will and must follow the establishment of a Southern republic. They expect a golden era, when Charleston shall be a great commercial emporium, control for the South as New York does for the North."

Lincoln told stories and seemed droll, almost gay, at a Cabinet state dinner the evening of March 28. The dinner was over and Russell of the London *Times* and all other guests had departed. The President then met his Cabinet in secret session. He read to them a memorandum from General Scott discouraging attempts to reinforce Sumter and advising, "The giving up of Forts Sumter and Pickens may be justified."

This amazed several members. Blair was first to find his tongue and blurted out that the head of the army was more than military, was "playing politician." Blair indicated that he blamed Seward's intrigue for this move.

All agreed, however, that the advice of the head of the army was not to be taken. The President asked the Cabinet to meet the next day.

And that night, said his secretaries, "Lincoln's eyes did not close in sleep." All night long his mind sought the realities behind multiple mirrors.

At noon next day the Cabinet met to discuss going to war. While the argument went on, Attorney General Bates wrote out his view. He would reinforce Fort Pickens, and "As to Fort Sumter, I think the time is come to either evacuate or relieve it." The President asked the others to write their views. The Secretary of State wrote: "I would at once, and at every cost, prepare for a war at Pensacola and Texas" and "I would instruct Major Anderson to retire from Fort Sumter forthwith." The Secretary of the Treasury would maintain Fort Pickens and provision Fort Sumter. The

Secretary of the Navy would make Fort Pickens impregnable, and as to Sumter, the Government was justified in "a peaceable attempt to send provisions to one of our own forts." The Secretary of the Interior seemed to believe that he would defend Fort Pickens and evacuate Fort Sumter, recognizing it as risky politically. The Postmaster General would hold Fort Pickens and fight "the head and front of this rebellion" at Fort Sumter. The Secretary of War was absent.

So the Cabinet stood three for and three against the evacuation of Sumter.

The Cabinet meeting over, the President brought out the memorandum written by Captain Fox and at the bottom wrote an order on the Secretary of War: "Sir: I desire that an expedition, to move by sea, be got ready to sail as early as the 6th of April next, the whole according to memorandum attached, and that you coöperate with the Secretary of the Navy for that object."

This with a signed duplicate to the Secretary of the Navy was delivered, and Captain Fox started for New York to get ready the expedition, which, Lincoln wrote later, "was intended to be ultimately used, or not, according to circumstances." Whether the ships would go to Pickens or Sumter, would land troops or merely food, would depend on "circumstances."

As the President was saying nothing publicly of some of the essential circumstances, he was numbered among those who could never know that a straight line is the shortest distance between two points. "The plans of President Lincoln in regard to the Southern imbroglio," said one newspaper, "are still wrapped in dense mist." Which was true. On land, at sea, there was mist.

"I feel like abandoning my country, moving off somewhere, I am sick down to my heel," wrote Captain Fox to Montgomery Blair on March 31 in a letter dated at the New York home of W. H. Aspinwall, Panama Railroad and Pacific Mail Steamer magnate. Mr. Aspinwall would consent to letting the Government have one of his ships, the *Baltic*, "but is evidently averse to the movement . . . the arguments of the opposition to this act of solemn duty are all political. . . . Mr. Aspinwall has written to the President advising no movement until the loan is taken and sends it with this note."

So to begin with Fox had learned that money for the Government might be slower in coming unless the Government would hearken closely to the advice of those who had money.

A messenger went from Lincoln that week to Richmond, where a convention of delegates, debating over secession and voting against secession, had been sitting since February 13. The messenger gave to Judge George W. Summers Lincoln's request to come to Washington for a conference. Summers consulted other delegates and chose for the errand John B. Bald-

READS THE PAPERS.

Our Friend, Mr. JONES, who is deeply interested in the condition of the country, takes
all the Papers, and reads them thoroughly. The following Dispatches puzzle him somewhat:
The Cabinet have issued the orders for the Evacuation of Fort Sumter.—*Herald.*
It is at last decided that Fort Sumter shall be reinforced.—*Times.*
Orders were sent off last evening to Reinforce Major ANDERSON at all costs.—*Tribune.*
It is believed that Major ANDERSON Evacuated Fort Sumter by order of the Government
last evening.—*World.*

Harper's Weekly shows a citizen limp from conflicting war rumors

win, who in a closed carriage arrived on April 4 at the White House, and
later told of what he saw and heard.

"Mr. Lincoln received me very cordially," wrote Baldwin, ". . . and
said he desired to have some private conversation with me. He started
through to a back room, opening into another room, but we found two
gentlemen there engaged in writing; he seemed to think that would not do,
and we passed across the hall into a small room opposite, and through that
into a large front room. There was a bed in it. He locked the door, and,

stepping around into the space behind the bed, drew up two chairs and asked me to take a seat." Lincoln then "took a seat on the edge of the bed, spitting from time to time on the carpet," during the conversation. (Of the various hundreds of persons who recorded private interviews with Lincoln, including the very frank Bill Herndon, who lived with him in the same law office for sixteen years, Baldwin was the first to say Lincoln liked to spit on a carpet and seemed to enjoy spitting while discussing a momentously solemn matter.)

Precisely what Lincoln said in the interview was not clear in Baldwin's later recollections. Lincoln did vaguely say "something about a withdrawal of troops from Sumter on the ground of military necessity," and whatever the point was, Baldwin replied: "That will never do under heaven. . . . Mr. President, I did not come here to argue with you. . . . I tell you before God and man, that if there is a gun fired at Sumter, war is inevitable." Also Baldwin offered his surmise that if the Virginia convention did dissolve and its members did go home, another convention would be called in short order.

Also Baldwin recollected that nine governors of Northern States were in the White House and it was arranged that he shake hands with them. Neither Washington nor New York newspapers that week told of nine Northern governors in Washington. At a later time they told of sixteen Northern governors, but the nine governors with whom Baldwin shook hands were his own invention.

Baldwin quoted Lincoln as saying: "Yes! your Virginia people are good Unionists, but it is always with an *if!* I don't like that sort of Unionism," holding Southern threats to be "a game of brag" by politicians, that when the Government showed its hand there would "be nothing in it but talk." Baldwin believed that "Lincoln's native good sense" was awakened and his eyes opened on Baldwin's solemn assurance that Virginia would join the seceded States the moment Lincoln opened a policy of force and coercion.

At this, according to Baldwin: "He slid off the bed, and began to stalk in his awkward manner across the chamber, in great excitement and perplexity. He clutched his shaggy hair, as though he would jerk out handfuls by the roots; he frowned and contorted his features, exclaiming, 'I ought to have known this sooner! You are too late, sir, *too late!* Why did you not come here four days ago, and tell me all this?' " and turned fiercely on Baldwin, who replied: "Why, Mr. President, you did not ask our advice. Besides, as soon as we received permission to tender it, I came by the first train, as fast as steam would bring me." "Yes, but you are too late, I tell you, too late!" Baldwin then pleaded with Lincoln that he might, if he so chose, be blessed and venerated forever as his country's savior, or execrated forever as its destroyer.

Another Virginian that week gathered Lincoln's version of what he told Baldwin in the bedroom conference. This Virginian was an antisecession Unionist, John Minor Botts, an old-line Whig who had been in Congress with Lincoln. As Botts had it from Lincoln, the President repeated to Baldwin the same offer he had made weeks before to the Border State committee, heightened by the dramatic fact that it was the last time he would ever be able to make the offer. The President had hoped that Judge Summers could come; he had an old congressional acquaintance with Summers, and faintly implied to Baldwin that he desired the presence of Summers rather than Baldwin. The President had wished to submit a proposition, saying to Baldwin: "But I fear you are almost too late. However, I will make it yet."

Then the President laid his cards on the table for Baldwin: "This afternoon a fleet is to sail from the harbor of New York for Charleston. Your convention has been in session for nearly two months, and you have done nothing but hold and shake the rod over my head. You have just taken a vote, by which it appears you have a majority of two to one against secession. Now, so great is my desire to preserve the peace of the country, and to save the Border States to the Union, that if you gentlemen of the Union party will adjourn without passing an ordinance of secession, I will telegraph at once to New York, arrest the sailing of the fleet, and take the responsibility of evacuating Fort Sumter."

Botts asked what was Baldwin's reply to this. "Oh," said the President, throwing up his hands, "he wouldn't listen to it at all; scarcely treated me with civility; asked me what I meant by an adjournment; was it an adjournment *sine die?*" To which question of Baldwin the President answered, "Of course, I don't want you to adjourn, and, after I have evacuated the fort, meet again to adopt an ordinance of secession."

Botts was hearing this recital from Lincoln on Sunday, April 7, 1861, and he plopped at the President: "Mr. Lincoln, will you authorize *me* to make that proposition? For I will start tomorrow morning, and have a meeting of the Union men tomorrow night, who, I have no doubt, will gladly accept it." The answer to Botts: "It's too late now. The fleet sailed on Friday evening."

Thus efforts at peace were going on the rocks. Baldwin had returned to Richmond declaring he had received from Lincoln "no pledge, no undertaking, no offer, no promise of any sort." Hay, Nicolay, Whitney, believed Lincoln gave Baldwin a message that Baldwin failed to deliver. They believed Judge Summers should have insisted on going to interview Lincoln, instead of letting Baldwin go. Summers may have believed it would be embarrassing to him to hear again what he had heard when with Rives and Morehead at Willard's he saw Lincoln leap from a chair and cry, "Mr. Rives, Mr. Rives, if Virginia will stay in I will withdraw the troops from Fort Sumter!"

On the afternoon of April 1, 1861, between five and six o'clock, Nicolay brought to Willard's Hotel a package of papers which he handed to Secretary Welles, who lived at Willard's. Welles opened the package, read the papers, said to himself they were "singular and remarkable." Then, as Welles told it: "Without a moment's delay I went to the President with the package in my hand. He was alone in his office and, raising his head from the table at which he was writing, inquired, 'What have I done wrong?' "

Then came the unraveling of a tangled affair. In Welles's hands were two papers signed by Lincoln, who after reading them said he was surprised he had sent such a document to the Secretary of the Navy; he had signed the papers without reading them, he told Welles; Seward with two or three young men had been at the White House through the day on a subject Seward had in hand. "It was Seward's specialty, to which he, the President, had yielded, but as it involved considerable details, he had left Mr. Seward to prepare the necessary papers."

Thus Welles heard Lincoln's explanation. "These papers he had signed, many of them without reading—for he had not time, and if he could not trust the Secretary of State he knew not whom he could trust. I asked who were associated with Mr. Seward. 'No one,' said the President, 'but these young men were here as clerks to write down his plans and orders.' I then asked if he knew the young men. He said one was Captain Meigs, another was a naval officer named Porter. . . . He seemed disinclined to disclose or dwell on the project, but assured me he never would have signed that paper had he been aware of its contents, much of which had no connection with Mr. Seward's scheme. . . . The President reiterated they were not his instructions, and wished me distinctly to understand they were not, though his name was appended to them—said the paper was an improper one—that he wished me to give it no more consideration than I thought proper—treat it as canceled—as if it had never been written."

The next day the tangle of orders and countermands became worse. Near midnight of April 6 Seward and his son came to Welles's room at Willard's bringing a telegram from Captain Meigs concerning the *Powhatan*, the flagship of the "expedition to move by sea" which had been ordered by President Lincoln to relieve Fort Sumter. Seward and Welles fell into an argument about the *Powhatan*, Seward saying that Lieutenant David D. Porter commanded it, Welles saying Seward was mistaken. So the three men went from Willard's to the White House.

On the way Seward told Welles that old as he was, he, Seward, had learned a lesson from this affair; he had better tend to his own business and keep in his own department. Welles said in his polite way it would be a good idea.

"The President had not retired . . . although it was nearly midnight," wrote Welles as to what he heard and saw. "On seeing us he was surprised, and his surprise was not diminished on learning our errand. He looked first at one and then at the other, and declared there was some mistake, but after again hearing the facts stated, and again looking at the telegram, he asked if I was not in error in regard to the *Powhatan*."

Welles then went to his office in the Navy Department and brought back and read to Lincoln the confidential instructions giving Mercer command of the *Powhatan*. Lincoln then told Seward the flagship of the Sumter expedition must be given back to Captain Mercer. Seward asked if the other expedition (one which he had originated with Lieutenant Porter of the navy and Captain Meigs of the army for the reinforcement of Fort Pickens at Pensacola, Florida) wasn't quite as important. Lincoln said the Pickens expedition could wait, but no time must be lost as to Sumter. He told Seward to telegraph without delay and return the *Powhatan* to its first commander, Mercer.

While this midnight and early morning conference was going on in the White House, the *Powhatan* got under way, steamed from the navy yard down East River, took an hour landing its former commander, Mercer, and was obeying orders from its new commander, Porter, to get out of New York Harbor in fast time. Then the quartermaster reported, "A fast steamer achasin' and signalin' of us, sir, and an officer wavin' his cap." The navy-yard commander had chartered the fastest little steamer out of New York and had it ready in case there came any last-minute telegram, which there did. It was handed to Lieutenant Porter. He read:

DELIVER THE POWHATAN AT ONCE TO CAPTAIN MERCER. SEWARD

Porter wrote a reply telegram:

HAVE RECEIVED CONFIDENTIAL ORDERS FROM THE PRESIDENT AND
SHALL OBEY THEM. D. D. PORTER

Then Porter ordered full steam on, steered his ship so as to throw pursuers off the track, and headed for Florida and Pensacola. "I was determined to go to Fort Pickens," he said later.

When the navy-yard commander, Captain Andrew H. Foote, saw the reply telegram of Lieutenant Porter, he snorted: "He's clean daft—or has run off with the ship to join the rebels. They would have tried him by court-martial anyhow. Well, I'll never trust anyone again. I have lost faith in human nature."

According to Porter, the crossed wires and misunderstandings in the affair traced back to his being requested by Seward to show how Fort Pickens could be reinforced and held. He and Captain Meigs of the army laid before Seward a plan that looked good; they would get a large steamer, load her with six or seven companies of soldiers, guns, munitions, land them outside Fort Pickens under the guns of a ship of war already down there. They took the plan to Lincoln, who said that if Pickens wasn't soon relieved there would be no holding it, and "Pensacola would be a very important place for the Southerners, and if they once get possession of Pickens, and fortify it, we have no navy to take it from them."

Porter replied: "Mr. President, there is a queer state of things in the navy department at this time. Mr. Welles is surrounded by officers and clerks, some of whom are disloyal at heart, and if the orders for this expedition should emanate from the Secretary of the Navy, and pass through all the department red tape, the news would be at once flashed over the wires, and Fort Pickens would be lost forever. But if you will issue all the orders from the Executive Mansion, and let me proceed to New York with them, I will guarantee their prompt execution to the letter."

"But," rejoined the President, "is not this a most irregular mode of procedure?" "Certainly," replied Porter, "but the necessity of the case justifies it."

"You are commander-in-chief of the army and navy," put in Seward, "and this is a case where it is necessary to issue direct orders without passing them through intermediaries."

"But what will Uncle Gideon say?" inquired the President. "Oh, I will make it all right with Mr. Welles," was the assurance of Seward.

However, Seward couldn't make it right with Welles. The bad feeling between them ran too deep. Lincoln had already sensed it. Porter wrote that in the discussion of the Fort Pickens relief plan and the overlapping authority of the State and Navy departments, Lincoln remarked: "This looks to me very much like the case of two fellows I once knew; one was a gambler, the other a preacher. They met in a stage coach, and the gambler induced the preacher to play poker. And the preacher won all the gambler's money. 'It's all because we have mistaken our trades,' said the gambler. 'You ought to have been a gambler and I a preacher, and, by ginger, I intend to turn the tables on you next Sunday and preach in your church.' Which he did."

Something of Navy Department feeling was reflected in Gustavus Vasa Fox's writing to his wife: "Mr. Seward got up this Pensacola expedition and the Prest signed the orders in ignorance and unknown to the depts. The Prest offers every apology possible and will do so in writing. So do the depts. I shall get it all straight in justification of myself and to place the blow on the head of that timid [word erased] W. H. Seward. He who paralizes [sic] every movement from abject fear."

Fox was in this reflecting his chief, Welles, and himself. For Seward in his anxiety to get action had made use of Porter, borrowing Porter from the Navy Department without asking, and seemingly unaware of bland, equivocal conduct on the part of Porter.

Among the papers Nicolay brought to Willard's for Welles to sign on April 1 were instructions to the Secretary of the Navy, in the handwriting of Captain Meigs of the War Department, with a concluding sentence, "Captain Samuel Barron will relieve Captain Stringham in charge of the Bureau of Detail," and the signature "Abraham Lincoln." Attached was a postscript in the handwriting of Lieutenant Porter, also signed "Abraham Lincoln," requesting of the Secretary of the Navy "that you will instruct Captain Barron to proceed and organize the Bureau of Detail in the manner best adapted to meet the wants of the navy, taking cognizance of the discipline of the navy generally, detailing all officers for duty, taking charge of the recruiting of seamen, supervising charges made against officers, and all matters relating to duties which must be best understood by a sea officer."

Not until later developments did these words sound ridiculous and even sardonic. The request proceeded: "You will please afford Captain Barron any facility for accomplishing this duty, transferring to his department the clerical force heretofore used for the purposes specified. It is to be understood that this officer will act by authority of the Secretary of the Navy, who will exercise such supervision as he may deem necessary."

Lincoln did not know when signing this appointment, nor Seward when advising Lincoln to sign it, that the man thereby appointed, Captain Samuel Barron, supposedly of the United States Navy, had five days before accepted a commission as a commodore in the Confederate States Navy!

Nor could Lincoln or Seward under the circumstances have guessed that two weeks later Captain Barron would go to Richmond, take the oath of Confederate loyalty, and enter actively into building coast fortifications to defend Virginia and North Carolina against ships whose officers would have been detailed by him had he managed to get into the place to which Lincoln appointed him, from which Lincoln removed him on the day Welles entered Lincoln's office in such anger that Lincoln's greeting was, "What have I done wrong?"

At a later time Welles commented: "President Lincoln believed the attempt to thrust Barron on the Navy Department was the fault of Porter rather than Seward, and he never thereafter reposed full confidence in Porter, though not insensible to his professional ability. . . . When from time to time I availed myself of Porter's qualities and gave him commands and promotion, the President expressed his gratification that I retained no resentment." This in Welles was not strictly correct, for at least one occasion came when Lincoln took the initiative in advancing Porter over Welles's disapproval.

On the very day of April 6 when Porter on the runaway ship, the *Powhatan*, was steaming south to relieve Fort Pickens, a naval lieutenant, Gwathmey, arrived in Secretary Welles's office and took from a belt strapped around his body under his shirt a letter from Captain Adams, the senior naval officer in command of Fort Pickens. Welles learned that Captain Adams was operating in obedience to an armistice negotiated by the Buchanan Administration by which the United States Government was not to reinforce Fort Pickens provided the Confederate forces did not attack it.

Taking the letter to Lincoln, they decided to send word back to Captain Adams to forget the armistice and to land troops. This message, however, could not be carried by Lieutenant Gwathmey; he was requesting that his resignation from the navy be accepted; he was going to join the Confederates; he had been sufficiently loyal to his oath as an officer. So John Worden, a naval lieutenant whose loyalty to the Union was vouched for, received from the Secretary of the Navy a dispatch and was advised to memorize it, burn it, and on arriving in Florida make a certified copy of it as he remembered it. Worden did this, and Fort Pickens was reinforced on the night of April 12.

The *New York Herald* spoke for a variety of powerful interests when on April 10 it declared: "Our only hope now against civil war of an in-

definite duration seems to lie in the over-throw of the demoralizing, disorganizing, and destructive [Republican] sectional party, of which 'Honest
Abe Lincoln' is the pliant instrument."

"The new pilot was hurried to the helm in the midst of a tornado,"
wrote Emerson of Lincoln's first weeks in office. As yet, however, the
tornado was merely beginning to get under way. It was, as yet, a baby tornado, its focal whirl in Charleston. There merchant ships from Boston and
Liverpool unloaded cargoes at the wharves. Telegraph, mail, and railway
services were much as usual.

The tall parapets of Fort Sumter, three miles out from the city of
Charleston, rising almost sheer with the rock walls of its island, were being
ringed round with batteries, guns, and the 5,000 troops recruiting under
General P. G. T. Beauregard. Daily the military was in touch with Governor F. W. Pickens of South Carolina and Secretary L. P. Walker of the
Confederate War Department at Montgomery. Visitors to the United States
Army officers or soldiers at Fort Sumter were challenged by Confederate
pickets, had to show passes from Governor Pickens. It was not quite war,
as yet. But the majesty of the United States Government was diminishing
at Charleston and her harbor.

Of the seceded Cotton States, South Carolina was the oldest, the proud-
est, the most aristocratic. Of all the larger cities in those States Charleston
could remember farthest back; her harbor had seen the War of the Revolution come and go; she had set up bronze statues to men who had met death
defending her harbor; the inscription read "These died of their wounds."
Her Robert Barnwell Rhett was the foremost Southern voice demanding
restoration of the African slave trade. Her lawyer and churchman, Christopher Memminger, who in 1832 had opposed and satirized secession, was
Secretary of the Treasury of the Confederate States. Since the day of Lincoln's election her streets had resounded with musket drill; the youth of the
city wanted war, and soon. It was Charleston who had given the South its
doctrine of secession, its now sanctified voice and intellect, John C. Calhoun,
whose figure in marble stood aloft and high on a single column of marble
over the drill ground of boys eager for war.

The North, the South, the civilized nations of the world, felt the drama
of this scene. For weeks the excitement of it had been intensifying. The
gambler's factor grew, and the dice of destiny were in the hands of Humpty
Dumpty. Fate and the intentions of History had faded into a fog of circumstance at which spectators flung the query "What next?"

Three Commissioners from the Confederate Government had arrived in
Washington before Lincoln was inaugurated, instructed to "play with"
Seward, which they did. And Seward had "played with" them. Seward's
incessant activity across this period would require heavy volumes to record;
his many spider-web proceedings, his masked assumptions and murmuring
fadeaways, his bold assumption that he spoke for Lincoln and knew the
intentions of the Government, his diplomatic maneuverings kept to himself
alone, which he justified to himself by his view that what he was doing

would either bring peace and Union or would achieve delay in which the Lincoln Administration could get ready for war. He had been more familiar than any other man with the group of Southern Senators in Washington in January who had met secretly and formulated plans looking toward secession. He had sat at the sickbed of Jefferson Davis, the leader of that group, and grasped their intentions, though he could not believe they would finally follow through on those intentions, and though, also, he had earned the lifelong ill regard of Varina Howell Davis that while he was outwardly the perfectly courteous gentleman he was inwardly a snake in the grass.

The Confederate Commissioners wrote and telegraphed their Government that the Lincoln Administration would give up Sumter. Their Alabama friend, Associate Justice John A. Campbell of the United States Supreme Court, who like Alexander H. Stephens was no thorough nor original secessionist, held conferences with Seward, and also went to the New Yorker Associate Justice Samuel Nelson of the Supreme Court, following which Nelson called on Seward with Chase and Bates. Justice Nelson as a loyal Union man told Seward that a policy of force in retaking forts would mean "very serious violation of the Constitution." Seward said in confidence that he was embarrassed by the demand of the Southern Commissioners for recognition of their Government. Nelson suggested that he should bring Campbell to Seward, went away and came back with Campbell, and the two of them argued with Seward for peace, conciliation, forbearance.

Seward got up from his chair gesturing. "I wish I could do it. See Montgomery Blair, see Mr. Bates, see Mr. Lincoln himself; I wish you would: they are all Southern men. Convince them! If Jefferson Davis had known the state of things here he would not have sent those Commissioners; the evacuation of Sumter is as much as the administration can bear." Campbell rejoiced to hear Seward say this last about Sumter, and passed on to the Confederate Commissioners assurances of Seward that Sumter would be evacuated. Assuming that Seward spoke for Lincoln, Justice Campbell gave one of the Commissioners on March 15 a note reading in part, "I feel entire confidence that Fort Sumter will be evacuated in ten days."

The ten days and more passed with the United States flag still flying from Fort Sumter. Justice Campbell went to Seward with a telegram from Governor Pickens, who believed he had heard Lamon say when leaving Charleston that he hoped to return in a few days to arrange for the removal of Anderson and the Sumter garrison. Beauregard had written his chief at Montgomery that Lamon had left "saying that Major Anderson and command would soon be withdrawn from Fort Sumter in a satisfactory manner." Both Fox and Lamon had given Major Anderson the impression, which he referred to in communications, that Sumter would probably be evacuated, that defense would probably not be ordered. And on March 30 the Governor of South Carolina was telegraphing the Confederate Commissioners in Washington asking why Sumter was still flying the Stars and Stripes.

Seward lost no time in showing this telegram of March 30 to Lincoln. And on April 1 Seward told Justice Campbell that "the President was concerned about the contents of the telegram—there was a point of honor involved; that Lamon had no agency from him, nor title to speak, nor any power to pledge him by any promise or assurance."

Lincoln asked that Campbell should question Lamon. This Campbell said he didn't wish to do. However, Seward and Campbell held two conferences on this day of April 1. Seward came to the second conference from an interview with Lincoln, and he wrote on a piece of paper which he handed to Campbell, "I am satisfied the government will not undertake to supply Fort Sumter without giving notice to Governor Pickens." Campbell asked: "What does this mean? Does the President design to supply Sumter?" And Campbell said Seward's reply was: "No, I think not. It is a very irksome thing to him to surrender it. His ears are open to everyone, and they fill his head with schemes for its supply. I do not think that he will adopt any of them. There is no design to reinforce it."

The next day, April 2, the Confederate Commissioners telegraphed their Government: "The war wing presses on the President; he vibrates to that side. . . . Their form of notice to us may be that of the coward, who gives it when he strikes."

Week by week the country had watched the emergence of Major Robert Anderson into a national figure. "Bob Anderson, my beau, Bob," ran a song line. He had kept a cool head and held on amid a thousand invitations to blunder. Nebraska legislators two thousand miles away had sent him a telegram of affection. Northern newspapers paid tribute to his patience and loyalty. Even the *Charleston Mercury* complimented him as a gentleman whose word was good. He was a West Pointer, a sober churchman, born and raised in Kentucky, saying, "We shall strive to do our duty." He had married a Georgia girl, had owned a plantation and slaves in Georgia and sold the slaves. He could see that his immediate duty was to obey orders from the United States Government but, according to one of his officers, if war came between the South and the North he "desired to become a spectator of the contest, and not an actor"; if his State of Kentucky should secede, he would go to Europe.

His wife had traveled from New York to bring him an old and tried sergeant who had served him faithfully in the Mexican War, and she had burst into tears at seeing the banner over Sumter, crying, "The dear old flag," as her husband ran from the sally port, took her in his arms and whispered, "My glorious wife." She told him, "The children are well, I return tonight." Such incidents had wrought for many people a picture of a man symbolizing Duty.

Anderson was nearly fifty-six years old, and in the Black Hawk War of long ago as a colonel of volunteers he had met Lieutenant Jefferson Davis and had sworn into service troops that included Private Abraham Lincoln. Now Lincoln was preparing a letter to serve as a guide for Anderson, a

CONSULTING THE ORACLE.

PRESIDENT LINCOLN. "And, what next?"
COLUMBIA. "First be sure you're right, then go ahead!"

Harper's Weekly in early April cartoons a puzzled Lincoln for its puzzled readers

letter that afterwards no one could have regrets about. Though in Lincoln's language, it was signed by the Secretary of War. Four copies were made, one sent by mail and three by other ways. It read:

Washington, April 4, 1861

Sir:

Your letter of the 1st instant occasions some anxiety to the President. On information of Captain Fox he had supposed you could hold out till the 15th instant without any great inconvenience, and had prepared an expedition to relieve you before that period. Hoping still that you will be able to sustain yourself till the 11th or 12th instant, the expedition will go forward; and, finding your flag flying, will attempt to provision you, and, in case the effort is resisted, will endeavor also to reinforce you.

You will therefore hold out, if possible, till the arrival of the expedition. It is not, however, the intention of the President to subject your command to any danger or hardship beyond what, in your judgment, would be usual in military life; and he has entire confidence that you will act as becomes a patriot and a soldier, under all circumstances. Whenever, if at all, in your judgment, to save yourself and command, a capitulation becomes a necessity, you are authorized to make it.

Major Anderson wrote a reply to this letter. He was now surprised at hearing reports that a relief expedition under command of Fox was preparing. "I ought to have been informed that this expedition was to come. Colonel Lamon's remark convinced me that the idea, merely hinted at to me by Captain Fox, would not be carried out. We shall strive to do our duty, though I frankly say that my heart is not in the war, which I see is to be thus commenced."

This sorrowful letter did not reach the War Department in Washington, nor Lincoln. It was seized and sent to the Confederate War Department at Montgomery. By now Anderson and the Sumter garrison were stopped from getting fresh meat and vegetables at the Charleston market. By now there had arrived in Charleston a War Department clerk from Washington, Robert S. Chew, who on the evening of April 8 read to Governor Pickens a notification from President Lincoln. And having read it, he left a copy for the Governor, its text:

Washington, April 6, 1861

Sir:

You will proceed directly to Charleston, South Carolina, and if, on your arrival there, the flag of the United States shall be flying over Fort Sumter, and the fort shall not have been attacked, you will procure an interview with Governor Pickens, and read to him as follows: "I am directed by the President of the United States to notify you to expect an attempt will be made to supply Fort Sumter with provisions only; and that, if such an attempt be not resisted, no effort to throw in men, arms, or ammunition will be made without further notice, or in case of an attack upon the fort." After you shall have read this to Governor Pickens, deliver to him the copy of it herein inclosed, and retain this letter yourself.

But if, on your arrival at Charleston, you shall ascertain that Fort Sumter shall have been already evacuated, or surrendered by the United States force, or shall have been attacked by an opposing force, you will seek no interview with Governor Pickens, but return here forthwith.

Thus the doubts of long months were at an end. Thus Lincoln framed an issue for his country and the world to look at and consider. Sumter now was a symbol, a Chip on the Shoulder. The Confederate Cabinet at Montgomery had now a specific challenge. Jefferson Davis called his advisers into session at Montgomery to consider Lincoln's message to Governor Pickens, which had been telegraphed on. Robert Toombs, Secretary of State, read Lincoln's letter, and said, "The firing on that fort will inaugurate a civil war greater than any the world has yet seen; and I do not feel competent to advise you." Toombs paced back and forth with his hands behind him, his head lowered in thought. After a time he gave his opinion on the proposed bombardment of Sumter: "Mr. President, at this time it is suicide, murder, and you will lose us every friend at the North. You will wantonly strike a hornet's nest which extends from mountains to ocean; legions, now quiet, will swarm out and sting us to death. It is unnecessary; it puts us in the wrong; it is fatal."

President Davis, however, decided in favor of attacking the fort, leaving to Beauregard the choice of time and method. He sent the order: "If you have no doubt of the authorized character of the agent who communicated to you the intention of the Washington Government to supply Fort Sumter by force, you will at once demand its evacuation, and, if this is refused, proceed, in such manner as you may determine, to reduce it."

Davis justified this bombardment order in writing later: "To have waited further strengthening of their position by land and naval forces, with hostile purpose now declared, for the sake of having them 'fire the first gun,' would have been as unwise as it would be to hesitate to strike down an assailant, who levels a deadly weapon at one's breast, until he has actually fired. He who makes the assault is not necessarily he who strikes the first blow or fires the first gun." His Commissioners had been assured they would be given notice of any military movement. The history of the negotiations is the narration of "a protracted course of fraud and prevarication practiced by Mr. Lincoln's Administration. . . . Every pledge made was broken, and every assurance of good faith was followed by an act of perfidy. Remonstrances, patient, persistent, and reiterated attempts at negotiation . . . by . . . South Carolina and by the Confederate States had . . . been met by evasion, prevarication, and perfidy. It was evident that no confidence could be placed in any pledge or promise of the Federal Government."

Thus Davis reasoned in offended dignity, as though revolutions can be reasonable and dignified in the mob slogans and mass actions that mark the first crisis and the last. For the wild humor, the headlong passion that ruled the hour, one must rather look at a tall man with blazing eyes and a long black mane of hair which he tosses as he speaks to a crowd serenading him in Charleston on the night of April 10. This man on the balcony is Roger A. Pryor. Only a few weeks ago he sat as a Virginia Congressman in Washington snarling a savage protest at a bill to give added military force to the

Lincoln Administration. As to his native State of Virginia, he was not speaking officially: "I wish to God I were; I would put her out of the Union before 12 o'clock tonight."

Pryor told them not to worry as to Virginia, the old Mother of Presidents: "Give the old lady time. [Laughter.] She cannot move with the agility of some of her younger daughters. She is a little rheumatic." Thus swagger and gaiety.

Then the solemn declaration: "Gentlemen, if Abraham Lincoln and Hannibal Hamlin were to abdicate their office tomorrow, and were to give me a blank sheet of paper whereupon to write the conditions of reannexation to the Union, I would scorn the privilege of putting the terms on paper. [Cheers.] And why? Because our grievance has not been with reference to the insufficiency of the guarantees, but the unutterable perfidy of the guarantors." Then Pryor spoke the words of passion and pride that were the key to the dominant action and tumult of that beautiful, lazy Southern city, with its Romanesque buildings, with its Revolutionary memories, with its pink and white marble walls:

"I thank you especially that you have at last annihilated this accursed Union, reeking with corruption and insolent with excess of tyranny. Not only is it gone, but gone forever. As sure as tomorrow's sun will rise upon us, just so sure will old Virginia be a member of the Southern Confederacy; and I will tell your Governor what will put her in the Southern Confederacy in less than an hour by a Shrewsbury clock. Strike a blow! [Tremendous applause.] The very moment that blood is shed, old Virginia will make common cause with her sisters of the South."

Pryor was the evangel of flame and blood required for revolution. His good partner and wife wrote that his mission in Charleston was part of the plan "to bring a popular pressure to bear upon the Government at Montgomery to make an assault on Fort Sumter."

On that same evening of April 10 when Pryor spoke his words, and stood ready for any sacrifice, Governor Andrew G. Curtin of the great steel, iron, and coal State of Pennsylvania was the recipient of a little note to him from President Lincoln. It read: "I think the necessity for being ready increases. Look to it."

And now while Lincoln's lonesome little relief ships moved down the Atlantic Coast and were daily, hourly, expected to heave into view off Charleston Harbor, there were notes and telegrams full of polite language sent back and forth. Beauregard on April 11 sent a little boat out to Sumter. Two men handed Anderson a note from Beauregard, his old-time affectionate pupil in artillery lessons at West Point: "I am ordered by the Government of the Confederate States to demand the evacuation of Fort Sumter. . . . All proper facilities will be afforded for the removal of yourself and command, together with company arms and property, and all private property, to any post in the United States which you may select. The flag which you have upheld so long and with so much fortitude, under the most trying circumstances, may be saluted by you on taking it down. Colonel Chesnut and Captain Lee will, for a reasonable time, await your answer. I am, sir, very respectfully, your obedient servant."

Major Anderson read this note and wrote a little answer: "I have the honor to acknowledge the receipt of your communication demanding the evacuation of this fort, and to say, in reply thereto, that it is a demand with which I regret that my sense of honor, and of my obligations to my Government, prevent my compliance. Thanking you for the fair, manly, and courteous terms proposed, and for the high compliment paid me, I am, general, very respectfully, your obedient servant."

However, as Major Anderson handed this note to Beauregard's aides, he made the remark, "Gentlemen, if you do not batter us to pieces, we shall be starved out in a few days." And Beauregard telegraphed this remark to his Government at Montgomery, and was told to get Anderson to fix a stated time for giving up the fort. Meanwhile the Confederate Commissioners at Washington telegraphed a newspaper report that a force would be landed at Sumter which would "overcome all opposition." Beauregard replied to the Commissioners that Sumter's evacuation would be demanded that day and "if refused hostilities will commence tonight."

Now four men from Beauregard went at night in a boat out to Sumter. At three-quarters of an hour past midnight they handed Major Anderson a note saying there would be no "useless effusion of blood" if he would fix a stated time for his surrender. Anderson called his officers; through the night hours from one o'clock till three they consulted. And at 3:15 that morning Anderson gave the four men his answer: "Cordially uniting with you in the desire to avoid the useless effusion of blood, I will, if provided with the proper and necessary means of transportation, evacuate Fort Sumter by noon on the 15th instant, and I will not in the meantime open my fire on your forces unless compelled to do so by some hostile act against this fort or the flag of my Government by the forces under your command, or by some portion of them, or by the perpetration of some act showing a hostile intention on your part against this fort or the flag it bears, should I not receive prior to that time controlling instructions from my Government or additional supplies. I am, general, very respectfully, your obedient servant."

Now the four men had full power from Beauregard to decide what to answer Anderson. They could take Anderson's reply back to Beauregard, have it telegraphed to their Government at Montgomery, and find out whether it would satisfy Jefferson Davis and his Cabinet to wait until April 15, three days more, to see whether Anderson's food was gone and whether he would then surrender.

It seemed almost as though the four men had decided before they came what they would tell Anderson. For within five minutes they gave him his answer, as follows:

Thaddeus Stevens of Pennsylvania, Chairman
of the House Ways and Means Committee

Senator and Mrs. James Henry Lane of
Kansas

Photograph from Frederick H. Meserve Collection

Photograph from U.S. Army Signal Corps

Thomas Corwin, Minister to Mexico

John Charles Frémont

From Frederick H. Meserve Collection

Kate Chase

Photograph from Library of Congress

The widowed Mrs. Stephen Arnold (Adèle Cutts) Douglas

Photograph from Oliver R. Barrett Collection

The actress Maggie Mitchell

The Confederate President's wife, Varina Howell Davis

Photographs from Oliver R. Barrett Collection

Fort Sumter, S. C., April 12, 1861–3:20 A.M.

Sir:

By authority of Brigadier-General Beauregard, commanding the Provisional Forces of the Confederate States, we have the honor to notify you that he will open the fire of his batteries on Fort Sumter in one hour from this time.

We have the honor to be, very respectfully, your obedient servant,

JAMES CHESNUT, JR.,
Aide-de-Camp.

STEPHEN D. LEE,
Captain, C.S. Army, Aide-de-Camp.

The four men got into their boat, with Chesnut musing over Major Anderson's parting words, "If we do not meet again on earth, I hope we may meet in Heaven."

An hour later they were at a battery commanded by Captain George S. James. And as Captain Lee reported it, the battery commander said to Roger A. Pryor, "You are the only man to whom I would give up the honor of firing the first gun of the war." Pryor, on receiving the offer, was shaken. With a husky voice he said, "I could not fire the first gun of the

Print showing the inside of Fort Sumter after bombardment

war." His manner, said Captain Lee, "was almost similar to that of Major Anderson as we left him on the wharf at Fort Sumter."

Pryor could not do it. But old Edmund Ruffin, according to Southern press accounts, could and did; a farmer from Virginia, soil expert, farm-paper editor, sworn for years to the sacred cause of perpetual separation from the Union, an ally of Rhett, sixty-seven years of age, his face framed in venerable white ringlets of hair—Ruffin pulled the first gun of the war, and swore he would kill himself before he would ever live under the United States Government.

Mrs. James Chesnut, Jr., whose husband had helped get the guns going, wrote in her diary of April 12 as the shooting began: "I do not pretend to go to sleep. How can I? If Anderson does not accept terms at four, the orders are he shall be fired upon. I count four, St. Michael's bells chime out and I begin to hope. At half-past four the heavy booming of a cannon. I sprang out of bed, and on my knees prostrate I prayed as I never prayed before."

It was a red dawn. The encircling batteries let loose all they had. The mortars and howitzers laughed. Wood fires on hulks at the inner harbor entrance lighted the distant lonesome relief ships from Lincoln; for a hundred reasons they could be of no help; if they could have crossed the sand bars at high tide they would have been bright targets for guns to shatter.

Through daylight of the twelfth and through the rain and darkness of the night of the thirteenth, the guns pounded Sumter with more than 3,000 shot and shell. Eight times the Confederates hit the flagstaff; at last they shot the flag off the peak; Sergeant Hart climbed up with a hammer and nailed it on again.

Wigfall, without authority from Beauregard, stepped from a rowboat under a flag of truce, asked surrender, rowed away.

Smoke, heat, vapor, stifled the garrison; they hugged the ground with wet handkerchiefs over mouths and eyes till they could breathe again. The last biscuit was gone; they were down to pork only for food. The storm and dark of the early morning on the thirteenth ended with clear weather and a red sunrise.

Again offered the same terms of surrender as before, Anderson, after thirty-three hours of bombardment, gave up the fort.

On Sunday, the fourteenth, he marched his garrison out with colors flying, drums beating, saluting his flag with fifty guns. They boarded one of the relief ships and headed north for New York Harbor. They had lost one man, killed in the accidental explosion of one of their own cannon.

In their last glimpse of Fort Sumter they saw the new Confederate flag, Stars and Bars, flying. In his trunk Major Anderson had the flag he had defended; he wished to keep this burnt and shot flag and have it wrapped round him when laid in the grave.

CHAPTER 8

THE CALL FOR TROOPS

ON that same Sunday of April 14, as Anderson marched out of Sumter the White House at Washington had many visitors. They filed in and out all day. Senators and Congressmen came to say that their people would stand by the Government, the President. The Cabinet met. A proclamation was framed to go the next day to the eyes and ears of millions of people, then around the world. It named the States of South Carolina, Georgia, Alabama, Florida, Mississippi, Louisiana, and Texas as having "combinations too powerful to be suppressed" by ordinary procedure of government.

"Now, therefore, I, Abraham Lincoln, President of the United States, in virtue of the power in me vested by the Constitution and the laws, have thought fit to call forth, and hereby do call forth, the militia of the several States of the Union, to the aggregate number of seventy-five thousand, in order to suppress said combinations, and to cause the laws to be duly executed."

He called on "all loyal citizens" to defend the National Union and popular government, "to redress wrongs already long enough endured." The new army of volunteer soldiers was to retake forts and property "seized from the Union." Also, "in every event the utmost care will be observed, consistently with the objects aforesaid, to avoid any devastation, any destruction of or interference with property, or any disturbance of peaceful citizens."

And as though a captain lifting an authoritative right hand to bring obedience and quiet to mutineers, Lincoln wrote, "And I hereby command the persons composing the combinations aforesaid to disperse and retire peacefully to their respective abodes within twenty days." Also the proclamation called both Houses of Congress to meet at twelve o'clock noon on the Fourth of July next.

Thus the war of words was over and the naked test by steel weapons, so long foretold, was at last to begin. It had happened before in other countries among other peoples bewildered by economic necessity, by the mob oratory of politicians and editors, by the ignorance of the educated classes, by the greed of the propertied classes, by elemental instincts touching race and religion, by the capacity of so many men, women, and children for hating and fearing what they do not understand while believing they do understand completely and perfectly what no one understands except tentatively and hazardously.

From day to day since Lincoln was sworn in as President he had moved toward war, seeing less bloodshed in one immediate war than in many smaller inevitable wars to follow. He could have joined with a majority of his Cabinet and ordered Anderson, as Anderson wished, to step quietly out of Sumter. He could have linked his sentiments with those of leading financiers and merchants of New York and the large Eastern cities—and compromised and mixed issues so that there would have been no proclamation of war.

"My policy is to have no policy," he said to John Hay.

Day to day events dictated. How did he explain Sumter? "The assault upon and reduction of Fort Sumter was in no sense a matter of self-defense on the part of the assailants," he wrote later. "They well knew that the garrison in the fort could by no possibility commit aggression upon them. They knew—they were expressly notified—that the giving of bread to the few brave and hungry men of the garrison was all which would on that occasion be attempted." Sumter was a symbol, a pawn, a token of power. Two governments each wanted its flag alone and supreme over that little spot of earth. "They knew that this Government desired to keep the garrison in the fort, not to assail them, but merely to maintain visible possession, and thus to preserve the Union from actual and immediate dissolution—trusting . . . to time, discussion, and the ballot-box for final adjustment; and they assailed and reduced the fort for precisely the reverse object—to drive out the visible authority of the Federal Union, and thus force it to immediate dissolution."

Lincoln had hoped, he said, to so manage the issues that in the finish he could point to his soft-spoken inaugural declaration, "You can have no conflict without being yourselves the aggressors." He took pains, so he said, "to keep the case so free from the power of ingenious sophistry that the world should not be able to misunderstand it." The world, however, began arguing the case, trying to answer the question: Who started the war? North and South on the American continent the argument was to run into millions of words.

The *Manchester Guardian*, issued from the district in England where employed men and spindles were fewer because of the shortage of cotton, commented as to Sumter and Lincoln: "The whole affair looks like nothing so much as a refusal on the part of the United States authorities to leave a place in which they did not desire to remain without the application of just as much force as would entitle them to all the advantages to be derived from an action for assault and battery. . . . It appears, we confess, to complete the character of Mr. Lincoln's policy as including every known kind of blunder. Morally he is to the full as responsible as the government of Montgomery for transferring the matters in dispute between them from the arbitrament of reason to that of arms, for his formal intimation to them that he was about to resort to force was a challenge that they could not be expected to disregard. . . . The only plausible explanation of President Lincoln's account is that he has thought that a political object was to be obtained by putting the Southerners in the wrong, if they could be manoeuvred into firing the first shot."

Lincoln had his way, said the South. He wanted a war and made one, they said. If he had wanted peace he could have had it, Lincoln knew well. He could have joined hands with all the forces of delay and compromise. It would have been easy. Compliments would have come thick and fast from the centers of restored commerce. Across a table papers could have been signed. The wayward sisters would have departed. No shooting. No boys thrusting bayonets into each other's vitals. Many States with many flags from coast to coast. Customhouses at the State borders. Many interstate treaties, ambassadors. Many collisions over fugitive Negroes at the border lines of Free and Slave States.

"Give a little finger and soon you will have to give the whole hand," a Western farmer had written Lincoln. For the sake of peace with Union there had been a series of compromises, the defense of which had led to what Lincoln described as "an insidious debauching of the public mind." Now instead of peace and one more compromise with further compromises just over the horizon—and further endless arguments as to what "the Fathers" meant when they wrote the Constitution—Lincoln issued a proclamation for troops of war.

The Southern combination had forced the issue, "immediate dissolution or blood," wrote Lincoln. Between the two Lincoln chose blood. Analyzing Lincoln the warmaker, his old-time friend Alexander Stephens, now Vice-President of the Confederate States, wrote long after: "Mr. Lincoln was kind-hearted (no man I ever knew was more so) but the same was true of Julius Caesar. . . . The Union, with him, in sentiment rose to the sublimity of a religious mysticism."

For Lincoln, the Union held a harassing dilemma of interest to "the whole family of man." He wrote it: "Must a government, of necessity, be too strong for the liberties of its own people, or too weak to maintain its own existence?"

This dilemma Lincoln and Douglas discussed at the White House that Sunday of April 14, just after the flag came down at Sumter. Among the afternoon callers was Congressman George Ashmun of Massachusetts, who had presided over the Chicago Republican National Convention of 1860. Ashmun agreed with Lincoln that the Administration should call to its support "the best men of the country," and one of these was Douglas. Ashmun went straightway to the home of Douglas and urged him to "go at once to the President and take him by the hand." Adèle Douglas put her hand on her husband's shoulder and said he ought to go—and he agreed decisively. He sent a message to the President, and the reply was that the Senator would be welcome early in the evening for an interview. Douglas and Ashmun drove to the White House near eight o'clock that evening, and Lincoln, noted Ashmun, met him "with outstretched hands and with a benignant smile."

Now Lincoln could be thankful that across the years of political strife between him and Douglas, the two of them had so spoken to and of each other that their personal relations had never reached a breaking-point. At the last November election Lincoln's total of votes stood 1,866,000 against the Douglas total of 1,375,000—and they talked this Sunday evening about what Douglas was going to tell the million or more men who would listen and consider anything he had to say, many thousands having an unquestioning faith that he could not go wrong.

The two foremost American political captains were closeted for a two-hour confidential talk, with only Congressman Ashmun in the room. Douglas read the proclamation to be published the next morning, gave it his approval, though advising that 75,000 troops would be insufficient and he would call for 200,000. He pointed on a map to strategic spots that required strengthening and Lincoln requested him to lay these views before General Scott. He predicted trouble in bringing Federal troops through Baltimore and suggested an alternative route. Throughout, noted Ashmun, Lincoln was "an earnest and gratified listener."

The interview over, Ashmun said to Douglas: "You have done justice to your own reputation, and to the President, and the country must know it. The proclamation will go by telegraph all over the country in the morning, and an account of this interview must go with it. I shall send it either in my own language or yours. I prefer that you should give your own version." Douglas, with his usual fast thinking, answered, "Drive to your room at Willard's and I will give it shape." And at Willard's he wrote out a dispatch, a short and pregnant statement, which the next day went to the country through the Associated Press.

He had called on the President, ran this statement, and had "an interesting conversation on the present condition of the country." The substance of this conversation was, on the part of Mr. Douglas, "that while he was unalterably opposed to the administration in all political issues, he was prepared to fully sustain the President in the exercise of all his constitutional functions, to preserve the Union, maintain the Government, and defend the capital. A firm policy and prompt action was necessary. The capital was in danger, and must be defended at all hazards, and at any expense of men and money." He added that he and the President "spoke of the present and future without any reference to the past."

Douglas was a hoarse and worn man of dwindling vitality, but he struck now with decisive words that sank deep in every one of his old loyal followers. He knew he had trumpets left, and he blew them to mass his cohorts behind Lincoln's maintenance of the Union.

Just how far Douglas in a few weeks had swung from his traditional viewpoint, and the extent of his hate for wreckers of the Union, was not told to the country but was given to Lincoln privately, according to the *New York Tribune* man, Albert D. Richardson, who had once met Lincoln on the prairies of Kansas and in a White House call now found "the same fund of humorous anecdote" but not "the old, free, lingering laugh." Richardson noted for his private record, but not for the American public of the hour: " 'Mr. Douglas,' remarked the President, 'spent three hours with me this afternoon. For several days he has been too unwell for business, and has devoted his time to studying war matters until he understands the military position better, perhaps, than any one of the Cabinet. By the way,' continued the President, with his peculiar twinkle of the eye, 'the conversation turned upon the rendition of slaves. "You know," said Douglas, "that I am entirely sound on the Fugitive Slave Law. I am for enforcing it in all cases within its true intent and meaning; but, after examining it carefully, I have concluded that a negro insurrection is a case to which it does not apply." ' "
The blunt meaning of this was that Douglas was telling Lincoln it would be all right with him if the Negroes anywhere in the South should suddenly organize and violently overthrow the power of their white masters and owners. It was a terrible thing to say, but it was a forecast of how under the changed conditions brought by the war men were stormy under their

sometimes smooth exteriors, and of how swiftly a war status can tear up by the roots an ancient point of doctrine and practice.

Now came the day of April 15, 1861, for years afterward spoken of by millions of people as "the day Lincoln made his first call for troops." What happened on that day was referred to as the Uprising of the People. Mass action ruled. The people swarmed onto the streets, into public squares, into meeting-halls and churches. The shooting of the Stars and Stripes off the Sumter flagstaff—and the Lincoln proclamation—acted as a vast magnet on a national multitude. The action was compared to Ezekiel's vision of the prophet's voice calling across a silent valley when the dry bones arose and walked, clothed with new flesh. It was likened to the mystic hosts that arose to go to fight for the tomb of Christ when Peter the Hermit called for Crusaders.

In a thousand cities, towns, and villages the fever of hate, exaltation, speech, action, followed a similar course. Telegrams came notifying officers, and militiamen to mobilize. Newspapers came, crying in higher or lower key the war song of the *Chicago Tribune:* "There is a republic! The gates of Janus are open; the storm is on us. Let the cry be, The Sword of the Lord and of Gideon!" with the instruction, "From this hour let no Northern man or woman tolerate in his or her presence the utterance of a word of treason," and the warning: "We say to the Tories and lickspittles in this community, a patient and reluctant, but at last an outraged and maddened people will no longer endure your hissing. You must keep your venom sealed or go down!"

Then came mass meetings, speeches by prominent citizens, lawyers, ministers, priests, military officers, veterans of the War of 1812 and the Mexican War, singing of "The Star-spangled Banner" and "America," fife-and-drum corps playing "Yankee Doodle." Funds were subscribed to raise and equip troops, resolutions were passed, committees appointed to collect funds, to care for soldier families, to educate or ostracize the unpatriotic. Women's societies were formed to knit and sew, prepare lint and bandages. Women and girls saw their husbands and sweethearts off to camp. Nearly every community had its men and boys marching away to the fifing of "The Girl I Left behind Me." In the farewell speeches at the home town they were told of heroic exploits of their fathers; they would do likewise.

In Pittsburgh, ropes hung from lampposts with signs "Death to Traitors"; men who had spoken Southern sympathies were beaten and told to hold their tongues. "A suspected secessionist was seized this evening and experienced some rough treatment," said a Wilmington, Ohio, dispatch. In Philadelphia on this April day masses of people gathered in the streets; leaders sprang up; calls were made on hotels, newspapers, and a postmaster who had forgotten to run up the Union flag. Mayor Henry told a crowd, "By the grace of Almighty God, treason shall never rear its head or have a boothold in Philadelphia." In New York a crowd of 2,000 swirled around the *Herald* office shouting threats and jeers till the Union banner flaunted from a window; likewise crowds arrived at the *Daily News,* Mayor Wood's pro-Southern newspaper, and at the *Express* and the *Journal of Commerce*, antiwar papers, and forced them to hang out the Stars and Stripes. In churches and saloons, in city crowds and at country crossroads, the talk was of the War and "What will the President do next?"

In the large cities military units of the foreign-born were formed. Irishmen of New York made up four regiments: the 69th, Irish Zouaves, Irish Volunteers, St. Patrick Brigade. The Italian Legion made ready, also the Garibaldi Guards. Germans supplied the Steuben Volunteers, the German Rifles, the Turner Rifles, the De Kalb Regiment. The English and Irish Home Guards were proposed for men of former service in the British Army and Irish constabulary, while the British Volunteers were to recruit from British subjects in New York.

Bishop Matthew Simpson of the Methodist Episcopal Church came to President Lincoln's office, the Bishop's friend Clinton B. Fisk reporting of it that Cabinet members dropped in, Bates, Blair, Cameron, Seward. "The bishop expressed the opinion that seventy-five thousand men were but a beginning of the number needed; that the struggle would be long and severe. Mr. Seward asked what opportunity a clergyman could have to judge of such affairs as these. Judge Bates replied that few men knew so much of the temper of the people as Bishop Simpson; Montgomery Blair sustained the view of Judge Bates. A Cabinet meeting followed. After it was over Lincoln and Simpson remained together quite a long time. The bishop gave him, in detail, his opinion of men throughout the country whom he knew."

A New York mother of five sons who enlisted wrote to her husband: "I was startled by the news referring to our boys, and, for the moment felt as if a ball had pierced my own heart. For the first time I was obliged to look things full in the face. But although I have always loved my children with a love that none but a mother can know, yet, when I look upon the state of my country, I cannot withhold them; and in the name of their God, and their mother's God, and their country's God, I bid them go. If I had ten sons instead of five, I would give them all sooner than have our country rent in fragments. . . . I hope you will provide them each with a Bible, and tell them our prayers accompany them night and day."

A Baltimore mother wrote to her son, a Boston clergyman, "My dear son: Your remarks last Sabbath were telegraphed to Baltimore and published in an extra. Has God sent you to preach the sword, or to preach Christ?" The reply was: "Dear mother: God has sent me not only to preach the sword but to *use* it. When this Government tumbles, look amongst the ruins for . . . Your Star-Spangled Banner Son."

"Patriotism, ambition, vanity, and the spirit of speculation, entered at once into competition and contributed, though unequally, to stimulate the national movement," wrote the French military observer, the Comte de Paris. "The ingenious, practical and calculating mind of the American neglected no means to hasten the organization so imperatively demanded by the national danger." In the days of swift decisions that followed soon,

Congressman Galusha Grow wrote a letter to Simon Cameron saying, "I saw many of the solid men of New York, and they will embark their all in this contest provided the Administration will prosecute it to the bitter end if need be to quell the insurrection so that no madcap will ever try the experiment again." The *New York Herald*, shifting its outlook, voiced the new viewpoint of powerful business interests in declaring: "The business community demand that the war shall be *short;* and the more vigorously it is prosecuted the more speedily will it be closed. Business men can stand

VOLUNTEER'S WANTED

FOR

COL. WILLIAM'S

REGIMENT!

NEARLY FULL. APPLY TO

Lieut. S. P. SIMPSON,

CAMDEN, DEL.

Type of handbill during the "Uprising." From the Barrett collection.

a temporary reverse. They can easily make arrangements for six months or a year. But they cannot endure a long, uncertain and tedious contest." An ideal and a motive lay back of Henry Ward Beecher's shout from his Brooklyn pulpit: "The country does not belong to us from the Lakes only to Washington, but from the Lakes to the Gulf of Mexico."

Senator Douglas at Bellaire, Ohio, in Chicago at the Wigwam, in Springfield before the Illinois Legislature, was saying that the shortest way to peace would be stupendous and unanimous preparation for war. The question was not union or disunion but the stability of the Government: "The proposition now is to separate these United States into little petty confederacies. First, divide them into two; and then, when either party gets beaten at the next election, subdivide again; then, whenever one gets beaten again, another subdivision."

Astor, Vanderbilt, Aspinwall, A. T. Stewart, Belmont of the House of Rothschild, the millionaires who had been at the breakfast to Lincoln when he came through New York, they and their cohorts and lawyers were now for war. From tottering ruins of politics came hesitant voices for war, ex-President Buchanan, his War Secretary, Lewis Cass, ex-President Franklin Pierce, John J. Crittenden, the reputable and adroit attorneys for vast property interests, William M. Evarts, David Dudley Field, Caleb Cushing.

None leaped so eagerly as the abolitionists at the ways now open for a war with slaveholders. "I was a Disunionist," said Wendell Phillips. "I did hate the Union, when Union meant lies in the pulpit and mobs in the streets, when Union meant making white men hypocrites and black men slaves." He told an audience: "The only mistake I made was in supposing Massachusetts wholly choked with cotton dust and cankered with gold. . . . How do we justify this last appeal to the God of Battles? Let me tell you how I do. I have always believed in the sincerity of Abraham Lincoln. You have heard me express my confidence in it every time I have spoken from this desk. I only doubted sometimes whether he were really the head of the Government. Today he is at any rate Commander-in-Chief."

Phillips drew a terrible contrast between the two sections of the country, voiced an arrogant pride of blood and breed: "The North *thinks*—can appreciate argument—it is in the Nineteenth Century—hardly any struggle left in it but that between the working class and the money kings. The South *dreams*—it is the thirteenth and fourteenth century—baron and serf—noble and slave." He was ready for tumult: "I rejoice that for the first time in my anti-slavery life, I speak under the Stars and Stripes, and welcome the tread of Massachusetts men marshalled for war. . . . Mr. Lincoln took office robbed of all the means to defend the constitutional right of the Government. He offered to withdraw from the walls of Sumter everything but the flag. . . . The right of a state to secede, under the Constitution of the United States—it is an absurdity; and Abraham Lincoln knows nothing, has a right to know nothing, but the Constitution of the United States. . . . South Carolina presents herself to the Administration at Washington and says, 'There is a vote of my Convention that I go out of the Union.' 'I cannot see you,' says Abraham Lincoln. [Loud cheers.] 'As President I have no eyes but constitutional eyes; I cannot see you.' [Renewed cheers.] He was right. . . . Today the question is, Shall Washington or Montgomery own the continent? And the North says, From the Gulf to the Pole, the Stars and Stripes shall atone to four millions of negroes whom we have forgotten for seventy years; and before you break the Union, we shall see that justice is done to the slave."

The requisite will for a long exhausting war was all there in the declaration of Gerrit Smith, an abolitionist of means who had given 120,000 acres of land to 3,000 colored men, who had spent $16,000 on the Kansas civil war, who had lost $12,000 bail money through refusal to return two slaves owned by Robert Toombs and Alexander Stephens, who was financially allied with John Brown's plan for an insurrection of armed slaves. He told an audience at his home town of Peterboro, New York, that the last fugitive slave had been returned. "A few weeks ago I would have consented to let the slave states go without requiring the abolition of slavery. . . .

HAMILTON'S
Light Cavalry

☞ A GOOD HORSE TO RIDE AND GOOD WEAPONS TO USE!!

ABLE-BODIED MEN

WANTED, to join the above Regiment, which is now in CAMP.

PAY AND RATIONS to commence on signing the Muster Roll.

Horses and Equipage Furnished.

IMMEDIATELY ON ARRIVAL AT CAMP.

Men sent to Camp within ten hours after signing the Roll.

For further particulars apply at the

RECRUITING STATION

A handbill. From the Barrett collection.

But now, since the Southern tiger has smeared himself with our blood, we will not, if we get him in our power, let him go without having drawn his teeth and claws."

Gerrit Smith was offering to equip a regiment of colored troops, and was sending his only son, Greene Smith, into the army, insisting it be without soldier's pay. As to the armed men going south, he told the audience: "They must still love the south. We must all still love her. Conquer her, and most completely too, we must, both for her sake and our own. But does it not ill become us to talk of punishing her? Slavery, which has infatuated her, is the crime of the north as well as the south. As her chiefs shall, one after another, fall into our hands, let us be restrained from dealing revengefully, and moved to deal tenderly with them, by our remembrance of the large share which the north has had in blinding them. The conspiracy of northern merchants and manufacturers, northern publishers, priests and politicians, against the slaveholders, carried on under the guise of friendship, has been mighty to benumb their conscience, and darken their understanding in regard to slavery."

The session of the New York East Methodist Conference opened with the prayer: "Let the forces that have risen against our Government, and Thy law, be scattered to the winds. Grant, O God, that those who aimed at the very heart of the republic may be overthrown. We ask Thee to bring these men to destruction, and wipe them from the face of the country." The old-school Presbyterian minister Dr. T. D. Wells preached to his New York congregation on the text "He that hath no sword, let him buy one."

Cheers and applause greeted the public reading of a letter of John Hughes, Archbishop of the Roman Catholic Church of New York, declaring for the Stars and Stripes: "This has been my flag and shall be till the end." At home and abroad, the Archbishop would have it wave "for a thousand years and afterward as long as Heaven permits, without limit of duration." The *New York Tribune* told its readers: "Father Rafina, priest of the Montrose Avenue Catholic Church, Williamsburg, New York, with his own hands raised the American flag upon the top of his church. The ceremony was witnessed by at least two thousand people. The reverend father addressed the assemblage in a few appropriate remarks." In Cincinnati, Archbishop Purcell unfurled with ceremonies a 90-foot Union flag from the spire of the Roman Catholic Cathedral. Father Creadon at Auburn, New York, called on "every Irishman who hears me to enlist, if he can; this is the first country the Irishman ever had that he could call his own."

Fifty thousand people made their way on April 20 to a Union mass meeting at Union Square in New York City, where those near enough could hear Daniel S. Dickinson's rephrasing of Daniel Webster's oratory: "When the timid falter and the faithless fly—when the skies lower, the winds howl, the storm descends, and the tempest beats—when the lightnings flash, the thunders roar, the waves dash, and the good ship Union creaks and groans with the expiring throes of dissolution, I will cling to her still as the last refuge of hope from the fury of the storm; and if she goes down

I will go down with her, rather than survive to tell the story of her ignoble end. I will rally round the star-spangled banner so long as a single stripe can be discovered, or a single star shall shimmer from the surrounding darkness." As William H. Appleton, publisher of books, stood at Broadway and Fourteenth Street watching the human swarm, he remarked to a friend, "We shall crush out this rebellion as an elephant would trample on a mouse."

Edward D. Baker, Senator from Oregon, shouted in his rich singing voice that New York was declaring to the world that she would sustain the Government to the last dollar in her treasury, to the last drop of her blood: "The national banners leaning from ten thousand windows in your city today proclaim your affection and reverence for the Union." Men from the Fort Sumter garrison, who had now arrived in New York, bowed to applause and cheers. Then arose little Robert J. Walker, one-time Senator from Mississippi, Secretary of the Treasury under Polk; it was long ago that Walker had started Jefferson Davis in the game as his protégé in politics; since then Walker had been a Douglas man, Governor of the Territory of Kansas. Now he was saying: "Where are we now? The world looks on with scorn and derision. We have no government—a mere voluntary association, a debating society, or a moot court, without any real power. We have no country, no flag, no Union." He mentioned politics: "A desperate effort is made to make this a party question, between Democrats and Republicans." He had never scratched a Democratic ticket in his life, and yet: "Much as I love my party, I love my country infinitely more. . . . This Union must, will, and shall be perpetuated; not a star shall be dimmed or a stripe erased from its banner."

Far from Union Square, beyond the Mississippi, in a cornfield near Iowa City, the farmer Governor Samuel J. Kirkwood saw an earnest man on a spent and foam-flecked horse. This corn-fed courier had been riding many miles and hours from Davenport on the Mississippi with a telegram he handed the Governor from the Secretary of War at Washington: "Call made on you tonight's mail for one regiment of militia for indefinite service." The Governor wrinkled his brow and gazed across a slope of cut cornstalks: "Why! The President wants a whole regiment of men! Do you suppose I can raise as many as that?" Yet a few days later, ten Iowa regiments were offered and Governor Kirkwood was telegraphing Washington: "For God's sake send us arms! We have the men."

At a Western religious conclave a psalm of jubilant hosannas came from a bishop of the Methodist Episcopal church, the Reverend Edward R. Ames: "There has been held a grand Union convention, the proceedings of which have not been reported by telegraph. It was held amid the fortresses of the everlasting hills. The Rocky Mountains presided, the mighty Mississippi made the motion, the Allegheny Mountains seconded it and every mountain and hill, valley and plain, in this vast country, sent up a unanimous voice; Resolved, that we are one and inseparable and what God has joined together, let no man put asunder." It was a week of distinguished and inflammatory oratory.

Here and there were men who listened to the oratory, read the editorials, and held the view of Nathaniel Hawthorne, author of books on the dark hearts of New England. He wrote to his wife, "It was delightful to share in the heroic sentiment of the time, and to feel that I had a country—a consciousness which seemed to make me young again." He had one regret and one thing to be glad of: "I am too old to shoulder a musket myself, and the joyful thing is that Julian [his son] is too young. He drills constantly with a company of lads, and means to enlist as soon as he reaches the minimum age. But I trust we shall either be victorious or vanquished before that time." Yet all was not clear in his mind.

Neither the orations nor the editorials, nor Lincoln's proclamation, had made it clear to Hawthorne: "Though I approve the war as much as any man, I don't quite understand what we are fighting for, or what definite results can be expected. If we are fighting for the annihilation of slavery, to be sure, it may be a wise object, and offer a tangible result, the only one consistent with a future union between North and South. A continuance of the war would soon make this plain to us, and we should see the expediency of preparing our black brethren for future citizenship by allowing them to fight for their own liberties, and educating them through heroic influences. Whatever happens next, I must say that I rejoice that the old Union is smashed. We never were one people, and never really had a country since the Constitution was formed." At the other extreme was Parson Brownlow, an editor in Knoxville, Tennessee, at the peril of his neck telling the world that though he was against abolition, he was for the Union and he would "fight the Secession leaders till Hell froze over and then fight on the ice."

Besides mere language, events of destructive violence added to the fury of the hour in the week of the Uprising. Three delegates came as a special committee from the Virginia convention to the White House. Their convention had in secret session voted 60 to 53 against seceding from the Union. They politely inquired of Lincoln as to his intentions. He replied politely that his intentions were still the same as he reported them in his inaugural. He read over part of his inaugural, as though they had not read it carefully enough, and as though by patience they might find new clews in it: "The power confided to me will be used to hold, occupy, and possess the property and places belonging to the government" and so on. They took their hats, reported back to their convention—and Virginia, the Mother of States, the Mother of Presidents, went out of the Union.

A story circulated that one member of the Virginia committee replied to Lincoln's question "What would you have me do?" by saying, "Mr. President, I would beg you to lend me your finger and thumb for five minutes." A few little words from his pen, dictated by them, as his finger and thumb moved over the paper, could have held Virginia in the Union.

On the day of April 17 when Virginia seceded, her troops were set in

motion for a surprise march on the United States fort and arsenal at
Harper's Ferry, the most dramatic point northward for raising her new flag.
They arrived on April 18 and took the fort and arsenal without fighting.
The 45 Union guards heard of their coming and quit the fort after using
gunpowder and fire to destroy munitions, guns, and war property worth
several million dollars. The barrels and locks of 20,000 pistols and rifles were
sent to Richmond to be remade. In a few weeks Professor Thomas J. Jackson, instructor in military tactics at the Virginia Military Institute, was in
charge at and near Harper's Ferry with 8,000 troops.

By what narrow chance Lincoln missed giving the enemy a fight at
Harper's Ferry was told by General John D. Imboden of the Confederate
expedition starting from Richmond: "Just before we moved out of the
depot, Alfred Barbour made an unguarded remark in the car, which was
overheard by a Northern traveler, who immediately wrote a message to
President Lincoln and paid a negro a dollar to take it to the telegraph office.
This act was discovered by one of our party, who induced a friend to
follow the negro and take the dispatch from him. This perhaps prevented
troops being sent to head us off."

Two days later the United States Navy Yard at Norfolk, Virginia, was
threatened, or the commander was afraid it was, and guns, munitions,
ships, and war property valued at $30,000,000 went up in smoke. Robert
E. Lee, Virginian, resigned from the United States Army, gave up his stately
home on Arlington Heights overlooking Washington, to take command of
the Army of Virginia; long ago he had opposed slavery; he favored the
Union but couldn't fight against his native State; before resigning he was
interviewed by Francis P. Blair, Sr., who said later: "I told him what
President Lincoln wanted him to do; he wanted him to take command of
the army. . . . He said he could not, under any circumstances, consent to
supersede his old commander [General Scott]. He asked me if I supposed
the President would consider that proper. I said yes. . . . The matter was
talked over by President Lincoln and myself for some hours on two or
three different occasions. . . . The President and Secretary Cameron expressed themselves as anxious to give the command of our army to Robert
E. Lee." Now Lee had gone to Richmond.

Lincoln had lost a commander that General Scott reckoned as worth
fifty thousand men. "Save in the defense of my native State I never again
desire to draw my sword," Lee wrote to Scott. Two months before, in
Texas, he had told army associates: "I fear the liberties of our country will
be buried in the tomb of a great nation. . . . If Virginia stands by the old
Union, so will I. But if she secedes (though I do not believe in secession
as a constitutional right, nor that there is sufficient cause for revolution)
then I will still follow my native State with my sword, and, if need be,
with my life."

The break came hard for Lee. "I know you think and feel very differently," he told a Union officer. "But I can't help it. These are my principles;
and I must follow them." Lee wrote later to Reverdy Johnson: "I never

intimated to anyone that I desired the command of the United States army, nor did I ever have a conversation with but one gentleman, Mr. Francis P. Blair, on the subject, which was at his invitation, and as I understand, at the instance of President Lincoln. After listening to his remarks I declined the offer he made me, to take command of the army that was to be brought into the field, stating, as candidly and courteously as I could, that, though opposed to secession and deprecating war, I could take no part in an invasion of the Southern states."

The seething of propaganda began. Southern newspapers reported elaborate plans in the North to stir up insurrections of slaves, with robbery, arson, rape, murder. Northern newspapers reported a Northern woman teacher in a New Orleans grammar school as being stripped naked and tarred and feathered in Lafayette Square "for abolition sentiments expressed to her pupils." North and South, horrors were exaggerated or fabricated. The North was arming Sioux Indian tribes for butchery and scalping of Southern women and children. Likewise the South was arming Cherokee Indian tribes for slaughter and pillage. So newspaper items ran.

While Northern organs predicted the capture and hanging of Jefferson Davis, "the monster," Southern papers told of Lincoln. The *Richmond Whig* of April 20 had "reliable information" that "Old Abe had been beastly drunk for the previous thirty-six consecutive hours, and that eight border ruffians from Kansas occupied the East Room, to guard his Majesty's slumbers." The *New Orleans Delta* of April 29 reported: "A gentleman arrived here this morning who, with several others, was arrested, while passing through Washington, for being Southerners, and were taken into the presence of the august Baboon. He declares that Lincoln was so drunk that he could hardly maintain his seat in the chair. It was notorious in Washington that he had been in a state of intoxication for more than thirty-six hours. The man is nearly scared to death; and few people, in that city, are in a better condition." The *Richmond Dispatch* offered doggerel:

> We'll hunt for Lincoln, Bess!—old tool—
> And take him half-and-half;
> We'll aim to *hit* him if a fool,
> And *miss* him if a calf!

While the *New York Tribune* declared "Jeff Davis & Co. will be swinging from the battlements at Washington at least by the 4th of July," the *New Orleans Delta* printed a letter from a Southern woman in Washington: "Old Lincoln sleeps with a hundred men in the east room to protect him from the Southern army. He is expecting them to attack the city every night; he keeps a sentinel walking in front of his bed-room all night, and often gets so frightened that he leaves the White House, and sleeps out, no one knows where. These are facts. Mrs. Lincoln, a few nights since, heard whispering in the hall in front of her room; she rose from bed, dressed, and sat up the remainder of the night, watching for the Southern army to blow up the White House, as they are confidently expecting it."

Jefferson Davis of Mississippi, President of the Confederate   Alexander Hamilton Stephens of Georgia, Vice-President
States of America   of the Confederate States of America

Photographs by McClees in author's collection

Robert Toombs of Georgia, Secretary of State, C.S.A.   Judah Philip Benjamin of Louisiana, Attorney General and later Secretary of State, C.S.A.

Photographs by McClees in author's collection

The *Petersburg* (Virginia) *Express* told how "Old Abe has his legs in perfect readiness to run. He does not so much as take off his boots." The
Picayune of New Orleans was pat and pertinent: "Mr. Lincoln is of a
Quaker family, and it is to be remarked that a Quaker President is the
first one to plunge the country into civil war, and within less than six weeks
after his accession to the office. Quakers are remarkable for approaching
their objects by indirect means."

Little Alexander Stephens in an Atlanta speech uttered the flaming faith
of the fresh-born revolution in saying: "Lincoln may bring his 75,000
troops against us," but "we fight for our homes, our fathers and mothers,
our wives, brothers, sisters, sons and daughters, and neighbors! They for
money!" As he visioned it, "God is on our side, and who shall be against
us?" He discussed man power: "We can call out a million of people, if
need be, and when they are cut down, we can call out another, and still
another, until the last man of the South finds a bloody grave." The *Raleigh
Banner*, urging a march on Washington, said, "The army of the South will
be composed of the best material that ever yet made up an army; while
that of Lincoln will be gathered from the sewers of the cities—the degraded,
beastly offscourings of all quarters of the world, who will serve for pay,
and run away as soon as they can when danger threatens." The *Mobile
Advertiser* printed lines from an Alabama self-styled Joan of Arc:

> Oh, Abraham Lincoln, we call thee to hark!
> Thou Comet of Satan! thou Boast of the Dark!
> Take off thy red shadow from Washington's land—
> Back! back! for thy footstep is slavery's brand.
> Future-eyed Prophecy cries to thee, DOWN!
> For she sees on thy forehead the hope of a crown;
> The fire that *sleeps* in our Southern eyes dark,
> Would *lighten* in battle—we're Joans of Arc.

Mrs. Chesnut, mistress of Mulberry Plantation, deep in South Carolina,
was writing in her diary, "I have been sitting idly today looking out upon
this beautiful lawn, wondering if this can be the same world I was in a few
days ago." She knew it wasn't.

The day of the President's call for 75,000 troops had passed, and not
a trooper arrived in Washington. And the next day and the next passed,
and not a regiment nor a company came—not a corporal's squad.

A volunteer White House Guard arose under Cassius M. Clay, who
would delay sailing as the new Minister to Russia, and Senator James H.
Lane, the new Senator from the new State of Kansas. Both these men had
commanded troops in the Mexican War, had faced mobs in their antislavery
careers; both expected the war to begin in Washington and were ready for
a last-ditch fight at the White House doors. Clay had sent his family to
Philadelphia, out of the war area, wore "three pistols and an Arkansas
tooth pick," while Jim Lane, "gaunt, tattered, uncombed and unshorn,"
wore "a rough rusty overcoat, a torn shirt, and suspenderless breeches."

He would growl, noted John Hay, "Baltimore will be laid in ashes," in a "husky, rasping, blood-curdling whisper." It was said that he "could stand up before five hundred men, two hundred and fifty of whom were ready to hang him to the next tree, and at the end of a half hour have them all cheering for him." With him now were gun fighters who had seen bloodshed on the Kansas border. Thus the Frontier Guards were at the White House. Mingled with adventure-hunting Jayhawkers were office-seekers, all sleeping on the carpets of the lower floor of the White House. At Willard's, Clay's battalion had rooms in a hotel that had seen better days; the ballroom now was a drill hall, "right, left, right, left."

"The White House is turned into barracks," wrote Hay. Alarmists and cranks flitted into the halls and corridors, demanded to see the President or whispered that they had information of plots, of attacks planned, of suspicious-looking steamers coming up the Potomac, of a mob that was to overwhelm the Executive Mansion, with picked men to seize and carry off the President. Hay and Major David Hunter were in charge of White House protection and guards. The Polish red-republican Count Gurowski, wild-eyed and growling, was among the guards, and an Italian exile, Vivaldi. Hay touring the house at midnight would see some of this band on duty, others quietly sleeping on the carpets of the East Room.

Three Potawatomi Indians in blankets and moccasins stepped in one day. "The Tycoon amused them immensely by airing the two or three Indian words he knew," noted Hay. "I was amused by his awkward efforts to make himself understood by speaking bad English . . . Where live now? When go back Iowa?"

As Lincoln lay in bed the night of the eighteenth, not yet asleep, John Hay came. Two very creditable women at the White House that evening had told of a young Virginian come into town that day for a new saddle. One of the women heard from him that he and a half-dozen other bold lads would "do a thing within forty-eight hours that would ring through the world." She told her story anxiously; perhaps she shouldn't have come, but she didn't want any harm done the President. "I told him the yarn," Hay wrote in his diary; "he quietly grinned."

Roger Pryor, the same firebrand whose balcony oratory had chimed with the taking of Sumter, was again on a balcony, now in Montgomery, crying with passion for "an immediate march on Washington." Albert Browne, reporting from Washington to Governor Andrew of Massachusetts, wrote: "The chances are that Virginia will go out and take the capital with her. . . . As matters stand ye chances are that ye next Congress of the United States will not meet at Washington."

Washington was hemmed in, its land and water approaches easy; the British in the 1812 war had no trouble taking it. Richmond and New Orleans newspapers were calling for its capture. The two great arsenals near by at Harper's Ferry and Norfolk were in the hands of Virginia troops. From the White House with a spyglass Confederate flags could be seen flying beyond on Virginia soil. "At night the camp-fires of the Confederates, assembling in force, could be seen on the Southern bank of the Potomac," wrote the journalist Ben Perley Poore. "It was not uncommon to meet on Pennsylvania Avenue a defiant Southerner openly wearing a large Virginia or South Carolina secession badge."

General Scott, at a little lunch with coffee served to the Cabinet around the President's green table, was asked about the defense of the Potomac below Washington. "What force is there at Fort Washington?" "I think, sir," he replied, in his precise military way, "I think, sir, that Fort Washington could be taken now with a bottle of whiskey. At last accounts, it was in charge of a single old soldier, who is entirely reliable when he is sober." The head of the army was cool, debonair, brave, loyal—and old, slow.

From the governors of Border States came warlike answers to Lincoln's dispatch asking for quotas of troops: "Kentucky will furnish no troops for the wicked purpose of subduing her sister Southern States," replied Governor Beriah Magoffin. "Your requisition, in my judgment," replied Jackson of Missouri, "is illegal, unconstitutional and revolutionary in its objects, inhuman and diabolical, and cannot be complied with." The Arkansas and Tennessee governors said they refused to join in "coercion" and "subjugation." Governor Letcher of Virginia replied, "You have chosen to inaugurate civil war," and he would meet the Lincoln Administration on that ground. Delaware would furnish one regiment. Governor Hicks of Maryland might assign four regiments to serve in their own State or for the defense of Washington.

President Davis at Montgomery announced that his Government would issue "letters of marque" giving authority to ships joining the Confederacy to seize United States vessels of commerce. Lincoln replied by proclaiming a blockade of ports of the seceded States. Vessels would be warned not to enter or leave Southern ports; failing to obey, they would be captured and sent to the nearest convenient Northern port. The forty wooden ships of the United States Navy then at hand would patrol 8,000 miles of seacoast— till there were more ships—and more. That was Lincoln's plan.

What was to happen now at Washington? At what moment would some free-going body of Southern troops ride into the capital, seize the city, and kidnap the Government? These questions were asked in Washington. Then and later this was regarded as an easy possibility. There were Southerners eager for the undertaking. Their wish ran with that of Leroy Pope Walker, Secretary of War at Montgomery, who in a balcony speech on the news from Sumter had said, "No man can tell where the war this day begun will end, but I will prophesy that the flag which now flaunts the breeze here will float over the dome of the old Capitol at Washington before the first of May."

At Gainesboro, Tennessee, a dummy figure labeled "LINCOLN" hung by a rope around the neck from an old courthouse with the inscription "May all abolitionists meet the same fate."

Each day in bureaus and departments at Washington came new resignations, Southerners leaving to go south to fight. On all sides were spies inter-threading North and South. Observers and reporters were free to come in or go out of Washington in any direction. Colonel Charles P. Stone, commanding thirty companies of volunteers raised in the District of Columbia, said these were the main defense of the national capital. The regular army "had already been distributed by the Southern sympathizers [under Buchanan] to the distant frontiers of the Indian country—Texas, Utah, New Mexico, Oregon and Washington Territory. Months would have been necessary to concentrate at Washington a force of 3,000 troops." Perhaps one-third of the regular-army total of 17,000 men and officers might soon be at hand to fight for the Government and its capital.

"Disaffection lurked, if it did not openly avow itself, in every department, and in every bureau, in every regiment and in every ship of war, in the post-office and in the custom-house, and in every legation and consulate from London to Calcutta," wrote Seward to Adams. "Of four thousand four hundred and seventy officers in the public service, civil and military, two thousand one hundred and fifty-four were representatives of states where the revolutionary movement was openly advocated and urged, even if not actually organized."

Lincoln later sketched the situation that week: "A disproportionate share of the Federal muskets and rifles had somehow found their way into these [seceded] States, and had been seized to be used against the government. Accumulations of public revenue lying within them had been seized for the same object. The navy was scattered in distant seas, leaving but a very small part of it within the immediate reach of the government. Officers of the Federal army and navy had resigned in great numbers; and of those resigning a large number had taken up arms against the government."

Thurlow Weed, arriving at the White House one morning to tell of danger to the navy yard at Norfolk, found that "Mr. Lincoln had driven out to visit some fortifications." When the next day he laid his information before Lincoln, the reply was, "Well, we can't afford to lose all those cannon; I'll go and see Father Welles myself." Which he did. And Welles sent an admiral who arrived just in time to see the navy yard highly illuminated at night, burning into ruins. And a few days later, troubled by a remark from Seward, Lincoln wrote Seward: "You astonish me by saying Mr. Weed understands there is some alienation, or enmity of feeling, on my part towards him. Nothing like it. I shall be glad to see him any time, and have wondered at not having seen him already."

On April 18 arrived 532 Pennsylvania boys from Pottsville, Lewistown, Reading, Allentown, whom Hay noted as "unlicked patriotism that has poured ragged and unarmed out of Pennsylvania." They had passed through Baltimore safely. Not so the 6th Massachusetts regiment the next day. As they marched from one station to another, changing trains, they met stones, bricks, pistols, from a crowd of Southern sympathizers. They answered with bullets. Four soldiers were killed, and twelve citizens.

Two by two the 6th Massachusetts marched up Pennsylvania Avenue that evening to the Capitol, in single file, their seventeen wounded on stretchers. Their dead at Baltimore were packed in ice and sent north for military burial and martyrs' monuments. The news of the street fighting, of heads broken with stones, of innocent bystanders meeting bullets, of taunts and howls and jeers, of shrieking women, went North and South; the war drums beat wilder.

The Mayor of Baltimore, George William Brown, and a committee called at the White House on Sunday morning, two days later, meeting with Lincoln, the Cabinet, and General Scott for a long conversation. The President agreed that no more troops should be sent through Baltimore if they could pass peaceably around it, the Baltimore officials promising to do their best to hold down the uprising people of their city.

As Lincoln began to write the committee a letter to this effect, he remarked, half in play, "If I grant you this concession, that no troops shall pass through the city, you will be back here tomorrow demanding that none shall be marched around it."

They left for the Baltimore two o'clock train, and then came back to the White House with a telegram that excitement was rising high in Baltimore on account of Northern soldiers approaching; the troops had arrived at Cockeysville, fourteen miles from Baltimore. They brought out the dispatch; it was from the president of the Baltimore & Ohio Railroad. The news caused Lincoln to send for Cabinet members and General Scott. After discussion, "The President at once, in the most decided way, urged the recall of the troops, saying he had no idea they would be there," ran Mayor Brown's statement to the public. "Lest there should be the slightest suspicion of bad faith on his part in summoning the Mayor to Washington and allowing troops to march on the city [Baltimore] during his [the Mayor's] absence, he [Lincoln] desired that the troops should, if it were practicable, be sent back at once to York or Harrisburg."

In the conversation of the day Mayor Brown had told Lincoln that Baltimore citizens regarded the proclamation calling for 75,000 troops as an act of war on the South and a violation of constitutional rights: "It was not surprising that a high-spirited people, holding such opinions, should resent the passage of Northern troops through their city." At these words, wrote Mayor Brown later, "Mr. Lincoln was greatly moved, and, springing up from his chair, walked backward and forward. He said, with great feeling, 'Mr. Brown, I am not a learned man! I am not a learned man!' that his proclamation had not been correctly understood; that he had no intention of bringing on war, but that his purpose was to defend the capital, which was in danger of being bombarded from the heights across the Potomac."

During the day's conference Mayor Brown was asked about an iron bridge on the Northern Central Railroad which had been disabled so that no trains could cross. "In my reply I addressed myself to the President," wrote Mayor Brown later, "and said, with much earnestness, that the disabling of this bridge, and of the other bridges, had been done by authority, and that it was a measure of protection to prevent bloodshed."

So now the railroad bridges between Washington and the North were down. Of the 75,000 men called for, a week ago, one Massachusetts regiment and five Pennsylvania companies had arrived. From the South came reports of a march on Washington; Beauregard, the hero of Sumter, would do this, that; he was coming with 10,000 men.

Now came word that the telegraph wires leading to the North were cut. The Baltimore telegraph office was in the hands of secessionists. The War Office said, "This stops all."

Now with mails stopped, railroads crippled, bridges down, telegraph wires dead, it was not easy in Washington to laugh away the prediction of the *New Orleans Picayune* that Virginia's secession would result in "the removal of Lincoln and his Cabinet, and whatever he can carry away, to the safer neighborhood of Harrisburg or Cincinnati—perhaps to Buffalo or Cleveland." Under command of Lee at Richmond in latter April were enough troops to take Washington had Lee believed immediate attack advisable. Lee's instructions for defense tactics drew the anger of Virginians, who telegraphed to Montgomery that President Davis was wanted at Richmond, that Lee temporized, feared collision, "wishes to repress enthusiasm of our people." A railroad superintendent telegraphed that they could carry 5,000 to 7,000 men 350 miles daily, and with Davis commanding, "One dash, and Lincoln is taken, the country saved, and the leader who does it will be immortalized."

More than idle wish or bluster lay back of the *Richmond Examiner's* declaring: "There is one wild shout of fierce resolve to capture Washington City, at all and every human hazard. The filthy cage of unclean birds must and will be purified by fire. . . . Our people can take it, and Scott the arch-traitor, and Lincoln the Beast, combined, cannot prevent it. The just indignation of an outraged and deeply injured people will teach the Illinois Ape to retrace his journey across the borders of the Free negro States still more rapidly than he came. . . . Many indeed will be the carcasses of dogs and caitiffs that will blacken the air upon the gallows, before the great work is accomplished. So let it be."

While Lincoln and his Administration were marooned in the little ten-mile-square District of Columbia surrounded by Slave States, the blame for it was put on Lincoln's "feeble" hands and a movement gained headway in New York for replacing Lincoln with a dictator. One George Law, engineer, railroad and canal builder, Panama Mail Steamship Company organizer and financier, stepped into the public eye with the stride and words of a man who could cut a Gordian knot, an executive who would go straight to the root of difficulties, saying it was demanded of the Government that it no longer permit traffic to be hindered at Baltimore. The lines of communication must be opened and kept so: "Unless this is done, the people will be compelled to take it into their own hands, let the consequences be what they may, and let them fall where they will."

Law added that this plain talk was not unkindly meant and assured the President that the Free States were behind the Administration. The *New York Times,* however, voiced a demand that George Law be made dictator, and it was evident that patience with Lincoln had completely run out among those who took part in this movement.

Nicolay and Hay noted that in greeting on May 1 a few 7th New York troops "The President, in the course of friendly conversation, spoke in a tone of amusement rather than harshness of the 'Times's' proposition to depose him; and said that just now the Government had three things to do: defend Washington, blockade the ports, and retake Government property. All possible dispatch was to be used in these matters, and it would be well if the people would cordially assist in this work before clamoring for more. The proclamation for calling out the troops, he said, was only two weeks old; no other people on earth could have surpassed what we had done in that time."

To Hay that week Lincoln talked about what seemed to him the key point of the hour: "For my own part, I consider the first necessity that is upon us, is of proving that popular government is not an absurdity. We must settle this question now,—whether in a free government the minority have the right to break it up whenever they choose. If we fail, it will go far to prove the incapability of the people to govern themselves. There may be one consideration used in stay of such final judgment, but that is not for us to use in advance. That is, that there exists in our case an instance of a vast and far-reaching disturbing element which the history of no other free nation will probably ever present. That, however, is not for us to say at present. Taking the government as we found it, we will see if the majority can preserve it."

Impatience was heard in the President's Cabinet, where Bates filed his written opinion that the Government seemed to lack force—"We frighten nobody, we hurt nobody"—and Chase on April 25 wrote to the President, "Let me beg you to remember that the disunionists have anticipated us in everything, and that as yet we have accomplished nothing but the destruction of our own property." Chase was in fear that a secession ordinance would be passed by the Maryland Legislature, the Baltimore customhouse be seized: "What next? Do not, I pray you, let this new success of treason be inaugurated in the presence of American troops. Save us from this new humiliation." In another letter, not to the President, Chase wrote a belief that the President in lieu of any policy had "merely the general notion of drifting, the Micawber policy of waiting for something to turn up."

Lincoln, however, was taking to himself one by one the powers of a dictator. He authorized a raid whereby at three o'clock in the afternoon of April 20 United States Marshals entered every major telegraph office in the Northern States and seized the originals of all telegrams sent and copies of all telegrams received during twelve months. Also the President dug into the Treasury of the United States for millions of dollars—without due and required authority of Congress. At a meeting held that Sunday of April 21 in the Navy Department away from any spies and all observers in the White House, the Cabinet members joined with Lincoln in the placing of immense funds.

"It became necessary for me to choose," said Lincoln later, "whether I should let the government fall at once into ruin, or whether . . . availing myself of the broader powers conferred by the Constitution in cases of insurrection, I would make an effort to save it." Also he detailed what he did that Sunday, as a man of authority, as the head of a Government nearly ready to go down: "I directed that an armed revenue cutter should proceed to sea, to afford protection to the commercial marine and especially the California treasure-ships then on their way to this coast. I also directed the commandant of the navy-yard at Boston to purchase, or charter, and arm as quickly as possible, five steamships for purposes of public defense." He directed three other port officials to get armed steamers. He named Governor Morgan of New York, William M. Evarts, Moses H. Grinnell, to be "especially empowered" to act for the Navy Department in forwarding troops and supplies. "I authorized and directed the Secretary of the Treasury to advance, without requiring security, two millions of dollars of public money to John A. Dix, George Opdyke, and Richard M. Blatchford, of New York, to be used by them in meeting requisitions necessary for the defense and support of the government, requiring them only to act without compensation, and to report their transactions when duly called upon."

These government money orders for million-dollar amounts Lincoln sent by private messengers, who went by way of Wheeling and Pittsburgh to New York, pursuing, as Lincoln said, "a circuitous way to the seaboard cities, inland, across the States of Pennsylvania and Ohio and the northern lakes."

A long week for the President ended with a long Sunday of hard work on April 21. Monday came—and no troops. The navy-yard commandant at Washington, Franklin Buchanan, resigned, taking with him nearly all his staff. John B. Magruder, commanding the battery of artillery most relied on for Washington defense, also resigned, Lincoln saying when told the news, "Only three days ago Magruder came voluntarily to me in this room, and with his own lips and in my presence repeated over and over again his asseverations and protestations of loyalty and fidelity."

For hundreds of Southern veterans of service in government departments it was moving day. Something told them they belonged farther south. Their papers from home reported an established Southern Confederacy and military forces that would soon capture Washington. "Lincoln the Usurper sleeps already with soldiers at his gate," said the Charleston Mercury. "Seeking the sword, in spite of all moral or constitutional restraints and obligations, he may perish by the sword." Of the clerks departing southward some said, "We'll be back in a few weeks." Perley Poore wrote, "An eloquent clergyman, among those who went to Richmond, left behind him in the cellar of his house, a favorite cat, with what he judged would be a three weeks' supply of water and provisions, so confident was he that President Davis would, within that time, occupy the White House."

Henry Villard, *New York Herald* correspondent, who had hired a horse at $5 a day and feed, rode on a leather saddle into Washington to find Willard's Hotel closed, its thousand guests dwindled to forty. Other hotels were empty. On Pennsylvania Avenue he could count on his fingers the people in sight. Many stores had closed their doors. "The telegraph did not work, the mails did not arrive or depart. . . . The Government remained without any intelligence from any quarter for several days. . . . It was as though the government of a great nation had been suddenly removed to an island in mid-ocean in a state of entire isolation."

Under these conditions it was interesting though not momentous news Villard brought Lincoln, that James Gordon Bennett on the day after Sumter fell had taken Villard to his home for dinner and told him to carry the message to Lincoln that "the *Herald* would hereafter be unconditionally for the radical suppression of the Rebellion by force of arms, and in the shortest possible time, and would advocate and support any war measure by the Government and Congress." Villard gave the added and more important news to Lincoln that "the *Herald* was obliged to make this complete change in its attitude, there having been ominous signs for some days in New York of danger of mob violence to the paper."

Off Annapolis troopships had arrived, General Scott reported to the President: "Their landing will be opposed by the citizens." Also, "the rails on the Annapolis road [twenty miles] have been taken up." Also, from 1,500 to 2,000 Virginia troops were building batteries four miles below Mount Vernon near a narrow neck of the Potomac River. Also, an equal force of Virginia troops was gathering on two sides of the river to attack Fort Washington. Also, "extra cars went up yesterday to bring down from Harper's Ferry about 2,000 other troops to join in a general attack on this capital." The General closed this Monday report, "I feel confident we can defend the Capitol, the arsenal, and all the executive buildings [seven] against 10,000 troops."

In the Treasury building now were howitzers. At the Mint were howitzers. In the marble corridors of the Capitol building were howitzers, muskets, provisions, munitions of war. In the Senate chamber slept the 6th Massachusetts boys. In the House of Representatives slept the Pennsylvania boys from Reading, Pottsville, Allentown, and Lewistown. The Georgetown flour-mills supply, 25,000 barrels, was seized as a war necessity. At each Capitol doorway was a ten-foot barricade of sandbags, cement barrels, iron plate.

Again Baltimore was heard from in thirty-five delegates of the Young Men's Christian Association. The Reverend R. Fuller, spokesman, told Lincoln that his duty as a Christian statesman was to "recognize the independence of the Southern States." Lincoln looked the spokesman and delegation over and remarked: "You, gentlemen, come here to me and ask for peace on any terms, and yet have no words of condemnation for those who are making war on us. You express great horror of bloodshed, and yet would not lay a straw in the way of those who are organizing in Virginia and elsewhere to capture this city. . . . You would have me break my oath and surrender the government without a blow. There is no Washington in that—no Jackson in that—there is no manhood or honor in that." He had no desire to invade the South. But he had to have troops to defend the capital and by geography and mathematics the troops had to cross Maryland. "Our men are not moles, and cannot dig under the earth; they are not birds and cannot fly through the air. There is no way but to march across, and that they must do. But in doing this there is no need of collision. Keep your rowdies in Baltimore and there will be no bloodshed. Go home and tell your people that if they will not attack us, we will not attack them; but if they do attack us, we will return it, and that severely."

And with these words in their ears the delegation left. The next day the Reverend Mr. Fuller wrote to Secretary Chase as a fellow churchman: "From Mr. Lincoln nothing is to be hoped, except as you can influence him. . . . I marked the President closely. Genial and jovial, he is wholly inaccessible to Christian appeals, and his egotism will forever prevent his comprehending what patriotism means."

Meanwhile newspaper items in the North were creating impressions of Lincoln: "President Lincoln said to a Baltimore deputation that if the passage of United States troops was again obstructed he would lay their city in ashes. One of the deputation said that 75,000 Marylanders would contest the passage of troops over her soil. To this the President said that he supposed there was room enough in her soil to bury 75,000."

One news-writer reported Lincoln's saying to a pair of the Fuller delegation, by way of illustration: "You have all heard of the Irishman who, when a fellow was cutting his throat with a blunt razor, complained that he *haggled* it. Now, if I can't have troops direct through Maryland, and must have them all the way round by water, or marched across out-of-the-way territory, I shall be *haggled*."

And now by some chance on the next day of April 23 a little mail arrived—and newspapers. Anderson and his garrison had arrived in New York and the town had gone wild over them! A Union Square mass meeting with 50,000 people shouting for the Union! Processions, speeches, enlistments of more men than the President called for! Million-dollar appropriations for the war! The Governor of Rhode Island sailing with troops and guns for Washington! The famous crack regiment, the dandy 7th of New York, had marched down Broadway between vast walls of living people, cheering crowds, heading south for Washington!

So the news ran. And out of it all nothing had reached Washington except the few boys now sleeping on their guns in the Capitol building. "I saw the President repeatedly," wrote Villard, "and he fairly groaned at the inexplicable delay of help."

"I think I saw three vessels go up to the Navy Yard just now," the

President scribbled to the Secretary of the Navy. "Will you please send down and learn what they are?"

On the afternoon of April 23 Lincoln was alone in his office in the White House—or believed he was alone, though John Hay, quiet and unobtrusive, was there. And Hay saw Lincoln "after walking the floor alone in silent thought for nearly half an hour," stop at a window and gaze long and wistfully down the Potomac in the direction of the expected ships. And as he gazed he broke out with irrepressible anguish in the repeated exclamation "Why don't they come! Why don't they come!"

By rail, wagon, horse, the son-in-law of Governor William A. Buckingham of Connecticut arrived at the White House to deliver the message that to the last man and the last dollar Connecticut would support the Union. "Mr. Lincoln was alone," noted this messenger, "seated in his business room upstairs, looking toward Arlington Heights through a widely opened window. Against the casement stood a very long spyglass which he had evidently just been using. I gave him all the information I could, from what I had seen and heard during my journey. He seemed depressed beyond measure as he asked slowly and with great emphasis, 'What *is* the North about? Do they *know* our condition?' I said, 'No, they certainly did not when I left.' This was true enough."

The Connecticut messenger then told Lincoln that he had his pockets full of money but could buy nothing with it in Washington: "New York city bank note values in Washington had suddenly and totally departed. They were good for their weight in paper, and no more. I remarked to the President that I had not a cent though my pockets were full of money. He instantly perceived my meaning, and kindly put me in possession of such an amount of specie as I desired."

On the next day, April 24, when as yet no troops had arrived, when Seward's messengers sent out by the dozen had not returned, wounded soldiers and officers of the 6th Massachusetts came to see the White House and the President. Lincoln spoke thanks to them for brave service, and wandered in his talk into the mystery of why the North allowed its Government to be isolated, imprisoned. It was a sad, ironic tone, noted Hay, in which he told them: "I don't believe there is any North! The Seventh Regiment is a myth! Rhode Island is not known in our geography any longer! You are the only Northern realities!"

A locomotive whistle shrieking hallelujah the next day, April 25, was followed by the marching—left, right, left, right—up Pennsylvania Avenue of the 7th New York. Then came 1,200 Rhode Islanders, and the Butler Brigade of 1,200 from Massachusetts. A crippled locomotive at Annapolis had been repaired by Massachusetts mechanics; volunteer tracklayers put the road from Annapolis in running order again. A troop route to the North had been found. In a few days Washington had 10,000 defense troops. Now, for a time, Lincoln knew that the capital would still be at Washington.

With the Butler Brigade had arrived Carl Schurz, the new Spanish

Minister, with pistols in his baggage and fight in his eyes. At the White House he told Lincoln it was revealed to him in his Wisconsin home that the Government needed every man at Washington and his duty was to hurry there. They talked long, and as Schurz reported it later: "He told

Headquarters Frontier Guard,

Washington City, April 27, 1861.

To Hon. S. Cameron. *Secretary of War*:

Sir: *In consequence of the arrival of large numbers of troops in this city, I am satisfied the emergency has ceased that called our company into service.*

If you concur in this opinion, I should be pleased to receive authority from you to disband said company, and to honorably discharge the members thereof from the service.

Very truly,

J. H. Lane

Capt Comdg.

War Department. April 27, 1861.

Gen. James H. Lane

Sir: *In reply to your letter of this day's date, stating that, in consequence of the arrival of large numbers of troops in this city, the emergency has ceased which called the company commanded by you into service, and that you would be pleased, therefore, to have authority to disband your company, and have an honorable discharge from service for it.*

Concurring fully with you, I readily grant you the authority asked for, and, in doing so, I beg to extend to you, and through you to the men under your command, the assurance of my high appreciation of the very prompt and patriotic manner in which your company was organized for the defence of the Capital, and the very efficient services rendered by it during the time of its existence.

Very respectfully,

Simon Cameron

Cheerfully approved

A. Lincoln

The White House defenders named the Headquarters Frontier Guard are mustered out, the President "cheerfully" approving. The ornate upper part of this document had a steel engraving of the White House, the lower section the signatures of J. H. Lane as "Capt." with an attest by M. W. Delahay as "1st Lieut." Original in the Barrett collection.

me of an incident characteristic of the situation, which I wish I could repeat in his own language. I give only the substance.

"One afternoon after he had issued his call for troops, he sat alone in this room, and a feeling came over him as if he were utterly deserted and helpless. He thought any moderately strong body of secessionist troops, if there were any in the neighborhood, might come over the 'long bridge' across the Potomac, and just take him and the members of the Cabinet—the whole lot of them. Then he suddenly heard a sound like the boom of a cannon. 'There they are!' he said to himself. He expected every moment somebody would rush in with the report of an attack. The White House attendants, whom he interrogated, had heard nothing. But nobody came, and all remained still.

"Then he thought he would look after the thing himself. So he walked out, and walked, and walked, until he got to the Arsenal. There he found the doors all open, and not a soul to guard them. Anybody might have gone in and helped himself to the arms. There was perfect solitude and stillness all around. Then he walked back to the White House without noticing the slightest sign of disturbance. He met a few persons on the way, some of whom he asked whether they had not heard something like the boom of a cannon. Nobody had heard anything, and so he supposed it must have been a freak of his imagination."

CHAPTER 9

JEFFERSON DAVIS—HIS GOVERNMENT

THE Confederate Government, strengthened by the finally seceded States of Arkansas, Tennessee, North Carolina, and Texas, had moved the last week in May from Montgomery, Alabama, to Richmond, Virginia, to be nearer the Border States and the expected heavy fighting. Into Richmond streamed regiments from all parts of the South. The cry in the South, "On to Washington!" snarled straight into the cry from the North, "On to Richmond!"

Among troops at Richmond were farmers and hillmen who never owned a slave nor an acre of ground, and young men from the First Families where a thousand acres and a hundred slaves was the unit. Dapper companies with shining blouses, brass buttons, uniform rifles of recent make, were regimented with other companies in butternut jeans, carrying shotguns and squirrel rifles.

"I was introduced to several privates by their captain, who told me they were worth from $100,000 to a half million dollars each," wrote J. B. Jones, diarist in the Richmond War Department. "These rich young men were dressed in coarse, gray homespun!"

From the Potomac River to the Gulf Coast and out where the Rio Grande trickled over New Mexico ran the recruiting ground of this Confederate Army. Its line zigzagged 1,500 miles from Chesapeake Bay through Kentucky and out to the corners of Kansas. Its brain and will centered in the capitol, the executive mansion, the departments, at Richmond. Its chief weapon of defense was an army of 100,000 troops. The controls of this Government were out of the hands of those who had first given it breath and fire. Rhett of the True Perpetual Separationists was now only a member of the Confederate Congress. The movement to elect him President and the efforts to appoint him Secretary of War had both failed. Yancey was shelved as a Commissioner to European nations, with no power to act and no special instructions; he was out of the way.

Down in Georgia and Alabama, Russell of the London *Times* asked why this outpouring of men from the South to test their blood against the North. "I am not prepared to say they are right or wrong," he wrote as to secession and Southern independence, "but I am convinced that the South can only be forced back by such a conquest as that which laid Poland prostrate at the feet of Russia." He saw the Southern women a factor in enlistments: "Here are many men who would willingly stand aside if they could, and see the battle between the Yankees, whom they hate, and the Secessionists. But there are no women in this party. Woe betide the Northern Pyrrhus whose head is within reach of a Southern tile and a Southern woman's arm."

Between Charleston and Savannah, wrote Russell: "Our fellow passengers were all full of politics—the pretty women being the fiercest of all— no! the least good-looking were the most bitterly patriotic, as if they hoped to talk themselves into husbands by the most unfeminine expressions toward the Yankees." In Charleston both sexes and all ages were for the war. "Secession is the fashion here. Young ladies sing for it; old ladies pray for it; young men are dying to fight for it; old men are ready to demonstrate it." Russell heard of a Mobile gentleman having a letter from his daughter: "She informs him she has been elected vivandière to a New Orleans regiment, with which she intends to push on to Washington and get a lock of Abe Lincoln's hair." Thus Russell in the Deep South, while J. B. Jones wrote in Richmond: "The ladies are postponing all engagements until their lovers have fought the Yankees. Their influence is great."

A new and a young Government it was at Richmond. "Where will I find the State Department?" an Englishman asked Robert Toombs, Secretary of State. "In my hat, sir," replied Toombs, "and the archives in my coat pocket." It was a good Toombs answer. He was a contradictory man, secondarily a politician and lawyer and firstly rather a gustatory artist and philosopher. It was his way and whim to oppose Stephens and win secession and then manage to get his old crony Stephens placed in high power.

The doctrine of secession and the heat of rebellion were in Toombs's

JEFFERSON DAVIS—HIS GOVERNMENT   239

May note of instructions to Confederate Commissioners Yancey, Rost, and others in Europe. "The President of the United States affects to consider that the Federal Union is still legally and unconstitutionally unbroken," read Toombs's note. "It matters not to him that, with the exception of three or four forts still occupied by United States troops, the Federal Government of the United States does not exercise jurisdiction of any kind over one inch of soil in the Confederate States. He still claims to be our ruler, and insists that he has the right to enforce our obedience. For this avowed purpose, he usurps the authority to call out large armies, make gigantic military preparations, equip powerful fleets, order the blockade of 2,000 miles of seacoast, and generally assume and exercise by himself the war-making power, which the Constitution that he pretends to be so anxious to preserve and force upon 12,000,000 people expressly denies to him. . . . War is declared and is now being carried on by the most flagrant violation of every principle, of every provision, and every mandate which that Constitution contains. . . . The authorized exponents of the sentiments of the party of which Mr. Lincoln is the leader, and whose policy he has resolved to carry out, avow that it is the purpose of the war to subjugate the Confederate States, spoliate the property of our citizens, sack and burn our cities and exterminate our citizens; and some are so lost to shame, so dead to every sense of humanity and civilization, as to stimulate the basest passions of those whom they desire to enlist by giving glowing allusions to the beauty of our women who are to become the prey of an infuriate soldiery."

Thus the impulsive Toombs, who was soon to resign and take to the camp and battlefield. He should have been Secretary of War, said many, but that place went to Leroy Pope Walker of Alabama, named by Yancey as his choice for the appointment by President Davis. Walker was a lawyer and politician, harassed by technical matters of how a people with ports restricted or closed, and with no gun nor arms factories nor powder mills, should create those requisites. He was soon to step from office to field service. Curiously enough, this Confederate War Department at Richmond took on as Acting Assistant Secretary of War one Albert Taylor Bledsoe, a West Point graduate who had become a Protestant Episcopal clergyman, later a professor of mathematics, though part of his ten years as a practicing lawyer was spent in Springfield, Illinois, with an office adjoining that of Lincoln & Herndon.

The finance head, Christopher Gustavus Memminger, an orphan-asylum boy, a German Lutheran born in Württemberg, a lawyer and politician, was the one South Carolina man in the Cabinet. He arranged with Gazaway B. Lamar, the Southern secessionist president of the Bank of the Republic in New York, for a contract with the American Bank Note Company to engrave and print in New York the bonds and treasury notes of the Confederacy. "The work was handsomely executed on the best of bank note and bond paper," wrote Memminger, "but with all the precaution taken by Mr. Lamar, the entire issue fell into the hands of the Federal Government and was seized as contraband of war." Engravers rushed from Europe were therefore to direct the printing of Confederate money on paper brought from Baltimore by agents who ran the Federal picket lines.

The Navy head was Stephen R. Mallory of Florida, once chairman of the Committee on Naval Affairs of the United States Senate, and having, as President Davis wrote, "for a landsman much knowledge of nautical affairs." Mallory was the one Roman Catholic of the Cabinet. The one Jew was Judah P. Benjamin of New Orleans, whose wife was a French Roman Catholic. He had twice been elected United States Senator from Louisiana, and in his advocacy of the legal grounds for slavery once came close to a duel with Jefferson Davis, the affair cooling down when Davis apologized for harsh words spoken; once when defending slavery Benjamin was classified by Senator Wade of Ohio as "a Hebrew with Egyptian principles." He had a rare legal mind, and as Attorney General and later as Secretary of State was one of the few trusted helpers of President Davis, toiled in his Richmond office from eight in the morning till past midnight, and was sometimes referred to as "the brains of the Confederacy." The one Texan in the Cabinet was the Postmaster General, J. H. Reagan, former Congressman, Indian-fighter, and Southwestern pioneer.

At the helm of this Cabinet was a strange, impressive figure chosen chiefly because he stood foremost of trained Southern statesmen as a military authority who should understand how to make war, because he stood in the public eye as a moderate rather than a radical secessionist, and because of rare personal integrity and distinctively Southern qualities. This was the Mississippi cotton planter, West Point graduate, Black Hawk War lieutenant, Mexican War veteran wounded in service, United States Senator, Secretary of War under the Pierce Administration, orator, horseman, man of fate—Jefferson Davis.

He and Lincoln were to feel out each other's strength as archantagonists before a clamorous world. Each would stand forth as a target and a symbol. Both were born in Kentucky, Davis a year earlier than Lincoln, one as a child carried north to free soil, the other as a suckling babe taken to the lower South. Each was a treader of lonely rooms enveloped by darkness broken with few and rare stars. The two of them carried under their hats the chief bewildering contradictions gathered around the words "aristocracy" and "democracy."

To the Confederate Congress at Montgomery, Davis said that he had convened it sooner than intended for action on "the declaration of war made against this Confederacy by Abraham Lincoln, the President of the United States. . . . In this extraordinary production, that high functionary affects total ignorance of the existence of an independent Government . . . over seven sovereign States, over more than five millions of people, and over a territory whose area exceeds half a million of square miles."

Lincoln's army of 75,000 volunteers Davis termed a posse comitatus to round up 5,000,000 outlaws, and in the "singular document" calling for that army "the President was usurping a power granted exclusively to Congress."

Of the other proclamation of Lincoln, announcing a blockade of Southern ports and threatening to punish as pirates those who under Confederate authority molested United States vessels, Davis said "it would seem incredible that it could have been issued by authority . . . it is hard to believe it could have emanated from a President of the United States."

These were opening verbal shots from Davis at Lincoln. He would coldly and with studied politeness at intervals point to Lincoln as an ignorant usurper and a bloodthirsty despot, while Lincoln, in the logic of his case, would refuse to acknowledge that a Confederate Government existed or that it had a constitutionally elected President named Davis. The roles of the two required that Davis on behalf of his people should, if he could, plaster Lincoln with infamy, while Lincoln must speak and write as though Davis were a nobody, not even the ghost of a glimmering hope.

The grandfather of Jefferson Davis was a Welsh peasant who arrived in Philadelphia with little more than a shirt to his back. Among his kinsmen was a John Davis who could not sign his name, who made his X-mark. They had no shield nor escutcheon, and their clan had lived by the labor of their hands; the family name of David was changed in America to that of Davis. On the one rare occasion when Jefferson Davis made for record a statement relating his ancestry, he began it: "Three brothers came to America from Wales in the early part of the eighteenth century. They settled in Philadelphia. The youngest of the brothers, Evan Davis, removed to Georgia, then a colony of Great Britain. He was the grandfather of Jefferson Davis. He married a widow, whose family name was Emory. By her he had one son, Samuel Davis, the father of Jefferson Davis." The details were scant. The genealogy faded into the short and simple annals of the poor, of the yeomanry of Europe who lived from year to year by selling their labor to those who would buy it.

Samuel Davis fought in the Revolutionary War, commanding a company of horsemen he recruited, and married Miss Jane Cook, a South Carolina woman of Scotch-Irish blood. They farmed a tract of wild land near Augusta, Georgia, then moved in 1792 five hundred miles north to Kentucky wilderness in Christian County, where for more than seventeen years they farmed 600 acres, raised tobacco, corn, wheat, horses, where were born the most of ten children given Bible names—Joseph, Samuel, Benjamin, Isaac—till the tenth child came in 1808 and was named after the great President, Jefferson. The father, a hard-shell Baptist and a Democrat, "grave and stoical," worked in the fields and at the barns alongside three or four slaves they owned. The baby Jefferson nursed at his mother's breast when in 1809 they moved southward a thousand miles, toward prosperous cotton lands, into Bayou Teche, Louisiana. From there they moved northward three hundred miles to their Poplar Grove farm near Woodville, Mississippi, where they stayed long, and as the older children married each was given a Negro slave as a wedding present.

At seven years of age his hard-shell Baptist father sent Jefferson with friends, with Negroes and pack mules, on a thousand-mile ride northward to enter the Roman Catholic St. Thomas Aquinas, in Washington County, Kentucky. There he asked venerable Father Wilson to let him become a Catholic. The Father was kind, told him to wait and learn. Of these two years at the Catholic seminary he said later, "I had been sent so young to school, and far from home without my mother's knowledge or consent, that she became very impatient for my return." Somewhat better days had come to the family and the boy grew up in the planter aristocracy culture. Once when he rebelled at going to school his father said he could not be idle and must work either with head or with hands. For two days he carried a bag with a cotton-picking gang, and as he told of it years afterward, "The heat of the sun and the physical labor, in conjunction with the implied equality with the other cotton pickers, convinced me that school was the lesser evil." From then on he looked on manual labor as giving a man an "implied equality" with others of a lower social class.

By this time his brother Joseph, twenty-four years older, had become a lawyer and a large landholder, soon to acquire reputation as one of the richest planters in the South. The big brother sent him to Transylvania University at Lexington, Kentucky, then got him an appointment as a cadet at West Point, where the boy said he would stay a year and then go to the University of Virginia. The boy, however, liked West Point, decided to be a soldier for life, stayed four years and graduated. For seven years he served, drilled, fought Indians and pranked at army posts in Wisconsin and Illinois, took a hand in the Black Hawk War, and had personal charge of the arrested rebel chief of the red men. Always on duty with him was his devoted manservant, the Negro slave James Pemberton.

At Transylvania when seventeen Jefferson had replied to a sister's letter telling him of his father's death: "The intelligence contained in yours was more than sufficient to mar the satisfaction of hearing from anyone. You must imagine, I cannot describe, the shock my feelings sustained at the sad intelligence." This formal manner, this icy perfection, was to stay with him. One of the rare times he dropped it was in his love letters to Sarah Knox Taylor, the sixteen-year-old daughter of Colonel Zachary Taylor at Fort Crawford, Wisconsin. "By dreams I have been lately almost crazy, for they were of you," he wrote to her, and again: "Kind, dear letter! I have kissed it often and often, and it has driven many mad notions from my brain." She was too young to marry, the father frowned; he disapproved of Davis, a soldier without a fortune, for a husband. But Miss Taylor visited a Kentucky aunt, the young Lieutenant resigned from the Army, the couple were married in Kentucky and went to Mississippi near Vicksburg, to Brierfield, an 800-acre plantation given them by Joseph Davis with fourteen Negro slaves on credit.

A summer of rich joys passed for the young couple. Then their plans were shattered. Malarial fever brought both of them down. In six weeks the bride of three months died in a delirium, singing an old hymn, "Fairy Bells," that she had from her mother. Her husband roused enough strength to rise from his bed and walk to her room to see her in her last moments, though she was too far gone to know his face or voice.

She had always said, it was recalled, that she would die young. He would probably follow her, said the doctors, but slowly he came out of it, racked and shaken, friends saying that in the after years he never lost the look of a fever convalescent. He sailed to Havana, Cuba, rested. He traveled to Washington, talked and drank with old West Point comrades who were rising in political power.

Then back in Mississippi, Jefferson Davis for ten years rested, read books by the shelf, learned all that approved literature could give him, held long discussions with his brother Joseph about history, Greek and Roman slavery, the latest views in the *National Intelligencer* and the New Orleans and New York newspapers. Jefferson read aloud to his brother the debates in the *Congressional Globe.* Joseph was fast becoming a millionaire, and the extent of their acres and slaves and ready cash, their personal abilities and social connections, were gradually placing these two grandsons of an illiterate Welsh peasant in the high exclusive circles of the Southern planter aristocracy. They belonged furthermore with that minority of large planters who kept no lash for their slaves, it was said, and maintained an exceptional decency and order. No nicknames were permitted slaves; James Pemberton was addressed as "James."

One visitor gave the tone of their establishment in its hospitality: "Your coffee in the morning before sunrise, little stews and soporifics at night, and warm footbaths if you have a cold. Bouquets of fresh flowers and mint juleps sent to your room, a horse and saddle at your disposal. Everything free and easy and cheerful and cordial . . . crowded with the roses of joy and hope." The Davis brothers took long horseback rides, hunted wild game and fowl, Jefferson once killing an alligator. The planter's life had isolation, half-barbaric charms "separated by a wide interval from the modern ideas of Europe," according to Russell of the London *Times,* who found the planter "a denomadised Arab," an Arab who had stopped wandering yet was still an Arab, who had "fixed himself with horses and slaves in a fertile spot, where he guards his women with Oriental care, exercises patriarchal sway, and is at once fierce, tender, and hospitable."

As a distinguished author writing for the foremost journal of the British imperialist class, Russell was an invited and honored guest at several of the largest and most distinctive plantations of the South, and noted the inner life of the planter's household as exceedingly charming "because one is astonished to find the graces and accomplishments of womanhood displayed in a scene which has a certain sort of savage rudeness about it after all, and where all kinds of incongruous accidents are visible in the service of the table, in the furniture, in the house, in its decorations, menials, and surrounding scenery."

An hour's ride from The Hurricane or Brierfield, at Natchez or Vicksburg, were arriving and departing steamboats, wharves and roustabouts, slave auctions, barrooms, brothels, high and low gambling-houses, and a roaring stream of people who earned or stole their livings. Jefferson Davis had done little or none of either; of growth from personal earning and struggling he had little. He had intellect, courage, many resources of personality, lived sparely as to food, drink, tobacco, yet lacked the sagacity to know that on some occasions when he believed he was holding fast to his personal integrity he was to others merely a marvel of obstinacy.

He could argue down other men and see them fumble as they failed to answer him, but what went on in the other man's mind he did not know or could not guess, for he had never formed the habit of trying to get inside other men in that way. If he said Yes and they said No or Perhaps, then they were wrong or queer and he was still right, and he would not dig with inquiry into why they had said No or Perhaps. One of his Welsh Quaker ancestors may have been related to the Quaker whom Ben Franklin quoted as saying to his wife, "Sometimes I think that all the world is queer but thee and me and sometimes I think thee is a little queer."

The older brother one day brought to the plantation Miss Varina Howell, a seventeen-year-old girl of a well-to-do planter family at Natchez, with soft liquid eyes, large curved eyebrows, with grace of speech and swift decisions; she was saved from mere prettiness by angular cheekbones and a full-lipped mournful mouth. She stood at windows of the Joseph Davis mansion and looked out on a long garden of rare roses and shrubs, flanked by eight acres of peach, fig, and apple trees. She stood at a high window overlooking the panoramic Mississippi River flowing a yellowish streak through gray forest. And she asked Joseph Davis why he named the place The Hurricane when people generally called it Davis Bend. "Yes," he said, "that is what people in Vicksburg call it but to me," and his eyes dimmed, "it will always be The Hurricane. Much has happened to give it that name—two children dead, two fine boys, a wife's health broken completely, and a storm that cost nearly all of us our lives as it shook the house down over our heads—that's enough surely to give it its name." Then a shortness of breath took him and he would say no more.

Of Jefferson Davis's twelve blooded saddle horses he chose a dark bay for Varina and they took long rides, and brother Joseph never overstayed in their company and left the two of them to get at each other. To her mother Varina Howell wrote her impression: "I do not know whether this Mr. Jefferson Davis is young or old. He looks both at times; but I believe he is old, for from what I hear he is only two years younger than you are. He impresses me as a remarkable kind of man, but of uncertain temper, and has a way of taking for granted that everybody agrees with him when he expresses an opinion, which offends me; yet he is most agreeable and has a peculiarly sweet voice and a winning manner of asserting himself. The fact is, he is the kind of person I should expect to rescue one from a mad dog at any risk, but to insist upon a stoical indifference to the fright afterward."

She was nineteen and he thirty-seven when they married, and testimonies ran that she was the rare and perfect wife of a difficult man. When he was away she could write him that it was lonely for her "and I wish you had never loved me, and then I should not have encouraged myself to thinking of you . . . if you cannot come at least write more often . . . have more charity for me, dearest, and set me a better example." She was health to him physically and mentally, in loyalty a tigress.

She followed him to Washington and shrank with horror when for the first time her husband was publicly called a scrub aristocrat. Discussing a pay-increase bill, Davis said "a common blacksmith or tailor" could not do the delicate work required of military engineers. Congressman Andrew Johnson of Tennessee, a former tailor, rose with the taunt that "an illegitimate, swaggering, bastard, scrub aristocracy" assumed to know much, but shorn of its pretensions had "neither talents nor information."

Against Varina's wishes her husband resigned from Congress and went away to the Mexican War, colonel of a regiment, the Mississippi Rifles, forming a flying-wedge V at Buena Vista that swung victory, taking a foot wound that put him on crutches for two years, confirming his belief that he was born to lead men in war. Pale and emaciated, he stood on his crutches at banquets in his honor in New Orleans, Natchez, Vicksburg, and tried to answer toasts that he was the idol of Mississippi, that when he had led his men sword in hand at Buena Vista, when he had pressed on with a broken foot and a boot filled with blood, he had inscribed his name high in the annals of war.

Crowds cheered him, Whigs and Democrats showered praise on him. In less than sixty days Governor A. G. Brown appointed him to the United States Senate. Not long after, another Mexican War hero, General John A. Quitman, who as a radical and violent secessionist stood close to Rhett and Yancey, was given a banquet, a private affair at which Southern steel and fire should find voice. One toast proclaimed "Colonel Jeff Davis, the Game Cock of the South" and another "Jeff Davis, the President of the Southern Confederacy," while Jeff Davis sat cold as marble. Thus ran the reports from mouth to mouth, and when they were carried to Davis with intimations that he was a secessionist he said, "To such a person I will make answer in one word and that a monosyllable," which was his way of saying, "It's a lie."

His national reputation in politics began with his service in the United States Senate in 1847, his clashes with Douglas, his denials of secession purposes clouded by arguments that States had a constitutional right to secede if and when it became necessary for their self-respect. After three years in the Senate he resigned to run for Governor of Mississippi, fell sick with dyspepsia, nervous attacks, and an inflamed eye, was defeated, and took up life again as a cotton planter in Brierfield. He had plenty to think about, could recollect Senator Sumner's repudiating the Fugitive Slave Law: "Be admonished, Sirs, by the words of Oriental piety: 'Beware of the groans of the wounded soul, oppress not to the uttermost a single heart, for a solitary sigh has power to overset a whole world.' Slavery! It is a crime against heaven and against God," and the reply from Clemens of Alabama begging no one to answer Sumner, as "The ravings of a maniac may sometimes do harm but the barking of a puppy never did any harm."

In his house and fields near by were the black men and women; they outnumbered the whites ten to one on the big plantations; and Sumner was telling them they were the human equals of the whites; Sumner was saying they should be set free; a horde of vagrant lecturers supported by moneyed men of the North were saying the same as Sumner. How far could this go without the Southern planters' rebelling and setting up their own government? Davis was asking that. In Santo Domingo the slaves had risen and slaughtered their masters.

What could result from this growing outcry that the South was barbaric in holding to slavery while the other civilized nations had abolished it? Could a solid array of Southern States be welded into a nation that would take its place among the powers of the earth? Davis played with that idea. It was complicated.

In Congress Colonel W. H. Bissell of Illinois had said in 1850 that the State of Illinois had sent nine regiments to Mexico, though only four were required, "and if it becomes necessary to put down secession and rebellion she will furnish four times nine regiments!" Bissell had gone further in the same speech, to say that Davis's command at Buena Vista was a mile and a half away from where the battle raged, whereupon Davis challenged Bissell to a duel, and Bissell for weapons chose muskets loaded with ball and buckshot at fifteen paces, wrote his last will and testament, and said he would be ready for Davis next morning to shoot it out. Friends and seconds stepped in; Bissell explained that his remarks alluded to another part of the battle than Davis inferred and he was not reflecting on Davis's personal bravery. These points satisfying Davis, the duel was canceled.

By now Varina Davis had heard of the will her husband wrote when he went off to the Mexican War. On the request of his brother, who had not yet given him clear title to Brierfield, he named his wife and sisters to share his Brierfield estate equally. For this Varina Davis hated her husband's brother and told him so. A breach began widening between Jefferson and Joseph, of whom Jefferson had written, "Materially and intellectually, I was more indebted to him than any other person in the world." Joseph had first brought him and Varina together and their marriage had clinched the place of the Davises in the untarnished aristocracy. Now Varina hated Joseph, and Jefferson sided with Varina. It was complicated.

Every corner of the United States military establishment, its materials and personnel, became known to Jefferson Davis in the four years beginning 1853 when he was Secretary of War under President Pierce, when he modernized tactics and equipment, brought the regular army up from 11,000 to 16,000, with pay increases for officers and men. As a Cabinet member he threw his influence toward a series of measures to advance Southern economic interests, held a considerable sway over the President, retarded free-homestead legislation, pressed for a Pacific railway if it could take a southern route and not the northern one projected by Senator Douglas, experimented with camel transport on Western deserts, pushed the Capitol building re-construction work, and chose the statue of a massive, fertile, warlike woman, in classic sculptural design, to surmount the Capitol—and with Mrs. Davis enjoyed bright years of Washington social life.

Into the newspapers went quarreling letters between him and General Scott, Davis claiming that Scott had overcharged $300 in a mileage expense account. In a long and blistering correspondence Davis alleged that Scott had violated several military regulations, that Scott's retorts showed him to be an enraged imbecile, that the only wounds Scott ever received were from falling off a horse in New York. Davis closed the incident by saying that he had received a hypocritical apology from Scott and "Having early in this correspondence stamped you with falsehood . . . I am gratified to be re-lieved from the necessity of further exposing your malignity and depravity." This resulted in Scott's judgment of Davis: "He is not a cheap Judas. I do not think he would have sold the Saviour for thirty shillings; but for the successorship to Pontius Pilate, he would have betrayed Christ and the Apostles and the whole Christian church."

Sam Houston of Texas more briefly set forth that Davis was "ambitious as Lucifer and cold as a lizard." Another Southerner had it Davis "could not forget what ought not to be remembered." Under an icy front his wrath blazed inside of him and found vent in politely calculated insults. His wife wrote, "If anyone differs with Mr. Davis, he resents it and ascribes the difference to the perversity of his opponent." For nothing much he challenged Senator Judah P. Benjamin of Louisiana to a duel; it was called off, Davis saying, "I have an infirmity of which I am heartily ashamed: when I am aroused in a matter, I lose control of my feelings and become personal." He lacked the skill to manage other men, but he was too positive a character to let others manage him, nor would he, as Lincoln did on occa-sion, let others believe they were managing him.

"The slavery agitation has ceased," President Pierce had said in a mes-sage to Congress. "A sense of repose and security pervades the land." The Whig party had gone under never to rise again from the Democratic ava-lanche that elected Pierce. Into the bosom of this tranquillity Douglas flung a bomb. On Sunday night, January 22, 1854, he called at the Davis home, explained a bill he had written, and Davis led the way by a back door of the White House for an interview with President Pierce. The Yes of the Presi-dent echoed the Yes of Davis to the bill—and it passed Congress, wiped out the Missouri Compromise, set up what Lincoln called squatter sovereignty, by which the people of any new Territory North or South could have slavery if they voted for it, laid the way for the Republican party, for the Lincoln-Douglas debates, for the wrecking of Southern power at Washing-ton in 1860. History would have required another channel of events had Davis or Pierce on that quiet Sunday evening said No to Douglas.

Again a United States Senator in 1857, Davis repeated his warnings that the slavery question was taking the country into danger, struck at both Seward and Douglas as hypocrites, and but thinly screened his belief that the South was a separate nation that would under pressure leave the Union. Buchanan's jugglery he could see through, but the civil war in Bleeding Kansas, the Lincoln-Douglas debates, the John Brown raid, had an alarming pitch and key.

While Lincoln and Douglas debated he said he wished they would tear each other to pieces like the Kilkenny cats. The debates over, Davis told the Mississippi Legislature that the election of an abolitionist as President "would be a species of revolution," the balloting an "observance of mere forms entitled to no respect." The sharper tone of exasperation in his speeches may have resulted from the new and baffling faces and issues rising in politics— or from neuralgia, nervous indigestion, laryngitis, and the old inflamed left eye, which he seemed about to lose. In 1860 he joined with Rhett and Yancey to split the Democratic party into Southern and Northern factions, finding perhaps only further mental confusion when one Massachusetts delegate, Ben Butler, voted fifty-seven times for the nomination of Jefferson Davis for President.

This haziness came again when for his health he and Mrs. Davis spent many weeks in Maine and Massachusetts and were overwhelmed with hospitality and with the public compliments of such Democratic wheel horses as Caleb Cushing and Robert C. Winthrop. He had stayed too long in Yankeedom and had been taken in, and did not speak his mind in Boston— so he heard from the South. They taunted him to finish his Faneuil Hall speech when he returned to Mississippi the day before Lincoln was elected President. He told them secession was the last remedy to apply. Nevertheless, they had Revolutionary ancestors. "I glory in Mississippi's star, but before I would see it dishonored I would tear it from its place to be set on the perilous ridge of battle as a sign around which her bravest and best shall meet the harvest-home of death!"

The audience stormed with applause. He then predicted that the election next day would be thrown into the House of Representatives, which might choose an abolition President. He also told of ex-President Pierce's having assured him the last summer that if a Northern army started South it would have to fight a war at home before it could move southward.

Then on November 6 Lincoln, though lacking a majority vote, carried the electors of every Northern State except New Jersey, and Davis on November 10 sent a letter to Rhett: "If South Carolina has determined to secede, I advise her to do so before the Government passes into hostile hands." He cautioned Governor Pettus of Mississippi that civil war would follow secession and therefore arms and munitions must be provided. He traveled to Washington, took his seat in the Senate, was argued by friends into sitting on the Committee of Thirteen to save the Union, opposed the Crittenden Compromise because it forbade slave property north of a certain line, wrote to Governor Pettus that the Black Republicans were bent on war.

When the Tennessee "poor white" Andrew Johnson thundered that whoever fired on the Union flag should meet a traitor's death, Davis pronounced Johnson "a degenerate son of the South unworthy to sit in the

Senate, an ally of Ben Wade, the foul abolitionist." Clashing with Senator Trumbull, he said a sense of honor dictated that the Government, to avert war, should let the South have its forts. "The man who would not have asked the return of the South Carolina forts to save bloodshed is a scoundrel."

They were sorry days in those last weeks of Jefferson and Varina Davis in the Washington they had loved and which had become so homelike. Their three growing children were with them, Jefferson, Jr., six years old, Margaret, three, and a year-old baby named Joseph Emory Davis after the elder brother. Jefferson and Joseph had forgiven each other, Joseph promising that a title deed would be given to Brierfield, though failing to keep the promise. Varina was still unforgiving of Joseph; she said she still hated him. In the Davis clan, as in the nation, was disunion.

On a sickbed racked by neuralgia, his left eye lost, Davis talked with Seward, and the news came that Lincoln had declared that he would concede almost every point at issue with the South except that no more Slave States could be made from Territories. Mississippi seceded January 9, and eleven days later Davis told the Senate that he was officially notified of the secession of his State and must resign. That the old Union and its associations still had a hold on him stood out from his speech delivered to crowded galleries, to doorways framing mosaics of brightly dressed ladies, to corners where bevies of women sat on the floor.

"Mr. Davis told me," wrote his wife, "that he had great difficulty in reaching his seat, as the ladies, of course, could not be crowded, and each one feared that the other would encroach on her scanty bit of room. . . . He glanced over the Senate with the reluctant look the dying cast on those upon whom they gaze for the last time. His voice at first low and faltering soon rang out melodiously clear, like a silver trumpet. Unshed tears were in it, and a plea for peace permeated every tone. The orator was too grief-stricken and too terribly in earnest to think of the impression he might create upon others. Had he been bending over his bleeding father, needlessly slain by his countrymen, he could not have been more pathetic or inconsolable."

Tears were in many eyes at his saying that they parted "not in hostility to others, not to injure any section of the country, not even for our own pecuniary benefit, but from the high and solemn motive of defending and protecting the rights we inherited, and which it is our duty to transmit unshorn to our children." "It only remains for me to bid you a final adieu." At night, said his wife, in his restless tossing came often the prayer, "May God have us in his holy keeping, and grant that before it is too late peaceful counsels may prevail."

Mrs. Davis and the children left Washington for their home in Mississippi. "Mr. Davis," she wrote, "remained a week in Washington, hoping that he might be arrested. A part of this time he was ill and confined to his bed." Resigned military and naval officers, Senators who like himself had spoken their farewells, came to see him, and his wife believed that in this hour he made efforts toward moderation, that "by telegrams and letters to every Southern State he endeavored to postpone their action." If as she believed he was at this time a moderate, "pursuing a pacific course," as he would put it, he had swung away from his militancy of November and December. Certainly his farewell speech had in it a pathos and tenderness, a touch of conciliatory spirit, not customary to him.

Returned to Mississippi, he accepted from Governor Pettus a commission as major general in chief command of the troops of the State. He gave a few days to military organization, then went to Brierfield for his last days there before taking his troops to the war front.

On February 10, with a warm spring sun pouring down on leaf and petal, he and Varina were in a rose garden trimming and cutting, as though roses were important, as though blood-red flowers carry ministrations.

A messenger threaded his way through the bushes and handed Jefferson Davis a telegram. He opened and read it, his wife trying to read his face while he read the telegram. His face took on grief and she was afraid evil news had arrived. "After a few minutes' painful silence he told me, as a man might speak of a sentence of death." The Montgomery delegates to the convention of the Confederate States of America had elected him provisional President—not Rhett nor Toombs nor Howell Cobb nor Stephens, but him. Both he and his wife knew he preferred campaign and battlefield to an administrative desk.

"I thought his genius was military," she wrote, "but that, as a party manager he would not succeed. He did not know the arts of the politician, and would not practice them if understood." He had hoped affairs might drift toward a dual Presidency, with two Chief Magistrates interchanging executive roles over the United States, but saw that as no longer practicable.

"In any case, I think our slave property will be lost eventually," he told her, and went on to speak of "the cordon of custom-houses which would be needful, if a commercial treaty of free trade could not be made [with the North], and of the immense standing army that would necessarily deplete the resources of the country if the slaves were still to be kept." They had vague hopes that after brief service as provisional President he would hold a high command under the later permanent Government of the Confederate States.

She wept a good-by and he rode to Montgomery, sleeping in his clothes, routed from his car by crowds roaring for their new President, calling for speeches, "bonfires at night, firing by day." After inauguration he wrote to her: "I thought it would have gratified you to have witnessed it, and have been a memory to our children. . . . The audience was large and brilliant. Upon my weary heart was showered smiles, plaudits, and flowers; but, beyond them, I saw troubles and thorns innumerable. We are without machinery, without means, and threatened by a powerful opposition; but I do not despond, and will not shrink from the task imposed upon me."

There was not time to write that some at Montgomery were disgusted with parading a President in a coach with four white horses, nor that after the inaugural one Mrs. Fitzpatrick poked Mr. Davis in the back with her parasol that he might turn and speak to her, someone commenting, "I am sure that was democratic enough."

At his left arm escorting him into the inaugural hall at Montgomery was Rhett of South Carolina, the extreme revolutionary secessionist. On his right as escort was Stephens of Georgia, who until the secession ordinance was passed had played every possible card politically to keep Georgia in the Union. Arm in arm these three men, with Davis as center, were the South. They embodied the controlling issues. The danger besetting Davis was a belief that he himself was the South, that his intellect alone could best light the way.

In the weeks Davis gave to raising an army and developing plans for what he hoped would become a nation among world powers, an opposition among his own people saw their revolution taking a wrong direction, one writing, "Having achieved one revolution to escape democracy at the North, it must still achieve another to escape it at the South."

The clause in the Constitution outlawing the African slave trade was "an infamous slur upon the whole institution, the lives and property of every slaveholder in the land," according to Rhett. The *Charleston Mercury* cried, "For what have we cast off the North as a rotten incubus, if we are thus to reenact all their swindles, outrages and insolences upon ourselves?" Rhett could sit in the Confederate Congress but could not publish its acts, and the *Mercury* muttered: "Laws are not only enacted in secret, but are vetoed in secret. It is time that the people knew, not only what laws they live under, but who are responsible for their passage." Privately Rhett estimated Davis as "an accomplished man, but egotistical, arrogant, and vindictive, without depth or statesmanship."

Russell of the London *Times* in a trip during May and June of '61 from Richmond through Charleston, Savannah, New Orleans, met everywhere a complete devotion to Davis: "Every Southern man I have as yet met, expressed unbounded confidence in Mr. Jefferson Davis. I am asked invariably as the second question from a stranger, 'Have you seen our President, sir? Don't you think him a very able man?'" Mrs. Chesnut, however, in her high inside circle was hearing of venomous old grudges held against the new President and wrote, "It seems to me already men are willing to risk an injury to our cause, if they may in doing so hurt Jeff Davis." She heard Mrs. Wigfall in a fling—"Jeff Davis is no seceder"—had been halfhearted about it at Washington, and the Confederacy had rewarded an "eleventh-hour man" with the Presidency.

When Southern gossip joined Northern propaganda in saying her husband was cold and icily unkind, Varina Davis recalled a young mother, a soldier's wife, coming to her Washington home when he was Secretary of War, and how Mr. Davis asked this young mother and two crying children into the house for breakfast with their own three children; to each child he gave a dollar, and after looking into their case gave them all railroad tickets home. Also Mrs. Davis recalled an old beggarwoman who sat knitting socks before the War Department door; each day Mr. Davis sent her a piece of money by an office messenger, one day insisting that Mrs. Davis get a cushion for the old woman to sit on. These were some of many gracious acts of her husband. Now from the Washington where they had lived happy years came a report that a reward of $100,000 was offered for the head of "the arch traitor, Jeff Davis." She took this war rumor as probably true, was "inclined to be angry," wrote Russell. "They are quite capable, I believe, of such acts," she told him.

Davis had a softer and more confused outlook than the public knew. "In Mrs. Davis's drawing room last night," wrote Mrs. Chesnut the last week in June, "the President took a seat by me on the sofa where I sat. He

Punch of London titles a cartoon "The American Brothers: or, How will they get out of it?"

talked for nearly an hour. He laughed at our faith in our own powers. We are like the British. We think every Southerner equal to three Yankees at least. We will have to be equivalent to a dozen now." Davis was sure from what he had seen of Southern fighting stuff in Mexico that pluck, muscle, dogged courage, dash, red-hot patriotism, would do all that could be done. "And yet his tone was not sanguine. There was a sad refrain running through it all. For one thing, either way, he thinks it will be a long war. Before the end came we would have many a bitter experience. He said only fools doubted the courage of the Yankees, or their willingness to fight when they saw fit. And now that we have stung their pride, we have roused them till they will fight like devils."

Davis was a chosen spear of authority heading eleven States committed to him as against twenty-three States formally still in the Union with Lincoln, one side reckoned as having 9,000,000 people (including 3,900,000 slaves) as against 22,000,000 Northern people.

Each in his Executive Mansion, one in Washington, one at Richmond, one hundred and twenty-two miles apart, Lincoln and Davis were to grapple and hurl destruction at each other.

Lincoln was at the prime of his powers, mentally in better form than at any period of his life. Davis had probably seen his prime in the years he was Secretary of War. His wife saw him with rasped nerves, careworn, "piteous" to look at, one eye gone. Yet others saw a steel exterior of perfect composure, and only himself knew how deep he was unbreakable, how far he could go before others would bend his will to theirs. Under his gun-metal surface he was something else that nobody knew, something he himself was afraid of, a stranger held leashed and never for a moment let loose to laugh or rage or talk free or be a plain fool; others might make monkeys of themselves, but not he; he would symbolize personal dignity. (Perhaps the war was all about personal dignity and the demarcation of it as between chattel slave and propertied aristocrat.) Northern preachers declaimed that Davis was a Beelzebub, a replica of the proud archangel who started a rebellion in heaven and tried to wrest control from the Almighty. The parallel, more comic than true, was not entirely false. He was not as crazy as Milton's insurrectionary archangel, but his personal dignity was peculiar and deep and he was ready to lose comparative paradise and go to superlative hell for it.

"Proud, indeed, must ever be to the Southern people," wrote F. H. Alfriend in the *Southern Literary Messenger*, "the contrast of the noble bearing of their chosen ruler with the display of vulgarity attending the journey of Mr. Lincoln from Springfield to Washington. These two men— one with the calm dignity of the statesman and the polished bearing of the gentleman; the other with coarse jests and buffoonery, upon the eve of the most important event in their individual history, and pregnant with significance to millions—were no bad indices to their respective sections."

"All we ask is to be let alone," Davis had said in his April 29 message to the Confederate Congress, a primitive heart cry that the South took for a slogan, that Northern sympathizers quoted often. Lincoln knew precisely and intricately what Davis meant, for Lincoln's elaborate Cooper Union speech had dealt with it, Lincoln saying toward the close: "What will satisfy them? Simply this: we must not only let them alone, but we must somehow convince them that we do let them alone. . . . Apparently adequate means all failing, what will convince them? This, and this only: cease to

THE SITUATION.

OFFICER LINCOLN. "I guess I've got you now, JEFF."
JEFF DAVIS. "Guess you have—well now, let us Compromise."

Officer Lincoln arrests the outlaw Jeff Davis, according to *Harper's Weekly*, a Northern
journal of the Unionist cause

call slavery wrong, and join them in calling it right. And this must be done thoroughly—done in acts as well as in words. Silence will not be tolerated—we must place ourselves avowedly with them."

In the event of the death of President Davis his place would be taken by a man who could himself have been President of the Confederate States by saying Yes to one condition. When Wiley P. Harris and Colonel A. M. Campbell had called on him in Montgomery, Alabama, and said that their State delegation preferred him for President and asked to present his name to the Confederate Congress, Alexander Hamilton Stephens told them that he had opposed secession and it would be bad policy to elect him President.

They urged that Stephens was the only man to whom Unionists were cordial. "You are the only man who can take away from this movement the character of a rebellion." They argued with him two hours and he said he would consider. Colin McRae and Judge Chilton of Alabama came likewise and he had demurred, then said he would consider. To Keitt of South Carolina and Toombs of Georgia he said, "Well, if I should be the unanimous choice of the delegates, as well as of the States, and if I can organize a Cabinet with such concert of ideas as will justify the hope of success, I will take it, but on no other conditions."

The provisional Congress had met, had adopted a provisional constitution, and was to elect a President and Vice-President, when on the evening of February 8 delegates from six States came to Stephens's room, their spokesman Robert Toombs, radiant, handsome, easily shifting from the air of solemn orator to quixotic comedian, smooth with always lurking angers, ever a warm personal friend of Stephens no matter how they disputed over politics.

"Aleck," said Toombs, "you are the choice of every man in Congress, and all of us are ready to pledge to help you form your Cabinet. There is only one point—those fellows from Virginia and the border States want you to promise to strike the first blow."

Aleck was looking his old friend in the eye. Toombs paused. Toombs went on: "Those fellows say their States are hanging in the balance, ready to turn with the first blow. They know Buchanan will never dare to strike. They believe Lincoln will be as cowardly. Now they want the question settled in their States, and they want you, when the first opportunity offers —say, if the administration should attempt to re-enforce or provision Fort Sumter—to strike the first blow."

The massive and bulking Toombs had spoken his portentous message to the little frail Alexander Hamilton Stephens. And there was silence. The shrunken and dwarfish figure sat composed, in his slow-burning hazel eyes a touch of clairvoyance and communion.

Then slowly and distinctly, "No, I will never strike the first blow."

And Toombs roared, "Aleck!" and with a long look into the unflinching eyes of Stephens turned on his heel and with the other men strode from the room to where nightlong caucuses were picking another man for President, a hard man, a man at the other extreme of temperament, a man eager to command armies, ready to strike the first blow and afterward ready to carry the war on into then unimaginable blood, ruin, ashes.

Stephens wanted retirement, peace, poetry, philosophy, time for friendly talks, time at his home in Liberty Hall to bathe the sore eyes of his old blind dog Rio. Yet Toombs and the others had gone ahead and made him Vice-President of the Confederacy, and at Savannah he had delivered an unprepared speech saying that slavery was the "corner-stone" of the Confederacy and the Negro was subhuman. It was garbled in reporting, and Stephens and his friends long regretted its proslavery tone, which failed to give any inkling of the little man who had been foremost to outlaw the African slave trade and who distinctly believed that the slavery institution would slowly rot and disintegrate from its own economic cancers.

So now the Confederacy had as Vice-President "a little, slim, pale-faced, consumptive man," as Lincoln had described him thirteen years back, when as fellow Whig Congressmen they were opposing the Mexican War, when Stephens brought tears to Lincoln's eyes with an antiwar speech. He was then, as Mrs. Chesnut accused him now, a sort of "half-hearted" patriot. At a reception in the Davis home he tried to tell Mrs. Chesnut, amid "frivle-fravle" interruptions, why he was gloomy. "He was deeply interesting," she wrote, "and he gave me some new ideas as to our dangerous situation. Fears for the future and not exultation at our successes pervade his discourse."

He understood the North and its Lincoln, once writing of old friendships in Congress, "I was as intimate with Mr. Lincoln as with any other man except perhaps Mr. Toombs."

"He had the look of being born out of season," said a woman of this Aleck Stephens, who had fought the Know-Nothings and the anti-Catholic movements of Georgia with an unequivocal hostility, under warnings that he was wrecking the Whig party; who had thrice challenged tall heavy men to duels and had the reply in substance, "Pick some man your size"; who had received verses of praise from ex-President John Quincy Adams of Massachusetts; who was sensitive as to what people were saying about him; who was the one man in the seething South to whom Lincoln had written the previous winter for counsel, Lincoln taking at face value Stephens's old-time declaration to the Know-Nothings: "I am afraid of nothing on the earth, or above the earth, or under the earth—except to do wrong." They had asked him then what he would do if his party were wrecked and he said, "I am toting my own skillet." Now too he was toting his own skillet, hoping for the best, though giving no encouragement to the mutinous spirit of his friend Thomas W. Thomas, writing to him: "All governments are humbugs, and the Confederate government is not an exception. Its president is the prince of humbugs. . . . He possesses not a single quality for the place save integrity. . . . Imbecility, ignorance, and awkwardness mark every feature of his management."

The United States had in fact now two governments taxing and ruling two sections. A chaotic, two-headed Lincoln-Davis governmental apparatus held dual sway over a divided country having of freemen some 2,500,000 farmers; 1,000,000 factory workers; 1,000,000 miscellaneous common laborers; 500,000 journeymen trades and craft workers, store clerks, miners; 100,000 sailors and fishermen; 20,000 house servants; 100,000 lawyers, ministers, priests; besides the rapidly swelling group of 25,000 government officeholders.

Eighty-six per cent of this population now to be violently shaken and shifted lived on farms and in villages and towns of less than 8,000 inhabitants.

Estimates in round numbers gave the Protestant religious denominations and sects 25,000,000 members and the Roman Catholic church 3,000,000 communicants. The Methodist Episcopal church had 1,000,000 members North, 500,000 in the seceded church South, and four other Methodist divisions had 200,000. Besides 1,000,000 regular Baptists there were 150,000 in related sects, Free Will, River Brethren, Dunkers, Mennonites. The last two taught that it was sin to take part in war and to kill other men in battle, which doctrine was also held by 50,000 orthodox Friends or Quakers and 40,000 Hicksites. Three hundred thousand Presbyterians were Old School, an equal number either New School or Cumberland, while seven other Presbyterian sects numbered roundly 100,000. The Disciples of Christ, Campbellite, had 333,000 members, the Lutherans 250,000, the United Brethren in Christ 100,000. Of Congregationalists there were 250,000. The Universalists, teaching that salvation was universal and there was no hell after death, comprised over 400,000, the Episcopalians 150,000, the German Reformed church 100,000, the Dutch Reformed 50,000. Two hundred thousand Jews held to their ancient rituals, while 60,000 Mormons looked toward their members undergoing desert hardships in Utah to establish their faith. Twenty thousand Second Adventists preached an early return of Christ to rear a new kingdom on earth.

The weaving and bobbing of these multifarious human pieces in 1861 was seen by the *Spectator* of London as the most stupendous real-life drama that history had staged in the modern era: "Every problem of the past, and every political difficulty of the present, is there working itself out visibly before our eyes. Evils which have perplexed the nations since the dawn of history demand their instant removal, while every form of government from mob-rule to the closest oligarchy is asserting by force its right, not only to exist, but to become supreme." The merits and evils of aristocracy and democracy were on show in a high-lighted flare "which affords to mankind the opportunity of a political education such as it has not enjoyed since Greece was submerged under the Roman wave." Venturing on the most painfully acute phase, the *Spectator* said, "The American people alone in history have to work out, not in the course of ages but at once, the problem which is older than any form of government now in existence, the extinction of human slavery."

The pace of invention would keep moving. Lincoln received on June 17, 1861, the first message ever telegraphed from a balloon: "This point of observation commands an area nearly fifty miles in diameter."

Unknown to the newspapers of the country, unknown to all its political leaders except two or three, unknown to all of Europe except a small group of Germans, some curious peace moves went on unofficially between the Washington and Richmond governments in final informal conversations aimed at stopping the war before it could start. The earnest and dutiful Rudolf Mathias Schleiden, knowing a war would play havoc with the profitable shipping trade of the Hanseatic Republic of which he was Minister, stepped into action.

The foreign diplomatic corps as a body planned mediation, with European nations as umpires of the American dispute, but this went on the rocks when Seward on April 23 published a statement from his department to the Governor of Maryland declaring that the differences between the States could not be submitted to foreign arbitrament under any circumstances.

Schleiden the next day proposed to Seward that he, Schleiden, should journey to Richmond and hold confidential discussions with Vice-President Stephens there. Seward favored Schleiden's plan on condition that "neither the President nor the entire Cabinet could expressly authorize" such discussions nor offer terms for an armistice. Later the same day Schleiden conferred with Lincoln and Seward.

Lincoln, as Schleiden reported to his Government at Bremen, expressed his hearty thanks that Schleiden was "willing to make an attempt of contributing to the prevention of bloodshed, and regretted that Schleiden had not gone to Richmond without consulting him or Seward." Schleiden explained that such a course would have laid him open to the suspicion of plotting with the South against the sole legitimately recognized Government at Washington. Lincoln agreed with Schleiden in this, and went on to say that his own designs for peace as offered in official statements had been misinterpreted and had brought charges of imbecility and fear, and he had resolved not to discuss the question further. The President repeated to Schleiden that "he did not have in mind any aggression against the Southern States, but merely the safety of the Government in the capital and the possibility to govern everywhere." On this account, Lincoln made clear, he could neither authorize negotiations nor invite proposals, but he promised to consider carefully all proposals which Schleiden might find himself called on to submit.

Schleiden took it that the President meant for him to go ahead and try negotiations with Stephens at Richmond without any special authorization. He then tried to get from Lincoln and Seward a statement as to whether they would accept a suspension of hostilities under condition of the two governments' simultaneously revoking "the two opposing proclamations," the one by Lincoln for the blockade of Southern ports, the other by Davis for seizure of Northern vessels flying the Union Jack. On this Lincoln would say nothing definite. Seward, however, urged Schleiden to go, without specific proposals, handed him a pass through the Union lines; and on the evening of April 24 Schleiden departed secretly for Richmond, arriving the next afternoon. What he heard on the trains to Richmond and from

Confederate volunteers crowding station platforms was war talk. They wanted fighting. What he heard in Richmond newspapers was more war talk, articles demanding an immediate attack on Washington and no attempts for a truce. The Virginia ordinance of secession had just been published, and on the day of Schleiden's arrival, the State convention ratified the provisional constitution of the Confederacy. Excited politicians in the lobby of his hotel were curious about what brought this stranger to their city in such an hour.

Vice-President Stephens replied to Schleiden's written request for an interview that he would be happy to see him immediately. During a three-hour talk behind closed doors Stephens told the Minister from the Hanseatic Republic that he believed all attempts at peace would be useless. The actions of Seward and Lincoln had filled the South with suspicion, in Stephens's view, though neither the Government at Montgomery nor the authorities of Virginia contemplated an attack on Washington. If the Confederate Secretary of War had said in a speech at Montgomery after the fall of Sumter that he hoped to be in Washington on May 1, it was merely a flowery phrase. "Public opinion in the South was embittered against the United States because of the strengthening of Fort Pickens and Fortress Monroe. Maryland's unexpected rising in favor of the South seemed to make it a condition of peace that Maryland be allowed to join the Confederacy." Stephens gave, too, the Southern opinion that the explosions and fires destroying vast war properties at Harper's Ferry arsenal and the Norfolk navy yard were deliberate acts of the North, for which the South in bitterness blamed the North.

In view of these matters Stephens favored a "de facto truce through tactful avoidance of an attack on both sides" rather than a formal armistice. He asked Schleiden to write him a letter on the subjects under discussion, which Schleiden did, Stephens replying that the Confederacy had resorted to every honorable means to avoid war, that the United States should indicate its willingness for amicable adjustment by some authoritative gesture. The objectives of the United States seemed to be "the recapture of former possessions looking to the ultimate coercion and subjugation" of the Southern people. Unless these objectives were changed, "no power on earth can arrest or prevent a most bloody conflict."

Schleiden held a last conference with Stephens, reached Washington on April 27, and sent a letter to Lincoln enclosing his correspondence with Stephens. He reported that the Southern States were arming in self-defense, that if the South were assured that the President would recommend to Congress when it assembled on July 4 a speedy and amicable adjustment of the differences, and the propriety of treating with Commissioners of the Southern States, there would not be any danger of a conflict. At the request of the President, Seward replied to Schleiden in an unofficial and confidential communication from the Department of State, with the information that the President was of the opinion that a continuance of the negotiations would be without any beneficial results. Schleiden then wrote to Stephens and to his Government at Bremen reporting this outcome of his errands. At a later time when Schleiden's Government refused to recognize the Confederate Government, Southern newspapers headlined items "Free Cities of Germany Aid the Lincoln Despotism."

On his Richmond trip Schleiden met with the typical war spirit in utterances such as that of the *Richmond Dispatch* saying that the Confederacy was "preparing with rapid strides to meet the Illinois baboon and his co-workers of iniquity," hurling at "the half starved Lincolnites" the défi: "Well, let them come—those minions of the North. We'll meet them in a way they least expect; we'll glut our carrion crows with their beastly carcasses. Yes, from the peaks of the Blue Ridge to tide-water, will we strew our plains, and leave their bleaching bones to enrich our soil." Lincoln and his batch of politicians would refuse Southern requests "until the Old Lion gets fully mad, springs to his feet, and brings a roar that will make the Ape quake with terror." In the Shenandoah Valley would be troops determined "to give Old Abe's canailles a warm reception." The Richmond newspapers agreed with the *Mobile Advertiser* that "starved, scurvy wretches from the back slums of the cities are not soldiers to meet the hot-blooded, thoroughbred, impetuous men of the South . . . dregs and off-scourings of the populace are the forces whom Lincoln suddenly arrays as candidates for the honor of being slaughtered by gentlemen."

More truly melancholy was James L. Petigru at Charleston, writing to a daughter in the North: "Jeff Davis has as complete control of the Southern mind as ever old Jefferson had and no matter what the moving cause may be, whether wounded vanity or groundless fears, our people, men and women and the women full as much as the men, are inflamed to the highest degree, and are under the hands of the rulers as malleable as melted ore. Nothing is more common than to hear people gravely talk of setting fire to the city if they cannot defend it."

More humble than Schleiden, and having no official standing, a former Roman Catholic priest went first to Lincoln, then to Governor Letcher of Virginia, then to Davis at Richmond, on what he guaranteed each of them beforehand was "important business." To Davis he began a talk about the horrors of war, and getting down to nothing specific, Davis asked him to put it in writing. The war clerk, J. B. Jones, received the manuscript of twenty pages of foolscap, Jones noting: "It consisted chiefly of evidences of the exceeding wickedness of war, and suggestions that if both belligerents would *only forbear to take up arms*, the peace might be preserved, and God would mediate between them. Of course, I could only indorse on the back 'demented.' " The old priest hung around for a week and then was seen no more, Jones philosophizing: "I think war is one of the providences of God, and certainly no book chronicles so much fighting as the Bible. War may be to the human race what pruning is to vegetation, a necessary process for the general benefit."

On May 1, 1861, the poet Longfellow up in Massachusetts wrote in his journal: "The word *May* is a perfumed word. It is an illuminated initial.

It means youth, love, song, and all that is beautiful in life. But what a May-day is this! Bleak and cheerless. And the little girls with bare necks, and rose-wreaths on their heads, remind me less of dancing than of death. They look like little victims. A sad thought for May-day."

A note came from George William Curtis to Longfellow that he should write a national song. The poet shrewdly wrote in his journal: "I am afraid the 'go to, let us make a national song,' will not succeed. It will be likely to spring up in some other way."

CHAPTER 10

TURMOIL—FEAR—HAZARDS

OUT of what sometimes looked like confusion confounded and many sorry kettles of fish the Lincoln Administration hammered away at shaping a new and huge war establishment. On May 3 the President issued a proclamation calling into service 42,034 three-year volunteers, 22,714 enlisted men to add ten regiments to the regular army, 18,000 seamen for blockade service—bringing the total of the army to 156,861 and the navy to 25,000. Day and night the President, Cabinet, departments, bureaus, military and naval officers, financiers, accountants, arms and supply divisions, worked on grand strategy and petty details of an organization having few precedents to guide it and tell it what to do and how and when.

From the windows of the White House Lincoln's spyglass caught the Confederate flag flying over the town of Alexandria eight miles down the Potomac River, where several heavy guns and 500 troops had been forwarded from Richmond. Batteries were getting set to blockade vessels up and down the Potomac. The provisional army authorized by the Virginia convention was drilling, and some of its detachments and their flags could be seen down-river. Farther away at Harper's Ferry, Colonel Thomas J. Jackson had 8,000 troops for Virginia service. Regiments from other Southern States had entered Virginia and were there on May 23 when the citizens of the State went through the motions of a free electorate that overwhelmingly ratified the ordinance of secession. These were the conditions that brought Lincoln's statement a little later: "The people of Virginia have thus allowed this giant insurrection to make its nest within her borders; and this government has no choice left but to deal with it where it finds it."

After this last week of May, 1861, the United States no longer ran its mail service into the seceded States. In this month too the Confederate Congress authorized all persons owing debts in the United States (except in Delaware, Maryland, Kentucky, Missouri, and the District of Columbia) to pay the amount of those debts into the Confederate treasury. According to

R. G. Dun & Company, the South owed Northern merchants about $211,000,000, of which $169,000,000 was due in New York City.

By May 9 some 20,000 troops were in Washington. They included Colonel Elmer E. Ellsworth and his regiment of Fire Zouaves recruited in ten

ROBBERY OF THE NATIONAL APPLE ORCHARD.

PRESIDENT LINCOLN. "I say, Jeff, this thing has been going on long enough. Suppose you drop those apples now and come down."
JEFF DAVIS. "Please don't shoot, Mr. Lincoln, ALL I WANT IS TO BE LET ALONE!" ·

Harper's Weekly gives a Northern point of view in May of '61

days by the Colonel from fire-department men of New York City. He could have had two regiments but was taking only as many as he had equipment for. New Yorkers had raised a fund of $60,000 for uniforms and arms. Ten different patterns of rifles were carried by Ellsworth's red-trousered ranks. In their stand of colors was a crimson silk flag presented by Mrs. John Jacob Astor, and another banner given by the actress Laura Keene. In the farewell parade in New York, 5,000 city firemen marched and cheered.

Arrived in Washington, the ex-firemen, quartered in a tall storehouse, let themselves down to the street by rope from the third story like so many monkeys. Some of them terrified tavern-keepers by charging meals to the Southern Confederacy. They hooted and frolicked, chased imaginary secessionists through the streets, held mock sessions in the Halls of Congress, dissolved the Union and reconstructed it, capered along perilous parapets of the Capitol building, knocked down the regularly assigned sentinels, hung like monkeys from the outer edges of the base of the dome two hundred feet in mid-air. Colonel Ellsworth paid for some of their damages out of his own pocket and took steps to discipline twelve rowdies on whom he blamed the pranks.

At the swearing in of the regiment, generals and Senators formed a group around the President standing hand in hand with young Tad.

When a small hotel next to Willard's broke into a big fire, the Fire Zouaves smashed doors of engine houses and had streams of water going before the regular department arrived. They formed pyramids on one another's shoulders, climbed up lightning rods like squirrels, suspended a man headfirst from the burning roof so that he could reach a hose sent up from below. Mr. Willard gave them thanks and a big breakfast. Then they were put in camp four miles south of the city. Meanwhile Ellsworth came and went at the Executive Mansion as one of the trusted favorites.

In a bright moonlight on May 24 at two o'clock in the morning, squads of cavalry crossed the bridges leading from Washington across the Potomac into Virginia, and were followed by infantry and by engineers, who began a work of crowning every hill for miles with defense trenches for the protection of the little ten-mile-square District of Columbia surrounded by Slave States. This advance Southern advocates termed the invasion and pollution of the sacred soil of Virginia, a Northern aggression more infamous than the Southern attack on Fort Sumter.

While a Michigan regiment marched toward the rear of Alexandria, Ellsworth's Fire Zouaves were to sail on transports down to that town of 10,000 and capture it. Ellsworth sat in his tent drenched in melancholy, writing to his father and mother that he expected the entrance to Alexandria would be "hotly contested," as a large force of the enemy had arrived there that day. "Whatever may happen, cherish the consolation that I was engaged in the performance of a sacred duty . . . my darling and ever-loved parents, good-bye."

To Carrie Spafford, his betrothed at Rockford, Illinois, his "own darling Kitty," he wrote that if anything should happen, "just accept this assurance, the only thing I can leave you—the highest happiness I looked for on earth was a union with you. . . . I love you with all the ardor I am capable of. . . . God bless you. Again good-bye." His favorite officer, Captain John Wildey of Company I, came into the tent and asked why the Colonel was delaying. The Colonel answered, "I was thinking in what clothes I shall die." Wildey started a line of cheerful talk but Ellsworth stayed blue, took from a trunk a new uniform fresh from the tailor, saying, "If I am to be shot tomorrow, and I have a presentiment that my blood is immediately required by the country, it is in this suit that I shall die."

In the midnight hustling and confusion of getting the regiment on board the transports, Ellsworth was among the gayest. Forty rounds of cartridges were issued to each man. The light of a clear gold moon glistened on the bayonets as twenty rowboats took them out to the transports. The moon faded to a white ghost and the sun's rim was edging up the horizon as the Zouaves arrived at Alexandria, where crowds of spectators lined a riverbank expecting the first battle of the war. A Union sloop of war had preceded the transports, under a flag of truce had sent a message giving the Confederate troops one hour to leave town. Ellsworth was told that the Confederate force of 500 had agreed to evacuate, and with a few straggling picket shots, had done so.

Ellsworth took charge of affairs by orders for control of railway traffic, and started personally for the telegraph office to stop communication southward, taking a squad with a sergeant, and his friends the regimental chaplain, the Reverend G. W. Dodge, Lieutenant H. J. Winser, and the *New York Tribune* man, E. H. House. A short walk and they came to the Marshall House, a second-class hotel, flying at the top of its flagpole the secession flag, which could be seen from the White House at Washington.

Ellsworth ordered the sergeant back for a company of troops, threw open the front door of the hotel, and walked in to ask a barefoot man arrayed only in shirt and trousers what sort of a flag it was over the roof. The man said he was only a boarder and knew nothing of it. Ellsworth sprang up the stairs, followed by his friends, to the third story, where with a ladder he mounted to the roof, cut down the secession flag with a knife loaned by Winser.

Then, as the *New York Tribune* man told it: "We turned to descend, Corporal Brownell leading the way, and Ellsworth immediately following with the flag. As Brownell reached the first landing-place, after a descent of some dozen steps, a man jumped from a dark passage, and hardly noticing Brownell, leveled a double-barrelled gun square at the Colonel's breast. Brownell made a quick pass to turn the weapon aside, but the fellow's hand was firm, and he discharged one barrel straight to its aim, the slugs or buckshot with which it was loaded entering the Colonel's heart, and killing him at the instant. I think my arm was resting on poor Ellsworth's shoulder at the moment; at any rate, he seemed to fall almost from my grasp. He was on the second or third step from the landing, and he dropped forward with that heavy, horrible, headlong weight which comes of sudden death."

The second barrel was aimed at Brownell and missed him because he sent his own rifle slug into the face of Ellsworth's killer. "Brownell did not know how fatal his shot had been, and so before the man dropped, he thrust his saber-bayonet through and through the body, sending the dead man violently down the upper section of the second flight of stairs."

Ellsworth's body was laid on a bed in a room near by, the secession flag wrapped about his feet. The *Tribune* man left for a few moments to make

Francis E. Brownell, who
killed Ellsworth's killer

*From stereograph in author's col-
lection*

The Marshall House, Alexandria, Virginia, where Ellsworth
was killed

Photograph from Oliver R. Barrett Collection

Elmer Ephraim Ellsworth

*Photograph from Frederick H.
Meserve Collection*

Sam Houston of Texas

Zebulon Baird Vance, Governor of North Carolina

Photographs by McClees in author's collection

sure of the seizure of the telegraph office, which had been Ellsworth's wish. "When I returned to the hotel, there was a terrible scene enacting. A woman had run from a lower room to the stairway where the body of the assassin lay, and cried aloud with an agony so heart-rending that no person could witness it without emotion. She flung her arms in the air, struck her brow madly, offered no reproaches, appeared almost regardless of our presence, and yielded only to her own frantic despair. It was her husband that had been shot—James W. Jackson, proprietor of the hotel." Also he was the partly dressed man who had told Ellsworth, "I am only a boarder here."

A coroner's jury of Alexandria citizens held an inquest over the remains of Jackson and gave a verdict—"The deceased came to his death at the hands of the troops of the United States while in defense of his private property, in his own house"—which was at variance with the telegram sent by Corporal Brownell to Troy, New York: "Father—Colonel Ellsworth was shot dead this morning. I killed his murderer. Frank."

On the morning of his death the body of Ellsworth arrived in Washington and was placed in a navy-yard building, where black crape and black bunting framed United States flags. The tolling of bells went on and the flags of public buildings were at half-mast. Around the casket stood a Zouave guard of honor.

In the White House a *New York Herald* man, with Senator Wilson of Massachusetts, entered the library and saw the President standing at a window looking out across the Potomac: "He did not move until we approached very closely, when he turned round abruptly, and advanced toward us, extending his hand: 'Excuse me, but I cannot talk.' We supposed his voice had given away from some cause or other, and we were about to inquire, when to our surprise the President burst into tears, and concealed his face in his handkerchief. He walked up and down the room for some moments, and we stepped aside in silence, not a little moved at such an unusual spectacle, in such a man and such a place. After composing himself somewhat, Mr. Lincoln sat down and invited us to him. 'I will make no apology, gentlemen,' said he, 'for my weakness; but I knew poor Ellsworth well and held him in high regard. Just as you entered the room, Captain Fox left me, after giving me the painful details of his unfortunate death. The event was so unexpected, and the recital so touching, that it quite unmanned me.' The President here made a violent effort to restrain his emotion, and after a pause he proceeded with a tremulous voice to give us the incidents of the tragedy that had occurred. 'Poor fellow,' he said as he closed his recital, 'it was doubtless an act of rashness, but it only shows the heroic spirit that animates our soldiers, from high to low, in this righteous cause of ours. . . . One fact has reached me which is a great consolation to my heart, and quite a relief after this melancholy affair. I learn from several persons that when the Stars and Stripes were raised again in Alexandria, many of the people in the town actually wept for joy. All the South is not secessionist.' "

Senator Chandler came in to tell the President of going with "his Michigan boys" to Alexandria and seeing them capture a company of Confederate dragoons. "Though by this time the President was quite himself again," wrote the *Herald* man, "we thought it was not a fitting moment to open a discussion of the matter which had brought us to the White House, so we took our leave without referring to it."

Mrs. Lincoln visited the navy yard in the afternoon, left flowers, and talked with Corporal Brownell about the tragedy. An hour later when the embalming was completed, she came again with the President, and they looked on the face of Ellsworth in death, Lincoln moaning, "My boy! my boy! Was it necessary this sacrifice should be made?" Lincoln invited the Zouave guards to take the body to the White House for the funeral services.

So they brought the body into the East Room, where on a Saturday morning came thousands to see a youth lying in state, clad in full uniform, while bells tolled on and flags drooped. Over the country likewise in many cities at the funeral hour bells tolled and flags were at half-mast. General Scott in full uniform, leaning on an aide, bestowed a long, inquiring look on the corpse, spoke distinct responses to the prayers of the church, and gave complete attention to the sermon. The Cabinet members attended, and leading military and naval officers, besides many Senators and Representatives. When at one o'clock an escort of Zouaves and a procession of carriages followed the hearse through immense crowds to the railroad station, the brass bands gave dirges of grief, again the bells tolled, and a salute of minute guns was heard from a battery at Arlington Heights. In New York City, at Albany, the body of Ellsworth lay in state and was viewed by thousands, had escorts with muffled drums and reversed arms.

Then home at last to Mechanicsville, New York, arriving in a gale of wind and wild rain. At Troy George W. Demers had spoken a requiem: "Sleep on, brave young warrior; narrow and silent is thy tent. The green mantle of thy mother earth shall enwrap thee. Thy nodding plume shall be the bent branches of the weeping willow. The robin shall sound for thee thy morning reveille. Thy bugle note shall be the sweet song of the oriole. All night long the watch-fires of heaven's dome shall burn above thy bed, whence no alarm shall rouse thee." Addressing a letter "To the Father and Mother of Colonel Elmer E. Ellsworth," the President wrote on May 25:

My dear Sir and Madam:

In the untimely loss of your noble son, our affliction here, is scarcely less than your own. So much of promised usefulness to one's country, and of bright hopes for one's self and friends, have rarely been so suddenly dashed as in his fall. In size, in years, and in youthful appearance a boy only, his power to command men was surpassingly great. This power, combined with a fine intellect, an indomitable energy, and a taste altogether military, constituted in him, as seemed to me, the best natural talent in that department I ever knew.

And yet he was singularly modest and deferential in social intercourse. My acquaintance with him began less than two years ago; yet through the latter half of the intervening period it was as intimate as the disparity of our ages and my engrossing engagements would permit. To me he appeared to have no indulgences or pastimes; and I never heard him utter a profane or an intemperate word. What was conclusive of his

Washington D.C.
May. 25. 1861

To the Father and Mother of Col.
Elmer E. Ellsworth:

My dear Sir and Madam,

In the untimely,
loss of your noble son, our affliction
here, is scarcely less than your own—
So much of promised usefulness

Above and below, the beginning and the close of a Lincoln letter in actual size of the handwriting

to address you this tribute to the
memory of my young friend, and
your brave and early fallen child.

May God give you that consolation which is beyond all earthly
power—

Sincerely your friend
in a common af-
fliction—
A. Lincoln

good heart, he never forgot his parents. The honors he labored for so laudably, and for which in the sad end he so gallantly gave his life, he meant for them no less than for himself.

In the hope that it may be no intrusion upon the sacredness of your sorrow, I have ventured to address you this tribute to the memory of my young friend and your brave and early fallen child.

May God give you that consolation which is beyond all earthly power.

Sincerely your friend in a common affliction,

A. Lincoln

So Ellsworth became a legend identified for all time with the United States flag, with patriotic valor. His pale eager face, delicately chiseled features framed in chestnut curls, fascinated gazing thousands who came for a look at him in his coffin, because to many he was the image of youth moving to drums and banners for the sake of emblems and mystic, inexplicable causes. Northern propaganda used him as a conspicuous and dramatic martyr, sunk his faults and vanities, his pretensions and ego, and held him up as "one of God's pet lambs." His grave foreshadowed a long row of the graves of comrade youths lying alongside, each of them taken off in an eyeblink.

The tears of Lincoln at the news of this one death were grief over the loss of a loyal young clansman—and were also unspeakable woe over the fate of mankind that brought blood and putrefaction into the sweet air of a Virginia May day. For a long time it would be in the Executive Mansion as the secretaries had it: "The echoes of Ellsworth's cheery and manly voice seemed to linger in the corridors and rooms."

Nine days after the funeral of Ellsworth came news of the death of the one man against whom Lincoln had carried on lifelong political warfare. In the Chicago Wigwam where Lincoln had been nominated, Stephen A. Douglas had told an immense audience, "Before God it is the duty of every American citizen to rally around the flag of his country," and then gone home, a physically worn and ravaged man, to die.

At his Oakenwald estate of 80 timbered acres between Thirty-first and Thirty-fifth streets, overlooking Lake Michigan, in hearing of the Illinois Central locomotives, at the last, downtown in the Tremont House, he argued stubbornly against the final unanswerable adversary. Once in a delirium he called, "Telegraph to the President and let the column move on." On the afternoon of June 3 his wife, holding his hand, asked him if he had any last word for his boys and he answered, "Tell them to obey the laws and support the Constitution of the United States." These were telegraphed and generally recorded as his last words, though Chicago and New York newspaper accounts agreed in substance with that of the *New York Herald:* "At about 5 o'clock Dr. Miller came into the room, and noticing the open shutters and windows inquired, 'Why have you all these windows raised and so much light?' Mr. Douglas replied, 'So that we can have fresh air.' His wife sat beside him, holding his right hand in both of hers, and leaning tenderly over him, sobbing. Dr. Rhodes remarked to Mrs. Douglas, 'I am afraid that he does not lie comfortable,' in reply to which Mr. Douglas said, 'He is—very comfortable.' These were his last intelligible words. From 5 o'clock he was speechless, but evidently retained his consciousness. When a few moments before his death, his wife leaned lovingly over him and sobbingly asked, 'Husband, do you know me? Will you kiss me?' he raised his eyes and smiled, and though too weak to speak, the movements of the muscles of his mouth evinced that he was making an almost dying struggle to comply with her request. His death was calm and peaceful; a few faint breaths after 9 o'clock; a slight rattling of his throat; a short, quick convulsive shudder, and Stephen A. Douglas passed into eternity."

His debate with Death was over. The fallacies of the opposition, his own fallacies, the fallacies of life, would no longer trouble him. His forty-eight years of life had taken his short, massive body through enough spectacular tumults, quarrels, and dramas to fill a life of many more years. Northern Democrats mourned over the lost giant of their party, while Republicans paid tribute to a leader who in a crisis had hushed mutiny among his followers. Cynical metropolitan editors saluted him as hero while country editors in black-bordered columns poured out grief. Memorial addresses of United States Senators were keyed to the words of Crittenden of Kentucky: "I know of no man who might have been more useful in this crisis."

Yet in a few days came news that Douglas died not merely poor but mortgaged and debt-ridden. "The lot in which now rest his ashes is in the center of that beautiful grove known as his long-chosen and favorite home, the surrounding portion of the tract is covered with mortgages," said a statement issued by fifteen prominent Democrats and Republicans of Illinois. "His children, his widow, and his countrymen to approach his grave must do so by permission of the sheriff, his creditors, and strangers. Shall the wife and children of Douglas go forth homeless, houseless wanderers from the State of Illinois?" So funds were being raised for the heirs of a master politician who had not had time nor methods for making money and keeping a fortune snugly out of politics.

The widow came to Lincoln at the White House later and he wrote a memorandum: "Yesterday Mrs. Douglas called, saying she is guardian of the minor children of her late husband; that she is being urged, against her inclination, to send them South on the plea of avoiding the confiscation of their property there [in North Carolina], and asking my counsel in the case." Lincoln advised her that he expected the United States would overcome attempts to confiscate property on grounds of loyalty to the Union, "but if not, I still do not expect the property of absent minor children will be confiscated," and she might act safely toward possession. But he gave the widow warning that "it is especially dangerous for my name to be connected with the matter, for nothing would more certainly excite the secessionists to do the worst they can against the children."

On a Mississippi River steamboat two women had traveled from Minnesota, where it was not yet summer, down to Memphis, where they saw bridal wreath and spirea whitening the bushes, and roses everywhere. One of the women, wife of an Alabama Senator, had begun weeping to the other over the sorrows of the land, stopping her tears, however, when the other mourned: "I was born in New Orleans and live in New York. One of my sons is in the 7th New York Regiment, and another in the New Orleans Zouaves."

Roll call of the Todd family of Lexington, Kentucky, found Mary Todd Lincoln, her eldest brother Levi, and her half-sister Margaret Kellogg for the Union, while her youngest brother George and her three half-brothers Samuel, David, and Alexander had joined the Confederate Army, and her half-sisters Emilie Helm, Martha White, and Elodie Dawson were the wives of Confederate officers.

To the White House had come Doctor Lyman Beecher Todd, cousin of Mrs. Lincoln. He asked for and was given the postmastership of Lexington, Kentucky, though friends of Lincoln in Lexington were urging another applicant. While Cousin Mary waited with a carriage to take him to the train, he shook hands with Lincoln and was advised: "Doctor, I wish you would see that the Lexington papers are sent here to the White House. The *Observer* has been coming to our home ever since Mary and I were married, and I reckon there's no better weather-cock for Kentucky politics just now." The *Observer* would be Lincoln's reliance in case the *Kentucky Statesman*, its Lexington rival, repeated its allegation that Lincoln declined to come to Kentucky "because he thought it a mere trap of the Kentuckians to catch him, tar and feather him, and set him on fire to make a torchlight procession of him."

"Good morning, my Confederate friend," said Lincoln in the tone of one Kentuckian who understood another. The caller, a regular-army officer, denied his request at the War Department, walked with the President to the office of Adjutant General Lorenzo Thomas.

"General Thomas, I would like to have a leave of absence granted to my Confederate friend, Captain Johnson, to enable him to accept the position of lieutenant-colonel of a Kentucky cavalry regiment."

"It cannot be done."

"But, I have not come over to discuss this question with you, General Thomas, but to order you to give the necessary instructions."

"Ah, well, it will be done."

To the White House on Lincoln's invitation had come Ben Hardin Helm, West Pointer, son of a former Governor of Kentucky, a Democrat, and the husband of Mary Todd Lincoln's "Little Sister" Emilie. The President offered Helm a commission in the United States Army, Mrs. Lincoln urging, "Emilie will be a belle at the White House receptions and we will be so proud of her, and we need handsome, dignified young men like yourself to ornament our army."

And Helm told the President that he had opposed him in politics, had no claims on him, though nevertheless, "You have been kind and generous to me beyond anything I have known." Helm was silent a moment, then thoughtfully: "I wish I could see my way—I will try to do what is right. You shall have my answer in a few days."

During those few days the White House guest talked with old West Point comrades, some of them resigned and packing to go South. He was still undecided when as he left the White House Lincoln handed him an envelope holding a major's commission in the United States Army, saying: "Ben, here is something for you. Think it over for yourself and let me know what you will do." Mary Lincoln gave him a kiss to carry to Emilie and said, "Good-by, we hope to see you both very soon in Washington."

After a long handclasp with Lincoln, Helm walked slowly down the stairs and out the door and was gone, and days passed and word came that he would wear the Confederate gray.

To Lexington, the heart of the Bluegrass Region, had returned John C. Breckinridge, Vice-President of the Buchanan Administration, the Southern Democrat who had received in the Electoral College 72 votes for President as against 180 for Lincoln and 12 for Douglas. On leaving Washington he had visited his cousin Elizabeth Grimsley at the White House, teasing her, "Cousin Lizzie, I would not like you to be disappointed in your expected stay at the White House, so I will now invite you to remain here as a guest when the Confederacy takes possession." Mary Todd Lincoln had interposed, "We will be only too happy to entertain her until that time, General."

Breckinridge had carried the home town of Mrs. Lincoln by a large plurality, while Lincoln received only 2 votes. The ten counties of the Bluegrass Region had cast only 15 ballots for Lincoln, and when the Kentucky-born Illinoisan won the election there was rage such as Horace Buckner wrote to John J. Frost: "Old Abe Lincoln is an infernal old Jackass. I should relish his groans and agonies if I could see him put to torture in hell or anywhere else. He has chosen to become the representative of the Republican party and as such I should like to hang him." This was the sort of material John C. Breckinridge was looking for, and he hoped to find enough of it, as he said, "to confront Mr. Lincoln with fifteen united compact States to warn him" against "his unholy war."

As if it were some book he knew by heart, Lincoln could picture Kentucky with her slave soil hemmed and wedged by free-soil strips, the Ohio River running along her northern border for hundreds of miles to the Mississippi, where at the two-river junction the Illinois Central Railroad terminus was a key to the Mississippi Valley. The Bluegrass Region, with Lexington as its center, was the predominant slaveholding section where the secession trend must be checked.

Out across that region rang the voice of a rugged original figure who became a rallying-point for Union sentiment. This was Robert Jefferson Breckinridge, sixty-one years old, a lawyer of eight years' practice who had taken to theology and for thirteen years was pastor of the Second Presbyterian Church of Baltimore, then becoming a college president, and later in Kentucky superintendent of public instruction. He had been a professor of theology, editor of religious journals, and had written one book titled *The Knowledge of God Objectively Considered* and another titled *The Knowledge of God Subjectively Considered*. His influence had been instrumental in stopping the American Bible Society from publishing a new and revised version of the Bible. As a high officer of the Presbyterian Synod he had a wide personal influence; his editorials in his *Quarterly Review* reached a large audience in the Border States; and across Kentucky he now roused a following that surprised the opposition. Secession, his argument began, was "utter madness," its pretexts "some futile, some false, some atrocious," not one of them becoming to a statesman, a philosopher, a patriot, or a Christian; "not one of them will endure the light of history, the judgment of mankind or the scrutiny of posterity."

When the Kentucky Legislature was preparing resolutions to recognize the seceded States in a plan approved by United States Senator John J. Crittenden and not disapproved by the other United States Senator, Garrett Davis, Dr. Breckinridge had called a mass meeting in Lexington, poured out his reasons for scorning the proposal, and sent the printed speech in thousands of copies to all parts of Kentucky. He asked: "Do you want the [African] slave-trade reopened? Do you want free trade and direct taxation? Do you want some millions more of African cannibals thrown amongst you broadcast throughout the whole slave States?" The aim of secession was "to make many nations out of one." Legally, he declared, it had no leg to stand on: "No States in the Union ever had any sovereignty at all independent of and except as they were *United* States."

The fierce old theologian kept his speech entirely in the realm of pure argument. He could not get personal with his opposition. It included two of his own sons who were going into Confederate gray (one of them organizing a company for service under the Stars and Bars) and such kinsmen as his nephew John C. Breckinridge, and such illustrious Kentuckians as James B. Clay, the son of Henry Clay. Of his three sons only one was choosing the Stars and Stripes to fight under.

Such mixed affairs in the War of Brothers were related to Lincoln by Cassius M. Clay, who in a conversation of several hours at the White House named Dr. Breckinridge and others as strong enough to stop Kentucky from seceding.

News of the Ellsworth killing had special interest in Lexington, Kentucky, as James Jackson, the killer of Ellsworth, was the youngest brother of a practicing physician in Lexington. The *Kentucky Statesman* referred to Ellsworth's killer as the "immortal hero who slew the ill-bred braggart at Alexandria" and exclaimed: "We rejoice in the death of Ellsworth and only regret that every man who followed him did not share the same fate. Mr. Jackson was too noble a man to fall a victim to the infamous thieves of Ellsworth's regiment." The tragedy was cited as an example of "Lincoln's despotism" and the many friends of Dr. Jackson were urged to avenge the death of his brother by joining the Confederate Army.

On the day of Ellsworth's death the Kentucky Legislature, after almost continuous session since January, adjourned sine die, proclaiming neutrality but still in the Union, and slowly drifting away from her sister Slave States to the south, who occasionally taunted Kentucky with "hesitation and cowardice." Joshua Speed and his brother James at Louisville had been allies of Dr. Breckinridge. Commissioned a brigadier general by Lincoln, Robert Anderson, who had said at Fort Sumter that if Kentucky seceded he would go to Europe, had set up headquarters in Cincinnati and given his best efforts to keep Kentucky in the Union. A naval lieutenant, William Nelson of Kentucky, had asked Lincoln to send him to his native State to stop secession. Nelson and others had distributed 10,000 rifles among Union men and Union military organizations. By stealth in the nighttime many a home-guard Unionist took to his arms his "Lincoln rifle" for use in emergency. Across the Ohio River on Ohio soil recruiting camps were set up, and some Ohio regiments had a fourth of their enrolled men from Kentucky. In the June balloting for members of the Congress Lincoln had called to meet on July 4, Kentucky elected antisecessionists in nine out of the ten districts, the Union majority in the State being 54,700.

At the Baltimore election of April 24, 1861, only one ticket was in the field, "States' Rights." Of 30,000 voters in the city only 9,244 went to the polls and they all voted for secessionist members of the Maryland Legislature, which was to assemble two days later. Plenty of advice came to Lincoln that he could now show decision, throw troops into Maryland, arrest the whole traitorous legislature and stop it from meeting. He wrote to General Scott that the question was submitted to him, and he had considered whether the General should arrest and disperse the members of the Maryland Legislature. It would not be justifiable nor efficient, the President had decided: "*First*, they have a clearly legal right to assemble; and we cannot know in advance that their action will not be lawful and peaceful. And if we wait until they shall have acted, their arrest or dispersion will not lessen the effect of their action. *Secondly*, we cannot permanently prevent their action. If we arrest them, we cannot long hold them as prisoners; and, when liberated, they will immediately reassemble and take their action. And precisely the same if we simply disperse them—they will immediately reassemble in some other place." Therefore, the President concluded, it was left the commanding General only to watch and wait, and if the Maryland Legislature acted toward arming their people against the United States, he should take counteraction, "even, if necessary, to the bombardment of their cities, and, in the extremest necessity, the suspension of the writ of *habeas corpus*."

What with Union regiments increasing daily at Annapolis, Governor Hicks could have pleased the secessionist element by calling the legislature to Baltimore. Instead he convened it at the town of Frederick, a Unionist community but without Union troops. Such decisions favoring the Unionists came regularly from Governor Hicks. His message to the legislature reported his personal interviews with President Lincoln and the Cabinet, and the President's insistence that while he wished to avoid collisions through bringing troops across Maryland, military necessity required that such troops be brought to the defense of the national capital. The Governor gave his own view "that the only safety of Maryland lies in preserving a neutral position between our brethren of the North and of the South," and while he admitted the right of Federal troops to cross Maryland, counseled "that we shall array ourselves for Union and peace," and observed, "The impending war has not come by any act or any wish of ours." Day by day the Maryland legislators saw more Federal regiments moved across Maryland toward Washington, heard of more regiments in reserve at Philadelphia and Harrisburg for quick transport to Baltimore. A Committee on Federal Relations reported its majority opinion that the Maryland Legislature did not possess the power to pass an ordinance of secession, a minority being of the opposite opinion; the legislature agreed with the majority of the committee by a vote of 53 to 13.

The senate of the legislature in secret sessions advanced a bill to put military control of the State in the hands of a secessionist Board of Public Safety. When the news of this action was made public, there was a flareback of opposition. Slowly it became clear that the strength of secession in Maryland lay chiefly in a furiously active minority in Baltimore. Whittingham, Episcopal bishop of Maryland, was not of this minority. He rebuked clergymen who had omitted the prayer for the President of the United States, and admonished them that the offense must not continue.

A commission appointed by the Maryland Legislature reported May 6 that they had been courteously received by President Lincoln at Washington, had exchanged full explanations with the Secretary of War and the Secretary of State, who were present, had set forth fully "the strength of sympathy felt by a large portion of our people for our Southern brethren in the present crisis," while also "acknowledging all the legal obligations of the State to the Federal Government." They had differed as to fact, but on the general principle at issue, said the report, "The President concurred in the opinion that so long as Maryland had not taken, and was not taking, a hostile attitude toward the Federal Government, that the exclusive military occupation of her ways of communications, and the seizure of the property of her citizens, would be without justification." They had insisted especially that the Federal Government must "abstain from all action in the transportation of troops that can be regarded as intended for chastisement or prompted by resentment," and had come away "not able to indicate to what extent the Executive discretion will be exercised in modifying relations" between Maryland and Washington; but they felt authorized "to express the opinion that some modification may be expected." They had brought up for discussion too "the particular matter of the commercial communications between the city of Baltimore and other parts of the country, brought to the attention of the General Assembly by the Mayor and City Council of Baltimore," meaning that the bridges burned and the railroads destroyed by secessionists had resulted in traffic's taking other routes and Baltimore was losing trade. In this matter too they expected that executive discretion would be exercised favorably.

John Hay noted in his diary Maryland disunionists calling on the President on May 4, and "They roared as gently as twere any nightingale. The only point they particularly desired to press was that there was no special necessity at present existing for the armed occupation of Maryland. . . . They also implored the President not to act in any spirit of revenge for the murdered soldiery. The President coolly replied that he never acted from any such impulse & as to their other views he should take them into consideration and should decline giving them any answer at present."

Day by day the boiling-point in Maryland receded as it became more evident that secession would result in devastating trade losses to Baltimore. Charleston at her distance could more easily be defiant.

The days passed till ten, twenty, thirty regiments had crossed Maryland to Washington. A military department under Brigadier General Benjamin F. Butler was set up at Annapolis. Under orders from Scott, General Butler on May 4 moved two regiments to Relay House, eight miles from Baltimore, took control of westbound rail traffic, cut off supplies and Maryland Confederate recruits from their route to Harper's Ferry.

In rain, darkness, and thunder Butler moved 1,000 troops to Baltimore on May 13, stacked arms on Federal Hill overlooking Baltimore, issued a proclamation that they were there to enforce respect and obedience to the laws of the United States. General Scott in a sharp note rebuked Butler for acting without orders, taking chances on a bloody collision with Maryland troops, militia, and police which might have put the Lincoln Administration in a bad light as overly eager for war. But the North cheered Butler. He gave them a spectacular picture. Among his troops were companies of the 6th Massachusetts regiment which had been mobbed in Baltimore. Butler himself, be it remembered, had been a Democratic delegate to the Charleston convention, where he had voted on fifty-seven ballots for Jefferson Davis for presidential nominee; furthermore, Butler had been the Breckinridge proslavery candidate for Governor of Massachusetts in 1860, and though he had polled only 6,000 proslavery votes out of a total of 169,000 in Massachusetts, it gave him a peculiar status in the State of Maryland with its $50,000,000 worth of slaves.

To circumvent the defiant minority in Maryland, the State and War departments had the President's order to General Scott on April 27 that "in suppressing an insurrection against the laws of the United States" he might at any point between Philadelphia and Washington where there was resistance "suspend the writ of *habeas corpus*." Under this order Butler arrested Ross Winans, a member of the legislature returning from Frederick to Baltimore, and had Winans locked up under guard at Butler's department headquarters in Annapolis. Ross Winans somehow did not strictly belong with the agricultural South, but rather with the industrial North, for he was born in New Jersey and during his sixty-five years had invented a plow, a friction wheel, and axle bearings for railway cars, had developed the eight-wheel car system, had built the first successful locomotive of the Baltimore & Ohio Railroad, had conducted in Baltimore the largest railway machine shops in America, had accumulated a personal fortune rated at $15,000,000. Yet Winans had also gone in for politics, favored secession and favored it to the extent that he manufactured 4,020 steel pikes of the type that John Brown had carried for arming the slaves, a very primitive weapon; also he had manufactured the Winans steam gun, a most modern and fantastic weapon, a cannon mounted on a four-wheel steam-propelled carriage, the cannoneers protected by a bulletproof cone; it was calculated to mow down infantry like a scythe, firing one-ounce or twenty-four-pound balls at the rate of one hundred to five hundred per minute. Winans had sent the first of this contraption on its way to Harper's Ferry for Confederate use; it was seized by the Federals and was found to be impractical for dealing out wholesale death.

The most eminent legal counsel of Baltimore, Reverdy Johnson, appeared before Lincoln requesting the release of Ross Winans. Lincoln had more than a passing acquaintance with Reverdy Johnson, since they had been opposing attorneys in the McCormick Harvester patent case in Cincinnati. Lincoln turned the Winans matter over to Seward, who issued an order for Winans's release, Butler protesting in telegrams that he could prove Winans's guilt, privately maintaining that part of Winans's $15,000,000 had "greased" the release. Lincoln knew, however, that Reverdy Johnson was not acting in Winans's behalf merely as an attorney, for Johnson had a month before come to the White House and asked Lincoln for some assurance that the President was not planning invasion or subjugation of the South. Lincoln had given Johnson a confidential letter on April 24, 1861, writing: "I do say the sole purpose of bringing troops here is to defend this capital. I do say I have no purpose to invade Virginia with them or any other troops, as I understand the word invasion. But, suppose Virginia sends her troops, or admits others through her borders, to assail this capital, am I not to repel them even to the crossing of the Potomac, if I can? Suppose Virginia erects, or permits to be erected, batteries on the opposite shore to bombard the city, are we to stand still and see it done? In a word, if Virginia strikes us, are we not to strike back, and as effectively as we can?"

To this note Reverdy Johnson replied the same day thanking the President for frankness, endorsing his policy, and writing, "In a word, all that your note suggests would be my purpose were I intrusted with your high office." This was worth having from an old-line Whig who had been United States Senator from Maryland and resigned to become Attorney General in President Taylor's Cabinet, whose capacity for analysis and statement had won him international distinction.

To Lincoln, Reverdy Johnson promised that Lincoln's specific written statement of his purposes should "be held perfectly confidential," but it seemed that he was careless and gave the substance of Lincoln's letter to Campbell of Alabama, not yet resigned from his seat as Associate Justice of the Supreme Court, Campbell within four days after Lincoln had written the confidential letter sending the substance of it direct to Jefferson Davis.

Butler was continuing in the national scene his Massachusetts record for ingenuity and expedients, for sheer nerve and audacity, for the calculated exhibitions of a careerist, for the chameleon shifts of a wily criminal lawyer suspected by his own clients of a shaded and always partly defensible treachery. Heavy of body and somewhat corpulent, with a well-rounded paunch, bald, sleepy-eyed with cunning, a cast in one eye, he was at every moment an actor with ready answers fitting his favorite combined role of the Man of the People and the Man Who Knows How. He had volunteered to arrest the Confederate Commissioners in Washington and prosecute them for treason. His militia troops in Massachusetts had elected him colonel, then brigadier general, and when Governor John A. Andrew of Massachusetts hesitated about giving a commission to a Breckinridge proslavery Democrat, Butler spread the word that when Governor Andrew did finally appoint him a brigadier it was because Butler had brought Boston banks to his support and it was banking pressure that wrung the unwilling appointment from Andrew.

Andrew, with a large group in Massachusetts, believed Butler to be crooked in law and politics, believed he would prove to be a "political general," but gave him his commission as brigadier on the two points that his troops had elected him and there would be advantages in having Massachusetts troops headed by a Breckinridge Democrat. "As a lawyer Butler was feared, both for the things he was able and the things he was willing to do," wrote a friend of Andrew. "He gave the world to understand that he held strong cards; but as yet no man knew what his game was." A friend of Butler noted: "He often believes his own sophistry, so ingeniously does he construct it. His fallacies are ingenious and difficult to unravel. His arguments always endanger the adversary—they often utterly overwhelm him. They abound in insinuations. His wit bites with a keen edge." When a West Point lieutenant criticized Lincoln's handing to Butler in May of '61 one of the few commissions given to major generals, Butler replied that the young lieutenant had never commanded a corporal's guard in active service, and "He forgot that putting an animal into a stable does not make him a horse, that point being better determined by the length of his ears."

As between two lawyers, Butler had told Lincoln that the order for him to leave with his brigade for Washington arrived when he was trying a case before a jury. He had quit his argument to the jury and got his case continued. It woke Lincoln to muse slowly, "I guess we both wish we were back trying cases."

To Carl Schurz, passing through Annapolis, the chunky-shaped Butler with squinting eye and a peculiar puffing of cheeks was a little grotesque, was most evidently enjoying his power, and "keenly appreciating its theatrical possibilities." While Schurz held a conversation with Butler, officers entered headquarters with reports or inquiries about orders. "Nothing could have been more striking than the air of high authority with which the General received them, and the tone of curt peremptoriness peculiar to the military commander on the stage, with which he expressed his satisfaction or discontent, and with which he gave his instructions. And after every such scene, he looked around with a sort of triumphant gaze, as if to assure himself that the bystanders were duly impressed. But he did expedite business, and, no doubt, he got over his theatrical fancies as the novelty of the situation wore off."

Butler was removed from the Maryland scene and put in charge of Fortress Monroe, to go his way as a sharp-tongued, resourceful, unscrupulous criminal lawyer who enjoyed power, with an itch for quarrels and unanswerable assertions of his personal correctness and authority, nursing the same delusion as his friend Jefferson Davis, that he was a military genius of the first rank, having, as Butler phrased it, "won his spurs." He protested his removal to a fort in letters cross-examining Secretary Cameron, and left Fortress Monroe for an interview with President Lincoln, to whom he said that the treatment of him implied reproaches. The President, according to Butler's report of their conversation, said very kindly and courteously, "The administration has done everything to remove every thought of reproach upon you; and I wish very much that you would accept the commission."

"Well, Mr. President," said Butler, "will you allow me to go to my room and consult with the mother of my children before I finally decide?"

"Certainly. You cannot do a better thing."

And Butler returned to say that his wife believed he would be unhappy and discontented at home, advised his accepting the commission. Butler then referred to himself as a Democrat who had opposed the President's election, "but I shall loyally support your administration as long as I hold your commission, and when I find any act that I cannot support I shall bring the commission back at once and return it to you."

"That is frank, that is fair," Lincoln broke out in his way. "But I want to add one thing: When you see me doing anything that for the good of the country ought not to be done, come and tell me so, and then perhaps you won't have any chance to resign your commission."

They shook hands and Butler left to spread the word that they were "the warmest personal friends." Not yet had Butler discredited himself. In fact his performances in Maryland had heartened the North, and he was on form worth the high commission Lincoln handed him. Yet he was basically an actor, a political general, and a military politician, so that eventually when John Hay should say to Lincoln that he believed Butler was the only man in the army to whom power would be dangerous, Lincoln would reply: "Yes, he is like Jim Jett's brother. Jim used to say that his brother was the damndest scoundrel that ever lived, but in the infinite mercy of Providence he was also the damndest fool."

The Butler gift for expedients rang across the country again when the last week in May fugitive slaves had flocked by hundreds into his camp and he held $60,000 worth of that form of property, black men, women, and children to whom he issued clothing and rations, and set the able-bodied to work. The legal question of returning these slaves to their former owners Butler disposed of by his decision, "The negro must now be regarded as *contraband* [like smuggled goods or anything forbidden to be supplied by neutrals to belligerents], since every able-bodied hand, not absolutely required on the plantations, is impressed by the enemy into the military service as a laborer on the fortifications." The country, the armies, editors, lawyers, and politicians picked up this word "contraband" as untying knots of the Fugitive Slave Law. It became a favorite of the Negroes, many a runaway after starving in timber and swamp arriving in the Union lines to say with jubilation, "I'se contraband."

The next flare-up in Maryland ended in the rare spectacle of the Chief Justice of the United States Supreme Court entangled in dispute and sharp controversy with the President of the United States. It began when General George Cadwalader, in command of Fort McHenry near Baltimore, sent a squad of soldiers who at two o'clock on the morning of May 25 roused one John Merryman from his bed in his home at Hayfields and took him to Fort McHenry and locked him up "in close custody." Lawyers for Merryman appeared the same day before Roger B. Taney, who made his home in Baltimore. They denied that Merryman was guilty of reported charges of treason, prayed for a writ of habeas corpus. Chief Justice Taney issued the writ prayed for and commanded that General Cadwalader appear before him "and that you have with you the body of John Merryman . . . and that you certify and make known the day and cause of the capture and detention of the said John Merryman; and that you, then and there, do submit to and receive whatever the said Court shall determine upon concerning you."

General Cadwalader's response to Chief Justice Taney was brought by a staff member, Colonel Lee, who explained that the General was busy with pressing matters and then read a statement from the General that the aforesaid John Merryman was charged with treason, was publicly known to be holding a commission as lieutenant in a company having in their possession arms belonging to the United States, and avowing his purpose of armed hostility against the Government. "He has further to inform you that he is duly authorized by the President of the United States in such cases to suspend the writ of *habeas corpus* for public safety. This is a high and delicate trust and it has been enjoined upon him that it should be executed with judgment and discretion. . . . He respectfully requests that you will postpone further action upon the case until he can receive instructions from the President of the United States, when you shall hear further from him."

"Have you brought with you the body of John Merryman?" inquired Taney.

"I have no instructions except to deliver this response to the Court," said the Colonel.

"The commanding officer declines to obey the writ?" asked Taney.

The Colonel replied, "After making that communication my duty is ended and my power is ended," and walked out of the room.

The Chief Justice then ordered "that an attachment forthwith issue against General George Cadwalader for a contempt in refusing to produce the body of John Merryman according to the demand of the writ of *habeas corpus.*" On the next day in a courtroom overflowing with people the Chief Justice heard United States Marshal Washington Bonifant certify that he had proceeded to Fort McHenry to serve the writ on General Cadwalader. "I sent in my name at the outer gate; the messenger returned with the reply 'that there was no answer to my card,' and therefore could not serve the writ as I was commanded."

"It is a plain case, gentlemen," remarked Taney, giving a written decision that "the President, under the Constitution and laws of the United States, cannot suspend the privilege of the writ of *habeas corpus*, nor authorize any military officer to do so." The Chief Justice added orally that the United States Marshal had legally the power to summon out a posse comitatus to seize and bring into Court the party named in the attachment, meaning General Cadwalader, "but it is apparent he will be resisted in the discharge of that duty by a force notoriously superior to the *posse comitatus*, and, such being the case, the Court has no power under the law."

To the crowd of fellow Baltimoreans who thronged the courtroom the Chief Justice made clear what he would do to General Cadwalader if that party were before him: "If he was before the Court, it would then impose the only punishment it is empowered to inflict—that by fine and imprisonment." Under the circumstances two things were left him to do: "I shall reduce to writing the reasons under which I have acted . . . and shall report them with these proceedings to the President of the United States, and call upon him to perform his constitutional duty to enforce the laws; in other words to enforce the process of this Court. That is all this Court has now the power to do."

The courtroom throng filed out. And the Chief Justice transmitted to the President a long written opinion on the ancient Anglo-Saxon custom of issuing writs of habeas corpus, with reminders and admonitions that the Executive himself should not violate law. Taney's majesty or authority as Chief Justice shrank somewhat as one by one, despite writs of habeas corpus, the active secessionist leaders in Baltimore were picked off and were no longer to be found at their usual haunts.

Police Marshal George P. Kane, who had resisted the surrender of forty wagonloads of muskets and other arms seized by Federal authorities and hauled from the city, and whose methods and evasions clearly allied him with the Confederacy, was arrested at dawn of June 27 and locked up at Fort McHenry. Four police commissioners, who were open and avowed secessionists, met and protested this action, and disbanded the city police force. So on July 1 the four police commissioners were likewise arrested and locked up in Fort McHenry. The secessionist trend in Maryland was definitely checked in June, when railroad schedules had been re-established, Unionists were elected to Congress in the six districts of Maryland, and Governor Hicks was having no difficulty enlisting four regiments of men to serve within the limits of Maryland or for the defense of the national capital.

Lincoln's reply to Chief Justice Taney's admonition that the Chief

Magistrate should not violate the Constitution he was sworn to administer was not made to Taney, but was given to the country in a message to Congress on July 4. In preparing the message Lincoln wrote as if he might be talking with a friend, using the words "I" and "my," and as he read it over he changed his mind about using "I" and "my." There was personal charm and attraction about using "I" and "my," more power, but some readers might believe that he considered Abraham Lincoln more important than the President of the United States. So he modified the sentence "In my opinion, I violated no law" into "It was not believed that any law was violated." This first draft of what he had to say on habeas corpus read:

Soon after the first call for militia, I felt it my duty to authorize the commanding general in proper cases, according to his discretion, to suspend the privilege of the writ of *habeas corpus*, or, in other words, to arrest and detain, without resort to the ordinary processes and forms of law, such individuals as he might deem dangerous to the public safety. . . . At my verbal request, as well as by the general's own inclination, this authority has been exercised but very sparingly. Nevertheless, the legality and propriety of what has been done under it are questioned; and I have been reminded from a high quarter that one who is sworn to "take care that the laws be faithfully executed" should not himself be one to violate them.

Of course I gave some consideration to the questions of power and propriety before I acted in this matter. The whole of the laws which I have sworn to take care that they be faithfully executed were being resisted, and failing to be executed, in nearly one-third of the States. Must I have allowed them to finally fail of execution, even had it been perfectly clear that by the use of the means necessary to their execution some single law, made in such extreme tenderness of the citizen's liberty, that practically it relieves more of the guilty than the innocent, should, to a very limited extent, be violated?

To state the question more directly, are all the laws but one to go unexecuted, and the Government itself go to pieces, lest that one be violated?

Even in such a case I should consider my official oath broken, if I should allow the Government to be overthrown, when I might think the disregarding the single law would tend to preserve it. But in this case I was not, in my own judgment, driven to this ground.

In my opinion, I violated no law. The provision of the Constitution that "The privilege of the writ of *habeas corpus* shall not be suspended unless when, in cases of rebellion or invasion, the public safety may require it," is equivalent to a provision— is a provision—that such privilege may be suspended when, in cases of rebellion or invasion, the public safety does require it.

I decided that we have a case of rebellion, and that the public safety does require the qualified suspension of the privilege of the writ of *habeas corpus*, which I authorized to be made. Now it is insisted that Congress, and not the executive, is vested with this power. But the Constitution itself is silent as to which, or who, is to exercise the power; and as the provision plainly was made for a dangerous emergency, I cannot bring myself to believe that the framers of that instrument intended that in every case the danger should run its course until Congress could be called together, the very assembling of which might be prevented, as was intended in this case by the rebellion.

The first momentous action of Lincoln's taking a hand in European diplomatic relations was in May of '61, when Seward read to Lincoln a long dispatch to be sent to Minister Adams at London with instructions that Adams was to hand the dispatch to Lord John Russell, Secretary of State for Great Britain. Usually Lincoln let such dispatches to foreign nations go as Seward wrote them. This one he held for careful reading and further attention.

The dispatch began by reciting that G. M. Dallas, Minister Adams's predecessor, had informed the State Department that in a conversation with Lord John Russell the British Secretary had said he had not yet seen the three representatives of the Southern Confederacy then in London but he was "not unwilling to see them unofficially." He further informed Dallas of an understanding between the British and French governments "which would lead both to take one and the same course as to recognition." Following the statement of this situation, Seward's dispatch read, "The President is surprised and grieved that Mr. Dallas did not protest," and Lincoln struck out the words "is surprised and grieved" and inserted the one word "regrets." At four places in Seward's dispatch where Lincoln considered the

[11]

Writing "Drop all from this line to the end," Lincoln strikes out from a note by Secretary Seward to Minister Adams at London closing paragraphs that could be construed as menacing, instructing Adams further that the paper was "for your guidance only, and not [to] be read, or shown to any one—"

tone needlessly warlike he enclosed a passage or phrase in brackets and put the words "Leave out" alongside.

At the end of Seward's dispatch were two long paragraphs that could easily be construed as welcoming a war with Great Britain. Seward pointed to a former war "between the European and the American branches of the British race," its result that "Europe atoned by forty years of suffering for the error that Great Britain committed in provoking that contest," and predicted drastic effects "if that nation shall now repeat the same great error." At the top line of these two warlike paragraphs Lincoln wrote "Drop all from this line to the end," to which he added for Minister Adams, "This paper is for your own guidance only, and not [to] be read or shown to any one."

As subdued and modified, the dispatch still had plenty of ready-to-fight spirit. Adams was to withdraw and desist from all intercourse, official or unofficial, with the British Government if it began unofficial intercourse with the domestic enemies of the United States. He was to play no favorites among European nations and take no notice of their alliances. "You will not insist that our blockade is to be respected if it be not maintained by a competent force. . . . As to the recognition of the so-called Southern Confederacy, it is not to be made a subject of technical definition. It is, of course, quasi direct recognition to publish an acknowledgment of the sovereignty and independence of a new power. It is quasi direct recognition to receive its ambassadors, ministers, agents, or commissioners officially. A concession of belligerent rights is liable to be construed as a recognition of them." Following this Seward had written, "No one of these proceedings will be borne unquestioned by the United States in this case," Lincoln changing "be borne unquestioned" to read "pass unnoticed."

Privateers would be treated as pirates, as American citizens raiding the commerce of their own country. "If Great Britain," wrote Seward, "shall choose to recognize them as lawful belligerents, and give them shelter from our pursuit and punishment, the laws of nations afford an adequate and proper remedy." To which Lincoln added for Adams's eye, "And while you need not say this in advance, be sure that you say nothing inconsistent with it."

Seward took the revised dispatch from Lincoln, added prefatory instructions that it was a confidential note not to be read or shown to anyone. With these changes Lincoln consented that the two final warlike paragraphs of Seward could be reinserted. When the dispatch reached Adams, he sought an interview with Lord John Russell to learn the status of the Confederate Commissioners, telling Russell that a continuance of their apparent relation with the British Government "could scarcely fail to be viewed by us as hostile in spirit, and to require some corresponding action accordingly." Russell replied that he had seen the Confederate Commissioners only twice and "had no expectation of seeing them any more." This was comforting to Adams, though not entirely so, for everyone knew Lord John Russell was "tortuous" in method and sometimes seemed to be coming when he was going.

Seward was still playing lingeringly with his old idea that a war with Great Britain might bring the Southern forces behind the old American flag in a solid Union. He believed nothing was to be lost by using a menacing tone to the British Government. His personal friend at London, Minister Adams, took his reckless threats and turned them into well-measured reproaches and courteous arguments. Adams was English-blooded and had instincts that were at home in London, one saying that his face could "outfreeze" that of any English gentleman with whom he had to dicker.

Believing Seward a great statesman and Lincoln still but a country lawyer unfortunately placed as President, Adams would have had a measure of enlightenment could he have read Seward's original draft of the May 21 dispatch with Lincoln's editorial interlinings and seen that Lincoln was doing the same as Adams in softening and modifying the Seward moods of menace. Further yet, he would have been enlightened if Seward could have told him in a long talk why Seward wrote his wife on June 5, 1861: "Executive skill and vigor are rare qualities. The President is the best of us."

Queen Victoria's proclamation of May 13, 1861, took notice of hostilities "between the government of the United States of America and certain States styling themselves the Confederate States of America" and declared the "royal determination to maintain a strict and impartial neutrality in the contest between said contending parties." The Queen and her consort, Prince Albert, the political liberals, and the masses of the English people leaned to the North in sympathy, while Prime Minister Palmerston, and the officials and imperialistic cliques voiced by the London *Times*, favored the South and in various technical rulings deviated far from strict neutrality. To the New York Rothschild agent, August Belmont, Palmerston said, "We do not like slavery, but we want cotton, and we dislike very much your Morrill tariff."

A queer obstacle, not easily defined yet definitely operating, known as British Public Opinion, was about all that stopped Palmerston from giving complete recognition to the Southern Confederacy and lending it the British fleet.

Schleiden of the Hanseatic Republic, in a letter of June 5, 1861, reported Lincoln fairly at ease regarding foreign relations: "The President last night entertained the whole diplomatic body at dinner, and told me in a very sensible manner, that it appeared to him as if this government had no reason to complain of any European power in this contest, all of them having, by the long-continuing want of any distinct policy on the part of the United States, been induced more or less to believe the Union weaker, and the seceded States stronger, than was really the fact."

To Carl Schurz departing for Spain Lincoln spoke about foreign affairs "with the same nonchalance with which he might have discussed an everyday law case at Springfield, Illinois." He told Schurz that if the Administration had so far "stumbled along," as was said, it had, on the whole "stumbled along in the right direction." To Schurz he expressed deep anxiety as to England, France, and the freshly arrived British Queen's proclamation of neutrality. He gave Schurz to understand that he deplored having given so little attention to foreign affairs and being so dependent on other people's judgment, and that he felt the necessity of "studying up" on the subject. He wished Schurz to watch public sentiment closely in Europe, and "whenever anything occurs to you that you want to tell me personally, or that you think I ought to know, you shall write me directly." A brother-in-law of Schurz, a young merchant from Hamburg, Germany, preceding a lunch at the White House was introduced to the President:

"He was astonished when Mr. Lincoln, instead of waiting for a ceremonious bow, shook him by the hand like an old acquaintance and said in his hearty way that he was glad to see the brother-in-law of 'this young man here.' "

Later in the year evidence was laid before Lincoln that the British Government was sending through its legation at Washington to the British consul at Charleston communications which were forwarded to President Davis at Richmond. Secret proposals, in which the French Government joined, were thus made that the Confederate Government should accede to only three of the four articles of the Declaration of Paris governing sea powers in maritime commerce and seizures of vessels, while the United States Government was invited to accede to all four of the articles. President Davis saw that these secret proposals were a quasi-recognition of his Government, and personally drafted resolutions, which the Confederate Congress passed, declaring that the Confederacy would accede to three articles, while as to the fourth, which would abolish privateering, they specifically "maintained the right of privateering." Thus Davis would have a measure of international sanction for his commissions to private individuals to arm vessels and raid United States commerce on the high seas.

The role of Robert Bunch, the British consul at Charleston, in these proceedings was regarded by Lincoln as a violation of the laws of the United States, to whose Government Bunch was officially accredited. So the exequatur, the authorization of Bunch to act as the consul of a foreign nation, was revoked. In long conversations between the British and United States governments neither side would concede any points, though the British Government did have a man-of-war leave Charleston Harbor carrying away the offensive Mr. Bunch.

The capture of the privateer *Savannah* in June raised the point whether the captain of the ship was a pirate to be given death by President Lincoln. "The capture will test Mr. Lincoln's nerve. Will he have the courage to hang the pirate captain?" asked *Harper's Weekly*. "Merchants and ship-owners, who have come forward nobly in support of the Government, are trembling in apprehension lest Mr. Lincoln should not have the nerve to carry out his policy, and nip piracy in the bud. Foreigners will decide, from Mr. Lincoln's action in this case, whether the President's proclamations are in earnest or mere bug-a-boos."

For all the prodding and veiled taunting, Lincoln refused to carry through a policy of hanging privateers as pirates, though his proclamation of April 19 had said plainly he would hang them. The *Jefferson Davis*, the *Dixie*, the *Bonita*, the *Lady Davis*, and other privateers commissioned by the Confederacy had by the end of May seized on the high seas and hauled into New Orleans Harbor eighteen vessels hailing from New England ports, with their cargoes of oil, fruit, sugar, salt, whale and sperm oil, ice, ballast. And the captures during June were bringing the total losses of Northern shippers and merchants into millions of dollars.

Therefore when the privateer *Savannah*, with captain and crew, was captured, a clamor arose that at least the captain be hanged as a pirate. The British view of the case was given by the Earl of Derby, who discussed Lincoln's proclamation and denied the right of the United States to make a definition of piracy not agreed upon by other nations: "The United States must not be allowed to entertain this doctrine, and to call upon Her Majesty's Government not to interfere. They must not strain the law so as to visit with the penalty of death, as for piracy, persons entitled to Her Majesty's protection." The Earl of Derby knew that the United States treated the Confederate States as mere rebels, and that as rebels the privateers were liable to all the penalties of high treason. That, however, was not the doctrine of Great Britain, "because we have declared that they are entitled to all the rights of belligerents."

When officers and seamen of the *Savannah* were to be put on trial in New York as pirates, Jefferson Davis sent an officer under a flag of truce through the Union Army lines into Washington to deliver into the hands of President Lincoln, on July 8, 1861, the first official communication Lincoln had received from the President of the Confederate States. The letter notified Lincoln that the schooner *Savannah*, a private armed vessel, had sailed under a commission of the Confederate States, and according to New York newspapers, the men captured on it were treated not as prisoners of war but as criminals, put in irons, confined in jail, charged in court with piracy and treason. "I could not, without grave discourtesy, have made the newspaper statements the subject of this communication," said the Davis letter, "if the threat of treating as pirates the citizens of this Confederacy, armed for its service on the high seas, had not been contained in your proclamation of 19th April last."

The Confederate President then said that his Government desired to conduct the war so as to mitigate its horrors, treat prisoners with "the greatest humanity and leniency," furnishing subsistence rations "such as are allowed to our own troops." Under painful necessity he must state that "if driven to the terrible necessity of retaliation by your execution of any of the officers or crew of the *Savannah*, that retaliation will be extended so far as shall be requisite to secure the abandonment of a practice unknown to the warfare of civilized man, and so barbarous as to disgrace the nation which shall be guilty of inaugurating it."

Lincoln read this letter carefully, and the Confederate messenger returned to Davis, who a week later reported to the Confederate Congress that his officer had been told that "a reply would be returned by President Lincoln as soon as possible" and "I earnestly hope this promised reply (which has not yet been received) will convey assurance that prisoners of war will be treated with regard for humanity."

When the captain and crew of the privateer *Jefferson Davis* were convicted in Philadelphia of piracy, the decision was finally put up to Lincoln whether they should hang as pirates, in which event an equal number of Federal officers in Southern prisons, chosen by lot, according to the Confederate Secretary of War would likewise be hanged. The Confederate

Secretary of War went so far as to name the thirteen Union officers, selected by drawing of numbers, who would go to the gallows.

The *Charleston Mercury* offered its belief that in spite of "the treachery and cruelty of Lincoln and his despotic horde of underlings and satraps," the convicted seamen would not be hanged, Lincoln knowing well that "we can erect the gallows or the gibbet as well as others."

The guess was correct. Lincoln refused to begin a competition in hanging. Jefferson Davis had outplayed him. He could not begin to consider hanging pirates when it was certain that for each pirate strung up one good Union officer would likewise dance on air from a rope. Had Lincoln been familiar with the fine points of international and maritime law which he learned through this affair, he would not have fallen in with Seward's claim that the United States alone had the power to define as a pirate a privateer on high seas that belong to all nations, and particularly to the British fleet. This was already vaguely in his mind when he had told Schurz that as to international matters he must "study up." Slowly and unwillingly the Lincoln Government moved toward a continuing policy of treating privateers as ordinary prisoners of war, which was internationally construed as at least a partial recognition of the belligerent rights of the Confederacy. Though Lincoln and his associates officially referred to the "pretended government" of "the so-called Confederate States of America," they knew they were doing this as a form and, howsoever it sounded, no other form was suitable. And in the specific matter of privateering they realized that hanging was less expeditious than other methods. Gradually as the blockade tightened and the navy outfitted cruisers for special attention to Confederate sea raiders, the terrors and losses of sea traffic for United States vessels grew less.

The days sped away and time was priceless amid blunders and vanities, John Hay on May 7 mentioning to Lincoln that one Singleton was behaving very badly: "He [the President] replied with emphasis that Singleton was a miracle of meanness; calmly looking out of the window at the smoke of two strange steamers puffing up the way, resting the end of the telescope on his toes sublime."

The President and the Cabinet through the new and often bungling personnels of their old departments were wrestling with crazy patterns of military organization, red tape, confusions of counsels, inpouring brigades, telegrams exchanged daily or hourly with governors recruiting troops, the direction of four grades of troops: (1) regulars; (2) three-month volunteers; (3) State militia; (4) three-year volunteers; besides independent troop units in Border States still neutral.

In the furious, complex, and driving labors of shaping effective armies for grand strategic campaigns against the prepared Southern States, the ailing, failing octogenarian Scott was slow, pompous, fussy, and his dropsy and vertigo were pathetic afflictions of a one-time hero. A group of Iowans called on the General in Chief, were ushered into his presence after much red tape, and at the mention of Iowa his eyes closed and he summoned reminiscences of buried soldiers and cholera at Rock Island during the Black Hawk War. His voice husky, eyes dull, he nodded assent to some question asked and then dozed off into a midday sleep. Senator Grimes of this group went to Lincoln with his opinion that an old imbecile headed the United States military establishment, and protracted war and disunion were probable. Congressman Josiah Bushnell Grinnell, also of this Iowa group, called on Lincoln later in the day, Lincoln saying: "You stirred up Grimes to swear in madness over the incapacity of our General. Now, candidly, did he color it?" Grinnell grinned. "He did sleep, and we retreated, not on bugle-call, but before he snored out in prologue."

On Scott more than anyone else Lincoln had to depend for information, advice, guidance in technical military matters and as to the merits of men whose commissions as major generals and brigadiers Lincoln must sign. Most of the troop bodies entering service, however, were volunteers raised by officers elected by their men. In giving such officers commissions Lincoln had to consider political matters, as also in the appointment of civilians of political merit yet unproved as to military ability. In many cases Lincoln and Secretary Cameron went directly over Scott's head and ordered action on political grounds, if not military. Carl Schurz, as an instance, proposed to Scott that he should be authorized to go to New York and among German friends there raise a regiment of cavalry for active service. In a series of questions and a final curt dismissal, Scott snubbed Schurz. He reported the conversation to Lincoln and Cameron, was handed the authority requested, went to New York, and had recruited several companies before leaving for his duties as Minister to Spain.

The new consul to Paris, John Bigelow, came to the White House, having in mind what he had heard from his friend Preston King, that Lincoln was "not only unequal to the present crisis, but [unequal] to the position he now holds at any time." Bigelow stayed in the President's private office more than a half-hour, hearing a conversation between Lincoln and a Senator on the army and field operations. "I observed no sign of weakness in anything the President said," noted Bigelow, "neither did I hear anything that particularly impressed me, which, under the circumstances, was not surprising. What did impress me, however, was what I can only describe as a *certain lack* of *sovereignty*. He seemed to me, nor was it in the least strange that he did, like a man utterly unconscious of the space which the President of the United States occupied that day in the history of the human race, and of the vast power for the exercise of which he had become personally responsible. This impression was strengthened by Mr. Lincoln's modest habit of disclaiming knowledge of affairs and familiarity with duties, and frequent avowals of ignorance, which, even where it exists, it is as well for a captain as far as possible to conceal from the public." Bigelow noted too that this impression which he formed, much like that of Preston King, was one he had constantly met in "men directly from Washington." There was "an almost uniform lack of that enthusiasm which usually accompanies the accession of a new dynasty and a new dispensation of patronage." Had Bigelow spoken frank private counsel to Lincoln, it would have been: "The authority of an executive officer largely consists in what his constituents think it is." Whether these valuations of Lincoln in the late spring and early summer of '61 were correct, time was to tell.

Amid furious political pressure, mental hysteria, and vocal bedlam, Lincoln "stumbled along" in selecting the guiding authorities for his sprawling and yet-to-be-tried military organization. In commissioning major generals of volunteers the President seemed to rest chiefly on the judgment of Scott, who favored John E. Wool, John A. Dix, Henry W. Halleck, Don Carlos Buell. The appointment of John C. Frémont as a major general was mainly political, as were the appointments of Benjamin F. Butler and Nathaniel P. Banks. David Hunter, Edwin V. Sumner, and John Pope, who had accompanied Lincoln from Springfield to Harrisburg, were commissioned as origadiers. Among the May and June appointees as brigadiers nearly all had West Point training and Mexican War service records. An exception was Robert C. Schenck of Ohio, once a professor, then a lawyer, Minister to Brazil under President Fillmore. He had stumped southern Illinois for Lincoln in 1860. Lincoln invited him to the White House, according to Schenck, for a short interview:

"Good morning, Mr. Schenck."

"Good morning, sir."

"We're having a devil of a time just now. Schenck, can you fight?"

"I don't know, sir, but I can try."

"And I am sure you will succeed. You have it in your blood, and I am going to give you a chance to try. You shall be made a brigadier-general."

That was all. Schenck walked out of the room with his commission.

William Tecumseh Sherman came on to Washington and found that "Mr. Lincoln had, without the sanction of law, authorized the raising of ten new regiments of regulars." Sherman left the White House one day with a commission to head one of these regiments. Sherman had amazed the President and given him a healthy laugh by refusing a brigadier's commission and saying that he would rather work up from colonel. On the White House steps Sherman met his old West Point friend Irvin McDowell, in a brand-new brigadier's uniform.

"Hello, Sherman, what did you ask for?"

"A colonelcy."

"What? You should have asked for a brigadier-general's rank. You're just as fit for it as I am."

"I know it," snapped Sherman.

Sherman sent the St. Louis horsecar street railways a word of good-by as superintendent; he would do his best for the war, though he was storm-tossed and haunted with impressions that men North and South were blind and crazy, that greedy politicians had too large a sway at Washington, and the war would end in a hundred years rather than the hundred days many people were predicting. Another West Pointer, Joseph E. Johnston of Virginia, of much the same feeling, in grief and tears had just resigned as quartermaster general of the United States Army to go into Confederate gray.

Sherman had said to Lincoln, "Why don't you nominate Thomas?" meaning George H. Thomas, a Virginian and a West Pointer of long army experience. Lincoln replied that Thomas was born in Virginia and there were doubts as to his loyalty. Sherman protested, "Mr. President, Old Tom is as loyal as I am, and as a soldier he is superior to all on your list." Lincoln inquired, "Will you be responsible for him?" Sherman snapped, "With the greatest pleasure." And Lincoln sent the nomination of Thomas as brigadier general to the Senate that day. When Sherman met Thomas later that day, he said: "Tom, there are some stories about your loyalty. How are you going?" "Billy, I am going South." "My God!" was Sherman's cry and he went on to explain what he had told Lincoln. "Give yourself no trouble, Billy," was the twinkling response. "I am going South, but at the head of my men."

Of a total of 1,108 United States Army officers, 387 had resigned to go South. These resigned Southerners, 288 of them West Point-trained, included the most promising officers, of actual field and battle service. General Scott in his long reign as head of the army had favored Southern men to a degree almost notorious. And partly for this reason and partly that the North offered wider opportunities to men of technical and engineering abilities, Northern men in much larger proportion had drifted out of the United States Army into other and better-paying jobs. When Scott a few years before had made his staff all Southern except one man, and was twitted about it, he had said, "If the Southern rascals have so much merit, how are we to deny them?"

Among West Pointers in Northern service were 162 born in Slave States. Among West Pointers gone South for service were 19 Northern-born men.

Whether or not Lincoln had time to examine these curious proportions, he was writing in a message to Congress: "It is worthy of note that while in this, the government's hour of trial, large numbers of those in the army and navy who have been favored with offices have resigned and proved false to the hand which had pampered them, not one common soldier or common sailor is known to have deserted his flag. Great honor is due to those officers who remained true, despite the example of their treacherous associates; but the greatest of honor, and the most important fact of all, is the unanimous firmness of the common soldiers and sailors. To the last man, so far as known, they have successfully resisted the traitorous efforts of those whose commands, but an hour before, they obeyed as absolute law. This is the patriotic instinct of the plain people."

As early as May 7, 1861, John Hay spoke to Lincoln about letters arriving thickly interspersed with suggestions on the race question, the slavery issue. The President was then, Hay noted, "engaged in constant thought upon his Message," what issues he would raise, how he would give the world his answer to the questions "What is the war for? Why are men going out to kill?" He would write in that message:

"On the side of the Union it is a struggle for maintaining in the world that form and substance of government whose leading object is to elevate the condition of men—to lift artificial weights from all shoulders; to clear the paths of laudable pursuit for all; to afford all an unfettered start, and a fair chance in the race of life. Yielding to partial and temporary departures, from necessity, this is the leading object of the government for whose existence we contend. . . . It is now for them [our people] to demonstrate . . . that when ballots have fairly and constitutionally decided, there can be no successful appeal back to bullets. . . . Such will be a great lesson of peace: teaching men that what they cannot take by an election, neither can they take it by a war; teaching all the folly of being the beginners of a war."

This passage would be often quoted by his opponents and set alongside another passage from a Mexican War speech of Lincoln's, holding: "Any people anywhere being inclined and having the power have the right to rise up and shake off the existing government, and form a new one that suits them better. This is a most valuable, a most sacred right—a right which we hope and believe is to liberate the world. Nor is this right confined to cases in which the whole people of an existing government may choose to exercise it. Any portion of such people that can may revolutionize and make their own so much of the territory as they inhabit."

In May and June of 1861, then, Lincoln was stressing popular government and maintenance of the Union above all issues. If the slavery issue was to come up front it would be through force of circumstances, through "yielding to partial and temporary departures, from necessity." This necessity had begun to work the moment the secession movement gained headway. It thrust the slavery issue forward for discussion and required that the millions of Negroes in the South be considered as a war factor, to be used by one side or both. The "contraband" would not down as an issue. It emerged in Douglas's suddenly telling Lincoln in effect that he would not care about the Fugitive Slave Law in case of a Negro insurrection. It was there in Jefferson Davis's telling his wife that the war would bring a new status to "our slave property." In one of his first interviews with the President, Senator Sumner said soon was the time to declare the Negroes free.

On May 7 Hay spoke to Lincoln about the Kentucky-born Browning of Quincy, Illinois, proposing to subjugate the South, establish a black republic in lieu of the exterminated whites, and extend a protectorate over them while they raised cotton. Hay seemed to believe Browning was speaking in earnest, whereas a study of Browning's diary would show that he was saying this in bitter sarcasm. Hay noted Lincoln's reply: "Some of our Northerns seem bewildered and dazzled by the excitement of the hour. Doolittle [Senator from Wisconsin] seems inclined to think that this war is to result in the entire abolition of slavery. Old Colonel Hamilton, a venerable and most respectable gentleman, impresses upon me most earnestly the propriety of enlisting the slaves in our Army."

Propaganda against slavery sprang up in unexpected quarters, the conservative Russell of the London *Times* sending his imperialistic journal the extremist Southern view that God had ordained slavery and it was justified not merely by necessity but in principle and doctrine, as though if slavery had not existed the South would have invented it for the Negro's benefit. Russell pictured an auctioneer selling a slave in Montgomery, Alabama: "Nine h'un'nerd and fifty dollars! Only nine h-hun-nerd and fifty dollars offered for him!" A bidder near by opened his mouth, spat, and said, "Twenty-five." The auctioneer: "Only nine hundred and seventy-five dollars offered for him! Why, 'at's radaklous—only nine hundred and seventy-five dollars! Will no one . . ." and so on. Beside the auctioneer Russell saw standing a stout young Negro man, twenty-five years of age, a bundle in his hand, muscular, broad-shouldered, wearing a coarse shirt, ragged trousers, and broken shoes. "His face, heavy and sad, was by no means disagreeable, in spite of his thick lips, broad nostrils and high cheek-bones. On his head was wool instead of hair. I am neither sentimentalist nor Black Republican nor negro-worshipper, but I confess the sight caused a strange thrill through my heart. I tried in vain to make myself familiar with the fact that I could, for the sum of nine hundred and seventy-five dollars, become as absolutely the owner of that mass of blood, bones, sinew, flesh, and brains as of the horse which stood at my side. There was no sophistry which could persuade me the man was not a man; he was, indeed, by no means my brother, but assuredly he was a fellow-creature. . . . The negro was sold to one of the bystanders, and walked off with his bundle, God knows where. 'Niggers is cheap,' was the only remark of the bystanders."

Russell compared this slave sale with others he had seen in Turkey, Smyrna, Egypt; among the Orientals it was something else. "Here it grated on my ear to listen to the familiar tones of the English tongue as the medium by which the transfer was effected, and it was painful to see decent-looking men in European garb engaged in the work before me."

A few weeks before Russell's first glimpse of a slave auction, Mary Boykin Chesnut of South Carolina was in Montgomery and herself saw one. She had been brought up to plantation life and had never gone out of her way to see slaves sold in competitive bidding. Her husband, one-time United States Senator from South Carolina, was one of the most loyal allies and co-workers of President Davis. She went with him to Montgomery. She strayed casually into a scene that suddenly amazed her. She wrote in her diary for March 4 of what she was doing and how she felt about it on the day Lincoln was sworn in: "I have seen a negro woman sold on the block at auction. She overtopped the crowd. I was walking and felt faint, seasick. The creature looked so like my good little Nancy, a bright mulatto with a pleasant face. She was magnificently gotten up in silks and satins. She seemed delighted with it all, sometimes ogling the bidders, sometimes looking quiet, coy, and modest, but her mouth never relaxed from its expanded grin of excitement. I dare say the poor thing knew who would buy her. I sat down on a stool in a shop and disciplined my wild thoughts. I tried it

Sterne fashion. You know how women sell themselves and are sold in marriage from queens downward, eh? You know what the Bible says about slavery and marriage; poor women! poor slaves! Sterne, with his starling—what did he know? He only thought, he did not feel.

"In *Evan Harrington* [a novel by George Meredith] I read: 'Like a true English female, she believed in her own inflexible virtue, but never trusted her husband out of sight.'

"The *New York Herald* says: 'Lincoln's carriage is not bomb-proof; so he does not drive out.' Two flags and a bundle of sticks have been sent him as gentle reminders. The sticks are to break our heads with."

The South had a secret the North knew little of. The South had many doubts about slavery. Those doubts were its secret. Over the South not yet did they dare speak this secret. As to white-race superiority the South had no doubts. While it defended black-race slavery as a living institution, the South was not sure but the institution was dying of some inherent malady. The brilliant and sensitive Mrs. Chesnut in her diary meditations touched a human phase of it that made her faint and heartsick, while the tougher-hearted Russell stood ashamed of his blood and language. They were highly civilized, upper-class persons. They embodied a deep trend. They recoiled shivering at the basic naked fact of an auctioneer's selling one human creature to another for a price bid, whether the creature sold was a muscular field hand in coarse clothing or a bright mulatto in silks and satins flashing her eyes at prospective buyers. The institution was complicated. So was the matter of race equality and of white-race superiority.

Up in Maine the little woman who had written *Uncle Tom's Cabin* received in the mail one day a pair of Negro ears sent by someone who loathed her race-equality ideas.

In his message to Congress Lincoln was writing no line or word dealing with any phase of the Negro and slavery.

The President kept an official loyalty to the Fugitive Slave Act. It had been embodied in a local commander's order that fugitive slaves in the District of Columbia or Virginia "under no pretext whatever be permitted to reside, or be in any way harbored" in troop camps or quarters, nor could such slaves accompany troops on march. Slaves from Maryland would slip down into the Union Army lines, their owners sending Senators and Congressmen from Maryland to ask Lincoln about the Fugitive Slave Law, which in his inaugural address he had said he was oathbound to uphold and execute. The President wrote to General Scott inquiring whether it would not be well "to allow owners to bring back" those who had crossed the Potomac with Union troops. The War Department communication to General Irvin McDowell, commanding in Virginia, urged him to "enter fully into His Excellency's desire" to carry out to the fullest his constitutional obligations: "Of course it is the General's wish the name of the President should not at this time be brought before the public in connection with this delicate subject."

So it seemed that fugitive slaves from Virginia, owned by secessionist

Virginians, who fled into Butler's camp at Fortress Monroe were easily held as "contraband," having no intercessors for their owners at Washington. But Maryland slaves who drifted down into District of Columbia and Virginia camps of the Union Army were immediately and hotly spoken for by Maryland Unionist members of Congress, sometimes speaking for slaveowners who could not be shown as disloyal. So Lincoln began slowly evolving a policy of letting commanders and localities develop their own method of treating fugitive slaves, military necessity always to govern the method.

On July 6, 1861, Secretary of War Cameron notified Lincoln that sixty-four volunteer regiments of 900 men each, besides 1,200 regulars, were in readiness around Washington, and the troops enrolled elsewhere over the North made a total of 225,000. Of this army, one of the largest the earth had ever seen, Lincoln was Commander in Chief. And he wrote his high pride of these volunteers in his message to Congress, for the world to know:

"So large an army as the government has now on foot was never before known, without a soldier in it but who has taken his place there of his own free choice. But more than this, there are many single regiments whose members, one and another, possess full practical knowledge of all the arts, sciences, professions, and whatever else, whether useful or elegant, is known in the world; and there is scarcely one from which could not be selected a President, a cabinet, a congress, and perhaps a court abundantly competent to administer the government itself."

This was in part Lincoln's reply to Pierre Gustave Toutant Beauregard, superintendent of the West Point Military Academy the previous winter just before he resigned, of continuous service in the United States Army for twenty-three years, a Mexican War veteran, a professor of the applied science of artillery, now commanding an army of 20,000 Confederate troops near Washington at Manassas Junction. He was a Louisiana Creole, born and bred in French traditions, immersed in Napoleonic legends, a short, compact, abstemious man of pride and temper not afraid to talk back to President Davis if the words came to him—and they did. As the hero who had shot away the flag at Fort Sumter and reduced it to ruins, he was called to Virginia to check Northern invasion. He began with a proclamation on June 1 inviting the freemen of Virginia to imitate their Revolutionary Fathers "and by the purity and sanctity of your domestic firesides, to rally to the standard of your State and country." The document opened in Gallic splendor of verbal anger:

"A reckless and unprincipled tyrant has invaded your soil. Abraham Lincoln, regardless of all moral, legal, and constitutional restraints, has thrown his Abolition hosts among you, who are murdering and imprisoning your citizens, confiscating and destroying your property, and committing other acts of violence and outrage too shocking and revolting to humanity to be enumerated. All rules of civilized warfare are abandoned, and they proclaim by their acts, if not on their banners, that their war-cry is 'Beauty and Booty.' Your honor and that of your wives and daughters, your fortunes, and your lives are involved in this momentous contest."

On July 4 when Congress assembled it was in the air that soon a battle would be fought near Washington. Greeley's *New York Tribune* clamored in headlines: "Forward to Richmond! Forward to Richmond! The Rebel Congress must not be allowed to meet there on the 20th of July! By that date the place must be held by the National Army!"

Business was worse, money scarce, loans slow. A short war was wanted. Everybody agreed on that. The time was already up for some three-month troops. The 4th Pennsylvania Volunteers and the 8th New York Artillery were calling for their discharges.

For weeks the picket lines of the opposing armies had been within rifle-shot of each other, and no fighting. "Why don't they fight?" was a query North and South.

Russell of the London *Times* told Lincoln of many "dropping shots" he had heard in the camps around Washington, an officer explaining, "They are only volunteers shooting themselves."

"Well," said the President, "that seems a waste of good material in every way; however, they will soon have a chance at making better use of their ammunition, I hope."

The House chaplain, the Reverend T. H. Stockton, offered the prayer: "O Lord, our God, if Thou dost indeed ordain and sanction war, may it not be a bloody and ruinous war. May it rather be an armed, mighty, irresistible migration—a migration of those who truly love liberty and civilization, who love the Union and the Constitution and the laws, retaking and repossessing and improving all that belongs to our Government."

Now came the first ceremonial of the House receiving a message from President Abraham Lincoln, a little drill ritual to be seen many times later, in both House and Senate. Mr. Nicolay enters the chamber and comes to a standstill near the door. The formal Sergeant at Arms with military precision marches to where Mr. Nicolay stands, and ranges himself alongside. The Speaker of the House interrupts whatever business is proceeding, declares that there is a message from the President. Then the President's private secretary announces that he has the honor to present a message from the President, giving its number and subject, and handing the document over to the Deputy Sergeant at Arms, who marches back to his place like an automaton.

In this message to Congress the President sketched the course of the Government since "four months ago," when his term of office began. The functions of the Federal Government were "generally suspended" in six Southern States, forts, arsenals, dockyards, customhouses, and armed forces organized in avowed hostile purpose: "A disproportionate share of the Federal muskets and rifles had somehow found their way into these States, and had been seized to be used against the government. Accumulations of public revenue lying within them had been seized for the same object. The navy was scattered in distant seas, leaving but a very small part of it within immediate reach of the government." The incoming Executive had chosen a policy that looked "to the exhaustion of all peaceful measures" before a resort to any stronger ones. "Of all that which a President might constitutionally and justifiably do in such a case, everything was forborne without which it was believed possible to keep the government on foot."

He gave a miniature history of the Fort Sumter affair, of how the fort was bombarded to its fall "without even awaiting the arrival of the provisioning expedition" and this act had forced the distinct issue of "immediate dissolution or blood." This issue embraced more than the United States and presented questions to "the whole family of man" as to whether democracy could maintain integrity against discontented individuals. It forced the questions: "Is there, in all republics, this inherent and fatal weakness?" "Must a government, of necessity, be too strong for the liberties of its own people, or too weak to maintain its own existence?"

No choice was left but "to call out the war power of the government." The response of the country was gratifying, surpassing expectation. Of the Border States of Maryland, Kentucky, Missouri, the message said nothing specific. In Virginia, North Carolina, Tennessee, Arkansas, the Union sentiment was "nearly repressed and silenced." Virginia's withdrawal from the Union was accomplished by a remarkable convention: "To this body the people had chosen a large majority of professed Union men." The seizures by Virginia of the Harper's Ferry arsenal and the Norfolk navy yard were followed by the transfer of the so-called Confederate States Government to the capital of Virginia, and "this government has no choice left but to deal with it where it finds it." As to those favoring "armed neutrality" in the Border States, they would "tie the hands of Union men" and bring disunion.

Besides his own view on habeas corpus, given in one long paragraph, the Attorney General would probably present a more extended argument, and legislation on the subject, if any, would be submitted to the better judgment of Congress.

Applause swept the House at the recommendation "that you give the legal means for making this contest a short and decisive one" and for the work at least 400,000 men and $400,000,000. "A right result at this time will be worth more to the world than ten times the men and ten times the money. The evidence reaching us from the country leaves no doubt that the material for the work is abundant, and that it needs only the hand of legislation to give it legal sanction, and the hand of the executive to give it practical shape and efficiency. One of the greatest perplexities of the government is to avoid receiving troops faster than it can provide for them. In a word, the people will save their government if the government itself will do its part only indifferently well."

The President then queried whether the Southern movement should be called "secession" or "rebellion," saying that the instigators of the movement understood the difference, in the beginning knowing well that "they could never raise their treason to any respectable magnitude by any name which implies violation of law," for "They knew their people possessed as much of moral sense, as much of devotion to law and order, and as much

Roger Brooke Taney, Chief Justice of the
Supreme Court

Photograph from U.S. Army Signal Corps

Abner Doubleday

Photograph from Oliver R. Barrett Collection

Robert Anderson, "Bob Anderson, my beau"   Winfield Scott, "Head of the Army"

From Oliver R. Barrett Collection

John Henninger Reagan of Texas, Postmaster
General, C.S.A.

Photograph by McClees in author's collection

Christopher Gustavus Memminger of South
Carolina, Secretary of the Treasury, C.S.A.

From Frederick H. Meserve Collection

Leroy Pope Walker, Secretary of War, C.S.A.

Photograph from Frederick H. Meserve Collection

Stephen Russell Mallory, Secretary of the
Navy, C.S.A.

Photograph by McClees in author's collection

pride in and reverence for the history and government of their common country as any other civilized and patriotic people."

The President revealed himself aware of the intricate processes of propaganda on a wide scale, and the technique for spreading of doctrine and viewpoint with irresistible infiltration. And he must have considered it important to notify the world that he was aware of such processes and technique, though he would reserve in silence other matters of which he was aware, and which he had voiced in once telling a Chicago crowd of workingmen and ordinary citizens in sarcasm, "Plainly, you stand ready saddled, bridled, and harnessed, and waiting to be driven." For now in his message to Congress when he referred to "they" he meant all those forces of the educated classes, the politicians, state officials, lawyers, clergy, editors, soldiers, slave-traders, who had created the mass sentiment that brought secession.

"They," ran Lincoln's sentences of high scorn, "knew they could make no advancement directly in the teeth of these strong and noble sentiments [of their people]. Accordingly, they commenced by *an insidious debauching of the public mind*. [Italics added.] They invented an ingenious sophism which, if conceded, was followed by perfectly logical steps, through all the incidents, to the complete destruction of the Union. The sophism itself is that any State of the Union may consistently with the National Constitution, and therefore lawfully and peacefully, withdraw from the Union without the consent of the Union or of any other State. The little disguise that the supposed right is to be exercised only for just cause, themselves to be the sole judges of its justice, is too thin to merit any notice. With rebellion thus *sugar-coated* they have been *drugging the public mind* [Italics added.] of their section for more than thirty years, and until at length they have brought many good men to a willingness to take up arms against the government the day after some assemblage of men have enacted the farcical pretense of taking their State out of the Union, who could have been brought to no such thing the day before."

Under the political necessities of the hour Lincoln could not have gone so far as to make it clear that in the debates with Douglas he had referred to the Northern public mind's being debauched no less than the Southern, that the masses of people in the North were no more difficult to drug with propaganda than those of the South, and that the North equally with the South had its instruments of rostrum, pulpit, press, for the spreading of the "ingenious sophism" and the dignifying of the "farcical pretense."

Again he went into a miniature history of the Union as a political whole, referred in satire to "some omnipotent and sacred supremacy pertaining to a State." The nation paid very large sums ("I believe, nearly a hundred millions") to relieve Florida of Indian tribes. "Is it just that she shall now be off without consent or without making any return? The nation is now in debt for money applied to the benefit of these so-called seceding States in common with the rest. Is it just either that creditors shall go unpaid or the remaining States pay the whole? A part of the present national debt was contracted to pay the old debts of Texas. Is it just that she shall leave and pay no part of this herself?" Lincoln at this point did not include the information that Southern Commissioners in Washington claimed that they were anxious to pay these debts and favored an arbitration board to adjudicate financial matters. The Southern reply generally on this matter was that their section had paid a fair share of Federal taxes and large areas in the North had been bought with its money as well as that of the North.

Lincoln said nothing on the point in his message, but pressed the argument: "If one State may secede, so may another; and when all shall have seceded, none is left to pay the debts. Is this quite just to creditors? [Lincoln knew England and Palmerston were listening for this.] Did we notify them of this sage view of ours when we borrowed their money? If we now recognize this doctrine by allowing the seceders to go in peace, it is difficult to see what we can do if others choose to go or to extort terms upon which they will promise to remain."

He forecast disintegration for seceders consistent to their principle: "To be consistent they must secede from one another whenever they shall find it the easiest way to settling their debts, or effecting any other selfish or unjust object." He referred to "the whole class of seceder politicians" as subtle and profound on the rights of minorities and not partial to the power speaking from the preamble to the Constitution, calling itself "We, the People." He would question "whether there is to-day a majority of the legally qualified voters of any State, except perhaps South Carolina, in favor of disunion."

On the side of the Union it was a people's struggle for a government in which "The people themselves, and not their servants, can safely reverse their own deliberate decisions." In full view of his great responsibility the Executive had done what he deemed his duty: "As a private citizen the executive could not have consented that these institutions shall perish; much less could he, in betrayal of so vast and so sacred a trust as the free people have confided to him. He felt that he had no moral right to shrink, nor even to count the chances of his own life in what might follow." The course was chosen: "without guile and with pure purpose, let us renew our trust in God, and go forward without fear and with manly hearts."

The message was a document of state, a brief for a client, a letter to the American people. The Northern press gave it greater approval than any utterance hitherto from Lincoln. The editor of *Harper's Weekly*, George William Curtis, who had been hissed down when he tried to have the Chicago Republican convention in 1860 endorse the Declaration of Independence with Jefferson's little proposition, "All men are created equal," vented his enthusiasm in a letter to a personal friend: "I envy no other age. I believe with all my heart in the cause, and in Abe Lincoln. His message is the most truly American message ever delivered. Think upon what a millennial year we have fallen when the President of the United States declares officially that this government is founded upon the rights of men! Wonderfully acute, simple, sagacious, and of antique honesty! I can forgive the jokes and the big hands, and the inability to make bows. Some of us who doubted were wrong. This people is not rotten. What the young men dream, the old men shall see." Not till the end of the letter did Curtis send kind remembrances from his wife and add, "We have a little girl, born on the day of the Proclamation."

The *Spectator* of London liked the ideas and decisions of the message, though uneasy about the language: "Mr. Lincoln writes like a half-educated lawyer, and thinks like a European sovereign."

The Senate confirmed the President's appointments. The House under Speaker Galusha A. Grow of Pennsylvania was accommodating. The Republicans had a decided majority. The Northern Democrats were in the main responsive to the back-home war sentiment. Applause rang to the President's call for a short, decisive war and 400,000 troops. A new army bill gave the President more than he asked, authorizing 500,000 three-year volunteers. His authority was broadened with powers to meet insurrection and "conspiracy to overthrow the Government of the United States," to punish piracy, to close insurrectionary ports by proclamation, to require government employees in any case to take the oath of allegiance. To the President's request for $400,000,000 Congress authorized a national loan of $250,000,000, levied a direct tax of $20,000,000 on States and Territories, and increased tariffs and income taxes. The Northern and Border Slave State Democrats, while giving support to the war, kept away from committing themselves to the Republican party, particularly on any trend of antislavery color.

A joint resolution to make legal and valid the extralegal, dictatorial, and proscriptive acts of the President in the emergencies since his proclamation of war in April met little direct opposition, but was held up and laid away amid unfinished business from day to day. He had gone out of his way to do so many things without authority from Congress, though the laws and the Constitution required that he should in those things have authority from Congress, that Congress was going slow about saying Yes to all he had done. Some of the murmuring took the form that he should have called Congress earlier and day by day asked its Yes or No.

Vallandigham of Ohio rose to say that Lincoln's inaugural address was "not written in the straightforward language expected from the plain, blunt honest man of the Northwest, but with the forked tongue and crooked counsel of the New York politician [meaning Seward], leaving thirty millions of people in doubt whether it meant peace or war." In the call for three-month troops he saw the President exercising "wicked and most desperate cunning." Andrew Jackson had acted with authority of Congress. Not so "our Jackson of today, the little Jackson at the other end of the avenue, and the mimic Jacksons around him." Lincoln as a usurper had stricken down personal liberty, free speech, the rights of home and private property. Freedom of religious belief would next go "under the polluting hoofs of an ambitious and fanatical clergy." Concerning "atrocious and shameless peculations and frauds" he would say that "the avenging hour for all these will come hereafter." Others had changed but he, Vallandigham, was still for peace. "I am for peace, speedy, immediate, honorable peace, with all its blessings." To the query of another member whether he believed in maintaining the Union, he responded that his votes in the House would speak for him. "I am answerable only to my conscience and to my constituents."

A memorial came to the Senate from three Baltimore police commissioners jailed at Fort McHenry. Writing from jail, they wished to know for what cause they were where they were. Senator Breckinridge of Kentucky, soon to join the Confederacy, said that a despot had always been defined as a ruler who took to himself the executive, legislative, and judicial departments of government—and this Lincoln had done. "What is the excuse? Necessity. I answer there was no necessity." And taking up each of Lincoln's warmaking acts, he argued that it was not necessary. Senator Powell of Kentucky rose to add, "There never was a king, potentate or sovereign, when he was assuming powers that did not belong to him for the purpose of crushing the liberties of his people, who did not do it under the plea of necessity." Senator Polk of Missouri, soon to join the Confederacy, set forth that only Congress had authority to declare war, and "a war monstrous in character and proportions" had been brought on by the President alone since March 4.

Senator Baker of Oregon rang out: "I want sudden, bold, forward, determined war; and I do not think anybody can conduct war of that kind as well as a Dictator." Amid stormy applause from the galleries Congressman Hickman of Pennsylvania shot his cry: "This government will be preserved, and the gallows will eventually perform its office."

CHAPTER 11

BULL RUN LOST '61—COMMANDER McCLELLAN

IN hotels and saloons along Pennsylvania Avenue in Washington on July 17, 1861, the London *Times* correspondent, Russell, heard of desperate fighting and the "rebel" army smashed. "I was rather amused," he wrote, "by the florid accounts given in the hall of Willard's by various inebriated officers." Freshly arrived New York newspapers gave him glowing descriptions of the Union troops in motion. And the next day a brigadier general told him the fighting had begun.

At the War Office, State Department, Senate, and the White House, messengers and orderlies ran in and out, military aides, civilians with anxious faces. Senator Sumner beamed to Russell. "We have obtained a great success; the rebels are falling back in all directions. General Scott says we ought to be in Richmond by Saturday night." Then an army officer riding past called out to him, "You have heard we are whipped; these confounded volunteers have run away."

Russell drove to Capitol Hill, having heard that he could see the smoke of the cannon from there, but it was a false lead. Russell heard Southern sympathizers along Pennsylvania Avenue saying, "Beauregard has knocked them into a cocked hat," and one good lady, "Believe me, the finger of the Almighty is in it."

And Russell wrote also of this July 18: "On my way to dinner at the British Legation I met the President crossing Pennsylvania Avenue, striding like a crane in a bulrush swamp among the great blocks of marble, dressed in an oddly cut suit of grey, with a felt hat on the back of his head, wiping his face with a red pocket-handkerchief. He was evidently in a hurry, on his way to the White House, where I believe a telegraph has been established in communication with McDowell's headquarters."

The marching Army of the Potomac, a cub of an army, was a little hilarious moving through Fairfax Court House and into Centerville, pulling down Confederate flags, looting houses, smashing pianos into kindling wood, carrying away any goods or articles they liked, in violation of regulations. They broke ranks and ran to pick blackberries or to take off their shoes and rest their feet under shady trees, while they talked slack to their officers.

At Centerville some of the men paraded in female attire plundered from citizens' homes, and one fellow traipsed up and down in the garb of a clergyman while he read the funeral service of Jefferson Davis. "Little save the general laxity of discipline" was proved by the march, as Colonel Tecumseh Sherman saw it. Goths and Vandals they were to him, and he could think of no greater curse than "invasion by a volunteer army."

The clamor of press and public for a battle had gone on till the President on June 29 gave way to political necessity, called a Cabinet meeting before which General McDowell laid his plans. His army of 30,000 was to fight the 21,900 Confederates at Manassas under General Beauregard. Another Confederate army over in the Shenandoah Valley was to be held by a Union army under General Robert Patterson, also in the valley, and stopped from joining Beauregard. General Scott approved McDowell's battle plan but favored waiting till a larger army, better trained and prepared, could win victories that would be destructive.

Lincoln and his Cabinet, as political authorities yielding to the demand of the country for fighting, and considering that the time of the three-month troops was almost run out, overruled Scott. On McDowell's asking for more time to drill and discipline his troops, Lincoln told him, "You are green, it is true, but they are green also."

The battle of Bull Run, Sunday, July 21, 1861, was to a large and eager public a sort of sporting event, the day and the place of combat announced beforehand, a crowd of spectators buggy-riding to the scene with lunch baskets as though for a picnic. A horse-owner in Washington held to a price of $1,000 for a spavined bay horse, telling a journalist: "Take it or leave it. If you want to see this fight a thousand dollars is cheap."

Russell of the London *Times* in the Senate gallery appreciated very much a message from a Federal officer informing him that "the army would advance very early next morning, left in front." He saw a similar note delivered to one Senator, who immediately told other Senators. On horseback, in buggies and gigs, Senators Trumbull, Wade, Chandler, Grimes, Wilson, McDougall, besides Congressmen with emergency navy revolvers and pretty ladies in crinoline gowns, rode out that afternoon or next morning to gaze on a modern battle. The word was that the Northern Shovelry would make Southern Chivalry bite the dust.

Lincoln went as usual that Sunday morning to the New York Avenue Presbyterian Church and heard a sermon by the Reverend Dr. Phineas D. Gurley. During the afternoon he read telegrams from the battlefield, telling nothing decisive. He went to General Scott's office, woke the aged veteran from a sleep. They discussed the telegrams. Scott looked for victory. Lincoln went away. The General turned for another nap.

More telegrams came to the White House, one every ten or fifteen minutes. A messenger from Scott arrived. All seemed favorable. The President went for a drive in his carriage, as usual of evenings.

At six o'clock came Seward, pale, worn, hoarse, asking Nicolay and Hay, "Where is the President?" He had gone to drive, they told Seward, showing telegrams indicating victory, one from Editor Hanscomb of the *National Republican* very positive of victory.

"Tell no one," came the words from Seward. "That is not true. The battle is lost." He had news that McDowell's army was retreating and calls were coming for General Scott to save Washington.

The President in his carriage returned a half-hour later. Nicolay and Hay told him the news. "He listened in silence, without the slightest change of feature or expression, and walked away to army headquarters." There a dispatch from a captain of engineers read: "The day is lost. Save Washington and the remnants of this army. The routed troops will not re-form." General Scott refused to believe it. The Cabinet was called. Now came a telegram from McDowell. His army had gone to pieces, and was "a confused mob."

Lincoln and the Cabinet decided to order all available troops rushed toward McDowell. The forts and batteries on the Potomac were notified to be ready for defense. Telegrams went north and west for troops to be hurried to Washington.

Robert L. Wilson had sought Lincoln that afternoon. As one of the six-footers of the Long Nine who had stuck close as brothers in Lincoln's early days in the Illinois Legislature, Wilson believed that Lincoln would tell him the news about the battle. In company with two Wisconsin Congressmen he hung around the White House, saw messengers and dispatch-bearers hurrying in and out, here and there a straggler from the army. Informed that Lincoln was at the War Office, they went there and mixed with the crowd milling about the doors and chattering questions about the news from the front. Lincoln and Nicolay stepped out heading toward the White House. Wilson left his companions, spoke to the President and walked along asking about the news. "These war fellows," said the President, "are very strict with me, and I regret that I am prevented from telling you anything; but I must obey them, I suppose, until I get the hang of things." "But, Mr. President," insisted Wilson, "if you cannot tell me the news, you can at least indicate its nature, that is, whether it is good or bad."

"The suggestion struck him favorably," wrote Wilson. "Grasping my arm he leaned over, and placing his face near my ear, said, in a shrill and subdued voice, 'It's damned bad.' It was the first time I had ever heard him use profane language but under the circumstances no other term would have qualified."

That night Lincoln lay on a lounge in the Cabinet room and heard eye-witnesses tell what they had seen from saddle, buggy, or gig on the twenty-mile ride from the battlefield. Strewn along roadways for miles were hats, coats, blankets, haversacks, canteens, rifles, broken harness, wagons upside down—the evidence of thousands of soldiers in panic and retreat to Washington.

At three o'clock that afternoon McDowell thought he had the battle won. He had good reason to think so. An hour later his army was going to pieces. Yet back of the enemy lines there was panic; and as Jefferson Davis came from Richmond toward the battle lines, he saw many runaways and asked an old man how the battle had gone. "Our line was broken," was the answer. "All was confusion, the army routed and the battle lost."

McDowell's staff man, James B. Fry, recorded 16 officers and 444 men killed, 78 officers and 1,046 men wounded, 50 officers and 1,262 men missing, not including Congressman Alfred Ely of New York captured and sent to Libby Prison at Richmond. General Johnston officially reported Confederate losses at 378 killed, 1,489 wounded, and 30 missing.

Back of these casualty figures lay personal incidents. A New York artilleryman flat on the ground among trampling horses raised himself as a cavalryman came toward him, lifted two bleeding stumps, and called out: "Don't ride over me! Both hands are gone!" A shell tore the leg of a Fire Zouave nearly off the trunk of the body; he took a photograph of his wife from a shirt pocket, handed it to another Zouave, saying, "Take this to my wife, good-by." A German of the 8th South Carolina regiment, taken prisoner, asked to say good-by to his wounded brother; they took him to the shade of a log hut where the brother lay in blood-soaked clothes covered with swarming flies and mosquitoes; the brothers spoke a few words in German, kissed each other, one as he left choking out the words, "You dying! and I a prisoner!"

To Colonel Sherman the anguish of mangled men writhing and crying was less horrifying than "horses running about riderless with blood streaming from their nostrils or lying on the ground hitched to guns, gnawing their sides in death." A Sherman aide saw a sixteen-year-old boy sink his bayonet in a horseman's side. "As the horse swerved, the musket was torn from his hands and bobbed away, fast between the Confederate's ribs; the boy sobbed, 'He took my gun.'" A 2d Wisconsin man from Kenosha, Henry Benson, getting a bullet through the hand, called out, "There goes one hand for the Union, boys!"; then another bullet cut through him near the heart and his last words were, "Tell my father I died like a man fighting for the Union." A surgeon probed the back of a boy for a bullet, a bystander remarking, "It's a bad place to be hit—*in the back*." And the boy twisted onto his back, showed a hole near his armpit, and said, "Here's where the ball went in."

Newspapers reported a North Carolina lad whose pocket Bible stopped a bullet that would have killed him, while a 1st Connecticut boy carried a deck of playing-cards that caught and held a slug of lead just over the heart. The story was widely told in verse form of a boy with a shattered arm, bleeding to death as he repeatedly murmured, "It grows very dark, Mother, very dark." A 69th New York man had seen an old woman, her white hair streaming, run out of a cottage near a line of fire, and wring her hands, crying, "Oh, God! oh, God! that I should live to see brothers shedding brothers' blood on American soil!"

One of the horse-and-buggy witnesses of the battle prattled to Lincoln of how the Federal troops had really won the victory and there was no reason to be discouraged. The President drawled, "So it's your notion that we whipped the rebels, and then ran away from them!" It was published that as one fleeing, panting Congressman arrived, Lincoln dryly offered, "I congratulate you on beating the race."

After the hot, sweltering Sunday of the battle came a Monday of drizzling rain. Across Long Bridge over the Potomac, from daylight on, came lines of bedraggled men. Hour by hour these silhouettes of defeat trod the bridge to the capital. Where was headquarters? When would they eat? Thousands were taken into homes and fed. Mother-hearted women made soups and meat stews in wash boilers, which were set out on sidewalks and the contents ladled to the hungry. Thousands dropped with their blistered feet and slept on sidewalks, lawns, porches.

The war censorship of telegrams had gone into effect and Senator Trumbull's dispatch to his wife reading "The battle resulted unfavorably to our cause" was received by her in the changed text "I came from near the battlefield last night. It was a desperately bloody fight."

Congress, the press, the pulpit, politicians, talkers, began fixing the blame. Patterson was to blame; if he had smashed at Johnston's army in the Shenandoah Valley, then Johnston's fresh regiments wouldn't have marched in and started the panic. The regulars were to blame for driving their caissons at top speed through the regimental ranks when heading to the rear for ammunition. The three-month troops were to blame; two of their regiments, claiming their time of service was over, marched off the field as the cannons began to sing. The shoulder-straps, political brigadiers, colonels, majors, were only tin soldiers good for sham battles; at four o'clock, as the rout was developing, more than 12,000 volunteers had lost their regimental organization. The Senators, Congressmen, politicians, correspondents, civilians, hack-drivers, ladies in crinoline, who had come to see the show ran like sheep first of all and started the stampede. The New York Sabbath Committee held fighting on Sunday to be unholy and the Reverend Stephen H. Tyng of St. George's Episcopal Church on Broadway, New York, cited as historical fact that "the party who attacks in war on Sunday has invariably been defeated." Muskets not worth shooting, bought in Belgium and sold to Cameron's War Department by swindling contractors, were to blame. Thus ran talk, alibis, explanations.

General Scott blamed himself. "Sir, I am the greatest coward in America," he told Congressmen in the White House, with Lincoln present. "I deserve removal because I did not stand up, when the army was not in a condition for fighting, and resist it to the last." "Your conversation seems to imply," said Lincoln, "that I forced you to fight this battle." General Scott replied, "I have never served a President who has been kinder to me than you have been."

Senator Richardson of Illinois, an old Douglas Democrat, reporting this conversation in a speech in the House, blamed the Cabinet, saying, "Mr. Speaker, standing here in my place, I desire to say of Abraham Lincoln—and I have known him from boyhood's hour till now—if you let him alone, he is an honest man; but I am afraid he has not the will to stand up against the wily politicians who surround him and knead him to their purposes."

At the first meeting with McDowell, Lincoln said, "I have not lost a particle of confidence in you." McDowell answered, "I don't see why, Mr. President, you should."

"All was lost—including honor," ran many an account of Bull Run. The blame was laid in some quarters on Lincoln. The Reverend Robert Collyer lecturing in Boston told of passing the White House one day: "I saw three pairs of feet on the sill of an open window; and pausing for a moment, a good-natured fellow said, 'That's the Cabinet a sittin', and them big feet's Old Abe's.'" The lesson of the lecturer was "That's about all they are good for in Washington, to point their feet out of the window and talk, but go nowhere and do nothing."

A letter came to Lincoln from Horace Greeley, written in New York at midnight of July 29, and noted as "in strict confidence and for your eye only." Greeley began, "Dear Sir: This is my seventh sleepless night—yours, too, doubtless—yet I think I shall not die, because I have no right to die. I must struggle to live, however bitterly. But to business. You are not considered a great man, and I am a hopelessly broken one. You are now undergoing a terrible ordeal, and God has thrown the gravest responsibilities upon you. Do not fear to meet them. Can the rebels be beaten after all that has occurred, and in view of the actual state of feeling caused by our late awful disaster?"

The foremost American editor was ready for an armistice, a national convention, peace, disbandment of forces. "The gloom in this city is funereal—for our dead at Bull Run were many, and they lie unburied yet. On every brow sits sullen, scorching, black despair." He would support any compromise Lincoln believed right. He closed, "Yours, in the depths of bitterness."

And to this letter from Greeley Lincoln made no reply. Once to Hay he spoke of it as "pusillanimous." Greeley, having helped bring on the tornado, was terrified at its first chaotic howlings.

S WEEKLY.   [AUGUST 10, 1861.

DICTATOR GREELEY dismisses the Cabinet, and Warns Lincoln that he will stand no more Nonsense.

"A decimated and indignant people demand the immediate retirement of the present Cabinet from the high places of power, which, for one reason or another, they have shown themselves incompetent to fill. The people insist upon new heads of Executive Departments."—*New York Tribune, July 23.*

Lincoln's Cabinet driven out by Greeley, as seen by a *Harper's Weekly* cartoonist (oddly unaware of the Lincoln beard), Greeley's editorial for the public being nearly as hopeless as his tremulous babblings in a private letter to the President

In later study of Bull Run, officers of skill and experience agreed with Sherman that it was one of "the best planned and worst fought" battles in history.

"As for blame and causes," wrote George William Curtis in a private letter, "they are in our condition and character. We have undertaken to make war without in the least knowing how. It is as if I should be put to run a locomotive. I am a decent citizen, and (let us suppose) a respectable man, but if the trains were destroyed, who would be responsible? We have made a false start and we have discovered it. It only remains to start afresh." (And from this public calamity Curtis turned to the private grief of Henry Wadsworth Longfellow's wife burned to death in the tragic swift blazing of a crinoline gown.)

Lincoln gave his personal attention to the camps around Washington, kept close to men and officers, mixed with them. He rode in an open hack with Seward one day across the Potomac. Colonel William Tecumseh Sherman at a roadside asked if they were going to his camp. "Yes," said Lincoln. "We heard that you had got over the big scare, and we thought we would come over and see the boys." He asked Sherman into the hack.

On the way to the camp Sherman advised Lincoln to "please discourage all cheering, noise, or any sort of confusion; we had enough of it before Bull Run to spoil any set of men; what we need is cool, thoughtful, hard-fighting soldiers—no more hurrahing, no more humbug." At the camp, noted Sherman, "Mr. Lincoln stood up and made one of the neatest, best, and most feeling addresses I ever listened to, referring to our disaster, the high duties that still devolved on us, and the brighter days to come."

At one or two points the soldiers began to cheer. Lincoln checked them. "Don't cheer, boys. I confess I rather like it myself, but Colonel Sherman here says it is not military, and I guess we had better defer to his opinion." As President he was Commander in Chief, he told the men; he was resolved that the soldiers should have everything that the law allowed. He called on one and all to appeal to him personally in case they were wronged.

William Thompson Lusk of the 79th New York regiment (Highlanders) wrote to his mother that having fought in battle and marched thirty miles, soaked from torrents of rain, with no food nor sleep for thirty-six hours, many of the men were chilled and shivering in lack of blankets and jackets they had thrown away. They clamored when Colonel Sherman ordered them out of a barn where they had taken shelter. "The men became querulous. Sherman grew angry, called them a pack of New York loafers and thieves." They were green troops who had yet to learn the art of war. Sherman too was to learn more of it.

The lurking mutiny of more than one regiment was expressed in Lusk's writing his mother: "Afterward Sherman visited the camp with President Lincoln. The men had grown sullen. As he drove by, they besieged his carriage, hooted him, and reminded him who it was that first basely deserted us on the battlefield, turning his horse's head from us, and leaving us to our fate. President Lincoln ordered his coachman to drive away."

Yet it was Sherman's men who under his orders had formed a hollow square and marched last of all from the wild confusion of the battlefield of Bull Run, covering the general retreat, and sending murderous volleys of rifle fire into Confederate cavalrymen who tried to break their ranks. Now they were sullen. Sherman had ordered some of them out of a barn, snapping, "I want to put my horses in here," a regimental scribe writing later, "The milk of human kindness was rather deficient in him at that time."

When Lincoln had finished a speech to this 79th New York regiment, with his usual appeal that they should present grievances to him, one Highlander stepped forward, "Mr. President, we don't think Colonel Sherman has treated us very well," and rehearsed their being driven out of a barn to make room for the Colonel's horses.

"Well, boys," said the President, "I have a great deal of respect for Colonel Sherman and if he turned you out of the barn I have no doubt it was for some good purpose. I presume he thought you would feel better if you went to work and tried to forget your troubles."

They drove to the camp of the 69th New York (Irish), who had fought with impetuous valor and whose Colonel Michael Corcoran was taken prisoner in the thick of the fighting. "Mr. Lincoln made to them the same feeling address," wrote Sherman, "with more personal allusions, because of their special gallantry in the battle under Corcoran." Here Lincoln again made his offer to hear willingly the grievance of any man. An officer stepped forward who had that morning tried to quit the service and leave camp, Sherman growling that he would shoot him like a dog. He said: "Mr. President, I have a cause of grievance. This morning I went to speak to Colonel Sherman, and he threatened to shoot me." Lincoln queried, "Threatened to shoot you?" "Yes, sir, he threatened to shoot me."

Lincoln looked at the officer, looked at Sherman, and then, stooping toward the officer as if to give a confidential message, and speaking in a stage whisper that could be heard for yards around, "Well, if I were you, and he threatened to shoot, I would not trust him, for I believe he would do it." The officer turned and vanished. The men whooped, laughed. Driving along in the hack, Sherman explained the mutiny, and Lincoln said, "Of course I didn't know anything about it, but I thought you knew your business best." Sherman thanked the President and said that what he had done would help discipline. It was one minor incident of mutiny, then common among the new troops.

Of the three division commanders of the Union army at Bull Run only one had ever seen a battle. Of nine Union brigadiers six had never seen smoke in open combat. The nine leading Confederate officers at Bull Run had all been under fire in the Mexican War or in Indian fights. The seventy-five-year-old General Scott quarreled with the sixty-nine-year-old General Patterson, the latter claiming that Scott's failure to send him orders resulted in his own failure to hold in the Shenandoah Valley Johnston's army, which had arrived at Bull Run to turn Confederate defeat into victory.

On the Confederate side arose disputes and the germs of costly enmities resulting from Bull Run, President Davis feeling himself ignored in Beauregard's official report of the battle, which said simply that the President arrived when the fighting was over; President Davis feeling himself equally ignored in Johnston's official report, which omitted any mention of the Confederate President. Officially Johnston could not tell of the Confederate soldiers who jubilantly left for home saying the war was over, of a dangerous overconfidence in Southern fighting superiority, though an opinion grew with him: "Exaggerated ideas of the victory, prevailing among our troops, cost us more than the Federal army lost by defeat."

Returned from Bull Run and speaking from the Spotswood Hotel balcony in Richmond to a serenading crowd, Jefferson Davis gave the counsel, "Never be haughty to the humble, never be humble to the haughty."

After the first few days of gloom and woe in the North came a second uprising. The raising of money, troops, supplies, proceeded toward the organization of the most gigantic army in history. On the night of Bull Run, noted his secretaries, Lincoln did not go to bed, stayed on the lounge in the Cabinet room all night. The next night, having heard more accounts of the lost battle, he lay on a sofa in his office and penciled an outline of what lay ahead to be done, a program for immediate action. Adding to it a few days later, he carefully copied it so that it read:

July 23, 1861

1. Let the plan for making the blockade effective be pushed forward with all possible despatch.

2. Let the volunteer forces at Fort Monroe and vicinity under General Butler be constantly drilled, disciplined, and instructed without more for the present.

3. Let Baltimore be held as now, with a gentle but firm and certain hand.

4. Let the force now under Patterson or Banks be strengthened and made secure in its position.

5. Let the forces in Western Virginia act till further orders according to instructions or orders from General McClellan.

6. [Let] General Frémont push forward his organization and operations in the West as rapidly as possible, giving rather special attention to Missouri.

7. Let the forces late before Manassas, except the three-months men, be reorganized as rapidly as possible in their camps here and about Arlington.

8. Let the three-months forces who decline to enter the longer service be discharged as rapidly as circumstances will permit.

9. Let the new volunteer forces be brought forward as fast as possible, and especially into the camps on the two sides of the river here.

July 27, 1861

When the foregoing shall be substantially attended to:

1. Let Manassas Junction (or some point on one or other of the railroads near it) and Strasburg be seized, and permanently held, with an open line from Washington to Manassas, and an open line from Harper's Ferry to Strasburg—the military men to find the way of doing these.

2. This done, a joint movement from Cairo on Memphis, and from Cincinnati on East Tennessee.

On the day before this memorandum of proposed action was given out—on Friday, July 26, 1861—the President had a call from his old law associate, Henry C. Whitney, fresh from Illinois. Stackpole, the messenger, carried Whitney's name in, and a few moments later Whitney walked in to find the President writing a card for an elderly gentleman who waited; he heard Lincoln read aloud from the card, which he had addressed to Secretary Chase telling Chase the bearer's recommendations were satisfactory and the fact that he was urged by the Methodists should be in his favor, as they were "complaining some of us." Whitney put in a joke: by the same philosophy Lincoln should treat the "rebels" better, for they too were "complaining of us" some. Lincoln replied dryly that they complained the wrong way. Stackpole happened in to interlard the remark that his particular religious denomination had received fewer offices than any other. Lincoln didn't seem to hear him. The elderly gentleman gave thanks for the card Lincoln had written for him, and withdrew. Whitney said he had no business except to pay his respects after being away three months on official errands.

Lincoln seemed glad to see his old associate and confidant, loosened, sat back, and talked about light and trivial matters of happier days. Whitney stayed the whole afternoon, with no callers admitted except Seward, who stepped in for a few moments. The President hailed Seward in a somewhat peremptory but good-natured manner: "Well, Gover-*nuer*, what is it now?" The Secretary of State was a mere trifle nettled but still amused at the abrupt greeting. His outline of some phase of New Mexican affairs brought the interruption from the President: "In other words New Mexico has no govern-*or* nor govern-*ment*," a few instructions, and Seward went out the door fully impressed that it was no day to lay constitutional issues before the President.

Later again came Stackpole with words that General, formerly Senator, James, of Rhode Island was outside and anxious; he must leave town that very afternoon. The President, carelessly: "Well, as James makes *canning* [cannon], I reckon I must see *him*." Then to Stackpole: "Tell him when I get through with Whitney I will see him." The hours sped, General James wasn't mentioned, Whitney held suspicions that General James's having *canning* (cannon) to sell was for the time a botheration to the President.

"As I left just before six o'clock," ran Whitney's narrative, "Stackpole told me that James waited till just before train time and then left soundly abusing the President and me; having heard that I was from Illinois he averred the President was amusing some back-woods railsplitter with stories." The only work the President did that afternoon was to sign his name to a mass of commissions for navy officers, talking all the while in a style that ranged from grave to gay, from lively to severe, estimates of leading men, the Cabinet, Bull Run, the future, old days on the Eighth Circuit, random monologues, the sublime and the ridiculous interwoven.

On Whitney's saying it was good that Lincoln seemed to have banished care for the time being, Lincoln's face saddened a moment. "I have.trouble enough; when I last saw you I was having little troubles; they filled my mind full: since then I have big troubles and they can do no more—what do you think has annoyed me more than any one thing?" "Bull Run, of course." "I don't mean an affair forced by events, and which a single man can't do much with, but I mean of matters wholly mine to arrange. Now, I will tell you; the fight over two post-offices—one at our Bloomington, and the other in Pennsylvania." Whitney put in that some politicians had already set up McClellan for his successor. Lincoln said with complete indifference that he was willing if McClellan would push the war and win it. Mutual friends in Illinois were mentioned. Whitney said of Judge David Davis, "You ought to make him a Supreme Judge," noting, "To this bit of vicarious electioneering, Lincoln vouchsafed no response at all but was thoughtful and silent for a few moments when he started out on a new subject, thus clearly rebuking me for obtruding office-seeking politics on his social pastime."

Lincoln mentioned a Border State man seeking appointment as quartermaster and asked Whitney's advice. Whitney recalled that this man and his associates in a business matter had employed Lincoln and Whitney as lawyers and had cheated both of them out of their fees. Whitney reminded Lincoln that he, Lincoln, had made elaborate research and written an extensive brief in the case, ending warmly, "A man who would cheat a lawyer out of pay for actual services would doubtless cheat the government if he got a chance." Lincoln reflected a minute, then slowly, "I rather reckon that is so." Whitney inclined to think Lincoln was intending to make the appointment but these reminders stopped it. As Lincoln dipped the pen and signed naval commissions Whitney suggested, "Everything is drifting into the army, and I guess you will have to put me in." Lincoln said in a day or two he would make Whitney a quartermaster.

The President spoke of disappointment that General Scott had not been able to wrangle a victory out of Bull Run, as though Scott might have met the necessity for immediate action more practically. Having outlined the immediate imperative steps, he added: "I hope ultimately they will get tired of it and arouse and say to their leaders and to their politicians, 'This thing has got to stop!' That is our only chance. It is plain to me that it's no use of trying to subdue those people if they remain united and bound they won't be subdued." The conversation ran on and Lincoln was suddenly giving a humorous account of the shifts and tricks by which a noted English statesman, Charles James Fox, managed to get out of paying his personal debts. The afternoon wore on. Hours sped. Congress was in session. War and revolution surged. The conversation ran from early afternoon till near sunset. The President needed a short holiday and took it. He didn't care a cornhusk, according to Whitney, for those "who think that a statesman, like a blind horse in a treadmill, needs no rest, or that, like the conventional whitewashed statue of justice, he must always *pose* for dignified effect."

In Congress the prowar spirit seemed to have been strengthened by the Bull Run result. In the Senate were 56 Republicans, 12 Democrats, and 4 Unionists; in the House 106 Republicans, 42 Democrats, 28 Unionists. On the day following the battle John J. Crittenden of Kentucky, now in the House of Representatives, by common consent offered a resolution framed to declare in a few words why the Lincoln Government was at war. It was hardly possible that Lincoln's hand and touch were absent from this declaration, so precisely did it stress what Lincoln had told Hay in meditations aloud and what Lincoln had put foremost in his message to Congress. The present deplorable civil war had been forced on the country "by the disunionists of the Southern States, now in arms against the constitutional Government, and in arms around the capital," said the resolution. In the national emergency Congress, "banishing all feeling of mere passion or resentment," would recollect only its duty to the whole country. The war was waged not for conquest or subjugation or interference with rights or established institutions, but "to defend and maintain the supremacy of the Constitution, and to preserve the dignity, equality, and rights of the several States unimpaired; and that as soon as these objects are accomplished the war ought to cease."

In the House only 4 Nays, in the Senate only 5, were recorded against this resolution. It became a refuge for those who wished to tell others why the war was on.

A little sister to the foregoing resolution met opposition from Crittenden and the Border Slave State members. Confiscation of the property of "rebels"—meaning chiefly slaves—was authorized by this measure. Slaves by the consent of their masters digging ditches or entrenchments, driving teams, carrying guns, or otherwise serving the Confederacy in war were thereby forfeited as property. Crittenden said that as a penalty given the slaveowner this was justice, but as a policy it was inexpedient and violated the Constitution.

Thaddeus Stevens replied that the Constitution as an instrument was already well in contempt of the "rebels" and "When a country is at open war with an enemy every publicist agrees that you have the right to use every means which will weaken him." The bill passed 60 to 48 in the House, one-third of the divided House not voting.

The President hesitated, "had some difficulty consenting to approve" this confiscation bill. Its antislavery animus would be confused with its military necessity. He signed it. The Confederate Congress at Richmond answered with a sequestration law for taking possession of the estates and property of "alien enemies," including authority over debts due Northern merchants by Southern people.

An author friend of Senator Sumner, Charles Edwards Lester, had from the Senator at this time an account of the President's refusal to begin a policy of emancipating the slaves: "The Senator said the President did not agree with him; that he still adhered to the policy of forbearance, believing that the country was not prepared to go as far as Mr. Sumner would advise.

Least of all did the President favor either of the two bills the Senator had introduced for confiscation of property and punishment of conspiracy. Mr. Sumner believed the hour had arrived for resorting to the full exercise of the War Power, desiring to have the President boldly lead. But Mr. Lincoln could not see it in that light." In the view of Lester and his friend Sumner "Mr. Lincoln's administration acted in superfluous good faith with the Rebels." A similar view was held by Senators Wade and Chandler, who pressed on Lincoln their hope that he would favor the immediate recruitment of Negro troops. He answered the time was not yet.

The Senate resolution to approve of the President's unconstitutional acts done without approval of Congress during the emergency weeks, when Congress was not in session and could not then approve, was introduced the third day of the session. It would declare legal and valid the President's first call for State militia troops, his proclamation of blockade and action therein, his call for three-year volunteers and his increase of the regular army and the navy, and not least of all his suspension of the ancient Anglo-Saxon writ of habeas corpus.

For weeks this resolution lay amid unfinished business. A few Peace Democrats openly opposed it as letting "the despot and usurper," Lincoln, have his way. Enough Republicans were mistrustful or jealous of the sweeping dictatorial acts of the President, his seizure of powers so long held exclusively by Congress, that they hesitated, refused to be interested, and the measure continued to lie amid unfinished business. Also those Republicans who favored giving the President complete approval, or a clean bill of health, did not care to press the matter till other more immediately practical legislation was out of the way. "There never was a moment it could have received my vote," said Senator Trumbull of Illinois on August 6, pointing to it as a personal matter brought up by Senator Wilson of Massachusetts, and denying that it was a "pet measure" of the Republican party. On August 5, the day before Congress adjourned, a bill to increase army pay came up for action and to this was added a rider, a section, declaring "that all the acts, proclamations, and orders of the President" relating to the militia and volunteers "are hereby approved and in all respects legalized and made valid, to the same intent and with the same effect as if they had been issued and done under the previous express authority and direction of the Congress of the United States." By a vote of 37 to 5 it passed the Senate, and by 74 to 19 the House, the Nays being Border States votes, with help from Ohio and Indiana.

Thus the President failed of full approval, was not yet by Congress whitewashed of guilt as a usurper in what he did with the regular army, with closing ports by blockade, and with the hoary and precious right of the writ of habeas corpus. Senator Preston King of New York made clear that he approved "the vigorous measures" of the Executive, "but I have a disinclination to pass upon a question the whole length and breadth and extent of which I do not entirely comprehend." Senator Fessenden of Maine was for complete approval, "without crossing a *t* or dotting an *i*," of what the President had done, though he believed Senate approval would amount to little and the people would not be deceived whatever action was taken.

Senator Henry S. Lane of Indiana was certain the Constitution in express terms said that the writ of habeas corpus could be suspended in case of rebellion and insurrection, the whole question coming to this: "Who is to judge? Where is the discretion lodged? Clearly with the President of the United States; and it can be safely lodged nowhere else." To which Senator John Sherman of Ohio presented his opposed opinion: "I do not believe the President of the United States has the power to suspend the writ of *habeas corpus*, because that power is expressly given to Congress, and to Congress alone. I do not believe the President of the United States has the power to increase the regular army, because that power is expressly given by the Constitution to Congress alone. Still I approve of the action of the President. I believe the President did right. He did precisely what I would have done if I had been in his place—no more, no less; but I cannot here, in my place, as a Senator, under oath, declare that what he did do was legal."

When Congress adjourned August 6, to stay away from Washington four months, it had given the President nearly all of the practical measures he needed to proceed with the war. One member said Congress had been "a giant committee of ways and means" serving the President. He was more of an executive than most of them had expected. Some were gauging him as too reckless about the fine line of authority that should run between the executive and legislative branches of the Government. They knew also that for the time, as Fessenden had said, the people endorsed his dictatorial emergency actions whether or not Congress did. Schleiden wrote to Sumner of the "illimited" power exercised by the Government: "Mr. Lincoln is, in that respect, the equal, if not the superior, of Louis Napoleon. The difference consists only in the fact that the President rests his authority on the unanimous consent of the people of the loyal States, the emperor his on the army."

On the day before Congress adjourned Senator Browning wrote in his diary, "Several of the Senators were quite drunk to day, especially McDougall of California and Saulsbury of Delaware, and some scenes were enacted which ought not to occur in a body occupying so exalted & dignified a position as the Senate of the U. S." To his wife John Lothrop Motley was writing: "A grim winter is before us. Gather you rosebuds while you may. The war is to be a long one." In the blouse of a dead Confederate soldier at Fairfax Court House was found a letter from a girl begging him to watch his own "precious life" while remembering "Kill a Yankee for me."

Day by day now the new regiments of the Army of the Potomac stepped off trains in the railroad yards, marched down Pennsylvania Avenue, sometimes halting on the White House lawn for a little reception with the President, then moving to camp in the tented cities that stretched farther on the river slopes and the hills beyond. Droves of beef cattle plodded through the streets toward the commissary department butchers. Miles boxes of hardtack, shoes, shirts, underwear, socks, uniforms, caps, lined warehouses and camps. A uniform of blue blouse and light-blue kersey trousers replaced the red shirts of the Fire Zouaves, the checked flannels of the Michigan lumberjacks, and other special garbs. The many varieties and contingents of troops were being shaped into one immense weapon, the

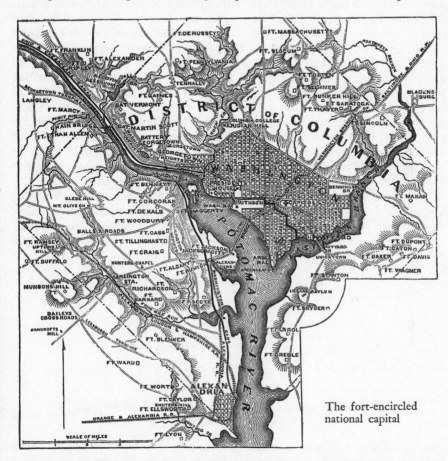

The fort-encircled
national capital

most colossal military unit the world had seen in modern historical times. This Army of the Potomac grew into 168,000 in November from 50,000 on July 22, when Washington had received its new commander, General George Brinton McClellan.

McClellan was the man of the hour, pointed to by events, and chosen by an overwhelming weight of public and private opinion. He looked the part, sat his saddle as a trained Man on Horseback, issued commands with a manner of authority, published proclamations modeled on Napoleon's style, thrust his right hand into his coat when photographed and gazed at the camera as though victory might lurk just beyond his well-modeled head and its genius of organization. "A neck such as not one man in ten thousand possesses," Dr. O. W. Holmes saw on a body "muscular as a prize-fighter's." His personal charm was a gift. Washington adopted him, the army took to him, correspondents nicknamed him "Little Mac" and "The Young Napoleon." He wrote his wife July 27: "I find myself in a new and strange position here: President, cabinet, Gen. Scott, and all deferring to me. By some strange operation of magic I seem to have become the power of the land."

Nicolay and Hay noted that "in everyone, from the President of the United States to the humblest orderly who waited at his door, he inspired a remarkable affection and regard." He was the courted, caressed "idol of Washington drawing-rooms," center of interests, ambitions, and germs of intrigue. Tecumseh Sherman and others were puzzled over the new commander's taking a house in Washington and maintaining headquarters in the city. "[He] told me," wrote Sherman, "he intended to organize an army of 100,000 men, with 100 field batteries, and I still hoped he would come on our side of the Potomac, pitch his tent, and prepare for real hard work, but his headquarters still remained in a house in Washington City."

Ten days before Bull Run, McClellan had been leading an army in West Virginia and with his portable printing press had published an address: "Soldiers! I have heard that there was danger here. I have come to place myself at your head and to share it with you. I fear now but one thing—that you will not find foemen worthy of your steel. I know that I can rely upon

Sõldiers! I hav. ieard that there
was danger here. I have come to
place myself at your head and to share
it with you. I fear now but one thing
—that you will not find foemen worthy of your steel. I know that I can.
rely upon you.
GEO. B. McCLELLAN,
Major Gen'l Commanding

Close of an address issued by McClellan in West Virginia.
Original in the Barrett collection.

you." As early as July 5 he wrote to a superior officer: "No prospect of a brilliant victory shall induce me to depart from my intention of gaining success by maneuvering rather than by fighting. I will not throw these raw men of mine into the teeth of artillery and intrenchments if it is possible to avoid it. I am trying to follow a lesson learned long ago—i.e., not to move until I know that everything is ready, and then to move with the utmost rapidity and energy."

Only the year before, he had married Ellen Mary Marcy, the daughter of a regular-army officer, to whom he was now writing, "Who would have thought, when we were married, that I should so soon be called upon to save my country?" He had left her and a $10,000-a-year job as president of the Ohio & Mississippi Railroad at Cincinnati; commanding an army of 18,000 in West Virginia, he had overcome about two-thirds that number, giving the North the only actions thus far having semblance of military victories. Farther back of this victory was a record. He had been chief engineer and then vice-president of the Illinois Central Railroad, entertained Douglas in his Chicago home, and in 1858 during the Lincoln-Douglas debates had loaned his private car, in which Douglas once passed Lincoln's sidetracked freight caboose. Politics thus far interested him little and the only ballot he had ever cast was for Douglas. He was an engineer, had read all the classics on how to win or lose a war, believed in preparations, maneuvers, strategy. What men who had directed armies in war had written about it, the military technic, filled his mind. His *Manual on the Art of War*, his translation of a French book on bayonet exercises, were reputable. He had improved an army saddle, making it more comfortable; it was called the McClellan saddle. He had directed engineer corps on construction jobs, explored the Red River, begun a survey for the Pacific railway in Oregon. He was chosen for responsible work in peacetime because he was considered a student, observer, writer, technician, an industrious manager having balanced judgment and integrity. At thirty years of age he was one of three army officers appointed by Jefferson Davis, then Secretary of War, to go to see Old World armies at drill, study the art of war, and report to America. They saw action in bloody Crimea and studied European styles in war.

The personal courage of McClellan had been tested. At Contreras in the Mexican War he had two horses shot from under him, grapeshot breaking his sword hilt. On a hunt with his father-in-law in the Northwest when a panther sprang at him he fired, missed, and then, using his rifle as a club, broke the animal's skull.

Now he faced a work that would call on all his courage and knowledge. What he had learned as a member of the Napoleon Club at West Point might now serve him. He was not quite thirty-five years old, would need all he had mastered of Napoleon's technic. He was writing his wife that he went to the Senate to get through "a bill allowing me to appoint as many aides as I please from civil life and from the army," and he found half a dozen of the oldest Senators remarking to him, "Why, how young you look, and yet an old soldier!" He noticed, "It seems to strike everybody that I am very young." Perhaps his mind went back to when he entered West Point. He was then only fifteen years and seven months old, but on account of his health, physique, and high standing in mental examinations, the regulation as to age was suspended in his case. Later he had graduated second in a class of 59 members. And looking back and thinking it over, he had not had a disgrace or a failure in his life. He wrote his wife: "They give me my way in everything, full swing and unbounded confidence. All tell me that I am held responsible for the fate of the nation, and that all its resources shall be placed at my disposal. It is an immense task that I have on my hands, but I believe I can accomplish it. . . . When I . . . stood in the library, looking over the Capitol of our great nation, and saw the crowd gathering around to stare at me, I began to feel how great the task committed to me."

After a week in Washington he wrote his wife, "I handed to the President to-night a carefully considered plan for conducting the war on a large scale." He wished her to know that when he planned war on a large scale it was "carefully considered" by him. He added for her assurance, "I shall carry this thing on *en grand* and crush the rebels in one campaign." The Napoleon whose campaigns and methods he had studied also carried things on *en grand* and crushed the opposition in one campaign. Also he added: "I flatter myself that Beauregard has gained his last victory. We need success and must have it." Thus on and on in long letters to his wife, pouring out news, information, gossip, complaints, fears, hopes, and comforts.

Other generals were writing to their wives, but none so mirror-gazing. On August 4 "some forty were present—Prince Napoleon and his staff, French minister, English ditto, cabinet, some senators, Gen. Scott, and myself." He seemed not to know that the newspapers would tell his wife as much and more. "It made me feel a little strangely when I went into the President's last evening with the old general [Scott] leaning on me; I could see that many marked the contrast." He was aware of himself as young and that all who had eyes could see the icy hand of death had nearly pulled the old veteran down. "I have Washington perfectly quiet now. . . . I have restored order very completely already." His self-assurance told him already he had won results. He was riding twelve hours a day and toiling on into the night and three o'clock in the morning organizing an army into the invincible instrument he wanted it. On August 8, however, he wished his wife to know he had been "pestered to death with senators, etc." and had "a row with General Scott." And did he mean to ease her fears as to the warrior's life in telling her, "I have scarcely slept one moment for the last three nights, knowing well that the enemy intend some movement"?

His daily bulletin home one day read: "On Sunday, instead of going to church, was sent for by the President immediately after breakfast, and kept busy until midnight, when I returned from a long ride too tired to talk even. Yesterday in the saddle from ten to five, and then persecuted until after midnight. Today the President sent for me before I was up; have been at work ever since, and soon start out to receive a brigade and some batteries."

The next day he was in the saddle at seven o'clock in the morning, rode in rain that drenched him, and stayed on his horse till nine o'clock at night. This did not close his "busy day," for it was one in the morning he dated the letter to his wife and told her, "Things are improving daily." New regiments, new batteries, cavalry, infantry; he wrote her the numbers of arrivals. Yet his path was not smooth. "Gen. Scott is the great obstacle. He will not comprehend the danger. I have to fight my way against him. To-morrow the question will probably be decided by giving me absolute control independently of him. I suppose it will result in enmity on his part against me; but I have no choice. The people call upon me to save the country. I must save it, and cannot respect anything that is in the way."

He was the Head of the Army. Fate and circumstance played with him. As he had gone that day on a slow gallop past thousands of men who saluted and cheered, his face was a mask. He looked cool, calm, collected. Yet under this composed bronze mask he was a dazzled, flustered man in the supreme hour that had come to him. He was writing his wife: "I receive letter after letter, have conversation after conversation, calling on me to save the nation, alluding to the presidency, dictatorship, etc. As I hope one day to be united with you for ever in heaven, I have no such aspiration. I would cheerfully take the dictatorship and agree to lay down my life when the country is saved. I am not spoiled by my unexpected new position. I feel sure that God will give me the strength and wisdom to preserve this great nation; but I tell you, who share all my thoughts, that I have no selfish feeling in this matter. I feel that God has placed a great work in my hands. I have not sought it. I know how weak I am, but I know that I mean to do right, and I believe that God will help me and give me the wisdom I do not possess. Pray for me, that I may be able to accomplish my task, the greatest, perhaps, that any poor, weak mortal ever had to do. . . . God grant that I may bring this war to an end and be permitted to spend the rest of my days quietly with you!"

Five days later, when he had an army twice the size of the enemy camped near Manassas, he wrote his wife that he was sleeping with one eye open at night "looking out sharply for Beauregard, who, I think, has some notion of making a dash in this direction." Nevertheless, "Gen. Scott is the most dangerous antagonist I have."

An illusion that the enemy outnumbered him kept growing. Day by day in personal interviews, in notes and letters, he called on the President, on Scott and others, for more and more men. "I am here in a terrible place; the enemy have from three to four times my force," he wrote his wife on August 16. . . . "If my men will only fight I think I can thrash him, notwithstanding the disparity of numbers." And though he had been chief of the Army of the Potomac only three weeks, he was writing, "I am weary of all this," adding a few days later, "I do not *live* at all; merely exist, worked and worried half to death." What he had learned in the Napoleon Club was no use. "I have no privacy, no leisure, no relaxation, except in reading your letters and writing to you."

One day in late September when hazy gray folded the blue hills and slashes of yellow and scarlet stood out on woodlands, McClellan rode with the President, the Secretary of War, and Governor Curtin to a ceremonial of presenting flags to fifteen Pennsylvania regiments. At a luncheon afterward McClellan invited the party to ride around his army and have a look at it. On the ride A. K. McClure noticed that McClellan impressed everyone favorably, "modest, but obviously self-reliant," showing "abiding faith in himself and his army." All in the party, believed McClure, saw that McClellan had wrought "most extraordinary results in the organization and discipline of his troops." At one point they halted to view a Confederate flag on

Munson's Hill, when McClellan "somewhat disturbed the equanimity of most of the party by saying we were just at that time outside of the Union lines." McClure noted Lincoln on a horse, "legs halfway between the under part of the girth and the ground, his long arms could have guided his horse by the ears," while the high silk hat somehow didn't go with a horse and had a touch of the comic.

They drew rein before regiments that lifted genuine cheers for Mc-Clellan. Lincoln was impressed. To McClure it seemed that Lincoln had "absolute confidence in McClellan" and a hope that Richmond would soon be captured and the war ended. McClure heard no anecdotes from Lincoln this day. The President was "unusually sober," hoped to end the war "without great effusion of blood," seemed to be thinking of hard sacrifices ahead for these boys under McClellan's complete direction.

Under his cool exterior McClellan now was writhing, and his wife found it a pleasant letter telling her that "the only comfort has been your father's arrival, which is a great relief to me. I like to see that cool, steady head near me." He appointed her father, Colonel Randolph B. Marcy, to be chief of staff. Colonel Marcy, as early as August, sent a recommendation to the War Department that conscription be enforced and enough men for McClellan's army be drafted. But the War Department considered it no time as yet for a draft of men. At least there should be one or two victories before trying conscription. "Yet," wrote McClellan, "the President, the old general [Scott], cannot or will not see the true state of affairs."

The old General complained of disrespect, of obedience wanting, and the President in early October met in General Scott's rooms opposite the War Office several of his key men. The question arose of the number of troops in and about Washington. According to Welles, "Cameron could not answer the question; McClellan did not; General Scott said no reports were made to him; the President was disturbed." Seward then read from a small paper how many regiments were in the various commands, including newly arrived troops, and a total. On Seward's appealing to McClellan, Mc-Clellan said Seward's figures were approximately correct. General Scott, with a frowning rampart of a face, considered it a remarkable state of things: "I am in command of the armies of the United States, but have been wholly unable to get any reports, any statement of the actual forces, but here is the Secretary of State, a civilian, for whom I have great respect but who is not a military man nor conversant with military affairs, though his abilities are great, but this civilian is possessed of facts which are withheld from me. Military reports are made, not to these Headquarters but to the State Department. Am I, Mr. President, to apply to the Secretary of State for the necessary military information to discharge my duties?"

Seward explained that he got his information by vigilance, attention, tabulating arriving regiments, and so on, Scott with a grim smile agreeing that the labors of the Secretary of State were arduous and he had not known the whole of them: "If you in that way can get accurate information, the Rebels can also, though I cannot." Cameron, half in earnest and half ironical, said all knew that Seward was meddling in all departments with what was none of his business and he thought "we had better go to our duties," which Welles considered "a pleasant way of breaking up an unpleasant interview."

The President had been "disturbed" at the opening turns of the conversation and was not at ease in its closing speech, with McClellan standing at an open door and General Scott addressing McClellan by name and saying much in few words: "You were called here by my advice. The times require vigilance and activity. I am not active and never shall be again. When I proposed that you should come here to aid, not supersede, me, you had my friendship and confidence. You still have my confidence."

In November General Winfield Scott was retired on pay, with honors, and with tributes from the President and others. In pitch-dark and a pouring rain at four o'clock in the morning of November 3, McClellan and his staff, with a squadron of cavalry, saw the old man off at the Washington depot. "He was very polite to me," ran McClellan's daily letter; "sent various kind messages to you and the baby; so we parted. . . . It may be that at some distant day I, too, shall totter away from Washington, a worn-out soldier, with naught to do but make my peace with God."

McClellan was now commissioned General in Chief, and at the White House Lincoln said to him, "I should be perfectly satisfied if I thought this vast increase of responsibility would not embarrass you." "It is a great relief, Sir!" said McClellan. "I feel as if several tons were taken from my shoulders today. I am now in contact with you, and the Secretary. I am not embarrassed by intervention."

"Well," said Lincoln, as John Hay heard him, "draw on me for all the sense I have, and all the information. In addition to your present command, the supreme command of the army will entail a vast labor upon you."

"I can do it all," McClellan said quietly.

He meant well, the new General in Chief. To the outside world he had to put up a front of courage and show all faith in himself. In his own heart he knew a personal test lay ahead of him. Beyond the drills and guard mount, the ritual of prayer to the flag at sunset, the bands playing, the grand reviews when platoons marched by hour on hour in glittering steel and brass—beyond this was monotony, mud, blood, the death rattle in men's throats, bloated horses with four feet to the sky. War was "Ugh!" and not "Ah!" Perhaps this was in the turmoil of his heart as he wrote home of the "gigantic dimensions" of the work ahead of him: "Even if I had the greatest intellect that was ever given to man, the result remains in the hands of God. I do not feel that I am an instrument worthy of the great task, but I *do* feel that I did not seek it. It was thrust upon me. I was called to it."

The bitter note in McClellan's letters to his wife now ran back to two things. First, he wanted more men for his army; he was planning a campaign to end with a decisive battle that would destroy the enemy and finish the war; yet such a campaign and battle could not be considered so long as the Confederate Army between him and Richmond outnumbered him. Second, the blame for his not getting all the men he wanted lay on the politicians. He wrote: "I . . . only wish to save my country, and find the incapables around me will not permit it. . . . Their reply to everything is, 'Impossible! Impossible!'" He had to deal with "unscrupulous, false" men. "I was obliged to attend a meeting of the cabinet at eight P.M., and was bored and annoyed. There are some of the greatest geese in the cabinet I have ever seen—enough to tax the patience of Job." He was peevish rather than bitter in writing, "I am becoming daily more disgusted with this administration—perfectly sick of it."

When Lincoln had suggestions for McClellan which he did not care to put in writing, he took another course. He dated and signed a card September 30, 1861, reading, "Will Gen. McClellan please see Pay-Master Whitney a moment?" On this Whitney commented: "This note grew out of an old habit Mr. Lincoln had of sending a verbal message on any subject he did not wish to put down in writing. He frequently used me in this way before he was President, and after he became President he frequently sent verbal messages by those he could trust."

As the weeks went by during autumn, McClellan found that the early suspicions he nursed against Lincoln as one of his enemies were not well founded; perhaps Lincoln was his friend. He wrote his wife, "I enclose a card just received from 'A. Lincoln'; it shows too much deference to be seen outside." One October day Lincoln and Seward arrived as he was writing the daily letter to his wife. "I have just been interrupted here by the President and Secretary Seward, who had nothing very particular to say, except some stories to tell, which were, as usual, very pertinent, and some pretty good. I never in my life met anyone so full of anecdote as our friend. He is never at a loss for a story apropos of any known subject or incident." Not always, however, was the visit of Lincoln given to anecdote. He was studying the art of war now, reading books, asking questions of military experts. A McClellan staff man said, "President Lincoln delighted in going to talk strategy with him."

One night as they parted at McClellan's house the General said: "I intend to be careful and do as well as possible. Don't let them hurry me, is all I ask." "You shall have your own way in the matter, I assure you," replied Lincoln as he and John Hay started on their walk to the White House. Two nights later, on October 12, a telegram was handed Lincoln from McClellan saying that the enemy was before him in force and would probably attack in the morning. "If they attack," he added, "I shall beat them." This expected attack, like others for which McClellan made preparations and waited confidently, failed to arrive.

In November Lincoln, Seward, and John Hay went to McClellan's house one evening. The General was at a wedding, said the servant, and would soon return. "We went in," wrote Hay in his diary that night, "and after we had waited about an hour, McC. came in and without paying any particular attention to the porter who told him the President was waiting to see him, went upstairs, passing the door of the room where the President and Secretary of State were seated. They waited about half-an-hour, and sent once more a servant to tell the General they were there; and the answer coolly came that the General had gone to bed."

Hay considered this deliberate snub the first sign of military authorities' overriding the civil government. "Coming home I spoke to the President about the matter, but he seemed not to have noticed it, specially, saying it was better, at this time, not to be making points of etiquette & personal dignity."

And the President said another day, "I will hold McClellan's horse if he will only bring us success."

Sometimes the President sent for McClellan to come to the White House. More often Lincoln called at McClellan's house. Once they met at Seward's house and McClellan's daily letter told the wife in Cincinnati: "The President is honest and means well. As I parted from him on Seward's steps he said that it had been suggested to him that it was no more safe for me than for him to walk out at night without some attendant. I told him that I felt no fear; that no one would take the trouble to interfere with me. On which he deigned to remark that they would probably give more for my scalp at Richmond than for his."

A few days later, however, McClellan felt the President, pressing for action, bothering him too much. At the home of Edwin M. Stanton he wrote, "I have not been at home for some three hours, but am concealed at Stanton's to dodge all enemies in shape of 'browsing' Presidents, etc."

McClellan's army now numbered more than 160,000; he had at least three times as many troops as the enemy at Manassas. There had been autumn weather on which many commented—mild, pleasant days and cool nights, perfect weather for an army movement to redeem Bull Run, to end the war. Thus ran hope and talk. Lincoln was trying to keep close to McClellan and get action. Toward the end of November, just before the first driving snowstorm came, McClellan was writing in his daily letter to the wife: "I am thwarted and deceived by these incapables at every turn. . . . I have one great comfort in all this—that is, that I did not seek this position, as you well know; and I still trust that God will support me and bear me out. He could not have placed me here for nothing."

The foreign influx among McClellan's attachés was satirized by one writer: "The Prince de Joinville's two sons are admirable additions to General McClellan's staff, and speak English so well that I can almost understand what they say. Two Arabs are expected here tomorrow to take command of Irish brigades, and General Blenker will probably have two Aztecs to assist him in the German division."

Twice in that autumn of 1861 the spick-and-span platoons of the Army of the Potomac had passed in grand review before President Lincoln, the Cabinet, governors of States, and ladies in silken crinoline. At one review McClellan had made a laconic Napoleonic address to the troops: "Soldiers! We have had our last retreat. We have seen our last defeat. You stand by me, and I will stand by you, and henceforth victory will crown our efforts." Now the soldiers were busy with axes, cutting down trees, building log huts, settling down into winter quarters. Soldiers, civilians, news-writers, used the words "All quiet on the Potomac." The phrase had several different meanings.

Ball's Bluff was bitter to remember. There on "a lovely, a rare October day," on high ground overlooking the Potomac, a few hundred Union soldiers were cornered, killed, captured. A few swam to the Maryland shore. Some were shot in the water. Their commander went down, a picked target of marksmen who sent several bullets into him as he came into the open calling to his troops to follow him. A grandson of Paul Revere, a son of Oliver Wendell Holmes, a nephew of James Russell Lowell, lay, two of them mortally wounded, Oliver Wendell Holmes, Jr., slowly recovering.

Near sunset of that day Lincoln, entering McClellan's headquarters, "spoke of the beauty of the afternoon" to a correspondent, who noted that "the lines were deeper in the President's face than when I saw him in his own home, the cheeks more sunken." The telegraph was clicking off Ball's Bluff. The name of the killed commander, General Edward D. Baker, Lincoln's "Ned" Baker, came through. "Five minutes passed," wrote a correspondent, "and then Mr. Lincoln, unattended, with bowed head and tears rolling down his furrowed cheeks, his breast heaving, passed through the room. He almost fell as he stepped into the street. We sprang from our seats to render assistance, but he did not fall."

Only a few days since Ned Baker had gone, "restless as an eagle," they said, to speak his good-by at the White House. From a woman of long friendship with him he accepted a bouquet of fresh blossoms, resting his eyes quietly on them as he said: "Very beautiful! These flowers and my memory will wither together." And at night he had scanned a batch of public and private papers, writing on each one what he wanted done "in case I should not return."

Gone now forever from Lincoln was a trumpet, a shield, an intimate companion and a bright light of loyalty, namesake of his second-born boy, his choice of all men to introduce him for a presidential inaugural address. Not again would the two of them laugh with glee over Baker's leaving California in 1860 to enter Oregon, form a combination of Republicans and Douglas Democrats, and wreck the political status of the secessionist United States Senator Joseph Lane. Their series of White House conferences on holding the Pacific Coast States to the Union was ended. Not again would Ned Baker refuse a brigadier general's commission, a major general's commission, from the President, knowing such appointment must in law be followed by his resignation as United States Senator from Oregon. Now with the namesake Lincoln boy, with Ellsworth, Baker was gone. And Lincoln was stunned, his breast heaving, "He almost fell as he stepped into the street" from a clicking telegraph room.

"Ah! what a scene was that," wrote Charles Carleton Coffin, "a few weeks later when President Lincoln, supported by Senators Trumbull and Browning of Illinois, entered the draped Senate chamber to attend the memorial services of his old friend! Again the tears rolled down his cheeks, as he heard the words of Senator McDougall recalling the by-gone scenes." Turning toward Lincoln, McDougall said, "He loved freedom, Anglo-Saxon freedom," and quoted from verses he had heard Baker recite one starlit night on a western plain: "Press where ye see my white plume shine amid the rank of war."

John Hay wrote in his diary of McClellan and Lincoln meeting after Ball's Bluff. They talked "sadly." McClellan said: "There is many a good fellow that wears the shoulder-straps going under the sod before this thing is over. There is no loss too great to be repaired. If I should get knocked on the head, Mr. President, you will put another man immediately into my shoes."

"I want you to take care of yourself," said the President.

Driving snow had come with the last week in November. Winter weather was on. Wool coats, heavy blankets, firewood, tents, huts, were the need. The war was costing more than $1,000,000 a day. A hazard was in the air. Would Little Mac, the Young Napoleon, slog through in a winter campaign and take Richmond? If he should, said men of the South at Richmond, he would find it as Napoleon did Moscow, a city in ashes.

The war was merely beginning to set in. The Four Horsemen of the Apocalypse had not come to their stride. There were portents, however.

"Women are in a bad box now," wrote Mrs. Chesnut at Richmond. "False hair is taken off and searched for papers. Bustles are suspect. All manner of things, they say, come over the border under the huge hoops now worn; so they are ruthlessly torn off. Women are used as detectives and searchers, to see that no men slip over in petticoats."

In Washington "rebels in crinoline" were given jail—it was clean and well ordered, yet jail. "These fascinating female secessionists," said the *New York Herald*, had during the previous Administration "held the government and the destinies of the country in their delicate little hands." The French Revolution had not produced "a circle of feminine politicians more accomplished, more sagacious and industrious." Their ramifications had run deep. "Every class and phase of society in Washington was so deeply affected by the soirées, receptions and fancy balls of these irresistible Southern ladies that the sudden transition in that city from all these social splendors and fascinations to the rough simplicities of 'Honest Old Abe' and his hordes of backwoods office-seekers, made Washington ripe for rebellion."

Eventually the jailed women were sent South to friends and relatives. During their weeks in prison they were an incessant topic in the North. The *Chicago Journal* correspondent wrote: "The elegant 'ladies' arrested for maintaining treasonable correspondence with the enemy, take the jail fare very unkindly. They are not used to such treatment and one of them keeps her position at the grated window of her cell calling out to passers-by and deriding this 'free country.' The arrests have had a wholesome effect upon the balance of their dangerous society and the other women are very quiet."

The role of woman in gathering military information, as well as her share in the intrigues of office-seekers, was a constant topic, Governor Dennison of Ohio writing to Chase, "It is the general impression here that women will accomplish anything with the authorities."

Of females in the Confederate secret service in Washington the widow Rose O'Neale Greenhow led in distinction. A tall brunette with slumberous eyes, wearing black dress, hat, and gloves, she was slightly horse-faced, having a gaunt beauty, education, manners, and resourceful speech. Her proud loyalty to the South and her will and courage set her apart as a woman who would welcome death from a firing squad if it would serve her cause. In her home at 398 Sixteenth Street a number of women were held under guard of the Sturgis Rifles, outfitted by the Chicago banker Solomon Sturgis. The mansion had costly furniture and carpets, a large rosewood piano, on the walls oil paintings of living and deceased members of the Greenhow clan. It had been a home and a center of Southern sentiment and social affairs before Mr. Greenhow, a State Department official, had died.

Now Mrs. Greenhow could not come downstairs in her house. She must live, with a servant, on the top floor, though her twelve-year-old daughter could go downstairs and play the piano. As associate spy suspects she had had the wife of ex-Senator Gwin of California and the wife of ex-Congressman Phillips of Alabama. With Mrs. Phillips, a Jewess, were a widowed sister and two daughters. Mrs. Betty A. Hassler, "fascinating in appearance but without decision of character," according to one reporter, had come under suspicion as the wife of a Southern officer and was paroled by order of the Secretary of War. Mrs. Jackson, mother of the killer of Ellsworth, had arrived clad merely in a flannel gown, stayed ten days, and was sent to Richmond. An Englishwoman, Mrs. Elena Lowe, had been arrested in Boston with her son, who carried an officer's commission in the Confederate Army, held in the Sixteenth Street mansion-prison, then returned to England while her son went to a cell in Fort Warren. A widowed Mrs. Baxter of Baltimore had been caught returning from Richmond with a commission for her sweetheart to serve as an officer in the Confederate Army; she relieved herself with tantrums and persistently refused to sleep under a blanket marked "USA." Mrs. Ellie M. Poole, alias Stewart, was the most closely watched. She had tied bed sheets together and let herself out of a jail cell at Wheeling, West Virginia, and was arrested a second time in Kentucky with incriminating papers on her person and $7,500 of Confederate money. It did not help her that she had been a correspondent of the *Richmond Enquirer* and the *Baltimore Exchange*.

In a driving rain, his shoes off and standing on the shoulders of one of his detectives, Allan Pinkerton had, before Mrs. Greenhow was arrested, raised a sash, turned the slats of a Venetian blind, and peered into a first-floor room of her home when one night she received as a caller a young

Union Army captain serving in a Washington garrison. As Pinkerton told it, the young captain was restless, furtive, yet evidently infatuated with the widow. After affectionate greetings the young captain and Mrs. Greenhow sat with a map before them and seemed to be discussing military information gleaned by the young captain. After a time they left the room into which gazed Pinkerton, his shoes off and standing on the shoulders of an assistant while the rain fell. For an hour the two detectives kept their vigil. Then suddenly the front door opened and the young captain came down the front steps and walked rapidly up the street. Pinkerton, not waiting to put on his shoes and not hesitating at shadowing his man in socks during a continuing downpour of rain, was arrested by a sergeant of the provost guard and taken to face the officer in command of the guard that night—who happened to be the identical young captain Pinkerton had seen affectionately going over war maps with Mrs. Greenhow! Eventually the young captain was given a year in a cell at Fort McHenry, and his death shortly after Pinkerton attributed to remorse and shame. Mrs. Greenhow was found to be the woman who sent in cipher to Beauregard on July 16, 1861, the message "Order issued for McDowell to move on Manassas tonight." On her more than anyone else Pinkerton blamed the Union disaster at Bull Run Creek.

Mrs. Greenhow was removed from her home to Old Capitol Prison, was later exchanged and sent to Richmond, commissioned a special Confederate emissary and propagandist to England. After service in Britain she returned to America and in running the Union blockade off the North Carolina coast, the boat in which she with others rode a high wild surf overturned. All the others spilled from the boat managed to survive. But Rose Greenhow perished, it was said, because of the down-drag of her heavy silk dress and the weight of many gold sovereigns belted around her waist, war funds she had hoped to deliver to the Confederate Government she had so loyally and desperately served.

After conference with President Lincoln and Cabinet members, Pinkerton had operated as chief of a secret-service bureau for "ascertaining the social, political and patriotic relations of the numerous suspected persons" in and about Washington. He continued in military and wartime fields the same methods he had employed as a railroad detective, assuming that the new field of espionage was not a particularly specialized one; a good private detective was, to Pinkerton, inferentially an expert secret agent in getting and relaying military information. It was a loose arrangement. Repeatedly the heads of departments stood off his "attempts to obtain satisfying particulars," he said. When later he organized and conducted a secret-service department under General McClellan (they had been old friends in the employ of the Illinois Central Railroad), he had more authority and resources. His reports to McClellan seldom failed to confirm the General's impression that the Confederate troops gravely outnumbered the Union Army.

In the Border Slave States spy was set against spy and the double-dealer paid extra, sometimes in cash or again with a coat of tar and feathers or perhaps a rope around his neck. Spite words and hate bullets sped from neighbor to neighbor in the borderland. The barn-burner was abroad in the night and railroad trains had run out on bridges where the trestles had been on fire just enough to send the locomotive and its cars toppling down. The secret Union Clubs of Kentucky were matched by the secret Knights of the Golden Circle spreading northward into Illinois, Indiana, Ohio. Union loyalists such as Andrew Johnson and Parson William G. Brownlow in Tennessee carried revolvers and had held their weapons ready when facing crowds that hooted them as treacherous rats. Senator Johnson had gone so far as to say of the secessionist leaders, "I would have all such arrested and tried for treason, and when tried and convicted, by the Eternal God I would hang them." In more than one community a mob had called to ask a man, "Are you secesh or abolitionist?" and getting the answer "I'm a Union man," had dragged their man to a near-by tree with a rope, telling him to say his prayers.

The war as such had not really set in as yet. Only that summer of '61 squads of Union recruits would march down one side of a street in Louisville while recruits on the other side headed for the Confederate Army. On a railroad train in central Kentucky one car held a company of troops going to a Union camp while in another car was a company of Confederates. The war was partly in the speechmaking stage. At recruiting camps the raw soldiery called for oratory. After four speakers had addressed the boys at a camp near Louisville, General George H. Thomas was called for. He blurted out: "Damn this speechmaking! I won't speak! What does a man want to make a speech for, anyhow?" and kept to his own quarters.

The Kentucky Senator, John C. Breckinridge, once a Vice-President of the United States, had called at the White House to bid good-by to his kinswoman, Elizabeth Todd Grimsley. He was resigning as United States Senator and joining the Confederate Army as a brigadier general. Northern soldiers under Tecumseh Sherman had reached Elizabethtown, Rolling Fork, Muldraugh's Hill; in September war dispatches were mentioning places of Lincoln's barefoot boyhood. He wrote in a military memorandum in October, "We have possession of the railroad from Louisville to Nashville, Tennessee, so far as Muldraugh's Hill, about forty miles, and the rebels have possession of that road all south of there."

"My distress," wrote Lincoln to General Buell, "is that our friends in East Tennessee are being hanged and driven to despair, and even now, I fear, are thinking of taking rebel arms for the sake of personal protection." He wanted the capture of Cumberland Gap, that mountain gateway through which his grandfather and grandmother had traveled. The operation would cut "a great artery of the enemy's communication" and would be performed "in the midst of loyal people who would rally around it." General Buell promised to take this line of action—repeated the promise—and then in the end moved toward Nashville and left the people to the ways of enemy troops, guerrillas, and bushwhackers.

Mrs. John Jordan Crittenden   Jefferson and Varina Howell Davis

Mrs. John Slidell   Mrs. William McKendree Gwin

Photographs from Frederick H. Meserve Collection

The McClellans at home

George Brinton McClellan, commanding the
Army of the Potomac

General and Mrs. George Brinton McClellan

Lincoln was groping for leaders who could combine military plans with governmental policy. Buell was a West Pointer, wounded in action and twice promoted for gallantry during the Mexican War—a brave man with his own viewpoint on where to fight in Tennessee. There was confusion and worse. Secretary Cameron returned from a trip west in November to say that General Sherman insisted 200,000 troops would be required to hold his 300-mile line and move that line southward. Sherman was "insane," related a Cincinnati newspaper item widely reprinted in the North. "Crazy" Sherman became a nickname. He was ordered removed from command; the order was recalled. There was confusion and worse. Seward started keeping a diary, and after one day of sketching chaos and analyzing paradoxes he handed it to his son, saying it was no time to write down half what he heard and saw each day.

Several weeks during the summer Northern newspapers were sprinkled with items daily about the death, demise, and decease of Jefferson Davis. The *Memphis Appeal* and other Southern journals retaliated with a hoax as follows:

ABE LINCOLN ASSASSINATED! ARREST OF THE ASSASSIN! GREAT EXCITEMENT!

Washington, August 7, 10 A.M.—Abe Lincoln was shot through the heart last night, just as he was entering his carriage, after leaving his cabinet in consultation. The assassin, a Southerner, is now in the hands of the authorities. There is great excitement, and "On to Richmond!" is the cry. Later—11 A.M.—Abe is still alive, but there is no chance for him to survive. The excitement here is great. Still later—12 M. —Abe was wounded in the abdomen and not in the heart. His physician thinks he will recover. The excitement is abating.

Later Still—1 P.M.—It is now currently reported that Abe was only slightly wounded in the leg. No excitement.

The Latest—2 P.M.—An investigation now proves that the bullet intended for Abe's heart missed its mark, and only killed one of his footmen. The people are returning to their business.

Later Still—3 P.M.—Abe's footman was not killed as reported but badly wounded. He will recover.

The Very Latest—4 P.M.—It has been officially announced from the capital that Old Abe's footman was very slightly wounded in the hand by the accidental discharge of a gun which he was cleaning. The President was not in consultation with his cabinet last night as first stated. "Nobody hurt."

Lincoln, Seward, McClellan, and Seward's son rode one September morning in a carriage out of Washington to Rockville, Maryland, headquarters of General Banks, commanding in Maryland. They were going, said the press, to inspect camps, forts, batteries. Reaching open country, Lincoln broke silence, and as Fred Seward heard it, remarked, "General Banks will be expecting us, I reckon." "Yes, sir," replied McClellan, "I have telegraphed him. He will provide a quiet place for conference. I suppose General Dix has his instructions also." "Yes," said Lincoln, "Governor Seward went over to Baltimore a day or two ago, and spent some hours with him at Fort McHenry. So he is fully informed." "Then he will take care of the members in that part of the State?" Seward smiled. "He can be depended on." With

Banks they worked out plans for the secessionist members of the Maryland Legislature to be turned back home, delayed, or arrested before the September meeting of the legislature. There would be little difficulty, Lincoln said at the conference, in "separating the sheep from the goats." It was so ordered and done.

The Maryland Legislature met on September 17. No secession ordinance was presented. No secessionist answered roll call. In their own circles the secessionist members of the legislature had said, "We are going to Frederick to take Maryland out of the damned Union and ally her to the Confederacy." In high Federal circles the word was, "They will never reach Frederick nor have a chance to legislate Maryland out of the Union." Nine secessionist members of the House of Delegates, with officers of both Houses, were arrested on September 16 by General Banks (as arranged at the conference with Lincoln, McClellan, and Seward) and taken to Fort Lafayette, New York, and Fort Warren, Boston. In Baltimore General Dix arrested ten members-elect of the Maryland Legislature, the Mayor of Baltimore, a Congressman, and two editors, who were also sent to Forts Lafayette and Warren, to keep company with similar political prisoners from Kentucky and Missouri. Union members of the Maryland Legislature were pleased, and Governor Hicks within four days wrote to General Banks: "We see the good fruit already produced by these arrests. We can no longer mince matters with these desperate people. I concur in all you have done."

The arrests were secret, the action sudden, illegal, unconstitutional, with no names given out, men lawfully elected to office vanishing into anonymous night as though smitten by a terror. An opposition found voice to say that the operation was "high-handed usurpation," Lincoln a tyrant and despot. The London *Saturday Review* believed the essential fact was that the arrests of the Maryland legislators took place "before they had time to meet, without any form of law or prospect of trial, merely because President Lincoln conceived they might, in their legislative capacity, do acts at variance with the American Constitution."

Lincoln gave the public three sentences of explanation to study: "The public safety renders it necessary that the grounds of these arrests should at present be withheld, but at the proper time they will be made public. Of one thing the people of Maryland may rest assured, that no arrest has been made, or will be made, not based on substantial and unmistakable complicity with those in armed rebellion against the Government of the United States. In no case has an arrest been made on mere suspicion, or through personal or partisan animosities; but in all cases the Government is in possession of tangible and unmistakable evidence, which will, when made public, be satisfactory to every loyal citizen."

Over the country steadily grew protest and clamor at the Government's arrest and jailing of political prisoners, the State and War departments replying that the arrested men and women were charged with giving "aid and comfort to the enemy" and the code of war was that they should be put away. When the Government was criticized as starting a reign of terror, some of its officials answered that they were merely throwing the fear of God and a healthy respect for the Government into the hearts of men who mocked it and plotted against it. The telegraph was busy. In Boston, New York, Buffalo, a seizure of mail or telegrams or a search of a man's home or hotel room would show him a disloyalist. A telegram to that effect would go to Washington. Back would come a telegram, often signed by Seward personally, "Arrest him."

Fort Lafayette at the gate of New York Harbor would fascinate the future historian, said the *New York Herald,* for it held within its walls "the Honorable Pierce Butler, for some years the husband of Fanny Kemble, also the handsome, amiable, but misguided secessionist Mayor Berret of Washington, Baltimore policemen, rebel financiers and diplomats, and maritime adventurers."

In too many cases the "evidence" sent to Washington was trumped up by citizens overanxious to show patriotism, by officers eager to make a record, by personal rivals or spiteful individuals who wanted their victim out of the way, by the dictates of little local tyrants who believed their authority challenged, by the operation of mob spirit which sought to quench any and all citizens who refused to kiss the flag and pronounce the Washington Government a perfect achievement of immortal heroes. Too many cases came under the ancient head of "persecution." Too many showed the work of fanatics endowed with authority clamoring their accusations with "the arrogance of elected persons." The handcuffs were clapped on Connecticut citizens organizing "peace meetings." A crippled newsboy selling his papers on the Naugatuck Railroad was thrust behind the bars because his newspapers included the *New York Daily News,* a disloyal sheet.

The mayor who had welcomed Lincoln to Washington was now a jailbird—having refused to take the oath of allegiance to the United States. Among his companions one Thomas S. Serrill had traveled from Liverpool to New York on the steamer *Persia* boasting that he was carrying for the use of the Southern Confederacy £40,000 in Bank of England notes, which money was found on him when he was searched. Another prisoner, Major Charles Kopperl of Carroll County, Mississippi, had made the rounds of hotels and saloons along Broadway, New York, wearing a revolver and a bowie knife, telling of how at the battle of Bull Run he had made mincemeat of Union soldiers. Another prisoner, Monsieur Louis de Bebian, had left the port of Wilmington, North Carolina, in a vessel that put into Newport, Rhode Island, for shelter, where letters of credit for $40,000 and papers concerning the purchase of clothing and arms for the Confederate Army were found on him. Samuel Aiken had been caught in Philadelphia buying raw material and seducing machinists for his cartridge and arms factory in Richmond, Virginia. Colonel Charles H. Tyler, another prisoner, had fought at Bull Run in the Confederate line, and being arrested in Cincinnati as a spy, found they wouldn't believe him when he said that he had come to Cincinnati to see his wife. When ex-Governor Morehead of Kentucky, with others, entered the prison the *New York Herald* on September 25 chronicled: "Three more candidates for the hospitalities of the Hotel de La Fayette passed through the city yesterday afternoon, en route for their winter quarters. The prisoners were permitted to take refreshments at the Astor House."

Thirty seamen on a naval vessel who refused to take the oath of allegiance were court-martialed and given prison. Sixty mutinous troopers of the 79th New York Highlanders were handcuffed and taken to the Dry Tortugas for hard labor at building forts.

Democrats had repeatedly warned Lincoln as did Ben Butler in a White House call: "Mr. President, you gave me permission to tell you when I differed from the action of the administration." Lincoln asked quickly, "You think we are wrong, do you?" "Yes," said Butler, "in this: you are making this too much a party war. You must get the Democrats in it." Butler pointed to the election for Congressmen coming next year. "And if you get all the Republicans sent out as soldiers and the Democrats not interested, I do not see but you will be beaten." And Lincoln replied, according to Butler, as if he had not thought of it before: "There is meat in that, General. What is your suggestion?" Then on hearing Butler's proposals Lincoln authorized Butler to enlist 6,000 men in sixty days in New England, Butler to command the division and follow his own devices. As officers he would choose all Democrats, Butler assured Lincoln, and "if you put epaulettes on their shoulders they will be as true to the country as I hope I am." Lincoln, according to Butler, told Butler to go ahead and arrange the presidential order to be signed: "Draw such an order as you want, but don't get me into any scrape with the Governors about the appointments of the officers if you can help it."

Butler headed an expedition of ships and men to Hatteras Inlet in August and at a cost of one man killed for five of the enemy, captured fortifications controlling a long line of seacoast, 715 prisoners, 1,000 muskets, 30 cannon, several ships, and 150 bags of coffee. The victory won, he decided to disobey orders and not sink two sand-laden schooners in the inlet. He also decided that his disobedience would be approved if he could get to Washington himself immediately with the news. He arrived at Postmaster General Blair's home opposite the White House late at night to find Blair in his study with the Assistant Secretary of the Navy, Gustavus Vasa Fox. They were glad to hear the news and asked Butler to step across and tell the President. "We ought not to get him up at this time of night," said Butler. "Let him sleep." "He will sleep enough better for it," was Fox's idea.

At the White House it took them about fifteen minutes to find the watchman and wake him. Butler remarked that it would have been a good night for the enemy to kidnap a President. Lincoln was called, and as Butler told it: "He immediately came in in his night shirt; and he seemed very much taller in that garment; and Fox was about five feet nothing. Fox communicated the news, and then he and Lincoln fell into each other's arms. That is, Fox put his arms around Lincoln about as high as the hips, and

Lincoln reached down over him so that his arms were pretty near the floor, and thus holding each other they flew around the room once or twice, and the night shirt was considerably agitated." Butler lay on a sofa and roared.

St. Louis with its 160,000 population, key city to Missouri and the Southwest, hung in the balance. Lincoln urged enrollment of 10,000 men in that city and signed a War Department order: "The President of the United States directs that you . . . will, if deemed necessary, proclaim martial law in the city of St. Louis." A notation of General Scott went on the order: "It is revolutionary times, and therefore I do not object to the irregularity of this."

To Congressman Frank Blair Lincoln wrote, "We have a good deal of anxiety here about St. Louis," and set forth: "I understand an order has gone from the War Department to you, to be delivered or withheld in your discretion, relieving General Harney from his command. I was not quite satisfied with the order when it was made, though on the whole I thought it best to make it; but since then I have become more doubtful of its propriety. I do not write now to countermand it, but to say I wish you would withhold it, unless in your judgment the necessity to the contrary is very urgent." He gave reasons why the politician should not be too sudden at stepping in and using his authority to change the military leadership at St. Louis: "We had better have him a friend than an enemy." They had taken command from Harney, a regular-army veteran, and given it back to him. "Now if we relieve him again the public will ask, 'Why all this vacillation?' Still, if in your judgment it is indispensable, let it be so." Within two weeks Blair believed it indispensable, changed commanders, and was sustained by Lincoln.

In August Lincoln had ordered a commission for Simon B. Buckner of Kentucky as a brigadier general of volunteers: "It is to be put into the hands of General Anderson, and delivered to General Buckner or not, at the discretion of General Anderson. Of course it is to remain a secret unless and until the commission is delivered." And since then General Buckner had become the ranking military officer of the Confederacy in Kentucky. In his case it could not be said that Lincoln had bought loyalty with epaulets.

To George Washington Morgan of Ohio Lincoln handed a brigadier's commission, not so much because Morgan was a West Pointer distinguished for leading a wild charge at Churubusco as for the reason that Congressman Riddle of Ohio came in with recommendations for the appointment from Senators Wade and Sherman (Republicans) and Representatives Vallandigham and Cox (Democrats). That Morgan was a Democrat free-spoken about Lincoln Administration mistakes was discounted. Morgan called on Riddle with thanks for using such powerful persuasion with the President.

Too many "shoulder-straps" were loafing around hotels and saloons, the newspapers chorused. One current satire had it that a boy throwing a stone at a dog on Pennsylvania Avenue missed but accidentally hit three brigadier generals. As Lincoln sat signing commissions one day he told a man whom he later made paymaster, "I'm making brigadier-generals today but I'll get around to your case later." In a few cases Lincoln made colonels and brigadiers of politicians, "to keep them from fighting against the war with their mouths," said Whitney, which wouldn't apply strictly to Lincoln's old-time dueling challenger, James Shields, now wearing the brigadier shoulder straps. Shields was one of the many Democrats given commissions. Illinois Republican editors complained that forty out of seventy Illinois regiments had Democratic colonels. Other Republican organs protested that out of six major generals appointed by Lincoln only one was a Republican—and among one hundred and ten brigadiers eighty were Democrats.

The case came before Lincoln of Philip Kearny, whose claims to appointment as brigadier general had been rejected by the War Department. Kearny in his forty-six years had never graduated from West Point, though he had served in Missouri dragoons, studied French cavalry tactics while serving with chasseurs in daring African exploits in the mountains of Algiers, had lost his left arm leading an impetuous charge against Mexicans at Churubusco, had learned of the ambush when fighting Rogue River Indians, had later again joined his old comrades of the Chasseurs d'Afrique, and at Solferino, Italy, "holding his bridle in his teeth," had led a cavalry charge that pierced the Austrian center and won for Kearny the first Grand Cross of the Legion of Honor the French Government ever pinned on an American soldier.

Seward brought to Lincoln an aide of Kearny's, J. C. Jackson, in company with a New Jersey Democrat who suggested that the President give Kearny command of a New Jersey brigade. The President listened through, turned sharply: "Mr. Jackson, what are General Kearny's politics?" Jackson replied, "I don't know, Mr. President, that he has any politics, but I do know that he is the best representative of the military spirit of the State of New Jersey and is so regarded." Jackson went away from this interview to gather opinions on Kearny's politics, to return alone to the White House, presenting his card, "Unfinished business," to be ushered where the President sat at a desk alone, with cordial greetings for Jackson. "Mr. President," he began, and reported of his inquiry resulting in confirmation as to General Kearny "that he has no politics, is a supporter of the government and this administration." And as Jackson heard it, the President exclaimed: "I thought so. I saw the predicament you were in as an aide of General Kearny. I knew General Kearny, too. He is my brigadier general. No one shall ever be appointed over him."

In many cases Lincoln commissioned politicians and adventurers because they could raise troops; they had followings. One was the Illinois Congressman John A. McClernand, a Douglas Democrat; another was John A. Logan, also a Douglas Democrat and a southern Illinois Congressman. In Logan's district a Pope County mass meeting declared for secession, and a mass meeting in Williamson County pledged itself to attach southern Illinois to the Confederacy. One of Logan's neighbors kept a bloodhound for hunting fugitive slaves. Dozens of young men from this district had gone south to the Confederate Army, Mrs. Logan's brother among them. The name of Logan was used for Southern recruiting; a speech of his against coercion of the South was circulated.

And Logan had returned from Washington with a commission as colonel of volunteers in the United States Army, had mounted a wagon in the public square of Marion and faced a crowd where men who sent word they would kill him watched with revolvers on their hips. "I trembled in every limb, my head swam, and I dared not speak to anyone," wrote Mrs. Logan, "though surrounded by acquaintances and friends." He spoke two hours, ending: "The time has come when a man must be for or against his country. The Union once dissolved, we shall have innumerable confederacies and rebellions. I, for one, shall stand or fall for this Union, and shall this day enroll for the war." A fifer and drummer of Logan's Mexican War regiment struck up "Yankee Doodle," the call to fall in was made, tears ran down Logan's cheeks, and a company of one hundred and ten men enlisted for three years or duration. "There was scarcely a dry eye in the whole crowd," wrote Mrs. Logan.

Lincoln had to gauge communities where uprisings die down and flare up again. The thermometer varied. Charles Francis Adams wrote his son in August: "We have now gone through three stages of this great political disease. The first was the cold fit, when it seemed as if nothing would start the country. The second was the hot one, when it seemed almost in the highest continual delirium. The third is the process of waking to the awful reality before it. I do not venture to predict what the next will be."

The *Salem Advocate*, far south in Illinois, gave its readers advice often heard among quiet men in the borderland: "If you have opinions in regard to the present fearful conditions, keep them to yourselves rather than express them and create bad blood among those who differ from you. Let us not now agitate by trying to make our neighbors believe as we do." The Methodist evangelist Peter Cartwright was nevertheless following no such counsel. He sent his war cry through the St. Louis *Christian Advocate* across Missouri: "If the Union men need help to kill traitors, call on Illinois. We can send you twenty thousand men, good and true. Rivers of blood will flow, but this Union must stand though the heavens fall."

As if the confusion required comic relief, the Chickasaw Indian tribe organized a house and senate, seceded from the United States, declared itself no longer "under the Lincoln Government," and called on neighboring Indian nations, the Choctaws, Cherokees, Creeks, Seminoles, Osages, Senecas, Quapaws, Comanches, Kiwas, together with the red brethren of the Delawares, Kickapoos, Caddoes, and Wichitas, to join in resistances to "Northern invasion by Lincoln hordes and Kansas robbers."

In New Mexico and the Indian country south of Kansas the tribes were "greatly disturbed," owing to the former Federal superintendents' having "espoused the insurrectionary cause," Lincoln noted in a memorandum for Congress. Repossession of the Indian country by Federal troops, believed the Great Father at Washington, would probably bring friendly relations again, several prominent Indian chiefs having written letters to the Commissioner of Indian Affairs expressing loyalty to the United States and a wish for Federal troops to protect them.

CHAPTER 12

FRÉMONT IN MISSOURI–JAMES GORDON BENNETT

IN Missouri during the summer and fall of 1861 civil war ran red and saw one battle of 5,000 Union troops against 11,000 Confederates where the slaughter nearly equaled Bull Run. The newspapermen were not present in numbers, nor Congressmen, Senators, ladies in crinoline. The round world heard less of it. Yet the warfare had raw bones, pointed a sinister forefinger toward the future, and had its weight in moving Lincoln to write in a message to Congress: "In considering the policy to be adopted for suppressing the insurrection I have been anxious and careful that the inevitable conflict for this purpose shall not degenerate into a violent and remorseless revolutionary struggle."

Four men had sat at a table in the Planter's House at St. Louis one day that summer. One was the Governor of Missouri, Claiborne Fox Jackson, who with a former governor, Sterling Price, had arrived in the city under a "safe conduct," a special permit granted by General Nathaniel Lyon, joined with Frank P. Blair, Jr., Republican Congressman representing the Union Safety Committee. In St. Louis and vicinity the regular State government of Missouri had been overthrown.

What the four men talked about several hours that day was whether Lyon as a Union commander could be free to march his troops anywhere in Missouri. Governor Jackson insisted that Missouri should be a neutral State and allow neither Union nor Confederate soldiers within its borders. In conclusion Lyon said he would see every man, woman, and child in Missouri under the sod before he would consent to Missouri's dictating to the United States Government. He clipped his words to the Governor: "This means war! One of my officers will conduct you out of my lines in an hour."

Then one day Lyon borrowed clothes from Blair's mother-in-law and with his red whiskers tucked under bonnet strings he rode in an open carriage through Camp Jackson, to make sure with his own eyes what was going on. The market basket on his arm held a dozen loaded revolvers; he rode past signs: Davis Avenue, Beauregard Street. The next day he surrounded Camp Jackson, took its 635 men prisoners of war. In street clashes of the military with crowds—or mobs—twenty-eight people were killed, two of them women.

A peculiar genius of conflict was this Nathaniel Lyon, short, bearded, with dark-red hair and fiery temperament, driving himself hard, some of his raw volunteer troops saying he talked to them the same as if they were mules and "He had no compliments for anybody." The son of a Connecticut Yankee farmer, a West Pointer, Indian-fighter in Florida, shot in the leg entering Mexico City with the American Army, Lyon handled regulars on the West Coast, at Forts Riley and Kearney, and came to St. Louis from Prairie Dog, Kansas. Congressman Frank Blair knew Lyon as a Union man and saw to it early that Lincoln appointed him commandant of the St. Louis arsenal. At the first signs of Governor Jackson's State troops' seizing the 60,000 muskets in his charge, Lyon used part of them to arm Blair's Home Guards and sent the rest across the river into Illinois. Keeping his force of 7,000 men on the hills around the arsenal, he watched the State troops assembling at Camp Jackson and waited till they had received arms and munitions sent upriver from the Confederate War Department at Baton Rouge; then he closed in.

The next day after his telling Governor Jackson at the Planter's House in St. Louis "This means war!" he started with 2,000 men for Jackson and the State government at the capital, Jefferson City. He ran them out of the capital to Booneville, scattered some 1,300 militia there, and sent the Governor and his guard of 200 or 300 men as fugitives southward. Governor Jackson was carrying the State seal with him, issuing proclamations and documents, yet for all its claims Lyon had made it look like a runaway government without a home to call its own.

Two men, Lyon and Frank P. Blair, had worked out their plans, which made it impossible for Missouri to secede from the Union. The Germans of St. Louis, who were mainly Union and antislavery, threw in their help as valuable allies.

From cornlands and sandhills came volunteers and State militiamen, thousands whetting to fight for the Southern cause of the neutrality of Missouri. Said one of their officers, "We had no tents, it is true, but tents would only have been in our way; we had no uniforms; the ripening corn fields were our depots of subsistence; the prairies furnished forage, and the people in defense of whose homes we were eager to fight gladly gave us of their stores." The foot soldiers were preceded by the "huckleberry" cavalry. Horsemen from Kansas and Texas threw in. The privates seldom saluted, called an officer "Jedge," and lacking bugles, the first sergeants called, "Oh, yes! Oh, yes! All you who belong to Captain Brown's company fall in here."

Lyon threw his army of 6,000 at more than twice that number of Confederates on August 10, 1861, at Wilson's Creek. Bullets struck him near the ankle, on the thigh; one cut his scalp to the bone; his horse was shot. Mounting another horse, his face white from loss of blood, he ordered a bayonet charge and led it, tumbling off his horse into the arms of his orderly with a bullet hole close to the heart. His army retired, the enemy not following. The losses were about 1,200 killed and wounded on each side. Missouri boys of both armies lay dead in the cornfields alongside Kentucky, Iowa, and Illinois boys.

The Confederates gave over the body of Lyon. Crowds came to gaze on his face as the coffin journeyed to Connecticut, where the General Assembly mourned its "beloved son" and the State received for safekeeping his sword, belt, and hat. Press stories, later denied by his family, said that his will left $30,000, nearly all of his estate, to the United States Government for carrying on the war.

An outcry arose when Congressman Frank P. Blair and others put the blame for Lyon's death, Wilson's Creek, and other losses on General John Charles Frémont, commander of the Department of the West, with headquarters, troops, and munitions at St. Louis.

Frémont, one of the first major generals appointed by Lincoln, was in 1856 the first Republican-party candidate for President. Born in Savannah, Georgia, expelled from college in Charleston, South Carolina, for "continual disregard of discipline," instructor of mathematics on a United States war sloop, and railroad surveyor in the Tennessee mountains, he became a lieutenant in the United States Topographical Corps, and at Washington fell in love with fifteen-year-old Jessie Benton, daughter of Senator Thomas H. Benton of Missouri. The Senator had him sent west of the Mississippi River on a surveying trip. He came back and ran away with Jessie; they were married, and thereafter the Benton home in St. Louis was his too, but he used it little. He led expeditions west, exploring the Rocky Mountains, South Pass, winning the first recorded climb up the highest point in the Wind River Mountains; Fremont Peak was named for him.

One fourteen-month trip took Frémont to Great Salt Lake, Fort Vancouver, and Sutter's Fort, California, with his men worn to skeletons and only thirty-three of sixty-seven horses and mules coming through. He clashed with the Spanish rulers of California, took a hand in overthrowing them and setting up the State of California, of which he was the first United States Senator. Though nicknamed "The Pathfinder," he was rather a pathmarker. His writings about the West gave him an international reputation. The Royal Geographical Society, the Prussian Government, voted him medals. His government reports were "fascinating as Robinson Crusoe," said admirers. He was moved by the "wild beauty," the "savage sublimity," the "terrible solitude," of the deserts and mountains. He spoke contempt for the man who would quit while there was a fighting chance, writing his wife: "Proue laid down in the trail and froze to death. In a sunshiny day and having with him means to make a fire, he threw his blankets down in the trail and laid there till he froze to death." Yet Frémont had such sentiment that "he would guide his horse so as to avoid crushing a flower or an anthill."

Then came land, gold mines, money pouring in at the rate of $75,000 a month, and Frémont's Mariposa estate of 46,000 acres, which had cost him

$3,000, was estimated worth $10,000,000. Then too came squatters, rival claims, and the details of management and finance. He was in Paris trying to sell half of his estate when the news came of Sumter. He offered his services and Lincoln immediately commissioned him a major general. At the White House he had talked with Lincoln of the plan for him to organize an army in the Northwest and go down the Mississippi and split the Confederacy in two.

Lincoln invited suggestions "in the unpretending and kindly manner which with him was characteristic," wrote Frémont of this interview. "When I took leave of him he accompanied me down the stairs, coming out to the steps of the portico. I asked then if there was anything further in the way of instructions that he wished to say to me. 'No,' he answered, 'I have given you carte-blanche. You must use your own judgment, and do the best you can.' "

After being placed in command of the Western Department on July 3, Frémont lingered in Washington and delayed in New York nearly three weeks, starting west amid the grief over Bull Run. He was getting muskets to be sent to St. Louis, he said. Others said he was tending to personal business affairs and taking his time.

At a White House reception, as General and Mrs. Frémont in their wraps were waiting for their carriage the President came up and asked the General if he would be presented to General McClellan. "With pleasure, but we are about leaving," said Frémont. The President countered: "Never mind that. I've got him in a corner in the other room and he's waiting for you." Then, followed by Senator Sumner and Mrs. Frémont, the General walked with the President the entire length of the East Room, "the observed of all the guests," who made a lane for them. On being introduced by the President, the Frémonts and the McClellans shook hands, exchanged a little conversation, and the Frémonts went for their carriage.

"The President questioned me every day about his movements," said Postmaster General Blair. "I told him so often that Frémont was off, or was going next day, according to my information, that I felt mortified when allusion was made to it."

At the Astor House in New York on July 15, Frémont received a telegram from Postmaster General Blair informing him, "The President is going in person to the War Department to arrange matters for you."

Frémont arrived in St. Louis on July 25, directed entrenchments thrown around St. Louis to make it safe from assault, wore out relays of telegraphers with messages to governors and troop commanders. He chartered eight steamboats, loaded them with artillery, stores, and 3,800 men bound for Cairo, where General Prentiss was threatened. The night before personally heading this expedition he went to bed at midnight, was at his desk at 4:30 in the morning and stayed there till afternoon, and rode the flagship *City of Alton* down to the relief of Cairo. Then back to St. Louis for war preparations.

Many days he worked from five o'clock in the morning till midnight.

Among those closest to him as guards, helpers, advisers, were three Hungarians, General Alexander Asboth, chief of staff, Colonel John Fiala, chief topographical engineer, Major Charles Zagonyi, head of a cavalry battalion; and Italians such as Captain Antonio Cattanco, Captain Ajace Saccippi, and Lieutenant Dominica Occidone. These dapper foreigners, trained in European tactics and methods, were to assist him in solving civil war in the State of Missouri, with a slang and a lingo of its own from the Iowa line to the Ozarks. (Frank and Jesse James were staying on in Missouri, though Samuel Clemens of Hannibal after two weeks of marching in mud and rain with Confederate warriors had gone west to Utah.) Some of Frémont's foreign aides carried titles queer in St. Louis: "adlatus to the chief of staff," "commander of the bodyguard," "military registrator and expeditor." At the other extreme as advisers he had a group of abolitionists, including Lincoln's good friend Congressman Owen Lovejoy, whose brother had been killed so many years ago by a mob just up the river at Alton, Illinois.

Should Frémont have known it would raise evil gossip for him to locate his headquarters in an elegant mansion at a rental of $6,000 paid to a relative of Mrs. Frémont, even though the rental was reasonable? Should he have known it would set unfriendly tongues buzzing for him to be surrounded by Hungarian and Garibaldian officers in trick uniforms, with ungodly titles? To reach his second-story office, callers passed guards at the street corner, at the gate, at the outer door, at the office door. He was a busy man wrestling with imponderable equations, protecting himself against fool interruptions and time-wasters. Yet his system didn't operate so as to put through the important items and get on with the war. He could handle oufits of one or two hundred men on the plains or desert or in unexplored mountains. Riding the human whirlwind in Missouri was another affair.

From the southwest corner of Missouri came a messenger from Lyon begging Frémont to send him men. Lyon was going to fight a battle whether or not Frémont sent the men. Frémont answered, "If he fights it will be on his own responsibility." Frémont had urged Lyon to retreat to Rolla, which would be falling back about halfway to St. Louis. And he started two regiments toward Lyon. But Lyon never saw them. For him war was fighting; he sought out the enemy. Lyon died in the drawn battle at Wilson's Creek. The memory rankled with men like Frank Blair.

"I will neither lose the state nor permit the enemy a foot of advantage," Frémont wrote Lincoln. "I have infused energy and activity into every department." A touch of the dictator was in his reference to $300,000 in the United States Treasury at St. Louis: "This morning I will order the treasurer to deliver the money in his possession to General Andrews, and will send a force to the treasury to take the money, and will direct such payments as the exigency requires. I will hazard everything for the defence of the department you have confided to me, and I trust to you for support."

To this letter Lincoln made no reply. Frémont got the money he wanted and needed, though his manner and tone were hardly required for the transaction.

Frémont addressed a telegram to "The President of the United States" inquiring, "Will the President read my urgent dispatch to the Secretary of War?" He received the reply on August 15: "Been answering your messages since day before yesterday. Do you receive the answers? The War Department has notified all the governors you designated to forward all available force. So telegraphed you. Have you received these messages?"

Lincoln's anxiety about Frémont and Missouri grew as the mail brought stories of extravagance, blunders, favoritism, corruption. Frank Blair went to St. Louis, which was natural, for Lincoln said later of the Blair brothers and their father, as John Hay noted it: "When this war first began they could think of nothing but Frémont; they expected everything from him, and upon their earnest solicitation he was made a general and sent to Mo. I thought well of Frémont. . . . He went to Missouri the pet and protégé of the Blairs."

Blair called on Frémont with General John M. Schofield, who wrote, "The general received me cordially, but to my great surprise, no questions were asked, nor any mention made, of the bloody field from which I had just come, where Lyon had been killed." Instead of wanting to learn any possible lessons from a tried soldier on the peculiar ways men may have of fighting pitched battles in Missouri, Frémont led Schofield to a table and pointed out on maps the triumphant line of march his army would take to southwestern Missouri and northwestern Arkansas, brushing aside all obstacles, and ending in New Orleans. It was a masterly campaign, as Frémont saw it, on paper. Blair and Schofield left Frémont's office. "We walked down the street for some time in silence. Then Blair turned to me and said, 'Well, what do you think of him?' I replied in words rather too strong to print. Blair said, 'I have been suspecting that for some time.'"

The fantastic tale arose that Frémont was scheming to set up a military republic, a Northwestern Confederacy, of which he would be the head. A young German, Emil Preetorius, who was at Frémont's headquarters and often talked with him, said this was idle chatter: "I had abundant proof that he was a patriot and a most unselfish man. The defect in Frémont was that he was a dreamer. Impractical, visionary things went a long way with him. He was a poor judge of men and formed strange associations. He surrounded himself with foreigners, especially Hungarians, most of whom were adventurers, and some of whom were swindlers. I struggled hard to persuade him not to let these men have so much to do with his administration. Mrs. Frémont, unlike the General, was most practical. She was fond of success. She and the General were alike, however, in their notions of the loyalty due between friends. Once when I protested against the character of the men who surrounded Frémont, she replied, 'Do you know these very men went out with us on horseback when we took possession of the Mariposa [Frémont's California estate]? They risked their lives for us. Now we can't go back on them.' It was the woman's feeling. She forgot that brave men may sometimes be downright thieves and robbers."

Gustave Koerner, appointed a colonel by Lincoln and one of Lincoln's friends to whom Frémont gave a degree of confidence, wrote: "There were plenty of very warm Union men who yet sought to make very large profits out of their patriotism. These clamored for all sorts of contracts for horses, beef, mules, hay, wagons, etc. And when they did not succeed, they naturally charged Frémont with favoring friends and acquaintances of his from the East or California."

Amid his difficulties Frémont held a theory he once wrote to his wife in a letter: "War consists not only in battles, but in well-considered movements which bring the same results." He recalled that during war it sometimes happens that spoken and written words have powerful effects. His veins ran with French blood and he may have heard of the Time of the Terror during the French Revolution. At any rate, he was dealing with a revolution in Missouri. And now he would bring out the Terror. Through the night of August 29 and past midnight and far into the morning of August 30 he worked on a proclamation. The gift of tongues had been bestowed on him, he believed. Daylight broke through the windows when Mrs. Frémont came and found him at his desk with a particular friend, Mr. Edward Davis of Philadelphia. "I want you two, but no others," murmured the General.

Then he read them the proclamation. And they, as wife and particular friend, said it was good, it was a stroke of genius, it would end the war, save the country, and send his name down the ages.

"Circumstances, in my judgment of sufficient urgency," ran the proclamation, "render it necessary that the commanding general of this department should assume the administrative powers of the State." In pompous terms and with threats he didn't have power to enforce, he declared "martial law throughout the State of Missouri." Drawing the line of the Union Army across half the State, he promised that all persons north of this line caught "with arms in their hands" would have court-martial and "if found guilty will be shot." Also "the property, real and personal, of all persons in the State of Missouri who shall take up arms against the United States, or who shall be directly proven to have taken an active part with their enemies in the field, is declared to be confiscated to the public use, and their slaves, if any they have, are hereby declared freemen." Thus he would bring the Terror to Missouri before marching his armies southward and subjugating the hostile populations between St. Louis and New Orleans.

Having written the proclamation in the night, he issued it in the morning. With so important a proclamation there should be no delay, in his judgment. It was too good to be laid aside and read over again on the chance that later judgment might revise it.

Lincoln, along with the country, first heard of the proclamation through the newspapers. After getting an authentic text he wrote Frémont on September 2: "Should you shoot a man, according to the proclamation, the Confederates would very certainly shoot our best men in their hands in retaliation; and so, man for man, indefinitely. It is, therefore, my order that you allow no man to be shot under the proclamation without first having my approbation or consent." Then Lincoln urged that "the confiscation of property and the liberation of slaves of traitorous owners will alarm our Southern Union friends and turn them against us; perhaps ruin our rather fair prospect for Kentucky." He asked Frémont to modify the proclamation so as to conform with an act of Congress passed on August 6 concerning confiscation of property used for insurrectionary purposes. "This letter is written in a spirit of caution, and not of censure. I send it by special messenger, in order that it may certainly and speedily reach you."

Frémont took six days to write a reply to Lincoln. "In the night I decided upon the proclamation and the form of it. I wrote it the next morning and printed it the same day. I did it without consultation or advice with anyone." He still believed it a first-rate piece of work as proclamations go, and he wouldn't change or shade it. It was equal to a victory in the field. "This is as much a movement in the war as a battle."

And this Frémont letter to Lincoln was carried by a special messenger—Mrs. Frémont herself. She left St. Louis on September 8 with her English maid, sitting two days and nights in a hot, overcrowded car, arriving in Washington the third day. And as she told it: "I had not been able to undress or lie down since leaving St. Louis. I had intended taking a bath and going to bed at once."

She changed her mind and sent from Willard's to the White House a written request to know when she might deliver Frémont's letter to the President.

A White House messenger brought back a card on which was written: "Now, at once. A. Lincoln."

It was nearly nine in the evening. She walked to the White House with Judge Edward Coles of New York, met the President in the Red Room: "I introduced Judge Coles, who then stepped into the deep doorway leading to the Blue Room—and there he remained walking to and fro, keeping in sight and hearing, just within range of the doorway. For he was struck at once, as I was, by the President's manner, which was hard—and the first tones of his voice were repelling. Nor did he offer me a seat. He talked standing, and both voice and manner made the impression that I was to be got rid of briefly. It was clear to Judge Coles as to myself that the President's mind was made up against General Frémont—and decidedly against me. In answer to his question, 'Well?' I explained that the general wished so much to have his attention to the letter sent, that I had brought it to make sure it would reach him. He answered, not to that, but to the subject his own mind was upon, that 'It was a war for a great national idea, the Union, and that General Frémont should not have dragged the negro into it,—that he never would if he had consulted with Frank Blair. I sent Frank there to advise him.' He first mentioned the Blairs, in this astonishing connection. It was a *parti pris*, and as we walked back Judge Coles, who heard everything, said to me, 'This ends Frémont's part in the war. Seward and Montgomery Blair will see to that, and Lincoln does not seem to see the injustice, the wrong of receiving secret reports against him made by a man authorized to do so, and as everyone knows, with his mind often clouded by drink and always governed by personal motives' [meaning Frank Blair]."

Thus ran Mrs. Frémont's memorandum of the interview. She added other details later. When she handed General Frémont's letter to Lincoln, "he smiled with an expression not agreeable," and stood under the chandelier to read it. As he read she took a seat—without invitation, travel-worn. He told her he had already written to the General, who knew the Administration's wishes. She said Frémont thought it would be well if Mr. Lincoln explained personally his ideas and desires, for "the General feels he is at the great disadvantage of being perhaps opposed by people in whom you have every confidence."

Lincoln seemed a little startled and asked: "What do you mean? Persons of different views?" Whereupon Mrs. Frémont began talking about the difficulty of conquering by arms alone; England and the wide world would welcome a blow struck against slavery. She thought there was "a sneering tone" in the President's voice as he remarked, "You are quite a female politician."

She had a caller the next day in the elder Frank Blair, an old friend of the Benton family and chief manipulator in 1856 of Frémont's nomination for President. He was sorry for her, wagged his head. "Who would have expected you to do such a thing as this, to come here and find fault with the President? Look what you have done for Frémont; you have made the President his enemy." His information was that Lincoln had received a letter from Frank Blair at St. Louis bringing charges against Frémont and that Postmaster General Montgomery Blair had been sent to St. Louis to make an examination.

She now wrote a letter to Lincoln asking for a copy of the charges against her husband. The President replied: "It is not exactly correct, as you say you were told by the elder Mr. Blair, to say that I sent Postmaster-General Blair to St. Louis to examine into that department and report. Postmaster-General Blair did go, with my approbation, to see and converse with General Frémont as a friend. I do not feel authorized to furnish you with copies of letters in my possession without the consent of the writers. No impression has been made on my mind against the honor or integrity of General Frémont, and I now enter my protest against being understood as acting in any hostility toward him." And Jessie Benton Frémont returned to St. Louis with contempt for Lincoln, hate for the Blairs, and a sharper eye for conspirators against her husband.

Some degree of her personal influence was indicated when Albert D. Richardson of the *New York Tribune* once wrote: "In a lifetime one meets not more than four or five great conversationalists. Jessie Benton Frémont is among the felicitous few, if not queen of them all."

When Lincoln spoke to Hay and others at a later time of his interview with Jessie Frémont, he said Frank and Montgomery Blair in the beginning had full and confidential relations with Frémont, thinking he would accomplish great things. "At last the tone of Frank's letters changed. They were pervaded with a tone of sincere sorrow, and of fear that Frémont would fail. Montgomery showed them to me and we were both grieved at the prospect. Soon came the news that Frémont had issued his emancipation order and had set up a Bureau of Abolition, giving free papers, and occupying his time apparently with little else. At last, at my suggestion, Montgomery Blair went to Missouri to look at and talk over matters. He went as the friend of Frémont. He passed, on the way, Mrs. Frémont coming to see me. She sought an audience with me at midnight and taxed me so violently with many things that I had to exercise all the awkward tact I have to keep from quarrelling with her. She surprised me by asking why their enemy, Monty Blair, had been sent to Missouri. She more than once intimated that if General Frémont should decide to try conclusions with me he could set up for himself."

And as Congressman J. B. Grinnell of Iowa heard Lincoln's version of the Jessie Frémont interview, she came "opening her case with mild expostulations, but left in anger flaunting her handkerchief before my face, and saying, 'Sir, the general will try titles with you! He is a man and I am his wife.'"

Donn Piatt wrote that the President demurred not so much to Frémont's excess of information as at the high valuation Frémont placed on it, the President with a merry twinkle in his cavernous eyes once saying, "John Charles knows too much."

Lincoln's letter to Frémont modifying the General's emancipation proclamation was dated September 11 and began: "Yours of the 8th, in answer to mine of the 2d inst., is just received." He was not saying that Frémont was slow and possibly insubordinate; he was indicating that Frémont took plenty of time in a matter of urgent policy. In mild language Lincoln's letter went on: "Assuming that you, upon the ground, could better judge of the necessities of your position than I could at this distance, on seeing your proclamation of August 30th, I perceived no general objection to it." Then, pointing to the clause relating to confiscation of property and liberation of slaves, he noted that particular clause "appeared to me to be objectionable in its noncomformity to the act of Congress passed the 6th of last August" and he had therefore written his wish to Frémont that the clause be modified: "Your answer, just received, expresses the preference on your part that I should make an open order for the modification, which I very cheerfully do."

Also this same week Lincoln wrote to a seasoned, sober, rather fatherly major general of Western experience, David Hunter: "General Frémont needs assistance which it is difficult to give him. He is losing the confidence of men near him, whose support any man in his position must have to be successful. His cardinal mistake is that he isolates himself and allows nobody to see him, and by which he does not know what is going on in the very matter he is dealing with. He needs to have by his side a man of large experience. Will you not, for me, take that place? Your rank is one grade

The following letter from the President to Gen. Fremont was transmitted to the latter by mail, on the 12th Inst.

Washington, D.C. Sept 11, 1861.

Major General John C. Fremont

Sir:

Yours of the 8th, in answer to mine of the 2d inst. is just received. Assuming that you, upon the ground, could better judge of the necessities of your position than I could at this distance, on seeing your proclamation of August 30th, I perceived no general objection to it.

At the top of this letter annulling Frémont's emancipation proclamation in Missouri Lincoln writes his memorandum for his personal file: "The following letter from the President to Gen. Fremont was transmitted to the latter by mail, on the 12th Inst." At the close of the letter, below, he signs in large script "Your Ob! Serv! A Lincoln," then in smaller handwriting adds his further memorandum: "The Act referred to commences on page 80. of pamphlet acts of Congress of late session."

said proclamation be so modified, held and construed, as to conform to, and not to transcend, the provisions on the same subject contained in the act of Congress entitled, "An act to confiscate property used for insurrectionary purposes," approved August 6, 1861; and that said act be published at length with this order.

Your Ob! Serv!
A Lincoln

(The Act referred to commences on page 80. of pamphlet acts of Congress of late session.)

too high to be ordered to it, but will you not serve the country and oblige me by taking it voluntarily?" And Hunter started for St. Louis.

From antislavery quarters now rose a sure breeze of hostile criticism. Press, pulpit, men and women of antislavery fervor, spoke and wrote their scorn of Lincoln. "My wife expressed the common feeling about Lincoln's letter to Frémont, by saying it seems to her to be the old conflict of Mr. Feeble-Mind and Mr. Ready-to-Halt with Mr. Greatheart," wrote George Hoadly, superior-court judge in Cincinnati, to Secretary Chase. "I have heard men of sense, such as are called conservative, advocate the wildest steps, such as the impeachment of Mr. Lincoln, the formation of a party to carry on the war irrespective of the President and under Frémont, etc. etc. For myself, I must say that if the letters of Mr. Lincoln to Magoffin [Governor of Kentucky] and Frémont are any fair indication of his character and policy, I pray God to forgive my vote for him. General Frémont is thus far the favorite of the Northwest, because he has come up to the standard. And if the election were next fall, to displace him would be to make him President."

Senator Sumner was writing Dr. Franz Lieber: "The London *Times* is right! We cannot conquer the rebels as the war is now conducted. There will be a vain masquerade of battle, a flux of blood and treasure and nothing done!" The President lacked vision. "Never has there been a moment in history when so much was all compressed into a single line and brought directly under a single mind. Our President is now dictator, imperator,— what you will; but how vain to have the power of a god and not to use it godlike! I am sad." Even Bill Herndon of the still existing law firm with the sign Lincoln & Herndon was writing from Springfield, Illinois: "Does the war go on to suit you? It does not suit me. Frémont's proclamation was right. Lincoln's modification of it was wrong."

These antislavery men clashed with such others as Montgomery Blair, who wrote, "The truth is, with Frémont's surroundings, the set of scoundrels who alone have control of him, this proclamation setting up the higher law was like a painted woman quoting Scripture."

Orville H. Browning of Quincy, Illinois, Kentucky-born, who had tried criminal and civil cases with Lincoln and who was appointed United States Senator to fill the unexpired term of Douglas, wrote a protest to Lincoln against the modification of the Frémont proclamation, Lincoln replying, "Coming from you, I confess it astonishes me." Browning had helped frame the very act of Congress on which Lincoln based his rebuke of Frémont. "That you should object to my adhering to a law which you had assisted in making and presenting to me less than a month before is odd enough." The proclamation raised the point of dictatorship as to principle. And as to policy: "The Kentucky legislature would not budge till that proclamation was modified; and General Anderson telegraphed me that on the news of General Frémont having actually issued deeds of manumission, a whole company of our volunteers threw down their arms and disbanded. . . . I think to lose Kentucky is nearly the same as to lose the whole game." With

Kentucky gone, Missouri and Maryland would go. "These are all against us, and the job on our hands is too large for us. We would as well consent to separation at once, including the surrender of this capital." As to shooting Missouri farmers caught with guns in their hands, "our adversaries have the power, and will certainly exercise it, to shoot as many of our men as we shoot of theirs. I did not say this in the public letter, because it is a subject I prefer not to discuss in the hearing of our enemies."

And it had happened that General Jeff Thompson, Confederate commander of the First Military District of Missouri, had issued a proclamation to meet Frémont's, announcing "most solemnly" that for every soldier of the State guard or of the Southern army put to death as ordered by Frémont he would "hang, draw, and quarter a minion of said Abraham Lincoln."

It was a saying, "When the Blairs go in for a fight they go in for a funeral." They had marked Frémont to be destroyed. Frémont fought back. Mrs. Frémont joined. Between them all there was "dirty work at the crossroads." Stories appeared in New York, Philadelphia, Chicago newspapers that Frémont was to be removed from command, that he lived in the style of a European monarch, that he ordered 500 tons of ice to be used in sherry cobblers for himself and staff, that vouchers showed $25 Colt revolvers bought for $35, $20 Enfield rifles bought for $26.50. Congressman Washburne headed a committee which investigated Frémont's department. Judges David Davis and Joseph Holt were appointed to direct an audit of accounts. War Secretary Cameron, with an adjutant general, went personally to St. Louis.

They all found extravagance, mismanagement, blunders, but no specific outstanding corruption. The total of contracts for food, guns, steamboats, uniforms, supplies, fortifications, ran to about $12,000,000. Nothing could be fastened on Frémont. He came through the search with a record for personal honesty. He let it be told that Frank Blair had asked him to give a contract for 40,000 uniforms to a friend of Blair and he had refused. He threw Blair into jail, let him go, arrested him a second time, and let him go. He suppressed the *St. Louis News*.

A secret agent of the Treasury Department, one B. Rush Plumly, went from Philadelphia to St. Louis. He wrote and telegraphed Lincoln that disorder and tumult were threatened in case Frémont was removed, took a train to Washington, and reaching the White House, told Lincoln he was calling out of respect, never having seen the President. Lincoln questioned him and remarked that telegrams and letters which had arrived seemed to come from "a set of speculators who would be disturbed if General Frémont was removed." Plumly protested, "I hope, sir, you do not include me in that category." "I do, sir," said Lincoln. "Mr. President," again protested Plumly, "I am not of them; I have no interest, remote or immediate, in contracts, and no other interest but to serve the government by sending the exact state of things; do you accept my statement, Mr. President?" "I think

I cannot," replied Lincoln. "Nobody has said anything to me against you, but my opinion was formed from your letters and despatches."

Of another White House caller about this time Thomas W. Higginson wrote to his mother. A friend of Frémont came on to smooth things over with the Government and talked till at last the President turned on him, saying, "Sir, I believe General Frémont to be a thoroughly honest man, but he has unfortunately surrounded himself with some of the greatest scoundrels on this continent; you are one of them and the worst of them."

Meanwhile in Missouri there was marching and countermarching of home guards, regulars, volunteers, Hungarians, hillbillies, and one killed, two, twenty, a hundred, in minor clashes at Monday's Hollow, Underwood's Farm, Big River Bridge, Springfield.

After the Fredericktown fight a volunteer wrote home of counting 142 dead men in a field, most of them with bullets through the head: "Col. Lowe was shot right in the forehead, his brains running out." Another had half his head blown away. A man climbing the top rail of a fence hung there with arms and legs dangling from the top rail: "I counted seven bullet holes in his body."

The Chicago Irish Brigade under Colonel James A. Mulligan defended Lexington eight days against 20,000 of the enemy and surrendered 1,600 men on September 20. Blamed for this fresh loss of good troops, Frémont notified General Scott at Washington: "I am taking the field myself. . . . Please notify the President immediately."

General Scott replied, "The President is glad you are hastening to the scene of action; his words are, 'he expects you to repair the disaster at Lexington without loss of time.'" Yet Frémont went on losing time. On October 7 he was at Tipton with 38,000 men, writing Jessie his dreams: "My plan is New Orleans straight, Foote [with gunboats] to join on the river below. I think it can be done gloriously, especially if secrecy can be kept." The dream reached some of his men. "New Orleans, and home again by summer!" was the word passed along. And for the winter would there be plenty of tents? "Is no need of tents," said General Asboth. "In Hungary we make a winter campaign and we sleep without tents, our feet to the fire—sometimes our ears did freeze."

And while Frémont sat with his dreams of war and glory, a man wearing clothes like a Southern planter got off a horse at the Frémont picket lines just beyond Springfield. And the man told the pickets he was a messenger with information from the rebel lines. They let him in. The officer of the day took the man to the chief of staff. No, he couldn't see General Frémont in person. But they would pass in anything he wanted to tell Frémont. The man in the Southern-planter clothes refused this offer. Hours went by. And late in the evening the chief of staff took him to the office where General Frémont sat at the end of a long table.

And the man ripped from his coat lining a paper and handed it to Frémont, who nervously unfolded it, read the name "A. Lincoln" signed to it, slammed the document down on the table, and frowned. "Sir, how did you get admission into my lines?" The man said he came in as a messenger bearing information from the "rebel" lines. Frémont waved him out. "That will do for the present."

Thus on November 2 Frémont was removed from command. Lincoln's removal order, dated October 24, had gone to General S. R. Curtis at St. Louis with instructions that the order was not to be handed Frémont if when reached by messenger "he shall then have, in personal command, fought and won a battle, or shall then be actually in a battle, or shall then be in the immediate presence of the enemy in expectation of a battle." Curtis made copies of Lincoln's order and sent three messengers by separate routes with it. Curtis had heard of Frémont's arrangements for no removal order to be delivered.

From German regiments came threats of mutiny; they had enlisted, men swore, to fight only under Frémont. He addressed them, asking for loyalty, praising his successor: "Soldiers! I regret to leave you. . . . I deeply regret that I shall not have the honor to lead you to the victory which you are about to win."

General Hunter temporarily took command. Other plans for reaching New Orleans were under way. Mrs. Frémont told Gustave Koerner: "Oh, if my husband had only been more positive! But he never did assert himself enough. That was his great fault."

Frémont had lasted in Missouri just a hundred days. In that time he made himself a hero in the eyes of nearly all the antislavery elements of the Northern States and of Europe. He gave freedom to the Negro slaves of his district—on paper, but the promise and the gesture gave gladness to all crusaders. As the abolitionist leaders such as Gerrit Smith and Wendell Phillips had swung in for the war and the Union, the antislavery movement had deepened and widened in power. Their hope was to abolish slavery and keep the Union. They were no longer merely martyrs. They were also patriots. They had acquired such footholds of political power now that old weatherworn wheel horses of politics were turning to them. They were an asset in votes. Nearly all the New England regiments in the field, and all the German battalions, were radical for abolition.

The process was under way by which the abolitionist, once so bitterly outlawed and hunted and mobbed, was to become recognized in the North as a respectable patriot of heroic quality. They now saw in Frémont a mouthpiece of their hopes. If Frémont yearned for distinction and leadership, it was now his. The good Quaker poet Whittier wrote:

> Thy error, Frémont, simply was to act
> A brave man's part, without the statesman's tact,
> And, taking counsel but of common sense,
> To strike at cause as well as consequence.

Sober citizens pulled the portraits of Lincoln from their walls and trampled under foot the face of the President, according to the *Cincinnati Gazette*. "He is not a genius," was Wendell Phillips's estimate of Lincoln.

"He is not a man like Frémont, to stamp the lava mass of the nation with an idea." At ceremonies honoring Frémont in person, Henry Ward Beecher in his Brooklyn church said, "Your name will live and be remembered by a nation of freemen." James Russell Lowell, Harriet Beecher Stowe's husband, Greeley and his *New York Tribune*, Bryant and the *New York Evening Post*, took deep offense at Lincoln's treatment of Frémont.

Worse in effect than another Bull Run disaster was the President's annulment of Frémont's emancipation edict: thus ran the pronouncement of Joseph Medill of the *Chicago Tribune*. In his opinion there was no law for "rebels," and Medill wrote to Chase on September 16 that he considered it "passing strange" that a Government with seven profound lawyers at its head should have overlooked that as a fact. The next day his newspaper editorially denounced the President's action and predicted grave humiliation unless the Administration took a more vigorous policy. A few weeks later Medill wrote to Chase that the country was tired of "boring auger holes with gimlets," and hoping that though the President ignored the cause of the war, Chase would not. Should Chase come out for a more radical dealing with confiscation of slaves and "rebel" property, "you will hit the nail squarely on the head." Medill seemed now to be so disappointed, even disgusted, with Lincoln that he was feeling out Chase as a prospective leader of the Republican party.

The *Springfield* (Massachusetts) *Republican*, however, did not trail along with the vehement defenders of Frémont; its editor, Samuel Bowles, wrote, "It is gratifying to know that we have a President who is loyal to law—when that is made to meet an emergency—as he is to meet an emergency for which no law is provided." This was a basic shift for the Samuel Bowles who seven months before had written that Lincoln was "a simple Susan."

Not so basic was the shift of the *New York Herald* with its brand-new presentation of Lincoln as the nation's hero: "The President, who has always been known as an upright man, of late months, has justly earned the reputation of a wise and energetic statesman." If Lincoln read a long editorial headed "President Lincoln Nobly Meeting the Crisis," his mood was partly that in which on the stump once he took a compliment from Douglas—"Not being used to it, it came to me all the sweeter."

The *Herald* editorial was historical, gratulatory, and not lacking in advice. "While contending in battle array with the insane faction of nigger-drivers at the South, and putting down with the strong hand their murderous and suicidal treason, Mr. Lincoln has been equally mindful that the original cause of evil began with the machinations of fanatical nigger worshippers at the North, and that to them are mainly owing our present troubles. The moderate and effective rebuke contained in his letter to Major-General Frémont is eminently worthy of admiration, both for the dignified and courteous language in which it is couched, and the death blow it strikes at all attempts of badly advised local commanders to overstep the legitimate sphere of their military duties."

Not for long could any man be the hero of the *New York Herald*. The "laughing Ishmael" who was himself that journal had been accused often of inconsistency and replied, "I print my paper every day," his version of Lincoln's "My policy is to have no policy." The foremost innovator in the journalism of his time, James Gordon Bennett, was studied by Lincoln as one of the powers to be kept on the Union side as far as possible. Greeley with his *New York Tribune* was an educator, a reformer, and a personal influence rather than a great editor or publisher. Raymond with the *New York Times* was a Republican-party man and a Unionist slowly coming to understand Lincoln and to sponsor the Administration.

As a strict newspaper, allied to no political party, no reforms nor isms nor special ideas, brilliant and even bawdy in its endless chatterings, the *New York Herald* was generally acknowledged to have circulation, resources, and prestige surpassing any other American journal. The Polish red-republican Count Gurowski wrote in his diary of August, 1861: "Mr. Lincoln has already the fumes of greatness, and looks down on the press, reads no paper, that dirty traitor the *New York Herald* excepted. So, at least, it is generally stated." The rumor was not correct, but may have arisen out of some chance remark of Lincoln on the news enterprise and editorial audacity of the *Herald*.

Daily printing 84,000 copies, the *Herald* announced itself on April 9, 1861, as "the most largely circulated journal in the world." Two days before the bombardment of Fort Sumter, be it remembered, the *Herald* said that the only hope against civil war seemed to lie "in the overthrow of the demoralizing, disorganizing, and destructive sectional party, of which 'Honest Abe Lincoln' is the pliant instrument." Bennett had been a stanch friend of Buchanan, had received from Buchanan confidential advance copies of messages to Congress, had pleaded for a second presidential term for Buchanan. Then in the uprising after Sumter mobs had surged around the *Herald* building, demanding that the American flag be run up, and Bennett had ordered Eddie Flynn, an office boy, to chase out of a back door and buy a piece of cloth known as the Stars and Stripes. Bennett from an upper window bowed smiling to the mob as the spangled cloth was for the first time hung out.

Bennett then telegraphed for Villard at Washington, and in Bennett's carriage driving up Broadway and Fifth Avenue through Central Park to Washington Heights, "he did nothing," wrote Villard, "but ask questions bearing upon the characteristics and doings of President Lincoln and the circumstances of my acquaintance with him." After dinner Bennett had given Villard the verbal message to Lincoln that the *Herald* would be unconditionally for suppressing the rebellion and for necessary war measures. A second message was to Secretary Chase, offering as a gift to the Government, for revenue service, a famous yacht of James Gordon Bennett, Jr., the son to be commissioned a lieutenant in the same service.

And a few days later Bennett, Jr., called at the White House and Lincoln penned a note to Chase, "The Secretary of State this moment introduces to me Mr. James Gordon Bennett, Jr., who tenders to the U.S. the service, a

fine Yacht of 160 tons burthen . . . allow him an interview, which I ask
for him." So Bennett, Jr., was commissioned a third lieutenant, and during
the summer cruised with a revenue cutter off the coast of Long Island.

The *Herald* was concededly the only American newspaper of considerable circulation and influence in Europe. Its insolent anti-British tone, and
its arrogant policy in general, misrepresented America, and Lincoln in his
anxiety about foreign goodwill picked Thurlow Weed to approach Bennett. Seward advised Lincoln not to send Weed. And Weed himself said
that he and Bennett for thirty years had been political and personal enemies, both rooming at the Astor House and never speaking as they met.
But Lincoln, when the matter narrowed down to a choice from several proposed emissaries, decided on Weed. Seward gave Weed a good breakfast
one morning and sent him to the White House.

"President Lincoln," wrote Weed, "remarked in his peculiar way, that
he understood I had had 'considerable experience in belling cats,' and with
this introduction proceeded to say that, in view of the influence the *Herald*
was exerting over Europe, he deemed it of the greatest importance that Mr.
Bennett should be satisfied that the course of the *Herald* was endangering
the government and the Union, adding his belief that if Mr. Bennett could
be brought to see things in that light he would change his course. While
appreciating the importance of the mission, I assured Mr. Lincoln I was the
last person in the country to be selected for such a duty, but he insisted that
I should make the trial, and I departed on the first train for New York."

At dinner and in a long evening of conversation Bennett and Weed
threshed over the issues, and the prominent feature of the discussion was
Bennett's continued and bitter denunciation of Greeley, Garrison, Seward,
Sumner, Wendell Phillips, and Thurlow Weed as having exasperated the
South into the war. Weed returned to Washington, reported the interview,
believed that the President and the Cabinet were "gratified" over his diplomacy. The results were slender, if any. The *New York Herald* went on har-
pooning the British Empire.

Self-announced as "daily daguerreotype of American manners and
thought" the *Herald's* sixty-six-year-old owner and editor, born of Roman
Catholic parents of French descent in Strathbogie, Scotland, had trained for
priesthood at Aberdeen, had starved as a bookseller in Boston, had lived
shabbily as a hack writer in New York, had served a year as Spanish translator for the *Charleston Courier*. In politics he had yoked himself to varied
flickering interests, receiving smooth words and saying he found President
Van Buren "cold, heartless, careless, and God knows what." He seemed to
have wept and to have studied his tears analytically and then become hard,
gay, elusive. He issued his first four-page penny *New York Herald* in 1835,
doing all the work except the printing himself, writing and shaping the
whole paper on an editorial desk of one board slung over two dry-goods
boxes, "one poor man in a cellar against the world," as he phrased it.

Then with years of toil from five in the morning till ten at night, scram-
bling, scandalizing, dramatizing, playing with a scale of shrieks and whispers

delicately manipulated, Bennett built a world-famed newspaper. "The newspaper's function," he said, "is not to instruct but to startle." Rivals were forced to imitate his elaborate legitimate news service, while his chameleon viewpoints, his breezy and idle chatter, his irresponsible gossip and lurid topics setting the town agog, were not so easy to match. He charmed, dazzled, shocked, so independently or flagrantly that his enemies agreed with Park Benjamin writing him as "obscene foreign vagabond, a pestilential scoundrel, ass, rogue, habitual liar, loathsome and leprous slanderer and libeller." The name of "Jenkins," his anonymous keyhole eyewitness and transom eavesdropper—or the writer with a flaring, overly lurid vocabulary —had entered American slang; any shameless blabber was a Jenkins.

Yet Bennett was first of newspaper editors to print financial news on a large scale, regularly to expose stock-market frauds, to publish lists of bankrupts, to mock at social functions and to satirize a "high society" he did not have time for, to print religious news, though his church items were at first resented and scorned. He was first to give large spreads to bawdy-house murders.

Under headlines "Declaration of Love," "Caught at Last" one June day in 1840 Bennett signed an announcement to his readers: "I cannot resist the divine instinct of honest nature any longer; so I am going to be married to one of the most splendid women in intellect, in heart, in soul, in property, in person, in manner, that I have yet seen in the course of my interesting pilgrimage through human life. . . . I can not stop in my career. I must fulfill that awful destiny which the Almighty father has written against my name. I must give the world a pattern of happy wedded life, with all the charities that spring from a nuptial love. In a few days I shall be married according to the holy rites of the most holy Christian church, to one of the most remarkable, accomplished, and beautiful young women of the age." He went on and on about the purity and good sense of his bride, without naming her, Henrietta Agnes Crean, a fine Irish colleen who was a music teacher. They could live on the *Herald's* "twenty-five thousand dollars per annum, almost equal to a President's salary," and *Herald* readers would notice improvements. "The holy estate of wedlock will only increase my desire to be still more useful. God Almighty bless you all."

The bridal couple went to Niagara Falls, to Boston, returned to New York, where threats of a boycott were made against the most fashionable Astor House if it permitted them to register. Some rival newspapers actually printed a statement that the James Gordon Bennetts were refused accommodations, the hotel-manager compelling corrections. On four occasions in public places Bennett was beaten with canes and cowhides, on each occasion giving his readers a full report of the event as he saw and felt it. His enemies overreached in hoping to destroy him. He was, as they printed it, "humbug," "venomous reptile," "instrument of mischief," "profligate adventurer," "venal wretch," "daring infidel," "prince of darkness," "ribald rascal," "cheat," "common bandit," "infamous slanderer," "veteran blackguard," "murderer of reputations," "nuisance," "black-hearted blasphemer," "turkey-buzzard," "villain," "forger," "ignorant hypocrite bloated with conceit," "immoral monstrosity." An advertisers' boycott of the *Herald* was attempted and failed.

Physical beatings, verbal castigation, social ostracism, attacks on credit and advertising income, all failed to stop the course of Bennett striding onward toward power, telling his readers he was "a friend of the human race" and "from my earliest days there were implanted in my burning soul those lofty principles of morals, honor, religion, that all the editors or bankers in Christendom cannot intimidate." He predicted that as newspaper abuse had made Martin Van Buren Chief Magistrate of the Republic, so "newspaper abuse will make me the chief editor of this country." He emphasized the role of the telegraph as adding to the power of the press: "The whole nation is impressed with the same idea at the same moment. This agency will be productive of the most extraordinary effects on society, government, commerce, and the progress of civilization; but we cannot predict its results."

As a central figure in the baffling human whirlpool of New York Bennett was playing with paradoxical forces that were to be a heavy anxiety to the Lincoln Administration. Though he mocked at New York aristocracy and held no individual reputation too clean for him to smutch, he kept close to the needs of business expansion and the widening streams of Northern capital that sought new fields and larger earnings. As a Catholic apostate and supporter of Know-Nothing principles he quarreled with Archbishop John Hughes, who proclaimed Bennett "a very dangerous man." As a Know-Nothing he was rather anti-Catholic than antiforeigner and took pleasure in printing statistics to show that 507,137 "poor emigrants" arriving in ten years had brought $21,900,000 into the country. He was metropolitan rather than rural, and had none of Greeley's influence with the farmers.

The *New York Times* cartooned Bennett in Scotch costume inflating the windbag of the *Herald*, and Bennett dismissed challenges of his two leading competitors with mocking: "Mr. Mephistopheles Greeley and that little villain Raymond are greatly moved upon the subject of the relative circulation of the *Herald* and their own petty papers; we are sorry for them." He had brought his newspaper to where internationally it was taken as America's answer to the London *Times*. Of its warlike threats John Bright of the British House of Commons wrote to Senator Sumner, "It is unfortunate that nothing is done to change the reckless tone of your *New York Herald;* between it and the [London] *Times*, there is great mischief done in both countries."

After the Bull Run disaster the *New York Herald* counseled fresh determination and further preparations, almost in the tone of Lincoln's memoranda for immediate action; no panic, no bewilderment, as in the case of Greeley. Then on Lincoln's revoking Frémont's personal proclamation of Negro emancipation had come the *Herald's* encomiums for Lincoln, praise in heaping measure, compliments that like fresh roses must soon wither and fade petal by petal.

Toward the end of that month of September, 1861, a *Herald* man came to the White House, and as Lincoln told it in his first letter, "private and confidential," to James Gordon Bennett, "Last evening Mr. Wikoff solicited me for a pass, or permission to a gentleman whose name I forget, to accompany one of our vessels down the Potomac today, as a reporter of the *Herald*, saying the Sec. of the Navy had refused, while he had given the privilege to reporters of other papers." Lincoln was aware that this procedure to any efficient publisher was nearly the same as a slap in the face. He explained to Bennett, "It was too late at night for me to see the Secretary, and I had to decline giving the permission, because he, the Sec., might have a sufficient reason, unknown to me."

Then he gave Bennett a sentence of grace and reservations: "I write this to assure you that the Administration will not discriminate against the *Herald*, especially while it sustains us so generously, and the cause of the country as ably as it has been doing." Rarely did Lincoln subscribe himself, as he did for Bennett, in the antique manner, "Your Obt Servant." Still more rarely did he depart from the signature of "A. Lincoln" into the more portentous one, as he did for Bennett, spelling his first name in full and signing "Abraham Lincoln." Customarily only his state papers were signed thus.

With no cessation Bennett would continue putting the blame for the war on "nigger worshippers," sprinkling his editorial page with that phrase, and steadily maintaining that antislavery agitators rather than heroes were hypocrites intoning I-am-holier-than-thou. The inexplicable involutions of the antislavery agitation were touched by George William Curtis, himself an antislavery man, in a letter of July 29, 1861, voicing what he could not say in his *Harper's Weekly* editorials: "There is very little moral mixture in the 'anti-slavery' feeling of this country. A great deal is abstract philanthropy; part is hatred of slave-holders; a great part is jealousy for white labor; very little is a consciousness of wrong done, and the wish to right it. How we hate those whom we have injured. I, too, 'tremble when I reflect that God is just.'"

A constant spur to the antislavery agitation was the increased fury at Negroes voiced by those who laid the blame for the war and all its misery on the Negro as the bottom cause. Had there been no Negro, there would have been no slavery and therefore no antislavery agitation, reasoned the *New York Express* in behalf of a motto: "Down everywhere, with the negro! Down with him as the pest of parties, and the curse of the country—when mixed up with politics."

To friends of Sumner who in September, 1861, urged Lincoln to issue a proclamation giving freedom to the slaves, he said, "It would do no good to go ahead any faster than the country would follow," Charles Edwards Lester writing that he heard the President add to this, "You know the old Latin motto, *festina lente*. How do the Italians, those bastard Romans, say the same thing now?"

"They have improved on it, Mr. President. They say, '*Andante adagio, perchè ho premúra*'—'Go slow, because I am in a hurry.'"

"That's it, exactly. I think Sumner and the rest of you would upset our applecart altogether, if you had your way. We'll fetch 'em; just give us a little time. We didn't go into the war to put down slavery, but to put the flag back; and to act differently at this moment would, I have no doubt, not only weaken our cause, but smack of bad faith; for I never should have had votes enough to send me here, if the people had supposed I should try to use my power to upset slavery. Why, the first thing you would see, would be a mutiny in the army. No! We must wait until every other means has been exhausted. This thunderbolt will keep."

"That reminds me, Mr. Lincoln. One fall in Connecticut we gave some apples to a neighbor of ours, with directions how to preserve them, laid down in a barrel of dry sand, headed up, and not opened till the 4th of July next year. On that morning he paid us a visit and announced he had opened his apples. 'Well, did they keep?' 'Yes,' said he, 'they kept; but they were all rotten!' "

Lester was pleased that Lincoln was kind enough to laugh at this. It was pat as to apples, but Lincoln would shift the comparison to powder and bombs: "The powder in this bombshell will keep dry; and when the fuse is lit, I intend to have them touch it off themselves."

Sumner in writing to Governor Andrew that Massachusetts, as always, should lead in antislavery action, urged that emancipation should be proclaimed "as an essential and happy agency in subduing a wicked rebellion." Sumner believed he was sending Governor Andrew timely information in writing that by stressing emancipation "you will help a majority of the Cabinet, whose opinions on this subject are fixed, and precede the President himself by a few weeks." This on the part of Sumner was misleading; it would have been correct had he written "minority of two" instead of "majority." He was sending simple and straightforward fact, however, in reporting to Governor Andrew, "He [the President] tells me that I am ahead of him only a month or six weeks."

Levi D. Boone, a physician who had once been Mayor of Chicago and handled the "lager-beer riots" that ensued when the saloon license rate was raised from $50 to $300 a year, came to exchange greetings with Lincoln. "The President seemed very much worn and anxious, and I could not help feeling, as he took my hand in both of his, and expressed his pleasure at seeing me, that he was thinking of matters that much more interested him than seeing an old acquaintance. Poor man! he is to be pitied."

CHAPTER 13

THE TRENT AFFAIR—"ONE WAR
AT A TIME"

THE Queen of England's proclamation on May 13 of '61, which recognized the Southern Confederacy as a belligerent power, also declared neutrality and warned Her Majesty's subjects not to enlist for land or sea service under the flag of either belligerent, not to supply munitions of war, nor to convey officers, soldiers, dispatches, arms, of either belligerent, nor to fit out ships for privateering or do any other act tending to give assistance to either belligerent. To the United States Government this was important and convenient, for the British Navy ruled the seven seas and patrolled far-flung colonial domains.

Her Majesty's Ministers had given unofficial hearings to the Confederate Commissioners, Yancey and Rost, and refused to go beyond the Queen's proclamation. Yancey had resigned in disgust and gone home to Alabama; accustomed to addressing thousands of plain people with his innermost thoughts, he had found it a trial to sit across a table from the bland, inscrutable diplomats of the British Empire and during extended conversations try to guess what they held.

"There are two nations in England," wrote John Bright to the American consul at Liverpool, "the governing classes and the millions who toil. The former dislike your Republic and their organs misrepresent and slander it. The latter have no ill-feeling towards you but are not altogether unaffected by the statements made to your prejudice."

Against the incessant propaganda of the powerful daily newspapers of the ruling class the British masses were holding to an instinct that the South stood for slavery and the North for human justice, even though the Lincoln Government thus far was committed in policy merely to preventing the spread of slavery into the Free States.

"The United States of America has ceased to be," said the London *Times*, amplifying its view that the North would never conquer the South and all incidents of the first seven months of war had favored the Confederate States. "So short-lived has been the American Union that men who saw its rise may live to see its fall."

The British Government had received from its Minister to the United States, Lord Lyons, reports that Seward was dangerous in his belief that the relations between Britain and the United States could be safely played with for political ends. Lincoln, in Lyons's judgment, would probably leave the whole management of foreign affairs to Seward. Lincoln had not given proof of possessing any natural talents to offset his ignorance of everything but Illinois politics. The President was well-meaning and conscientious, in the measure of his understanding, but not much more, according to Lyons's appraisal.

In November of '61 came the explosion known as the Trent Affair, a dramatic clash of English-speaking nations. The *Trent*, a British Royal Mail packet, one day out from Havana, was steaming serenely along the Bahama Channel. At noon of November 8 she came to where the channel narrows to a width of fifteen miles. There the *San Jacinto*, a screw sloop of the American Navy, was waiting.

The *Trent* hoisted the British colors. The *San Jacinto* ran up the Union Jack. Also the *San Jacinto* fired a shot across the bow of the *Trent*.

And as the British steamer showed no signs of slowing down, the American sloop sent a shell that burst in front of the bow of the *Trent*. This brought her to, as the sailors say.

Captain Moir of the *Trent* stood on the deck, lifted a trumpet to his lips, and sang out, "What do you mean by heaving my vessel to in this way?" No answer came to his cry.

Three boats were leaving the *San Jacinto* with officers, sailors, marines. It seemed as though they would bring word to Captain Moir of what was up. The sea was smooth and they rowed to the *Trent* in a few minutes.

Lieutenant D. MacNeill Fairfax, aboard the *Trent* and speaking for Captain Charles Wilkes, commander of the *San Jacinto*, asked for the passenger list of the *Trent*. He had information that James M. Mason and John Slidell, newly appointed Confederate Commissioners to Great Britain and France respectively, were on board.

Mr. Slidell happened to be standing near when his name was mentioned and he stepped up to Lieutenant Fairfax, saying, "I am Mr. Slidell; do you want to see me?" And Mr. Mason, also being near, stepped up, and as he and Lieutenant Fairfax had been introduced years before on land there was no need for him to say who he was. Next the Lieutenant asked for the secretaries to Messrs. Mason and Slidell and they were lined up.

At this point the American Lieutenant informed the British Captain that he had been sent by his commander to arrest Messrs. Mason and Slidell and send them as prisoners on board the United States vessel near by.

The passengers meanwhile crowded around with such cries as "Pirates! villains!" and "Throw the damned fellow overboard!" Lieutenant Fairfax knew they meant him, and reminded them that every move was being watched through spyglasses from the *San Jacinto*, heavy guns were bearing on them, and he couldn't answer for consequences in case they should try to throw him overboard as they suggested.

Among those with spyglasses on the *San Jacinto* was a heavy-jawed man with a dangerous eye and wavy locks of hair—Charles Wilkes, sixty-three years old, scientist, experimenter in astronomical observation, explorer of south-polar ice fields, authority on meteorology, author of eleven volumes and atlases, sea rover at home anywhere in the Western Hemisphere. He was a strict disciplinarian, and once when charges were preferred against him by fellow officers he was acquitted on all counts except one of illegally punishing members of the crew, for which he was reprimanded.

Mrs. Slidell inquired who was the commander of the *San Jacinto*. "Your old acquaintance, Captain Wilkes," said Fairfax, which surprised Mrs. Slidell. She had sipped tea with him in Washington. "He is playing into our hands!" said Mrs. Slidell spunkily. Mr. Mason offered her the hint not to discuss the matter at this time. When she and the wives and daughters of the prisoners were offered the use of the commander's cabin on the *San Jacinto* they declined with thanks; they would stay on the *Trent* and go to London.

"Good-by, my dear, we shall meet in Paris in sixty days," said Mr. Slidell as he bade farewell to his wife. Lieutenant Fairfax went with him to his cabin for his luggage. There Slidell's daughter clung to him and begged to go with him. She wept as he was rowed with the three other prisoners on the path of the smooth sea to the *San Jacinto*.

During the whole operation there was the best of feeling between Lieutenant Fairfax and Captain Moir. It was only the passengers and the families of the prisoners who had talked rough. On parting from Captain Moir, Lieutenant Fairfax stood on the main deck, hat in hand, and said, as Commander Williams, the British naval agent on board, heard the parting words: "Sir, I have a painful duty to perform, and if, in the excitement of the moment, I have said aught that by possibility can be construed into a personal offence, or an insult towards you, I most humbly beg your pardon, sir, for I never meant it."

And Captain Moir, hat in hand and equally courteous, replied: "I have had a painful scene to witness—a scene of degradation to my country's flag. I do not deny that my feelings have been greatly excited; but if by any gesture I have done aught to offend you, as a man, there is my hand, sir, and I crave your forgiveness."

The two ships moved away from each other toward different horizons and soon each was alone in the silence of the sea.

When the *Trent* passengers reached London on November 27, they found themselves accepted heroes and heroines who had undergone severe tests. Commander Williams, the royal naval agent, proved quite a witness. His testimony, in part, concerned the fifteen-year-old daughter of the Slidells: "Miss Slidell was with her father in the cabin, with her arm encircling his neck, and she wanted to be taken to prison with him. Mr. Fairfax [the United States lieutenant] attempted to get her away with inducements. In her agony, then, did she strike him in the face three times." He told of "the marines rushing with the points of their bayonets at Miss Slidell," how she screamed, and it was then that he, Commander Williams, had just time "to put his body between her and the bayonets of the marines."

England went into an uproar. The London *Times* fastened on Captain Wilkes: "He is an ideal Yankee. Swagger and ferocity, built on a foundation of vulgarity and cowardice, these are his characteristics, and these are the

James Murray Mason of Virginia

Photograph from National Archives

Charles Ferguson Smith

From author's collection

John Slidell of Louisiana

Photograph by McClees in author's collection

Samuel Ryan Curtis

From author's collection

Nathaniel Lyon

Edward Dickinson Baker

From Oliver R. Barrett Collection

David Dixon Porter

From author's collection

David Glasgow Farragut

From Oliver R. Barrett Collection

Gideon Welles

John Adolph Dahlgren

From Oliver R. Barrett Collection

An English cartoon of mixed motives

most prominent marks by which his countrymen, generally speaking, are known all over the world. To bully the weak, to triumph over the helpless, to trample on every law of country and custom, wilfully violate all the most sacred interests of human nature, to defy as long as danger does not appear, and, as soon as real peril shows itself, to sneak aside and run away— these are the virtues of the race which presumes to announce itself as the leader of civilization, and the prophet of human progress in these latter days. By Captain Wilkes let the Yankee breed be judged."

The London *Morning Chronicle* tore its hair and gave the war party its cues: "Abraham Lincoln, whose accession to power was generally welcomed on this side of the Atlantic, has proved himself a feeble, confused and little-minded mediocrity. Mr. Seward, the firebrand at his elbow, is exerting himself to provoke a quarrel with all Europe, in that spirit of senseless egotism which induces the Americans, with their dwarf fleet, and shapeless mass of incoherent squads, which they call an army, to fancy themselves the equal of France by land, and of Great Britain by sea. While these mischief-makers stagger on at the head of affairs, their only chance of fame consists in the probability that the navies of England will blow out of the water their blockading squadrons, and teach them how to respect the flag of a mightier supremacy beyond the Atlantic."

And Britain did more than talk. Lord Palmerston, the Prime Minister, and Lord John Russell, Secretary for Foreign Affairs, framed a note to the United States Government, a scrap of paper for Seward and Lincoln to read. Mainly it asked whether Captain Wilkes had done what he did by his own wish and whim or at the command of his Government. If it was a government order and in line with United States policy—then war! The language was elegant, but held the essence of the psalmist—"The words of his mouth were smoother than butter, but war was in his heart."

The ships of the best and biggest navy in the world were made ready. Eight thousand picked troops were put on transports and set sail for Canada.

By this time the United States had gone into an uproar. Yankee Doodle tore his shirt. The eagle was brought out to scream. "The Star-spangled Banner" blared its sonorous patriotism from multitudinous brass instruments.

Captain Wilkes arrived at the port of New York with his prizes, marched down Broadway for a City Hall reception. Banquets were spread for Wilkes; in New York, Boston, he was dined, wined, toasted. Secretary Welles wrote him, "Your conduct was marked by intelligence, ability, decision and firmness, and has the emphatic approval of this department." Congress met and thanked him for "brave, adroit and patriotic conduct." General McClellan let it be known that he endorsed Wilkes.

Benson J. Lossing, the historian, in the War Office at Washington when the telegram came telling of Wilkes's exploit, wrote that he could never forget the scene as the Secretary of War led cheers in which Governor John Andrew of Massachusetts joined. Andrew said Benedict Arnold was a saint compared with Mason and Slidell. That the United States Government had in its clutches John Slidell was exciting to antislavery men, for Slidell had led in repealing the Missouri Compromise, was an author of the Fugitive Slave Law, had lengthily examined John Brown in jail, seeking information that might convict New England financial backers of Brown. Mason's record ran close to that of Slidell. The two of them personified the doctrines justifying slavery.

America trembled with war fever. Famous lawyers such as Caleb Cushing and Edward Everett justified Wilkes as having the law with him. Many experts on international law bobbed up. Anthony Trollope wrote that it "was pretty to hear the charming women of Boston as they became learned in the law of nations." As to what Great Britain would say, the *New York Tribune* remarked, "We do not know and we do not greatly care."

Near midnight on December 18 the Queen's messenger delivered to the British Minister in Washington the note from Her Majesty's Government. And there were waiting and wonderment as to what the United States Government would answer as to the release of Mason and Slidell. The London *Times* correspondent heard that General Scott was returning from a European trip to conduct a campaign on the Canadian border. "Press, people, soldiers, sailors, ministers, senators, Congressmen, people in the street, the voices of the bar-room—all are agreed. 'Give them up? Never! We'll die first.'" A general was heard to say that he would "snap his sword, and throw the pieces into the White House, if they were given up." At a cotillon party given by M. de Lisboa, the correspondent met Seward "in very good humor and inclined to talk."

Seward without a doubt was feeling extra good that evening. "We will wrap the whole world in flames!" he told W. H. Russell, the Prince de Joinville, and others. "No power so remote that she will not feel the fire of our battle and be burned in our conflagration." Russell asked one of the guests if Seward was showing fight. "That's all bugaboo talk," was the explanation. "When Seward talks that way, he means to back down. He is most dangerous and obstinate when he pretends to agree a good deal with you." And the young French princes, and the young and pretty Brazilian and American ladies, danced and were happy.

Harper's Weekly of November 16 printed verses in parody of the English national song, "God Save the King." One read:

> God save me, great John Bull!
> Long keep my pockets full!
> Great John Bull!
> Ever victorious,
> Haughty, vainglorious,
> Snobbish, censorious,
> Great John Bull!

In Britain the war fever kept up. "We knew not what was to come," wrote Thackeray. "Everywhere, at every fireside, all over the three Kingdoms [of England, Scotland, Wales] myriads of hearts beat with the thought, 'Will they give up the men?'" The liberal Cobden estimated three-fourths of the House of Commons as "glad to find an excuse for voting for the dismemberment of the great republic."

Young Henry Adams at the American legation in London wrote on December 13 to a brother in America: "Good God, what's got into you all? What do you mean by deserting now the great principles of our fathers, by returning to the vomit of that dog Great Britain? What do you mean by asserting now principles against which every Adams yet has protested and resisted? You're mad, all of you. It's pitiable to see such idiocy in a nation.

There's the *New York Times* which I warned only in my last letter against such an act, and its consequences; and now I find the passage erased, and editorial assurances that war was *impossible* on such grounds."

During the weeks of this fury Lincoln gave no inkling of what he would do. In his December message to Congress he made no reference to the matter. When the news arrived in November, he had walked into Attorney General Bates's office, where Titian Coffey heard him say: "I'm not getting much sleep out of that exploit of Wilkes's, and I suppose we must look up the law of the case. I am not much of a prize lawyer, but it seems to me pretty clear that if Wilkes saw fit to make that capture on the high seas he had no right to turn his quarter-deck into a prize court." To a White House caller he said he feared the captured diplomats would turn out to be "white elephants." Galt, the Canadian financial Minister, in a White House visit asked the meaning of fortifications and depots of arms on the Great Lakes, Lincoln replying, "We must say something to satisfy the people." And what about the Mason and Slidell case? Galt inquired.

"Oh, that'll be got along with," was the brief and equivocal response. Minister Lyons treasured the anecdote, and it was rehearsed in many legations that to a portentous diplomatic inquiry the American President had answered, "Oh, that'll be got along with."

So often the White House callers were asking, "Is it to be peace or war?" The President could ease the public mind by speaking just a few words, he was reminded. One politician kept pressing and received a Lincoln parable: "Your question reminds me of an incident which occurred out west. Two roughs were playing cards for high stakes, when one of them, suspecting his adversary of foul play, straightway drew his bowie-knife from his belt and pinned the hand of the other player upon the table, exclaiming: 'If you haven't got the ace of spades under your palm, I'll apologize.' "

Sumner wrote to Bright that he had spoken to Lincoln of how this was the time to drive out distrust and win the confidence of the British Government. "The President said at once with perfect simplicity, 'I never see Lord Lyons. If it were proper I should like to talk with him, that he might hear from my lips how much I desire peace. If we could talk together he would believe me.' " Sumner had shown Lincoln letters from Bright and Cobden, and wrote to Bright: "The President is much moved and astonished by the English intelligence. He is essentially honest and pacific in disposition, with a natural slowness. Yesterday he said to me, 'There will be no war unless England is bent on having one.' "

Charles Darwin wrote from England to his American fellow scientist Asa Gray: "When you receive this we may be at war, and we two be bound, as good patriots, to hate each other. How curious it is to see two countries, just like two angry and silly men, taking so opposite a view of the same transaction!"

Language and ink in quantity were spilled on precedents and similar cases, the rights of neutrals and belligerents, paradoxes of natural claims.

"One war at a time," was Lincoln's word to Seward. Blair was the only Cabinet member with Lincoln from the first.

"The English didn't give us time to turn around," was a later comment of Lincoln's. "It was very humiliating, but we had one big war on hand and we didn't want two at the same time. England in the end will be the only one hurt."

Schleiden wrote to his Government at Bremen of Seward, Welles, and Blair in disagreements and animosities, and the only hope of peace lay in the judgment of Lincoln. "The President has stated that no instructions were sent to Wilkes [to seize Mason and Slidell on the high seas] and he is incapable of an intentional untruth."

Notes from the French, Austrian, and Prussian governments were read to the Cabinet, advising the release of Mason and Slidell. Yet the tone of the press and of public opinion over the North was decidedly for war rather than a "backdown" to Britain. The *New York Herald* leaped at the chance to please its readers by twisting the British lion's tail.

At one Cabinet meeting Lincoln had all his counselors but one against him. He was reminded of a revival meeting in Illinois when a fellow with a few drinks too many in him had walked up the aisle to a front pew. All eyes were on him, but he didn't care, joined in the singing, droned Amen at the close of prayers, and as the meeting proceeded dozed off in sleep. Before the meeting ended the pastor asked the usual question: "Who are on the Lord's side?" and the congregation arose en masse. When the pastor asked, "Who are on the side of the Devil?" the dozing sleeper came to, heard part of the question, saw the parson standing, arose to his feet to say: "I don't exactly understand the question but I'll stand by you, parson, to the last. But it seems to me," he added reflectively, "that we're in a hopeless minority."

After one of the Cabinet meetings that December, Lincoln asked Seward to write a reply to England giving reasons why Mason and Slidell should be given up. "I have a mind to try my hand at stating why they ought *not* to be given up; we will compare points." Thus the younger Seward heard it. And when later Lincoln and the Cabinet approved Seward's note, the two had quiet words, Seward asking, "You thought you might frame an argument for the other side?" Lincoln smiled with a shake of the head. "I found I could not make an argument that would satisfy my own mind. And that proved to me your ground was the right one."

When the Cabinet met at 10 A.M. on Christmas Day, the war fever still ran high. Sumner, as chairman of the Senate Committee on Foreign Relations, read to the Cabinet letters he had received from John Bright, the great English liberal. He had shown these letters to Lincoln, who wanted the Cabinet to have the English view revealed in them. The tremendous excitement in England had been "fed, as usual, by newspapers, who seem to imagine a cause of war discovered to be something like a treasure-trove," wrote Bright. After the first explosion there was a calming down, but movements of the army and navy pointed to trouble. Certain parties were hunting "any decent excuse" for a quarrel. "You know the instinct of aristocracy and of powerful military services, and an ignorant people is easily led astray on questions foreign to their usual modes of thought." Yet for all the war spirit among the masses, "the great majority of the people will be delighted if some way can be found out of the present difficulty."

Never did spoken words of the orator John Bright find a more important audience than the nine or ten men gathered in the White House Cabinet room at Washington that Christmas morning. Shrewd phrases out of hard life were in Bright's letters. "Nations *drift* into wars—as we drifted into the late war with Russia—often through the want of a resolute hand at some moment early in the quarrel. So, now, a courageous stroke, not of arms, but of moral action, may save you and us. . . . It is common here to say that your government cannot resist the mob violence by which it is surrounded. I do not believe this, and I know that our government is often driven along by the force of the genteel and aristocratic mob which it mainly represents." An odd echo rang in some of the Bright sentences read to the Cabinet. "I know nothing but what is in the papers, but I conclude this government is ready for war if an excuse can be found. I need not tell you that at a certain point the moderate opinion of a country is borne down by the passion which arises and which takes the name of patriotism, and that the good men here who abhor war may have no influence if a blow is once struck."

Of all the persons involved in the negotiations no one had more trying days and embarrassing moments than Charles Francis Adams. He put up a brave front and told the British Government he was sure that his Government was not responsible for Captain Wilkes's act. He was asked to produce evidence on oath. But he couldn't swear to anything, because he didn't know anything worth swearing to; he had to play a waiting game. "He could safely infer nothing, assume nothing, imagine nothing," wrote his son Charles Francis, Jr. "He must possess his soul in patience, be enigmatical—and wait!" He was thankful it took from sixteen to twenty days to send a message from London to Washington and receive a reply. He told the British Ministers his information was confidential but reliable.

"He said we ought nevertheless to act on his assertions and suspicions," sneered Palmerston. "What would happen if we were to act in that way?" Thus from week to week Adams was helpless till one day mail arrived with Seward's note replying to the British challenge. It called for arbitration and said that the captured Southern Commissioners "will be cheerfully liberated." Discussion of this note had run two days in Lincoln's Cabinet, and Bates wrote in his diary, "There was great reluctance on the part of some of the members of the cabinet—and even the President himself"—to give up the Southern Commissioners. However, it was so ordered. The British reply later took exception to minor points and acknowledged satisfaction as to "the reparation which Her Majesty and the British nation had a right to expect."

In a cartoon titled "Up a Tree," *Punch* of London gave the informational line "President Lincoln ordered the release of Messrs. Mason and Slidell after short deliberation," and between "Colonel Bull and the Yankee Coon" had a dialogue. Coon: "Air you in arnest, Colonel?" Colonel Bull: "I am." Coon: "Don't fire—I'll come down."

Minister Adams received tributes for his patience and skill in many difficult negotiations. John Hay wrote an elegant sonnet of admiration for Seward. Lord Lyons for his services was created a Knight Grand Cross of the Bath by the Queen of England. Mason and Slidell were let out of their comfortable jail at Boston, placed on board a British war vessel, and as they journeyed across the Atlantic the London *Times* set forth: "The four American gentlemen who have got us in our late trouble and cost us probably a million apiece, will soon be in one of our ports. How, then, are we to receive these illustrious visitors?" Slidell arrived exactly twenty days later than he had estimated when he told his wife, "Good-by, my dear, we shall meet in Paris in sixty days."

Lincoln had mixed feelings over the way the Trent Affair ended. To Horace Porter and others, on their request, he later gave what he regarded as the essentials. "Yes," he said, "Seward studied up all the works ever written on international law, and came to Cabinet meetings loaded to the muzzle on the subject. We gave due consideration to the case, but at that critical period of the war it was soon decided to deliver up the prisoners. It was a pretty bitter pill to swallow, but I contented myself with believing that England's triumph in the matter would be short-lived, and that after ending our war successfully we would be so powerful that we could call her to account for all the embarrassments she had inflicted on us." Then came a fable:

"I felt a good deal like the sick man in Illinois who was told he probably hadn't many days longer to live, and that he ought to make peace with any enemies he might have. He said the man he hated worst of all was a fellow named Brown in the next village and he guessed he had better begin on him. So Brown was sent for, and when he came the sick man began to say, in a voice 'as meek as Moses,' that he wanted to die at peace with all his fellow creatures, and he hoped he and Brown could now shake hands and bury all their enmity. The scene was becoming altogether too pathetic for Brown, who had to get out his handkerchief and wipe the gathering tears from his eyes. It wasn't long before he melted and gave his hand to his neighbor, and they had a regular love-feast. After a parting that would have softened the heart of a grindstone, Brown had about reached the room door, when the sick man rose up on his elbow and said, 'But, see here, Brown, if I *should* happen to get well, mind *that old grudge stands!*' "

"I here publicly record my inextinguishable hatred of the British Government," said the pastor of the Congregational church of Princeton, Illinois, Congressman Owen Lovejoy on the House floor. "I mean to cherish it while I live, and bequeath it as a legacy to my children when I die." If the next war with England came while he was alive he would carry a musket in it. He would teach his three sons never to "kiss the rod of chastisement" swung by England. He had wept tears, he said, over the surrender of Mason and Slidell, and only an exalted Christian could "cheerfully smile at this chalice drugged with the bitterest ingredients that were ever pressed to human lips." In the traditional hostility of his countrymen against England he had never shared, said Lovejoy, but for Palmerston, Russell, the London *Times*, and associated imperial interests he would prepare a revenge to wreck their "proud empire" and "darken every jewel that glitters in her diadem."

This was the embitterment Lincoln had in mind in telling of the sick man who if he got well would let the old grudge stand. In Cabinet discussions, in official action, in the long meek silence of weeks in which he refused to yield an inch to the public clamor and the press outcry for war, Lincoln held with a tenacious humility to his policy declared in five words—"One war at a time."

CHAPTER 14

THE USES OF PATRONAGE

WILLIAM H. HERNDON arrived at the White House on his first visit to Washington, his mission, as he wrote, "intended to promote the prospects of a brother-in-law, Charles W. Chatterton, who desired to lay claim to an office in the Bureau of Indian Affairs. Mr. Lincoln accompanied me to the office of the Commissioner of Indian Affairs, told a good story, and made the request which secured the coveted office, an Indian agency, in an amazingly short time. This was one of the few favors I asked of Mr. Lincoln, and he granted it 'speedily, without delay; freely, without purchase; and fully, without denial.'"

Of a visit of several days in Washington Herndon wrote that Lincoln, "notwithstanding the pressure of business, made me spend a good portion of the time at the White House." One subject recurred in Lincoln's talk: "He could scarcely cease from referring to the persistence of office seekers. They slipped in, he said, through the half-opened doors of the Executive Mansion; they dogged his steps if he walked; they edged their way through crowds and thrust papers in his hands when he rode; and taking it all in all, they well-nigh worried him to death. He said that, if the Government passed through the Rebellion without dismemberment, there was the strongest danger of its falling a prey to the rapacity of the office-seeking class."

Herndon noted ominous words as from Lincoln: "This human struggle and scramble for office, for a way to live without work, will finally test the strength of our institutions."

The visit of the law partners ending, Lincoln on the rear portico of the White House shook hands with "William," spoke a warm good-by and put his wayward friend into a carriage for the ride to the railroad depot.

Other Illinois friends called. Henry C. Whitney wrote: "I had no hesitation at all in asking Lincoln the square question: what place he thought I ought to take under the government; he told me his advice would be to take contracts for surveying the public lands. I said I knew nothing about it; he said he did, as he had thought at one time, under Taylor's administration, of procuring such contracts, in order to make some money, which he needed then, and supposed I needed now; he asked me if I had ever surveyed at all. I told him I had some, chiefly in an amateurish way. 'That won't make any difference,' he said. 'You need not do the actual work: of course, you will have to organize surveying parties.' He then went on in detail to inform me what I would have to do; and how much I could make during his term;

William H. Herndon writes a memorandum for two friends explaining that he was a bank commissioner of the State of Illinois "at the solicitation and request of Mr. Lincoln," and that under Lincoln's Federal Administration it was distinctly understood that he "wanted to hold no office." Original in the Barrett collection.

he said I could make $50,000 during his term. I asked how I could secure these contracts. 'Leave that entirely to me,' he said. 'I'll see that you get the contracts,' he said with emphasis. 'If I was a young man like you: that would be exactly what I would go at, if I had the opportunity that you now have.' I declined it, as it would keep me out on the frontier away from my family: and asked him to appoint me as Register of the Fort Scott [Kansas] Land Office: that he said he would do, and it would give him great pleasure to do it."

Meanwhile came two Senators from Kansas presenting their lists for the offices due that State, Lincoln saying: "These are all right, except the Fort Scott land office. That I have promised to a young friend in Illinois and until he releases it, it is not at my disposal otherwise." By this time Whitney didn't want the Kansas land office, taking instead a job as army paymaster.

Old and tried friends had to be gently reminded they were going too far. "Give up your restlessness for new positions," Lincoln wrote Senator Browning; his friends must join to hold back the rush of place-hunters. A single diary entry of Browning in Quincy, Illinois, read: "Very fine day, but some what windy & dusty In the office writing letters on behalf of other persons—Have written to President Lincoln for Robt L Browning—to Kasson 1st Asst: PM Genl. for D I Caldwell & old man Burchard, and to Mr. Bates for Lee & others."

A commission as paymaster of all Federal troops in the Pacific Northwest, with the rank of major, went to Simeon Francis, who had mixed in a street fight with Douglas, who had been editor of the *Sangamo Journal,* whose wife had brought Mary Todd and Abraham Lincoln together after a quarrel. Now they were at Fort Vancouver in Washington Territory, a six weeks' journey from their old home.

From Leavenworth, Kansas, came a letter beginning "Dear Lincoln," Mark Delahay writing, the Jayhawker whose electioneering expenses at the Chicago convention were paid by Lincoln. Delahay and his faction had overthrown one governor and elected a new one in Kansas. Meanwhile the old governor was holding over a month and Delahay's long letter was filled with intimations that Governor Charles Robinson, the holdover, would misuse opportunities at hand in connection with two regiments being raised in Kansas. "The appointments and outfits for these regiments involve an immense amount of patronage, which will all be used to perpetuate Robinson in office against the overwhelming vote of the people." Delahay ended the letter: "Pardon me for troubling you, yet these reflections are of great moment to us here."

One day came a letter from the once well-to-do Ninian W. Edwards, whose father was the third Governor of Illinois. Lincoln and Edwards had married Todd sisters. He replied to Edwards: "My dear Sir: It pains me to hear you speak of being ruined in your pecuniary affairs. I still hope you are injured only, and not ruined. When you wrote me some time ago in reference to looking up something in the Departments here, I thought I would inquire into the thing and write you, but the extraordinary pressure upon me diverted me from it, and soon it passed out of my mind." He had lacked time for inquiries as to his brother-in-law's proposals. "And yet I am unwilling, of course, that you should be deprived of a chance to make something, if it can be done without injustice to the Government, or to any individual." Two months later he commissioned Edwards a captain commissary of subsistence. And Mrs. James C. Conkling at Springfield wrote her boy Clinty, at Yale, "The appointment is thought very strangely of."

The sculptor Leonard W. Volk had waited for news from Lincoln. At Springfield in the winter he had asked Lincoln for appointment as consul at Leghorn and believed Lincoln had said he would take care of him. But another man had been appointed, and Volk in Chicago was saying, "He probably forgot the promise."

From Springfield had come one T. Yateman asking an office of Lincoln, his case recited by Mrs. James C. Conkling to her son at Yale: "Your friend Mrs. T. Yateman is at St. Louis. Her husband has gone South to secure an appointment in the *Southern* army. His wife is very much opposed to it, and feels very badly about it. . . . If disappointed South his friends say, he will be willing to return and apply for something in the *Northern* army."

In the Senate objection was raised that one appointee named by the President was a drunkard. A leading Senator appeared and made an argument closing: "No, gentlemen, he is not a drunkard. He may, occasionally, as I do, take a glass of wine, but I assure you on the honor of a gentleman, he never gets drunk." Thereupon the appointment was approved. "It was soon evident," wrote Ben Perley Poore, "that the person was an incorrigible sot, and when it became absolutely necessary to remove him, it leaked out that he had retained and paid the Senator for vouching for his temperance habits."

Offices were for sale, could be negotiated, it was believed in many quarters. An Ohio merchant wrote in a letter to Congressman Riddle his offer of $2,000 for a postmastership. And the Congressman politely refused the money. In the *New York Herald* of October 9, 1861, was a want ad reading:

> $100—NAVY.—The Advertiser, being desirous of obtaining the position of master's mate in the Navy, will give $100 to any person of influence who will secure him the appointment. All communications confidential. Address Navy, box 101 Herald Office.

Among many wanting office was a belief that either money or influence could bring it, while Lincoln guessed he had "ten pegs where there was one hole to put them in." Often his salutation to a White House caller was, "Well, sir, I am glad to know that you have not come after an office."

A delegation of active Republicans arrived one day and Lincoln kept up a running fire of questions about politics in their State. They sought a port-collectorship for their man. Lincoln held the talk to politics until at last the chairman of the delegation edged in with a speech: "Mr. President, we have come here today to present to your favorable consideration our distinguished townsman. He is preëminently qualified for the position—not only for his administrative ability, but his invincible loyalty and attachment to Republican principles. No honors, sir, could be showered on him that could elevate him higher in the estimation of his fellow-men."

Lincoln dismissed the delegation with a response: "Gentlemen, it gives me much gratification to hear the praise bestowed. Such a man needs no office; it can confer on him no additional advantage, or add prestige to his well-earned fame. You are right, Mr. Chairman, 'No honors could be showered on him that would elevate him higher in the estimation of his fellowmen.' To appoint so good and excellent a gentleman to a paltry place like this would be an act of injustice to him. I shall reserve the office for some poor politician who needs it." Thus Mrs. John A. Logan heard this incident.

The factional enmity of Weed and Greeley in the Republican party of New York faded in a curious joint recommendation. Lincoln wrote Secretary Chase about an architect's position in the Treasury Department held by a man named Young and wanted by a man named Adams: "Ought Mr.

Young to be removed, and if yea, ought Mr. Adams to be appointed? Mr. Adams is magnificently recommended; but the great point in his favor is that Thurlow Weed and Horace Greeley join in recommending him. I suppose the like has never happened before, and never will again; so that it is now or never. What say you?"

In some quarters was a constant murmuring, such as that of Senator Sumner writing to an applicant for a foreign post: "Nobody who wishes to succeed should hail from Massachusetts or New York. Their claims are said to be exhausted."

Out of one rough-and-tumble affair Lincoln wrote to Chase a letter that sounded like Lincoln talking in a hurry and hoping to get aggravating minor details out of the way for major strategy. The letter might stand as typifying the conversational statement, inquiry, instruction, explanation, that Lincoln often delivered across his desk regarding an appointment. It read:

(Private)

Executive Mansion, July 18, 1861

Hon. Secretary of the Treasury.
My dear Sir:

I can scarcely avoid an "unpleasantness," not to say a difficulty, or rupture, respectively with Mr. Senator King and Mr. Speaker Grow, unless I can find a place for each a man. Mr. Grow, knowing I have Mr. King on hand, as well as himself, was here this morning, insisting that the second and fifth auditorships are still open, and that I might give them to Mr. King's man and to his. Is the fact so? Are those places open? If they are, you would both oblige and relieve me by letting them go as indicated. Grow's man is Joseph E. Streeter, really of Illinois (no acquaintance of mine), but, as Grow says, to be charged to Pennsylvania. King's man is —— Smith, of Minnesota. I neither know him nor remember his Christian name as given by Mr. King.

Yours as ever,
A. Lincoln

Advice and philosophy crept into notes to department heads. "This man wants to work—so uncommon a want that I think it ought to be gratified," began a note of introduction. A similar one read: "The lady bearer of this says she has two sons who want to work. Set them at it if possible. Wanting to work is so rare a want that it should be encouraged."

The President sometimes ordered department heads and office chiefs to make places for men whose appointments he considered necessary. "Because of his relationship to the late Senator Douglas, I wish James Madison Cutts, Jr. to be a Captain in some part of this new corps. At the very urgent solicitation of Hon. Mr. Van Wyck, I wish Horatio B. Reed to be a Second Lieutenant in this new corps. I also wish Francis E. Brownell, who stood by Col. Ellsworth at his death, to be Second Lieutenant in this corps." He pressed a young man from Illinois for a lieutenancy: "The father of the young man is a very highly valued friend of mine, of long standing." A place for another young man from Illinois "would greatly oblige me" for the reason that "his father is one of my best friends whom I have not, so far, been able to recognize in any substantial way."

Not often was the tone peremptory, as in one note: "You must make a job for the bearer of this—make a job of it with the collector and have it done. You *can* do it for me and you *must*." A rebuke might go, as in a note to "Hon. Sec. of Interior" reading: "How is this? I supposed I was appointing for register of wills a *citizen of this District.* Now the commission comes to me 'Moses Kelly, of *New Hampshire!*' I do not like this."

Of a steamboat inspectorship at Baltimore Lincoln wrote to Chase that he was "somewhat interested" in the applicant. "As the place is in your department, if you will look into the question of his qualification for the place, and shall be satisfied with him, I will appoint him,—no matter how soon." Also he informed Chase that he had refused the Washington post office "to my old friend, Nathan Sargent, which wounds him, and consequently me, very deeply." Sargent had found a Treasury Department office which the incumbent wished to vacate. "I will be much obliged if you agree for me to appoint Mr. Sargent to this place."

As to Thomas Doyle, backed by Governor Sprague of Rhode Island for the Providence post office, Lincoln had to write the Governor that both Senators and Representatives from Rhode Island favored Walter C. Simmons. "I therefore beg you to be assured that if I follow the rule in this case . . . it will be with pain, and not with pleasure, that you are not obliged."

For Albert Brooks the President wrote a note to Secretary Smith requesting appointment of Brooks to a certain position in the Interior Department. To Lincoln the abilities of Brooks were known out of their acquaintance in Illinois. To Smith, Brooks was "a small inferior looking man with a decided cast in one eye." After weeks of waiting Brooks made his second call on the President, who was more than surprised to hear that Smith had not appointed Brooks. The Secretary of the Interior soon called on the President, and with other persons present, Lincoln asked why Brooks had not been appointed. Smith declared Brooks incapable, the office requiring a good lawyer.

LINCOLN. How long have you known Brooks?

SMITH. I never have known him but the looks of the man is sufficient evidence of his incapacity.

LINCOLN (*rising from his chair*). I have known Albert Brooks twenty years and I know him to be capable of filling any position in the Interior Department from Secretary down. Appoint him to the position he seeks or I may find occasion to appoint him Secretary of the Interior.

A young newspaperman who had written a campaign biography, William Dean Howells, came seeking a consulate where he would see the world and have time to write books. Howells wrote to his father: "I went to see Mr. Nicolay, the President's private secretary. He said he would see if the Consulate at Venice were vacant. I should call again the next day. I called, the place was vacant, he thought I could have it." Which soon happened. Later came Hinton Rowan Helper, who wrote that terrorizing book *The Impending Crisis;* he was sent as consul to Buenos Aires.

Also there came to the White House one of the greatest of American literary artists, Herman Melville, whose *Moby Dick* was like its author, neglected and little known. Nicolay, Hay, Lincoln, none, knew that a vast audience was later to salute Melville as a genius of priceless creative imagination. So Melville, though poor and needing a good government job, went away from Washington as one more office-seeker who couldn't solve the connections. He stood in line at a reception, shook hands with Lincoln, and wrote to his wife: "Old Abe is much better looking than I expected and younger looking. He shook hands like a good fellow—working hard at it like a man sawing wood at so much per cord."

From William W. Richmond of Louisiana came a long letter in elegant antique script alleging that he was a wronged Southern Union man, denying transactions brought against him when in consular service, as charged by Senator Simmons of Rhode Island, denying he was "either a scamp or an interloper," and holding that the President would so brand him unless he were appointed to a consulate. "When you, Mr. Lincoln, take away from me my good name, never giving me the slightest opportunity for its vindication, I am not to be censured for feeling myself more deeply wronged than if I had been robbed, in the night, of a priceless treasure. You have the surname of 'Honest'; if you would live as the 'Just' in the present and future—I say it fearlessly—you must condemn no one without hearing their defence." The letter proceeded to say that his frustrated hopes of serving the Government of his forefathers resulted from heads of that Government's "vilifying and traducing a character heretofore kept unsullied." The letter ended: "May Providence, which seems to beset me in every way, give me other force than I now have to bear up under these ills and to your heart a proper appreciation of my position and so incline it that you may repair the great wrong done me."

Lincoln read this long letter and pierced to the core of the matter with a notation he wrote on the back of it: "Will Mr. Richmond distinctly declare that he did not write a letter to Mrs. L. giving Senator Simmons' name, as one of his backers for a consulate? A. L." It seemed that the pleader had written to Mrs. Lincoln and had named as a backer one who was opposed to the President, which made his case something other than he represented in his lengthy letter and elegant script.

An Indiana Congressman, Albert S. White, asked Lincoln to appoint a certain man postmaster of Lafayette, Indiana. Lincoln promised that he would. Later another man got the job. Congressman White went to the White House and faced Lincoln, who gave White a story: "In one of our large towns in Illinois a new hotel was opened and many people were invited to a banquet. One guest ate ravenously and later went to the landlord and told him he had received no invitation, neither had he any money to pay for his food, but had entered and eaten because he was hungry and would feel that the debt was satisfied if the landlord would kick him out. Now, White, I promised you that La Fayette appointment, I admit it. Just before I left Springfield an old friend came to see me and I asked him if I could do anything for him, but he said there was no office he wanted. Well, the other day this good old friend of mine came on, and of course was my guest, and before he left he asked me for the La Fayette post-office for a friend, and I had to give it to him. Now if you will kick me out of the door and go quits I shall feel greatly obliged to you."

Thus White told it. He may have invented the close of the incident, alleging that the President parted his coattails and waited for the kick. Whatever the action, Lincoln won his point with White. On one important policy he later had thorough and continued co-operation from White, and eventually appointed White a Federal judge for the District of Indiana.

One disgruntled place-hunter snorted, "Why, I am one of those who made you President!" And Lincoln started to dig into a pile of papers on his desk. "Yes, and it's a pretty mess you got me into!"

The Minister to Japan, Townsend Harris, had returned to be replaced by Robert H. Pruyn. With Harris was his Japanese interpreter, Joseph Heco, who was returning to Japan and called on Seward to thank the State Department for having permitted him an enjoyable term of service as translator. "Wait a while and I will introduce you to our Chief Executive," said Seward to Heco. "You must not leave without meeting our great man. You can tell the folks back home about it." Heco wrote an account of his interview, which was translated by a Japanese:

As we entered the chamber, we found the President occupying an easy chair, with legs crossed at the ankles and placed on a foot-stool, listening attentively to the plea of a military man who referred to some documents. Seeing us come, the President did not turn his attention to us. Mr. Seward first offered me a chair and then took some newspapers and began reading them on a couch. After I look around ornaments of the room and listening to the talk of the President and army officer I cannot hear what exactly saying, but could hear this much, that the officer discharged by superior officer suddenly was complaining to the President and wanted to come back to the same office and begging but the President tired listening to repeated petitions. And the President turning head to officer, "I listened, I heard your plea. However, major, I never met with the so often repeating the same thing."

When he, the officer, hear the President talk so, he hurriedly stood up in chair, then he gathered the papers by the trembling fingers and put them in his pocket. Then officer said, "Mr. President, I must beg your pardon for the trouble I give to you but I simply begged your sympathy toward me." And the President nodded his head. Then major opened door and left like an arrow. The President stood gazing at door a moment.

Then the President proceeded toward us, he took Mr. Seward's hand, shook, then Mr. Seward pointed at me and said to the President, "I am very honored introducing to your excellency, my young friend Japanese gentleman, Heco." The President said to us, "I am very glad see a gentleman come from far away," then opened a very big hand and gave me the etiquette of shaking hands.

Then he asked Japan's condition. And while in the course of talking with the President, he asking and I answering, Mr. Chase come in, also Secretary of the Navy come to the Cabinet meeting. Then I thanked the President about my appointment. Then I paid my adieu. Then I paid my same respects to all Cabinet members. They returned kind words to me and I retired from the White House. . . . The President's appearance was very tall and thin, large palm of hand, hair black, upper lip shaved clean, wearing a black coat. May I say he is manly but not severe or harsh looking? Sincerity and honesty mark his kind and tolerant appearance.

CHAPTER 15

DECEMBER '61 MESSAGE
COMMITTEE ON THE CONDUCT
OF THE WAR

THE war cost was mounting toward $1,500,000 a day as the winter of 1861 set in. Over $500,000,000 would be spent the coming fiscal year, the Treasury Department estimated; a $250,000,000 loan must be arranged in the next six months. Money was pouring in and out in larger aggregates, bigger numbers, than Federal bookkeeping ever before recorded. Of Federal loans of $197,000,000 up to December 1 Eastern banks had taken $146,000,000, and to the remainder "the people subscribed freely," reported Secretary Chase. So freely, in fact, had they drawn out their bank savings to support the war that the banks in December decided no longer to pay out gold or silver. Gold was beginning to hide out, and its shifting price interested speculators and gamblers.

A long-drawn battle, with money as ammunition, had been fought between the North and the South in Great Britain and on the continent of Europe. The fighting—with gold, moneybags, credit—was over war supplies. The North won. It outbid and outbought the South. One Northern agent wrote to Seward in November of '61, "I have now in my hands complete control of the rebel contracts on the continent." He itemized 206,000 yards of cloth moving to the port of Le Havre, cloth "gray, but can be dyed blue in 20 days." He listed 100,000 yards of light-blue army cloth, 100,000 blankets, 40,000 guns, 20,000 saber bayonets. He mentioned options that if taken would equal a great victory, the winter clothing for 100,000 enemy troops "taken out of their hands." This battle of the dollars went on quietly, nothing of its grim extent reaching the press. It was one of the state secrets not discussed in public state papers.

Lincoln's message to Congress in December, 1861, swept the national horizons and maintained in austere tone throughout that the Union was intact and its Government would ride the crisis and enforce its will. The loyal, disloyal, half-loyal, and doubting were by millions to read this message shaped with a balancing eye. He opened with "great gratitude to God for unusual good health and most abundant harvests," and declared it "gratifying to know that the expenditures made necessary by the rebellion are not beyond the resources of the loyal people." He dealt with the seeming assumption of the insurgents that foreign nations would act solely and selfishly for the most speedy restoration of commerce, including especially the acquisition of cotton. "If we could dare to believe that foreign nations are actuated by no higher principle than this, I am quite sure a sound argument could be made to show them that they can reach their aim more readily and easily by aiding to crush this rebellion than by giving encouragement to it."

The Trent Affair was raging in tumultuous discussions and crazy challenges in the very hour Lincoln's message went to Congress, but the only dim reference he gave it was in saying, "I venture to hope it will appear that we have practised prudence and liberality toward foreign powers, averting causes of irritation, and with firmness maintaining our own rights and honor." When the message arrived in Paris and speculators on the Bourse scrutinized it for what it would tell them as to where to put their money, they were amazed that the event that had the world by the ears was not touched by the American President. "Mr. Lincoln forgot it!" cried one speculator, and the word was passed along in far-flung press discussions: "Mr. Lincoln forgot it!" With a paralysis of oceanic commerce setting in and prices fluctuating, the head of the American people neglected to mention the matter. As a joke it was chilling. People swore while they laughed, said French newspapers. "Was there ever such a people on the face of the earth? *Ils ne se doutent de rien!* They fiddle while Rome is burning."

Though the Trent Affair was given silent treatment, the Border States were dealt with categorically. Kentucky "is now decidedly, and, I think, unchangeably," ranged on the side of the Union. Missouri had passed beyond seizure by the insurrectionists. The three States of Maryland, Kentucky, and Missouri, "neither of which would promise a single soldier at first, have now an aggregate of not less than forty thousand in the field for the Union, while of their citizens certainly not more than a third of that number, and they of doubtful whereabouts and doubtful existence, are in arms against it." The Union people of western Virginia after bloody struggles were masters of their own country. An insurgent force of 1,500 dominating the narrow peninsular region known as the Eastern Shore of Virginia had laid down their arms. "This leaves no armed insurrectionist north of the Potomac or east of the Chesapeake." The President intimated there were yet many good Union men in North Carolina and East Tennessee engaged in "popular movements." These loyal regions should be connected with Kentucky and other faithful ports of the Union by railroad. Footings had been secured on the Southern coast at Hatteras, Port Royal, and Tybee Island near Savannah, Georgia.

The President paused to salute General Winfield Scott as having brilliantly served the country in a time far back "when few of the now living had been born." The old veteran deserved recognition. "I cannot but think we are still his debtors."

The Southern debt of $200,000,000 owing to the North had brought urgent solicitation of the President to establish, by military power, courts to adjudicate the collection of lawful claims. He had thus far declined to do this and would refer the whole matter to Congress, being "fully aware of the delicacy, not to say the danger, of the subject."

Noticeable in this message of December, 1861, was Lincoln's departure from his custom in the previous July and March messages of referring to himself as "he" or "the executive." After nine months as President he was "I." Where in March and July he had written "The executive deems it of importance," he now wrote "I deem it of importance." In unbroken array sentences began "I venture to hope," "I recommend," "I venture to say," "I repeat," "I respectfully refer," "I refer with pleasure," "I presume," "I would invite special attention," "I may remark," "I am informed," "I ask attention," "I could scarcely be justified," "It seems to me," "It is not my purpose." For reasons best known to himself he had decided that the President of the United States, the magistrate, and Abraham Lincoln, the person, were so identical that the stiffness of discourse in the third person could be dispensed with.

Over and again this message of the President traveled along as though sometime soon or late the Union would again be what it had been, as though the war on hand were a brief interlude in a long national life. He mentioned to the Congress three vacancies on the Supreme Court bench, two of the outgoing judges residing "within the States now overrun by revolt." He had forborne making nominations to fill the vacancies, "unwilling to throw all the appointments northward, thus disabling myself from doing justice to the South on the return of peace."

Three Territories created by the last Congress, Colorado, Dakota, Nevada, had been organized, with civil administrations inaugurated. Their abundant resources would invite a large immigration when peace was restored. In pointing to this, and in other gestures, the President gave the impression of a young pioneer country striding into a vast and irreckonable future. In the seventy years since the taking of the first census "we find our population at the end of the period eight times as great as it was in the beginning" and "The increase of those other things which men deem desirable has been even greater." He could see, with the Union maintained, promises for the future. "There are already those among us who, if the Union be preserved, will live to see it contain 250,000,000. The struggle of to-day is not altogether for to-day—it is for a vast future also."

From some of "the most grave and maturely considered public documents," as well as in "the general tone of the insurgents," Lincoln would deduce a denial to the people of all right to participate in the selection of public officers except the legislative, joined with labored arguments to prove that large control of the people in government is the source of all political evil. (This Lincoln knew would go for Davis, Benjamin, Rhett, though not for Stephens, Toombs, and Governor Joseph E. Brown of Georgia.) Rhett and the South Carolinians who told Russell of the London *Times* it would be glorious to have a king, or again to be under the dominion of the British

Crown, were among sources of Lincoln's sentence "Monarchy itself is sometimes hinted at as a possible refuge from the power of the people." Mention of these matters was beyond escape for him. "In my present position I could scarcely be justified were I to omit raising a warning voice against this approach of returning despotism."

Then followed an extraordinary little treatise on what Lincoln considered the basic point of the American economic and political system as related to the common man. "It is not needed nor fitting here that a general argument should be made in favor of popular institutions," he wrote; "but there is one point, with its connections, not so hackneyed as most others, to which I ask a brief attention. It is the effort to place capital on an equal footing with, if not above, labor, in the structure of government." A rough-hewn sketch of American society placed the farmer and the free laborer as the living and controlling element in a government of the people.

Translated into journals of the International Working Men's Association in France, Germany, Italy, Russia, the argument gave added force to the statements of Karl Marx, one of the organizers of the International, in an article the previous month declaring: "The present struggle between the North and the South is . . . nothing but a struggle between two social systems, the system of slavery and the system of free labor. Because the two systems can no longer live peacefully side by side on the North American continent, the struggle has broken out. It can only be ended by the victory of the one or the other system." Lincoln's argument read:

It is assumed that labor is available only in connection with capital; that nobody labors unless somebody else, owning capital, somehow by the use of it induces him to labor. This assumed, it is next considered whether it is best that capital shall hire laborers, and thus induce them to work by their own consent, or buy them, and drive them to it without their consent. Having proceeded so far, it is naturally concluded that all laborers are either hired laborers or what we call slaves. And, further, it is assumed that whoever is once a hired laborer is fixed in that condition for life.

Now, there is no such relation between capital and labor as assumed, nor is there any such thing as a free man being fixed for life in the condition of a hired laborer. Both these assumptions are false, and all inferences from them are groundless.

Labor is prior to, and independent of, capital. Capital is only the fruit of labor, and could never have existed if labor had not first existed. Labor is the superior of capital, and deserves much the higher consideration.

Capital has its rights, which are as worthy of protection as any other rights. Nor is it denied that there is, and probably always will be, a relation between labor and capital, producing mutual benefits. The error is in assuming that the whole labor of the community exists within that relation. A few men own capital, and that few avoid labor themselves, and with their capital hire or buy another few to labor for them. A large majority belong to neither class—neither work for others nor have others working for them. In most of the Southern States, a majority of the whole people, of all colors, are neither slaves nor masters; while in the Northern, a majority are neither hirers nor hired.

Men with their families—wives, sons, and daughters—work for themselves on their farms, in their houses, and in their shops, taking the whole product to themselves, and asking no favors of capital on the one hand, nor of hired laborers or slaves on the other. It is not forgotten that a considerable number of persons mingle their own labor with capital—that is, they labor with their own hands and also buy or hire others to labor for them; but this is only a mixed and not a distinct class. No principle stated is disturbed by the existence of this mixed class.

Again, as has already been said, there is not, of necessity, any such thing as the free hired laborer being fixed to that condition for life. Many independent men everywhere in these States, a few years back in their lives, were hired laborers. The prudent, penniless beginner in the world labors for wages awhile, saves a surplus with which to buy tools or land for himself, then labors on his own account another while, and at length hires another new beginner to help him. This is the just and generous and prosperous system which opens the way to all—gives hope to all, and consequent energy and progress and improvement of condition to all.

No men living are more worthy to be trusted than those who toil up from poverty—none less inclined to take or touch aught which they have not honestly earned. Let them beware of surrendering a political power which they already possess, and which, if surrendered, will surely be used to close the door of advancement against such as they, and to fix new disabilities and burdens upon them, till all of liberty shall be lost.

When first issued, it was not known that this explanation of the American system would be kept and cherished as portentous, that from year to year there would be reprints of it in liberal journals and the labor press, that it would find its way to the family of man in all corners of the earth.

In a single sentence presenting neither information nor argument, Lincoln declared his plain friendship for the two foremost Negro national governments of the earth, one near the Gulf of Mexico having been established by the most bloody and ferocious Negro insurrection of record in the Western world, the other in Africa instigated by the American Colonization Society for the use of such freed Negroes of the United States as wished to live in an exclusively Negro country. "If any good reason exists why we should persevere longer in withholding our recognition of the independence and sovereignty of Hayti and Liberia, I am unable to discern it."

Unusual success in suppression of the "inhuman" African slave trade could be reported. Five vessels being fitted out for the slave trade had been seized and condemned. Two mates of vessels engaged in the trade had been convicted. One captain "taken with a cargo of Africans on board his vessel" had been convicted of the highest grade of offense, punishable with death.

The operation of the Confiscation Act by which Negroes belonging, as property, to disloyal slaveholders became freemen was scrupulously recited in terms of law. "The legal claims of certain persons to the labor and service of certain other persons have become forfeited." In such numbers had these liberated Negroes come into the Union Army lines and become Federal dependents, and so sure was it that more of them would arrive for disposal, that it now became necessary to have a permanent policy for their disposal.

The message drew more approval and perhaps less hostile comment in general than either the first inaugural or the July 4 message to Congress. Emerson found it very good reading and wrote in his journal: "He speaks his own thought in his own style. All thanks and honor to the Head of the

State! The message has been received throughout the country with praise, and we doubt not, with more pleasure than has been spoken."

Its most original feature concerned Negro freedom. Delicately, tentatively, and in the strictest of legal terms pertaining to the management of property, Lincoln projected his policy of gradual compensated emancipation. Had it been a case for plain words, Lincoln could have said that in effect and substance his proposal was that the Border Slave States might enact laws for selling their slaves to the United States Government, which in turn should free the slaves and then take steps to colonize them. The idea was momentous to Lincoln. His political ingenuity was at work on it more deeply and actively than he cared to tell the country just then.

A combination of Bell Democrats and Lincoln Republicans having made one George P. Fisher attorney general of Delaware, Lincoln and Fisher had agreed on a scheme for gradual compensated emancipation for Delaware, $400 to be paid per slave, so that the slaveowners of Delaware would receive $719,200. Lincoln had written out with his own hand two drafts of bills embodying the details for the Delaware Legislature to consider. Fisher tried to interest the twenty-one members of the Delaware Legislature in this scheme. They could not see it. The bill was not even introduced. Proslavery legislators of the little tidewater State presented a resolution, which failed of passage, declaring that Congress had no right to buy slaves, that abolitionists would be encouraged, that their use of so much money looked like a bribe, and that when the people of the State of Delaware desired to abolish slavery they would do so in their own way.

This controlling group in Delaware could not see that soon Necessity would dictate as to slavery. As the armies slogged deeper south, as the cannon, horses, and wagons found their way deeper into the Cotton Belt, the question would demand answer: Are these people slave or free? Either way, pitiless consequences.

A letter came to Lincoln from a historian and politician, once a member of President Polk's Cabinet, George Bancroft, who had heard radical speeches at a meeting in New York to raise funds for the relief of loyalists in North Carolina. He wrote: "Your administration has fallen upon times which will be remembered as long as human events find a record. . . . Civil war is the instrument of Divine Providence to root out social slavery. Posterity will not be satisfied with the result unless the consequences of the war shall effect an increase of free States. This is the universal expectation and hope of men of all parties."

Out of the brooding of many minds over the war was coming a more decisive viewpoint as to slavery. As the year closed, *Harper's Weekly* speculated on Lincoln's changing viewpoint: "If anybody supposes that Slavery is going to survive this war he seems to us not rightly to understand human nature. The military hand, which knows no rule but necessity, will loosen its roots; and the hand of law will afterwards tear it up and cast it into the fire. Probably there is no man in the country who sees this more clearly than the President." Lincoln's reply to Bancroft would have suited *Harper's*

Weekly: "The main thought . . . in your letter is one which does not escape my attention, and with which I must deal in all due caution, and with the best judgment I can bring to it."

Though the President had reported progress in suppression of the African slave trade, the *New York Times* estimated that 30,000 Africans landed in Cuba the current year. "The price for the clearance of a slaver is as well known to those in the trade as the price of a barrel of pork," said the *New York Leader*, a Tammany organ reporting information in its circles that in searching ships for slave-trade evidence officers would find gold in sums ranging from $2,500 to $4,000, depending on the size of the vessel, and thereupon authorize departure of the vessel.

Corruption, bribery, secret influence bought and paid for, marked each step of a slave ship's cruise from its first port clearance to the purchase of Negro tribesmen at the African Gold Coast on to permissions to sell in Cuba and later to smuggle the slaves into the Cotton States on the Gulf of Mexico. The American Anti-Slavery Society credited reports of a slave-dealer named Mitchell in a ninety-day voyage landing 1,300 Negroes on one of the Windward Islands north of Cuba, boasting in New York that he had sold his cargo at auction in the square of a Cuban city for $1,000 a head, paying $50 a head to "certain authorities," reaping a profit of $1,000,000 on a three-month cruise.

In the Cotton States restrictions were clamped tighter on free and slave Negroes. The free Negro in South Carolina must wear a copper badge with his number on it; caught without it, he was fined $20 or jailed. Also each free Negro must have a white guardian; caught without a guardian, he could be publicly auctioned as a slave. A fire in Charleston in December burning $7,000,000 worth of property was generally credited to Negroes. In Texas "any free person, who shall, in the hearing of any slave, utter words calculated and intended to render him discontented with slavery" was subject to a term of from two to seven years in the penitentiary. Advertisements similar to one in a Georgia newspaper were common:

> *For Sale.* Negroes, bacon, flour, corn, groceries,
> &c. Valuable negroes for cash, or on time. 40,000
> pounds choice bacon, including sides, shoulders,
> and extra hams.

The organized abolitionists expected little from President Lincoln. The executive committee of the American Anti-Slavery Society in its twenty-eighth annual report scored Lincoln as "under the delusion that soft words will salve the nation's sore." In his plea for law enforcement, including the Fugitive Slave Law, he was helping men-stealers to chattels which had got away. In a scrutiny of Lincoln's record on slavery, they found him "a good enough Republican for the party's purposes, but far from being the man for the country's need."

They analyzed him in a scrupulously careful paragraph: "A sort of bland, respectable middle-man, between a very modest Right and the most arrogant and exacting Wrong; a convenient hook whereon to hang appeals at once to a *moderate* anti-slavery feeling and to a timid conservatism practically pro-slavery, half-way assertions of human rights, and whole-way concessions to a wicked prejudice against dark-colored manhood, arguments against slavery extension, and apologies for continued complicity in slaveholding. He thinks slavery wrong, but opposes the immediate abolition of it; believes it ought to be kept out of the Territories, but would admit it to the Union in new States; asserts the power of Congress to abolish it in the District of Columbia, but would have leave asked of the slave-holders for the exercise of that power; considers slave-catching as a 'distasteful' business, but would enforce it by Congressional enactments, not only under but beyond the Constitution's warrant for it; dislikes the slave trade, but is not ready to forbid it between the States; affirms the equality of white men and black in natural rights, but is 'not in favor of negro citizenship'; in short, if we rightly understand him, regards impartial justice as a most excellent thing, but as somewhat too fine and costly for everyday wear."

Hoping to widen the cleavage between Lincoln and the antislavery people, a crafty opposition set going an item printed in the *Pittsburgh Gazette*, the *Boston Herald*, and many other newspapers: "A gentleman who recently visited Washington City informs me that, in a conversation with the President, the latter remarked, 'I hate Abolitionists as much as you do. I hold them in utter contempt.'"

Wendell Phillips, at the Massachusetts Anti-Slavery Society annual meeting in Boston, held that Lincoln was honest but "as a pint-pot may be full, and yet not be so full as a quart, so there is a vast difference between the honesty of a small man and the honesty of a statesman." There was pathos in Governor John Andrew with Mrs. Andrew, Julia Ward Howe, and James Freeman Clarke calling at the White House, sitting under the Stuart portrait of Washington in a drawing-room, and talking with the President "mostly on indifferent topics." They took leave and "were out of hearing," as Julia Ward Howe wrote it, when Clarke said of Lincoln, "We have seen it in his face; hopeless honesty—that is all!"

Harper's Weekly printed on December 21, 1861, its estimate: "The President is an honest, plain, shrewd magistrate. He is not a brilliant orator; he is not a great leader. He views his office as strictly an executive one, and wishes to cast responsibility, as much as possible, upon Congress." This almost tallied with Attorney General Bates's writing in his diary, "The President is an excellent man, and in the main wise, but he lacks will and purpose, and I greatly fear he has not the power to command." The patience of William H. Herndon had run out on November 21, 1861, when he wrote to Senator Trumbull that Lincoln was trying "to squelch out this huge rebellion with pop-guns filled with rose-water," and Lincoln "ought to hang somebody and get a name for will or decisiveness of character." Herndon was nothing if not explicit: "Let him hang some child or woman if he has not the courage to hang a *man*."

There came before Lincoln the case of Nathaniel Gordon of Maine, captain of a ship which had sailed to Africa and at the mouth of the Congo River had taken on board some 900 Negroes. Captured on the high seas and convicted as a slave-trader, Gordon was sentenced to death by a judge declaring, "You are soon to pass into the presence of that God of the black man as well as the white man." Lincoln read the evidence, scrutinized many respectable names on a petition for pardon. Then he wrote a death sentence giving the doomed man an extra two weeks to live. The language of the document was strange and austere. It recited:

Whereas, it appears that at a term of the Circuit Court of the United States of America for the southern district of New York held in the month of November A.D. 1861, Nathaniel Gordon was indicted and convicted for being engaged in the slave-trade, and was by the said court sentenced to be put to death by hanging by the neck on Friday the 7th of February, A.D. 1862;

And whereas a large number of respectable citizens have earnestly besought me to commute the said sentence of the said Nathaniel Gordon to a term of imprisonment for life, which application I have felt it to be my duty to refuse;

And whereas it has seemed to me probable that the unsuccessful application made for the commutation of his sentence may have prevented the said Nathaniel Gordon from making the necessary preparation for the awful change which awaits him;

Now, therefore, be it known that I, Abraham Lincoln, President of the United States of America, have granted and do hereby grant unto him, the said Nathaniel Gordon, a respite of the above-recited sentence until Friday the 21st day of February, A.D. 1862, between the hours of twelve o'clock at noon and three o'clock in the afternoon of the said day, when the said sentence shall be executed. In granting this respite it becomes my painful duty to admonish the prisoner that, relinquishing all expectation of pardon by human authority, he refer himself alone to the mercy of the common God and Father of all men.

Thus was sent to death the first and only slave-trader in the history of the United States to be tried, convicted, and hanged in accordance with the Constitution and Federal law. One of the prosecuting attorneys, Ethan Allen, told of extraordinary pressure on Lincoln to pardon Gordon. From District Attorney Smith he heard of Smith's arriving in Lincoln's office and Lincoln's taking from his desk a reprieve already prepared. "He picked up a pen, which he held in his hand while he listened to the argument of Mr. Smith on the imperative necessity of making an example of this man Gordon, in order forever to terrorize those who were engaged in this business. Mr. Lincoln listened to him very patiently and with a sort of wail of despair (as it was afterward described), flourishing the pen over the reprieve he said, 'Mr. Smith, you do not know how hard it is to have a human being die when you know that a stroke of your pen may save him.' He threw down the pen, however, and Gordon was executed in New York."

The Reverend Henry Ward Beecher, the Reverend Dr. Henry W. Bellows, and the Boston merchant and abolitionist John Murray Forbes had together called on Lincoln to urge the hanging of Gordon. Possibly Forbes was as vehement toward the President as he was in a letter to the New York Evening Post, saying of the convicted slave-ship captain: "Is he, like the rattlesnake in camp . . . to have the oath put to him, and to be released? . . . The great want of the hour is to see one spy—the higher his social position the better—hanged, and thus begin to protect the lives of our soldiers from these secret enemies. But if this wish of the nation can not be gratified, can we not at least hang one of the pirates who have sacrificed such hecatombs of Africans?"

Rather tenderly, the poet Longfellow wrote on February 21, 1862: "To-day Captain Gordon, the slaver, is to be hanged. It seems to me very illogical to hang him, and yet to protect by the Constitution all our international slave-traders."

Resolved, That John C. Breckinridge be, and he is hereby, expelled from the Senate.

When this resolution was offered in the Senate by Chandler of Michigan, Senator Lazarus W. Powell of Kentucky rose to say that Mr. Breckinridge had already resigned from the Senate, the inference being that a resigned Senator could not be expelled and it was like trying to throw somebody out who was not in. Trumbull questioned Powell and learned that the resignation consisted of Breckinridge's declarations to the press that he was joining the Confederate Army as a brigadier general. Trumbull then offered a new and revised substitute resolution, which passed the Senate by 18 votes to o, reading:

Whereas, John C. Breckinridge, a member of this body from the State of Kentucky, has joined the enemies of his country, and is now in arms against the Government he had sworn to support; therefore,
Resolved, That the said John C. Breckinridge, the traitor, be, and he is hereby expelled from the Senate.

Two Senators from Missouri, Waldo P. Johnson and Trusten Polk, and a member of the House, John W. Reid, were also formally declared expelled from Congress. Henry C. Burnett of Kentucky, who had said that by indorsing and ratifying the illegal acts of the Administration "you are writing one of the saddest, blackest pages in the history of this country," was likewise declared out. Resolutions for the expulsion of Senators Benjamin Stark of Oregon, James F. Simmons of Rhode Island, and Lazarus W. Powell of Kentucky failed of the necessary votes to expel.

The country was interested most of all in the case of Senator Jesse D. Bright of Indiana, who was summarily ejected rather than formally expelled. He had written a polite and cordial letter to Jefferson Davis introducing a friend who had improved firearms to sell. The sudden production of the letter in the Senate seemed to embarrass all concerned except Senator Bright, who was thereupon given leave of absence and time to think it over.

Besides its routine grist of legislation Congress considered new land offices and new branch mints in the West, polygamy in Utah, street-railway horsecars for Washington, impeachment of judges, compensation for horses lost in battle, contracts for horses, government manufacture of cannon and projectiles, Negroes unjustly jailed in Washington. The name of the ship *Sally McGee* was changed to *Ocean Eagle*. The Senate requested the President to furnish copies of the court-martial hearing of a regular-army colonel who was reported by a superior officer to have been drunk at the battle of Bull Run. "It will be exceedingly interesting," said Senator Grimes of Iowa, "to learn how drunk a man may be to justify another in applying that opprobrious term to him, and yet not drunk enough to warrant his removal from command."

From day to day as Congress met and in discussion, inquiry, report, touched every living and immediate question shaking the American people, the President had no special collaborator and spokesman in that body. To many of them he was a twilight and hazy figure framing his tentative and hesitant policies out of far and vague echoes which he wished to set forth as the will of the nation, when more often it was the influence of this or that faction or adviser. This sheet of haze and tone of twilight was as much the creation of Lincoln as of Congress. His personal power was too vast and his responsibility too far-spread for any final intimacy. To Senator Browning, whom the Governor of Illinois had appointed in the place of Douglas, Lincoln sometimes spoke as though he were thinking aloud, though it was plain that he had reservations with Browning which were dropped in the offhand chats with the whimsical and debonair young John Hay. To Fessenden, Collamer, Preston King of the Senate, and to Riddle, William Kellogg of Illinois, William D. Kelley of Pennsylvania of the House, he spoke in confidence occasionally. Both Blair of Missouri and Washburne of Illinois undertook for the President matters of legislation and politics in which the President was not to be mentioned.

Owen Lovejoy of Illinois and Albert Gallatin Riddle of Ohio were the only radical antislavery Congressmen—and Isaac N. Arnold of Chicago the only moderate—who never forsook faith in the President.

The battle of Bull Run was fought all over again, with words, in Senate and House in December of '61, five months after it happened. The discussion arose partly out of the personal writhing of Senators and Representatives under the laughter and lampoons flung at them for running when the army ran; partly from a suspicion that too many Democrats—including General McClellan—conservative on the slavery question were directing the war; partly from an insistence that the executive branch of the Government should be held strictly responsible to Congress for unnecessary blunders. Regarding the Bull Run and Wilson's Creek disasters, queried Senator Lane of Kansas: "Who has been guilty? The President of the United States or some subordinate officer?" Lane desired full investigation. He attached no blame. "No one has a more exalted opinion of the ability, the honesty, and the patriotism of the President of the United States than myself."

House and Senate members inquired and disputed whether the President had overruled the judgment of General Scott that the battle should not be fought, Blair repeatedly insisting that he could vouch for his accurate information that when a telegram had arrived to Scott from Patterson, who had just learned that Johnston had eluded him and would reinforce Beauregard at Bull Run, the President had suggested to Scott that the attack be delayed. Blair was the one member to step constantly into the clashes with points that would have otherwise let the blame for Bull Run fall squarely on the President.

Measures to emancipate the Negro and to exterminate the slaveholder were pressed on Lincoln with courteous and pertinent appeals, or again with taunts and threats of what would happen if he didn't go the full route. The tone of Hay's diary indicated that the President felt that this cleavage between him and the extremists might never be finally closed and their strained relations would become a habit and custom. Shortly before Congress met Hay noted: "This evening the Jacobin club, represented by Trumbull, Chandler and Wade, came up to worry the administration into a battle. The wild howl of the summer is to be renewed. The President stood up for McClellan's deliberateness."

In some circles the talk still went on about the need for a dictator. The radicals would have preferred Frémont in supreme control, and said so, in conversation and letters.

When in December Congress appointed a Committee on the Conduct of the War, Lincoln saw it as one extreme intended to check another. Its members, chiefly radical antislavery Republicans, were headstrong men of brains, courage, ability, of long training in politics and the antislavery struggle. Nothing less than genius shone and coruscated from some facets of this committee. They were to help Lincoln, and more often interfere with him, for a long time. They sniffed out waste and corruption; they cleared away stenches; they muddled, accused men wrongly, roused fear and suspicion, and left ranklings; they wrangled and bombinated; they played with the glory and despair of democracy.

The chairman of the committee, Benjamin Franklin Wade of Ohio, strode into the White House one day and stormily told Lincoln he must throw McClellan overboard. Lincoln asked who should then be put in McClellan's place. Snorted Wade, "Anybody!" Lincoln, coolly: "Wade, anybody will do for you but I must have somebody."

Short, deep-chested, defiant-looking Ben Wade was sixty-one years old, of Puritan stock, his father a Revolutionary War soldier. Day laborer on the Erie Canal, farm hand, cattle-driver, schoolteacher, prosecuting attorney of Ashtabula County, he entered the Ohio Legislature and put through a bill forbidding that body to grant divorces. He fought passage of the Fugitive Slave Law and then fought its enforcement. He entered the United States Senate in 1851 as one of the small group of antislavery men who first dared, on broad policy grounds, to challenge the Southerners then in control. When Senator Badger of North Carolina argued he should not be forbidden to take his old black mammy with him if he emigrated to Kansas, Wade replied: "We have not the least objection to the Senator's migrating to Kansas and taking his old mammy with him. We only insist that he shall not be permitted to sell her after he has taken her there." He listened to Toombs's speech approving the act of Preston Brooks in beating Sumner nearly to death, and rose to say that if the principle announced was to prevail, "let us come armed for the combat, and although you are four to one, I am here to meet you." It was believed Toombs would challenge Wade to a duel. It was known also that Wade had brought his squirrel rifle and two pistols from Ohio to Washington. It was also known that Wade was a dead shot and would reply to a challenge, "The rifle and thirty paces."

Three days later, Toombs put his hand on Wade's shoulder and said, "Wade, what is the use of two men making damned fools of themselves?" Wade answered, "None at all," and they were on speaking terms again. When Douglas in debate remarked, "The gentleman from Ohio entertains a different code of morals from myself," Wade returned: "Morals? My God, I hope so!" He was fierce, scornful, profane, blustering—and enjoyed sitting by the hour and listening to his wife at home under the evening lamp reading to him. A Negro boy asked him for money to buy freedom and he gave the boy $10, saying, "Why don't you run away?" He welcomed the war as an opening to abolish slavery and punish the South for what he called its many sins. With Senator Chandler and three Congressmen at the battle of Bull Run he had helped stop the rout, according to the *National Intelligencer*: "These gentlemen, armed with Maynard rifles and navy revolvers, sprang from their carriages some three miles this side of Centreville, and presenting their weapons, in loud voices commanded the fugitives to halt. Their bold and determined manner brought most at that point to a standstill. Many on horseback, who attempted to dash by them, had their horses seized by the bits." For years he had been called "Old Ben" Wade; in some of his moves was a tincture of his wanting to be President.

Senator Zachariah Chandler of Michigan, another member of the Committee on the Conduct of the War, had driven from the Bull Run battlefield to the White House, told of the battle, and urged the President to call for a half-million more troops to show the country that the Government was "just beginning to get mad." Millionaire dry-goods merchant and landowner, "Zach" Chandler was of the breed of restless, rawboned New England Yankees who had pushed west, settled up the country, made money, and were restless to make history and more money. He opened his store in Detroit in 1833, when stage lines between Chicago took five days. He fostered the underground at Detroit by which fugitive slaves took farewell of the United States for the free soil of Canada. In 1856 he headed with $10,000 a subscription fund to buy rifles and supplies for the abolitionists in the civil war in Kansas. A founder of the Republican party, elected United States Senator in 1857, he signalized the overthrow of Lewis Cass and Democratic control of Michigan. When the Cotton States left the Union, he told the Senate he would rather sell out his properties and go live among the Comanches than stay in a Union that was a rope of sand. His letter saying that "without a little blood-letting the Union was not worth a rush" had kicked up a wide commotion; he wrote it as a private letter, but when it became public said he would stand for every word of it. His emotions were often more tempestuous than he let the public know.

Lyman Trumbull, another member of the Committee on the Conduct of the War, had outplayed Lincoln for election to the United States Senate from Illinois in 1855. Cold, shrewd, scholarly, humanitarian though no friendly mixer, accurate in statement, no demagogue, a clean politician whose word was dependable, he often suspected Lincoln as cunning if not Machiavellian, and seldom was a colaborer for Lincoln's measures in their beginnings. Often he joined those who spread distrust of Lincoln, though "he [Lincoln] never misled me," wrote Trumbull. Though they were Illinois neighbors and Julia Jayne, whom Trumbull married, was a bridesmaid for Mary Todd at Lincoln's wedding, the two men had barriers between them; Trumbull was always dead in earnest, solemn and meticulous, never bantering, colloquial, risqué. Of a clan that had given Connecticut three Trumbulls as State governors, he had a precise mind which occasionally wrought out beautifully independent moves in politics. Often, too, plain luck had been with him as man and boy. When he was thirteen his feet slipped from under him one day and he went headfirst into a well, and where others might have broken a neck or drowned, he came to the top of the water, got into the bucket, and was hoisted up by playmates. At eighteen he quit farm work, taught school in New Jersey, took a steamer to Charleston, South Carolina, went by train to Georgia and there walked seventy-five miles from Milledgeville to Pike County. For three years he was principal of the Greenville Academy in Merriwether County, earning $200 a year and fees from pupils. Meanwhile he studied law, saved his money, bought a horse, and with $1,000 in cash belted to his waist he journeyed north, crossing Kentucky alone, arriving at Shawneetown, Illinois, with letters of introduction from Georgia friends. Joining the Democratic party, he was a member of the Illinois Legislature with Lincoln in 1840, became Illinois secretary of state, then supreme court justice, and parting with the Democrats on the slavery-extension issue, he was elected United States Senator.

In the letters passing between him and Lincoln as Republican-party leaders was no sign of the bad feeling which so easily and so often followed such a rivalry as theirs for high place. Now that Lincoln was President, Trumbull naturally could not give Lincoln his opinion that he found the President too slow, "most unmethodical in all his ways," lacking "executive ability, resolution, prompt action." Trumbull could hope for more from Lincoln if he did not see "an influence almost if not quite controlling," probably having in mind Seward's influence over Lincoln. This influence, he feared, was "looking more to some grand diplomatic move for the settlement of our troubles than to the strengthening of our arms." He wrote this in November of '61 to M. Carey Lea, along with his sincere judgment as an Illinois man for many years a close observer of Lincoln: "I have entire confidence in the integrity and patriotism of the President. He means well and in ordinary times would have made one of the best of Presidents, but he lacks confidence in himself and the will necessary in this great emergency, and he is most miserably surrounded."

An intangible factor in the relationship of Trumbull and Lincoln was the unrelenting hatred of Mrs. Lincoln for Mrs. Trumbull. As young unmarried women Julia Jayne and Mary Todd had been chums and had continued to be the most intimate of friends until that session of the Illinois Legislature in 1855 when Trumbull in a close contest with Lincoln was elected United States Senator. A fierce unreasoning anger rode Mrs. Lincoln, and since that night she had never spoken to Julia Jayne Trumbull nor by any nod of recognition admitted her existence.

The Southern Union man on the Committee on the Conduct of the War was Senator Andrew Johnson, whose hammer-and-tongs oratory had rung across Tennessee in loyalty to the Lincoln Administration, declaring in September of '61: "If Mr. Lincoln administers the laws according to the Constitution, I will sustain him, and so will you, my friends. If he does not, impeach him and hurl him from his seat. But he has done well thus far." With never a day of regular school in his life, it was said, he had learned to read while sitting cross-legged at his trade of tailor in Greenville. Marrying the sixteen-year-old Eliza McCardle in 1827 turned out to be one of the blessings of his life; she was comely, knew more of books and reading than he did, and was a helper in the efforts that made him lawyer, Congressman, Governor of Tennessee, leader of mountain people lacking slaves and loyal to the Union. He wore democracy as a garment, and to Jefferson Davis's question, "What do you mean by the laboring classes?" had replied, "Those who earn their bread by the sweat of their face and not by fatiguing their ingenuity." On coming to Washington his daughter Martha said: "We are plain people from the mountains. I trust too much will not be expected of us." For sheer physical courage and audacity of opinion he was equal to

Andrew Johnson autographs his sentiment: "Show me the man who makes war on the Government, and fires on its vessels, and I will show you a traitor. If I were President of the United States, I would have all such arrested, and when tried and convicted, by the Eternal God I would hang them."

the immortal Andrew Jackson of Tennessee, though he lacked Jackson's sagacity and sense of melodrama. He was striving in the Jackson tradition now in his writing on March 2 of '61 that any man firing on the American flag was a traitor, and "If I were President of the United States, I would have all such arrested, and when tried and convicted, by the Eternal God I would hang them."

Johnson had toiled without ceasing for a law to open public lands for free homesteads. He had urged popular election of United States Senators; he advocated that Federal judges be appointed for twelve-year terms instead of life. Supporting the Breckinridge ticket in 1860, he had fought secession tooth and nail and flaunted the Union banner in a Slave State nearly encircled by Slave States. More than once he had brought out his loaded revolver facing crowds ready to lynch him. "They will never take us out of the Union or make us a land of slaves—no, never!" he had shouted. "We intend to stand as firm as . . . our own majestic mountains."

Then there was the Republican floor-leader of the House of Representatives, chairman of the Committee on Ways and Means, a gnarled thorn-tree of a man, "the master mind of the House." He was not a member of the Committee on the Conduct of the War, but he helped create it and over and again he would be found manipulating issues, measures, and men where his hand was not in evidence.

And what was Thaddeus Stevens like? And who could read Thaddeus Stevens's heart? No one. He was as impenetrable as Abraham Lincoln, and as lonely and incessant in his broodings on the fate of man on the cold planet Earth. One crazy piece of gossip, widely published, gave him the French master intriguer Prince Talleyrand as a sire. All those who knew him even a little knew that his mother was the high priceless memory of his life. He talked of her often. "She worked day and night to educate me." And when he became a lawyer with practice and money he said, "I really think the greatest gratification of my life resulted from my ability to give my mother a farm of 250 acres, and a dairy of fourteen cows, and an occasional bright gold piece which she loved to deposit in the contribution box of the church she attended." He spoke of her as "kindly disposed to the sick and poor of every class" and of her being a "ministering angel" relieving needs of pain and poverty during a spotted-fever plague in their Vermont neighborhood. He kept his memory of her in a heart highly sensitized to the pain, poverty, and tragedy of life.

Though Stevens limped with a clubfoot, he was a horseman and a swimmer and said he could have swum the Hellespont as did the clubfooted English poet Byron. His tongue was often sharp and, men said, malicious and arrogant. He had lights of intellect; it was, besides political sense, his mind with a rare capacity for analysis, summary, and statement of involved governmental problems that had made him chairman of the Ways and Means Committee of the House.

On hundreds of *Congressional Globe* pages the short speeches of Stevens stood alone and apart as terse, direct, bare. And he knew politics from practice. In the Pennsylvania Legislature he had put through bills that won him the name of father of the free school system of the State. The Pennsylvania school law, which accorded education only to families who admitted they were too poor to pay their way at private schools, he declared was founded on poverty and should be entitled An Act for Branding and Marking the Poor. He won a legislature, at first hostile, into a new outlook and policy as to education. He had formed a movement to destroy the Freemasons, had tried to pass a bill forbidding any Mason from sitting on a jury where the defendant was a Mason—then he dropped this issue and never came back to it.

Petitioners clamoring against Stevens at one legislative session were hired, he alleged, at $15 the head. "The most respectable of them were keepers of disorderly houses in Kensington. Then came journeymen butchers, too worthless to find regular employment; next, professional boxers, who practice their pugilistic powers for hire; low gamblers, who infest the oyster cellars of the suburbs; dog-keepers who, in Spring Garden and Southwark, raise and train a ferocious breed of dogs, whom they fight weekly for wages. Their troop was flanked by a few professional thieves and discharged convicts, gathered up from the hotels and hovels and refitted with such cast-off clothes as their employers could command."

In law practice, investments, iron and furnace projects, Thaddeus Stevens had made one fortune of $200,000, lost it, made another, and had a reputation for paying his debts to the last dollar, declining to take advantage of the bankruptcy law when to do so would have netted him $90,000. As a member of the Pennsylvania Legislature he logrolled and promoted a $5,000,000 State-built railway that would loop its route around his Maria Iron Furnace in Franklin County, winding and turning on itself thirty-five miles where a wagon road took only twenty-two miles between Gettysburg and Waynesboro. "The Tapeworm," laughed a Democratic opposition, who sold the railway without completing it, saying its serpentine contortions twisted like the political career of its patron Stevens. Citizens of Gettysburg were grateful for the better transportation that Stevens brought them, but no one denied that his real-estate holdings would have risen in value and his hauling cost for ore and coal at his furnace works would have been lowered had "The Tapeworm" been finished as originally projected by him. He could be coldly and ruthlessly practical when he wanted certain results.

As a young lawyer on his way to Baltimore to buy lawbooks he stopped at a Maryland hotel, became interested in a slave there, bought the slave's freedom for $300, and returned home without lawbooks. As a member of the 1837 Constitutional Convention of Pennsylvania he was one of the few who refused to sign the new constitution; he had proposed that any "free man" in Pennsylvania could vote, but the word "white" was inserted. When prominent citizens served notice that abolitionists would not be permitted to speak in Gettysburg, Stevens addressed a mass meeting, clung to one issue, served notice that he would defy and resist any attempt to limit the constitutional right of free speech. And as he was not merely a crusader but also the foremost lawyer and real-estate taxpayer in the community, he won his point, and abolitionist lecturers came and went freely in Gettysburg. In several fugitive-slave cases he donated his services, once helping get acquittal for two white men charged with treasonably aiding fugitive slaves from Maryland who had shot and killed their pursuing owner.

His law office in Lancaster always had more students than any other. He was known as particularly considerate, even deferential, to young attorneys. To one young man who wrote asking under what terms he could study law in Stevens's office, he replied, "Two hundred dollars. Some pay; some don't."

Terror-struck by the drunken death of a long-time drinking companion, he smashed the kegs and bottles of liquor in his cellar, signed a total-abstinence pledge, and predicted, "Slavery's twin, the dram-shop, will stir the nation next." He admonished a slack nephew against laziness and rum. "There is no hope for one who even tastes strong drink."

His recreation was gambling. An old stager said he lost and won and didn't seem to care. "He played with consummate coolness, never lost his temper, and never increased the amount of his bet. His sarcastic remarks upon the discomposure of his fellow-players, who sometimes exclaimed with rage and profanity at their ill-luck, were always witty as well as cutting. While they were eating and drinking with the voracity of cormorants, he never indulged in anything more stimulating than a cracker and a sip of water. The contrast between his coolness and apathy and the fierce excitement of others sitting at the same table was amazing." One acquaintance saw him lose $2,000 in one night of "bucking the tiger," but he was at the game again the next night. Once in the earlier days when he was the largest real-estate holder in Gettysburg, a tenant farmer of his drove a load of hay to the front of a hotel where Stevens late of an afternoon was playing euchre. Twice, three times, the farmer called from the street up through a window to Stevens, asking where to put the hay. Finally to the farmer's clamor Stevens shouted down, "Bring it in and bet it on the ace." At poker once he won from a young Irishman $500 that had been saved across years for a wedding-trip and a start in married life. Sadly the young Irishman went to his bride-to-be and told her that the wedding-trip planned for the next week was all off because his money was gone. She told him, "We'll get married and take the trip anyhow; I have the money to pay for it." And on the honeymoon she explained to the bridegroom that Mr. Stevens had brought her the money lost at poker, saying that her future husband needed the lesson that he was no born gambler.

His home people liked Stevens to the extent that his re-election to Congress in 1860 was by a vote of 12,065 to his opponent's 470.

Whether playing poker at home or speaking in the House, Stevens threw off epigrams and flung a hard, cynical wit. Meeting a Lancaster lawyer who had double-crossed him, he leaned on his cane, stood still, and slowly clipped his words: "You must be a bastard, for I knew your mother's husband and he was a gentleman and an honest man!" In a dry high-keyed voice he would say to the House, "My organism is not favorable to retreat, and I must leave to my friends the honors to be won by the arts of locomotion backward." Of Federal purchase of a run-down railroad in Central America he said the offer of it arose "by the example of the ancient speculator who from the top of a high mountain offered the kingdoms of the earth which he did not own an inch of." The railroad was "more upon paper than any-where else," he believed, with half-apology: "I do not know that I know anything about railroads myself, although it has been my fortune to be the president of one for about six or seven years."

Sleeping through a dispute of sticklers for parliamentary procedure, Stevens would arise to acknowledge, "I slept an hour in blissful ignorance and am ready for business if the skirmishers will allow it." In contested-election cases he had sometimes broken from his party, and once, being told that the opposition-party man was a scoundrel, Stevens answered, "They say the other is and I must know which is worse." The nickname of "The Old Commoner," occasionally "The Great Commoner," was given him by ad-mirers. He was reputed an infidel, but a freethinker saluting him as such was answered: "My mother was a soft-shell Baptist, a reputable thinker in her time, and, as I remember, held the Ten Commandments good law and the Sermon on the Mount as orthodox. I am one of her poor disciples; good-morning, sir." His ready knowledge of the Bible once brought the question whether he had not at one time prepared himself for the ministry. His answer went only, "Well, I have read the books."

When in 1842 he had moved from Gettysburg to Lancaster, he had brought with him one who became the most-talked-of woman in Lancaster. Lydia Smith was the widow of a Gettysburg Negro barber, by whom she had two children. She was a comely quadroon with Caucasian features and a skin of light-gold tint, a Roman Catholic communicant with Irish eyes, her maiden name Hamilton. For twenty years she was the clean, efficient, careful housekeeper of the bachelor attorney Thaddeus Stevens, herself quiet, discreet, retiring, reputed for poise and personal dignity. Some news-papers referred to her as "Mrs. Stevens," insisting that that title was used by some who had speaking acquaintance with her.

Senator Grimes of Iowa saw Stevens as "a debauchee in morals and politics," while the equally pure and upright Congressman Josiah B. Grin-nell of Iowa noted that "never marrying, his bachelorship was the occasion of many a comment, often cruel." Grinnell believed with others who told of it that Stevens as a youth had fallen in love with a rich man's daughter whom he could look at only from a distance. He nursed to himself a secret that he would offer himself only when he had made a name and money. That hour came and he sought her, but she was pledged to another. It was like a timeworn melodrama with the ancient finale that she married, was hardly out of the freshness of youth when she was laid in an early grave, and Thaddeus Stevens lived on sworn to her memory—"A death that brooded over him with raven wings," wrote Grinnell.

To a woman who wrote verse effective toward getting free schools

Stevens gave a farm. Money and a gold watch and chain went to a Vermont farmer who had years back lost a cow through college mischief of Stevens and others. He wrote a tragedy in college days, and through life studied the classics of tragic literature.

"Homer informs us that the moment a man becomes a slave, he loses half the man," said Stevens in Congress in 1850, "and a few short years of apprenticeship will expunge the rest, except the faint glimmerings of an immortal soul." The life of a slave brings the slave look. "Take your stand in the swamp, spade and mattock in hand, and uncovered and half naked, toil beneath the broiling sun." He meant white men. "Go home to your hut at night, and sleep on the bare ground, and go forth in the morning unwashed to your daily labor, and a few short years, or a generation or two at the most, will give you a color that will pass muster in the most fastidious and pious slave market in Christendom." Yet all slaves did not have so hard a life, it was urged. He would answer that: "Dante, by actual observation, makes hell consist of nine circles, the punishments of each increasing in intensity over the preceding. Those doomed to the first circle are much less afflicted than those in the ninth, where are tortured Lucifer and Judas Iscariot—and, I trust, in the next edition will be added the Traitors to Liberty. But notwithstanding this difference in degree, all from the first circle to the ninth inclusive, is hell, cruel, desolate, abhorred, horrible hell."

To a Negro preacher who came asking money to build a church Stevens gave $50 in bills which he had just won at poker, and said dryly to a friend, "God moves in a mysterious way his wonders to perform." Though Jeremiah S. Black said of Stevens that his mind was "a howling wilderness, so far as his sense of obligation to God was concerned," he wore an ascetic face dented with processes of thought acting on experience and realistic history; men used seriously all the words of contempt for him except that of hypocrite.

A Gettysburg newspaper printed an item that Stevens had administered the Holy Sacrament to a dog, whereupon Stevens sued the newspaper, won the suit, and dryly welcomed the Governor of the State handing a pardon to the lying editor. He was not atheist nor skeptic in such degree that the theological seminary at Gettysburg could not with grace name him to its board of trustees. By his handling of a witness he changed the color of testimony so it appeared his client, on killing a man, did not cry, "By God, I've *shot* him!" but had moaned, "*My God!!* I've shot him," which words, rightly inflected for the jury, won acquittal. He was quoted as saying he had defended fifty men in murder trials, won acquittal for forty-nine, and the one man convicted was the only innocent one of the lot. What he had actually said was that he had often set up the plea of insanity for an accused murderer but in only one case was he sure the man was insane and in that case the man was convicted. He was a familiar of the hearts of murderers and at home in the chicanery of courts and the skulduggery of evidence.

After Daniel Webster's famous speech on the Compromise of 1850 Stevens's quiet wrath found words: "As I heard it, I could have cut his damned heart out." To a savage personal attack on himself as "over-rated," "stentorious," "impudent," and much else, he once responded: "During the greater part of his personal tirade I was at a loss to know what course had driven him beside himself. I could not imagine on what boiling cauldron he had been sitting to make him foam with all the fury of a wizard who has been concocting poison. . . . I shall fearlessly discharge my duty however low and indecent abuse may be heaped upon me by malignant wise men or gilded fools."

During Stevens's headstrong career in politics, especially during his radical anti-Masonic maneuvers, nearly all the crimes, follies, and lapses in the calendar were alleged against him, including murder, carnal association with Negro women, and bastardy. A criminal indictment against him, charging bastardy, was returned by a Gettysburg grand jury in 1838. Stevens told his friend Edward McPherson that five men had visited the girl's father with assurances that he could recover $20,000, Stevens saying he would fight the case, regretting it "more for the sake of the weak girl, the instrument of her father's cupidity." The case was continued, the suit finally withdrawn, rumor saying that Stevens had made a settlement out of court.

He received in 1848 a letter from Congressman Lincoln at Washington saying: "I am now about to start for home and I desire the undisguised opinion of some experienced person and sagacious Pennsylvania politician, as to how the vote for that state, for governor, and president, is likely to go. In casting about for such a man, I have settled upon you." This approach from Lincoln, however, had led to no particular political co-operation.

Entering Congress in 1849, Stevens quoted the text "He hath made of one blood all nations of men" and would account for the variations of color, form, and intellect among men by the effects of climate, habit, food, education. He assailed clerical defenders of slavery who were quoted. "These Reverend Parasites do more to make infidels than all the writings of Hume, Voltaire, and Paine. If it were shown that the Bible authorized, sanctioned and enjoined human slavery, no good man would be a Christian." Had not New England sold slaves? The question came. Stevens answered: "Yes, she had; she was very wicked, but has long since repented. Go ye and do likewise." He became known to his opposition as a devastating debater and an evangel of hate, using "language that Southern gentlemen would not use to a respectable negro." Stanly of North Carolina said that if Stevens and his like were "let alone, they would in a few years be universally despised and buried with the burial of an ass, drawn and cast forth beyond the gates of Jerusalem."

Squirming under verbal shafts, Stevens one day compared his opponent to "a little spotted, contemptible animal armed by nature with a volatile, penetrating virus . . . no insult shall provoke me to crush so filthy a beast." He had lost his customary poise, apologized to the Chair, trusted he would never again so digress "even to brush off these invading vermin." He flashed with unexpected sarcasm; even Southern members laughed with him. Giving the floor to another member, he closed his speech: "I now yield to Mr. B, who will make a few feeble remarks." Entering the House when a vote was being taken in a contested-election case, and hearing from a party member that it was a case of "two damned rascals," he asked, "Which is *our* damned rascal?"

One orator pacing up and down the House aisle as he spouted at length, Stevens mildly inquired, "Do you expect to collect mileage for this speech?" One habitually uncertain House member asking for leave of absence, Stevens rose, not to object, "but to suggest that the honorable gentleman need not ask this favor, for he can easily pair off with himself!"

When a factional quarrel raged in the Democratic party and a member proposed that all opposed to the Republican party should caucus and frame an organization, Stevens said it would work out like the happy family described in a Cooper novel where "the prairie wolf, the owl and the rattlesnake all live in one hole." At Franklin Pierce went the fling, "If he ever did fall into the path of rectitude, it was momentary and accidental, for which he is not to be held responsible."

"What do you think of John Brown?" a Virginia member asked Stevens after the Brown fiasco. "A fool, sir!" "Why, I thought you would call him a hero." "A fool, sir! Think of going to capture the State of Virginia with *twenty-two* men. Why didn't he take *thirty?* Then he'd have *done* it!" Accused of voicing a fanatic cause, he said fanaticism is *excessive* zeal. "There may be fanatics in false religion, in superstition. But there can be no fanaticism, however high the enthusiasm, however warm the zeal, in true religion, or in the cause of national, universal liberty."

Irony lurked in some of his smooth sentences, as when he spoke of the secessionist "threat of rending God's creation from turret to foundation" and added, "I give them credit for repeating with grave countenances that which they have so often found to be effective when operating upon timid men." He would sign a disputative letter to a political associate "Your faithful if not obedient servant." With the passing years he choked down expressions that might seem to be sentimental attempts at flowery oratory. This arose partly in some quirk of his pride; he was a cripple but asked no favors. And it rested partly on his practical mind, on his saying, "Congress is composed of men, not angels." His peak in emotional flood of language was in his free-schools speech to the Pennsylvania Legislature, admonishing those who would acquire popularity "to build not your monuments of brass or marble, but to make them of ever-living mind! . . . Who would not rather do one living deed than to have his ashes forever enshrined in burnished gold?"

When Lincoln had declared a blockade of the seceded States, Stevens in a White House call made the point that a nation did not blockade its own ports and therefore the declaration of blockade was a tacit acknowledgment of Southern independence. According to Stevens, Lincoln said mildly: "Yes, that's a fact. I see the point now, but I don't know anything about the Law of Nations and I thought it was all right."

STEVENS. As a lawyer, Mr. Lincoln, I should have supposed you would have seen the difficulty at once.

LINCOLN. Well, I'm a good enough lawyer, in a western law court, I suppose, but we don't practice the Law of Nations out there, and I supposed Seward knew all about it and I left it to him. But it is done now and can't be helped. So we must get along as best we can.

Born in 1793, Stevens had seen Jackson, Clay, Calhoun, Webster, and Douglas rise and pass out. Nearly seventy now, he was bald and wore a heavy wig of black hair. An emphatic shake of the head sometimes jiggled the wig over one ear. When an abolitionist woman asked him for a lock of hair, he took off the wig and offered it to her. He rose from his seat in the House when about to speak, "rising by degrees as a telescope is pulled out." He swept a large bony right hand in gesture at an offender of party discipline "as if he would clutch and shake him." Perley Poore noticed that he would "often use invectives which he took care should never appear printed in the official reports."

As the hurricane of the war loomed, he saw it as the end of an era, the start of a new chapter, in which the slave had nothing to lose but his shackles and maybe freedom to win. He stood for a short time almost alone in refusal to vote for the Crittenden Compromise; he led in putting through the bill at the summer session for confiscating slave property found in use for "insurrectionary purposes." Now in December he had brought up a bill to free all slaves; this was one way "to subdue the rebels." He knew the bill could not pass, but he knew, in gambler's lingo, that it was a good card to play, and that though he lost the trick now, the day would come when the card might be trumps. He spoke a forecast: If the war went on, the time would come when all slaves would be called to make war on their masters and owners.

Mr. Seward's course, wrote Stevens to Chase, "has mortified and discouraged me. . . . Can we stand against such a Prime Minister? Will Lincoln have nerve enough to resist? Will he have a Cabinet who will resist? . . . With him [Seward] in the State department, and with Cameron to make whatever department he may occupy a den of thieves, I have but little hope." He wished Lincoln would "imitate Jackson," and not seek "to purchase peace by concessions, and ignoring platforms à la mode Seward."

The Blairs, Stevens feared, had "inoculated our sainted President" with reactionary follies. Frank, Jr., he saw as "a political Ishmael . . . except [in] his own family circle." Montgomery Blair he rated a polluting meddler who should be driven from the Cabinet.

Scholar, wit, zealot of liberty, part fanatic, part gambler, at his worst a clubfooted wrangler possessed of endless javelins, at his best a majestic and isolated figure wandering in an ancient wilderness thick with thorns, seeking to bring justice between man and man—who could read the heart of limping, poker-faced old Thaddeus Stevens?

Early he had gone to warn Lincoln that Cameron had taking ways and might not be the man for War Department head. "You don't mean to say you think Cameron would steal?" Lincoln asked. "No," was the reply, "I don't think he would steal a red-hot stove."

Lincoln repeated this to Cameron as good wit and perhaps a warning to be careful. Cameron insisted that Stevens must take it back, retract. So Stevens at the White House said, "Mr. Lincoln, why did you tell Cameron what I said to you?"

"I thought it was a good joke and didn't think it would make him mad."

"Well, he is very mad and made me promise to retract. I will now do so. I believe I told you he would not steal a red-hot stove. I now take that back."

CHAPTER 16

OPINION-MAKERS

ONE dark night Lincoln with four other men climbed up the tower of the Smithsonian Institution. Toward hills encircling Washington they flashed signals. The next day an army officer marched into Lincoln's office a prisoner, Professor Joseph Henry, secretary and director of the Smithsonian Institution, the most eminent man of learning in the employ of the United States Government. "Mr. President," said the officer, "I told you a month ago Professor Henry is a rebel. Last night at midnight he flashed red lights from the top of his building, signaling to the Secesh. I saw them myself."

Lincoln turned. "Now you're caught! What have you to say, Professor Henry, why sentence of death should not immediately be pronounced upon you?" Then, turning to the army officer, Lincoln explained that on the previous evening he and others had accompanied Henry to the Smithsonian tower and experimented with new army signals.

The officer thereupon released from his custody a physicist of international repute, a creative genius in science, probably America's foremost experimenter and discoverer in electrical transmission and electrodynamic power, credited with constructing in 1831 the first electromagnetic telegraph, sending signals and ringing a bell at the other end of a wire more than a mile long. Soon the government was to begin issuing daily weather forecasts based on meteorological data gathered by Joseph Henry and his associates. His family home had been in Washington since 1846; he had toiled to make the government-supported Smithsonian Institution a true national center of learning. The University of Pennsylvania offered him the chair of natural philosophy at double his government salary; Princeton (College of New Jersey) wanted him as president; he was staying where he believed he was most useful, one friend saying, "He never engaged in an investigation or an enterprise which was to put a dollar into his own pocket, but aimed only at the general good of the world."

Yet evil talk ran on about Joseph Henry. He said he could not forget that Jefferson Davis had for years been a steadfast friend of the Smithsonian and that his family and the Davises had had pleasant parties; he could not learn to hate them now and to speak that hate. He was a scientist, with a theory difficult to explain in wartime—that true science is for all mankind and works by an international partnership.

Lincoln joined his request to others approving the use of the Smithsonian amphitheater for a lecture course that winter, and Professor Henry consented. Aware of its antislavery promoters, Henry stipulated that they must announce at each lecture that the government institution would not be committed to the opinions expressed.

Horace Greeley came to lecture and a *New York Tribune* correspondent, William A. Croffut, asked Lincoln if he would attend. "Yes, I will," Croffut quoted Lincoln. "I never heard Greeley, and I want to hear him. In print every one of his words seems to weigh about a ton; I want to see what he has to say about us." Welles, Bates, Chase, sat with Lincoln on the platform as the chairman's introductory speech proceeded: "Ladies and gentlemen: I am requested by Professor Henry to announce that the Smithsonian Institution is not in any way responsible for this course of lectures. I do so with pleasure, and desire to add that the Washington Lecture Association is in no way responsible for the Smithsonian Institution." The second sentence was drowned in merriment that swept the 2,000 people in the hall. Lincoln asked where the laugh came in and learned that this introduction had become a custom at which the audience habitually laughed. The President joined those still laughing. Backstage later he remarked, "The laugh was rather on you, Henry."

Greeley's lecture that evening proposed the destruction of slavery as the first real objective, "the one sole purpose of the war." He turned and faced toward the President as he said it. Most of the audience stood up and joined in a wild cheer. Lincoln sat with an impassive face, later saying, according to George W. Julian, "That lecture is full of good thoughts and I would like to take the manuscript home with me and read it over carefully some Sunday."

For months Lincoln had been trying to get something like co-operation from Greeley. Once he had asked, said Homer Byington, a *New York Tribune* correspondent: "What in the world is the matter with Uncle Horace? Why can't he restrain himself and wait a little?" Byington replied that one man did not write all that was printed in the *Tribune*. "Well," said Lincoln, "I do not suppose I have any right to complain; Uncle Horace agrees with me pretty often after all; I reckon he is with us at least four days out of seven."

On the matter of co-operation from Greeley came two quite unusual men to interview Lincoln. One was James R. Gilmore, well-to-do head of a cotton and shipping firm in New York. His many trips South had given the material for a book of sketches, *Among the Pines*, written under the pen name of Edmund Kirke; moderately emancipationist in viewpoint, vividly reporting scenes of Negro life, it was widely read. In company with Gilmore was Robert J. Walker, Pennsylvania-born, a young lawyer in Pittsburgh who migrated to Mississippi, where he was once elected governor, twice elected United States Senator, and after serving as Secretary of the Treasury under President Polk had fallen out of power in Mississippi, opened a law office in Washington, campaigned for Buchanan, was appointed Governor of the Territory of Kansas, where he sensationally broke with Buchanan and joined himself to Douglas.

Walker now served as special adviser to the Treasury Department and had confidentially told Gilmore (according to Gilmore) that when Greeley and others had urged him for a Cabinet place, preferably that of Secretary of State, "I told Mr. Lincoln that it would not be wise. . . . I could be of most use in a private capacity."

In the Trent Affair, on finance, on emancipation policy, on the political outlook, the President continuously sought the counsel of this living encyclopedia of Southern and Northern politics, once nicknamed "The Wizard of Mississippi." In Walker's time Mississippi had sold bonds for a $10,000,000 loan, repudiated payment, and earned a hard name among British holders of the promises to pay. Under Walker's management Jefferson Davis was handpicked and sent to Congress. Under Walker's instigation, in part, President Polk began the war with Mexico, and if Polk had accepted Walker's advice, the war would have gone on till the United States took permanent possession of lands reaching to Central America and the Isthmus of Panama.

Politically discarded in the Cotton Belt, as lawyer and lobbyist in Washington Walker still adventured, went to England and sold about $1,000,000 of railway securities in exchange for thousands of tons of railroad iron resold in New York for "good American money." Some called him a fisher in muddy waters, worth watching; they said his voice was "squeaky." Others, like Greeley and Gilmore, compared him to Benjamin Franklin for sagacity; to them his voice sounded "high and tremulous." A somewhat shriveled-looking little man, well-spoken, nervous, dyspeptic, adroit, shrewd rather than subtle, Walker had become an unofficial member of Lincoln's Cabinet. Though associated with proslavery forces all his life, he had in 1838 given freedom to all his own slaves and, never trafficking with the secession doctrine, had been as strict a Union man as Douglas. Walker had sent a note asking the President what time he and Gilmore could have an interview and, according to Gilmore, a messenger returned with a narrow slip of paper addressed to "His Highmightyness, Governor Walker, late of Kansas Territory" and the penciled message, "I shall be glad to see you both—come at 3 P.M. A.L."

After compliments between Lincoln and Walker, Gilmore brought out a proposal from Greeley that all information of the inner workings of the Administration which Lincoln gave to Walker should be transmitted through Gilmore to Greeley for the use or guidance of the New York Tribune. In exchange it would be expected that Greeley give such aid as he could to a new magazine, the Continental Monthly, to be issued by Gilmore and Walker; also Greeley would allow the use of his *New York Tribune* columns to Walker for feeling out or forestalling public opinion. According to Gilmore, Lincoln wrote a letter during the interview, addressing it to Walker, reading it aloud to the two of them, setting forth the terms of the arrangement, and closing with high confidence in Greeley: "Having him firmly behind me will be as helpful to me as an army of one hundred thousand men." Gilmore in reproducing the letter from memory failed to convey Lincoln's style, and overstressed Lincoln's appraisal of Greeley, though the letter may have closed in the words rendered by Gilmore: "Now, Governor, this is a longer letter than I have written in a month—longer than I would have written for any other man than Horace Greeley."

This letter of Lincoln's Gilmore carried to New York and handed to Greeley in the *Tribune* office. According to Gilmore, Greeley read the letter twice, "his face beaming with simple joyousness" as he remarked of the President: "He is a wonderful man—wonderful. I can never harbor a thought against him, except when I keep away from him. You must let me keep this letter. . . . I want it just to look at when I am downhearted." Which Gilmore said would be very well unless Lincoln objected.

Whatever the specific terms of the bargain, whatever it was in strict language that Lincoln wrote in this letter, and whether or not Greeley's face beamed with simple joyousness on reading it, there could be little doubt that Lincoln transmitted to Greeley through Walker and Gilmore some such points as Gilmore ascribed to the letter: "That Greeley has ever kicked the traces has been owing to his not being fully informed. Say to him that, if he ever objects to my policy, I shall be glad to have him state his views frankly and fully. I shall adopt his if I can. If I can not, I will at least tell him why. He and I should stand together, and let no minor differences come between us; for we both seek one end, which is the saving of the country."

Among the 50,000 and more subscribers of the *New York Tribune* were all the unburied and living editors and news-writers of America, besides influential personages in Europe. The man Greeley hungered and thirsted to teach humanity better ways through the printed word. More than any American since Benjamin Franklin he was compared with that printer, philosopher, writer, politician, diplomat. He had arrived in New York a greenhorn from Vermont farms who had picked up the trade of printer, a stick and bundle over his shoulder, $10 in his pocket; twenty years old. His first work was on a job no other printer in the city would take, setting the type on a 32mo New Testament with Greek references and supplementary remarks. He edited the *New Yorker*, the *Jeffersonian*, the *Log Cabin*, and in 1841 started his penny morning paper, the *New York Tribune*, which for twenty-one years was at the forefront reporting, if not advocating, every reform, radical idea, and "ism" that came to view. His *Tribune* writers had included Charles A. Dana, George William Curtis, William Henry Fry, Bayard Taylor, Margaret Fuller, George Ripley, Count Gurowski, Henry J. Raymond. "I have been branded aristocrat, communist, infidel, hypocrite, demagogue, disunionist, traitor, corruptionist, and so forth and so forth," he once declared in urging a friend not to class him also as a poet. He kept close to workingmen's movements, leaned to the ideas of the French Utopian Socialist Fourier and in the first year of the *Tribune* said, "We have written something and shall yet write more, much more, in illustration and advocacy of the great social revolution which our age is destined to commence, in rendering all useful labor at once more attractive and honorable, and banishing want and all consequent degradation from the globe." Greeley printed in 1842 a front-page column daily by a leading Fourierite, Albert Brisbane. He made the *Tribune* Whig in policy, then anti-Whig, then Republican. Yet as a Republican he had so leaned toward Douglas for President that Lincoln in anxiety had urged Herndon on an Eastern trip to interview Greeley, Herndon finding that Greeley believed he would be fighting the devil with fire if with Republican alliance they could send Douglas to the White House. "Mr. Greeley," commented one of his staff men, John Russell Young, "would be the greatest journalist in America if he did not aim to be one of the leading politicians of America." He often refused to print important speeches of Democrats as news, saying he would do so when Democratic newspapers began printing equally important addresses of Republicans. His personal ways, plain and queer, his abrupt manners and peculiar clothes, made him a half-myth that the country talked about. When topics of conversation lagged, Greeley was brought up. In a sense he embodied the vague, grandiose ambitions and hopes of Americans from coast to coast; the overseas world looking on would yet copy American democracy and be redeemed. He had elusive intentions, mind quality. As a boy playmates nicknamed him "The Ghost"; he was fair, pink-skinned, baby-faced, blue-eyed with a stare of innocence; with light, silky, almost albino hair—just a little diaphanous: people could see through him—and then again could not.

As a vegetarian Greeley sometimes broke the rule and when he did, ate three and four times the regular portion of a meat-eater; as a teetotaler he occasionally drank a glass of beer. Offered a cigar, he replied, "No, thank you, I haven't got down that low yet, I only drink and swear." At an evening party in Chautauqua, New York, he sat "lost in thought," ate a plate of doughnuts, ate till the last cube was gone on a plate of cheese, and showed that he had for that evening the digestion of a horse. To a letter requesting an autograph he signed a reply in spluttery handwriting that he never under any circumstances wrote an autograph for anybody. Next to writing for the public he enjoyed lecturing to it, and often took the platform. Henry Ward Beecher asked him what he called "success" in a lecture and he answered, "Where more folks stay in than go out." He was the first president of Typographical Union No. 6 in New York, though he later fought the union when a strike was ordered on the *Tribune* to stop the publication of an advertisement for printers by a rival paper. Though a member of the Universalist Church teaching that there is no hell, when he was once asked to subscribe to a fund that would save sinners from going to hell, he told the solicitor: "I won't give you a cent. There don't half enough go there now."

He owned a farm at Chappaqua, thirty-three miles from New York, and liked to call himself a farmer; his farmer readers knew well enough that Greeley could not run the country and a farm, both.

To a young man who wanted a newspaper job he said: "If I were to advertise in my paper tomorrow for fifty young men to go on a pirate ship and for five men to work on my farm, there would be five hundred applications for the situation on the pirate ship and not one for the farm. Would you believe that?" "Yes, sir," responded the young man. "I think I'd rather sail on a pirate ship than work on a farm." Up, down, and across America had gone such tales of Horace Greeley, a national asset of folklore. "Go West, young man," was his repeated advice, and in the westward flow of settlers a famous slogan.

Greeley shuffled rather than walked, wore his cravat in disorder, one pant leg stuffed in one boot. His smooth cherubic face rose out of an under-chin beard, the voice a high squeak. He wore a linen duster in summer, a large baggy overcoat in winter, and summer or winter across the years a wide-brimmed white hat. They knew him a block off by the white hat. His handwriting gave rise to dozens of stories, half of them true. A joker dipped a chicken's feet in ink, walked the chicken across a sheet of paper, and took the script to Greeley; he deciphered it as one of his own editorials. A young man carrying Greeley's letter of angry dismissal from the *Tribune* employ used it as a letter of recommendation. He scolded the printing-room foreman for a mistake in a Board of Trade article; the foreman said they had followed copy strictly; the man who wrote the copy should be kicked, squeaked Greeley; they showed him that he had written the copy, and

Horace Greeley "makes a few scratches"

Greeley begged pardon and said to the foreman, "Tom Rooker, come here and kick me quick."

Once, making a political denial, he declared: "I never said all Democrats were saloon-keepers. What I said was that all saloon-keepers were Democrats." His office was open to the public, and occasionally a man came in and bawled at Greeley for the *Tribune's* sins and errors as Greeley quietly scratched away at his two daily columns of writing. Once when such a caller had about used up his profanity and vituperation and was leaving, Greeley squeaked to him, "Come back, my friend, come back and relieve your mind."

Closer to the masses of people than most of his staff men were aware, Greeley rebuked a managing editor for printing, while he was away, eleven columns of arguments on sustaining opera in New York. "What would it cost to burn the Opera House?" he asked. Eleven columns about opera! "I don't believe three hundred who take the *Tribune* care one chew of tobacco for the matter!" His bald round head carried nearly all the colossal information and statistics of the row of *Tribune* annual almanacs. His scissors hung from a cord over his desk and couldn't get lost. Also over the desk dangled a bell cord which summoned a copy boy for a rush editorial.

Once when a caller stood talking near the desk Greeley never looked up, scratched away at his editorial. Then as he reached the bottom of the page and got ready to scratch away at another page, he turned to the man and said, "I'll be damned if I'm going to spend my time getting New York offices for Jerseymen"—and the caller left.

The softer and finer lights of him shone in his handling of beggars and borrowers, who knew he was easy. Hundreds had come one by one and got money from him and never paid it back. He classified them as casual, chronic, or systematic, and usually let them know that he knew they were lying about paying back the loan. A clerk from New Hampshire, penniless, with his wife in New York, asked for money to get back to his father's house. "Stranger," said Greeley, "I must help you get away. But why say anything about paying me? You know, and I know, you will never pay a cent."

To one borrower who paid him $20 which was owing he said, "You are the first one that has disappointed me." In twenty years some $50,000 at least had gone this way, so Greeley associates estimated. He preached often and long that men should stay out of debt. His soft heart for borrowers kept his funds low, and he would have gone into debt himself if he hadn't lived plainly, economically. Though he suavely told Congress how to run the government finances, he had sold his interests in the *Tribune* until in 1860 his ownership was only three-twentieths. Often when told of good speculations and chances to make money he said: "I haven't any time to make money; and I don't want any anyhow. Money is more trouble than it's worth."

For good reasons or none at all, Greeley had lent thousands of dollars to the son of Commodore Vanderbilt, steamship and railroad magnate. And as he sat at his desk writing one day a visitor tried to make him look up, saying, "I am Commodore Vanderbilt." Greeley went on writing. The Commodore cleared his throat and went on: "I understand you are lending money to my son, Cornelius. I wish you to know that if you expect me to be responsible for it you are mistaken. I will not pay one cent." Greeley kept his head down and his pen traveled along scratching away at an editorial as he squeaked, "Who the hell asked you to?" The Commodore left. Years later the loan was paid.

A half-dozen Republicans from upstate came to his office one day to tell Greeley how to run the paper. Without looking up from his writing he knew who they were and their errand. The spokesman several times said that they were influential party men, "of the highest standing," and so on.

Greeley, without pausing in his writing, blurted: "A set of confounded asses, I know that. They are wasting their time, and trying to waste mine, by coming here."

At twenty-five he married Miss Mary Y. Cheney, a Connecticut schoolteacher whom he met at a vegetarian Grahamite boardinghouse in New York. She was slight, girlish-looking, a brunette with long curls falling below her shoulders. Their first child was fair, with notable complexion and hair that fell as "a shower of ruddy gold" to his shoulders; he died at five in an Asiatic cholera plague that infected New York in 1848. Another boy died at six from croup. One girl died at six months of age. Two infants died at childbirth. Of the seven Greeley children two daughters were alive.

"I didn't raise my children for this world but for the next," said the mother, whose beauty and charm faded with tragedy and years. Her freezing manners and sharp words kept many from making a second visit to the Chappaqua farm. They spoke of "domestic fury," of Mrs. Greeley's snatching manuscripts from his hand and throwing them in the fire so that he took to hotels occasionally to finish his editorials. And they spoke of him as being patient and not answering back.

Though Whittier in a verse alluded to Greeley as "our later Franklin," Greeley lacked men and women who truly cared for him. Greeley scolded, argued, set off bombs of language, where Franklin smiled, persuaded, or kept quiet and waited. Between Bennett's *Herald* and Greeley's *Tribune* was the distinction that one emphasized news and the other opinion. The viewpoints and crusades of Greeley had given him a personality and a place as teacher and leader whom millions believed worth hearing. Theodore Parker had called him on the whole the greatest of Americans, a type and an embodiment. He favored the ballot for woman as a "natural right," to be given her when she demanded it, but first she must "emancipate herself from the thraldom to etiquette, and the need of a masculine arm in crossing the street." Greeley crowded the *Tribune* with the latest scientific information, advocated constantly a Pacific railway and a free-homestead law, praised the conquests of the McCormick harvester; he predicted steam engines for farm work; he rang the bell for Irish freedom; he preached old-fashioned honesty, frugality, simplicity. He published his eleven lectures, written in six years, under the title *Hints toward Reform*.

Thousands of "self-made men" echoed his saying, "Of all horned cattle the most helpless in a printing office is a college graduate." Junius Henri Browne, of many years' service under Greeley, noted him "a character combining numerous antagonisms," wayward, moody, undisciplined. "His friends could not be certain of him, for he could not be certain of himself. He was not only unlike other men—he was unlike himself often. General rules failed to apply to him."

Indicted in Virginia for circulation of "incendiary documents," Greeley's *Tribune* was seen by slaveholders as inflammatory; on the other hand, abolitionists denounced him as coward and temporizer on the slavery issue. Senator Charles Sumner had visited him at Chappaqua in the summer of 1861 and discussed issues—and reached for the personal influence of Greeley and the power of the *New York Tribune* in swaying the American masses.

Gilmore quoted Greeley in late '61: "We are all going to the devil . . . all owing to stupidity at Washington. . . . It pains, it grieves me to think of it. For you know it is said that but for my action in the convention, Lincoln would not have been nominated. It was a mistake—the biggest mistake of my life." Gilmore rated Lincoln as better than Seward, the only other choice, and referring to Seward's hand fixing the call for 75,000 men when a majority of the Cabinet would have called for 500,000, Greeley squeaked, "If I had known the facts at the time I would have unseated Seward." Whereupon Gilmore ventured: "Pardon me, Mr. Greeley, if I doubt your ability to do that. Mr. Lincoln has an overestimate of Seward,—a sort of blind confidence in his judgment." Gilmore referred to his warning Lincoln that Seward would run the country on the rocks, "but all I said had no more effect on him than water upon a duck's back."

Greeley recalled having seen Lincoln at the White House about two weeks after inauguration. And he had felt that Lincoln was too bland, too easygoing as he parceled out post offices and consulates. He had told Lincoln then, "Mr. President, do you know that you will have to *fight* for the place in which you sit?" And Lincoln answered "pleasantly—I will not say lightly," wrote Greeley. Lincoln could not see that a terrible war was ahead; he was not serious, busy, and active, as Greeley took his measure. His moaning letter to Lincoln just after Bull Run beginning "This is my seventh sleepless night" reflected his fear that Lincoln was not losing enough sleep over the war. Greeley asked Gilmore's impression of Lincoln.

GILMORE. I have met him but once. I think him thoroughly honest, and anxious to do his duty.

GREELEY. And could you not so win his confidence that he would disclose to you, from time to time, his views on certain lines of policy?

GILMORE. I don't think I could, for, if I read him aright, he is a very politic man,—one of the hear-all-and-say-nothing sort. It amused me to see how adroitly he drew out of me just what I was most anxious to tell. He could have no motive for confiding his views to me; but with Governor Walker it will be different. Mr. Lincoln has the highest opinion of his judgment, and will naturally seek his advice on all important subjects that may, from time to time, come up. He will be forced to be open with him, and thus I shall know all the inner workings of the administration.

GREELEY. For Walker will tell you all such things?

GILMORE. Of course. He has Mr. Lincoln's permission to do so. Now, Mr. Greeley, you have asked my impression of Lincoln, and I have told you only the half. He has the reputation of being the frankest of men, but there never was a bigger mistake. With all his apparent transparency, he is as deep as a well.

And their talk went on till it ended in some sort of a cordial proposed arrangement by Lincoln for the most practical of courtesies to be given Greeley.

On the revolutionary advances in communication an *Atlantic Monthly* writer had noted, "Today newspapers multiplied by millions whiten the whole country every morning like the hoar frost."

Westward from Omaha gangs of linemen had strung wires to the coast. "The President's message," said a dispatch in December of '61, "read in Congress at 12 o'clock on Tuesday, was received by telegraph at San Francisco, and published early on Wednesday morning."

The *Crisis* at Columbus, Ohio, refused to marvel: "One-half of what is sent over the country as telegraph news is nothing but the invention of men hired to keep up sensations. The public mind becomes bewildered and no one knows what to believe."

Multiple steam-power printing presses were pouring out fresh editions of Mrs. Stowe's *Uncle Tom's Cabin*, Helper's *The Impending Crisis*, and a martyrizing biography of John Brown by Frank B. Sanborn.

The Uprising of a Great People, translated by Mary Louise Booth from the French of Count Agénor de Gasparin, published in 1861, went to hundreds of thousands of readers in America, though aimed by its author at a European audience. Gasparin, a distinguished liberal, stressed human slavery as the cause of the war and urged the support of all civilized countries for the North.

In a closing page the Frenchman pleaded: "Ah! courage, Lincoln! the friends of freedmen and America are with you. Courage! you have to resist your friends and to face your foes; it is the fate of all who seek to do good on earth. Courage! You will have need of it tomorrow, in a year, to the end; you will have need of it in peace and in war."

A letter of cordial thanks went from Lincoln to Mary Louise Booth for her translation. She had been swept by the solemn written oratory of Count de Gasparin, saw his book as keen propaganda material, and toiled feverishly almost twenty-four hours a day for a week to give the North an English version that it bought in successions of printings, that it welcomed and quoted.

Propaganda ran riot, often in crazily amusing patterns that roused healthy laughter rather than diabolical hate. Editors enjoyed spreading for their readers a toast to which Michigan troops had raised their glasses: "Jefferson Davis—may he be set afloat in an open boat without compass or rudder, may that boat and contents be swallowed by a shark, and the shark swallowed by a whale, the whale in the devil's belly, and the devil in hell, the door locked and the key lost; and further, may he be chained in the southwest corner of hell, and a northeast wind blow ashes in his eyes to all eternity." *Vanity Fair* printed a "Mother Goose for Jefferson Davis" with lines

> Davis is a traitor;
> Davis is a thief;

rambling through much unimaginative nonsense that concluded:

One of the Zouave Butcher Boys
Will chop off Davis' head!

An Elizabethan stylist on the *Charleston Mercury* raged in a Shakespearean soliloquy on Lincoln: "A horrid looking wretch he is!—sooty and scoundrelly in aspect—a cross between the nutmeg dealer, the horse-swapper and the nightman—a lank-sided Yankee of the uncomeliest visage, and of the dirtiest complexion, and the most indecent comparisons. Faugh!"

Hate was sought, sown, cultivated, prayed for. In the Senate, Sumner said that the gallows could not do the work needed to civilize the South. "The conspirators should not be only punished to the extent of our power, but they should be stripped of all means of influence, so that, should their lives be spared, they may be doomed to wear them out in poverty, if not in exile." The property and lands of the leaders must be taken, and the large plantations "broken-up, partitioned into small estates" for slaves, homeless whites, and Northern soldiers. With the "peculiar and overbearing social influence" of the planters destroyed, brave Northern soldiers, "resting at last from their victories and changing their swords into plowshares, will fill the [Southern] land with Northern industry and Northern principles."

Miss Anna Ella Carroll, daughter of Thomas King Carroll, Governor of Maryland in 1830-31, visited the White House on request of the President. Her pamphlet on *The War Powers of the Government* had elaborately defended the President's right to suspension of the writ of habeas corpus; one edition had been published under "Seal of the Department of State" and copies placed in the hands of all members of Congress. After her discussion with the President Miss Carroll went away and wrote an argument on *The Relations of the National Government to the Revolted Citizens*, which was published, given to members of Congress, and put in general circulation. Having quoted from Sumner's doctrine of confiscation, Miss Carroll commented, "I cannot recall to memory any instance surpassing the atrocity of this proposition in all the annals of despotism."

She challenged as a threat the position of Senator Jacob M. Howard of Michigan that "the President is our general and bound to execute our behests, and liable for disobedience to be reduced at once to the condition of a private citizen and incapacitated to hold any office or emolument under the Government." Against one Senator's claim, "There is *no limit* over the power of Congress," she presented her own view: "I do not charge that there is a conspiracy in Congress to grasp the sword and overthrow republican institutions and establish upon its ruins a legislative despotism; but certain it is that unless this claim is rebuked by the country it will end in one. Grant the power during war, and Congress will continue the war for the sake of the power. . . . Despotism is inevitable wherever power is lodged in a single body."

A handsome daughter of Maryland, bright with personal style and decency in dispute, Miss Carroll had free rein from Lincoln and Seward, who seemed to consider her writings pertinent and portentous enough to be laid on the desks of Senators and Congressmen. They read her, and to some it was rather novel that anyone could be saying that a legislative body might become as despotic as an executive department.

Senator James Grimes of Iowa arose in the Senate to remark, "The President of the United States saw fit, in the plenitude of his wisdom, to import to this District from the State of Illinois Mr. Ward H. Lamon, and to appoint him the marshal!" Grimes charged that Lamon had paid little attention to the District jail, which "a humane and Christian man might make a Bethesda." Grimes charged further that though at first Christian men and women had visited the jail and distributed tracts and books among the prisoners, this practice had been stopped. In fact, he himself, a United States Senator, had tried to get into the jail and learned that "this foreign satrap, Mr. Lamon, made a peremptory order, that no person—not even members of Congress—should be admitted to the jail without first supplicating and securing a written permission to do so from him."

Then Grimes went to the White House: "When, for the first time in six months, I attempted to approach the footstool of the power enthroned at the other end of the avenue, I was told that the President was engaged." Thus there was sarcasm, and men of importance played peanut politics.

Crying that the Administration must listen to the voice of the people, though giving no clew to what the voice of the people was saying, Senator Hale of New Hampshire set forth that the President and his aides would find themselves "engulfed in a fire that will consume them like stubble; they will be helpless before a power that will hurl them from their places."

One cruel piece of ignorant officialism came before Lincoln's eyes in part —and he failed to gather the whole of it. Into his hands arrived a letter beginning, "Mr. Lincoln, Dear Sir," signed by Ellen Sherman, the wife of General Tecumseh Sherman. She recited grave discriminations against her husband and reflections on him, her statements later proving to be entirely true. Both McClellan and the Adjutant General, Lorenzo Thomas, had made a record for plain arrogance and toplofty ridicule of a fighter seeking merely a chance to prove himself. She enclosed with her letter some of the falsely based newspaper accounts of her husband's "insanity," mentioned army conspirators maneuvering through press attacks as timing their operations well. Although contradictions had been published, "Who gives credence to them?" No official contradiction had appeared. The wife appealed to Mr. Lincoln: "As the minister of God to dispense justice to us and as one who has the heart to sympathize as well as the power to act, I beseech you by some mark of confidence to relieve my husband from the suspicions now resting upon him. He is now occupying a subordinate position in General Halleck's department which seems an endorsement of the slander. I do not reproach Gen. Halleck, for Gen. Sherman's enemies may have shaken the confidence of the men in him by the suspicions that he is insane and thus rendered it impolitic to appoint him to a command there."

She hoped malice would not prevail over justice, looked for relief "from the sorrow that has afflicted me in this trial of my husband." If she were sure there was to be no forward movement of troops down the Mississippi, she would ask Mr. Lincoln to telegraph her husband to come to Washington, "when you could dispose of him in your wisdom." It was a moving plea. "Will you not defend him from the enemies who have combined against him?" She saw her husband harassed by the cruel press stories. "Newspaper slanders are generally insignificant, but this, you will perceive, is of a peculiar nature and one which no man can bear with stoicism, particularly one who is so sensitive and nervous."

And Lincoln's decision seems to have been that amid the miasmic army politics of the hour, he would not in this single matter set himself at cross-purposes with General McClellan. That is, he would take no action. He had previously endorsed a letter from a pro-Union railway president in Kentucky, James Guthrie, requesting him to send Sherman "back to Kentucky to serve under Buell." The endorsement was qualified, and read: "If General McClellan thinks it proper to make Buell a major general, enabling Sherman to return to Kentucky, it would rather please me." McClellan was joined with the War Department clique, including Secretary Cameron, who refused to contradict the newspaper stories that Sherman was "insane." A. K. McClure found Cameron and others assuming that Lincoln credited these stories. On hearing of Sherman's removal, McClure had gone to the War Department and asked Thomas A. Scott, the Assistant Secretary of War, what it meant. Scott had a short answer: "Sherman's gone in the head." And McClure found on further querying "that Scott simply voiced the general belief of those who should have been better informed on the subject."

The gentle and quaint Attorney General Bates wished that Lincoln would step out and assert himself more, writing in his diary on December 31, 1861: "If I were President, I *would* command *in chief*—not *in detail*, certainly—and I *would* know what army I had, and what the high generals (my Lieutenants) were doing with that army." For months past, wrote Bates, he had "pressingly urged" the President "to have some military organization about his own person," to have three or four aides around him to carry his orders, to collect information, to keep papers and records, "and to do his bidding generally, in all Military and Naval affairs." Earnestly the Attorney General made his points: "I insisted that, being 'Commander in chief' by law, he *must* command—especially in such a war as this. The Nation requires it, and History will hold him responsible." Again ten weeks later Bates wrote of a private talk with the President. The pressure to remove Marshal Lamon, and to crush McClellan, Bates saw as ominous. "Warned him that extreme men in Congress were lying in wait agst him, anxious to catch him in some error—and striving to *make precedents* against him, especially in regard to both the appointing and removing power. . . . I warned him to stand firm on his present *rock* [as to the slavery question] and not yield an inch either to the fierce rush of the northern abolitionists or the timid doubters of the border slave states. I told him that nothing valuable was ever won by timid submission. 'You have taken your positions cautiously (said

I), now maintain them bravely, and I will sink or swim with you.' He answered me very kindly and frankly &c."

To the White House one winter evening came by appointment a sixty-nine-year-old man who had made a name for himself and wished to talk with Lincoln about why he was losing his good name. As an infantry line officer in the War of 1812 his record was good. As a major general commanding a division he led cavalry in hot action at Cerro Gordo in the Mexican War and was honorably mentioned. As a commander of state militia quelling riots newspapers had praised his firm hand and steady head. As the owner of large textile mills he was highly spoken of in the business world. And now politicians, generals, newspapers, were blaming him and ridiculing him, General Robert Patterson, for the shameful Northern defeat at Bull Run. More than any other he was blamed. His good name was dragged low and become a byword.

To Lincoln he read orders, telegrams, letters, which he believed cleared him of failure. "The President attentively listened," and after some conversation the President addressed him in nearly the following words, according to Patterson's notes: "General Patterson, I have never found fault with or censured you; I have never been able to see that you could have done anything else than you did do. Your hands were tied; you obeyed orders, and did your duty, and I am satisfied with your conduct."

To this Patterson replied that so far as the President and the War Department were concerned he was satisfied, but he must have a trial by his peers in order to win public approval of his conduct and to stop the daily abuse laid on him. "The President replied that he would cheerfully accede to any practicable measure to do me justice, but that I need not expect to escape abuse as long as I was of any importance or value to the community, adding that he received infinitely more abuse than I did, but he had ceased to regard it, and I must learn to do the same."

CHAPTER 17

EXPECTATIONS OF McCLELLAN

SPEAKER GALUSHA A. GROW with Representatives Schuyler Colfax and Reuben E. Fenton in December of '61 had called on Lincoln about getting McClellan's army into action. Lincoln said Providence with favoring sky and earth seemed to beckon the army on, but General McClellan, he supposed, knew his business and had reasons for disregarding these hints of Providence. "And, as we have got to stand by the General, I think a good way to do it may be for Congress to take a recess of several weeks, and by the time you get together again, if McClellan is not off with the army,

Providence is likely to step in with hard roads and force us to say the army can't move." Fenton was sure he quoted "nearly the words" of Mr. Lincoln saying to them: "You know Dickens said of a certain man that if he would always follow his nose he would never stick fast in the mud. Well, when the rains set in it will be impossible for even our eager and gallant soldiers to keep their noses so high that their feet will not stick in the clay mud of Virginia."

During the winter of 1861-62 Lincoln probably considered one concrete question more than any other: "Why doesn't McClellan move with his army and how can we get him to fight?" Six months had gone in January of 1862 since McClellan had been put at the head of the Army of the Potomac. Weeks had dragged on without fighting, though he had three men to one in the Confederate army near by at Manassas. He had told Speaker Grow: "I have no intention of putting the army into winter quarters. I mean the campaign will be short, sharp, and decisive."

Money, men, bread, beef, gunpowder, arms, artillery, horses, had been given McClellan on a colossal scale. The army under him was published and spoken of as the largest and finest known in modern history. That he drilled, maneuvered, practiced, two, three, four months was understood—without murmuring. But when he settled into winter quarters, with an enemy army only two days' easy march away, there was exasperation.

His army was made up mainly of boys in the early twenties, thousands of them nineteen and under. They wrote to the folks back home, letters about their winter huts, pork and beans, coffee and soup from tin cups, epidemics of measles and mumps, digging trenches, putting up telegraph wires, clearing range for artillery with pick and shovel, throwing up earthworks, driving beef to camp, hauling military stores, dysentery, sore feet, roaches in hardtack, target practice, washing shirts and underwear in creeks and rivers. And what the folks back home did not hear from the boys they did from the newspapers and their Congressmen.

Lincoln's December message to Congress made clear why McClellan was given high command, saying: "It is a fortunate circumstance that neither in council nor country was there, so far as I know, any difference of opinion as to the proper person to be selected. The retiring chief repeatedly expressed his judgment in favor of General McClellan for the position, and in this the nation seemed to give a unanimous concurrence. The designation of General McClellan is, therefore, in considerable degree the selection of the country as well as of the executive, and hence there is better reason to hope there will be given him the confidence and cordial support thus by fair implication promised, and without which he cannot with so full efficiency serve the country." An old saying held that one bad general is better than two good ones. "The saying is true, if taken to mean no more than that an army is better directed by a single mind, though inferior, than by two superior ones at variance and cross-purposes with each other."

Shortly after this message to Congress the *New York Herald* correspondent Malcolm Ives wrote a letter following a three-hour talk with McClellan, noting, "His language concerning the President is enthusiastic. He thinks his [the President's] apparent weakness the result of a bonhomie which hurts nothing." Some slant at this bonhomie, or joking and storytelling, was in McClellan's mind on September 6 of '61. Major General Heintzelman wrote in his diary: "When General McClellan had seen the President to the door [and] as he pushed the door to, looking back he said—'Isn't he a rare bird?' "

So in September McClellan, finding the President "a rare bird," had at first probably suspected weakness behind the President's "bonhomie" and then with several months' further study had decided the bonhomie was merely the President's "apparent weakness." And in November McClellan wrote to his friend Barlow: "The President is perfectly honest and is really sound on the nigger question—I will answer for it now that things go right with him." Thus besides his heavy and terrific responsibilities as a military commander McClellan was going further and assuming it was also his province to formulate and spread judgments of whether the Commander in Chief was "sound" or "unsound" on the politically involved slavery and race issue, terming it "the nigger question" and revealing himself totally unaware of the forces Seward had in mind when telling Steve Douglas, "No man will ever be President who spells 'negro' with two g's."

Early in December Lincoln had handed McClellan a carefully worked out memorandum asking specific and technical questions about a forward movement. McClellan kept the memorandum ten days and sent it back with replies scribbled in pencil and a note dismissing all of Lincoln's suggestions: "The enemy could meet us in front with equal forces nearly, and I have now my mind actively turned towards another plan of campaign." General Joseph Johnston of the enemy army at Manassas was reporting to Richmond an "effective total" of about 47,000 men, while McClellan was claiming that Johnston's force was three times its actual size. When officers of other armies called for more troops McClellan was surprised, sometimes shocked. General Tecumseh Sherman wired for 75,000 men to help the Western forces drive south, and McClellan handed the dispatch to Lincoln, then at his headquarters, with the remark, "The man is crazy."

When George Bancroft came to the White House, Lincoln asked if he had as yet seen McClellan. Bancroft said No. "I will take off my slippers," said Lincoln, "and draw on my boots and take you over." Which he did. And they walked over to McClellan's headquarters, Lincoln and America's then most-distinguished historian, a sixty-year-old man who had studied German, French, Italian, Arabic, and Hebrew literatures, earned the degree of Doctor of Philosophy at Göttingen University, talked with Goethe, taught Greek at Harvard, almost won the Governorship of Massachusetts on the Democratic ticket, served as Secretary of the Navy under Polk and initiated the national naval academy at Annapolis. Why shouldn't Lincoln take this nationally distinguished and learned man to look at McClellan? Lincoln rang the bell and told the servant that Mr. George Bancroft and the President were waiting to see him. The General came in. They talked about the war, the army, and prospects. Bancroft wrote his wife: "Of all silent, uncommunicative, reserved men, whom I have ever met, the general stands first among the first. He is one, who if he thinks deeply keeps his thoughts to himself."

Possibly Lincoln had so often met a refusal of McClellan's to see him when he called that he took along a famous historian, a competent witness, on one occasion just to see what would happen. Possibly also he believed it would be interesting to see how McClellan would talk in the presence of the foremost American historian, who also happened to be a good Democrat highly respected by the navy. McClellan, however, who could chatter end-lessly when in the mood, and whose letters to his wife gave his fathoms of depth, merely gave Bancroft the impression that "if he thinks deeply [he] keeps his thoughts to himself." Also it may have been a day when McClellan felt that his enemies had, as he put it, "succeeded in sowing the seeds of distrust in Mr. Lincoln's mind." Possibly, too, he was a little tired of editors' and politicians' speaking of his "masterly inactivity." Or he may have heard Lincoln quoted as saying, "McClellan is a great engineer, but he has a special talent for a *stationary* engine." Or he may have been thinking over a story Lincoln had told him and have held a slight suspicion that Lincoln wished him to be more careful with his figures about the size of the Confederate army at Manassas. A notorious liar, ran Lincoln's venerable anecdote, in-structed a servant to step on his feet when he was spreading it on too thick. And as the liar was one day telling of a building which he had seen in Europe, a mile *long* and a half-mile *high*, he felt another foot crushing his toes. And he suddenly stopped telling about this big building. But a listener asked how *wide* the building was and he answered, "About a foot!"

Or again McClellan may have been restless under the rising murmurs about his headquarters' being in an aristocratic mansion in Washington in-stead of the field; his panoplied cavalry guard that always rode the streets of Washington with him; his infantry bodyguard and numerous orderlies; two French princes, heirs to the throne of France, who were staff members; his volunteer staff member John Jacob Astor, wealthiest of New Yorkers, who paid his own expenses and lived by himself in a rented house with a valet, a chef, and a steward.

From week to week the contact grew worse between the political power, as embodied in Lincoln and Congress, and the military branch that asked for what it wanted. The political power tried to give it but the mili-tary branch did not seem to know that this process was getting tiresome to the political end of the Government, which was closer to the people and the taxpayers. The atmosphere about McClellan had not changed since the No-vember day when Lincoln had told the General to "draw on me for all the sense I have, and all the information . . . the supreme command of the Army will entail a vast labor upon you," and McClellan had replied quietly, "I can do it all." He still believed he could do it all, carried himself as though he could, and when there was murmuring that he was doing nothing much at all, he blamed politicians for not giving him what he needed or for interfering with his plans.

Late in December McClellan fell sick with typhoid fever and took to his bed for three weeks. During those weeks he ran his armies, from the Atlantic to the Mississippi and beyond, from his bed. Lincoln wrote Chase a card on January 2, 1862: "I have just been with General McClellan and he is much better." Days followed, however, when others came to McClellan's bedside and did business. But the President was kept outside, and failed to get polite entry. It was during this illness that Lincoln decided to make calls on Little Mac no longer. Part of what happened was later told in McClellan's version: "My malady was supposed to be more serious than it really was; for although very weak and ill, my strong constitution enabled me to retain a clear intellect through the most trying part of the illness, so that I daily transacted business and gave the necessary orders, never for a moment abandoning the direction of affairs. As is often the case with such diseases, I sometimes passed days and nights without sleeping, and it more than once happened that the President called while I was asleep after such intervals of wakefulness, and, being denied admittance, his anxiety induced him to think that my disease was very acute and would terminate fatally. The radical leaders represented to the President that I kept my own counsels, acted entirely on my own high judgment, and should my malady terminate fatally, great confusion would ensue."

McClellan was correct in his belief that Lincoln feared great confusion would ensue if the head of the national armies should die. What flitted through Lincoln's mind at this time was merely hinted at in an entry in the diary of the very responsible Senator Orville H. Browning on January 12, 1862: "Sunday Jany 12 A very warm day. Went to Dr Gurleys Church in A.M. with dress coat & no overcoat. After night went to the Presidents in same way & returned at 9 perspiring freely with walking. Had long talk with the President about the war—He told me he was thinking of taking the field himself, and suggested several plans of operation. One was to threaten all their positions at the same time with superior force, and if they weakened one to strengthen another seize and hold the one weakened &c. Another was to shell them out of their intrenchments with guns that would throw very large shell over two miles—the enemy having none of that size."

Lincoln had been reading military treatises drawn from the Library of Congress, had held long conversations with officers widely versed in the theory of war, and considered himself as having grasped a few of the essentials. In a letter to General Buell while McClellan lay sick abed Lincoln said he did not offer his views on strategy as military orders. "While I am glad to have them respectfully considered, I would blame you to follow them contrary to your own clear judgment, unless I should put them in the form of orders. As to General McClellan's views, you understand your duty in regard to them better than I do." He then sketched a general principle emphasizing the advantage Northern forces had over the South: "I state my general idea of this war to be that we have the greater numbers, and the enemy has the greater facility of concentrating forces upon points of collision; that we must fail unless we can find some way of making our advantage an overmatch for his; and that this can only be done by menacing him with superior forces at different points at the same time, so that we can safely attack one or both if he makes no change; and if he weakens one to strengthen the other, forbear to attack the strengthened one, but seize and hold the weakened one, gaining so much."

In the Department of Missouri, General Halleck wrote Lincoln, mutinous "foreign" regiments calling for Frémont to command them had been disarmed; high officers were in the plot with the soldiers, Halleck believed; public property was robbed and plundered; discipline was going to pieces. Lincoln wrote on Halleck's letter: "It is exceedingly discouraging. As everywhere else, nothing can be done." By "foreign" regiments Lincoln knew Halleck meant the Germans; Frémont was dear to them because of his bold stand for immediate abolishment of slavery. And Lincoln wrote to Halleck, "The Germans are true and patriotic, and so far as they have got cross in Missouri it is upon mistake and misunderstanding." So he gave Gustave Koerner, an able attorney and one-time Lieutenant Governor of Illinois, to Halleck, saying that Koerner could be made a brigadier general. "He is an educated and talented German gentleman, as true a man as lives. With his assistance you can set everything right with the Germans. . . . He does not wish to command in the field, though he has more military knowledge than many who do. If he goes into the place he will simply be an efficient, zealous, and unselfish assistant to you."

In memoranda kept by General Irvin McDowell were glimpses of Lincoln at the time McClellan lay sick and directing his armies. McDowell wrote of January 10, 1862: "Repaired to the President's house at eight o'clock, P.M. Found the President alone. Was taken into the small room in the north-east corner. Soon after we were joined by Brigadier-General Franklin, the Secretary of State, Governor Seward, the Secretary of the Treasury, and the Assistant-Secretary of War.

"The President was greatly disturbed at the state of affairs. Spoke of the exhausted condition of the treasury; of the loss of public credit; of the delicate condition of our foreign relations; of the bad news he had received from the West, particularly as contained in a letter from General Halleck on the state of affairs in Missouri; of the want of coöperation between Generals Halleck and Buell; but more than all, the sickness of General McClellan.

"The President said he was in great distress, and as he had been to General McClellan's house, and the General did not ask to see him; and as he must talk to somebody, he had sent for General Franklin and myself to obtain our opinion as to the possibility of soon commencing operations with the Army of the Potomac.

"To use his own expression, 'If something was not soon done, the bottom would be out of the whole affair; and if General McClellan did not want to use the army, he would like to borrow it provided he could see how it could be made to do something.'"

They discussed what could be done immediately in a forward movement of the 130,000 effective troops of the Army of the Potomac. General Franklin, a constantly loyal friend of McClellan, was asked for his views and said he was "in ignorance of many things necessary to an opinion on the subject." The President then asked him "if he had ever thought what he would do with this army if he had it." Being pressed, Franklin said he favored a plan for the army to be taken by water to York River and the Peninsula for operations on Richmond.

Two nights later somewhat the same group met—with McClellan present, up and out of bed and functioning. He refused to discuss proposed movements of the army. When McDowell, at the request of the President, presented a plan of campaign to commence in three weeks, McDowell ended with an apology for the necessity of offering his opinion. To which McClellan coolly remarked, "You are entitled to have any opinion you please!" This was all that came from McClellan during a long discussion in which the President kept asking what and when anything could be done, again going over ground they had been over before.

"Much conversation ensued, of rather a general character," ran McDowell's memorandum. "The Secretary of the Treasury then put a direct question to General McClellan to the effect as to what he intended doing with his army, and when he intended doing it?" After a long silence McClellan said a movement in Kentucky was to precede any from Washington. "After another pause he said he must say he was very unwilling to develop his plans, always believing that in military matters the fewer persons who were knowing them the better; that he would tell them if he was *ordered* to do so. The President then asked him if he counted upon any particular time; he did not ask what that time was, but had he in his own mind any particular time a movement could be commenced. He replied he had. Then, rejoined the President, I will adjourn this meeting."

The hesitation of McClellan at making any one of the several movements open to him reminded Lincoln of a man in Illinois whose attorney was not sufficiently aggressive. "The client knew a few law phrases and finally, after waiting till his patience was exhausted by the nonaction of his counsel, he sprang to his feet and exclaimed, 'Why don't you go at him with a *fi fa demurrer*, a *capias*, a *surrebutter*, or a *ne exeat*, or something, and not stand there like a *nudum pactum* or a *non est?*'"

Now that McClellan was up where they could get at him, the Committee on the Conduct of the War called him for a consultation. Senator Zachariah Chandler bluntly asked McClellan why after five months' training he did not take his army and attack the enemy. McClellan replied that there were only two bridges across the Potomac to Washington and made an extended explanation of how military strategy requires that a commander should safeguard any retiring movement he might have to make while attacking an enemy.

"General McClellan, if I understand you correctly, before you strike at the rebels you want to be sure of plenty of room so that you can run in case they strike back," was Chandler's thrust, seconded by Wade's snorting,

"Or in case you get scared." McClellan then went into a lengthy and patient explanation for the Senators of how wars are fought and how necessary it is for generals to have always available lines of retreat as well as lines of communication and supply.

"General," said Wade, "you have all the troops you have called for, and if you haven't enough you shall have more. They are well organized and equipped, and the loyal people of this country expect that you will make a short and decisive campaign. Is it really necessary for you to have more bridges over the Potomac before you move?" "Not that," was the answer. "Not that exactly, but we must bear in mind the necessity of having everything ready in case of a defeat, and keep our lines of retreat open."

After McClellan had left the committee room, Chandler sniffed to Wade, "I don't know much about war, but it seems to me that this is infernal, unmitigated cowardice."

Six days later Senator Browning wrote in his diary that it was "a rainy dismal day" and "At night Mrs Lincoln on whom we had called during the day, sent her carriage and I went up there and staid till 10 O'clock. I spent an hour or two in the Presidents room in conversation with him upon public affairs. He expressed great confidence in Genl. McClelland."

This may have meant merely that Lincoln wished to indicate to his old associate in law that in case Wade, Chandler, and their cohorts should on the floor of the Senate bear down too hard on McClellan, Browning could then make any reply he felt reasonable. For Lincoln, while refusing to remove McClellan from command, as urged by radicals, was getting ready to let McClellan know who held authority and who was responsible to the people of the country. He issued on January 27 his General War Order No. 1. His secretaries, Nicolay and Hay, said that Lincoln wrote it "without consultation with any one, and read it to the Cabinet, not for their sanction, but for their information." The order fixed February 22, 1862, as "the day for a general movement of the land and naval forces of the United States against the insurgent forces." The language was tinted with a suggestion that fighting was wanted, whatever the cost or losses, and that where discipline was lacking officers would be held accountable. He named the Army of the Potomac, the Army of Western Virginia, the army near Munfordville, Kentucky, the army and flotilla of gunboats at Cairo, Illinois, and a naval force in the Gulf of Mexico as ordered to "be ready to move on that day." Department heads, commanders, and subordinates "will severally be held to their strict and full responsibilities for prompt execution of this order." Four days later he followed this with "President's Special War Order No. 1" commanding that the Army of the Potomac, after providing for the defense of Washington, move on February 22 to seize and occupy Manassas Junction, "all details to be in the discretion of the commander-in-chief." To this last he added a note to McClellan on February 3 urging his plan for a land attack on the Confederate army near Washington rather than an expedition by water for a Peninsular attack on Richmond:

. . . If you will give me satisfactory answers to the following questions, I shall gladly yield my plan to yours.

First. Does not your plan involve a greatly larger expenditure of time and money than mine?

Second. Wherein is a victory more certain by your plan than mine?

Third. Wherein is a victory more valuable by your plan than mine?

Fourth. In fact, would it not be less valuable in this, that it would break no great line of the enemy's communications, while mine would?

Fifth. In case of disaster, would not a retreat be more difficult by your plan than mine?

Now instead of waiting ten days, as he had in December, to answer a few reasonable inquiries from a patient and friendly Executive, McClellan replied on the same day with a long letter showing his belief that by rapid enveloping movements on the Peninsula near Richmond he could take the Confederate capital. A direct land attack on the Confederate army near Washington he could not approve. But he did have a mental picture of what he was going to do, for he came to Secretary Chase on February 13 and said, "In ten days I shall be in Richmond." Chase's memorandum ran on: "A little surprised at the near approach of a consummation so devoutly to be wished, I asked, 'What is your plan, General?' 'Oh,' said he, 'I mean to cross the river, attack and carry their batteries, and push on. All I want is transportation and canal boats, of which I have plenty that will answer.'" Chase's memorandum closed: "I did not think it worth while to reply, but made a note of the date and waited. The ten days passed away; no movement, and no preparation for a movement, had been made."

McClellan gave consent to Lincoln's plucking Frémont from his retirement and putting him in charge of a project the President had often stressed. Henry C. Bowen, owner of the *Independent*, a leading religious weekly, happened to be passing Lincoln's office in the White House and Lincoln called, "Come in, you are the very man I want to see." He told Bowen he had been thinking a great deal lately about Frémont. "And I want to ask you, as an old friend of his, what is the thought about his continuing inactive." Bowen said a large class of people felt that Frémont had been badly treated and he ought to have an appointment measuring up to his rank and ability. "Well," said Lincoln slowly, "I have had it on my mind for some time that Frémont should be given a chance to redeem himself. The great hue and cry about him has been concerning his expenditure of the public money. I have looked into the matter a little and I cannot see as he has done any worse or any more, in that line, than our eastern commanders. At any rate, he shall have another trial."

So there was created the Mountain Department in West Virginia, where Frémont took command of 25,000 men, later reinforced by 10,000. He was to follow a pet plan of Lincoln's, which he approved. The idea was to march over the mountains into East Tennessee, lend strength to the Unionist sentiment which dominated there, and seize the railroad at Knoxville. McClellan had no objections. And for the time being Lincoln had found a niche for the political and military figure about whom there clung such an aura of romance that thousands of boy babies were named for him in families where they counted him a rare hero.

Lieutenant David D. Porter, with Secretary Welles, presented to Lincoln one day an argument for the capture of New Orleans. Lincoln was reminded of an old woman in Illinois who suspected a skunk of killing some of her chickens. Her husband sat up with a shotgun all night and in the morning brought her two dead rabbits. "Thar's two of them skunks I killed."

"Them ain't skunks," said the old woman. "Them's my pet rabbits. You allers was a fool!"

"Well, then," returned the old man, "if them ain't skunks I don't know a skunk when I sees it."

"Now, Mr. Secretary," said the President, as Porter noted it, "the navy has been hunting pet rabbits long enough; suppose you send them after skunks. It seems to me that what the lieutenant proposes is feasible. He says a dozen ships will take the forts and city, and there should be twenty thousand soldiers sent along to hold it. After New Orleans is taken, and while we are about it, we can push on to Vicksburg and open the river all the way along." Seward coming in, they all went to McClellan's headquarters, where the General spoke to Porter as an old acquaintance, Lincoln commenting: "Why, do you two fellows know each other? So much the better." He outlined the plan for troops to hold New Orleans after the navy took it. "Time flies, and I want this matter settled. I will leave you two gentlemen to arrange the plans, and will come over here at eight o'clock this evening to see what conclusion you have arrived at." And the President was informed at McClellan's headquarters that evening that the General would spare 20,000 men for the expedition.

CHAPTER 18

CORRUPTION—STANTON REPLACES CAMERON

A JOBBER from Vermont, Jim Fisk by name, twisted his swagger mustache ends and grinned with a cock of his eye, "You can sell anything to the government at almost any price you've got the guts to ask." His suite at Willard's particularly welcomed Congressmen to a Havana cigar, a favorite drink, and any kind of a dicker that would pay. Fisk had sold a stock of blankets to the War Department at prices three times what the Vermont factory had expected. *Vanity Fair* satirized:

I, Lieutenant-Colonel Graham,
Of the Twelfth, depose and say,
That the coats contractors gave us,
Were of shoddy cloth of gray;
Only for a day we wore them,
And they came to pieces then.

The hardheaded millionaire landowner and legalist from Bloomington, Illinois, Judge David Davis, was chosen by Lincoln to head a committee to investigate purchasing methods of the military department in Missouri. The committee, having sworn and heard 1,200 witnesses, signed a report giving praise to the usually straight methods of merchants, manufacturers, and mechanics when dealing directly with the Government. Yet it also related that when commissions or contracts were let without open competition and then relet, cliques were formed to pass along favors to friends and relatives; the public treasury was looted. A pontoon bridge across the Ohio River at Paducah, Kentucky, costing $120,000 to build went downstream as a total loss when the river rose. One dealer bought discarded tents from the Government and resold them to the Government at profits of from 3 per cent to 33 per cent. For tugboats worth $1,500 in open market the Government paid $4,000 each; for 38 mortar boats in open market worth $5,000 each the Government paid $8,250 each.

Captain E. M. Davis, assistant quartermaster at St. Louis, bought from his son H. C. Davis of Philadelphia blankets to the amount of $14,283. Before the Committee on Government Contracts Captain Davis testified that the receipted bill which he produced was mistakenly itemized and his son had been paid $3.25 per blanket instead of $3.25 per *pair* of blankets. The word "pair" should have run through the whole bill. The Government had paid for two blankets and received one, thereby paying twice the price named by Davis before a board of survey which authorized the purchase. He testified that it was a "mistake" on his part to omit the word "pair" and through that omission to double the price of the blankets to the Government. Representative William M. Davis in the House was a brother of Captain E. M. Davis, and with pathos alleged that the committee had wrongly branded his brother as a scoundrel. Representative Henry L. Dawes of Massachusetts presented the testimony of Captain E. M. Davis, with the itemized receipted bill, and commented, "He who says we have undertaken to stab Captain Davis in the back, does not know all the facts." Representative Davis of Pennsylvania had not been aware of the facts, it was evident, and rose to say briefly of his brother, "If he is guilty punish him."

Frémont had testified at Washington and disproved all charges of personal dishonesty; the stealing was by traders, commission men, contractors; he was naïve and convincing. Greeley filled an extra sheet of the *New York Tribune* with Frémont's testimony, and gave his editorial opinion that evil partisans were hounding the deposed commander. Frank Blair took the floor in Congress for a long speech lambasting Frémont, Schuyler Colfax of

Indiana replying to Blair. Newspapers bristled with attack and defense of Frémont. The drift was in his favor. At the Astor House and later at an apartment on Fourth Avenue in New York he and his wife had received antislavery Congressmen, Senators, publicists, many saying they wished such a man as he were at the head of affairs in Washington. Here and there secret meetings had been held to further his cause. In his new command in West Virginia he was expected to excel his Missouri record.

On taking command in place of Frémont in Missouri, General Hunter on November 11 of '61 arrested Major Justus McKinstry, who had come to Frémont with twelve years of regular-army experience as quartermaster. "Furnished by the Administration to the Department of the West, which was supposed to be a guarantee for his faithfulness and integrity; trusting confidingly, Frémont watched him not closely," said Representative Van Wyck. For three months McKinstry was under close confinement in the St. Louis arsenal, then paroled, later court-martialed, dismissed from the army for neglect and violation of duty. He left St. Louis to set up as a stockbroker in New York. One hardware firm through which McKinstry worked sold the Government nearly $1,000,000 worth of goods, evidence showing that no prices were asked or bid beforehand; the fixing of prices came after delivery and ranged from 25 per cent to 50 per cent over the current quotations. "In building the forts at St. Louis," said Van Wyck, "more than $100,000 was squandered upon profligate, unprincipled favorites."

As if to gain strength by plain confession and to clarify his mind for immediate problems, Lincoln one midautumn day had meditated aloud to Nicolay on what confronted the Administration. Nicolay wrote a memorandum and sealed it in an envelope marked: "A private paper, Conversation with the President, October 2, 1861." It was a catalogue of the main and immediate troubles of the Administration, in a skeleton sketch that read:

Political
Frémont ready to rebel.
Chase despairing.
Cameron utterly ignorant and regardless of the course of things, and the probable result. Selfish and openly discourteous to the President. Obnoxious to the country. Incapable either of organizing details or conceiving and executing general plans.

Financial
Credit gone at St. Louis. ⎫ Immense claims
" Cincinnati. ⎬ left for Con-
" Springfield. ⎭ gress to audit.
Over-draft to-day, Oct. 2, 1861, $12,000,000.
Chase says new loan will be exhausted in 11 days.

Military
Kentucky successfully invaded.
Missouri virtually seized.

October here, and instead of having a force ready to descend the Mississippi, the probability is that the Army of the West will be compelled to defend St. Louis.

Testimony of Chase
                Bates
        the Blairs
                Meigs
                Gower
                Gurley
                Browning
                Thomas, that everything in the West, military and financial, is in hopeless confusion.

Demands for Cabinet reorganization came from the press and from political circles. Attorney General Bates confided to his diary: "There is no quarrel among us, but an absolute want of continuity and of intelligence, purpose and action. In truth, it is not an administration, but the separate and disjointed action of seven independent officers, each one ignorant of what his colleagues are doing." In the Administration teamwork others could stray, while the President was "the lead-horse which mustn't kick over the traces," Lincoln remarked to Nicolay.

A report to Congress in December by the Committee on Government Contracts threw light on curious commissions and special favors, exorbitant prices charged the Government, and low-quality goods and articles delivered to the army and navy. Corruption so underlay the Government, wrote General Tecumseh Sherman in a private letter, that "even in this time of trial, cheating in clothes, blankets, flour, bread, everything, is universal." New York and Pennsylvania traffickers had sold the Government "rotten blankets, rusty and putrid pork" for army use, alleged the *New York Tribune*, suggesting, "Wellington gave 'em the gallows." The Michigan Legislature too asked the gallows for "traitors in the disguise of patriots" who had paralyzed war efforts "by a system of fraud and peculation." The Ohio Legislature viewed congressional disclosures of wastefulness and deep corruption "with surprise, anxious alarm, pain and regret." Grimes of Iowa wrote to another Senator that imbecility and corruption were carrying the country to destruction, the flood of it "perverting the moral sense of the people."

The devious course by which the ship *Catiline* was chartered as a War Department transport at a rate of $10,000 per month paid to men who bought her for $18,000; the recommendation of its owner by Thurlow Weed; the hazardous transactions of Alexander Cummings, who left essentials and details to his clerk James Humphrey, who had been recommended to him by Thurlow Weed; the deposit by Cummings to his personal bank account of $160,000 taken from the $2,000,000 sent to New York by Lincoln for emergency use in forwarding troops and provisions to Washington in latter April; the vague explanations of Cummings, his failure to furnish vouchers, the number of things which he as former publisher of the *Phila-*

delphia Evening Bulletin and later publisher of the *New York World*
should have been expected to know but did not know—these were covered
in but part of the testimony and findings in the eleven-hundred-page report
of the Committee on Government Contracts. From the statement "The
Committee have no occasion to call into question the integrity of Mr.
Cummings" one inference among others was that he had meant well and
was led astray by Cameron. Also committee members made it clear that
having heard Mr. Cummings testify as to the constantly reappearing Thurlow Weed in the *Catiline* affair, they would have summoned Mr. Weed as
a witness but for the fact that Mr. Weed was on a State Department mission
in England "assisting to counteract the machinations of the agents of treason
against the United States in that quarter."

They had expected to ask Weed why powder-manufacturers and cattle-
sellers figured in testimony to the effect that Weed had established himself
as some sort of an auxiliary to Cameron. One powder-maker said his propositions were carried by Weed to Cameron, resulting in an understanding
that he was to pay Weed 5 per cent of the sums the contract called for.
Another powder-maker testified that his firm demurred at paying Weed
5 per cent, "that Weed gave them authority to make one thousand barrels
of powder but they preferred having the authority direct from the government."

Secretary Welles had given to his merchant-millionaire brother-in-law,
Governor Edwin Dennison Morgan of New York, the responsibility of buying ships for the navy at 2.5 per cent commission. And the Government
had paid Morgan $90,000 in commissions. As a buyer of ships Mr. Morgan
did well by his country, but it was claimed that if his commissions had
been less the Government would have benefited to the extent that they were
less. "Secretary Welles, honest himself, would not take a farthing from the
Treasury," said Republican Representative Charles H. Van Wyck of New
York. "It is no answer to say that Mr. Morgan is honest. Grant it. Mr.
Morgan is fond of money, or he would not, he could not consent to take
nearly ninety thousand dollars of the money which has been paid to him in
five months. A man who is thus greedy of gain evidently is more zealous
of his own than his country's interests." In Boston the customary commission on ship sales of more than $20,000 was 1 per cent, and Secretary Welles
could have insisted on that per cent; or the Secretary could have paid a
salary of $5,000 a year for Mr. Morgan's services as a ship-purchaser. The
skill and shrewdness of Mr. Morgan in choosing good ships to buy and in
buying them for the lowest possible prices should have been turned to the
advantage of the Government. "If the men owning vessels have been compelled or induced to sell them at small prices, what right has the Secretary
to allow his brother-in-law to put his hands in the pocket of each seller,
and realize the immense sum of $90,000 in a few months? That money really
belonged to the Government. As an agent, he takes it; and if it be an unconscionable amount, it belongs to his employers. The Secretary must have
known this transaction was liable to the criticism it has received, or he

would not, as he says he did, in advance, feel he might receive some censure because this great bounty was bestowed on a brother-in-law." These points in many variations were urged by the nonpartisan *Leslie's Weekly*, which for many weeks featured its demand that the President throw Welles out of the Cabinet.

To a resolution directing that the Secretary of War furnish the Senate with information as to contracts, amounts, names of contractors, dates, payments of money, Cameron made no reply. Months passed and Cameron sent neither information nor excuses nor regrets nor acknowledgments to the Senate. Again the Senate passed its resolution calling for information, Trumbull on January 14 of '62 inserting in the discussion a piece of current history: "Hall's carbines were originally sold by the Government [as useless and condemned property] at about two dollars apiece. Seven hundred and ninety were purchased back by Mr. Cummings in April or May at fifteen dollars apiece. In June the Government sold them again [as useless and condemned property] for $3.50 apiece. Afterwards, in August [having been altered and repaired], they were purchased by an agent of the Government at $12.50 apiece, and turned over to the Government at twenty-two dollars apiece; and the committee of the House are trying to prevent this last payment to the agent who purchased them for the Government at $12.50." That, said Trumbull, was one transaction, and Congress was not unreasonable in requesting further information regarding other transactions. Several cases were cited of politicians' getting contracts from Cameron to deliver firearms to the Government and taking these contracts to musket-manufacturers and dickering for commissions. The Senate kept pressing Cameron for information as to the extent that this system had been used in Cameron's buying $22,000,000 worth of firearms for the Government.

Part of the clamor that arose was political and aimed at smearing the Administration. Part of it traced to the jealousy of contractors and special interests not in favor with Cameron. Of this Lincoln was keenly aware. A delegation of New York and Boston bankers called on him and urged the removal of Cameron. "They talked very glibly," said Lincoln later to the painter Carpenter. One from Boston was "especially" glib, and Lincoln finally had to tell them so in effect, adding too that he was not convinced, and furthermore: "Gentlemen, if you want General Cameron removed, you have only to bring me *one proved* case of dishonesty, and I promise you his 'head.' But I assure you I am not going to act on what seems to me the most unfounded gossip."

Van Wyck in the House Committee set forth as to the Hall's carbine deal that Simon Stevens, the Government agent, had relations "of a warm personal character" with General Frémont, had gotten some sort of approval from the upright, trusting but deluded commander for the purchase of the firearms. "The bargain was an unconscionable one, whereby Stevens was to make about $50,000 in one day, without incurring any risk or investing any capital," said Van Wyck. The exposé by the House Committee and the clamor of Van Wyck, Trumbull, and others eventually stopped payment on part of the fraudulent firearms, which inspection proved were so defective they would shoot off the thumbs of soldiers using them. It helped none that Simon Stevens, while not a relative, was a protégé of Thaddeus Stevens and an occupant of his law office. It helped none that young J. Pierpont Morgan, the rising financier in New York, loaned $17,486 to Simon Stevens for the purchase of Hall's carbines from the Government for immediate resale to the Government for $109,912, and that Morgan presented to Congress in connection with this firearms sale exorbitant claims for money due him as a lender, while he refused to answer questions that would disclose the terms on which he had entered the deal. An array of respectable citizens presenting extortionate demands was the target of the committee's declaration: "He cannot be looked on as a good citizen, entitled to favorable consideration of his claim, who seeks to augment the vast burdens, daily increasing, that are to weigh on the future industry of the country, by demands upon the treasury for which nothing entitled to the name of an equivalent has been rendered. . . . Worse than traitors in arms are the men who pretending loyalty to the flag, feast and fatten on the misfortunes of the nation."

Cameron, it was evident, had paid off old political debts and smoothed out organization quarrels and fortified himself for the future by his favors to Pennsylvania in the matter of horses and railway transport. Some of the results of the horse contracts instigated by Cameron were related by Representative Dawes to the House on January 13, 1862:

A regiment of cavalry has just reached Louisville, one thousand strong, and a board of Army officers has condemned four hundred and eighty-five of the one thousand horses as utterly worthless. The man who examined those horses declared, upon his oath, that there is not one of them worth twenty dollars. They are blind, spavined, ringboned, with the heaves, with the glanders, and with every disease that horse-flesh is heir to. Those four hundred and eighty-five horses cost the Government before they were mustered into the service $58,200, and it cost the Government to transport them from Pennsylvania to Louisville more than ten thousand dollars more before they were condemned and cast off. . . .

There are, sir, eighty-three regiments of cavalry, one thousand strong, now in or round about the army. It costs $250,000 to put one of those regiments upon its feet before it marches a step. Twenty millions of dollars have thus been expended upon these cavalry regiments before they left the encampments in which they were gathered and mustered into the service. They have come here and then some of them have been sent back to Elmira; they have been sent back to Annapolis; they have been sent here and they have been sent there to spend the winter; and many of the horses never sent back have been tied to posts and to trees within the District of Columbia and there left to starve to death. A guide can take you around the District of Columbia to-day to hundreds of carcasses of horses chained to trees where they have pined away, living on bark and limbs till they starve and die; and the Committee for the District of Columbia have been compelled to call for legislation here to prevent the city wherein we are assembled from becoming an equine Golgotha.

Kentucky, proverbial for splendid horses, had loyal citizens who would have benefited by sales to the cavalry regiments. "Who will pretend," inquired Van Wyck, "that the public exigency required that when cavalry regiments were to be forwarded from the State of Pennsylvania to the land of the dark and bloody ground, it was necessary to transport, at great expense, the remaining disabled, diseased horses left in the Keystone State?" By the express order of the Secretary of War a contract was made for 1,000 horses to be delivered at Huntingdon, Pennsylvania.

Such a horse market the world never saw. The first inspector—an honest man—of the first hundred rejected three in five. The next day owners refused to present themselves, and by some legerdemain he [the honest inspector] was removed and others substituted; then horses of all ages, from two to thirty; of all diseases and defects, secret and open, were from day to day received. The whole neighborhood were in arms. The people remonstrated. Lawyers and clergymen were present at the inspection, and sought to deter the buccaneering crew by open condemnation; the inspectors heeded not this clamor, but ordered the horses to be ridden upon the crowd to drive them away, if possible. Horses with running sores, which were seen by the inspectors, were branded, and if one outraged common decency he would be rejected, and an opportunity sought the same day to pass and brand him. Immediately the horses were subsisted by private contract to favorites, at thirty-nine cents per day, and they sub-let to farmers from twenty-four to twenty-six. Over four hundred of these horses were sent with Colonel Wynkoop's regiment, and the papers at Pittsburg report some actually so worthless they were left on the docks. The remaining five hundred were left at Huntingdon for the benefit of contractors. In that single transaction fifty thousand dollars were stolen from the Government.

While the horse-traders went drolly on hoodwinking Uncle Sam with plugs and spavins, Secretary Cameron still refused to give the Senate or the public any inkling of how he felt about it. He dryly and drolly dismissed the entire subject of horses and cavalry with two sentences in his annual report to Congress, December 1, 1861: "While an increase of cavalry was undoubtedly necessary, it has reached a numerical strength more than adequate to the wants of the service. As it can only be maintained at a great cost, measures will be taken for its gradual reduction." In substance, then, whatever wrong might have been done through buying horses would be corrected by not buying any more.

The firearms scandals were disposed of in a single sentence that, coming from Cameron with no facts or data beyond the single sentence, might be read in several ways: "Combinations among manufacturers, importers, and agents, for the sale of arms, have, in many cases, caused an undue increase in prices." In the item of cannon the Secretary was more specific. He recommended that Congress authorize establishment of a national foundry for the manufacture of heavy artillery, the knowledge of costs thus obtained being of advantage in dealing with private manufacturers. And as to his administration in general, he would characterize it as "strictly economical."

Leslie's Weekly voiced a prevalent feeling and re-echoed the talk of millions in its comment on the disclosures of the House Committee on Government Contracts: "Fraud, falsehood, and favoritism are exposed on every one of the 1,100 pages of the published report of the Committee. It is a sickening catalogue of vessels bought by Government agents, through the intervention of third parties, straw men, at twice and three times their value, the difference between the actual cost and the price charged to the Government going into the pocket of the agent; it tells how contracts for cattle were given out to favorites or parasites, men utterly unacquainted with the purchase of cattle, at prices so exorbitant that they were turned over, half an hour afterwards, to practical dealers, at such prices as to enable the favorites to realize from $10,000 to $40,000 by a single stroke of the pen."

The able Assistant Secretary of War, Thomas A. Scott, could not find the report of the Committee on Government Contracts pleasant reading. He had testified that his salary as vice-president of the Pennsylvania Central Railroad had stopped when he became Assistant Secretary, but that he had kept his railroad office and title because he considered it of more value to himself than the Federal position. The committee held it highly improper for him to have a double allegiance when the Pennsylvania railroad was selling transportation to the Government and he was the buyer who fixed rates; there was the added embarrassment too that Secretary Cameron, to whom he owed his appointment, was a stockholder interested in the Northern Central Railroad to the extent that it was commonly called "Cameron's road." Quoting from testimony, Representative Van Wyck condemned as reckless expenditure the War Department order issued by Scott allowing 2 cents per mile for the transportation of troops, whether carried in passenger cars or in boxcars, whether taken as single passengers or by regiments. Scott had issued the order without consulting Quartermaster General Montgomery C. Meigs of the army, who testified that he first saw the order in the hands of a subordinate. The rate charged for soldiers was nearly double that for immigrants, and without the immigrant's allowance of 80 pounds of baggage free. "So enormous were the profits," said Van Wyck, "that railroad companies in the West bid and paid from fifteen to twenty-five hundred dollars to nearly every regiment for the privilege of transportation."

Representative William S. Holman of Indiana read the schedule of rates fixed by Scott, observed, "Those prices are enormous," and that through them the railroads were realizing "unprecedented profits from the Government." Two-thirds of an extravagant claim of the Illinois Central for troop transport had been paid by the War Department notwithstanding the request of the House that it be delayed until the House had received full information regarding it. Holman in this connection pointed to Federal grants to the Illinois Central of land now valued at $43,000,000, and as the railroad had cost its owners only $32,000,000, it had profited $11,000,000 through the generosity of the Government. Holman considered it noteworthy too that "a great body of its stock is held at this time by European capitalists."

In order to let the overreaching railroad-managers know there was a war on, Holman introduced bills and resolutions from the Committee on Government Contracts which set up the principles that the Government could withhold payments of railroad charges considered extortionate, that the railroad prices should be computed at or near cost, that the Government should be indemnified against failure of the railroads to transport troops and supplies promptly. Unless prices and service were placed on a more equitable basis, the Government would seize the railroads and operate them whatever the consequences. "Nothing herein shall be so construed as to prevent the Secretary of War from taking possession of said railroads and their appurtenances, and applying the same to the exclusive use of the Government, whenever, in his judgment, the public interests may require it, without, in such case, compensation to the said companies."

Rather than pay the "enormous profits" hitherto required by the railroads Holman would risk Government seizure and operation, while being well aware of "the very uncertain and expensive agencies to which a Government must ever resort."

The catalogue of frauds and extortions was, said several journals, sickening. In the speeches of Holman, Trumbull, Dawes, Van Wyck, was no tone of persecution or of political maneuvering. They were Republican-party men who wanted to get on with the war and win it, and they were sickened by the job of having first of all to combat men of their own party within the Administration whom they termed "public enemies." They said they were well aware that disturbers, gossips, spies, informers, disgruntled competitors, jealous rivals in politics and business, not to mention newspaper sensationalists, were spreading exaggerated stories and rumors; it was no time for idle chatter but one for sticking strictly to the documentary record. Interruptions of their speeches were usually requests for further information. The methods and findings of the Committee on Government Contracts were almost universally accepted. The longer addresses of Representative Charles H. Van Wyck of New York had lamentation, depth of woe. No sooner did he begin a melancholy abstraction derived from facts than he was led back into more of the stark and grinning facts. "The whole sky has been wrapped in gloom, and men go about the streets wondering where this thing will end," he said. "The mania for stealing seems to have run through all the relations of Government—almost from the general to the drummer-boy; from those nearest the throne of power to the merest tide-waiter. Nearly every man who deals with the Government seems to feel or desire that it would not long survive, and each had a common right to plunder while it lived." Then he launched into the case of two New York men selling two sailing vessels to the Government, adding larceny to perjury "that they might rob from the Treasury $8,000"; and the case of the president of the New Haven Propeller Company selling a ship named *The Stars and Stripes* to the Government for $19,000 more than she had cost him and of that profit pretending that it was necessary for him to pay $8,000 to bribe an ex-Congressman and a bureau head to let him the contract of sale.

Even at the Treasury Department, noted Van Wyck, were speculators of no standing in the business world who were bidding in contracts they could not fill, and all concerned knew the contracts would be sublet. Methods were in use that no good businessman would sanction. "Even in the Treasury Department—pure and upright as I believe the Secretary to be—what business man could justify, or who, in his own transactions, would allow that a contract of over half a million expenditure should be competed for by only two firms, who could combine and unite? It is no answer to say that the work is done as cheaply as before; the spirit of the law has been violated and the millionaire enriched." In a banknote contract and in other matters underlings were in control. "They say who shall approach within the charmed circle, they say whose papers shall be put on file, and whose shall be gladdened by the eyes of the Secretary."

Then again Van Wyck came to one of his abstractions: "The soldier who, borne down by disease and overcome with fatigue, is found sleeping at his post, you punish with death; while the miscreant who holds his festival at this carnival of blood rides in his carriage, drinks champagne, and dines with Cabinet ministers, you treat with deferential respect. Do you say Government cannot banish treason and punish crime?" He spoke his apology for what might appear severity of tone: "I am not harsh; I only speak what, standing in the mighty and august presence of stirring times, contemplating a bleeding, suffering country, I feel it my duty."

Van Wyck called the roll of rascals, gave cases and names, with the amounts stolen or the extortionate profits garnered, and alluded to them as the equivalents of incendiaries, horse thieves, dancing harlots. Was it a truth or a masked traitor's lie that every star of the sky stands as a sentinel over the graves where the patriot dead sleep? "The pirates who infest the ocean are not more deserving the execration of mankind than the gang who, on land, are suffered to feast upon the sweat of the poor and the blood of the brave."

Henry Laurens Dawes of Massachusetts in terse speeches tinted with satire insisted that the Government should require strict accounting, had the right to question and to claim unevasive answers, from its servants in the war establishment. Dawes referred to public enemies who, having a reputation for "masterly financial ability," nevertheless refused to produce a few simple vouchers concerned with the spending of immense sums of money. As a member attending all sessions of the Committee on Government Contracts, and having traveled six thousand miles without compensation in gathering evidence, Dawes set forth that he had done much hard work, had no desire to blacken men's names as charged, and that his purpose was to show that enormous expenditures were affecting the national credit. He knew more than he cared to tell of politicians suddenly gone into the military-supply business. "Why, Mr. Speaker, an ex-Governor of one State offered to the ex-judge of another State $5,000 to get him permission to raise one of these regiments of cavalry, and when the ex-judge brought back the commission the ex-Governor took it to his room at the hotel, while another co-plunderer sat at the keyhole watching like a mastiff for his dinner. He counted up $40,000 profit upon the horses, $20,000 on the accouterments, and like profits for the other details in furnishing the regiment."

Dawes plucked at the stuffed-shirt front of Alexander Cummings and brought a burst of laughter from the House at the ridiculous motions and notions of a man suddenly entrusted with vast funds and no ideas. The entire Cabinet had joined with the President during the April crisis, when the Government was ready to take flight from Washington, in naming Alexander Cummings as one of two men in New York to have the use of $2,000,000 of United States Treasury cash for the hurrying of troops and supplies to the immediate relief and defense of Washington until mail and telegraph communications were re-established. Dawes referred to the grotesque squanderings of Cummings and the bland innocence of Cummings in telling the committee he had no vouchers to put in evidence. The *Congressional Globe* read:

MR. DAWES. On the 21st of April, in the city of New York, there was organized a corps of plunderers upon the Treasury, and $2,000,000 was put at the discretion of a poor unfortunate—honest, I think—but entirely incompetent editor of a newspaper. He went straightway to purchase linen pantaloons and straw hats and London porter and dried herrings and such like provisions for the Army, including Hall's carbines, until he had used up $240,000 of the money, and then he got scared and stopped. [Laughter.]

MR. HOLMAN. My friend has made a slight mistake. He expended $390,000 instead of $240,000.

MR. DAWES. With the eye of my friend from New York upon me, I would rather keep a little under. [Laughter.]

Not for a moment could any charges of dishonesty stand against Secretary Welles or Secretary Chase, according to Dawes, but Welles nevertheless had played favorites, and as to Chase, "I accord to him legal and political sagacity; but looking to the deplorable condition of the Treasury and public credit, I fail to see any evidence of financial skill or ability." Secretary Cameron, however, he found hopelessly leagued with rats and scoundrels, playing politics and furthering his own Pennsylvania organization at Federal expense. At a sumptuous banquet given by Cameron to old henchmen, to new henchmen hitherto hostile to him, to horse-traders and firearms dealers, Dawes said that "the hatchet of political animosity was buried in the grave of public confidence and the national credit was crucified between malefactors." The first year of the Lincoln Administration and the last year of the Buchanan Administration were contrasted when Dawes said the evidence was beyond doubt "that somebody has plundered the public Treasury well nigh in that single year as much as the entire current yearly expenses of the Government which the people hurled from power because of its corruption."

The question was thrust at Dawes why he and his committee had not called as witnesses some of the unnamed thieves and malefactors alluded to in testimony taken. He replied that, three or four years before, Congress had passed a law "to screen offenders" with a provision that any man called before an investigation committee and examined was thereby immune from prosecution. "This committee has omitted to call men before it, because it was possible that it might be necessary to investigate their official conduct further."

At times in their speeches Dawes, Van Wyck, Holman, Trumbull, faltered for words, and it was evident that they were staggered more by incompetence than by corruption. Between human greed and human stupidity the Government's will to action was paralyzed. The historian would have difficulty and hesitation, it was noted, in placing the guilt as between respectable thieves seeking personal bounty for their personal benefit and equally respectable though honest dummies who sat at their desks and put on airs of importance and didn't know the immediate and commanding thing at hand to do. To Nicolay, Lincoln said one day amid the furore: "It is a good thing for individuals that there is a Government to shove their acts upon. No man's shoulders are broad enough to bear what must be."

The ordinarily gentle and well-poised Maine Senator, William Pitt Fessenden, wrote to his wife that winter, "When a man feels as if he could cut everybody's throat, and that everybody wants to cut his, he is in a pretty bad condition." As chairman of the Senate Finance Committee, Fessenden had to help find $10,000,000 a week to pay for the war, and he wrote his wife of everybody's grumbling over nothing done. "The truth is that no man can be found who is equal to this crisis in any branch of the government. If the President had his wife's *will* and would use it rightly, our affairs would look much better. Favoritism has officered the army with incapables. . . . The Treasury has been plundered and mismanaged (not by the secretary) until there is little left in it, and God only knows how we are to replenish."

In the *Atlantic Monthly* Edward Everett referred to "miscreants" who had "robbed the people directly or disguised their thefts under the euphonism of 'commissions.'" The *Boston Transcript* said that they would find it very hard to be "respectable" and at the same time to be known as "miscreants."

In the War Department Cameron personally was slovenly as to method, seemed to have no files nor records in his office, and according to Representative Riddle "in any official matter he would ask you to give its status and what he had last said about it." On being informed, "he would look about, find a scrap of paper, borrow your pencil, make a note, put the paper in one pocket of his trousers and your pencil in the other." Once a caller had to tell him, "The last thing you did in this case, Mr. Secretary, was to put my pencil in your pocket." After fussing with the often vague and indirect Cameron it was a relief, said Riddle, to go to Assistant Secretary Thomas A. Scott and meet an "electric brain and cool quiet manner."

Of like tone was a letter in late August of William Cullen Bryant to J. M. Forbes: "A man who wants to make a contract with the government for three hundred mules, provided he be a Pennsylvanian, can obtain access to him, when a citizen of East Tennessee, coming as the representative of the numerous Union population of that region, is denied. There are bitter complaints too of Cameron's disregard of his appointments and engagements. . . . Mr. Lincoln must know, I think, that Cameron is worse than nothing in the Cabinet."

Slowly the President had arrived at his appraisal, given to Nicolay, that Cameron was utterly ignorant and regardless of the course of things, obnoxious to the country, selfish, incapable of organizing details, and—least of all—"openly discourteous to the President." To Sumner, A. B. Ely was writing: "Thaddeus Stevens said Cameron would add a million to his fortune. I guess he has done it."

The first open break between Lincoln and Cameron came in December of '61 when the Secretary issued his annual report. The President was making ready to send to Congress the usual batch of reports from the executive to the legislative department when he was surprised to find that the report of the Secretary of War had been printed, and without having been submitted to him or read by him, it had been mailed to the postmasters of all the larger cities for release to the newspapers as soon as the telegraph brought word that the President's message had been read to Congress. This first surprise was followed by a second one, which came in the closing paragraph of Cameron's report. There Cameron for the first time in his life took his stand alongside the crusading abolitionists. On an issue where the President was treading as if on eggs Cameron came down flatfooted. There Cameron was recommending that Federal forces moving into enemy territory should free and arm the slaves. Without having consulted the Executive who headed the Administration and by whom he had been chosen as a confidential adviser, Cameron was thrusting himself forward as a spokesman of Administration policy. The slave property of rebels should be confiscated, declared the paragraph that surprised and offended the President. "It is as clearly a right of the Government to arm slaves, when it may become necessary, as it is to use gunpowder taken from the enemy. Whether it is expedient to do so is purely a military question. . . . If it shall be found that the men who have been held by the rebels are capable of bearing arms and performing efficient military service, it is the right, and may become the duty of the Government to arm and equip them, and employ their services against the rebels."

With this reasoning of Cameron as to the legal right of the Government regarding Negroes the President did not disagree. It was a matter of timing. Whether the hour had arrived for throwing abandoned or fugitive Negroes into regiments to be hurled at the enemy was still another question, one of policy and one so momentous that its announcement should come from the President and not from a Secretary who would launch it without consulting the Administration chief, through postmasters and a press release.

The *New York Tribune* had printed this "incendiary" passage. Of course it drew much comment. One abolitionist wrote, voicing many of the same view, that to Cameron would go the honor "of being the first man connected with the Administration to strike an official blow at the great cause of the war." But as Lincoln first glanced at the copy from the public printer placed in his hands, and his eye rested on the passage about arming the slaves, he was instantly aroused. And as the incident later came to the portrait-painter Frank B. Carpenter, Lincoln spoke decisively: "This will never do! General Cameron must take no such responsibility. That is a question which belongs exclusively to me!"

Telegrams went to the postmasters of the leading cities. The Cameron report was mailed back to Washington. A new edition was printed with the closing paragraph of the first edition omitted and a new paragraph substituted which raised the question of what should be done with the slaves abandoned by their owners to advancing Federal troops: "They constitute a military resource, and, being such, that they should not be turned over to the enemy is too plain to discuss."

Newspapers of course had easily gotten copies of the Cameron report, and they published the suppressed paragraph alongside the final official one. The difference between the two was that the first sounded as though the Administration was about ready to throw Negro troops into the war, while the later one suggested that the Administration was still hesitating and asking the question as to abandoned and fugitive Negroes, "What can be done with them?" and answering that they constituted a military resource, implying that they might yet be used as troops.

Bursts of approval came from the antislavery ranks for Cameron, not as vociferous as the applause for Frémont when he proclaimed freedom to the slaves of Missouri, yet loud and prolonged enough so that John Bigelow of the Paris consulate had to write home, "Are Cameron and Frémont to be canonized as martyrs?" Still other spectators, such as the *New York Herald*, were not impressed, and explained the incident as a craftily calculated stroke by which Cameron expected to rally the rapidly increasing antislavery forces behind him, to the confusion of those who were pressing allegations of fraud and corruption against him. It seemed on the part of Cameron too sudden a conversion to the cause of the Negro, in which he had hitherto been no radical; in the crusader's mantle he was a comic.

Both Lincoln and Cameron knew that they had come to the parting of the ways as President and Cabinet Minister. "Having corrected his minister's haste and imprudence," wrote Nicolay and Hay, "the President indulged in no further comment, and Cameron, yielding to superior authority, received the implied rebuke with becoming grace. From the confidential talks with his intimates it was clear enough that he expected a dismissal. But Lincoln never acted in a harsh or arbitrary mood. For the time being the personal relations between the President and his Secretary of War remained unchanged. They met in Cabinet consultations, or for the daily dispatch of routine business, with the same cordial ease as before. Nevertheless, each of them realized that the circumstance had created a situation of difficulty and embarrassment which could not be indefinitely prolonged."

Cameron began to hint that his War Department duties wearied him and he would prefer a foreign mission. Lincoln said nothing for several weeks.

The affair seemed to have blown over. Then a note of January 11, 1862, written by Lincoln to Cameron was made public:

> Executive Mansion, Washington, January 11, 1862
>
> Hon. Simon Cameron, Secretary of War
> My dear Sir:
> As you have more than once expressed a desire for a change of position, I can now gratify you consistently with my view of the public interest. I therefore propose nominating you to the Senate next Monday as minister to Russia.
>
> Very sincerely, your friend,
>
> A. Lincoln

In a private letter of the same date Lincoln wrote to Cameron that he had not been unmindful of Cameron's long-expressed wish to resign. "I have been only unwilling to consent to a change at a time and under circumstances which might give occasion to misconstruction, and unable till now to see how such misconstruction could be avoided." But Cassius Marcellus Clay was returning from the post of Minister to Russia to fight for his country as a major general, and therefore the President could now offer that post to Mr. Cameron. "Should you accept it, you will bear with you the assurance of my undiminished confidence, of my affectionate esteem, and of my sure expectation that, near the great sovereign whose personal and hereditary friendship for the United States so much endears him to Americans, you will be able to render services to your country not less important than those you could render at home." This letter, subscribed "Very sincerely, your friend, A. Lincoln," could be used by Cameron either at the court of the Czar or in Pennsylvania political circles for the information of any who wished to know how matters stood between him and the President.

Cameron's reply of the same date "with profound respect" acknowledged the "kind and generous tone" of the President's letter. "When you invited me to Springfield, Illinois, and presented me with the choice of one of two named places in the list of your constitutional advisers, I could not, for grave public reasons and after great reflection, refuse a trust so trying and laborious." He had been devoted to his office duties. "I have done my best. It was impossible in the direction of operations so extensive, but that some mistakes should have happened and some complications and complaints should have arisen. . . . I thank you for the expression of your confidence in my ability, patriotism, and fidelity to public trust. Thus my own conscientious sense of doing my duty by the executive and by my country is approved by the acknowledged head of the government himself." The proffer of the new post abroad, Cameron said to Lincoln, was "illustrative of your just and upright character."

Behind the scenes of these public interchanges something else went on. Of several accounts given of how Lincoln dismissed Cameron none was wholly correct and most of them were vitally incorrect, according to A. K. McClure of Pennsylvania. An earlier letter shifting Cameron from Washington to St. Petersburg was written by the President and delivered to Cameron by Chase without Chase's knowing what was in the letter, ran McClure's account. Spending an evening with Assistant Secretary Scott, McClure saw Cameron arrive near midnight for a visit with Scott after having just received Lincoln's letter. Cameron's nerves were on edge and he was close to tears. "He laid the letter down upon Scott's table and invited us both to read it, saying that it meant personal as well as political destruction, and was an irretrievable wrong committed upon him by the President. We were not then, and indeed never had been, in political sympathy, but our friendly personal relations had never been interrupted. He appealed to me, saying, 'This is not a political affair; it means personal degradation; and while we do not agree politically, you know I would gladly aid you personally if it were in my power.' Cameron was affected even to tears, and wept bitterly over what he regarded as a personal affront from Lincoln. I remember not only the substance of Lincoln's letter, but its language, almost, if not quite, literally, as follows: 'I have this day nominated Hon. Edwin M. Stanton to be Secretary of War and you to be Minister Plenipotentiary to Russia.' Col. Scott, who was a man of great versatility of resources, at once suggested that Lincoln did not intend personal offense to Cameron, and in that I fully agreed; and it was then and there arranged that on the following day Lincoln should be asked to withdraw the offensive letter; to permit Cameron to antedate a letter of resignation, and for Lincoln to write a kind acceptance of the same. The letter delivered by Chase was recalled; a new correspondence was prepared."

McClure believed that Cameron had "no knowledge or even suspicion" of Stanton's succeeding him. Nicolay, however, was told by Cameron that Lincoln asked him whom he wished for his successor in the War Department and when Cameron answered, "Stanton," Lincoln said, "Well, go and ask Stanton whether he will take it." On his way to see Stanton, Cameron met Chase, told his errand, and Chase said: "Don't go to Stanton's office. Come with me to my office, and send for Stanton to come there and we will talk it over together." Thus Nicolay said he had it from Cameron. Chase with a lead pencil wrote in his diary for January 12, 1862:

At church this morning. Wished much to join in communion, but felt myself too subject to temptation to sin. After church went see Cameron by appointment; but, being obliged to meet the President, etc., at one, could only excuse myself.

At President's, found Generals McDowell, Franklin, and Meigs, and Seward and Blair. Meigs decided against dividing forces, and in favor of battle in front. President said McClellan's health was much improved, and thought it best to adjourn until tomorrow, and have all present attend with McC. at three. Home, and talk and reading.

Dinner. Cameron came in. Advised loan in Holland, and recommended Brooks, Lewis, and another whom I have forgotten. Then turned to department matters, and we talked of his going to Russia and Stanton as his successor, and he proposed I should again see the President. I first proposed seeing Seward, to which he assented. He declared himself determined to maintain himself at the head of his department if he remained, and to resist hereafter all interferences. [This would indicate that Cameron was still waiting to hear whether the President had determined to keep him in Washington or send him to St. Petersburg.] I told him I would, in that event, stand by him faithfully. He and I drove to Willard's, where I left him and went myself to Seward's. I told him [Seward], at once, what was in my mind—that I thought the President and Cameron were both willing that C. should go to Russia. He seemed to receive the matter as new, except so far as suggested by me last night. Wanted to know who would succeed Cameron. I said Holt might embarrass us on the slavery question, that Stanton was a good lawyer, and full of energy. . . . Finally, he agreed to the whole thing [of approving Stanton for Secretary of War], and promised to go with me to talk with the President about it to-morrow.

Just at this point Cameron came in with a letter from the President, proposing his nomination to Russia in the morning! He was quite offended, supposing the letter intended as a dismissal, and, therefore, discourteous. We both assured him it could not be so. Finally he concluded to retain the letter till morning, and then go and see the President. . . . C. [and I] went off together, I taking him to his house. Before parting, I told him what had passed between me and Seward concerning Stanton, with which he was gratified. I advised him to go to the President in the morning, express his thanks for the consideration with which his wishes, made known through me as well as by himself orally, had been treated. . . .

We parted, and I came home. A day which may have—and, seemingly, must have—great bearing on affairs. Oh! that my heart and life were so pure before God that I might not hurt our great cause. I fear Mr. Seward may think Cameron's coming into his house prearranged, and that I was not dealing frankly. I feel satisfied, however, that I have acted right, and with just deference to all concerned, and have in no respect deviated from the truth.

Chase, Seward, Cameron, each believed he was taking a hand in picking the next Secretary of War, it seemed. Lincoln, in the Nicolay and Hay view, was guiding the situation with a strong will and a delicate tact, encouraging each to believe that his advice counted and thus holding the Cabinet in health and harmony as it rode through the crisis of the first polite removal of an unsatisfactory Minister. Others believed that in the particular case no voice was more influential with Lincoln than that of General McClellan, who favored Stanton and knew him so well that he had once used Stanton's home as a hideout to avoid an interview with Lincoln.

The President named Cameron for the post of Minister to Russia, which roused Dawes in the House and Trumbull in the Senate; they raked out materials not before presented and raised points not to be laughed off. Sumner, having been impressed with Cameron's new leanings to the antislavery cause, took Dawes's speech to Cameron and asked what answer should be made to such accusations. Cameron replied that he had never himself made a contract since he had been Secretary of War, leaving all contracts for supplies to the heads of bureaus, who were regular-army officers. He put this statement in writing and addressed it to Vice-President Hamlin, president of the Senate, with the added point that he had "not found any occasion to interfere" with such heads of bureaus. Dawes in reply produced Executive Document No. 67 listing all arms contracts made by the War Department, with a final summary:

	Muskets and Rifles
Contracts by order of Secretary of War	1,836,900
Contracts by Chief of Ordnance	64,400
Contracts by order of Major-General Frémont	1,000
Contracts by order of Major P. V. Hagner	1,500

Thus it was less clear than before what Cameron might mean by his written statement to Hamlin: "I take this occasion to state that I have myself not made a single contract for any purpose whatever, having always interpreted the laws of Congress as contemplating that the heads of bureaus, who are experienced and able officers of the regular army, shall make all contracts for supplies for the branches of the service under their care respectively." An added item was produced by Dawes to show that two days after Cameron had resigned as Secretary of War, before his successor had entered office and while his nomination as Minister to Russia was pending in the Senate, and against the advice of the Chief of Ordnance, Cameron made a contract for an unlimited number of swords and sabers, all that could be furnished in the ensuing six months by Messrs. Horstman of Philadelphia.

For the first time a long wrangle took place in the Senate over the confirmation of a major appointment by President Lincoln. Four days the Senate wrestled behind closed doors on the matter of naming Cameron Minister to Russia. Trumbull led the opposition, saying that confirmation would be an immoral act, like giving an unfaithful servant a good "character" or recommendation, and that the new office would be a whitewash to enable Cameron to recover his seat in the Senate, which was Cameron's design. Cameron was confirmed on January 17 by a vote of 28 to 14, Trumbull handing to Horace White, a newspaperman, a list of the six Republicans who voted against confirmation, saying that they wished their names published: Foster, Grimes, Hale, Harlan, Trumbull, and Wilkinson. Equally upright, and moral in their own view, in favoring Cameron were Sumner, Ben Wade, Zach Chandler, Fessenden, and Lane of Kansas; they held that the line of right and wrong was not as clear-cut as Trumbull would have them believe.

Opinion rose and flourished in antislavery quarters that, as the *New York Evening Post* said, while there had been fraud and corruption in the War Department, Cameron had "no participation in these robberies." Greeley framed a chromo, editorially joining Frémont and Cameron as wronged heroes, saying in the *New York Tribune:* "General Cameron has been surrounded and pressed upon by troops of noisy well-wishers who would have scorned the idea of selling their God for thirty pieces of silver so long as there was the faintest hope of making it forty. These have bored him into signing contracts by which they have made enormous profits at his expense as well as the country's." *Vanity Fair* blandly cartooned the President as saying to Cameron: "I am resolved what to do, Simon. I will send you to

St. Petersburg where you may serve nobly the cause of your country at the Court of the Kezzar."

Schleiden of Bremen noted that Cameron a few days before departing for Russia said the national outlook was extremely unfavorable, and added, "We want a great man and have not got him—but I ought not to have said that." In loose-hung gray clothes, a fox wariness on his face, the smooth and adroit manipulator often mentioned as politically the Czar of Pennsylvania sailed on his journey to meet the Czar of all the Russias at Peterhof Palace beyond the Baltic Sea in a city where James Buchanan of Pennsylvania had complained that the tall wood stoves failed to heat decently the big rooms. There amid droshkies, troikas, balalaikas, and muzhiks he might forget transactions in horses, muskets, blankets, not yet out of mind in the Congress at Washington, which concerned itself more than once that winter with unfinished business relating to the removal of dead horses, whose numerous carcasses were a detriment to the health of the community. *Leslie's Weekly* put a heading "The Exiles of Siberia" on a paragraph: "Mr. Lincoln has a wide reputation as a humorist. The nomination of Mr. Cameron to St. Petersburg, which is a long way on the road to Siberia, looks as if he were also addicted to practical joking. It would be no joke for the ex-Secretary of War, however, if the Czar were to take his appointment as a hint to 'pass him on' to that land of penance, and the companionship of that goodly company of army contractors and speculators whose exploits in the Crimean war failed to receive the imperial approval!" A cartoon in *Harper's Weekly* pictured Cameron holding a packed carpetbag standing at the desk of the Secretary of the Navy, saying: "Good-by, Welles. I'm off for Russia! There's too much talk of hanging here to suit me!"

No other member of Lincoln's Cabinet seemed to have the complete approval accorded Edwin McMasters Stanton from a variety of Republican and Democrat factions. The Senate confirmed the President's appointment of Stanton. Sumner said: "I urge that confirmation. Mr. Stanton, within my knowledge, is one of us." Ben Wade agreed. So did General in Chief McClellan.

A Jackson Democrat, with the record hazy as to whether he was in 1860 under the proslavery Breckinridge banner or in the squatter-sovereignty camp of Douglas, Stanton was an extraordinary figure of a man. Replacing an ousted secessionist in President Buchanan's Cabinet as the Cotton States were seceding, he confidentially advised Seward and other Unionists of what went on in Cabinet meetings. Buchanan, hearing of Lincoln's newly appointed Secretary of War, wrote to his niece Harriet Lane, "He was always on my side, and flattered me ad nauseam."

Seward in March of '61 had urged Lincoln to appoint Stanton district attorney at Washington, vouching for Stanton's loyalty. Chase joined his endorsement to that of Seward. Lincoln was cordial, waited, and after several Cabinet discussions said the subject would have to be disposed of, Welles noting: "The President remarked he thought it judicious to conciliate and draw in as much of the Democratic element as possible, and he was willing to try Stanton, though personally he had no special reason to regard him favorably." The office came within the province of the Attorney General, the President noticed; he would therefore turn the matter over to Bates. And Bates appointed another man.

Before inauguration the suggestion had come that Stanton should be Secretary of War, Representative Riddle of Ohio telling Lincoln that he had often called at Stanton's house during the winter weeks of secession and "I found him to be heart and soul against the conspirators, that he fully understood their movements, and was ready and anxious to defeat their plots." Riddle added that one night after a long interview Stanton shook hands with him and said, "Stand firm; you men have committed no blunder yet." Riddle believed he made a favorable impression on Lincoln and flatly said that he was disappointed at not finding Stanton's name in the Cabinet the President announced.

Since then Stanton had been legal adviser to McClellan, to Cameron, Dix, and others. As the days passed he wrote letters to Buchanan, to Dix, to others, referring to "the painful imbecility of Lincoln," mentioning "distrust in the sincerity of Lincoln," which he had noticed rising, telling of "reports of the trepidation of Lincoln." He heard this and that and sped it onward in letters. "It is said that Lincoln takes the precaution of seeing no strangers alone." Bull Run was "another imbecility of the administration"; it was "the result of Lincoln's running the machine for five months." The day after Lincoln's secret night ride through Baltimore, the Public Man wrote in his diary: "As I was crossing Fourteenth Street, I met the Attorney-General [Stanton], who stopped me to ask if I had seen the President-elect since he 'crept into Washington.' Every word was a very ill-suppressed sneer, and it cost me something to keep my temper in talking with him even for a few moments. When he found that I had only met Mr. Lincoln once, to my recollection, he launched out into a down-right tirade about him, saying he 'had met him at the bar, and found him a low, cunning clown.'" This referred to Stanton's meeting Lincoln in the McCormick Reaper case at Cincinnati. Donn Piatt wrote of how Stanton "described, in wrath, the long, lank creature from Illinois, wearing a dirty linen duster for a coat, on the back of which the perspiration had splotched two wide stains that, emanating from each arm-pit, met at the centre, and resembled a dirty map of a continent." And Piatt, a lifelong friend and admirer of Stanton, further told of Stanton's snorting, "I said that if that giraffe appeared in the case I would throw up my brief and leave." McClellan wrote as though amused and somewhat baffled by Stanton's frequently referring to Lincoln as the "original gorilla" and adding a twist in declaring that Du Chaillu "was a fool to wander all the way to Africa in search of what he could so easily have found at Springfield, Illinois." The evidence was not meager that Stanton had a habit of entertaining himself and others with his musings on the simian traits of Lincoln.

Often in handling people Stanton seemed to manage a fierce glare and a domineering, tempestuous manner. He was crazy or sick, more often just plainly difficult, according to various people. In fact asthma was the lesser of his afflictions. Donn Piatt wrote of Stanton that in the years just before entering Lincoln's Cabinet he had been "subject to a determination of blood to the brain, and had been warned by his capable physician, that, unless he found entire quiet in abstinence from all excitement, he might die at any moment. This disorder, added to his mental strain, overwhelmed his nervous system, and not only deepened the gloomy spells to which he was addicted, but made him irritable and impatient." Once Piatt had stepped into Stanton's room at the National Hotel without knocking, finding Stanton seated at a table, his face hid in his arm. "As I touched his shoulder he looked up. To my amazement his face was distorted with grief, while tears seemed to blind him." Piatt stammered out a message he had come to deliver. "Yes, yes," said Stanton, wiping his eyes. "It is very kind of you, Donn, but not now, please, not now."

Though Stanton was often fussy, peevish, petty, letting himself go in brainstorms of anger and arrogance, he had an instinct for place and power that guided him. As a lawyer he had been more than "astute." As an official he practiced statecraft with the accent on craft. He could, for instance, be found guilty of nothing in particular in the personal touches by which Cameron went out and Stanton came in as head of the War Office. Yet what happened was curious and had the color of what was usually termed "Washington intrigue."

Before Cameron sent to Lincoln his report favoring the arming of Negroes for Union service, he called in his legal adviser, Stanton. And Stanton gave approval to this clause and wrote an additional paragraph which Cameron adopted and inserted. And the lawyer who had been sufficiently non-abolitionist, on his record so inoffensive on the slavery issue, as to win an appointment to sit at President Buchanan's Cabinet table, used this language in the paragraph accepted by Cameron:

"Those who make war against the Government justly forfeit all rights of property, privilege, and security derived from the Constitution. . . . As the labor and service of their slaves constitute the chief property of the rebels, such property should share the common fate of war. . . . It is as clearly the right of this Government to arm slaves when it may become necessary as it is to use gunpowder or guns taken from the enemy."

Stanton may have penned this paragraph for Cameron in sincerity. In the tumults and shifting viewpoints of the hour, he may have been genuinely convinced of what he wrote for Cameron to give to the public before Lincoln could annul it. Stanton may, furthermore, have been innocent of any belief that his few well-chosen words would light a blowup hoisting Cameron out of his Cabinet seat beyond recall. If Stanton was innocent of any such intention, it would not accord with many pieces of action likewise having his personal touch. A friend, admirer, biographer, and close student of Stanton's record arrived at this impression:

"Interesting, indeed, is the fact that Lincoln was unaware that the iron-willed giant he was putting in was more stubbornly in favor of enlisting and arming the slaves of rebellious masters than the man he was putting out. Lincoln was also unaware that the recommendation which, with his own hand, he had expunged from Cameron's report and which was the means of forcing its supposed author out, was conceived and written by the very man now going in—but so it was; and so it may be said that Stanton wrote his own appointment!"

By a tortuous path this nervous, asthmatic, strong man of many contradictions had come to be head of a War Department having authority over 600,000 soldiers; moderates or conservatives like Seward, Cameron, and McClellan endorsed him while in the same moment the radicals Chase, Wade, and Sumner were saying, "He is one of us."

Stanton was the son of a widowed mother, and at thirteen years of age, seeing her tears over being helpless, threw his arms around her crying, "Never mind, mother, I'll take care of you." Which he did—he took care of her and a family of five. Working his way through Kenyon College, clerking in a bookstore in Columbus, Ohio, he met Mary Lamson, daughter of an Episcopal clergyman, carefully educated and, like himself, poor. They took their honeymoon in a 125-mile sleigh ride from Columbus to Cadiz, Ohio, where he began law practice, made money from the start, was known as stiff and proud rather than sociable, and on occasion was designated as "cheeky." In trying a case where a physician, his Quaker uncle, testified, he made out for the jury that the witness was a liar and an ignoramus. His later apology to the uncle that it was a way lawyers had drew the reply, "Well, Edwin, if thy profession requires thee to tell such lies, I think thee had better choose another." Employed to defend a man under a charge of murdering a family with poison, Stanton swallowed some of the drug in the presence of the county sheriff. Emetics brought up the poison, or the self-willed Stanton would have died from the test.

Charging a farmer a $1,000 fee for winning a $2,000 suit, he inquired, "Do you think I would argue the wrong side for you for less?" He recovered $1,000 damages in a slander suit against a physician who had blathered around that he had delivered Rectina McKinley, a spinster, of a child. However, one William Ralston married Miss McKinley and came to Stanton inquiring if the $1,000 damages had been collected. "Yes, Billy," replied Stanton. "It is all paid in. You now have a good wife. I have proved to all the world that she is without a blemish. I charged only $1,000 for sending her out of court with a good character." And Stanton kept the money. Elected prosecuting attorney, he left the county before his term was ended, settling in Steubenville, building a practice, moving on to Pittsburgh, then Washington, District of Columbia.

The Erie Railway, Wheeling Bridge, McCormick Reaper, and other cases brought him national reputation. His friend Jeremiah Black, first Attorney General under Buchanan, sent him to California to combat land sharks who through fraudulent titles sought to swindle the Government out of large tracts of valuable land. After months of hard work and steady resistance to bribery, inducements, and skulduggery, he re-established government title to its property. "He is accounted the first lawyer in America," said the *Chicago Tribune* as Stanton took over the War Office. That, however, took no account of the moody and hectic Stanton, of the weird undergrowths of behavior swarming behind his black whiskers and black bushy hair, his spectacled nearsighted eyes with a vehement stare, his stocky and deep-chested body. As a boy he trained snakes, and once horrified a quiet family of women and children by entering their home with two large wriggling snakes wound around his neck. When his child Lucy died, after her body had been buried a year he had it exhumed, cremated, and placed the ashes in a metal box which he kept in his own room.

The wife of his youth died in childbirth in 1844 and Stanton insisted that she must wear her wedding-clothes for burial. He wept while hours passed and he moaned, "She is my bride and shall be dressed and buried like a bride." He gathered her rings, jewels, and letters, threw them into the coffin, and when friends of the dead woman removed the keepsakes he put them back. Then for years he went twice a week to decorate her grave, on Sundays always going alone, "to meet her," he said. At the head of the grave he put a sprig of weeping willow which a friend had brought from Napoleon's burial place at St. Helena.

Twelve years passed before he married the daughter of a wealthy merchant in Pittsburgh. Just before this marriage he gathered all the letters he had written his first wife before and after their marriage and arranged them in a neat pile on the fireplace grate. But he could not set a match to them. "Alfred," he called to his gardener, a long-time aid, "you light them for me, please." He walked back and forth weeping and wringing his hands. Alfred told of it later: "I turned my back so Mr. Stanton could not see I was crying too."

The favorite relaxation of Stanton was to leave home of a morning with a market basket on his arm, walk slowly along to the grocer's and huckster's, and shop for the home pantry and icebox. He knew the Constitution and the price of eggs and was solemn about both. "We never heard him sing a note," said one who saw him at close range. Religion steadily deepened in him. Born of a Quaker strain, he was raised a Methodist and became a devoted communicant of the Episcopal Church. In odd intervals he was writing a book to be called *Poetry of God,* he told Donn Piatt in vacation days at Piatt's country place in Ohio. "I want to call attention to the fact," he said to Piatt, "that God, in all his communications with man, clothed his language in the highest imagery. All light, and all color, that make life beautiful are the affair of a little nerve God has endowed us with to enjoy his precious gifts that after all live only in our brain." Then the book had faded and dwindled before law and politics. A vortex of action called. He sat in Buchanan's Cabinet across a table from John B. Floyd, secessionist and Secretary of War, as Floyd urged withdrawal of troops from Charleston Harbor. Stanton exploded with wrath, declaring that the surrender of Fort Sumter would be a crime equal to treason and all who took a hand in it should be hanged. Then months had passed with history in a whirligig, events seen in a mist, and he sat in Donn Piatt's room in Washington reply-ing to a query from Mr. and Mrs. Piatt. "Yes, I am going to be Secretary of War to Old Abe." "What will you do?" was asked. "Do? I intend to accomplish three things. I will make Abe Lincoln President of the United States. I will force this man McClellan to fight or throw up; and last but not least, I will pick Lorenzo Thomas [Adjutant General of the War Depart-ment] up with a pair of tongs and drop him from the nearest window."

A telegram from Harper's Ferry called for large guns. Stanton ordered the guns sent that day. After office hours he went to the arsenal, found it closed, hunted up a subordinate, learned that no guns had been sent, ordered the door of the arsenal broken open, helped drag the guns out, went with the guns to the railway, and saw them pull out for Harper's Ferry. The arsenal officer came to Stanton the next morning saying, "It was not con-venient, Mr. Secretary, to despatch those guns yesterday, but if you think it is at all urgent, I will attend to it at once this morning." Stanton: "The guns are now at Harper's Ferry, and you, sir, are no longer in the service of the United States Government."

Executive ability had arrived at the War Department, it was reported. At ten o'clock in the morning a room 15 by 20 feet was opened and began to fill up with claim agents, contractors, relatives of soldiers, and Senators and Congressmen, all unable to get a private interview with the department head. At eleven there was a buzz and a stir and Stanton walked in, speaking to no one till he reached a high desk opposite the entrance. Then he picked out one by one those he would do business with. To a gushing office-seeker he might say, "Sit down, sir, I'll attend to you by-and-by." He might roar at an officer, even a major general in brass buttons and gold stars: "Come, sir, what are you doing in Washington? You are not needed here. I'll see about mustering you out." Many a caller was soon frozen to his seat, cer-tain that he wouldn't speak until spoken to. Then Stanton might move from the desk and walk free from interruption, perhaps saying to a cripple or a widow, "What brings you here?" When he talked with contractors, dealers, jobbers, his clerks and stenographers took down the proposals and terms. Interviews with the Secretary alone were almost impossible; he insisted on witnesses. "He went at me like a tiger," said more than one caller. For energy, incessancy, he was likened to a steam engine in pants. He installed the telegraph office in the War Department library, and in a day's routine would read telegrams and dictate answers for hours. Lincoln nicknamed him "Mars."

"This army has got to fight or run away," he wrote Charles A. Dana. "And while men are striving nobly in the West, the champagne and oysters on the Potomac must be stopped." He swore he would get McClellan's army into action. He believed he was infusing earnestness into the Lincoln Ad-ministration and wrote Dana after a week in office: "I feel a deep, *earnest* feeling growing up around me. We have no jokes or trivialities, but all with whom I act show that they are in dead earnest."

Some were troubled over the new titan who might go too far and try to run away with the whole concern, they told Lincoln. He drawled: "We may have to treat him as they are sometimes obliged to treat a Methodist minister I know of out West. He gets wrought up to so high a pitch of excitement in his prayers and exhortations, that they are obliged to put bricks in his pockets to keep him down. We may be obliged to serve Stanton in the same way, but I guess we'll let him jump awhile first."

To the White House one day came Senators who had caucused and decided that the President would do well to reorganize the entire Cabinet and set up a new one. "Gentlemen," said Lincoln, "your request for a change of the whole cabinet because I have made one change reminds me of a story." He told of an Illinois farmer pestered by skunks. The farmer's wife was especially wrought up and kept after him to get rid of them varmints. One moonlight night he loaded his shotgun and went out while the wife waited in the house. She heard the shotgun blaze away. And soon her husband came in. "What luck?" she asked. "I hid myself behind the woodpile," said the farmer, "with the shotgun pointed toward the henroost, and before long there appeared not one skunk but *seven*. I took aim, blazed away, killed one and he raised such a fearful smell that I concluded it was best to let the other six go." The Senators got no farther on their proposal than that.

Every day Stanton had his errands at the White House. At any hour he might be seen walking from the War Office taking telegrams, letters, official business, to the President. Likewise Lincoln stepped over to the War Office nearly every day, sometimes during large troop movements or battles spending hours with his War Secretary over the latest wire news. "There grew up between them," said Nicolay and Hay, "an intimacy in which the mind and heart of each were given without reserve to the great work in which they bore such conspicuous parts." The personal allusions of Stanton comparing Lincoln to the baboon, the gorilla, the giraffe, were heard no more.

The President gave wide and free play to Stanton's capacity for hard work and Stanton's enjoyment of actual personal power. In a trifling routine matter the Secretary would on occasion stride and gesticulate as though he were a ship's captain ordering manacles on mutineers. In giving assignments to others he usually had fears and reservations. He would have liked to be enough men himself to run the whole War Department. Then others could not complain if he drove them as ruthlessly as he drove himself.

Stanton was at first considered the tough actor required for the hour. Seldom, however, had any lashing, abrupt, tough actor, insisting on his way of doing things, been so endowed with a vast knowledge of legal technicalities added to a piety that gushed forth as a wellspring of orthodox faith when there was glory or despair in events ticked off on the War Office telegraph. Where the ambition of Chase was rather polished and conventional and he always considered what men might be saying about him, Stanton cared little so long as he got practical results and held a guiding hand on the war machine. His overanxiety to guide the machine, to have his hand and brain in the whole works, was the point where he was least strong and to his own advantage could have been less truculent and dominering.

Cameron had twice curtly refused to give the House information it requested concerning the Ball's Bluff disaster, writing once that the General in Chief (McClellan) believed that it would "be injurious to the service," and again that it was "not deemed compatible with the public interest." Stanton, in office less than two weeks, gave out no information, but with an iron hand in ruthless action gave complete satisfaction to those clamoring for punishment of one they believed false and guilty at Ball's Bluff in particular and elsewhere in general.

On representations by men in Congress who believed that the dead General Edward D. Baker was a sacrifice to either stupidity or treachery, and on the basis of evidence taken by Senator Wade for the Committee on the Conduct of the War, Stanton on January 28 of '62 took action. He issued through the War Department an order directing General McClellan to arrest Brigadier General Charles P. Stone, commander of a division of 10,000 troops in the Army of the Potomac, West Pointer of gallant and meritorious conduct in the Mexican War, an able engineer and technician. McClellan kept the order twelve days without making the arrest, until a report from one of his detectives on an examination by himself of a witness convinced him that he should act in the premises. So he arrested General Stone, saying at the same time to the Secretary of War that the case was too indefinite to warrant the framing of charges.

And General Stone was taken from Washington to Fort Lafayette in New York Harbor, put in solitary confinement, his clothes and effects searched, his letters and papers examined. This was the officer entrusted with direct management of the inauguration parade of March 4, 1861, commander of all troops in defense of Washington in the weeks immediately after Lincoln became President. And friends of Stone said that when Lincoln was first told of charges to be brought against the officer of misconduct at Ball's Bluff, of returning fugitive slaves to their owners, of familiar greetings between himself and his wife to Virginia slaveholders, of correspondence with the enemy, of receiving rebel officers in his camp, of treacherous execution of orders so as to throw victory to the enemy, Lincoln met the news with an incredulous smile. "Oh! I could never believe General Stone would be disloyal!"

Good Massachusetts soldiers who fought valiantly and lost overwhelmingly at Ball's Bluff had written to their Governor John A. Andrew that their commander, General Stone, was in the habit of returning escaped slaves to their masters, forwarding Confederate mail, and associating with secessionists. Andrew replied to his Massachusetts boys that Stone's orders in respect to such matters as returning fugitive slaves should not be obeyed. General Stone wrote to the Adjutant General of the War Department protesting against State interference. The Adjutant General sent the protest on to Governor Andrew. Andrew forwarded it to Senator Sumner, who took the Senate floor and denounced General Stone. Stone wrote a letter to Sumner calculated to bring on a duel, if possible, so that one of the two could kill the other. This letter, seething and alive with contempt for Sumner and for abolitionists as troublemakers, was shown to Lincoln. And a friend of Sumner wrote that Lincoln heard a long story in connection with the letter, pondered, and remarked, "I don't know that I should have written such a letter; but if I had wanted to, I think, under the circumstances—under the circumstances, mind you—I would have had a right to do so."

Unless there were military reasons, said Sumner in the Senate, General Stone "ought to be confronted with his accusers at an early day." He had no opinion on the case, "for I know nothing about it." He was not aware of evidence on which the Senate could act. "Sir, I have seen in various newspapers a most persistent attempt to accord to me and my imagined influence the credit or the discredit of it. This is a mistake. I have been from the beginning an absolute stranger to this arrest. The arrest was made originally without suggestion or hint from me, direct or indirect. I knew nothing about it at the beginning, and know nothing about it now." Seldom did Sumner speak in such forthright Anglo-Saxon with so little of classical phrasing.

The one man who stood out foremost as responsible for throwing General Stone into a cell at Fort Lafayette, and holding him there for months, was Stanton. It was his first notification to the military wing that a political department had power to interfere and punish and stood ready to do so.

On Stanton's announcing to him the news of the arrest of General Stone, the President said, "I suppose you have good reasons for it; and having good reasons, I am glad I knew nothing of it until it was done." Willie Lincoln lay sick with fever, and at a later time in connection with the Stone affair the President wrote, "Owing to sickness in my family, the Secretary of War made the arrest without notifying me that he had it in contemplation." To a Senate request for information three months later the President answered:

In relation to Brigadier-General Stone, I have the honor to state that he was arrested and imprisoned under my general authority, and upon evidence which, whether he be guilty or innocent, required, as appears to me, such proceedings to be had against him for the public safety. I deem it incompatible with the public interest, as also, perhaps, unjust to General Stone, to make a more particular statement of the evidence.

He has not been tried because, in the state of military operations at the time of his arrest and since, the officers to constitute a court martial and for witnesses could not be withdrawn from duty without serious injury to the service. He will be allowed a trial without any unnecessary delay; the charges and specifications will be furnished him in due season, and every facility for his defense will be afforded him by the War Department.

And Stone was held in Fort Lafayette prison one hundred eighty-nine days, released without trial and without charges having been preferred against him, then again restored to his brigadier shoulder straps. He rendered loyal service under a Union commander, a former Massachusetts Governor,

Nathaniel P. Banks, who endorsed a letter from Stone to Lincoln asking that "some act, some word, some order, may issue from the executive which shall place my name clear of reproach." Lincoln began the writing of a letter to Banks, the general tone of the unfinished draft indicating that he believed there was no conclusive evidence against Stone. Had he finished the letter, it might have included Stanton's viewpoint: "To hold one commander in prison untried is less harmful in times of great national distress than to withdraw several good officers from active battle-fields to give him a trial. Individuals are nothing; we are contributing thousands of them to save the Union, and General Stone in Fort La Fayette is doing his share in that direction."

Stanton on February 14, 1862, issued "by order of the President" a document the two of them had worked over. It began with a short history of the outbreak of the war: "every department of the government was paralyzed by treason"; armies, ships, navy yards, arsenals, one after another betrayed or abandoned to the enemy; unexpected political combinations and secret societies furthering the disloyalists; municipal authorities powerless and judicial machinery embarrassed; the national capital besieged and cut off from the States. "In this emergency the President felt it his duty to employ with energy the extraordinary powers which the Constitution confides to him in cases of insurrection. He called into the field such military and naval forces, unauthorized by the existing laws, as seemed necessary. He directed measures to prevent the use of the post-office for treasonable correspondence. He subjected passengers to and from foreign countries to new passport regulations, and he instituted a blockade, suspended the writ of *habeas corpus* in various places, and caused persons who were represented to him as being [engaged] or about to engage in disloyal or treasonable practices to be arrested by special civil as well as military agencies, and detained in military custody, when necessary, to prevent them and deter others from such practices. Examinations of such cases were instituted, and some of the persons so arrested have been discharged from time to time, under circumstances or upon conditions compatible, as was thought, with the public safety."

Meantime a favorable change of public opinion, a plainer definition of the line between loyalty and disloyalty, had arrived. "The whole structure of the government is firm and stable; apprehensions of public danger and facilities for treasonable practices have diminished with the passions which prompted heedless persons to adopt them." The insurrection was "believed" to be declining.

"The President," continued this order, "in view of these facts, and anxious to favor a return to the normal course of the administration, as far as regard for the public welfare will allow, directs that all political prisoners or state prisoners now held in military custody be released on their subscribing to a parole engaging them to render no aid or comfort to the enemies in hostility to the United States." To all persons so released and keeping their parole the President granted amnesty for any past offenses of treason or disloyalty. The Secretary of War, however, would at his discretion still hold in jail "any persons detained as spies" or others whose release might be deemed as operating against the public safety. And the sweeping and arbitrary power lodged in the hands of the new Secretary of War was told in a final sentence: "Extraordinary arrests will hereafter be made under the direction of the military authorities alone."

The foresight that had won for Cameron a reputation for wizardry was revealed in the number of unquestioned antislavery Republicans—Owen Lovejoy, George Julian, and A. G. Riddle among them—who were joined to nimble jugglers such as Schuyler Colfax in voting against censure of the ex-Secretary of War. Riddle was puzzled by the course of Thaddeus Stevens, whom he heard "professing to forgive Cameron in consideration of the radical grounds taken against slavery by the Secretary in his annual report." Not many weeks before, recorded Riddle: "I was present when someone announced to Stevens Cameron's appointment as Minister to Russia. 'Ugh! ugh! Send word to the Czar to bring in his things of nights,' was Stevens' response."

The ghost of Simon Cameron stalked Washington when resolutions were passed by Congress ordering payment stopped on certain fraudulent contracts or exorbitant claims and declaring for the principle that "open and fair competition invited by reasonable advertisements for proposals" should be in practice. Members who through the winter had withheld comment on the Committee on Government Contracts rose to criticize and denounce it, Thaddeus Stevens leading. In an eleven-hundred-page report a misprint for which a proofreader was to blame, and one mistake in identification as between two men having the same name, were the only flaws at which Stevens could fling his verbal harpoons. Whether, like Sumner, Stevens had revised his estimate of Cameron since Cameron had taken moderate antislavery ground, or whether Stevens was roiled by the committee's plastering of his protégé Simon Stevens in the Hall's carbine deal, or whether several motives joined, he repeatedly urged that since the eleven-hundred-page report was false in one particular, it was false in all. On the resolution ordering the Secretary of the Treasury to pay for Hall's carbines $12.50 apiece instead of $22 as contracted through Simon Stevens, Thaddeus Stevens moved to lay on the table, moved to amend, and was defeated by a vote of 103 to 28. On a resolution that censured Simon Cameron for "a policy highly injurious to the public service" and for negligence in requiring no guarantees from Alexander Cummings, whom he invested with large moneys, the vote was 79 for to 45 against.

Lincoln's response to the formal record of censure of Cameron was unexpected and took the form of a long message to Senate and House. The House had not struck at him; its language implied Lincoln had been betrayed by two men he had trusted. Yet Lincoln defended those men. He reviewed the outbreak of the war, treason in all departments, and Washington beleaguered, and then gave Congress tumultuous autobiographical paragraphs which were really extended statements of what he had before told Congress in explanation of why he had assumed dictatorial powers. The paragraphs read:

I thereupon summoned my constitutional advisers, the heads of all the departments, to meet on Sunday, the 21st day of April, 1861, at the office of the Navy Department; and then and there, with their unanimous concurrence, I directed that an armed revenue cutter should proceed to sea, to afford protection to the commercial marine and especially the California treasure-ships then on their way to this coast. I also directed the commandant of the navy-yard at Boston to purchase, or charter, and arm as quickly as possible, five steamships for purposes of public defense. I directed the commandant of the navy-yard at Philadelphia to purchase, or charter, and arm an equal number for the same purpose. I directed the commandant at New York to purchase, or charter, and arm an equal number. I directed Commander Gillis to purchase, or charter, and arm and put to sea two other vessels. Similar directions were given to Commodore Du Pont, with a view to the opening of passages by water to and from the capital. I directed the several officers to take the advice and obtain the aid and efficient services in the matter of his Excellency Edwin D. Morgan, the Governor of New York, or, in his absence, George D. Morgan, William M. Evarts, R. M. Blatchford, and Moses H. Grinnell, who were, by my direction, especially empowered by the Secretary of the Navy to act for his department in that crisis, in matters pertaining to the forwarding of troops and supplies for the public defense.

On the same occasion I directed that Governor Morgan and Alexander Cummings, of the city of New York, should be authorized by the Secretary of War, Simon Cameron, to make all necessary arrangements for the transportation of troops and munitions of war, in aid and assistance of the officers of the army of the United States, until communication by mails and telegraph should be completely reëstablished between the cities of Washington and New York. No security was required to be given by them, and either of them was authorized to act in case of inability to consult with the other.

On the same occasion I authorized and directed the Secretary of the Treasury to advance, without requiring security, two millions of dollars of public money to John A. Dix, George Opdyke, and Richard M. Blatchford, of New York, to be used by them in meeting such requisitions as should be directly consequent upon the military and naval measures necessary for the defense and support of the government, requiring them only to act without compensation, and to report their transactions when duly called upon.

The several departments of the government at that time contained so large a number of disloyal persons that it would have been impossible to provide safely through official agents only for the performance of the duties thus confided to citizens favorably known for their ability, loyalty, and patriotism.

The several orders issued upon these occurrences were transmitted by private messengers, who pursued a circuitous way to the seaboard cities, inland, across the States of Pennsylvania and Ohio and the northern lakes. I believe that by these and other similar measures taken in that crisis, some of which were without any authority of law, the government was saved from overthrow. I am not aware that a dollar of the public funds thus confided without authority of law to unofficial persons was either lost or wasted, although apprehensions of such misdirection occurred to me as objections to those extraordinary proceedings, and were necessarily overruled.

He was recalling these transactions because his attention had been called to the House resolution reading:

Resolved, That Simon Cameron, late Secretary of War, by investing Alexander Cummings with the control of large sums of the public money, and authority to purchase military supplies without restriction, without requiring from him any guarantee for the faithful performance of his duties, when the services of competent public officers were available, and by involving the government in a vast number of contracts with persons not legitimately engaged in the business pertaining to the subject-matter of such contracts, especially in the purchase of arms for future delivery, has adopted a policy highly injurious to the public service, and deserves the censure of the House.

He closed with a paragraph of explanatory comment which took all censure off Cameron and placed it on the entire Administration, and which seemed to assume that the situation had been so chaotic and the action so furious that it was a time to let some bygones be bygones.

Congress will see that I should be wanting equally in candor and in justice if I should leave the censure expressed in this resolution to rest exclusively or chiefly upon Mr. Cameron. The same sentiment is unanimously entertained by the heads of departments who participated in the proceedings which the House of Representatives has censured. It is due to Mr. Cameron to say that, although he fully approved the proceedings, they were not moved nor suggested by himself, and that not only the President but all the other heads of departments were at least equally responsible with him for whatever error, wrong, or fault was committed in the premises.

Nicolay and Hay noted: "Cameron gratefully remembered this voluntary and manly defense of his official integrity. He remained one of the most intimate and devoted of Lincoln's personal friends."

The great industrial, iron-coal-and-oil State of Pennsylvania, nearest to Washington and most liable to invasion, was not to be torn by the political warfare and disruption that would have followed the particular sort of degradation Cameron's enemies would have put on him. So many others in the Federal service hoped to get something for nothing out of the Government that to make an example of Cameron alone would be unjust, and to spend time on all who emulated Cameron would leave no time for the Administration to fight the war on hand. A new Secretary of War had been installed who was so equitably just and so feverishly anxious to be exact and open in all government buying and selling that men feared that faults might underlie his marvelous scruples. The unblemished abolitionist Congressman Owen Lovejoy, with a curiously steady light of conscience for a lamp to his feet, might have dropped the word to Lincoln to try Cameron longer. Certain it was that not again, as a year earlier, would Thaddeus Stevens walk in to tell the President that Cameron would steal anything except a red-hot stove.

Yet the unremitting quest of individual profits and personal fortunes, behind war fronts where men were dying for proclaimed sacred causes, made a contrast heavy for the human mind to hold and endure. Van Wyck had not yet learned the answer to his riddle: "The soldier who, borne down

by disease and overcome with fatigue, is found sleeping at his post, you punish with death; while the miscreant who holds his festival at this carnival of
blood rides in his carriage, drinks champagne, and dines with Cabinet ministers, you treat with deferential respect. Do you say Government cannot
banish treason and punish crime?"

CHAPTER 19

WHITE HOUSE CHILDREN

THE boys Tad and Willie, joined by two playmates from Cincinnati, Bud
and Holly Taft, took rags and old clothes and made a doll they named
Jack. In red baggy trousers, with a tight blue jacket and a red fez on his
head, this Jack was a Zouave. And they sentenced Jack to be shot at sunrise
for sleeping on picket duty. They were burying Jack when the head gardener asked, "Why don't you have Jack pardoned?"

Into the White House chased the four boys, upstairs to a desk where
a man dropped his work, heard them, and soberly wrote on a sheet of
Executive Mansion stationery:

> The doll Jack is pardoned.
> By order of the President
> A. Lincoln

To Julia Taft, sister of Bud and Holly, Tad gave this pardon paper, saying there would be no burying of Jack. In a week, however, Jack was hanging by the neck, dangling from the branch of a big bush in the garden, Tad
saying, "Jack was a traitor and a spy."

From Bud, Julia heard one day that the President had sent Bud out to
buy him a pair of rubbers. Bud asked what size. The President glanced at his
feet a moment and said, "The biggest pair you can find." Willie Lincoln
asked Bud, "Why do you call pa 'Mr. President'? You don't call ma 'Mrs.
President.'" Bud explained what he considered proper. The four boys sat
at the foot of the table through a state dinner, talked later about "those
'bassadors all tied up with gold cord," pa looking plain in black, and ma all
dressed up. They discussed why the preacher at the Fourth Presbyterian
Church, as Willie said, "always prayed so long for pa." Bud Taft answered:
"You know your father is President of the United States. 'Course they have
to pray for him a lot." Tad sang:

> Old Abe Lincoln,
> a rail-splitter was he,
> and that's the way
> he'll split the Confederasee.

Willie held that this was "disrespectful to pa." Tad excused himself: "I don't care. Everybody knows pa used to split rails."

The Taft boys one summer Sunday showed Tad and Willie their collection pennies; Sunday school had broken up without the usual collection. Willie Lincoln flashed: "Pa says there is a battle in Virginia. That's big cannon going off that sounds like slamming doors."

The bright, serious, sweet-sixteen Julia Taft kept this on the print of her remembrance. She saw Tad in the vestibule of the White House crash a new ball into a tall mirror. Tad kicked a piece of shattered glass: "Well, it's broke, I don't believe pa'll care." Willie regretted: "It is not pa's looking glass. It belonged to the United States Government." Tad on hearing he would have bad luck for five years, and what to do about it, got a handful of salt and threw it over his left shoulder to sprinkle a velvet carpet. Then he tried saying the Lord's Prayer backward, but gave it up when news came that his goat Nanko had escaped from the stables.

At church one Sunday the Lincoln and Taft families had heard of a lieutenant of the provost guard on the previous Sunday warning some of the worshipers that anyone disturbing the service or leaving before it was over would be arrested and put in the guardhouse. Near by them the children caught sight of the lieutenant sitting in a pew with a straight back and a straight face, rigidly military and stern as a clock of doom.

JULIA TAFT (*to Tad*). See the lieutenant, how still he sits.

TAD (*to Julia*). I bet he wouldn't sit so still if a bee stung him.

JULIA (*to Tad*). Yes, he would.

TAD (*to his father*). Do you think he would sit so still, pa, if a bee was stinging him?

THE PRESIDENT. Yes, I think he would, Tad.

Tad was dashing, valorous, often impudent, Willie the more thoughtful and imaginative. All the main railroad stations from New York to Chicago were in Willie's memory and at his tongue's end. He could call them off, including Troy, Schenectady, Utica, Rome, including Ashtabula, Cleveland, Sandusky, Toledo. He spent hours drawing up timetables and would conduct an imaginary train from Chicago to New York with perfect precision. Also Willie spent hours curled up in a chair enjoying books, a grave, delicate boy. He wrote after Ball's Bluff his "Lines on the Death of Colonel Edward Baker," which he sent to the *National Republican* editor with a note:

> Dear Sir:
> I enclose you my first attempt at poetry.
> Yours truly,
> William W. Lincoln

The verses read:

There was no patriot like Baker,
  So noble and so true;
He fell as a soldier on the field,
  His face to the sky of blue.

His voice is silent in the hall
  Which oft his presence graced.
No more he'll hear the loud acclaim
  Which rang from place to place.

No squeamish notions filled his breast,
   The Union was his theme;
"*No surrender and no compromise,*"
   His day-thought and night's dream.

His Country has her part to play,
   To'rds those he left behind;
His widow and his children all,
   She must always keep in mind.

Thus the eleven-year-old William Wallace Lincoln wrote his first verse and called it an "attempt." When a nine-year-old Willie had gone on a trip with his father and to a playmate wrote a letter describing a room:

Me and father have a nice room to ourselves. We have two little pitchers on a washstand. The smallest one for me, the largest one for father. We have two little towels on top of both pitchers. The smallest one for me, the largest one for father.

We have two little beds in the room. The smallest one for me, the largest one for father. We have two little wash basins. The smallest one for me, the largest one for father.

The formal methods of officialdom and perhaps something of his father's desire for accuracy of statement influenced Willie and he wrote one letter:

Washington, D.C., September 30, 1861
Executive Mansion

Dear Henry,

The last letter you sent to me arrived in due time, which was on Saturday. My companions and I are raising a battalion. When I came here, I waited until the beginning of June, and then joined another boy in trying to get up a regiment. We failed, however, and I then attempted to muster a Company. That soon broke up. Thereafter a boy stated he commanded a battalion, and my Company and I at once joined, believing that he spoke the truth, but we found out that was not the case. Disappointed in every way we set to work and raised one, which is in a high state of efficiency and discipline.

    I am
       Dear Henry
          Yours Sincerely
               William W. Lincoln

In his diary Attorney General Bates wrote that the boy Willie was too much "idolized" by his parents. The boy had rare lights—and the father and mother made much of him.

Willie Lincoln went riding on his pony in a chilly rain and fell sick with a cold and fever in February of '62, at a time when a White House ball and reception was planned. In Washington society ran a rumor that Mrs. Lincoln had shown a friend eighty declinations to attend the ball, Senator Wade writing on a card: "Are the President and Mrs. Lincoln aware that there is a civil war? If they are not, Mr. and Mrs. Wade are, and for that reason decline to participate in feasting and dancing."

The President spoke of the ball to Miss Dorothea Dix, wanted to stop it, had it announced officially that there would be no dancing. "But the Marine band at the foot of the steps filled the house with music while the boy lay dying above," wrote one woman. "A sadder face than that of the President I have rarely seen. He was receiving at the large door of the East Room, speaking to the people as they came, but feeling so deeply that he spoke of what he felt and thought, instead of welcoming the guests. To General Frémont he at once said that his son was very ill and he feared for the result. On seeing his sad face and grieved appearance, the feeling with which we had gone gave way to pity, and after expressing our hopes for the lad's recovery we passed on to make our respects to the President's wife. The ball was becoming a ghastly failure."

Earlier that evening Mrs. Elizabeth Keckley, a comely mulatto who served as dressmaker and maid, had arranged Mrs. Lincoln's hair and helped her into a dress of white satin trimmed in black lace, with a surprise of a long trail in the height of daring fashion. In this new apparel she entered the guest room where Willie Lincoln lay abed. Mrs. Keckley noted: "As she swept through the room, Mr. Lincoln was standing with his back to the fire, his hands behind him, and his eyes on the carpet. His face wore a thoughtful, solemn look. The rustling of the satin dress attracted his attention. He looked at it a few moments; then, in his quaint, quiet way remarked, 'Whew! our cat has a long tail to-night!' Mrs. Lincoln did not reply. The President added: 'Mother, it is my opinion, if some of that tail was nearer the head, it would be in better style.'"

And, noted Mrs. Keckley, he glanced at her bare arms and neck. "She had a beautiful neck and arm, and low dresses were becoming to her. She turned away with a look of offended dignity, and presently took the President's arm, and both went down-stairs to their guests, leaving me alone with the sick boy." During the hours of the reception Mrs. Lincoln several times left the party below to come upstairs and stand over Willie's bed.

During the next few days Willie called for Bud Taft, who came and held his hand in Willie's. The President would come in, lean over, and stroke Willie's hair. "Better go to bed, Bud," he said one night. Bud answered, "If I go he will call for me." Still another night Lincoln came in, found Bud asleep, picked him up and carried him off to another room.

A few days later the mystic and inevitable messenger came for the boy. Elizabeth Keckley wrote, "The light faded from his eyes, and the death-dew gathered on his brow." She had been on watch but did not see the end, telling of it: "I was worn out with watching, and was not in the room when Willie died, but was immediately sent for. I assisted in washing and dressing him, and then laid him on the bed, when Mr. Lincoln came in." He lifted the cover from the face of his child, gazed at it long, and murmured, "It is hard, hard to have him die!" The mother wept long hours, moaned and shook with grief.

They closed down the lids over the blue eyes of the boy, parted his brown hair, put flowers from his mother in his pale, crossed hands, and soldiers, Senators, Cabinet officers, foreign Ministers, came to the funeral. The mother could not come. She was too far spent.

The body was later sent west to Illinois for burial. And the mother clutched at his memory and if his name was mentioned her voice shook and the tears came. "She could not bear to look upon his picture," said Mrs. Keckley. "And after his death she never crossed the threshold of the Guest's

Room in which he died, or the Green Room in which he was embalmed."

Also Mrs. Keckley told of a scene: "In one of her paroxysms of grief the President bent kindly over his wife, took her by the arm, and gently led her to the window. With a stately, solemn gesture, he pointed to the lunatic asylum. 'Mother, do you see that large white building on the hill yonder? Try and control your grief, or it will drive you mad, and we may have to send you there.'" And though his words may not have been as direct and abrupt as Mrs. Keckley recalled them, he gave her a warning of tragedy impending for herself. She had wet with her tears a clipping pasted in a scrapbook telling of the funeral: "He was his father's favorite. They were intimates—often seen hand in hand. And there sat the man, bent now with the load at both heart and brain—staggering under a blow like the taking from him of his child. His men of power sat around him—McClellan, with a moist eye when he bowed to the prayer, as I could see from where I stood."

Then Tad lay abed—and Senator Browning wrote in his dairy: "The President's youngest Son is very ill, and they would not consent for Mrs Browning to leave them this morning I remained till 12 O'clock . . . leaving Mrs Browning there. Returned at night and sat up part of night"

With Tad's recovery the White House began to resume a normal tone, though the Taft children came no more. The President had sent for Bud to have a last look at Willie before his old playmate was put into the casket. And Bud had to be carried from the room and was not well for days. At a later time Julia Taft went to a White House Saturday afternoon reception given by Mrs. Lincoln; and Julia saw that when Tad's eyes lighted on her, on Bud's sister, he threw himself on the floor and screamed and kicked till he was carried out by the servants. "You must excuse him," said Mrs. Lincoln to her guests. "You know what he remembers."

Tad had seen bright and strange moments in the companionship of the Taft children. The sudden appearance of Julia Taft shocked him with vivid memories. He may have recalled such moments as Julia had in mind when she later wrote: "Willie gave me a little watch charm someone had given him. He said, 'I will give you my little gold dog, Julie, because I love you, and you must keep it always.' Dear Willie! He was pure gold if the little dog was not. But I have always kept it."

A *New York Evening Post* reporter said of the President as he saw him then, "Since his late bereavement he looks sad and careworn, but is in very good health again," available for public business about eighteen hours out of twenty-four. "He is frequently called up three or four times in a night to receive important messages from the West."

The grief over Willie was hard to shake off, however, for a month later in answering a letter which should have had an earlier reply the President wrote of "a domestic affliction" which "has delayed me so long."

A fire alarm rang out one night many weeks after Willie's death. The White House stables were burning. A guard saw a tall and hatless man come running from the White House, spring like a deer over a boxwood hedge, and call, "Have the horses been taken out?" Getting the answer No, he asked why not, and with his own hands burst open the stable door. Inside everything seemed on fire. He hesitated a moment, then was making ready to rush in when men caught him and held him back. One suddenly had the idea that the man they were holding was the President of the United States and it might be that the stables had been set on fire to lure him outdoors for assassination. Captain Bennett of the Union Light Guard and others hurried him back into the Executive Mansion, his home. There from a window of the East Room he looked at the dwindling walls as they fell from fire. "He was weeping," said one of the guards. Tad told why. In the stable was a pony that had been Willie's favorite companion. And the man had rushed out hoping to save the pony.

CHAPTER 20

DONELSON—GRANT—SHILOH

INTRODUCING a West Coast man to President Lincoln one day, Senator McDougall of California said, "Mr. President, this is General Ryan, a loyal neighbor of mine, who can build a cathedral and preach in it, a ship and sail it, or an engine and run it." The North had this versatility.

Lincoln called to Washington a St. Louis man who had spent many days on the bottom sand and mud of the Mississippi River, salvaging ships with a diving bell he invented. Born in Indiana, this man as a boy had seen the family lose everything by fire in St. Louis; and he peddled apples on the street, became a dry-goods clerk, worked as a purser on a river boat, designed new and powerful machinery to pump out sand and water and lift a sunken boat, cargo and hull, to where it could be refitted and operate again. Selling this business, he started a glassworks, the first west of the Ohio River, went bankrupt to the tune of $25,000, and with cash from his creditors started once more in steamboat-salvaging. He had paid off his debts, taken a trip to Europe with his wife, and was doing very well when he came to the White House to see Lincoln. They talked about the best way to carry on the war on the Western rivers.

James B. Eads, for that was the man's name, went back to St. Louis and under government contract got 4,000 men scattered over the country working on his plans. In one hundred days he had ready eight iron-plated, steam-propelled gunboats.

These gunboats and more, carrying over 140 large-caliber guns, made up a flotilla commanded by Andrew H. Foote, a Connecticut Yankee Puritan sea dog, who in 1856 had lost 40 of his own men and killed 400 Chinese in the Canton River of China, who never swore nor drank nor allowed intoxicating liquor on shipboard, and whose prayer meetings and systems of religious instruction among seamen were often discussed in naval and other circles. When a preacher was sick Foote mounted the pulpit and delivered a sermon. An earnest man was chief skipper of the iron turtles of Uncle Sam's inland navy.

On February 6 of '62 Commodore Foote and his gunboats escorted a line of steamboats up the Tennessee River carrying eighteen regiments under Brigadier General Ulysses S. Grant. They crowded the decks watching the scenery, 18,000 troops, cornhuskers, teamsters, rail-splitters, shop-

Fitting out gunboats at Cincinnati

men, factory hands, college students, from Iowa, and Nebraska, from Illinois, Indiana, Ohio, Missouri, many of them not yet old enough to vote. They had heard, these boys, that the hard life of war with its danger, hunger, sleeping in the rain and snow, tries out a fellow so that he finds whether he's a real man or not. Also they had heard of adventure, bravery, glory, history, and many believed that war would tell them things no man can explain to another—he must go for himself. Also many of them had a mystic belief that the Mississippi River should fly one flag from upper Minnesota to the Gulf, and the Union of States should be held together from Atlantic to Pacific. From the decks these prairie boys watched the river scenery.

The gunboats stopped at Fort Henry, filled it with exploding shells, and troops marched in and took its Confederate flag. The garrison had left for Fort Donelson, twelve miles away on the Cumberland River. Grant marched his army this twelve miles across country to Fort Donelson in fair weather, so warm and balmy that thousands of soldiers threw away their blankets, overcoats, or both.

Foote took his gunboats up to the Ohio River, up the Cumberland, and exchanging shots with the Fort Donelson guns was disabled so that he had to steam upriver. This left Grant with 27,000 troops, counting new arrivals, to contest with 18,000 troops inside a fort. Commanding his right wing he had John A. McClernand, Illinois lawyer and Congressman whom Lincoln had appointed a brigadier; in the center was Lew Wallace, an Indiana man who hoped when the war was over to write novels; at the left was General Charles F. Smith, a hard drinker and a profane man who had been an instructor at West Point when Grant was a cadet. Heading the first brigade was Lincoln's old associate in politics and law, Richard J. Oglesby. Heading one Illinois regiment was John A. Logan, who expected to meet among the Southern troops some of the boys from his home county in southern Illinois.

Before the fighting began a cold wind came, snow fell, the roads froze, and in ten-above-zero weather men fired and loaded their muskets, and in the night huddled and shivered, seeking fences, brush, trees, logs, to keep off the wind. Neither side dared light a bivouac fire. Men and boys were found next morning frozen stiff.

Grant went aboard Foote's flagship to arrange for the gunboats, though disabled, to keep up the best fire they could from a distance so as to worry the cannoneers in the fort. Riding back from this conference, Grant found his right wing battered and wavering. Some word dropped led him to order Confederate prisoners searched. They were carrying three days' rations in their haversacks. Grant sent word along the line that the enemy in desperation was trying to cut its way out and retreat. "Gentlemen, the position on the right must be retaken."

General Charles F. Smith, sober but profane, made a speech telling his troops he was a regular-army man and could not help going into the war, but they had volunteered to fight and now was the time. He led his lines into withering fire that dropped hundreds of his men. Sharpshooters in rifle pits tried to bring him down, but he carried a charm. He had been accused of disloyalty to the Union and had answered, "Wait till we get into battle." He was showing what military reports call gallantry; handsome, erect, a soldier at sixty. "I was nearly scared to death," a soldier said, "but I saw the old man's white mustache over his shoulder, and went on."

Nearly all the correspondents mentioned the personal quality of the individual soldiers on both sides. They had come for fighting and they fought. "Cold and hungry, with garments stiff with frost, the soldiers were still hopeful and firm," wrote one. "I did not find a single discouraged man, or one who, if he were so, would admit it. The universal sentiment was, as bluff Colonel Oglesby expressed it, 'We came here to take that fort, and we will take it.' Our troops fought with the coolness of veterans and the desperation of devils. In the thickest of the fight, where officers had to remove the dead bodies of their men out of the way of the backward wheels, regiments coolly performed maneuvers which Scott in his tactics pronounces impossible to be made on the battlefield. . . . When one regiment ran out of cartridges and was ordered back to be replaced, soldiers, grim with smoke and powder, would angrily inquire for what, and beg to be allowed to use the bayonet." The *Richmond Dispatch* correspondent wrote, "The enemy are represented to have fought nobly, far better than the Northern soldiers have ever fought before; but most, if not all of them, were from the West, sturdy farmers and backwoodsmen, and, like ourselves, accustomed to the use of arms."

On Sunday, February 16, 1862, telegrams began trickling into the War Department at Washington. General Simon B. Buckner, commanding Fort Donelson, had sent a messenger to Grant asking for "terms of capitulation" and Grant replied: "No terms except an unconditional and immediate surrender can be accepted. I propose to move immediately upon your works." And the Confederate commander was surrendering the fort and 13,828 prisoners. The battle losses were: Union, 500 killed, 2,108 wounded, 224 missing; Confederate, 231 killed, 1,534 wounded.

The victory clinched Kentucky to the Union, gave a foothold in Tennessee, sent Union armies two hundred miles forward into enemy territory. More than anything else it lighted up the gloom of the North. Over the country were outpourings of people to celebrate with bonfires, fireworks, bells ringing, whistles blowing, meetings, speeches, subscriptions for the wounded. "Men embraced each other on the street."

Through the columns of the *New York Tribune* Stanton gave the country a letter saying: "The glory of our recent victories belongs to the gallant officers and soldiers that fought the battles. No share of it belongs to me." Much had been said of "military combinations and organizing victory" and the War Secretary heard such phrases with apprehension. "They commenced in infidel France with the Italian campaign, and resulted in Waterloo. Who can organize victory? Who can combine the elements of success on the battlefield? We owe our recent victories to the Spirit of the Lord, that moved our soldiers to rush into battle, and filled the hearts of our enemies with dismay. The inspiration that conquered in battle was in the hearts of the soldiers and from on high; and wherever there is the same inspiration there will be the same results. . . . Battles are to be won now and by us in the same and only manner that they were ever won by any people, or in any age, since the days of Joshua, by boldly pursuing and striking the foe."

Lincoln had first taken particular notice of the Donelson victor when he read the proclamation Grant issued in September to the citizens of Paducah, Kentucky: "I have come among you, not as an enemy, but as your friend and fellow-citizen, not to injure or annoy you, but to respect the rights, and to defend and enforce the rights of all loyal citizens. . . . I have nothing to do with opinions. I shall deal only with armed rebellion and its aiders and abettors. . . ." Lincoln commented, "The modesty and brevity of that address show that the officer issuing it understands the situation, and is the proper man to command there at this time." Also Lincoln heard from Swett one day of Grant's threatening to shoot speculators in hay and army supplies who came to Cairo and interfered. Lincoln told Swett to "look out," as Grant generally kept his word.

The country listened to hear what kind of a man this Ulysses S. Grant was. He broke over the rules of war, seemed to be an original. When he left Fort Henry marching to Fort Donelson he had only about as many soldiers as there were in Fort Donelson, while military theory required that he should have five men to one in the fort to be taken. He expected reinforcements, of course, but they might not arrive. Also he fought in winter weather over mud and through ice, sleet, and snow, even though spring was only a few weeks off. It looked a little Napoleonic, but on close-up scrutiny of Grant nobody could say he was another Napoleon without laughing.

He was an Ohio boy who graduated at West Point as number 21 in a class of 39. He was marked down for being late at roll call, for not having his coat buttoned or brushed, for not keeping his musket clean, and for wearing another coat, jacket, or cap than required by regulations. He slouched at West Point, saying before he went there that he did not hope to get through. He slouched afterward. The way he made war was slouchy. He had not studied Napoleon nor joined the Napoleon Club. He was an original. As a boy twelve years old hauling logs for his father's tanyard at Georgetown he made a trip for a final load but arrived when the gang of workers who lifted the logs onto the wagon with handspikes had gone home. The boy slanted a sugar tree from the wagon, hitched a horse to one log after another and snaked it onto the wagon. The father was amazed. Not even the grown men in that neighborhood had thought of so simple a way of getting a load of logs onto a wagon.

At West Point he rode a horse over a hurdle 6 feet 6, a new record. At Monterey in the Mexican War he went for ammunition relief, riding under fire in Comanche style, clinging to the saddle with one leg while holding his head and body close to the side of the horse away from the enemy. He could break horses and had tried his hand at breaking troops who had not learned discipline. An odd number. He loved horses, dogs. But he never hunted, could not shoot animals. He was 5 feet 8 in height, wore whiskers, was nearly always a little disheveled, even sat for his picture with coat or hair in disorder. He had quiet manners, gravity, gray eyes, and a face with economy of expression. At Fort Vancouver on the West Coast in 1854 no works nor projects challenged him. He was homesick, carried in his inside coat pocket a worn pack of letters from his wife, one day showing the men at this army post a letter page inked with a baby handprint—his second boy, Ulysses, Jr., two thousand miles away with the mother.

Grant had married her without a regular proposal; they were buggy-driving across a flooded bridge when she cried, "I'm going to cling to you no matter what happens," and safely over, he asked, "How would you like to cling to me for the rest of your life?"

One day there came to Fort Vancouver a locket holding a long thin braid of a woman's hair interwoven with a little curl of a child's hair; this Grant wore around his neck. Why did he drink harder at this time? Was it loneliness for home? For he was warned that as a captain his drunkenness was bad for the regiment. He wrote out a blank resignation and gave it to the colonel; it was to be dated and sent to the War Department if whisky again got the best of him, which it did. He quit the army, saying, "Whoever hears of me in ten years will hear of a well-to-do old Missouri farmer."

Grant cleared land on 80 acres near St. Louis let to him by his wife's father. He became accustomed to two slaves given to his wife by her father, a slaveholder. He hauled wood ten miles into St. Louis at $10 a cord, wearing blue army overalls tucked into his boots, sometimes eating, drinking, and talking over old times with some West Point or Mexican War comrade of old days. He built himself a two-story house of logs, a masterpiece of simple design and craftsmanship, and named the place Hardscrabble. The word would pass for a nickname; it was hard scrabbling he had fallen on. His hands grew hard and horny, his shoulders bent from work. Ague and rheumatism came on him as he tried to make that farm pay in the year that Abe Lincoln was wrestling in debates with Douglas just across the river. Casting a ballot for Buchanan in 1856, he said he did it to vote against Frémont.

They traded Hardscrabble for a house and lot in St. Louis. As a real-estate salesman Grant failed. Friends said ague and rheumatism still held him; chills shook him on spring afternoons, weakened him so that he was dizzy and had to be helped to the omnibus he rode home in. He looked glum and felt useless. Applying for the job of county engineer, with thirty-five exceptionally solid and respectable citizens vouching for his able and sober qualities, he was rejected; he was a Democrat and the Republican county commissioners picked a nice German of the right party. His father advanced money. The family moved to Galena, Illinois, where he was selling hides to shoemakers and harness- and saddle-makers, his income $800 a year, when the war commenced. At a public meeting in Galena after Sumter Captain Grant was elected chairman. He wrote the Government at Washington offering his services, and the Government not answering, he went to Springfield, Illinois, was made colonel, and took a regiment to Missouri.

Chaplain James B. Crane, bringing him the *Missouri Democrat* one day in August, said, "I see that you are made brigadier-general." "Well, sir," said Grant, "I had no suspicion of it. It never came from any request of mine. That's some of Washburne's work. I knew Washburne in Galena. He was a strong Republican and I was a Democrat, and I thought from that he never liked me very much. We never had more than a street or business acquaintance. But when the war broke out I found that he had something to do with having me commissioned colonel and I suppose this is more of his work." (Congressman Washburne was closest of all Illinois Congressmen to Lincoln—the lone man who met Lincoln at the Washington depot after the secret night ride through Baltimore.)

Slow in getting a uniform, Grant wrote his sister Mary weeks after his appointment, "If I get a uniform and get where I can have my daguerreo-type taken, your wish in that respect shall be gratified." She had asked him how long the war would last, and he wrote on August 12, 1861: "I have changed my mind so much that I don't know what to think. That the rebels will be so badly whipped by April next that they cannot make a stand any-where, I don't doubt. But they are so dogged that there is no telling when they may be subdued." He had made a trip back to Galena and when one citizen said, "Some day you will be a candidate for high civic honors," he answered, "I would like to be Mayor of Galena, then I might get a sidewalk built from my home to the depot." When first asked about being a colonel, he murmured, "I would rather like a regiment, yet there are few men really competent to command a thousand soldiers, and I doubt whether I am one of them." Having been in Frémont's office, Grant commented: "He sat in a room in a full uniform with his maps before him. When you went in he would point out one line or another in a mysterious manner, never asking you to take a seat. You left without the least idea of what he meant or what he wanted you to do."

When ordered by Frémont to "make a demonstration" against Confed-erates at Belmont, he did more than ordered. He was expected merely to harass them so that they would not send reinforcements to another Confed-erate command. As he took 3,000 troops on steamboats down river he changed his intentions. "I saw that the officers and men were elated at the prospect of at last having the opportunity of doing what they had volun-teered to do—fight the enemies of their country. I did not see how I could maintain discipline, or retain the confidence of my command, if we should return to Cairo without an effort to do something." So he landed them, marched through cornfields and scrub timberland, charged, and drove the Confederates out of camp. And while the cornhuskers and shopmen were looting the camp, yelling, cheering, making patriotic speeches, some drink-ing whisky, the reinforced Confederates came back, and an officer rode up to Grant calling, "We are surrounded and will have to surrender." And Grant was cool. "I guess not. If we are surrounded we must cut our way out as we cut our way in." Which they did. And Grant was the last man to ride his horse up the gangplank of the last boat to leave. Of his 3,000 men against an enemy force of 7,000, Grant lost 90 killed, 173 wounded, 235 missing, while the enemy lost 261 killed, 427 wounded, 278 missing.

A horse was shot from under him during the fighting, and he wrote his sister Mary: "It was my bay horse (cost me $140) that was shot. I also lost the little pony, my fine saddle and bridle, and the common one. What I lost cost about $250." To his wife he wrote: "I feel proud to command such men. . . . We accomplished all that we went for, and more." He did not write his wife that after boarding the steamer he had lain down a few mo-ments on a sofa in the cabin and had no sooner got up than a bullet crashed into the head of the sofa where his own head had been.

Grant did not like show-off. He seldom swore; admirers said, "No im-pure word ever escaped his lips." His profanity was mostly limited to "dog-

gone it" and "by lightning." A near relative put in an application for a contract to supply the Cairo district with leather, Grant writing on the paper a
request that it be *not* granted, as the applicant was a kinsman of his.

Where Napoleon's big word was "glory," Grant's was "duty." He asked
little for himself, writing his father, "While on duty at Springfield [Illinois]
I there saw so much pulling and hauling for favors that I determined never
to ask for anything, and never have, not even a colonelcy." On his brigadier
appointment the officers of his regiment requested to be attached to his
command, and he wrote to his father, "This I do not want you to read to
others, for I very much dislike speaking of myself." To a letter from his
sister and children he would reply with a closing paragraph: "Tell the children to learn their lessons, mind their grandma, and be good children. I
should like very much to see them. To me they are all obedient and good.
I may be partial, but they seem to me to be children to be proud of."

Something of the essential of his slouching, backward, toiling ways was in
the letter he wrote his sister on February 9 just before taking Donelson.
"What the next few days may bring forth I can not tell you. I intend to
keep the ball moving as lively as possible. . . . You have no conception of
the amount of labor I have to perform. An army of men all helpless, looking
to the commanding officer for every supply. Your plain brother, however,
has as yet no reason to feel himself unequal to the task, and fully believes he
will carry on a successful campaign. I do not speak boastfully but utter a
presentiment." He had known General Gideon J. Pillow, who ran away
from Fort Donelson after it was attacked, giving over command to Buckner;
and Grant had written his sister months before as to Pillow: "I do not say
he would shoot himself, ah, no! I am not so uncharitable as many who served
under him in Mexico. I think, however, he might report himself wounded
on the receipt of a very slight scratch, received hastily in any way, and
might irritate the sore until he convinced himself that he had been wounded
by the enemy."

The country had now nicknamed him "Unconditional Surrender" Grant.
When he wrote the Confederate commander the famous note using those
words he had been waked out of a sleep in a Negro cabin at gray dawn,
with snow blowing outside and no fire within. General Charles F. Smith,
sober but profane, was with him. Grant read Buckner's request for "terms
of capitulation" and asked, "Well, what do you think of it?" Smith: "I
think, no terms with the traitors, by God!" Then Grant wrote swiftly on
a cracker-box desk and handed the note to the white-mustached West Point
instructor of old days, who blurted, "By God, it could not be better!"

Then had come the surrender. Buckner told Grant, "If I had been in
command you would not have reached the fort so easily." "If you had," rejoined Grant, "I should have waited for reinforcements. But I knew Pillow
would never come out of his works to fight."

And Grant had walked away from the Union officers and followed
Buckner till the two of them were alone. Then he offered Buckner his purse,
all the money he had. Thus Buckner told it at a later time. It was the first

day Grant had seen Buckner since 1854 in San Francisco, when Buckner lent him the money to get back home and try farming in Missouri. Of this minor incident, naturally, the wide world knew nothing.

Grant wrote to Congressman Washburne: "I feel very grateful to you for having placed me in the position to have had the honor of commanding such an army and at such a time. I only trust that I have not nor will not disappoint you." Underhand work against Grant started with speculators and contractors who had been refused passes, favors, and been dealt with sternly. Grant had gone so far as to suggest officially to Halleck the need of a law providing that "all fraudulent contractors be impressed into the ranks, or, still better, into the gunboat service, where they could have no chance of deserting." These war-profit-seekers had the collusion of high military men in the spreading of stories to discredit him. "General Grant left his command without any authority and went to Nashville," Halleck wired McClellan. "His army seems to be as much demoralized by the victory of Fort Donelson as was that of the Potomac by the defeat of Bull Run. It is hard to censure a successful general immediately after a victory, but I think he richly deserves it. I can get no returns, no reports, no information of any kind from him. Satisfied with his victory, he sits down and enjoys it without any regard to the future." McClellan believed he understood the case, and wired back, "Do not hesitate to arrest Grant at once if the good of the service requires it and place C. F. Smith in command." Halleck wired again: "A rumor has just reached me that since the taking of Fort Donelson General Grant has resumed his former bad habits [meaning drink]. . . . I do not deem it advisable to arrest him at present but have placed General Smith in command of the expedition up the Tennessee." Still later, when it was shown that Grant had gone to Nashville to see the commander of forces there, Buell, and to get on with the war, Halleck told Grant it was McClellan who had directed Smith to be put at the head of Grant's forces. Of his own telegrams to McClellan, Halleck chose to say little.

The batch of wire communications between Halleck and McClellan showed nothing so peculiarly human as jealousy, a strange gnawing worry on the part of Halleck and McClellan because suddenly a fresh unknown performer had eclipsed them each as a military artist, had dimmed their luster.

Against intrigue, connivance, and slander, Lincoln gave to Grant the stars of a major general. The President was more than interested in this plain fighter who had given the Union cause its first victories worth mentioning. Lincoln saw among the driving motives in the Fort Donelson victory the passion of the Northwest, his own region, for nationalism, for an unbreakable Union of States. The geographical necessity involved was pointed out as early as May, 1861, in the publication *Once a Week* in London: "What the reason is we hardly know; but there seems to be a disposition on both sides the water to disparage Mr. Lincoln. Not only is he blamed for inaction; but the quality of his action is found fault with in a way which appears to really impartial people, unjust. . . . The share that the great North-West is claiming in the struggle seems not to be attended to on our side the water; but it is highly important. The stout and prodigious population there have learned by the Kansas question how to appreciate the South,—or its aggressive forces at least. Their pride in their first President renders them intensely loyal. Their commerce is imperilled by the secession of the lower Mississippi States; and it is certainly the opinion of good judges in the older parts of the Union, that when the Western men begin to swarm down the Mississippi, and attack the seceding States in rear, while a blockade is instituted at sea, they will leave little to be done elsewhere."

The laughter at McClellan now was wry, bitter. The Western forces had battled and won big points sooner than commanded in Lincoln's general order setting February 22 as the day for a general movement of land and sea forces. Washington's Birthday came while McClellan's colossal Army of the Potomac kept to its tents and winter huts around Washington. Johnston near by at Manassas had in his Confederate army less than one man for McClellan's three. Jefferson Davis was aware Johnston was far outnumbered, for he wrote to Johnston on February 28, 1862, "Your opinion that your position may be turned whenever the enemy shall choose to advance, and that he will be ready to take the field before yourself, clearly indicates prompt effort to disencumber yourself of everything that would interfere with your rapid movement when necessary." Davis wrote more in this vein, adding, "I am making diligent efforts to reinforce your columns." It was not strange Johnston should write one of his generals, "McClellan seems not to value time especially."

A clerk who handled much of the White House mail, William O. Stoddard, noted that Lincoln was "intensely, absorbingly interested" in the February 22 advance which he had ordered and that he expected some kind of a forward movement. A staff officer from McClellan was let in by the doorkeeper and began respectful explanations of why the advance could not be made on February 22. "Why?" asked the President. The officer murmured, "The pontoon trains are not ready," and was interrupted by the outburst, "Why in hell and damnation *ain't* they ready?" and as Stoddard saw it: "The officer could think of no satisfactory reply, but turned very hastily and left the room. Mr. Lincoln turned to the table and resumed the work before him, but wrote at about double his ordinary speed. Little apology is called for by the precise manner of his expression; entirely at variance from his habit of speech, it was extorted from him by the awful pressure of months concentrated in the intense irritation of an instant."

Lincoln now stepped publicly into the handling of the Army of the Potomac, to the extent of publishing on March 7 and 8 his General War Orders No. 2 and No. 3. One directed McClellan to organize his army for active field operations into four corps, Lincoln naming the generals to command. The second ordered that whatever the field operations might take, enough troops should be left in and about Washington to leave the capital secure. This and other matters brought McClellan to the White House for a call on the President. Affairs had changed since the weeks when Lincoln sat with his hat in hand in the reception room at McClellan's headquarters, sometimes being let in to see his General in Chief, sometimes not. It was Sunday, March 9, 1862, and while McClellan sat in conference with Lincoln and Stanton a message came which upset McClellan, though it was no surprise to the others. The news was that the rebel batteries on the Potomac River were abandoned, and Johnston's army at Manassas had moved out of its entrenchments, broken from winter quarters, and moved southward, leaving as mementoes many "Quaker guns"—logs on wheels, painted to look like cannon.

McClellan was shocked into action. That very Sunday he ordered his army to march on the enemy's deserted camp. From the field at three o'clock the next morning he telegraphed Stanton, "The troops are in motion." He arrived at Bull Run Creek, at Manassas, and found it as reported—empty. Then he marched his army back again to Washington. For the benefit of those asking why he did not push on, find the enemy, and attack, he let it be known he was giving his troops a practice maneuver; they were learning to relieve themselves of "impediments" and move in light marching order. Also he passed the word to inner circles that the enemy had learned of his plans to attack from the Peninsula and was therefore hurrying toward Richmond for its defense. Nathaniel Hawthorne, then in Washington, wrote his impression: "On their march toward Manassas, and almost with their first step into Virginia mud the phantasmagoria of a countless host and impregnable ramparts, before which they had so long remained quiescent, dissolved quite away. It was as if General McClellan had thrust his sword into a gigantic enemy, and, beholding him suddenly collapse, had discovered to himself and the world, that he had merely punctured an enormously swollen bladder."

Shouts, cheers, an eager uproar from the ranks and lines of troops, had greeted McClellan when Hawthorne went out to see a review. "If he is a coward, or a traitor, or a humbug, or anything less than a brave, true, and able man," wrote Hawthorne to his wife, "that mass of intelligent soldiers, whose lives and honor he had in charge, were utterly deceived, and so was the present writer; for they believed in him, and so did I; and had I stood in their ranks, I should have shouted with the lustiest of them." This was the dress-parade McClellan. He had a way with him. Soon after this review Hawthorne wrote to his daughter Rose: "Tell mamma that the outcry opened against McClellan, since the enemy's retreat from Manassas, is really terrible, and almost universal; because it is found that we might have taken their fortifications with perfect ease six months ago, they being defended chiefly by wooden guns. Unless he achieves something wonderful within a week, he will be removed from command, and perhaps shot—at least I hope so; for I never did more than half believe in him."

Besides delays there were peculiar blunders. McClellan, for instance, planned a permanent bridge at Harper's Ferry to be made of canalboats. He telegraphed for cavalry, artillery, and a division of infantry, intending that they should cross the bridge and move up the Shenandoah Valley. So far, so good. But when the canalboats came up the Potomac and arrived at the lift locks at Harper's Ferry it was found that they were 6 inches too wide to pass. Therefore no bridge—and $1,000,000 thrown away. When McClellan came back to Washington saying he was "well satisfied with what had been accomplished," he wrote in a memorandum for the War Department, "While up the river I learned that the President was dissatisfied with the state of affairs; but, on my return here, understood from the Secretary of War that upon learning the whole state of the case the President was fully satisfied."

When McClellan later tried to make clear what was wrong in the situation, he emphasized the point that Stanton had a regular policy "to prevent personal interviews between the President and myself"—this from the man who had during the previous winter more than once refused the President admittance to his headquarters for an interview! By keeping the President and him apart "he [Stanton] was thus enabled to say one thing to the President and exactly the opposite to me."

On March 8, however, which was the day the President issued his general order that of whatever troops went into field action enough should be left to hold Washington secure, McClellan had his chance to get as long and full an interview as he liked with the President. He was sent for and arrived at the White House at 7:30 in the morning. "I found him in his office," wrote McClellan. "He appeared much concerned about something, and soon said that he wished to talk with me about 'a very ugly matter.' I asked what it was; and, as he still hesitated, I said that the sooner and more directly such things were approached the better." And the interview, as reported by McClellan, went on:

"He referred to the Harper's Ferry affair (the boats being too wide for the lift-locks, etc.), upon which I found that the secretary had deceived me when he said the President was satisfied. I told him what had passed between the secretary and myself, at which he was much surprised. He told me that he had never heard of my memorandum or of any explanation on my part. I then gave him my statement of the matter, with which he expressed himself entirely satisfied.

"He then adverted to the more serious—and ugly—matter, and now the effects of the intrigues by which he had been surrounded became apparent. He said that it had been represented to him (and he certainly conveyed to me the distinct impression that he regarded these representations as well founded) that my plan of campaign . . . was conceived with the traitorous intent of removing its defenders from Washington, and thus giving over to the enemy the capital and the government, thus left defenceless.

"It is difficult to understand that a man of Lincoln's intelligence could give ear to such abominable nonsense. I was seated when he said this, concluding with the remark that it did look to him much like treason. Upon this I arose, and, in a manner perhaps not altogether decorous towards the chief magistrate, desired that he should retract the expression, telling him that I could permit no one to couple the word treason with my name.

"He was much agitated, and at once disclaimed any idea of considering me a traitor, and said that he merely repeated what others had said, and that he did not believe a word of it. I suggested caution in the use of language, and again said that I would permit no doubt to be thrown upon my intentions, whereupon he again apologized and disclaimed any purpose of impugning my motives."

It was the next day that McClellan was at the White House with Lincoln and Stanton when the news came of Manassas evacuated, and McClellan for the first time moved his army as if to fight and make war—returning as fast as he went and explaining it as a practice march for soldiers who had as yet much to learn.

McClellan had outcamped Beauregard, wrote one newspaper satirist: "It was a contest of inertia and our side out-sat the other."

Some bond of loyalty between the President and his general however still held, for McClellan wrote his friend Barlow on March 16 of '62, "The President is all right,—he is my strongest friend."

Ben Butler recruited troops in New England to join with the navy, steam down to the Gulf, and take New Orleans. But McClellan interfered, wanted the troops for himself. Lincoln held Butler in Washington and asked him one day whether if he had an army of 100,000 he would move across the Potomac and attack the enemy. "Certainly I would, Mr. President, and if it was of any use I would ask for the privilege." But what he most wanted was to go and take New Orleans. "I won't say, General, whether I will let you go or not," replied Lincoln. Butler pleaded. Later he sailed south under orders.

Among powerful financial, transportation, and industrial interests gathered around such individuals as August Belmont, William H. Aspinwall, Cyrus McCormick, James Gordon Bennett, there was still faith in McClellan. They could not hold it against McClellan, as did the Republican antislavery radicals, that he was a Democrat in politics with a frank contempt for abolitionists and their methods. Their newspapers still favored McClellan and their news-writers still found him a live figure to write about. Stanton threw into jail, as a spy suspect, a *New York Herald* correspondent, Dr. Ives. "The agents of the Associated Press and a gang around the Federal Capitol appear to be organized for the purpose of magnifying their idol," wrote Stanton to a New York man, with reference to McClellan. Slowly Stanton was drifting completely away from the General in Chief who had agreed to his name for War Secretary. Slowly too the impression was taking root in many circles that McClellan was interfered with too much by Stanton, by War Office bureaucrats, by the suspicious antislavery radicals. The abolitionist Anna Dickinson lost her position in the Philadelphia mint for accusing McClellan of treason at Ball's Bluff. The city council of Philadelphia presented an ornamented sword to McClellan and received his words: "The war can not be long. It may be desperate. I ask in the future forbearance, patience, and confidence."

Congress gave the President authority to take over any and all railroad and telegraph lines whenever, in his judgment, the public safety required it. Stanton under this power was tightening a censorship of press and commercial dispatches. Where the War Department suspected information might leak, wires were tapped. The technique of conveying or intercepting intelligence was developing. In the garments of women, in pies and cakes, in hat linings and hollow umbrella handles, in false trunk bottoms, in the soles of shoes, messages North and South had been intercepted. Northern newspapers referred to women spy suspects in detention at Washington as "malignants in petticoats," as "she Secesh." From one of the latter was taken a petticoat weighing 50 pounds, mostly silk intended for an army balloon at Richmond. Mrs. Rose O'Neale Greenhow was still a prisoner in her own house in Washington, on evidence indicating that she had relayed to Beauregard about all he needed to know as to when the battle of Bull Run would begin. Hidden in a cake sent to her was a note arranging for her escape. "Lieutenant Sheldon," said *Leslie's Weekly*, "brought her a nice new cake and she threw it downstairs."

Treason lurked, shadows whispered, and phantoms mocked with macabre laughter among the cornerstones of the Government and its walls and rafters. Stanton on the night of April 2, 1862, came to the White House and showed Lincoln a letter filled with explicit and detailed statements that General McClellan was in 1860 initiated by Jefferson Davis into a secret society favoring Southern secession, that Davis still held power over McClellan, and that McClellan would feel himself bound by his oath to the secret Knights of the Golden Circle. Stanton and Lincoln agreed that the letter was morbid, its statements fabricated and false. Yet both knew also it was not good that people should be spreading and believing such stories about the foremost Union commander, and that the letter was sufficiently sinister for Stanton to have left the War Office to hold a discussion with Lincoln about it.

Browning on the night of April 2 asked Lincoln if he still had confidence in McClellan's fidelity. Browning wrote in his diary of Lincoln's reply: "He assured me he had, and that he had never had any reason to doubt it. That he [McClellan] had now gone to Fortress Monroe with his Command, with orders to move on Richmond without delay, and that only on yesterday when McClelland came to take leave of him preparatory to marching, he shed tears when speaking of the cruel imputations upon his loyalty, and defending himself against them The President added that Genl Scott, and all the leading military men around him, had always assured him that McClelland possessed a very high order of military talent, and that he did not think they could all be mistaken—yet he was not fully satisfied with his conduct of the war—that he was not sufficiently energetic and aggressive in his measures—that he had studied McClelland and taken his measure as well as he could—that he thought he had the capacity to make arrangements properly for a great conflict, but as the hour for action approached he became nervous and oppressed with the responsibility and hesitated to meet the crisis, but that he had given him peremptory orders to move now, and he must do it."

Eight days later Browning wrote in his diary: "Then went to Presidents [sic], but he was sick and in bed, and I did not see him. Went up again at night, and sat with him an hour or more. He was comfortable and in very good spirits—having been out riding in the evening. He told me he was becoming impatient and dissatisfied with McClellan's sluggishness of action, and read me a letter he had written him in reply to his demand for more troops." This Lincoln letter of April 9, 1862, began: "My Dear Sir: Your despatches, complaining that you are not properly sustained, while they do not offend me, do pain me very much." He explained about troops assigned to Frémont and now demanded by McClellan. "Blenker's division was withdrawn from you before you left here, and you knew the pressure under which I did it, and, as I thought, acquiesced in it—certainly not without reluctance." Blenker was a favorite under Frémont in Missouri and Frémont had insisted that he must have Blenker and Lincoln had given him Blenker and had talked over with McClellan just exactly why Blenker could not go along with McClellan. But McClellan no sooner was away from Washington than he again clamored for Blenker's division precisely as though he and Lincoln had not had a long enough discussion about it to end any further talk about Blenker.

More serious, however, in this letter was the point that McClellan had stripped Washington of all defense troops except some 20,000. Therefore Lincoln had ordered McDowell with 40,000 to stay in and near Washington. He tried to remind McClellan of the written decision of a council of McClellan and corps commanders that enough troops should be left to protect the capital city, "to give an entire feeling of security for its safety from menace." The estimate was that 40,000 to 55,000 men would be necessary. In both political and military circles it was agreed that the capture of Washington by the enemy would probably bring Britain and France to recognize the Richmond Government, the blockade would be broken, arms and supplies would pour into the South, and the South would win the war hands down. So Lincoln wrote McClellan: "My explicit order that Washington should, by the judgment of all the commanders of [army] corps, be left entirely secure, had been neglected. It was precisely this that drove me to detain McDowell."

Then came bickering. Over and again across the coming weeks and months McClellan was to claim he had only so many troops—giving the number—and he must have more. The War Office would answer that so many troops—giving the number—had been sent him and asking why he did not have more than he claimed. "There is a curious mystery about the number of troops now with you," wrote Lincoln. "When I telegraphed you on the 6th, saying you had over 100,000 with you, I had just obtained from the Secretary of War a statement, taken as he said from your own returns, making 108,000 with you and *en route* to you. You now say you will have but 85,000 when all *en route* to you shall have reached you. How can the discrepancy of 23,000 be accounted for?"

He tried to prod McClellan gently into moving forward and fighting. "Once more let me tell you it is indispensable to you that you strike a blow. I am powerless to help this." Whether the troops went by a water route to the Peninsula and moved on Richmond or whether they went overland would not change the essential difficulty. "We would find the same enemy and the same or equal intrenchments at either place. The country will not fail to note—is noting now—that the present hesitation to move upon an intrenched enemy is but the story of Manassas repeated." Lincoln closed the letter: "I beg to assure you that I have never written you nor spoken to you in greater kindness of feeling than now, nor with a fuller purpose to sustain you, so far as in my most anxious judgment I consistently can; but you must act."

McClellan wrote his wife: "I have raised an awful row about McDowell's corps. The President very coolly telegraphed me . . . that he thought I had better break the enemy's lines at once! I was much tempted to reply that he had better come and do it himself." It also troubled McClellan that the President issued an order limiting his command to that of the Army of the Potomac. He would like to be managing other armies too. He wrote his wife of "rascality" and "traitors" at Washington.

In such a mood McClellan in April of '62 headed the Army of the Potomac, which lay on the Peninsula before the Confederate entrenchments at Yorktown. Moving this army from Washington by water had required 113 steamers, 188 schooners, 88 barges, hauling for three weeks 121,500 men, 14,592 animals, 1,150 wagons, 44 batteries, 74 ambulances, besides pontoon bridges, telegraph materials, equipage, cattle, food, supplies. John Tucker, in charge of this transport for the War Department, reported, "The only loss of which I have heard is eight mules and nine barges which went ashore in a gale, the cargoes being saved."

McClellan kept his army at Yorktown for weeks while he threw up entrenchments, built batteries, installed big guns. "Do not misunderstand the apparent inaction here," he wrote to Lincoln. "Not a day, not an hour has been lost. Works have been constructed that may almost be called gigantic." To an admiral he wrote, "I am probably weaker now than they are, or soon will be." Of a river to be crossed by the army, he wrote that "it grows worse the more you look at it." John Hay was writing Nicolay: "The little Napoleon sits trembling before the handful of men at Yorktown, afraid either to fight or run. Stanton feels devilish about it. He would like to remove him if he thought it would do." General Joseph E. Johnston was writing Robert E. Lee, "No one but McClellan would have hesitated to attack." For when McClellan landed and began his gigantic works, the Confederate entrenchments were held by 5,000 men. During the weeks McClellan was getting ready to fight the Confederates recruited thousands of troops, partly through the use of a conscription act passed by the Richmond

Government. And when at last McClellan's big guns were set to blow the enemy off the map, when finally Union troops moved out to capture the foe, they found nobody to fight. Again he had not heard Lincoln's warning: "the present hesitation to move upon an intrenched enemy is but the story of Manassas repeated."

At unfailing intervals McClellan called to Washington for more men, more guns. He was given a division from McDowell's army. He telegraphed Lincoln, "Would be glad to have the 30-pounder Parrotts in the works around Washington. Am very short of that excellent gun." Lincoln wired back: "Your call for Parrott guns from Washington alarms me, chiefly because it argues indefinite procrastination. Is anything to be done?" When at last after a month of siege the empty Confederate entrenchments were captured, McClellan telegraphed: "Yorktown is in our possession. . . . No time shall be lost. . . . I shall push the enemy to the wall." The total force under Johnston, who had evacuated, numbered 55,633 men, about one to two of McClellan's. They had waited till McClellan had finished building elaborate batteries, till McClellan was perfectly satisfied that he could shell and shatter all opposition. Then they drew off.

During the weeks McClellan was moving to the Peninsula and entrenching at Yorktown, other actions were staged elsewhere and with different results. Three days' fighting went on at Pea Ridge in the northwest corner of Arkansas between Missouri, Iowa, Illinois, and Ohio regiments against Missouri, Arkansas, and Texas regiments along with three Red Indian regiments. The Union forces lost 203 killed, 972 wounded, 174 missing, as against 800 to 1,000 killed, 200 to 300 missing, of the Confederates. The Southern commander had planned to carry the war to St. Louis and on into Illinois, but the prolonged and bloody combats at Sugar Creek, Leesville, Elkhorn Tavern, dispersed his army, freed Missouri from all but guerrilla warfare, and broke Southern military power west of the Mississippi.

Near Santa Fe, New Mexico, Texas and Colorado cavalry clashed, with 32 Union killed and 36 Confederate. Fort Pulaski, Georgia, was captured, with 360 prisoners. On the Mississippi River Commodore Foote and General John Pope took Island No. 10 with over 2,000 prisoners, threatening all down-river traffic of the South.

An action came as "a thrust into the vitals of the Confederacy." The sea dogs Commodore David Glasgow Farragut and Commodore David Dixon Porter, with battleships and mortar boats, along with Major General Ben Butler heading an army of land troops, ran and battered their way through the forts and batteries at New Orleans and captured the largest seaport and the most important metropolitan center of the South, a city of 168,000. An army of 10,000 Confederates left the city, their torches lighting 15,000 bales of cotton, a dozen large ships, several fine steamboats, unfinished gunboats, and property worth millions of dollars.

In charge of the city as its military governor came Ben Butler of Lowell, Massachusetts, the Breckinridge proslavery Democrat who had at one time striven to nominate Jefferson Davis for the Presidency of the United States.

Butler handed the editor of the *True Delta* a proclamation to print. The editor refused. Butler arrested him, put in printer boys from Massachusetts, and published the proclamation telling the citizens what they could and could not do. He sent for the Mayor, the city council, and the chief of police, and read to them a paper telling them what they could and could not do. Then Butler tried to regulate the town newspapers, the food supply, money, flags permitted and prohibited.

Regulating the women was no simple affair. They drew aside their skirts when they met Union officers and soldiers. They grimaced and taunted. They spat on the Union flag. They stepped off the sidewalk rather than pass a Yankee. They exercised subtle ingenuity to make the conquerors feel like barbarians. Butler issued Order No. 28 whereby "any female" who "by word, gesture or movement" should "insult or show contempt for any officer or soldier of the United States" was thereafter "to be regarded and held liable to be treated as a woman of the town plying her vocation." The Mayor told Butler he could not keep the peace under such a law. Butler arrested the Mayor, the chief of police, and others, and put them in the guardhouse of a captured fort. In time the new governor was to be known among all loyal Southerners as "Beast Butler" or "Butler the Beast," or in token of stolen silverware, "Spoons Butler."

On the Tennessee River near the Mississippi State line at Shiloh Church and Pittsburg Landing, General Albert Sidney Johnston had hurled 40,000 Confederate troops in attack on 36,000 under Grant. In the Sunday morning sun Johnston had told his staff men, "Tonight we will water our horses in the Tennessee River." To generals who advised other plans Johnston said, "I would fight them if they were a million." His troops sent the Union front lines reeling. One Union division fell back to its eighth position during the twelve hours of combat that day. Grant came on the field several hours after the fighting began; he was at breakfast nine miles up the river when he first heard the firing. At times the battle seemed to be the swaying and surging of many mobs, the gray and the butternut-brown against the blue. Men fought from tree to tree, with sometimes the cry, "How about Bull Run?" met by the answering cry, "How about Fort Donelson?" One Union division was cut off and 2,200 were taken prisoner.

The Union lines were steadily forced back. Would night find them driven to the bank of the wide Tennessee River and no bridge to cross? Tecumseh Sherman had three horses shot under him, got a bullet in the hand, another through his hat; a third grazed his shoulder. One tree about as thick as a lean man received ninety bullets, another tree sixty. In a clearing between woodlands dead men lay so thick that careful walking was required not to step on corpses. One soldier lay on his back holding in a rigid hand a daguerreotype of a woman and child he had been gazing on when death came. Another soldier, with encased photographs of his wife and his mother in a blouse pocket, found that they had neatly stopped a lead ball from entering his heart. A private who kept a diary recorded seeing a soldier who had been killed while taking aim; he lay with one eye open, the other closed, his hands clutching a rifle. "Another died while in the act of placing his hand in his haversack for food. Some were disembowelled by cannon-balls, others with half their heads off lay in the midst of brains and blood. During the engagement riderless horses were flying in all directions. Wounded were borne off the field by hundreds, some with arms and legs off, writhing in agony." Two Kentucky regiments fought each other with fury and hatred, one of the Union soldiers wounding and taking prisoner his own brother. As the Confederate brother was started toward the rear he took notice of his Union brother firing at a man near a tree and shouted, "Hold on, Bill, don't shoot there any more! That's father!"

Toward evening Grant sat his horse, watching the Confederates try to take a hill guarded by a battery and Union gunboats. Someone asked him if things looked gloomy. He answered: "Delay counts for everything with us. Tomorrow we shall attack them with fresh troops, and drive them, of course."

Darkness fell on the Sabbath slaughter. Rain came in torrents on the tentless soldiers of the two armies. Grant lay under a tree and tried to sleep, but a swollen foot and ankle, caused by a horse's slipping in mud and falling on him, kept him awake. He went to a log house near by where it was dry and where wounded soldiers came to surgeons for treatment. Their cries of pain kept him awake and he went back to his tree under the rain.

In the gray of dawn the Union troops moved in attack and that day, reinforced by 20,000 under Buell and 6,000 under Lew Wallace, drove the enemy to retreat. Albert Sidney Johnston, counted one of the most brilliant of Confederate commanders, was killed the day before, it was learned. The Union army lost 13,047 in killed, wounded, and missing, the Confederates 10,694.

One lesson sank home to the Union troops at Shiloh: From then on they dug trenches; even a 1-foot ditch with another foot of dirt piled in front of it reduced the human-target area to be shot at by the enemy.

Sherman wrote home: "I still feel the horrid nature of this war, and the piles of dead and wounded and maimed makes me more anxious than ever for some hope of an end, but I know such a thing cannot be for a long, long time. Indeed I never expect it, or to survive it." Grant likewise felt that a hard long war was ahead. He had seen the Confederates lose an army at Fort Donelson and then had seen them collect a new army, take the offensive, and show courage and endurance beyond all expectation. The motives that drove the Southern men and women on lay deeper than was generally believed in the North. "I give up all idea of saving the Union except by complete conquest," was Grant's thought after Shiloh.

Nineteen melancholy steamboats loaded with thousands of gashed and perforated Union soldiers moved north and brought the war home to Peoria, Chicago, Detroit. Still other steamboats carried thousands of men clothed in butternut and gray—to be held in Camp Douglas at Chicago as prisoners of war.

The President at Washington issued a proclamation saying, "It has pleased Almighty God to vouchsafe signal victories to the land and naval forces engaged in suppressing an internal rebellion, and at the same time to avert from our country the dangers of foreign intervention and invasion." Therefore he recommended to the people of the country that "at their next weekly assemblages in their accustomed places of public worship" they should "especially acknowledge and render thanks to our Heavenly Father for these inestimable blessings." He spoke of hope for peace, harmony, and unity in his own country, and beyond that "the establishment of fraternal relations among all the countries of the earth."

At first the joy over victory ran high in the North. Then this was modified by a widely spread story that Grant was drunk at Shiloh, that he could not sit on his horse while directing the battle, that he was a butcher who without a heart sent men to sacrifice. "There is much feeling against Grant, and I try to defend him, but with little success," Tecumseh Sherman wrote to his brother, John, the Ohio Senator.

Also Grant was no general, could not manage a battle, it was alleged. An Illinois officer, George T. Allen, wrote to Senator Trumbull on April 25, "Good generalship would have saved us thousands of valuable lives and have carried our army in triumph into Corinth." A former Illinois State Senator, now a brigadier general, John M. Palmer, wrote to Senator Trumbull, "No sadder day will, I hope, ever come for Illinois than that sad Sunday when the flower of her soldiers were decimated at Pittsburg unless the day that Grant was made a Brigadier-General."

Lincoln received at the White House one night at 11 o'clock his friend A. K. McClure, who as spokesman for a number of Republicans talked for nearly two hours on how "the tide of popular sentiment" was against Grant and Grant should be dismissed from the service so that the President could retain the confidence of the country in the Administration. McClure said this course seemed to be "the almost universal conviction of the President's friends."

Lincoln let McClure talk with few interruptions. Then, as McClure reported it afterward: "When I had said every thing that could be said from my standpoint, we lapsed into silence. Lincoln remained silent for what seemed a very long time. He then gathered himself up in his chair and said, in a tone of earnestness that I shall never forget, 'I can't spare this man—he fights!' "

In Richmond on February 22, 1862, Jefferson Davis and his wife rode in a carriage toward Capitol Hill. As the newly elected head of the permanent Government of the Confederate States of America, he was to take his inauguration oath for a six-year term of office.

Walking alongside the Davis carriage Mrs. Davis saw two Negroes dressed in formal black clothes, high top hats, and white gloves. She asked the coachman who these men were. "Well, ma'am, you told me to fix everything up like it ought to be, and dis yere's de way we do in Richmond at fun'rals and sich-like." Thus Mrs. Davis, not lacking humor, gave the anecdote.

Heavy and unremitting rain poured on the equestrian statue of George Washington at the top of Capitol Hill while President Davis near by under a canvas cover addressed a big crowd holding umbrellas: "After a series of successes and victories . . . we have recently met with serious disasters." He was referring to Fort Donelson; pale, worn, resolved, and around him men also resolved. They would consecrate their toil, property, lives, to a nation of their own. Tears trickled down the faces of gray-headed men of the planter aristocracy. They joined in silence in the prayer of Davis spoken across the rain: "Acknowledging the Providence which has so visibly protected the Confederacy during its brief but eventful career, to Thee, O God! I trustingly commit myself, and prayerfully invoke Thy blessing on my country and its cause."

CHAPTER 21

FAREWELL, WOODEN WARSHIPS!

ON Sunday, March 9, 1862, news came to the Navy Department that sent Secretary Welles hurrying to President Lincoln, who at once called the Cabinet to the White House for quick thinking and emergency action. The facts were that a United States 40-gun frigate, the *Merrimac*, sunk at Gosport about a year before, had been raised by the Confederates, fitted with a cast-iron ram, and covered with 4-inch iron plates. Moving out from Norfolk on Saturday afternoon, she had met in battle two Union war vessels, the *Congress* and the *Cumberland*, and shot and rammed their wooden hulls till they were helpless. Another Union war vessel, the *Minnesota*, also wooden, had been run aground. And the news was that the *Merrimac* would smash her on Sunday morning and then be free to move on Washington or New York.

"Sitting in my office about ten thirty in the morning, when I should have been in church, the President was announced at the door," wrote Admiral Dahlgren in his diary for this March 9. The Admiral rose and met Senator Browning and the President, who was saying, "Frightful news!" and reporting that the *Minnesota* was ashore after having tried to attack the *Merrimac*, while the only other immediately available ship, the *Roanoke*, was hugging close to the guns of Fortress Monroe, one of her shafts broken. "The President did not know whether we might not have a visit here, which would indeed cap the climax," added Dahlgren in his diary. "I could give but little comfort."

The dignified, bearded, and bewigged Secretary of the Navy wrote of that morning, "Although my Department and the branch of the Government entrusted to me were most interested and most responsible, the President ever after gave me the credit of being, on that occasion, the most calm and self-possessed of any member of the Government." Welles took pride in being so calm when others were so frantic. "The President himself was so excited that he could not deliberate or be satisfied with the opinions of non-professional men, but ordered his carriage and drove to the navy yard to see and consult with Admiral Dahlgren and other naval officers." And Dahlgren turned the President over to Welles for advice and opinion. Welles told the President of their one hope, their one chance, the *Monitor*, a new type of sea fighting craft, arrived at Hampton Roads the night before.

When Welles mentioned to Stanton that the *Monitor* carried only two guns, "his mingled look of incredulity and contempt cannot be described," wrote Welles. . . . "To me there was throughout the whole day something inexpressibly ludicrous in the wild, frantic talk, action, and rage of Stanton as he ran from room to room, sat down and jumped up after writing a few words, swung his arms, scolded, and raved. He could not fail to see and feel my opinion of him and his bluster,—that I was calm and unmoved by his rant, spoke deliberately, and was not excited by his violence. . . . The *Merrimac*, he said, would destroy every vessel in the service. . . . Likely the first movement of the *Merrimac* would be to come up the Potomac and disperse Congress, destroy the Capitol and public buildings; or she might go to New York and Boston and destroy those cities." Thus Welles wrote: "In all that painful time my composure was not disturbed."

Stanton telegraphed Northern seacoast governors and mayors of danger from the *Merrimac;* they should be ready to obstruct their harbors. Also Stanton got Admiral Dahlgren to make ready sixty rock-laden canalboats to be sunk in the Potomac and obstruct the *Merrimac* when she came to Washington to blow the dome off the Capitol. But Dahlgren refused to take further orders from the Secretary of War; he was in the navy and that department had its own Secretary.

In Lincoln's room Welles and Stanton met, and according to Welles: "Stanton, with affected calmness but his voice trembling with emotion, inquired if I had given orders to prevent the boats which he had provided from being prepared and loaded. I replied that I had given no orders to prepare and load any boats, nor did I intend to. . . . Stanton said he had given the order to Meigs and Dahlgren, and had done it to protect Washington and with the approval of the President, to whom he turned. The President confirmed his statement, or remarked that Mr. Stanton had thought it imperative that something should immediately be done for our security; that those officers, Meigs and Dahlgren, one or both, were present, and he thought no harm would come of it, if it did no good. . . . Mr. Stanton said the War Department would bear both the expense and the responsibility. The passages were sharp and pungent. . . . Stanton claimed that, instead of consulting and asking, the military could order naval assistance, and that it was the duty of the Secretary of the Navy and of naval officers to render it. President Lincoln would not, however, lend himself to this view of the subject."

Then from Hampton Roads came the story of what happened. Towed by a tug out of New York Harbor three days before, the little *Monitor* met rough weather; water broke over the engines, down the blower pipes and smokestacks; hand pumps were rigged and worked; then the wind and high waves went down, or the *Monitor* would have gone to sea bottom. Once again fighting rough sea in shoals the captain and crew wondered if the hawser running to the tug would hold. It did. That was luck, or Providence. They rode out two storms. So far, so good.

At last they came to Hampton Roads, saw the shattered ship *Congress* burning, took a pilot on board and steamed near the *Minnesota*, a wooden frigate. They were a tired crew on the *Monitor*, twice nearly sunk, no food but hard sea biscuit on a storm-soaked vessel, and no sleep in forty-eight hours. Their commander, Lieutenant John Worden, said no captain ever had a better crew; the crew swore their captain was the best that ever walked a deck. As the *Merrimac* came on toward the *Minnesota* the next morning, the little *Monitor* made straight for her, a David against a Goliath, ten guns on the *Merrimac* against two on the *Monitor*. "A cheesebox on a raft," "a tin can on a shingle," that was the *Monitor*, equipped with a revolving steel tower or turret, so that she could shoot from any position; and her raftlike deck was so low that the big *Merrimac* could not ram her.

During the shooting the tiny *Monitor* moved and maneuvered around the giant *Merrimac* like a fast bantamweight boxer circling a ponderous heavyweight. The big one crashed its ten guns against the little one. And the little one did not move except to answer with its two guns. A deep thrill went round the hearts of the men handling the guns in the *Monitor* turret when the first heavy slugs of the *Merrimac* thundered their impact on the outside of the turret. The men looked gladly into each other's faces as if to say, "She's a tough giant but this shortboy is tougher."

Sometimes it was hard to start the turret revolving. They hoped it would not snarl.

"Once the *Merrimac* tried to ram us," wrote S. Dana Greene, lieutenant commander, "but Worden avoided the direct impact by skillful use of the helm, and she struck a glancing blow which did no damage. At the instant of collision I planted a solid 180-pound shot fair and square on the forward part of her casemate. Had the gun been loaded with thirty pounds of powder, which was the charge subsequently used with similar guns, it is probable that this shot would have penetrated her armor; but the charge being limited to fifteen pounds, in accordance with peremptory orders from the Navy Department, the shot rebounded without doing any more damage than possibly to start some of the beams of her armor-backing."

The *Monitor* turret ran out of shells and she drew off for fifteen minutes to bring up fresh ammunition. The *Merrimac*, drawing 22 feet, could not follow the *Monitor*, which could steam into water a little over 12 feet deep.

The *Monitor* came back. Again the two guns against ten trying to cripple or kill each other.

"Again she came up on our quarter and fired twice," said a Confederate on the *Merrimac* after the fight. "The impact forced the side in bodily two or three inches. All the crews of the after guns were knocked over by the concussion, and bled from the nose or ears. Another shot in the same place would have penetrated."

The *Merrimac* ceased firing, and a gunnery officer was asked by his superior, "Why are you not firing, Mr. Eggleston?" "Why, our powder is very precious," called the lieutenant, "and after two hours' incessant fir-

Some called it "David and Goliath"

ing I find that I can do her about as much damage by snapping my thumb at her every two minutes and a half."

At ten yards' distance a shell from the *Merrimac* hit the sighthole of the pilothouse, stunning Commander Worden, filling his eyes with powder and blinding him, his face covered with blood.

The *Monitor* drew off to care for its commander and to examine how badly the pilothouse was wrecked.

The *Merrimac* drew off and steamed to Norfolk.

After six hours it was a drawn battle. Each side made its mistakes. If the *Merrimac* had concentrated its entire fire on the *Monitor* pilothouse from the first, it would have destroyed the *Monitor's* control. If the *Monitor* had shot at the *Merrimac's* water line, where the armor was weak, it would have sunk the *Merrimac*.

However, the two ships had taught the navies of the world a lesson. London and Paris declared that the era of wooden fighting craft was over. The Washington Government would now begin building a fleet of monitors. The blockade of Southern ports would go on.

In the crews of both ships were men writing home, as did S. Dana Greene, of being worn. "My men and myself were perfectly black with smoke and powder. All my underclothes were perfectly black, and my person was in the same condition. . . . I had been up so long under such excitement that my nervous system was completely run down. . . . My nerves and muscles twitched as though electric shocks were continually passing through them. . . . I lay down and tried to sleep—I might as well have tried to fly."

News of the battle came with pleasure to John Ericsson, the Swede who designed the *Monitor*. He was type and symbol of the industrial, mechanical North, the machine-age man from whose head incessantly sprang new tools, wheels, devices. He grew up among mines and ironworks in Sweden, became a captain in the army, resigned, invented an instrument for taking sea soundings, a hydrostatic weighing machine, artificial drafts that decreased smokestack size and economized fuel, a self-acting gunlock for naval cannon, a steam carriage in 1829 which ran thirty miles an hour. He came to the United States in 1839, and two years later furnished designs for a screw warship, the *Princeton*, "the first vessel having propelling machinery below water-line, out of reach of hostile shot." He improved gun carriages, optical instruments, won medals for innovations "in the management of heat, particularly as shown in his caloric engine of 1858."

His wife came from Sweden, joined him in New York, was as proud of his genius as he was of her beauty. And while she filled her time as best she could Ericsson worked at the shop all day and stuck to his drawing-table till midnight. After a time he found that she was, as he said, "jealous of a steam-engine."

So she went to England, Ericsson sent her an allowance, they wrote letters to each other, never meeting again. He sent her passage money to cross the Atlantic and begin over their home life; it arrived to find her on a deathbed, a sister writing to Ericsson her last message for him: "I have always been a trouble to you. Forgive me." She could not quite gather his passion for tools, wheels, progress, man's quest in the material world.

Ericsson's very bodily strength was a curious item. He asked two workmen in his shop one day to remove a bar of iron he had tripped on. They said it was too heavy. He looked at them, picked it up, carried it and threw it on the scrap pile. They later put it on a scale and found that it weighed six hundred pounds.

This granitic man of quiet pride had written to the President in August of '61 that "steel-clad vessels cannot be arrested in their course by land batteries" and New York would be "at the mercy of such intruders," wherefore he would offer plans. "Attachment to the Union alone impels me to offer my services in this fearful crisis—my life if need be—in the great cause which Providence has called you to defend." Respectfully he stated, "I seek no private advantage or emolument of any kind." In the event that his plans were approved he could within ten weeks construct a vessel to destroy the "rebel" fleet at Norfolk, leaving stolen ships sunken "and the harbor purged of traitors." Having planned upward of one hundred marine engines, designed naval structures for thirty years, and feeling at home in the science of artillery, he trusted his anxiety to serve would be understood. He was fifty-eight years old when in '61 he laid before a Naval

Board of three commodores his plans for "an impregnable steam-battery of light draught," which he had been perfecting for eight years. They told him that his plans had been considered when previously presented by a friend of Ericsson—and they were rejected.

Ericsson came near walking out of the room and letting the whole matter slide; his New York shop was filled with more contracts than he could handle. Then he stopped and asked why they rejected the plans. Mainly, it turned out, they were afraid that the *Monitor* as designed would upset; it lacked stability. So Ericsson talked about stability of vessels that day, and one commodore told him, "Sir, I have learned more about the stability of a vessel from what you have now said than all I knew before."

At one session of the Naval Board President Lincoln and Cabinet members were present. "All were surprised at the novelty of the plan. Some advised trying it; others ridiculed it." A naval captain who was hostile said that to worship the little model would not be idolatry "because it was in the image of nothing in the heaven above or in the earth beneath or in the waters under the earth." The session closed with Lincoln holding a pasteboard model of the *Monitor* in his hand and remarking: "All I have to say is what the girl said when she put her foot into the stocking. It strikes me there's something in it."

Finally they gave Ericsson a contract with a clause saying that if the *Monitor* did not prove "invulnerable" he was to refund all government money paid him. He did not read this clause, being in a hurry to get to work, or he might have handed the contract back instead of signing it. He asked to build 12-inch guns, but the naval experts told him 11-inch were plenty big. He asked to use thirty pounds of powder instead of fifteen for a shot, but the ordnance chief said No. He was told that "the concussion in the turret will be so great that men cannot remain in it and work the guns." Others had "calculated her displacement" and could prove that the *Monitor* would not float. These and other croakings were in his ears as he went to New York, drew his final plans, and saw the ship built in exactly one hundred days. When she went into action the final government payment on her had not been made. Now he could read a letter from the chief engineer of the *Monitor* saying: "Thousands have this day blessed you. I have heard whole crews cheer you." The New York Chamber of Commerce offered to raise a fund which would be "suitable return for his services" and "evince the gratitude of the nation." Ericsson replied: "All the remuneration I desire for the *Monitor* I get out of the construction of it. It is all-sufficient."

On the day after the *Merrimac-Monitor* battle Lincoln wrote advising the Secretary of the Navy that the *Monitor* could be easily boarded and captured, her turret wedged, her machinery drowned by pouring water. He passed on the advice from Lieutenant Worden that "she should not go sky-larking up to Norfolk."

A naval lieutenant the day after the battle arrived at a Cabinet meeting to tell the President that the wounded Commander Worden was at his house. The President dismissed the Cabinet. "There will be no further business today. I am going around to see the brave fellow."

Ushering Lincoln into an upstairs room at his house, the naval lieutenant said, "Jack, here is the President come to see you."

The President stood gazing down on Worden in bed, the scorched eyes closed, the torn face bandaged. "You do me great honor," murmured Worden. No answer came.

The lieutenant turned to see Lincoln in tears with nothing to say for the moment. When he did find words he said: "It is not so. It is you who honor me and your country, and I will promote you." And he made Worden a captain that very day.

Carl Schurz, meeting Lincoln that day, noted: "His mind was still so full of the great event that it gave him evident delight to tell me the whole story."

Captain Worden a few days later informally received the President, Assistant Secretary of the Navy Gustavus Vasa Fox, and personal friends on board the *Monitor* in the Washington navy yard. Again, so they said, tears were in the President's eyes as he stood handshaking amid the seamen and their commander, whose face on one side was to be black and purple for life with powder driven into it from a cannon shot twenty yards away. On request Worden told the story of the fight, answered questions, and apologized for not having the customary refreshments for distinguished visitors aboard a naval vessel. Lincoln smiled, and as L. E. Chittenden noted, he replied to Worden: "Some uncharitable people say that old Bourbon is an indispensable element in the fighting qualities of some of our generals in the field. But, Captain, after the account that we have heard today, no one will say that any Dutch courage is needed on board the *Monitor*." Fox made a short talk that closed with the remarks: "I never fully believed in armored vessels until I saw this battle. I know all the facts which united to give us the *Monitor*. I withhold no credit from Captain Ericsson, her inventor, but I know the country is principally indebted for the construction of this vessel to President Lincoln, and for the success of her trial to Captain Worden, her commander."

A few weeks after the great battle of the ironclads President Lincoln, with Stanton and others, went down the Potomac River in a steamer. Near Kettle Bottom Shoals they saw a long line of boats. Someone asked what those were. "Oh," said the President, as Welles noted it, "that is Stanton's navy. That is the fleet concerning which he and Mr. Welles became so excited in my room. Welles was incensed and opposed the scheme, and it has proved that Neptune was right. Stanton's navy is as useless as the paps of a man to a sucking child. They may be some show to amuse the child, but they are good for nothing for service."

An admiral of the United States Navy at a later time sketched the *Monitor* as the crystallization of forty centuries of thought on attack and defense at sea: "She exhibited in a singular manner the old Norse element of the American navy; Ericsson (Swedish, *son of Eric*) built her; Dahlgren

(Swedish, *branch of a valley*) armed her. . . . How the ancient skalds would have struck their wild harps in hearing such names in heroic runes!" And an added Norse name was that of Gustavus Vasa Fox, whose insistence in the face of doubters gave Ericsson his chance to launch an idea that junked the wooden navies of the world.

At times in his diary Welles was critical of Fox as officious and too ready to make decisions without consulting others. In the main, however, the head of the Navy Department seemed to rely on Fox, seldom interfered, and considered the Swedish-blooded Yankee from Massachusetts indispensable. Of loyal Administration men Fox seemed to be the chief link with the country's foremost shipowner, William H. Aspinwall. To this magnate Fox wrote in November of '62 that, as requested, he would take care of a nephew of Aspinwall in an appointment to the Annapolis naval academy. "I will keep the name of your Nephew before me. Another class is formed in February and the Secretary of the Navy will make no further appointments for a couple of months." Also Fox was so busy that he would have to defer the pleasure of a visit to Aspinwall's country house.

"My wish, and my advice is, that you do not allow any ordinary obstacle to prevent his appointment," Lincoln had written to Welles the year before when he had heard of opposition to Fox as chief clerk of the Navy Department. "He is a live man, whose services we cannot well dispense with."

To Browning and to Hay in rambling and familiar conversation Lincoln had told of his impulse to step out and take charge of the Army of the Potomac himself and see what he could do as a field commander. He had checked this impulse, and the nearest he had come to active field service was in the week of May 5, 1862. On May 4 Stanton telegraphed Major General John E. Wool, commanding at Fortress Monroe: "The President desires to know whether your force is in condition for a sudden movement, if one should be ordered under your command. Please have it in readiness." With Secretaries Stanton and Chase and two transports loaded with troops, Lincoln rode down the Potomac by night in a drizzle of rain and the next morning had breakfast amid the tossing salt waters of Chesapeake Bay. Lincoln was no sailor, lacked stomach for the sea, Chase writing to his daughter Janet: "It would have amused you to see us. The President gave it up almost as soon as he began [luncheon], and, declaring himself too uncomfortable to eat, stretched himself at length upon the locker [of the cabin]. The rest of us persisted in eating, but the plates slipped this way and that, the glasses tumbled over, and rolled about, and the whole table seemed as topsy-turvy as if some spiritist were operating upon it. But we got through at last, and the Secretary of War followed the example of the President."

They arrived at Fortress Monroe, not far from Yorktown, where McClellan was then campaigning. They were at the mouth of the James River, a direct water route to Richmond and a practical highway for hauling supplies and reinforcements to McClellan's army if he should shift his base and locate his headquarters on that river, as he later did. Stanton sent a message to General John E. Wool, commanding. Wool with his staff came clanking on board the *Miami*. After a conference with the President, it was determined that Lincoln, Stanton, Wool, Chase, and General Egbert L. Viele should visit Commodore Louis M. Goldsborough on his flagship the *Minnesota* for a talk. A tug carried the five important men through a pitch-dark night to within hailing distance of the *Minnesota*.

"Ship ahoy! flagship ahoy!" shouted the tug captain. But his voice was feeble, didn't carry to the flagship, and Chase had a notion that the tug captain was bashful about hollering as loud as he could in the midst of such government dignitaries as were on his tug. No reply came from the flagship. General Viele then tried his lungs with the hail, "Ship ahoy!" and out of the pitch-dark came the cry, "What do you want?" "General Wool wishes to go on board." "Come round on the port side." The tug slowly chugged to the port side, where by searching sharply the eyes could make out a narrow steps with guide ropes. "It seemed to me," wrote Chase, "very high to the deck and the ascent a little fearful. Etiquette required the President to go first, and he went. Etiquette required the Secretary of the Treasury to follow, and he followed. We got up safely . . . and it did not seem so much of a 'getting up-stairs' after all." After a long conference with the Commodore they were towed back to the *Miami*, slept to a gentle sea rocking that night, and the next day saw action. By orders of the President the fleet moved to attack Confederate batteries at Sewell's Point. The roar of the first cannon broke upon a Sabbath silence. Enormous shot and shell were hurled three miles.

The *Merrimac* came out, wavered, hesitated. Beyond and waiting stood her old antagonist the little *Monitor*. The old outmoded wooden ships moved out of the way. The *Merrimac* retreated and refused to give battle.

Ashore and on horseback, the President rode with General Wool inspecting troops at the camp two miles from Fortress Monroe, riding through the burned and blackened walls of what had been the village of Hampton, destroyed by the Confederates when retiring before Union forces. The stately old home of ex-President John Tyler and a few other residences of Southern loyalists had not met the torch. Of the first regiment in the review of troops at the camp, Chase noted: "The colonel and his troops were made glad by the President, who rode along their line alone, uncovered, and inspiring a great enthusiasm. It is delightful to observe everywhere the warm affection felt and expressed for the President."

Commodore Goldsborough was summoned ashore by the President. Again an attack on the Sewell's Point batteries was ordered. The bombardment put one battery out of commission and revealed that a second battery was not as effective as supposed. The *Merrimac* steamed out slowly, paused, stood a while, again turned back, and looked as if she would fight only when she had to.

Lincoln had talked with a pilot, studied a chart, and found a landing-place nearer to Norfolk than the one considered by General Wool. The President in a tug was scouting the shore line; Chase was aboard the *Miami*.

"Several horsemen who seemed to be soldiers of the enemy, appeared on the beach," wrote Chase. "I sent to the President to ask if we should fire on them, and he replied negatively." Returning to General Wool and discussing plans for taking Norfolk from the Confederates there, the President allowed Wool to use the landing the General preferred.

Six regiments were put on shore, marched to Norfolk, found it evacuated by the Confederates, with smoking ruins of large stores of military supplies. The Mayor of Norfolk formally surrendered the city to General Wool. General Viele and others were agreed that the operation was delayed by disputes between two general officers as to rank and by slow movement of the troops. While the expedition was moving Generals Viele and Mansfield, with a Colonel Carr, were summoned to Fortress Monroe by the President. Lincoln's first question, according to Viele, was:

"Colonel Carr, where is your command?"

"At Camp Hamilton, sir."

"Why are you not on the other side of Norfolk?"

"I am awaiting orders."

Turning to Mansfield, Lincoln said: "Why are you here? Why not on the other side?"

"I am ordered to the fort by General Wool."

Then, as Viele noted: "President Lincoln with vehement action threw his tall hat on the floor, and, uttering strongly his disapproval and disappointment, he said finally, 'Send me someone who can write.' Colonel Le Grand B. Cannon of Wool's staff responded, and Lincoln dictated an order to General Wool requiring that troops at Camp Hamilton be at once ordered to Norfolk, and that troops already there be pushed rapidly forward. The delays in forwarding and pushing the troops allowed the Confederates time to burn the navy yard at Portsmouth, and to destroy the shipping."

The President had been "greatly alarmed for our safety" by the report of General Mansfield, wrote Chase, "and you can imagine his delight when we told him Norfolk was ours. Mr. Stanton came into the President's room and was equally delighted. He fairly hugged General Wool."

The President, with Stanton and Chase, the next day rode through the streets of the captured Norfolk and gazed on the ruined hulk of the *Merrimac*, which the Confederates had blown up rather than risk another fight with the *Monitor*.

Then the party sailed back to Washington on the steamer *Baltimore*, Chase writing long letters to his daughter Janet giving details of what he regarded as a big performance. Neither before nor after did Chase write such praise of Lincoln. "So ended a brilliant week's campaign by the President; for I think it quite certain that if he had not gone down, Norfolk would still have been in the possession of the enemy, and the *Merrimac* as grim and defiant, and as much a terror as ever. The whole coast is now virtually ours."

A curious week it was for Lincoln with his first experience at directly

John Ericsson

Steel engraving from author's collection

John Lorimer Worden, battle commander of the *Monitor*

From author's collection

Crew of the *Monitor* in its fight with the *Merrimac*

Photograph from Oliver R. Barrett Collection

Gustavus Vasa Fox, a sponsor of the *Monitor*

Photograph loaned by Scandinavian American Foundation

John Ericsson, inventor of the *Monitor*

Photograph loaned by J. O. Peterson of Brooklyn, New York

handling sea and land forces, with fleet and field headquarters under his hat, and the event somewhat under the eye of McClellan farther up the Peninsula. In no other week of Lincoln's life, that he or his friends told of, had he been seasick one day and on another day so angry that he took his silk hat off his head and threw it on the floor.

On the results of the week he had not failed in holding to the theory that the sea dog D. D. Porter quoted as hearing from him: "It's a good rule never to send a mouse to catch a skunk or a pollywog to tackle a whale." Porter had given the President a venerable anecdote of an old Revolutionary farmer, meeting the musketry fire of the red-coated British at Bunker Hill, feeling the sting and burn of a bullet in the calf of his leg and roaring to his son: "Dang it, Jim, they're firin' bullets. We must fire back at 'em."

CHAPTER 22

SEVEN DAYS OF BATTLES—SUMMER OF '62

McCLELLAN'S army having had nine months of organization, practice, drill, instruction in theory, saw its first active field service and went under fire in April of '62. Leaving his elaborate defenses at Yorktown to follow the retreating Confederates, McClellan fought a rear-guard action at Williamsburg, and moved to White House Landing, twenty miles from Richmond. Meanwhile he renewed his calls on the War Department and the President for more men and guns. Also he continued, with some of his generals, an undiminished political activity.

Long letters passed between McClellan and Lincoln on the corps organization of the army, Lincoln writing once in reference to three high officers: "I am constantly told that you have no consultation or communication with them; that you consult and communicate with nobody but General Fitz-John Porter and perhaps General Franklin. I do not say that these complaints are true or just; but at all events, it is proper you should know of their existence. Do the commanders of corps disobey your orders in anything?" On his own judgment the President did not pretend to understand the subject. "I ordered the army corps organization not only on the unanimous opinion of the twelve generals whom you had selected and assigned as generals of division, but also on the unanimous opinion of every military man I could get an opinion from (and every modern military book), yourself only excepted." The President considered it indispensable for McClellan to know how his struggle against the present corps system was received in quarters that could not be disregarded. "It is looked upon as merely an effort to pamper one or two pets and to persecute and degrade their supposed rivals." The President intimated that if General McClellan continued to pay attention to political criticism from Washington he should be practical. "When you relieved General Hamilton of his command the other day, you thereby lost the confidence of at least one of your best friends in the Senate. . . . The success of your army and the cause of the country are the same, and of course I only desire the good of the cause." McClellan's high officers seemed to have excess dignity. "Let me say, not as applicable to you personally, that senators and representatives speak of me in their places without question, and that officers of the army must cease addressing insulting letters to them for taking no greater liberty with them."

One corps commander, E. D. Keyes, wrote from the Peninsula a long letter, a treatise that took one or two days to write, addressing it to Senator Ira Harris. It advised that for successful invasion "you must have one line of operations and one army, under one general," implying that the one general should be McClellan. It closed: "Please show this letter to the President." These instances multiplied.

Rain, mud, heavy roads, bogged his army, McClellan complained to Lincoln, as though the enemy had fair weather and smooth going. Lincoln remarked to Hay that "he seemed to think, in defiance of Scripture, that Heaven sent its rain only on the just and not on the unjust."

To McClellan's handicap of always believing he was outnumbered was added a fear that enemies among his own officers were leagued with enemies at Washington in plots against him. He wrote his wife on May 1: "I shall be very glad when we are really ready to open fire, and then finish this confounded affair. I am tired of public life; and even now, when I am doing the best I can for my country in the field, I know that my enemies are pursuing me more remorselessly than ever." He described his predicament—"the rebels on one side, and the abolitionists and other scoundrels on the other."

The wounded Confederate commander Joseph E. Johnston was replaced by Robert E. Lee, and the issue was whether McClellan could outguess Lee. Lee sent Stonewall Jackson to the Shenandoah Valley, let his best fighter go away, on a job that Lee guessed Jackson could accomplish while McClellan delayed, waited. Jackson with 17,000 men swept hither and yon in the valley region and in fourteen days marched his army one hundred and seventy miles, routed 12,500 of the enemy, captured $250,000 worth of supplies and property, took 3,000 prisoners and 9,000 rifles. It was a Napoleonic raid and foray on a large scale, which threatened Washington so seriously that Lincoln called off McDowell from co-operation with McClellan. Lincoln sent orders to some 60,000 men under McDowell, Frémont, and Banks, three different armies, and tried to surround Jackson. Frémont, however, disobeyed two of Lincoln's orders, "resting" his men one day when they were ordered to march, and another day taking a route different from the one ordered by Lincoln. On paper the strategy worked out by Lincoln, for bagging Jackson's army in the clutch of three Union armies, was logical enough. But Jackson was an illogical phantom, got away with his supplies and prisoners, and joined Lee at Richmond—as Lee had guessed he would.

McClellan guessed that Lee must have at least 200,000 troops or he would not have dared to detach Jackson for the Shenandoah Valley operation. Lee had less than 83,000 when reinforced by Jackson, but this McClellan neither knew nor could guess. Clearly in McClellan's dispatches to Washington and his letters to his wife stood out the appalling fact that he himself believed that Lee with 200,000 men was perfectly willing to wait and delay battle while McClellan came on with one soldier to Lee's two. McClellan pushed his troops to a point four miles from Richmond, still believing he was short of troops, still calling to Washington for more men. On a day when his army outnumbered the enemy by 30,000 to 40,000 he telegraphed to the War Department: "The rebel force is stated at 200,000. I regret my inferiority in numbers, but feel that I am in no way responsible for it, as I have not failed to represent repeatedly the need for reinforcements." Lincoln wired him: "The probability of your being overwhelmed by 200,000, and talking of where the responsibility will belong, pains me very much. I give you all I can, and act on the presumption that you will do the best that you can with what you have, while you continue, ungenerously I think, to assume that I could give you more if I would. I have omitted and shall omit no opportunity to send you reinforcements whenever I possibly can."

In telegraphing Lincoln "The rebel force is stated at 200,000," McClellan was taking as correct the report of his secret-service chief, Allan Pinkerton, Illinois Central Railroad detective when McClellan was chief engineer. "My shrewd and daring operatives," wrote Pinkerton, "moved in and out among the Rebel troops at all times." They reported to him that by June 26 the enemy numbers were "swelled to nearly 200,000 effective men. . . . General McClellan knew from the reports I laid before him, the fearful odds against which he had to contend." And yet—the overwhelming evidence of Confederate officers and their records affirmed that with all the new troops secured through their conscription law passed in April, and with the reinforcements of Stonewall Jackson arriving from the Shenandoah Valley, the Confederate forces before and around Richmond were never over 90,000 in number.

Lincoln understood with McClellan that if the Army of the Potomac could smash the enemy army, take Richmond, and send the Confederate Government a fugitive flying southward, it would set big bells ringing over the North. On the other hand, the wreck of McClellan's army might mean the end of the Union cause. The hazards affected McClellan's mind. Over and again in the many letters to his wife, written often at midnight and "1 A.M.," he told her of his courage, his resolution, how firm he was. He mentioned his faith and his fearlessness often enough to show his own doubt of himself.

These phases of McClellan haunted Lincoln, Stanton, Ben Wade, Zach Chandler. "He's got the slows," was one comment of Lincoln.

In April the War Department ordered recruiting stopped, as though the forces in the field were enough to win the war. Weeks passed, and it was seen that more men were needed—and more money; that perhaps desperate years lay ahead.

Lincoln wrote a letter for Seward to use among men of financial and political power who were insisting that they must know precisely where the President stood, whether he really meant to carry on a war, and if so for how long, and what were his immediate intentions. Lincoln's letter outlined immediate plans "to hold what we have in the West, open the Mississippi, and take Chattanooga and East Tennessee" besides going on with the Virginia campaign. "Then let the country give us a hundred thousand new troops in the shortest possible time, which . . . will take Richmond."

Then came in this letter a manner of oath: "I expect to maintain this contest until successful, or till I die, or am conquered, or my term expires, or Congress or the country forsake me." He would appeal to the country at once for new forces "were it not that I fear a general panic and stampede would follow, so hard it is to have a thing understood as it really is." The President was convincing. Seward and others got the governors of the North to sign a request that more troops be raised.

Lincoln on July 1 made a call for 300,000 three-year men—wondering how the country would take it. He wrote to McClellan, who was calling for 50,000 more soldiers, to be patient. On July 4 he sat through a long talk with McClellan's father-in-law and chief of staff, R. B. Marcy, who wired McClellan: "I have seen the President and Secretary of War. Ten thousand men from Hunter, 10,000 from Burnside, and 11,000 from here have been ordered to re-enforce you as soon as possible. Halleck has been urged by the President to send you at once 10,000 men from Corinth. The President and Secretary speak very kindly of you and find no fault."

Meanwhile Lincoln's circular letter to the Northern governors was going out, telling them that even with 50,000 troops raised in a month, 20,000 would be leaving and the gain would be only 30,000. "Time is everything. Please act in view of this."

The raising of new troops came addedly hard now because of McClellan's handling of his army. The enemy struck at his White House Landing base of supplies, where food, guns, powder, wagons, mules, arrived from Washington. And McClellan ordered a change of base to Harrison's Landing on the James River. And during the Seven Days' battles, on McClellan's retreat Lee put in every last man and gun he had and tried to crumple up McClellan and capture his army. In the finish, and after bloody fighting, McClellan still held Harrison's Landing and had lost only 16,000 men as against 20,000 Confederate losses.

A complex and weary McClellan, after the first of the Seven Days' battles, telegraphed to Secretary Stanton: "I have seen too many dead and wounded comrades to feel otherwise than that the government has not sustained this army. If you do not do so now the game is lost."

Then McClellan used accusing words: "If I save this army now, I tell you plainly that I owe no thanks to you or any person in Washington. You have done your best to sacrifice this army."

And of these words, McClellan wrote his wife: "Of course they will never forgive me for that. I knew it when I wrote it."

And it happened that Lincoln and Stanton never saw the last final accusing words of the telegram till a much later time. For Colonel E. S. Sanford, supervisor and censor of telegraphic messages, found these words to be outrageous, infamous, treasonable, designed by McClellan "to reach the public as a means of shifting the cause of defeat from his own to other shoulders."

Colonel Sanford took on himself the duty of cutting out from the telegram what he regarded as treason. "The telegram, minus the offensive words, was then recopied, and the copy handed by him to Stanton and taken by Stanton to the President," said Major A. E. H. Johnson, custodian of telegrams, when the facts were later uncovered. Neither the Secretary of War nor the President knew of its mutilation. "Both acted upon it in perfect ignorance of the terrible charge it had previously contained against them."

Lincoln replied to the mutilated telegram: "Save your army, at all events. Will send reinforcements as fast as we can." As it was a two-hundred-mile water route, he added, "Of course they cannot reach you to-day, to-morrow or next day." He would comfort McClellan, reason with him: "I feel any misfortune to you and your army quite as keenly as you feel it yourself. If you have had a drawn battle, or a repulse, it is the price we pay for the enemy not being in Washington. We protected Washington, and the enemy concentrated on you. Had we stripped Washington, he would have been upon us before the troops could have gotten to you."

McClellan's effort in the Peninsula had a world audience. His campaign was a commanding historic event. He was the first man in the Western world to command 100,000 men. He was extraordinarily outfitted and supplied, in tents, clothes, shoes, blankets, guns; his men were far better off than the enemy troops, who after a battle took the shoes off dead men for the living barefoot troops. Hundreds of miles of logs laid over mud, corduroy roads, had been built by McClellan's men. Their pontoon bridges by the score had been torn away by rising rivers and rebuilt by the laughing engineer corps. They had wrestled in rain and deep red clay with mules and wagons bringing up cannon, ammunition, coffee, hardtack, pork and beans. In artillery and rifles they surpassed the enemy in numbers and in late models.

At Malvern Hill a Confederate artilleryman sat in comfort behind a tree. "A moment later," noticed General D. H. Hill, "a shell passed through the huge tree and took off the man's head. This gives an idea of the great power of Federal rifled artillery." A Federal balloon, piloted by its inventor, Professor T. S. C. Lowe, rose 1,000 feet above Richmond, sending balloon telegraph and signal messages to McClellan; it was beyond range of the Confederate guns, but with their steady fire at it Lowe became known as "the most shot-at man in the war." A Confederate creation known as the Silk Dress Balloon, made from hundreds of wedding-gowns and evening dresses sent with prayers to Richmond by the women who had worn them, it was said, drifted onto a sand bar and was captured on the way to its first flight.

At one time, as McClellan came near Richmond, the gold and the archives of the Confederate Government were loaded on railroad cars ready to move in case McClellan reached the city.

On both sides was courage, tenacity. A correspondent saw a Federal soldier brought into a field hospital, "both legs torn off by a shell, both arms broken by bullets, the film of death glazing his eyes," but when spoken to he cried out, "I trust to God we are licking them!" At Malvern Hill a Confederate colonel had shouted: "Come on, come on, my men! Do you want to live forever?"

Surgeon Daniel W. Hand of the 1st Minnesota Volunteers told of a day of work at amputations in a field hospital: "It was late in the night before my own cares allowed me to rest, and then, where should I lie down? A cold wind was blowing, and we shivered in our scanty clothing. Every foot of sheltered ground was covered with sleeping men, but near the operating table, under a tree in the house-yard, there lay a long row of dead soldiers. My steward, Cyrus Brooks, suggested we make a windbreak by piling them up against the remnants of a fence. We did so, and then lying down behind them, we slept soundly until morning."

Gay humor lighted grim incidents. General O. O. Howard's right arm was shattered, and when he met General Phil Kearny, who had lost his left arm in Mexico, the two men shook hands on Howard's saying, "Hereafter we buy our gloves together."

At White House Landing, in order to keep supplies out of the enemy's hand McClellan ordered railroad trains loaded with powder and food run off an embankment into the deep mud of the Pamunkey River; other trains of cars were burned where they stood on the tracks. A South Carolina regiment gathered 925 rifles thrown away in a wheat field at Shirley; these were part of 35,000 small arms that fell to the Confederates as McClellan retreated. Strewn for miles were broken army wagons, axes, shovels, camp kettles, medicine chests, blankets, overcoats, stacks of flour barrels and mess beef, much of it burned or spoiled to make it useless to the enemy.

Not with pride did Northern people read of Confederate cavalry under the twenty-nine-year-old General J. E. B. Stuart making a ride that took them around the whole of McClellan's army, with no interruptions. It was just after this ride that James F. Wilson, calling at the White House with other officials, asked the President, "Have you any news from the army?" The reply was mournful, noted Wilson: "Not one word. We can get no communication with it. I don't know that we have an army. It may have been destroyed or captured, though I cannot so believe, for it was a splendid army. But the most I can do now is to hope that serious disaster has not befallen it."

Yet for all his losses of men and material McClellan had won a victory. His cannon mounted tier on tier at Malvern Hill had mowed down the repeated lines of Confederates ordered up by Lee. Moving from Yorktown toward Richmond, McClellan had killed more of the enemy forces than they had of his. And now, having broken the fiercest blow the enemy could bring against him, he shrank under the protection of his gunboats at Harrison's Landing. When the order came to fall back, Chaplain Marks heard the one-armed New Jersey army officer who had fought among Indians, Arabs, Italians, say to other high officers: "I, Philip Kearny, an old soldier, enter my solemn protest against this order for retreat; we ought, instead of retreating, to follow up the enemy and take Richmond. And in full view of all the responsibility of such a declaration I say to you all, such an order can only be prompted by cowardice or treason."

The collapse of this campaign staggered Lincoln, who remarked of it later, "I was as nearly inconsolable as I could be and live."

And in a lighter vein he told Lamon: "It seems to me that McClellan has been wandering around and got lost. He's been hollering for help ever since he went south, wants somebody to . . . get him out of the place he's got into." Lincoln was reminded of an Illinois man who with some friends visited the state penitentiary. They wandered everywhere and saw everything in the big jailhouse, and this man got separated from his friends and couldn't find his way out. He meandered farther till at last he came across a convict looking out from between the bars of his cell door. And he asked the prisoner, "Say! How do you get out of this place?"

McClellan wrote the War Department, "To accomplish the great task of capturing Richmond and putting an end to this rebellion reinforcements should be sent to me rather much over than much less than 100,000 men." His wish was that Lincoln should get him these troops, outfitted and equipped. As yet he could not estimate his losses but, he wrote, "I doubt whether there are today more than 50,000 men with their colors."

Lincoln said, "Sending men to that army is like shoveling fleas across a barnyard—not half of them get there." Still again, when another request came for more men, he said: "If I gave McClellan all the men he asks for they could not find room to lie down. They'd have to sleep standing up."

With Stanton, Lincoln started for Harrison's Landing, spent a day there, talked with McClellan, quizzed his generals, and found that McClellan had 86,500 troops present for duty, 34,000 absent by authority, 3,700 absent without authority, his command including more than 120,000.

Lincoln and Stanton, on this visit, rode horseback alongside McClellan reviewing troops. As they passed the tens of thousands of men lined up in marching order they might have wondered a moment how they looked to the men and officers while reviewing them. Part of it was told in a letter of Chaplain Joseph Twichell of a Connecticut regiment, who wrote his father on July 9 of '62: "So far as I can judge, the troops are in excellent humor—especially with themselves. McClellan does well to be proud of his command, whether or not the pride is reciprocal. His proclamation [telling the troops they fought with unparalleled bravery] was received with as much quiet complacency, as a man would pocket a debt duly paid. It was somewhat so yesterday when President Lincoln and Secretary Stanton paid us a visit. As they rode along the lines the boys cheered stoutly, like good, loyal soldiers, but there was the feeling—'We are the chaps to be admired! It is you, Abraham and Edwin, that ought to do the cheering!'

"The visit of our good President was a surprise. At about the middle of the afternoon, a salute fired by the gunboat announced his coming. We were called out into line and before night fell he went the rounds. I have seldom witnessed a more ludicrous sight than our worthy Chief Magistrate presented on horseback yesterday. While I lifted my cap with respect for the man raised up by God to rule our troubled times, I lowered it speedily to cover a smile that overmastered me. McClellan was beside him, stout, short, and stiffly erect, sitting his horse like a dragoon, and the contrast was perfect. It did seem as though every moment the President's legs would become entangled with those of the horse he rode and both come down together, while his arms were apparently subject to similar mishaps. . . . That arm with which he drew the rein, in its angles and position resembled the hind leg of a grasshopper—the hand before—the elbow away back over the horse's tail. The removal of his hat before each regiment was also a source of laughter in the style of its execution—the quick trot of the horse making it a feat of some difficulty, while from the same cause, his hold on it, while off, seemed very precarious.

"But, the boys liked him, in fact his popularity with the army is and has been universal. Most of our rulers and leaders fall into odium, but all have faith in Lincoln. 'When he finds it out,' they say, 'it will be stopped.' I heard officers yesterday make the earnest remark, 'With all their palaver and re- views, and Dukes and Princes [meaning McClellan's contingent of foreign nobles], I don't believe they'll be able to pull the wool over old Lincoln's eyes.' His benign smile as he passed us by was a real reflection from his hon- est, kindly heart, but deeper, under the surface of that marked and not all un- comely face were the signs of care and anxiety. God bless the man and give answer to the prayers for guidance I am sure he offers."

The one little speech of the President on this trip to the Peninsula was reported by various journals, the *Harper's Weekly* account running:

During his visit he made a speech to the serried masses of army men who had just come out of seven days terrific combat. Dismounting from his horse and mounting upon a rail fence, he addressed the army in these words: "Be of good cheer; all is well. The country owes you an inextinguishable debt for your services. I am under immeasurable obligations to you. You have, like heroes, endured, and fought, and con- quered. Yes, I say conquered; for though apparently checked once, you conquered afterward and secured the position of your choice. You shall be strengthened and re- warded. God bless you all!"

Lincoln returned to Washington carrying a letter written by McClellan. It was something to think about. McClellan had met the presidential steamer at Harrison's Landing and himself handed the letter to Lincoln, who read it with McClellan looking on, told McClellan he was much obliged, and put the letter in his pocket. It was a long letter and must have taken McClellan several hours, more likely a day or two, to write.

McClellan coolly unfolded for Lincoln his ideas on how the country ought to be run, what policies should guide the Government. The war should be "conducted upon the highest principles known to Christian civilization." Private property should be respected; "radical views, especially upon slavery," would melt away the armies. Free advice on broad questions was dealt out for the President. McClellan believed it healthy advice, for he wrote his wife: "I have written a strong, frank letter to the President. . . . If he acts upon it the country will be saved."

And while the letter was neither strong nor frank, and any current editorial of the *New York Herald* was keener and more specific in the same field, McClellan was sincere in believing that it would save the country. His sincerity was incomplete, however, else he would have informed Lincoln that Fernando Wood, the Mayor of New York who in '61 tried to get his city to secede from the Union and set up as a Free City, had called on him in camp to talk politics. With Wood was another Democrat of national influence—and they told McClellan, as between Democrats, that he ought to be his party's candidate for the Presidency in the next campaign. They went away and McClellan wrote out a letter stating his views. Before mailing it, he read it to one of his generals, "Baldy" Smith, who broke out, "General, do you not see that looks like treason, and that it will ruin you and all of us?" So McClellan tore up the letter, before Baldy Smith's eyes, and thanked Baldy Smith. And since then he had been more than ever haunted by his responsibility; over and again in letters to his wife he referred to himself as the one man to save the country.

Of the letter he handed Lincoln McClellan wrote to his wife: "I will send you a copy to-morrow, as well as of the other important letters which I wish you to keep as my record. They will show, with the others you have, that I was true to my country, that I understood the state of affairs long ago, and that had my advice been followed we should not have been in our present difficulties." And later: "The President, of course, has not replied to my letter, and never will. His reply may be, however, to avail himself of the first opportunity to cut my head off."

Donn Piatt, long after the event, said that McClellan's Judge Advocate Key rode through a camp where the soldiers gathered and cheered Little Mac, and after a long silence McClellan broke his reverie by saying to Key: "How these brave fellows love me, and what a power that love places in my hands! What is there to prevent my taking the Government in my own hands?" And Key hurried to reply: "General, don't mistake those men. So long as you lead them against the enemy, they will adore you and die for you; but attempt to turn them against their Government and you will be the first to suffer." Ben Perley Poore, a fairly responsible correspondent, wrote, "A prominent politician, more outspoken than some of those around him, is quoted by General Custer as having said, 'It is not on our books that McClellan shall take Richmond.' " This may have been a Washington wartime rumor, idle chatter. Both McClellan and his friends, however, were using questionable language, accusations, gestures.

McClellan spoke of "saving" his army almost as though by some slight whim of mind or caprice of heart he might not choose to save it—and what then? His chief of staff and father-in-law, R. B. Marcy, deepened misgivings in Washington when in a talk with Stanton he remarked that he would not be surprised if McClellan's army should be forced to "capitulate." The lingo could mean anything. Browning noted in his diary: "This excited Stanton very much, and he went directly to the President and reported what had been said. It also excited the President, whereupon he sent for Marcy and said to him sternly, 'Genl I understand you have used the word "Capitulate"—that is a word not to be used in connection with our army &c.' Marcy blundered out some kind of explanation, excuse or apology."

The habit of blaming others for mistakes, accidents, fate, had grown on McClellan. He wrote to his wife of being humble, nothing in himself, an instrument of the Almighty, but such acknowledgments were lost in his flow of words blaming others. "I am tired of serving fools. God help my country!" Or, "I am satisfied that the dolts in Washington are bent on my destruction." There was a "game" against him. There were "pretexts" to persecute him. He saw "incompetents" at Washington doing "injustice" to him. This, that, was "infamous."

McClellan's viewpoints and vocalisms won him enemies, who now stepped out of hiding. Zach Chandler of Michigan rose in the Senate on July 16 and snarled and roared accusations of "wholesale murder"; of Northern traitors "who will come behind you and cut your throat in the dark" under the pretense of patriotism; he named McClellan, in effect, as the leader of all high treasons.

McClellan was writing to his old friend William H. Aspinwall, Panama Railroad and Pacific Mail Steamship magnate, for a position at "some comparatively quiet pursuit." He indicated, "I really need rest."

Lincoln had called General Halleck from the West to serve as General in Chief of all land forces. And Lincoln was through with gathering more troops for McClellan, telling Browning, as noted in that Senator's diary, "That if by magic he could reinforce McClelland with 100,000 men to day he would be in an ecstasy over it, thank him for it, and tell him that he would go to Richmond tomorrow, but that when tomorrow came he would telegraph that he had certain information that the enemy had 400,000 men, and that he could not advance without reinforcements."

Halleck was asking McClellan's generals whether they ought to stay before Richmond on the Peninsula. Some said No, some Yes. Fighting Joe Hooker told McClellan that they could take Richmond and ought to, with no waiting. He, Hooker, would handle the advance and lead the way. And according to Hooker, two hours afterward he had orders from McClellan to get ready three days' rations and be ready to march the next day at two o'clock for Richmond. But before that hour McClellan countermanded the order.

Slowly the news had trickled out, and at last the whole story had to be told to the country of the Seven Days' battles, of superb valor and endurance, of beating the enemy and then retreating, of a great army that seemed to have everything in men and material foiled, thwarted, sent shrinking to the protection of its gunboats.

Out over the country, in homes where had been faith, doubts crept in. The national mood reached the White House, where the President sat in his library writing, "with directions to deny him to everybody." But the old friend Senator Browning stepped in a moment and in the evening wrote of the moment: "He looked weary, care-worn and troubled. I shook hands with him, and asked him how he was. He said 'tolerably well' I remarked that I felt concerned about him—regretted that troubles crowded so heavily upon him, and feared his health was suffering. He held me by the hand, pressed it, and said in a very tender and touching tone—'Browning, I must die sometime,' I replied, 'your fortunes Mr President are bound up with those of the Country, and disaster to one would be disaster to the other, and I hope you will do all you can to preserve your health and life.' He looked very sad, and there was a cadence of deep sadness in his voice. We parted I believe both of us with tears in our eyes."

And now the Army of the Potomac, its sick and wounded, its cannon and horses, its mules and wagons, its trophies and battle flags, its farm hands, shopmen, college boys, store clerks, ditch-diggers, all in uniform, was brought back from the Peninsula to old places on the Potomac River within sight of the Capitol. And McClellan was relieved of command in the field and told to report himself for orders at Alexandria.

While this army was moving off the Peninsula, where it had done titanic fighting and failed of its objectives, the country wondered why, and nearly every discussion ranged around three men. These were McClellan in field command, Stanton with his War Department, and the President who had authority over both of them. What were the secrets of mismanagement, jealousy, quarrels, and blunders among these three? The country asked. And the President on August 6, 1862, made a speech at a war meeting in Washington answering the question in a familiar manner as though he might be talking to some one man who had casually dropped into his office. Without any tone of complaint over disaster, even with touches of dry humor that drew laughter, he spoke as though he were a referee, an umpire, who could make a delicate decision in a mixed affair. He seemed to wish to give an impression that he knew what he was talking about and would correct himself the moment more facts and light came to him. He seemed almost to be under the spell of an idea that the people wanted their President to step straight into the center of a scandalous intrigue and give an interpretation that might help stem further disaster. What he set out to say could not be said in any comprehensive way, and when he had finished, what he had said amounted to a patient and good-humored warning that there was too much loose talk and the troubles at hand could not be met by idle chatter. Newspapers gave their readers this report of the speech with interpolations:

Fellow-Citizens,—I believe there is no precedent for my appearing before you on this occasion—[Applause.]—but it is also true that there is no precedent for your being here yourselves—[Applause and laughter.]—and I offer in justification of myself and of you that, upon examination, I have found nothing in the Constitution against it. [Renewed applause.] I, however, have an impression that there are younger gentlemen who will entertain you better—[Voices—"No, no: none can do better than yourself; go on!"]—and better address your understanding than I will or could, and therefore I propose but to detain you a moment longer. [Cries—"Go on! Tar and feather the rebels!"]

I am very little inclined on any occasion to say any thing unless I hope to produce some good by it. [A voice—"You do that. Go on!"] The only thing I think of just now not likely to be better said by someone else is a matter in which we have heard some other persons blamed for what I did myself. [Voice—"What is it?"]

There has been a very wide-spread attempt to have a quarrel between General McClellan and the Secretary of War. Now, I occupy a position that enables me to believe at least these two gentlemen are not nearly so deep in the quarrel as some presuming to be their friends. [Cries of "Good!"] General McClellan's attitude is such that in the very selfishness of his nature he can not but wish to be successful—and I hope he will—and the Secretary of War is precisely in the same situation. If the military commanders in the field can not be successful, not only the Secretary of War, but myself, for the time being the master of them both, can not but be failures. [Laughter and applause.] I know General McClellan wishes to be successful, and I know he does not wish it any more than the Secretary of War for him, and both of them together no more than I wish it. [Applause and cries of "Good!"]

Sometimes we have a dispute about how many men General McClellan has had, and those who would disparage him say he has had a very large number, and those who would disparage the Secretary of War insist that General McClellan has had a very small number. The basis for this is, there is always a wider difference, and, on this occasion, perhaps a wide one between the grand total on McClellan's rolls and the men actually fit for duty; and those who would disparage him talk of the grand total on paper, and those who would disparage the Secretary of War talk of those at present fit for duty. General McClellan has sometimes asked for things that the Secretary of War did not give him. General McClellan is not to blame for asking for what he wanted and needed, and the Secretary of War is not to blame for not giving when he had none to give. [Applause, laughter, and cries of "Good, good!"]

And I say here, so far as I know, the Secretary of War has withheld no one thing at any time in my power to give him. [Wild applause, and a voice—"Give him enough now!"] I have no accusation against him. I believe he is a brave and able man—[Applause.]—and I stand here, as justice requires me to do, to take upon myself what has been charged on the Secretary of War as withholding from him. I have talked longer than I expected to do—[Cries of "No," "No"; "Go on!"] and now I avail myself of my privilege of saying no more.

Lincoln himself was not sure what he was accomplishing by this speech, though one evident intention was to give the country a picture of a President in contact with the irresistible force Stanton and the immovable obstacle McClellan. A second, third, and fourth reading of the speech would yield further intentions, one of which was to let the people know that in the hotbed of cliques, factions, whispering circles and clamoring gangs, at Washington, the President was actually presiding, was an understanding spectator of clashing temperaments, and was trying to weld all parties and factions possible into a united front.

Harper's Weekly commented: "The peril of the nation annihilates party, and whoever forgets that fact, the President does not. He is the most purely national and loyal Chief Magistrate we have had in many a year. Removals from office have been made from patriotic and not upon partisan grounds." Besides McClellan were other Democrats in high station. "Mr. Jeremiah S. Black, the last Secretary of State under James Buchanan, has been named Reporter to the Supreme Court. General Dix, the last Secretary of War in the same Cabinet, is now Major-General in command at Baltimore."

Stanton was gaining results in department organization. Yet it was more often by sheer driving, head-on force than by smooth, intelligent co-ordination. Donn Piatt of Frémont's staff, taking tea at Stanton's home, was asked how he was "getting on under that little mountebank of the Mountain Department." Piatt resented the question, saw Stanton's short lip curling up from white teeth in a sneer. Piatt squirmed, felt insulted. He said Frémont had more military ability in his little finger than McClellan had in his entire body. "That may be," and Stanton's lip curled again, "and not say much either. What has the husband of Jessie done to impress you with his ability?" Piatt's reply did not interest Stanton, though Stanton knew Piatt as one of his profoundest and most sympathetic admirers.

Stanton went into a discussion of McClellan. Piatt remembered vividly one remark: "This fellow with his gang is as busy as the devil impressing on the men he is murdering to no purpose, that the abolitionists at Washington, as he calls us, have abandoned them to death in the swamps of the Chickahominy. We are today in more peril from the Army of the Potomac than the rebels at Richmond."

Hate, fear, jealousy, were rampant. To a man who came complaining against his superior officer, rather loose-mouthed, Lincoln merely said, "Go home and read Proverbs xxx, 10." And the man hunted up his Bible and read the verse "Accuse not a servant unto his master, lest he curse thee, and thou be found guilty."

Amid the somber days arose a folk fable to pass the time. It epitomized much. Lincoln had scolded McClellan, the drollery ran, for not sending more complete and detailed reports of his army's progress. So McClellan sent a telegram to Lincoln one day: "Have captured two cows. What disposition should I make of them?" Lincoln: "Milk 'em, George."

The President spoke of fog in a little informal address at Jersey City on June 24, when he was returning from a conference with General Winfield Scott at West Point. He had left Washington suddenly, stayed a day at the military academy, talked long with the dim-eyed, asthmatic, venerable veteran of 1812, and he took the country into his confidence only so far as his statements went to the Jersey City crowd, which insisted on a speech.

"When birds and animals are looked at through a fog, they are seen to disadvantage," he remarked. "And so it might be with you if I were to attempt to tell you why I went to see General Scott. I can only say that my visit to West Point did not have the importance which has been attached to it, but it concerned matters that you understand quite as well as if I were to tell you all about them. Now, I can only remark that it had nothing whatever to do with making or unmaking any general in the country."

The President was strictly conversational. "The Secretary of War, you know, holds a pretty tight rein on the press, so that they shall not tell more than they ought to; and I'm afraid that if I blab too much, he might draw a tight rein on me."

The shrewdest performer among Union secret-service operatives was the subject of a special Cabinet session in April of '62. Allan Pinkerton had hurried from McClellan's field headquarters with the information that his best spy, a man whom he regarded as the greatest secret agent of all times, had at Richmond been caught in meshes of treachery and blunder, a death warrant read to him that on April 29 he would be hanged by the neck till he was dead.

The President and Stanton agreed with Pinkerton that the Cabinet should seek to determine whether any official intervention, threat of retaliation, or other recourse might be adopted to save Timothy Webster from hanging. In many corners of the South Webster was supposed to be a trusted spy of Jefferson Davis's. Webster had encouraged this impression, had studied the role of a Southern "fire-eater," could act the part of the impassioned loyal Southerner. More than once a suspicious barroom questioner had begun asking, "Haven't I seen you before?" and leading on with inquiries till Webster knocked him down, pulled a revolver, and then delivered such a fierce, indignant Confederate speech that the crowd was with him.

Once in Pittsburgh a mob came near lynching Webster as a Confederate spy. He was known in Richmond for his escapes from the clutches of Union military officials who sought him as a Confederate spy. He had delivered to the Confederate Government military information of some value, the information having been agreed on beforehand with Pinkerton and McClellan. While Webster lay sick in his room at the Monumental Hotel in Richmond, weakened by inflammatory rheumatism, Pinkerton worried about him and sent two operatives, John Scully and Pryce Lewis, who offered themselves for the dangerous errand of finding Webster. In sending these two, Pinkerton acted in mistaken judgment, for Scully and Lewis had searched homes and personally questioned many suspected rebels in Washington. Their faces were known to at least a score of secessionist sympathizers and two or three Confederate secret-service operatives.

Scully and Lewis arrived in Richmond, went to Webster's bedside, and found him a pathetic invalid under the care of Mrs. Carrie Lawton, also a Pinkerton operative. Had they then left Richmond and gone straight back with a report to their chief all would have been well, for Timothy Webster had dug himself deep into the confidence of many Confederates, had covered his tracks; searches of his room and effects had disclosed nothing to incriminate him or throw doubt on him. But Scully and Lewis went back to Webster's bedside again and again, though he told them, "Get out of this town as fast as you possibly can." They aroused suspicion, were arrested, identified, court-martialed, sentenced to be hanged. The Confederate press announced that two Yankee spies would meet their deserved doom.

Lewis and a gang of prisoners overpowered a jailer, escaped, straggled along the streets of Richmond, two by two, far apart. In chilly winds and drenched with rain they made their way to the banks of the little muddy Chickahominy River near the Army of the Potomac. But roving squads of Confederates picked them up one by one. And Lewis was taken back to Richmond in irons.

Then with the death rope but a few days away for Scully, a Confederate spy impersonating a Roman Catholic priest heard admissions from Scully that implicated Timothy Webster. Pryce Lewis on being told of Scully's admissions corroborated them. A court-martial put Webster on trial. A worn and weak-voiced invalid, he sat and listened and saw Scully and Lewis, word by word, to save their necks from the rope swear away his life. The press announced that on April 29 Webster would be hanged.

President Lincoln and his Cabinet considered the situation. The resulting action was a message sent by telegraph and by flag-of-truce boat to the Confederate Government reciting the lenient course of the Union Government in dealing with Confederate spies, how many had been released after short prison terms, and none thus far tried for life or sentenced to death. Pinkerton believed that the closing part of the message might be effective, with its intimation that if Webster were put to death the Union Government would retaliate. Stanton had written the message and framed it in a legal and diplomatic tone. Had it delivered a plain and unmistakable threat that if Webster were hanged a Southerner of equal dignity and importance in some Northern prison would likewise be given the rope, the Confederate Government would at least have delayed and held conversations about the matter.

As it was, Timothy Webster on April 29, in broken health, so weak that he had to be lifted into the carriage that took him from his prison to the gallows yard, met his fate serenely. He had asked that he might face a firing squad like a soldier, but this was denied him. At the steps leading up to the gallows he summoned strength enough to walk alone to where a nervous hangman, unaccustomed and inexpert, was slow, allowed the noose to slip. The crowd of onlookers was curious and silent, made no mockery, and witnessed Timothy Webster dancing on air and taking leave of life as unafraid as he had lived it.

Pinkerton regarded Webster as unsurpassed in the annals of detective art, considered his work in unearthing a Baltimore plot to assassinate Lincoln, and his reports to McClellan's headquarters on the numbers and movements of Confederate forces around Richmond, as noteworthy achievements. Jefferson Davis took the ground that in the case of Major André, General

George Washington had recognized the valor and personal worth of the condemned man and had put him to death with sincere regret.

"Belle Boyd, the Secesh Cleopatra, is caged at last," said *Leslie's Weekly* one summer day of '62. "It appears that she has red hair and large teeth, and a loud coarse laugh." This was mere propaganda, for Belle Boyd had moderate-sized teeth and could laugh pleasantly when she chose. She was, however, the brightest approach of the South to a "Secesh Cleopatra." She used her looks and charm, her woman's prerogatives, to worm information out of Union officers and soldiers. A letter of hers intended for General Jackson was intercepted. Stanton ordered her arrest; she was seized at Front Royal, Virginia, her room searched, her person stripped, and incriminating papers found, with a handsome pistol and belt given her by a Union officer.

Under heavy guard she was taken to Old Capitol Prison in Washington and lodged in cell No. 6, with an outlook on houses where she had mixed in gay parties of the Buchanan Administration. She scraped a hole through plaster and exchanged notes with gentlemen of the Army of Virginia in the next cell. She received messages from others on the floor above, who loosened a plank in the floor and talked with her. She hung on the wall of cell No. 6 a half-length portrait of the Confederate President with the inscription "Three Cheers for Jefferson Davis and the Southern Confederacy." On the evidence she could have been legally convicted as a spy, shot at sunrise, and heard of no more, but she became one of two hundred prisoners exchanged and sent to Richmond. Also she resumed her spy activities and became a Southern legend, flirting pitilessly in behalf of her cause.

CHAPTER 23

THE DRAFT—DECISIONS—PATHOS

IN the year since the first battle at Bull Run, the Union armies had cleared their way into 100,000 square miles of enemy territory. Lincoln in a letter to the friendly Frenchman, Count Agénor de Gasparin, then in Switzerland, gave his explanation, in part, of why the Southern armies with fewer numbers so often held off the Federals: "The enemy holds the interior and we the exterior lines; and . . . we operate where the people convey information to the enemy, while he operates where they convey none to us." The American soldier was not a peasant conscript. "With us every soldier is a man of character, and must be treated with more consideration than is customary in Europe. Hence our great army, for slighter causes than could have prevailed there, has dwindled rapidly. . . . The moral effect was the worst of the affair before Richmond, and that has run its course downward. We are now at a stand, and shall soon be rising again, as we hope."

The Count should not be alarmed to hear of men being drafted. "It seems strange even to me, but it is true, that the government is now pressed to this course by a popular demand. Thousands who wish not to personally enter the service are nevertheless anxious to pay and send substitutes, provided they can have the assurance that unwilling persons, similarly situated, will be compelled to do likewise. Besides this, volunteers mostly choose to enter newly forming regiments, while drafted men can be sent to fill up the old ones, wherein man for man they are quite doubly as valuable."

Part of an "order of the President" written by Seward, corrected by Stanton, August 5 of '61, calls for "a draft of three hundred thousand militia" for nine months' service. The final sentence: "The Regulations will also provide for ridding the service of such incompetent persons as now hold commissions in it." Original in the Barrett collection.

On the day of August 4, 1862, when he wrote so cheerfully to the Count de Gasparin regarding a draft, Lincoln issued a second call for 300,000 troops. The first call in July had brought no such mass meetings and cheers as the call in the spring of 1861. Crops were being harvested, business reviving, wages going up, many jobs beckoning to workmen. The war, as an adventure, was getting monotonous.

The government plan now called for the governors of Northern States to furnish their quota, whether or no the State militia held enough men. This meant conscription by the States, "the draft." Sheriffs and commissioners took lists of all men between eighteen and forty-five years of age in counties and cities. Names written on folded ballots were shaken in a revolving wheel or drum-shaped box. A blindfolded man drew out the names of those who were to go to war for nine months, or else inside of five days pay a substitute to go.

Men who did not want to go to war, by thousands, filed papers, exemption claims—they were physically unfit to go; they were aliens, citizens of other countries; they held to a religious belief that war was a sin. In ten days, 14,000 claims were filed in New York City. Thousands were crossing into Canada or buying steamship tickets for Europe. One steamer was over-hauled at sea and all men passengers were taken back to New York. Six hundred passengers ready for two boats, the *Etna* and the *Saxonia*, were stopped from sailing. Five hundred crossed from Detroit to Windsor, Canada, on August 8, four days after Lincoln's call for troops.

Loyal Irish in Cincinnati issued rallying cries for their clan to organize a regiment. Loyal Germans held a mass meeting and cried shame on all who had lived in the United States five years and were evading the draft. The *Cincinnati Commercial* printed the names of 500 citizens seeking exemption. An examining surgeon at New Fairfield, Connecticut, reported five cases of young men each cutting off a forefinger so as to classify among the physi-cally unfit. Others had all their teeth extracted. An eastbound train from Chicago was stopped by the chief of police and 26 men on their way to Detroit were taken off. In rural Iowa disorders arose, and the editor of the *Dubuque Herald* was arrested for obstruction to enlistment. In New York, Baltimore, and St. Louis aliens crowded the consulate offices. Some of these had made snug fortunes in the new country, had signed declarations

Drawing names of drafted men

of intention to become citizens—and Seward had to rule that they were not considered citizens and were exempt.

Here and there the native-born showed their temper. In Cleveland, Ohio, a crowd tried to smash the boxes from which the names were to be taken by the blindfolded man. And this Cleveland crowd sent five picked men in to look over the lists, to make sure that no pets of government officials, rich merchants, or war contractors were left out, and to see that the lottery was fair. In Port Washington, Wisconsin, a crowd smashed the boxes, chased out the commissioner, and rioted so that troops had to be called. In Mary-land and southern Indiana draft commissioners and United States Marshals had to run for their lives while mobs tore up the enlistment rolls and broke the boxes. Drafted men in Bucyrus, Ohio, on their way to camp halted in the public square and gave three cheers for "the Constitution as it is, and the Union as it was," and three cheers "that we don't fight to free the niggers."

In many cities special efforts were made to enlist enough volunteers so that no draft would be required. At public meetings funds were raised to pay enlisted men a bounty above the $100 government bounty. Commission brokers sprang up who advertised that they would furnish substitutes for those who could pay. Stanton warned newspapers that these advertisements were obstructive and brokers and editors were liable to arrest. Resistance and evasion of the attempts of the State governments to draft soldiers spread so far that President Lincoln issued a proclamation that "all persons discouraging volunteer enlistments, resisting militia drafts, or guilty of any disloyal practice affording aid and comfort to rebels against the authority of the United States" would come under martial law—and the writ of habeas corpus would be useless in any jail where they were held.

The rolling drums, the patriotic appeals, and the offers of bounty money brought 91,000 volunteer enlistments. James S. Gibbons offered verses for the hour and a tune, composed by the famous and beloved Stephen Foster, was taken up by millions, one stanza going:

> If you look all up our valleys where the growing harvests shine,
> You may see our sturdy farmer boys fast forming into line;
> And children from their mother's knees are pulling at the weeds,
> And learning how to reap and sow against their country's needs;
> And a farewell group stands weeping at every cottage door:
> We are coming, Father Abraham, three hundred thousand more!

At the fighting fronts near Washington the record held blunders, grief. In the civil populations to the rear was anxiety, tumult. Lincoln had spoken of "fog" in his Jersey City address. Fog it was. At times it was in spots a storm, a red tornado, as at Shiloh or in the Seven Days. But more often it was fog.

In an after-supper group on a revenue cutter one evening Secretary Chase spoke worry over an important letter he had forgotten to write that day. Lincoln said that a man was sometimes lucky in such forgetting; he seldom knew what a letter contained until some day again it confronted him with an indiscreet word or expression. This reminded Stanton of a telegram received that day from a general with a little army down in northern Alabama. The telegram was vague; no telling what the general wanted, yet an immediate reply was demanded. So the Secretary of War telegraphed back, "All right; go ahead." Stanton termed it a dilemma. "I suppose you meant," added Lincoln, "that it was all right if it was good for him, and all wrong if it was not," and told of the boy riding a horse for sale who was asked if the horse had the splints and answered, "Well, mister, if it's good for him he has got it, but if it is not good for him he hasn't." That was the position of the general down in Alabama. "I guess he'll come out all right; but at any rate you can't help him now."

Decisions—every day telegrams, letters, callers, committees. And the answer had to be Yes or No. Often a plan or a movement was sheerly an experiment, a tryout, and the White House approval of it was as much of a gamble as Stanton's reply, "All right; go ahead," to a telegram he could not make sense of.

While General Halleck at Corinth, Mississippi, called for more men to be sent to him, Governor Sprague of Rhode Island asked Lincoln for a note or letter of introduction to Halleck. Sprague was going to travel from

GENERAL ORDERS, ⎱   WAR DEPARTMENT,
                            ADJUTANT GENERAL'S OFFICE,
   No. 71.   ⎰   *Washington*, June 21, 1862.

In every case of prisoners taken in arms against the United States, who may be tried and sentenced to death, the record of the tribunal before which the trial was had will be forwarded for the action of the President of the United States, without whose orders no such sentence, in such cases, will be executed.

BY ORDER OF THE SECRETARY OF WAR:

                                    L. THOMAS,
                                       Adjutant General.

OFFICIAL:

                    Assistant Adjutant General.

To safeguard against the extremes or follies of martial law, military trials, and executions of enemy prisoners—and toward the exercise of some degree of control over a trend to "remorseless revolutionary warfare"—the President directed an order be issued as above.

Washington far down into Mississippi. Lincoln knew that Sprague wanted to get part of Halleck's force transferred east—and took sides with neither Sprague nor Halleck in a letter agreeable to both, the body of it saying:

This introduces, Gov. William Sprague, of Rhode Island. He is now Governor for the third term, and Senator elect of the U.S. I know the object of his visit to you— He has my cheerful consent to go, but not my direction—He wishes to get you and part of your force, one or both, to come here—You already know I should be exceedingly glad of this if, in your judgment, it could be, without endangering positions and operations in the South-West; and I now repeat what I have more than once said by Telegraph, "Do not come or send a man, if, in your judgment, it will endanger any point you deem important to hold, or endangers, or delays the Chattanooga expedition—
Still, please give my friend, Gov. Sprague, a full and fair hearing—

To Bill Herndon, Pete Halstead, and several other Western men, Lincoln one evening in early '62 spoke of his method. While groaning as pleasantly as he could over pain from a tooth extraction, he said that in military affairs he found it necessary "to yield here a little and there a little in order to keep peace in the family." If he interfered in a plan not essential nor vital, then the West Pointers, the regular-army officers having execution of all his plans, would in some way or other obstruct or defeat the execution of his scheme. "Therefore," noted Herndon, "inasmuch as they had to be depended on at *last*, he found it best to trust them at *first* and rely on events and the power of persuasion to rectify errors."

Halleck, for instance, the new General in Chief, what would he do? Could he tell field commanders how to ride the whirlwind? Maybe he could. Anyhow, he was the pick of the lot on their present records. If he fell down, someone else would step in. He was forty-seven years old, a New York boy, a West Pointer, an engineer with artillery in the Mexican War. He not only understood army regulations but could write them. Twelve lectures at Harvard on the science of war were for Halleck merely introductory. He wrote a book justifying war, telling how it should be carried on: *Elements of Military Art and Science*. A four-volume translation from the French, on how Napoleon made war, came with his signature. He helped occupy California and organize it as a Territory, was lieutenant governor, and wrote most of the State constitution. Resigning in 1854, he went into law; when the war opened in '61 he was head of the leading law firm of San Francisco and major general of the State militia. He and Stanton were opposing lawyers in California land-fraud cases where Stanton won for the Federal Government; the low respect of Stanton for Halleck was said to date from the trial of these cases.

On the word of General Scott that Halleck had extraordinary military talent Lincoln appointed him a major general. He took over the Department of Missouri when Frémont stepped out. In St. Louis those who liked him nicknamed him "Old Brains." His department got results, whether it was his work or his management or the rising genius of Grant and Sherman. After Shiloh he took the field, replacing Grant, heading 100,000 men against the Confederate 50,000 at Corinth. The message from Stanton at Washington was: "I have no instructions to give you. Go ahead and all success attend you." Outnumbering the enemy two to one, Halleck advanced with pick and shovel, entrenching, bridge-building, road-making. Meanwhile he called for reinforcements. Four armies had been joined into his one. And Halleck asked for a fifth army, one off in Arkansas.

"I beg you to be assured we do the best we can," Lincoln wrote Halleck, with explanations of how no more troops were available. "My dear general, I feel justified to rely very much on you. I believe you and the brave officers and men with you can and will get the victory at Corinth." Halleck moved slowly onward with pick and shovel, entrenching, making sure that his 100,000 would bag the enemy 50,000. After six weeks he arrived at Corinth when the enemy had slipped out and was fifty miles away again. He reported this to Washington as a victory.

Yet for all of Halleck's failings as a field commander he had proved an efficient administrator at St. Louis, and Nicolay and Hay believed he made a mistake in leaving his Western department headquarters for the field. "He was a thinker and not a worker; his proper place was in the military study and not in the camp. No other soldier in the field equalled him in the technical and theoretical acquirements of his profession."

Instead of sending to the Library of Congress for books on military science, Lincoln could now call in Halleck and ask the living encyclopedia. Like McClellan, like Stanton, Grant, and others in high place chosen by Lincoln, Halleck was not a Republican. He bothered Secretary Chase by remarking at the first Cabinet meeting he attended, "I confess I do not think much of the negro." He was suave, learned, lacking in wisdom, habitually scratched his elbows.

McClellan, reading in the newspapers that Halleck had been appointed General in Chief, reached new depths of scorn for Lincoln. He wrote to Mrs. McClellan: "In all these things the President and those around him have acted so as to make the matter as offensive as possible. He has not shown the slightest gentlemanly or friendly feeling, and I cannot regard him as in any respect my friend—I am confident that he would relieve me tomorrow if he dared to do so. His cowardice alone prevents it. I can never regard him with other feelings than those of contempt."

Senator Chandler came away from the White House one day and told a colleague, "Old Abe is mad now and the war will go on." Chandler may have met Lincoln in the mood of the letter written to August Belmont, who had sent on to the President complaints received from New Orleans. Lincoln advised the New York agent of the House of Rothschild: "Broken eggs cannot be mended; but Louisiana has nothing to do now but to take her place in the Union as it was, barring the already broken eggs. The sooner she does so, the smaller will be the amount that will be past mending. This government cannot much longer play a game in which it stakes all, and its enemies stake nothing. Those enemies must understand that they cannot experiment for ten years trying to destroy the government, and if they fail still come back into the Union unhurt."

Governor Andrew telegraphed he could not get "quick work" out of United States paymasters delaying transport of regiments. Lincoln wired: "Please say to these gentlemen that if they do not work quickly I will make quick work with them. In the name of all that is reasonable, how long does it take to pay a couple of regiments?"

Some decisions came easy, such as signing the Pacific Railway Bill on July 1, 1862. Rails were to be laid from the western Iowa line to San Francisco Bay. The Union Pacific corporation, already organized, was to build the road, getting ten sections of land per mile alongside its right of way, and loans through United States bonds of $16,000 per mile of track. As the bill stood now it was under "military necessity" an offer to railroad financiers to push through a job that would tie the two coasts closer.

Also it was easy to sign the Homestead Bill on May 20, 1862, giving a farm free to any man who wanted to put a plow to unbroken sod. Immense tracts of land were thrown open in the Western Territories. Anyone a citizen of the United States or taking out first papers declaring intention of citizenship, paying a registration fee of $10, and staying on the same piece of ground five years could have title papers making him the owner of a quarter-section of land, nothing less than 160 acres.

"Can it be true? A big farm of rich land for nothing except your promise that you stay on it and work the land five years?" Such questions flew when the news spread to Europe, bringing to America, below decks of sailing vessels, tens of thousands of Britons, Irish, Germans, Scandinavians, many exclaiming, "What a strange new country where they give away farms!"

While the war raged the beginnings of a vast agricultural domain were laid. Years back the Homestead Act would have passed Congress but for the Know-Nothing fear that Roman Catholic immigrants would monopolize free lands, the fear of high-tariff interests that revenue from land sales would make customs revenue less necessary, and above all the Southern fear of increased Northern political strength. As a war measure touching enlarged food supply, and as an act fulfilling a Republican-party pledge, Lincoln found it easy to sign the bill.

Decisions—every day hundreds of decisions—Yes or No—take it or leave it—right or wrong—heads or tails—six of one and a half-dozen of the other.

Telegrams from Natchez and Cairo published in New York newspapers in May of '62 reported that Farragut's squadron, instead of steaming up the Mississippi River, had returned to New Orleans. "This information may not be true," Fox of the Navy Department wrote to Farragut, "but the probability of it has distressed the President so much" that Fox had ordered a vessel from Hampton Roads to proceed with all speed to notify Farragut of instructions to move up the Mississippi and take that river if possible.

A committee from Baltimore told the President of straggling soldiers in numbers, "half sick, half well," turned from hospitals with no definite directions where to go. "Is this true?" he wrote to the Surgeon General. "Are men turned from hospitals without knowing where to go?"

General Wetmore of New York introduced to Lincoln on June 17 Dr. Horace Green, a leader in the medical profession, who had come from the Lee estate, White House on the Peninsula. In charge of sick and wounded he had seen hundreds of the soldiers on steamboats on the muddy, miasmic Pamunkey River and others in hospital tents pitched on muddy ground. "Mr. Lincoln received us very kindly, and heard my statements patiently," Dr. Green wrote in his diary of his requesting authority to use the White House estate and grounds for hospital service. The Doctor and Lincoln could not forget a tradition that the White House estate had belonged to Mrs. George Washington, that the wife of General Robert E. Lee was the present owner, that any misuse and defacement of it would not look well.

Dr. Green finished a brief plea for its hospital use and Lincoln replied: "Gentlemen, I understand all this matter perfectly well. It is only a political raid against General McClellan. General McClellan does not choose to give up these grounds, and a political party is determined that he shall be compelled to do it. There is no necessity that this property should be used for this purpose. I have within three days seen a telegram from General Mc-Clellan to the Secretary of War, declaring that there was plenty of ground outside of the White House property suitable for hospital tents, and plenty of water elsewhere."

A little disturbed, Dr. Green determined not to be put down. When he spoke he was cool and decided: "Mr. President, you must allow me to un-deceive you so far as I myself am concerned. I, sir, am no politician. I speak as a *medical man*. And so far from being opposed to General McClellan, he is the son of one of my old professors at Philadelphia, and I have always been his friend, and am so up to this hour. I speak of what I *do know;* and on my reputation as a medical man I assure you, sir, that our soldiers are dying there daily for the want of just such a place, and such accommoda-tions as the grounds, especially those about the White House, can supply. At present the hospital tents are placed on the damp, low, and marshy grounds surrounding the place; sick and wounded are constantly breathing the malarious and damp atmosphere, drinking the muddy waters of the Pamunky—an atmosphere and water which would, in this hot weather, make a well man sick in less than a week."

The President said he was told the house would hold only some twenty-five or thirty patients at the most. The house had rooms for double that number, Dr. Green estimated, and at any rate he cared little about the house. "It is the fine, dry and shaded lawn about the house, and the spring of ex-cellent water there, that are needed. Hospital tents of the present day, pitched on good ground, furnish the best and healthiest hospitals in use. And all the injury that would accrue to this place, to use the grounds for this purpose, would be the loss of the grass from shaving the lawn. I believe, sir, it would be the means of saving many valuable lives of your soldiers."

The President was impressed and said: "Well, Dr. Green, I will tell you the truth of this case. General McClellan promised Mrs. General Lee that those grounds should be protected from all injury, and that is the reason he does not want them used." Dr. Green at once put his view briefly and sharply. "I admire, sir, the gallantry of the General in this matter; but, sir, are our brave soldiers to die off like rotten sheep there because General Mc-Clellan chooses to protect the grounds of a rebel?"

"Well, such is the case," said the President. "McClellan has made this promise, but I think it is wrong. I believe what you say in reference to this matter. He does not want to break the promise he has made, and (with emphasis) *I will break it for him*." And turning to General Wetmore, he said the Secretary of War would direct the grounds to be used for hospital purposes if the Surgeon General would make the requisition. "Go and get and bring me these papers. This business must be settled now, done up at once!" The result was an order requiring McClellan to relinquish the ground, now for weeks picketed by Union troops guarding it from molestation.

Decisions—hundreds of them every day—on matters public and private. John P. Usher, Assistant Secretary of the Interior, stepped in to tell Lin-coln that the railroad from Baltimore to Harrisburg, the Northern Central of Pennsylvania, was bound to be good property for investment. The war would increase traffic on it. "The stock was then worth only a few cents on the dollar," Usher said in telling of the incident later. "I knew that from the necessity of the case it would advance in value to par or nearly so. I bought large blocks of it, and told Mr. Lincoln that if he would give me $10,000, I would make him all the money he wanted." But Lincoln said No. Usher considered the investment proper, but Lincoln seemed to think otherwise. Usher seemed blissfully unaware the railroad was known to many investors as "Cameron's road."

Decisions—as to politics—suffering soldiers—money investments.

Colonel Scott of a New Hampshire regiment came with his story. He had fallen sick and his wife nursed him in a hospital. In a steamboat collision off Hampton Roads she was drowned. Her body was found, and he asked the Secretary of War for a permit to go to make arrangements for the burial. The Secretary said No. A great battle was near and every officer was wanted.

Lincoln sat and listened to Scott's story. It was a Saturday night. Lincoln was alone, his coat off. And as Colonel Scott recalled his words, Lincoln broke out: "Am I to have no rest? Is there no hour or spot when or where I may escape these constant calls? Why do you follow me here with such business as this? Why do you not go to the War Office, where they have charge of all this matter of papers and transportation?"

Colonel Scott told of Stanton's refusal. And Lincoln went on: "Then probably you ought not to go down the river. Mr. Stanton knows all about the necessities of the hour; he knows what rules are necessary, and rules are made to be enforced. It would be wrong for me to override his rules and decisions in cases of this kind; it might work disaster to important movements. And then, you ought to remember that I have other duties to attend to—heaven knows, enough for one man!—and I can give no thought to questions of this kind. Why do you come here to appeal to my humanity? Don't you know that we are in the midst of war? That suffering and death press upon all of us? That works of humanity and affection, which we would cheerfully perform in days of peace, are all trampled upon and outlawed by war? That there is no room left for them? There is but one duty now—to *fight!* The only call of humanity now is to conquer peace through unrelenting warfare. War, and war alone, is the duty of all of us. Your wife might have trusted you to the care which the Government has provided for its sick soldiers. At any rate, you must not vex me with your family troubles. Why, every family in the land is crushed with sorrow; but they must not each come to me for help. I have all the burdens I can carry. Go to the War Department. Your business belongs there. If they cannot help you, then bear your burden, as we all must, until this war is over. Everything must yield to the paramount duty of finishing the war."

Colonel Scott left the room. What was there to say? In his hotel room he brooded over his wife's body, her drowning, how suddenly tragedy may arrive, whether her body would have decent burial. Early the next morning he sat in his hotel room with his thoughts when he heard a rap at the door, opened it. There stood the President, who took Scott's hands and holding them, broke out: "My dear Colonel, I was a brute last night. I have no excuse to offer. I was weary to the last extent; but I had no right to treat a man with rudeness who had offered his life for his country, much more a man who came to me in great affliction. I have had a regretful night, and come now to beg your forgiveness." He had arranged with Stanton for Scott's permit to go to his wife's body. He took Scott to the steamer wharf in his carriage and wished him Godspeed.

CHAPTER 24

SECOND BULL RUN AUGUST '62 — CHAOS

THE popular Orpheus C. Kerr (Robert H. Newell and "Office Seeker") and his nonsense relieved for occasional moments the gloom of some of his readers. Among those who took him as sure entertainment was Lincoln. "Rejoice with me, my boy, that I have got back my Gothic steed, Pegasus, from the Government chap who borrowed him for a desk," wrote Kerr. "The splendid architectural animal has just enough slant from his backbone to his hips to make a capital desk, my boy; and then his tail is so handy to wipe pens on. In a moment of thirst he swallowed a bottle of ink, and some fears were entertained for his life; but a gross of steel pens and a ream of blotting paper, immediately administered, caused him to come out all write."

Into a horseplay world Kerr took his readers. Of Pegasus producing "architectural illusions" he wrote: "He was standing on the hill-side the other day, with his rear-elevation toward the spectators, his head up and ears touching at the top, when a chap noticed him afar off, and says he to a soldier, 'What church is that I behold in the distance, my fellow worm of the dust?'" Then Kerr would swing back to reality and tell of a walk across Long Bridge to Arlington Heights. "How pleasant it is, my boy, to escape occasionally from the society of Congressmen and brigadiers, and take a lazy sprawl in the fragrant fields."

And one of Orpheus C. Kerr's letters opened: "Patriotism, my boy, is a very beautiful thing. The surgeon of a Western regiment has analyzed a very nice case of it and says it is peculiar to this hemisphere. He says that it first breaks out in the mouth, and from thence extends to the heart causing the latter to swell. He says that it goes on raging until it reaches the pocket, when it suddenly disappears, leaving the patient very Constitutional and conservative."

Lincoln had his laugh at Kerr's letter of August 9, 1862, which set forth: "Notwithstanding the fact that President Lincoln is an honest man, my boy, the genius of Slumber has opened a large wholesale establishment here, and the tendency to repose is general." Equally bland three weeks later, Kerr wrote: "As every thing continues to indicate, my boy, that President Lincoln is an honest man, I am still of the opinion that the restoration of the Union is only a question of time, and will be accomplished some weeks previous to the commencement of the Millenium."

During that desperate, hammering summer of 1862 Lincoln revolved often in his mind the curious failure of his 200,000 men in Virginia against half that number. Would he have to try one general, another, and still another, and for how long?

A new combination named the Army of Virginia, formed by the three commands of McDowell, Banks, and Frémont, was headed by General John Pope, whom Frémont detested as a plotter against him in Missouri operations. Frémont had hoped command would be given back to him. His hope failing, he requested Lincoln to relieve him of field duty, which Lincoln did. Frémont with his personal staff returned to New York City, where he and Mrs. Frémont established a headquarters for Republican radicals. Repeatedly came friends of Frémont urging on Lincoln his claims, pleading for justice, but Lincoln refused to give him another army to play with. And Frémont bided his time and maneuvered politically.

John Pope, the new commander, was a dashing horseman, a figure to look at, his valor in battle impetuous and undisputed. He had been one of Lincoln's military escort en route to inauguration, was Kentucky-born, a graduate of Transylvania University at Lexington, his father a United States judge whom Lincoln had met in law practice in Springfield, Illinois. A West Pointer, a Mexican War officer promoted for gallantry on the field, an engineer, a surveyor, an explorer, an 1860 Republican, John Pope had been continuously an army man, soldiering his lifework. His victories had brought in 1,300 prisoners at Blackwater, Missouri, and some 6,000 at Island No. 10 on the Mississippi. In his new Eastern command it was supposed or hoped that he embodied somehow the fighting quality or luck of the Western armies. To his men and generals he offered maxims: "Success and glory are in the advance, disaster and shame lurk in the rear." He wrote letters from "Headquarters in the Saddle." He issued an address to his new command. "I have come to you from the West, where we have always seen the back of our enemies." The Western policy was attack and not defense, he would have them know. "I presume that I have been called here to pursue the same system and to lead you against the enemy. It is my purpose to do so, and that speedily."

Was General Pope strutting to scare the enemy, or blustering to hide his personal embarrassment over the job just ahead of him? His soldiers must dismiss from their minds "certain phrases" which, he notified them, "I am sorry to find so much in vogue amongst you." As to "lines of retreat" and "bases of supplies," which he was hearing of constantly, he said: "Let us discard such ideas. . . . Let us study the probable lines of retreat of our enemies, and leave our own to take care of themselves." From his "headquarters in the saddle" he meant well. His overconfidence ran into bombast almost inconceivable unless possibly it served to ease his own misgivings. For Pope was facing two great proved fighters, two strange captains of men, Lee and Jackson.

One of these, Robert Edward Lee, fifty-five years old, had become the most portentous personality with whom Lincoln would have to contend in the months ahead. For Lee had two rare gifts, patience with men and patience with unforeseen circumstance. His training in handling and understanding men had been long, hard, varied, and thorough. The smooth reciprocal functioning of Lee with Davis was almost startling as a contrast to Lincoln and McClellan. Militarily Lee and Davis were one head of the Army of Virginia. Where Jefferson Davis would often fail to read the enemy mind Lee supplied the deficiency. Neither jealousy nor envy nor ambition, in any ordinary sense, gnawed at the heart of Lee. He sacrificed personal pride or ease to immediate ends in his handling of men, whether dealing with the President of the Confederacy or with staff generals or with barefoot privates. Of his father, Henry ("Light-Horse Harry") Lee, an uncle said that he seemed "to have come out of his mother's womb a soldier." After earning a reputation for brilliant fighting in the American Revolution, Light-Horse Harry spent thirty years in wild money affairs, failed of fortune, was jailed for debt at Westmoreland and Spotsylvania, was beaten, crippled, and disfigured in defense of a Baltimore newspaper that in 1812 opposed war with Great Britain, sailing away from America in his last years; for the sake of health and peace from creditors he lived an exile's life. Contemplation of his father's ways seemed always to counsel the son, "Patience, patience."

Robert E. Lee's elder half-brother, Henry ("Black-Horse Harry") Lee, had served as Assistant Postmaster General under President John Quincy Adams, had mismanaged and squandered an inherited estate, had become impoverished and entered the service of Andrew Jackson as a political writer, living at The Hermitage in Tennessee and winning favor from Jackson. With President Jackson's appointment as consul to Morocco in his portfolio, Black-Horse Harry Lee sailed for Africa while scandals were aired. He had married a young woman of property, had been swept into an affair of passion with his wife's younger sister; in view of this and other admitted facts not one member of the United States Senate would vote for his confirmation—and Black-Horse Harry lived in Italy, in Paris a few years, and died an exile. On this tradition too Robert E. Lee had contemplations.

With depths of affection for his valiant father, with charitable silence for his wayward brother, Robert E. Lee had followed the vagrant ways of neither. He sank himself in another tradition, that of George Washington, who had been in his near-by tomb at Mount Vernon only ten years when Lee arrived in a family coach at Alexandria, Virginia, a baby to grow up as a boy hearing of General Washington's letter to his father wishing him "all imaginable success and happiness," to live near the post office where Washington often came in person, and to walk in the market place where

Washington had drilled troops, to pass the hall where Washington had pronounced the responses of the Masonic ritual, and to see the old doctor who was physician and intimate friend of Washington. This could only fascinate the boy whose father had spoken in eulogy of Washington as "first in war, first in peace, first in the hearts of his countrymen." The boy later, grown to manhood, sojourned at Arlington Heights with George Washington Parke Custis, grandson of Mrs. Washington and adopted son of George Washington, and married the daughter, Mary Ann Randolph Custis.

So he became further immersed in the shadows, legends, and personal testimonies of George Washington. What this did to the inside of Lee no man could say, but men who studied him closely said that one of his secrets was a grip on the character of Washington as a model, a hope, and a light. The reserve, the tenacity, the scruples, the exactitude in petty detail, the piety, the patience and forbearance, the balances of justice and fair dealing, the bearing of distinction touched with aristocratic outlook—these ways of Washington he pondered. They haunted him.

Robert E. Lee's mother, Ann Hill Carter Lee, was the daughter of Charles Carter, whose James River plantation and other possessions gave him reputation as the richest man in Virginia except George Washington. Her inheritance had dwindled so far that West Point was the advisable place for her son's education. On the basis of his father's brilliant Revolutionary War record, John C. Calhoun signed his appointment, and he went away to West Point with his mother saying: "How can I live without Robert? He is both son and daughter to me"—her acknowledgment as a chronic invalid of his loyalty in the years he had served and nursed her. After graduation with high standing, he was married to Mary Custis, a frail blonde girl of whom it was said that she had "features aristocratic but not beautiful." In the Arlington Heights mansion overlooking Washington, D.C., which for many years was to be the home of Lee, were relics and mementos of George Washington, his bookcase, his camp equipment, the bed in which he died. And one kinsman commented that in the eyes of the world the marriage of Robert E. Lee had made him "the representative of the family of the founder of American liberty." Of Mary Custis Lee it was written, "She loved wildflowers and old gardens and evening skies"; she bore seven children in fourteen years, and became a chronic invalid.

Once, apologizing in advance to expected guests, General Lee wrote: "Tell the Ladies that they are aware Mrs. L. is somewhat addicted to laziness and forgetfulness in her Housekeeping. But they may be certain she does her best. Or in her Mother's words 'The spirit is willing but the flesh is weak.'" The years passed with no deviation of his interest in her. He was tall, handsome, gracious, attractive to women, it was often noted; at thirty-five his confession to a friend ran: "You are right in my interest in pretty women. It is strange that I do not lose it with age. But I perceive no diminution." About the same time to one of his cronies he said, "I would not be unmarried for all you could offer me."

On leaving West Point Lee was flung into the realities of handling engineers and work gangs to cut ditches in Georgia mudbanks, to blast rock from the bed of the Mississippi for river-channel improvement at St. Louis, to repair casemates in New York Harbor, to run pile-drivers in Baltimore Harbor. He came to know measurably that odd bird, the regular-army soldier, and that enigma, the American workingman. His reputation for fair dealing spread far, and once when he assured an offending soldier, "You shall have justice," the answer was quick—"That is what I am afraid of." From his first assignment of duty in 1829, which put him to his armpits in mud while building fortifications at Cockspur Island in the Savannah River, through his duties thirty-one years later policing Indian tribes and fighting Mexican bandits on the plains of Texas, he was a military man to whom the word "duty" had peculiar meaning. "Duty," he wrote, "is the sublimest word in the language."

Many times as a court-martial judge Lee rode hundreds of miles from case to case, hearing hundreds of witnesses and advocates by the score, learning in detail of neglects, faults, jealousies, among army officers. Youth and the cub officer taught him in the two years he was superintendent of the West Point military academy. Advising a father to let his son resign before examinations, he wrote, "I consider the character of no man affected by a want of success, provided he has made an honest effort to succeed." Of one dawdling cadet he asked: "How is your mother? I am sure you must be devoted to her; you are so careful of the health of her son." Having made the best possible effort, he would be calm and let the record stand: this was his philosophy.

Lee's only leave of absence during thirty years in the army was an annoying year in which he acted as executor of the tangled estate of his wife's father, about that time writing, "I have no enjoyment in life now but what I derive from my children." Seeing his daughter Annie in 1859 weeping together with her departing guest, a Georgia girl, he gaily called: "No tears at Arlington. No tears!" Seldom had he been longer than three months continuously away from his family. He would write a daughter "My Precious Annie," saying, "I inclose some violets I plucked," and to his wife of a garden he saw "filled with roses and beautiful vines" and among them "the tomato-vine in full bearing, with the ripe fruit on it." He wrote that it did him good "to see the mules walking around and the corn growing," signs multiplying that he hankered for a farm or plantation of his own to manage, with a big house to entertain guests, as a country gentleman.

Like his ancestors, Lee referred to England as "the old country," wrote impressed as "imprefsed," show as "shew." Life at any moment might be lacking conveniences wanted by the individual, he learned, and wrote his daughter Agnes: "You must expect discomforts and annoyances all through life. No place or position is secure from them, and you must make up your mind to meet with them and bear with them." He gave advice that was prosaic and dull unless shined up with practice, such as "The true man of honor feels humbled himself when he cannot help humbling others." Grave and self-composed outwardly, he wrote home of a little daughter, "She is like her papa—always wanting something," from far in the Southwest wrote once, "I walk alone with my thoughts."

At West Point it had been noted Lee could laugh in the face of some cadet who had slipped in folly, and it was taken he was laughing at the folly and not the cadet. The other fellow didn't get sore. Strictly responsible personally, Lee had a sober-faced tolerance of the incompetent, the stupid and blundering. This connected partly with a religious understanding that all men are sinners and none is perfect, partly with a nurse nature that had made him the affectionate caretaker of his invalid mother and languishing wife, and also with an instinct that men, women, and children would usually, though not always, do better when gentled. Cold and austere he seemed on parade in his official uniform, panoplied for duty, though in the bosom of his family "he was very fond of having his hands tickled, and what was still more curious, it pleased and delighted him to take off his slippers and place his feet in our laps to have them tickled," said one of the sons. They would ask for more stories and he teased them. "No tickling, no story!"

With a physical frame "solid as oak," trained to hardships and loneliness, Lee sipped wine occasionally, drank no hard liquor, cared nothing for tobacco, once wrote a son: "I hope you will always be distinguished for your avoidance of the 'universal balm,' whiskey. Its temperate use is so difficult." Knowing the boy had heard this before, he apologized for giving advice: "You must pardon a fault which proceeds from my great love and burning anxiety for your welfare and happiness." He gave an odd incident of himself and whisky through the Mexican War. "A lady in Virginia prevailed on me to take a bottle of fine old whiskey, which she thought I could not get on without. I carried that bottle all through the war and on my return home I sent it back to my good friend, that she might be convinced that I could get on without liquor."

After the butchery at Cerro Gordo, Lee had said to a brother, "You have no idea what a horrible sight a field of battle is." Two years on the staff of General Scott during the Mexican War had been his high test. His record then and since led Scott to say openly that Robert E. Lee was "the best of American soldiers," in discretion and valor "the very best soldier I ever saw in the field."

Lincoln in March of '61 had signed a commission appointing Lee a colonel in the United States regular army at the same time that the Confederate Government offered Lee a commission as brigadier general. Scott and Old Man Blair had made it plain that Lee was the choice for high command of the Union armies, Blair having authority from President Lincoln to "ascertain Lee's intentions and feelings," and the consent of Secretary Cameron to offer high command. Lee had waited through Lincoln's inauguration, through the bombardment and evacuation of Fort Sumter. It was April 18, with the "Uprising of the North" at its height of fury, when Lee rode up Pennsylvania Avenue, dismounted at the younger Blair's home opposite the State, War, and Navy buildings, and behind closed doors talked with Blair. "I declined the offer he made me," wrote Lee, "stating as candidly and courteously as I could, that though opposed to secession and deprecating war, I could take no part in the invasion of the Southern States." At the office of his lifelong friend and beneficent elder comrade, General Scott, he heard the words, "Lee, you have made the greatest mistake of your life," and sadly, as between old associates with a difference beyond scope of language, he advised that if Lee were going to resign he must not delay. Not that day did Lee resign. Virginia had not yet seceded. He would wait.

The next day in Alexandria he read the news that the Virginia convention in secret session had gone out of the Union. To a druggist in Alexandria he had remarked the day before, "I must say that I am one of those dull creatures that cannot see the good of secession." As an officer of the United States Army, however, he could be ordered to defend Washington by invading Virginia, which duty to him would be a species of blasphemy.

So Robert E. Lee sent Secretary Cameron his resignation the next day, wrote to Scott: "I shall carry to the grave the most grateful recollections of your kind consideration, and your name and fame will always be dear to me. . . . Save in defence of my native State, I never desire to again draw my sword." To his sister Ann, whose West-Point-trained son was staying with the United States Army, Lee wrote of "a state of revolution" in the whole South, "and, though I recognize no necessity for this state of things, and would have forborne and pleaded to the end for a redress of grievances, real or supposed, yet in my own person I had to meet the question whether I should take part against my native state." His sister would blame him, he knew, "but you must think of me as kindly as you can . . . may God shower upon you everlasting blessings." The pivot of his decision was stated: "With all my devotion to the Union and the feeling of loyalty and duty as an American citizen, I have not been able to make up my mind to raise my hand against my relatives, my children, my home." To his brother Smith he wrote: "I wished to wait until the Ordinance of Secession should be acted on by the people of Virginia, but war seems to have commenced, and I am liable at any time to be ordered on duty, which I could not conscientiously perform. . . . I had to act at once. . . . I am now a private citizen, and have no other ambition than to remain at home."

In the hill-set house at Arlington overlooking the Federal capital a gloom hung as though death had walked in and made dark promises. "My husband has wept tears of blood over this terrible war, but as a man of honor and a Virginian, he must follow the destiny of his state," wrote Mary Custis Lee of that week and others following. Though Virginia was dear, wrote a daughter, "the army was to him home and country." And when the voters of Virginia balloted in favor of secession, one of Lee's sons said that the people had lost their senses, while another son declared that if he could dictate policy he would call the secession movement revolution and seize and fortify Arlington Heights. In the old family pew of George Washing-

Robert Edward Lee, 1852   The wartime Robert Edward Lee

George Washington Custis Lee, son of R. E. Lee   The Lee family residence in Richmond, Virginia

From Oliver R. Barrett Collection

John Pope

From author's collection

Fitz-John Porter

From Oliver R. Barrett Collection

The younger and older Thomas Jonathan ("Stonewall") Jackson

From Oliver R. Barrett Collection

ton in Christ Church in Alexandria Robert E. Lee sat with a daughter one Sunday in April of '61; he left the services a sorrowful man who could not join his fellow worshipers in jubilation over their revolution, which they believed had the spirit of 1776 and the nod of approval from George Washington's ghost. From Christ Church to Arlington to Richmond and to war he had gone in what he saw as inescapable duty.

Into the smoke of battles and onto slopes strewn with the corpses of Southern and Northern boys Lee had gone because, as he said with an undeniable sincerity, he could not do otherwise: the first step was his decision that he could not fight against Virginia; the second and inevitable other step for him was his decision that, Virginia invaded, he must fight for her and against her invaders. Yet he was neither a revolutionist nor a secessionist nor a Union-hater nor temperamentally joined to the men who had created the Confederacy and then asked him to fight for it. Lee was a conservative whose instincts favored a strong government to hold down disorder, tumult, and insurrection, his measure of doubt in the American experiment being reflected in a letter home in January of '61 saying that he had read Nicholls Everett on Washington: "How his spirit would be grieved could he see the wreck of his mighty labors! . . . It has been evident for years that the country was doomed to run the full length of democracy. . . . I fear that mankind will not for years be sufficiently Christianized to bear the absence of restraint and force."

In another letter home in January of '61 Lee wrote words that, had they been spoken before the Confederate Congress at Montgomery that winter, would have been hissed as treason to the basic doctrine of States' Rights and followed by suspicion and mistrust: "Secession is nothing but revolution. The framers of our Constitution never exhausted so much labor, wisdom and forbearance in its formation, and surrounded it with so many guards and securities, if it was intended to be broken by every member of the Confederacy at will. It was intended for 'perpetual union' so expressed in the preamble, and for the establishment of a government, not a compact, which can only be dissolved by revolution, or the consent of all the people in convention assembled. It is idle to talk of secession."

Then his instinct carried Lee to the question where he would go if secession became a fact. "A Union that can only be maintained by swords and bayonets, and in which strife and civil war are to take the place of brotherly love and kindness, has no charm for me. I shall mourn for my country and for the welfare and progress of mankind. If the Union is dissolved, and the Government disrupted, I shall return to my native State and share the miseries of my people, and save in defence will draw my sword on none." A few weeks before this he had written a son, "While I wish to do what is right, I am unwilling to do what is wrong, either at the bidding of the South or the North." Of his hope for preservation of the Union he wrote, "I will cling to it to the last." He felt and resented "the aggressions of the North," though "I am not pleased with the course of the 'Cotton States'" and he could see no benefit in "their selfish, dictatorial bearing, the threats they throw out against the 'Border States.'" On the South Carolina proposals to legalize and reopen the African slave trade he was decisive, writing a son: "One of their plans seems to be the renewal of the slave trade. That I am opposed to on every ground."

And on this question of slavery, which at last had exploded into the secession upheaval, where did Robert E. Lee stand? One of his uncles, Richard Henry Lee, member of the Virginia House of Burgesses from 1761 to 1788, spoke deep hatred of slavery and sought passage of a motion "to lay so heavy a duty on the importation of slaves as effectually to put an end to that iniquitous and disgraceful traffic with the colony of Virginia." Lee knew that George Washington held the institution to be an involved menace that must be dealt with delicately. As a boy in Alexandria he saw the jail chimney where stood iron pikes from which once had gazed the bloody heads of Negroes who had tried to raise an insurrection against their masters and owners. On duty at Fortress Monroe when the Nat Turner slave revolt took place, he had noted, in a letter, the extraordinary fact that more whites had been killed than blacks and that the insurrection had been organized at religious meetings by Negro preachers supposed to be expounding the teachings of Jesus.

On Lee's first assignment as a lieutenant on fortification work in Georgia he had taken with him a faithful sick and worn old Negro slave, for rest and healing in a warmer climate. As executor of the estate of his wife's father he had his first experience at managing slaves in which he had property title, some half-dozen. One later result of this was publication in the *New York Tribune* of letters written by anonymous antislavery agitators— they alleged on hearsay that Robert E. Lee had personally taken charge of the discipline of a captured runaway Negro girl, alleging further, with no slightest evidence, that Lee had stripped the girl slave and given her thirty and nine lashes.

At Leavenworth on court-martial duty Lee had seen civil war and "Bleeding Kansas." He had directed the troops and marines who captured John Brown at Harper's Ferry, looked into the eyes of a militant abolitionist seeking martyrdom. One report told of an old Negro's saying to Lee, "Even ef po' Marse John did bre'k de law, don't you think, suh, dat hangin' him would be a li'l abrupt?" and Lee's replying, "I think that just about expresses the sentiment not only of the colored people but of many others."

With John Brown, Lee believed in Jesus, in the redemption of mankind by the Galilean Saviour who represented the Divine Will. Like John Brown, Robert E. Lee was unfailingly devout and pious, daily kneeling in prayer and meditation. What Lee might have told John Brown, had they talked at length as between two Christians and churchmen, was in a letter to his wife three years before in which he approved of President Buchanan's first message to Congress. Nowhere else did Lee seem to have shown so fully what was in his head and heart as to slavery and abolitionists. He hated slavery enough to want it abolished. He hated abolitionists enough to call them evil, strange, intolerant, unfit to have a hand in government. To his wife in late 1856 from western Texas he wrote his views:

In this enlightened age, there are few I believe, but what will acknowledge, that slavery as an institution, is a moral & political evil in any Country. It is useless to expatiate on its disadvantages. I think it however a greater evil to the white than to the black race, & while my feelings are strongly enlisted in behalf of the latter, my sympathies are more strong for the former. The blacks are immeasurably better off here than in Africa, morally, socially & physically. The painful discipline they are undergoing, is necessary for their instruction as a race, & I hope will prepare & lead them to better things. How long their subjugation may be necessary is known & ordered by a wise Merciful Providence. Their emancipation will sooner result from the mild & melting influence of Christianity, than the storms & tempests of fiery Controversy. This influence though slow, is sure. The doctrines & miracles of our Saviour have required nearly two thousand years, to Convert but a small part of the human race, & even among Christian nations, what gross errors still exist!

While we see the Course of the final abolition of human Slavery is onward, & we give it the aid of our prayers & all justifiable means in our power, we must leave the progress as well as the result in his hands who sees the end; who Chooses to work by slow influences; & with whom two thousand years are but as a Single day. Although the Abolitionist must know this, & must See that he has neither the right or power of operating except by moral means & suasion, & if he means well to the slave, he must not Create angry feelings in the Master; that although he may not approve the mode by which it pleases Providence to accomplish its purposes, the result will nevertheless be the same; that the reasons he gives for interference in what he has no Concern, holds good for every kind of interference with our neighbours when we disapprove their Conduct; Still I fear he will persevere in his evil Course. Is it not strange that the descendants of those pilgrim fathers who Crossed the Atlantic to preserve their own freedom of opinion, have always proved themselves intolerant of the Spiritual liberty of others?

When offered high command of the Union armies, Lee had said, according to Old Man Blair, "If I owned the four million slaves of the South I would sacrifice them all to the Union," and then asked a question that Blair couldn't answer: "But how can I draw my sword against Virginia?" The very asking of the question included its answer.

So he had gone to Richmond, organized to defend Virginia, had supervised, without command, dismal military operations in West Virginia and returned to find himself unpopular. Newspapers nicknamed him "Evacuating Lee." He wrote his wife of the journalistic military critics: "I know they can regulate matters satisfactory to themselves on paper. I wish they could do so in the field." Patiently he had served as the right arm militarily of Jefferson Davis. They had been cadets at West Point when Davis was near dismissal on the charge of frequenting a drinking-place and imbibing. They had become better acquainted when Lee as superintendent at the academy had found his wishes cordially and understandingly met by Davis, the Secretary of War. Now there began between Lee and Davis a rare and peculiar partnership that rested chiefly on Lee's understanding of Davis, on his gift of taking what he could get and never complaining because he was not given more. Davis's talent for loyalty was also a factor, and as little by little he saw how completely unselfish was Lee's devotion to the cause, how utterly mere personal ambition was sunk, he gave Lee wider and wider powers. Where Lee went jealousy and friction were minimized. The criticism was to rise that he was too amiable, too ready to yield to a determined lieutenant. His patience with men and with unforeseen circumstance, his cool resilience and adaptability, were thus far the main slender personal factor that had kept the Lincoln Government from getting an army into Richmond.

"The war may last ten years," Lee had written his wife shortly after arriving in Richmond. He warned soldiers and politicians they were "on the threshold of a long and bloody war," advising that they must plan with that expectation, saying "that he knew the Northern people well, and knew that they would never yield except at the conclusion of a long and desperate struggle." Standing before the Houdon statue of George Washington, with its notable head and remarkably sensitive mouth done from the living man, Lee mused gravely, "I hope we have seen the last of secession," as though some of the States seceded from the Union might secede from the Confederacy, as though it was not yet certain that Washington's lessons on the value of unity and cohesion had been learned in the South. In his first month at Richmond, in sending back home boys under age for service he said: "Those are beautiful boys, sir, and I very much disliked to refuse them; but it will not do to let boys enlist now. I fear we shall need them all before this war is over."

To an officer who protested against the outdated arms issued to his company Lee said, "Sir, your people had better write Mr. Lincoln and ask him to postpone this thing for a few months until you can get ready for him." To his wife, to his sons, went the admonitions "In God alone must be our trust," "God's will be done," "Be content and resigned to God's will." The news of the Fort Donelson surrender to Grant he said was "not favorable," but "we must make up our minds to meet with reverses and to overcome them," and "I hope God will at last crown our efforts with success."

An officer delivered an opinion of another officer and tried to draw out Lee, who smiled. "Well, sir, if that is your opinion of General ——, I can only say that you differ very widely from the general himself." Recommending an officer for promotion, he was informed that the officer customarily spoke of him with disrespect, and replied quickly, "The question is not what he thinks or is pleased to say about me, but what I think of him." Riding on a field where one of his sons was fighting, he remarked, "That's right, my son, drive those people back." Or again he would refer to the enemy as "our friends across the river."

Suddenly, when General Joseph Johnston was wounded, Lee had been sent forward to take in hand four different armies, weld them into a unit for action. In a four months' campaign, at times outnumbered two to one, he had stopped McClellan and earned a name as the savior of Richmond and the Confederacy. To a doubting inquirer one of Lee's generals had said his first name was "Audacity," that he would tower head and shoulders above all others in audacity. In a conference with generals just before the Seven Days' battles, one of them, busy with pencil and paper, was showing that McClellan with superior forces could sweep on to Richmond. "Stop, stop!" said Lee. "If you go to ciphering we are whipped beforehand." His items inserted in Richmond newspapers helped to mislead Pinkerton and McClellan as to his numbers and designs. He sent one of his old West Point cadet students, J. E. B. Stuart, to get information as to McClellan's actual strength, and Stuart's 1,200 horsemen made their estimates in a ride around McClellan's entire army. He approved Magruder's marching the same 10,000 men back and forth on a level of ground, into the woods and out again, giving an imitation for McClellan's observers of a vast horde preparing to slaughter its foe.

Lee read in Lincoln a diplomatic sensitivity about the capture of Washington, knew what the loss of the Union capital would mean in the eyes of London and Paris, and sent Jackson on threatening operations that kept troops near Washington and away from McClellan. "Profoundly grateful to Almighty God," he telegraphed President Davis after one victory on the Chickahominy, at the end of the campaign, in an official summary saying "correct and timely information" might have enabled better results, "but regret that more was not accomplished gives way to gratitude to the Sovereign Ruler of the Universe for the results achieved." His patience was required to stand up under the *Richmond Examiner's* sneer at "the bloodless and masterly strategy of Lee," while his General D. H. Hill officially reported of an attack under fierce artillery fire at Malvern Hill, "It was murder, not war."

Line after line Lee had hurled at the tiers of artillery planted by McClellan at Malvern Hill. And the lines broke under shattering fire and the hillsides in the gloaming and the moonless night were ghastly with the moans and writhing of the wounded. Lee admitted failure and, riding among bivouacs of troops, asked, "General Magruder, why did you attack?" The answer was: "In obedience to your orders, twice repeated." In one battle a Texas regiment lost nearly 600 of its 800 men. The losses during the Peninsular campaign in Lee's army of 85,000 and McClellan's army of 150,000 were officially tabulated:

Killed	*Wounded*	*Missing*
Confederate 3,286	Confederate 15,909	Confederate 946
Union 1,734	Union 8,062	Union 6,053

Lee had won victories, though McClellan had killed nearly two for one of Lee's men. Lee had stopped McClellan from getting to Richmond and had persuaded McClellan's mind into calling for more troops and guns from Washington. Lee knew better than McClellan that war is a conflict of wills, and had imposed his will on McClellan to the extent that McClellan believed he was a loser when he was not, which was why McClellan did not try to push through and take Richmond after Malvern Hill, which was why Mc-Clellan retreated to Harrison's Landing after murderously punishing Lee at Malvern Hill. And while Lee's mind was concentrated entirely on the point of whether he could drive McClellan into the James River in spite of gunboat protection, leaving all Southern politics to Jefferson Davis, McClellan concentrated his mind for many hours on the political difficulties of the North and wrote the long letter instructing Lincoln in the matter of government policy which he duly handed over immediately on Lincoln's arrival at Harrison's Landing.

Usually Lee planned a battle (using the method of Scott in Mexico), left the action to his corps and division commanders, and kept his serenity. "As soon as I order them into battle, I leave my army in the hands of God." Outnumbered nearly two to one by McClellan, he took his chances, once writing his view of an emergency: "This is a case where possible error is better than probable wrong." He would have his officers use independent judgment, under given circumstances even disobeying orders. He told them of General Twiggs in Texas with a staff that often made changes in orders and of the General's saying to one, "Captain, I know you can prove that you are right, and that my order was wrong, in fact you gentlemen always are right, but for God's sake, do wrong sometimes!"

More than once in the campaign before Richmond Lee's army had outslugged and outplayed the heavier opponent and then come to a standstill, bleeding and too weak to follow up the advantage gained. This weakened condition Kearny and Hooker had stressed in urging McClellan to press Lee into Richmond, and McClellan had hesitated and desisted. Lee had burned up more of the available man power of the South than was good for his cause. He was not unmindful of what his General D. H. Hill later noted: "The attacks on the Beaver Dam intrenchments, on the heights of Malvern Hill, were all grand, but of exactly the kind of grandeur which the South could not afford." The matter was complicated and psychological.

Enfolded in the churchman and the Christian gentleman, Robert E. Lee was the ancient warrior who sprang forth and struck and cut and mangled as if to tear the guts and heart out of the enemy, as if like his father Light-Horse Harry Lee he seemed "to have come out of his mother's womb a soldier." He was comparatively silent on why men fight, on why fighting is one of the most ancient games of man, on the secrets in the blood of men that respond to the fife and drum, to the wild plunge of primitive spear or modern bayonet into the pink viscera of the other man, the foeman. Lee could not have been so expert, so smooth and profound in the demands and tests of maneuver and combat, without having moments when his breath of life told him he was born to it and it was for him the supreme and incomparable game for a living man. Of such moments he said little. This composed part of his personal mystery. On one shell-torn field where stumps and butts of men quivered half alive and half dead, he quietly commented, "It is well that war is so terrible, or else we might grow too fond of it."

Lee's right-hand man Thomas Jonathan Jackson too was born for war.

His valley campaign up and down the Shenandoah, in which he captured half of one Union army, beat off three other armies with which Lincoln was trying to trap him, and slipped through for a rapid march to join Lee, had become one of the shining chronicles of the Confederacy. Lincoln from the White House undertook to direct continuously from day to day the field movements of several armies. To Frémont, to Banks, to McDowell, with forces three times that of Jackson, Lincoln sent telegrams giving the reported movements of Jackson's "foot cavalry." During three weeks in a series of telegrams there glimmered Lincoln's hope that from his assorted varieties of armies in and about the Shenandoah, he might set up one little combination that would cross Jackson's path somewhere and damage or break that adventuring zealot. The opening telegrams on the same day advised Frémont: "Much—perhaps all—depends upon the celerity with which you can execute it. Put the utmost speed into it. Do not lose a minute"; and McDowell, "Everything now depends upon the celerity and vigor of your movement."

But Jackson was putting on a campaign that for swift troop movement amazed the world and was later soberly and in detail compared to the famous performances of Napoleon of France and Charles XII of Sweden. Thirty miles in twenty-four hours his infantry marched. "Mystify, mislead and surprise," was his counsel of approach, and then "hurl overwhelming numbers at the point where the enemy least expects attack." With 17,000 men in this one month he won five battles, took many prisoners, sent to Richmond great wagon trains of muskets, munitions, medicines, and supplies, threw Washington into a scare, made McDowell's army of 40,000 hug Washington so close that it could not co-operate with McClellan. An order from Lincoln to McDowell that he should detach 20,000 men to reinforce Frémont for fighting Jackson, McDowell termed "a crushing blow" that he obeyed with "a heavy heart."

Why Lincoln at such a distance should have undertaken what he did was not clear, particularly when Frémont was the key and he knew from Missouri experience of Frémont's "celerity." His seriously telegraphing Frémont "Put the utmost speed into it. Do not lose a minute," was not in accord with his usual judgment of men. He wrote to Frémont: "I think Jackson's game—his assigned work—now is to magnify the accounts of his numbers and reports of his movements, and thus by constant alarms keep three or four times as many of our troops away from Richmond as his own force amounts to. Thus he helps his friends at Richmond three or four times as much as if he were there. Our game is not to allow this." Lincoln read with accuracy the main design of Lee and Jackson in the Shenandoah Valley campaign. Regarding reports that Jackson was being reinforced from Richmond he telegraphed McClellan, "This may be reality, and yet may only be contrivance for deception, and to determine which is perplexing."

Amid the perplexities, Jackson accomplished precisely what he set out for, Stanton telegraphing several governors of Northern States: "Intelligence from various quarters leaves no doubt that the enemy in great force are marching on Washington. You will please organize and forward all the militia and volunteer force in your State." Regiments hurried forward amid excitement that in Massachusetts was referred to afterward as "the great scare" and "the great stampede," and "the Third Uprising." Lessons were learned, Lincoln never again attempting to direct the field movements of several armies a long way from the White House.

Two conditions had to do with Lincoln's role in this matter. One was that neither he nor Lee, nor Davis, nor Jackson himself was as yet acquainted with the phenomenal cunning and mobility of Jackson and his "foot cavalry." Had Lincoln been aware of it as fact, he would have hardly dared match the melancholy military tortoise Frémont against a phantom demon that broke all the regular and applied rules of warfare. A second point was that Lee had imposed a psychology, a frame of mind, on McClellan that counseled in effect "Do nothing but what can be safely done and go slow and careful in strategy and logistics." Lincoln seemed to have decided that Jackson was a "contrivance for deception," a scarehead and a bugaboo, and he would apply Lee's rule: "This is a case where possible error is better than probable wrong." The Shenandoah Valley scene connected with the stupendous triple scene of Washington, Richmond, the Peninsular armies, and the shaded personalities of Lincoln, McClellan, Frémont, Lee, and Jackson. Frémont under Lincoln's instruction "Do not lose a minute," lost a whole day "resting" his troops while Jackson pressed a ragged and barefoot army through storm and mud.

Lincoln, advising with McDowell about starting to destroy Jackson, heard McDowell say that he could begin marching the next Sunday but he had been excoriated all over the country for fighting Bull Run on a Sabbath. And Lincoln hesitated and smiled. "Get a good ready and start on Monday," seemingly unaware that one day might be as decisive as death when hunting Jackson, even one Sabbath day.

Jackson's reverence for the Sabbath went so far that he would not mail his wife a letter to be carried in the mails on a Sunday nor would he open a letter received from her on a Sunday. But "with the blessing of an ever-kind Providence" he would fight, slay, and deliver doom to the enemy if on a Sabbath the enemy looked ready for punishment. Jackson joined Lee for the defense of Richmond, he and his men in main decisive actions before Richmond fighting poorly, the general explanation being that they were too worn with their valley campaign. They were soon to perform again, under their leader nicknamed "Stonewall" from a story that a Confederate general at Bull Run had pointed at him while the bullets were flying and men fleeing and said, "There stands Jackson like a stone wall." The tale was a "sheer fabrication," said D. H. Hill, Jackson's fellow general and brother-in-law, and "the name was least suited to Jackson, ever in motion, swooping like an eagle on his prey; but the name spread like wild-fire." An orphan boy who managed to get into West Point, Jackson had graduated far below the class leader, George B. McClellan. His Mexican War record bright, he became professor of natural philosophy and artillery tactics in the Virginia Military Institute at Lexington. Tall, rawboned, with big hands and a peculiar stride, he would walk alone, raise his right hand high over his head and let it down; he was either praying or easing himself physically—the onlookers could not tell which. He had many books and two favorites, which he always carried in his mess kit—the Bible and a volume of Napoleon's maxims on war. His spiritual guide was Jesus of Nazareth, his professional and military inspiration the Little Corsican, whose eighty-eight campaigns he had mastered from A to Z.

The dyspeptic Jackson had taken a water cure in the North, worn a wet shirt next to his body, lived on a diet of stale bread and buttermilk; for years he went to bed at nine o'clock, leaving any party or meeting so as to reach his bed at that hour. "His dyspepsia caused drowsiness," said D. H. Hill, "and he often went to sleep in conversation with a friend. At church I have seen his head bowed down to his very knees during the sermon. He always heard the text of our good pastor, and a few opening sentences; after that all was lost." His eyes went bad; he was ordered to do no reading by lamplight, and sat one hour, two hours, of an evening in silence with closed eyes or staring at the wall, concentrating on points arisen in his mind during the day. Alongside Negroes on his farm near Lexington he worked with his hands. His students would see him going or coming from a long walk, and he would suddenly stop, gaze into the distance at seemingly nothing at all, then resume his walk. He was practicing for better eyesight, but the students thought he was just queer. "They played tricks upon him, made sport of him, teased him, but he went straight on in his own ways," said D. H. Hill. "As he was passing by the tall Institute building one day, a vicious cadet who hated him, let drop a brick from the third story window. It fell close by his feet, and his escape was almost miraculous. He did not deign to look up, and stalked on with contemptuous indifference."

In his first address at a debating society Jackson stammered out a sentence and quit, the local paper saying that he was "nervous"; he kept on practicing till he was a tolerable orator; praying publicly he learned slowly after many attempts. In Mexico he read the Bible from cover to cover, made notes, sought the Roman Catholic archbishop in Mexico City and had long talks on that faith. Later he was baptized, but not confirmed, in the Protestant Episcopal church at Fort Hamilton, Long Island, New York. Still later he joined the Presbyterian church at Lexington, became a deacon, conducted a Sunday school for Negroes. He married Eleanor Junkin and a year later saw her and a newborn child to their double grave. Four years afterward he married Mary Anna Morrison, and their household ran like clockwork in its daily program.

Letters of Jackson to his wife gushed with little excesses of romance. "When I gave my darling the last kiss" was a moment. He saluted her as "darling," "precious pet," "sunshine," "little jewel of mine," "esposita." He brandished swords about her head in play or leaped from hiding behind a door to take her in his arms. "When my sweet one writes let the letters be long. . . . You are very precious to somebody's heart. . . . I hope that my little somebody is feeling lively as a lark. . . . I wish you could see with me the beautiful roses in the yard and garden, and upon the wall of the house here."

Cadets of Jackson stood guard at the hanging of John Brown, and he wrote his wife: "I sent up a petition that he might be saved. Awful was the thought that he might in a few minutes receive the sentence, 'Depart, ye wicked, into everlasting fire.' I hope that he was prepared to die, but I am doubtful." From the field he sent his wife scraps of news. "It was your husband that did so much mischief at Martinsburg. To destroy so many fine locomotives, cars, and railroad property was a sad work, but I had my orders, and my duty was to obey. If the cost of the property could only have been expended in disseminating the gospel of the Prince of Peace, how much good might have been expected!" He wrote her from Bull Run of a finger broken by a bullet, and "Whilst great credit is due to other parts of our gallant army, God made my brigade more instrumental than any other in repulsing the main attack. . . . I am glad that the battle was fought on your birthday, so you can never tell me any more that I forget your birthday." Gulping hard to get down whisky ordered by a physician, he said: "I like it; I always did, and that is the reason I never use it." Refusing a glass of brandy, he said to a fellow officer, "I am more afraid of it than of Yankee bullets."

Why the saying arose that "Stonewall's men will go anywhere he leads them" was not clear. He shot deserters more swiftly and ruthlessly than any other general North or South. No other major commander was more secretive as to where going or what doing. Jackson would ask many questions about one route and then take another. His men were drilled to say "I don't know" as to where they were headed. He preferred to camp at night on a crossroads, so that enemy spies or scouts could have their choice as to which of four routes he might march the next morning.

An elder general, Ewell, said he never saw one of Jackson's couriers arriving that he did not expect an order to attack the North Pole. There was no doubt of Jackson's military genius or of his lunacy, Ewell used to say with a mischievous twinkle. He once heard Jackson insist seriously that he never ate pepper because of a weakening effect on his left leg. For digestive aid Jackson sucked lemons. Often on march, in battle, officers rode up to Jackson and received his orders between lemon sucks.

Years back Jackson had told his wife that it was "better for the South to fight for her rights *in* the Union than *out* of it." But now his Shenandoah Valley was invaded, *his* valley, whose corners he knew as he knew his favorite Bible verses. "If this valley is lost then Virginia is lost." His brother-in-law, General Rufus Barringer, told of hearing Jackson in July of '62 lay down a program for "light movable columns" to counterinvade the North: "I would hurl these thunderbolts of war against the rich cities and teeming regions of our Federal friends. I would seek to avoid all regular battles. I would subsist my troops, as far as possible, on the Northern people. I would lay heavy contributions in money on their cities. I would encumber my marches with no prisoners, except noted leaders held for ransom or retaliation." Of all Southern commanders who had the ear of Lee and of Davis none was more fiercely in favor of defending by taking the offensive, of striking deep into Northern territory. Of his chief he said: "Lee is a phenomenon. He is the only man I would follow blindfold."

As Jackson now marched toward Pope he was told, "The new general claims your attention." He replied, "And please God, he shall have it." Lee in one dispatch alluded to the "miscreant Pope," who had directed his army to live off the country and reimburse only loyal citizens, who had ordered instant destruction of any house from which any soldier was shot, who had further ordered the arrest of all male noncombatants within the Federal lines and the expulsion of those who refused to take an oath of loyalty to the Union and to give security for their good behavior. This to Lee was not civilized warfare, and he was saying, "Pope must be suppressed." In a letter to Mrs. Lee he mentioned the son of his sister Ann, Louis Marshall, a captain serving on General Pope's staff: "I could forgive [his] fighting against us, but not his joining Pope."

In the last week of August, 1862, Lincoln sat up till late every night, and one night all through into a bitter dawn. In the telegraph office at the head of the first stairway in the War Department building on August 27 he telegraphed Colonel Hermann Haupt, railroad chief in the field with Pope's army, "Is the railroad bridge over Bull Run destroyed?" He received a reply at 4:25 A.M. saying of the bridge "if it is not destroyed . . . probably will be," and wired Haupt, "What became of our forces which held the bridge till twenty minutes ago, as you say?"

Minutes counted. Lee and Jackson were performing around Pope. Lincoln queried Burnside at Falmouth, "Any news from General Pope?" He wired Banks at Manassas Junction, "Please tell me the news." He asked Haupt, "What news?" on August 30 and in a second telegram the same day, "Please send me the latest news." He telegraphed McClellan: "What news from direction of Manassas Junction? What generally?" McClellan replied that he was clear that only two courses were open: first, to help Pope with all available forces; "second, to leave Pope to get out of his scrape, and at once use all our means to make the capital perfectly safe."

Lincoln puzzled over such words as "leave Pope to get out of his scrape." Did McClellan possibly mean that if Pope's army could win with men sent from the Army of the Potomac, then such men should *not* be sent? He answered McClellan: "I think your first alternative—to wit, 'to concentrate all our available forces to open communication with Pope'—is the right one, but I wish not to control. That I now leave to General Halleck, aided by your counsels."

McClellan was writing his wife: "I fancy that Pope is in retreat, though this is only a guess of mine. . . . I don't see how I can remain in the service if placed under Pope; it would be too great a disgrace. . . . I . . . don't know what is going on in front; am terribly ignorant of the state of affairs, and therefore somewhat anxious to know. . . . I shall keep as clear as possible of the President and cabinet; endeavor to do what must be done with Halleck alone; so I shall get on better. . . . I have just telegraphed very plainly to the President and Halleck what I think ought to be done. I expect merely a contemptuous silence. . . . I am heart-sick with the folly and ignorance I see around me. . . . I have seen neither the President nor the secretary since I arrived here; have been only once to Washington, and hope to see very little of the place. I abominate it terribly. . . . I have no faith in anyone here. I expect I got into a row with Halleck to-night. He sent me a telegram I did not like, and I told him so very plainly. He is not a refined person at all, and probably says rough things when he don't mean them."

And what with jealousy, spite, bickering, officialism, politics, pride, sloth, ignorance, a large army of troops stayed quiet and safe along the Potomac while Pope farther off was outguessed, flanked, surprised, hacked and harassed, and driven off from Bull Run Creek with slaughter. In combat and retreat he lost 14,000 out of 80,000; Lee lost 9,000 out of 54,000.

John Hay wrote in his diary of a horseback ride from the Soldiers' Home to the White House with Lincoln, and of matters that made public would have farther torn the country: "We talked about Bull Run and Pope's prospect. The President was very outspoken in regard to McClellan's present conduct. He said that it really seemed to him McC. wanted Pope defeated. He mentioned to me a despatch of McC.'s in which he proposed, as one plan of action, to 'leave Pope to get out of his own scrape.' He spoke also of McC.'s dreadful cowardice in the matter of Chain Bridge, which he had ordered blown up the night before, but which order had been countermanded; and also of his incomprehensible interference with Franklin's corps which he recalled once, and then when they had been sent ahead by Halleck's order, begged permission to recall them again & only desisted after Halleck's sharp injunction to push them ahead till they whipped something or got whipped themselves. The President seemed to think him a little crazy. Envy, jealousy and spite are probably a better explanation of his present conduct. He is constantly sending despatches to the President and Halleck asking what is his real position and command. He acts as chief alarmist and grand marplot of the Army. The President, on my asking if Halleck had any prejudices, rejoined, 'No! Halleck is wholly for the service. He does not care who succeeds or who fails so the service is benefited.'"

Stanton took Lincoln and Hay to his house. "A pleasant little dinner and a pretty wife as white and cold and motionless as marble, whose rare smiles seemed to pain her. Stanton was loud about the McC. business. . . . He said that nothing but foul play could lose us this battle & that it rested with McC. and his friends. Stanton seemed to believe very strongly in Pope. So did the President for that matter."

Back at the War Department, Lincoln and Hay found Halleck quiet and confident. "He said the greatest battle of the century was now being fought. He said he had sent every man that could go, to the field."

Everything seemed to be going well on Saturday, August 30, as Lincoln and Hay saw it. "We went to bed expecting glad tidings at sunrise. But about eight o'clock the President came to my room as I was dressing and, calling me out, said, 'Well, John, we are whipped again, I am afraid. The enemy reinforced on Pope and drove back his left wing and he has retired to Centreville where he says he will be able to hold his men. I don't like that expression. I don't like to hear him admit that his men need holding.'"

On Sunday things began to look better. "The President was in a singularly defiant tone of mind. He often repeated, 'We must hurt this enemy before it gets away.'"

On Monday when Hay spoke of the bad look of events, the President said: "No, Mr. Hay, we must whip these people now. Pope must fight them. If they are too strong for him, he can gradually retire to these fortifications. If this be not so, if we are really whipped we may as well stop fighting."

"Dark days are upon us," wrote Fox of the Navy Department confidentially to S. P. Lee commanding the North Atlantic blockading squadron. Fox and Lee had married Blair girls, and Fox was writing as he would talk at a family gathering. "Pope, a lying braggart, without brains of any kind, has been driven into Washington. The rebels again look upon the Dome of the Capitol, and the flag of disunion can be seen on the neighboring hills. . . . We shall come out of it and wheel into line, dispirited and determined. The President is most anxious and you know the people are."

By now McClellan regarded Washington as unsafe, believing that Lee's army stood a chance of taking the capital. McClellan was writing his wife, "If I can slip over there I will send your silver off." Army gossip ran riot. Officers who felt McClellan was wronged, Lieutenant Colonel Richard B. Irwin for one, spread stories that army stragglers poured into Washington, took possession of streets and public places and held high jinks. "The Government ordered arms at the arsenal and money in the treasury to be shipped to New York, and the banks followed; a gun-boat with steam up, lay in the river off the White-House," ready to carry away the President.

Stormy tides rocked Washington as the broken pieces of a defeated army straggled in. Outbound railroad trains were packed; thousands fled the national capital. Jackson's foot cavalry would cross the Potomac at Georgetown, ran a rumor. The Federal Treasury building was barricaded with hundreds of barrels of cement. By order of the President clerks in the civil departments enrolled and began military drill. Stanton had important papers gathered into bundles to be carried away on horseback, if necessary. This was the day that General M. C. Meigs saw Stanton issuing volleys of orders for the safety of the city.

And Meigs wrote: "Lincoln, on the other hand, dropped into my room on his weary way to see Stanton, drew himself way down into a big chair, and, with a mingled groan and sigh exclaimed, 'Chase says we can't raise any more money; Pope is licked and McClellan has the diarrhoea. What shall I do? The bottom is out of the tub, the bottom is out of the tub!' I told the President to meet his generals with Stanton, fix the bottom back in the tub, rally the army, and order another advance at once. This seemed to brace him up a little and he went on to the War Department; but for the moment he was completely discouraged and downhearted. Stanton, on the other hand, was more full of power and vehement energy than ever."

Mourning was heard. Eulogies were spoken of Fighting Phil Kearny, the one-armed. In a gray rain at Chantilly he rode out of his own skirmish line, suddenly was among Confederates, who called on him to surrender. He wheeled his horse, lay flat on the animal's back, dug in his spurs and dashed off, then fell to the ground, a bullet in his spine. He was carried into the Confederate lines, where General A. P. Hill saw the face and said, "Poor Kearny! he deserved a better death than this." And Lee ordered the body carried to the Union lines under a flag of truce, with a courteous note to General Pope: "The possession of his remains may be a consolation to his family."

In the trail of the Union Army were thousands of wounded. Fletcher Webster, son of Daniel Webster, leading a regiment he had raised, fell with a bullet in his lungs. Six soldiers lay in an orchard, not in the shade but in a broiling sun, each with a leg off, and with them a corporal with both legs off. A surgeon, heavy with liquor, was doing nothing for them. Still another of this orchard squad had his side torn by a shell, and he heard the boys with legs off wishing for ripe apples. He dragged himself inch by inch through long grass till he reached apples and threw them to comrades. Then he faded out.

The dying colonel of the 1st Michigan Cavalry wrote to his brother and sister saying: "I die midst the ring and clangor of battle, as I could wish. . . . I am one of the victims of Pope's imbecility and McDowell's treason. Tell the President would he save the country he must not give our hallowed flag to such hands." The letter was published, discussed.

Three thousand convalescent soldiers were moved from Washington to Philadelphia to make room for serious cases from Bull Run. Floors in the Capitol, in the Patent Office building, were cleared for torn and mutilated men. Signs went up on street walls calling for volunteer nurses, each to bring a bucket and a tin cup, a bottle of brandy, and if possible, transportation toward the battlefield. Colonel Haupt received a telegram from Washington that five passenger cars and two freight cars were starting with "hundreds of men who want to go to the battlefield," many probably "to satisfy a morbid curiosity." A crowd of perhaps 1,000 gathered at the War Office and started by rail, in hacks, in ambulances. An officer in charge of military railroads wrote McClellan's chief of staff the next day of "the drunken rabble who came out as nurses" and were of no use. Of one contingent of 200 volunteer nurses only 16 reached their point at Centerville; a few of these were taken prisoner, sent to Libby Prison, and later paroled. Of another contingent of 1,000 only 75 reached the battlefield, where under a flag of truce they worked among wounded men who had lain on rainy ground twenty-four hours and more. A few did competent, even heroic, service in dressing wounds, loading ambulances, and starting the cases on the rough overland haul to Washington.

The War Department call on Northern cities for surgeons, lint, linen bandages, liquor, hospital supplies, was answered by volunteer medical men, by gatherings of women scraping lint and tearing sheets to make bandages, by public meetings to raise funds. New York City rushed 2,100 cases of supplies, guarded on their way to Washington by the Mayor of New York, aldermen, and twenty policemen.

In this second panic at Bull Run one man satisfied Lincoln in everything, so John Hay wrote in his diary. This was Haupt, the railroad man. He took on himself many duties outside his particular job, advancing supplies and munitions, rebuilding bridges, watching transport, telegraphing the President, working day and night with little food or sleep. "The President is particularly struck with the business-like character of his despatch, telling in the fewest words the information most sought for." It was some weeks earlier that Lincoln had told members of the War Committee that he had seen "the most remarkable structure that human eyes ever rested upon," and explained: "That man Haupt has built a bridge across Potomac Creek, about 400 feet long and nearly 100 feet high, over which loaded trains are running every hour, and upon my word, gentlemen, there is nothing in it but beanpoles and cornstalks." From a distance the green, new-cut timbers did look just so. When Haupt returned from his Bull Run service and called at the War Office, the Cabinet was in session, but Stanton shouted, "Come in, Haupt!" and took the hero's two hands. And they commissioned him a brigadier general.

Haupt told of a slightly drunken general disputing about orders and saying and repeating, "I don't care for John Pope one pinch of owl dung." This reflected in degree the disgust of many officers and soldiers. Pope now came to the White House and read to Lincoln and Welles a long paper, a manifesto, on why he failed of victory, on how other generals would rather see the country ruined than that he should win a victory. About this piece Pope had written for the country to hear, Secretary Welles wrote in his diary: "It certainly needs modifying before it goes out, or there will be war among the generals who are now more ready to fight each other than the enemy." The President and the Cabinet took up Pope's report, decided against publication; it would be bad for the country to hear just then. Yet it was published, with all of Pope's excuses and accusations. And how was not so clear.

The matter of Pope, his record and all, came up as a topic in the Cabinet, and Welles wrote of it in his diary: "Smith complimented Pope's patriotism and bravery, and the President joined in the encomiums. Said that Halleck declared that Pope had made but one mistake in all the orders he had given . . . but no harm came of his error. Blair was unwilling to concede any credit whatever to Pope; said he was a blower and a liar and ought never to have been intrusted with such a command as that in front. The President

[handwritten manuscript text]

Cuts on two opposite pages reproduce one page from the diary of Gideon Welles on September 7, 1862, wherein he quotes Lincoln in a critical hour. The passage reads: "the army from the vicinity of Richmond I thought wrong and I know it was in opposition to the ["judgement" crossed out] opinion of the best military men in the service. Placing Pope over them roused the indignation of many. But in this Stanton had a purpose to·accomplish, and in bringing first Pope here—then by Pope's assistance and Genl Scotts advice bringing Halleck—and correcting measures which followed, he succeeded in breaking down and displacing McClellan but not in dismissing and disgracing him. This the President would not do or permit to be done, though he is more offended with McC. than he ever was before. In a brief ["talk" crossed out] consulta-

admitted Pope's infirmity, but said a liar might be brave and have skill as an officer. He said Pope had great cunning. He [Pope] had published his report, for instance, which was wrong. . . . 'But,' said he [the President], 'it can never, by any skill, be traced to him.' 'That is the man,' said Blair. 'Old John Pope, his father, was a flatterer, a deceiver, a liar, and a trickster; all the Popes are so.' "

Pope was relieved of command and assigned to the Northwest to curb Indian tribes. Welles noted in his diary that the President "spoke favorably" of Pope. Lincoln clearly believed that the departing general had not had a fair chance. "Pope," said the President, "did well, but there was an army prejudice against him, and it was necessary he should leave. He had gone off very angry, and not without cause, but circumstances controlled us." Lincoln probably told Pope and Halleck, as he did Welles, "We had the enemy in the hollow of our hands on Friday, if our generals, who are vexed with Pope, had done their duty; all of our present difficulties and reverses have been brought upon us by these quarrels of the generals."

Welles also recorded in this week following Second Bull Run that his

[Handwritten facsimile of the following transcribed text]

tion with him as we were walking together on Friday, the President said with much emphasis—'I must have McClellan to reorganize the army and bring it out of chaos. But there has been a design—a purpose in breaking down Pope, without regard of consequences to the country. It is shocking to see and know this, but there is no remedy at present. McClellan has the army with him.' My convictions are with the President that McClellan and his generals are, this day, stronger than the Administration with a considerable portion of this Army of the Potomac. It is not so elsewhere with the soldiers, or in the country where McClellan has less favor. The people are disappointed in him, but his leading Generals have contrived to strengthen him in the hearts of the soldiers in front of Washington." Original in the Library of Congress.

convictions joined those of the President "that McClellan and his generals are this day stronger than the Administration with a considerable part of this Army of the Potomac." On a walk with the President, Welles noted the words: "I must have McClellan to reorganize the army and bring it out of chaos, but there has been a design—a purpose in breaking down Pope, without regard of consequences to the country. It is shocking to see and know this, but there is no remedy at present. McClellan has the army with him." Others, like Lincoln, felt a sinister code operating among generals and politicians. Others too were saying it was "shocking." And rumors arose. Senator Wilson came to Welles telling of "a conspiracy on foot among certain generals for a revolution and the establishment of a provisional national government." Lincoln agreed with Welles as to how this rumor began traveling, Welles saying, "Wilson is doubtless sincere, but . . . is influenced by Stanton, who is mad with the army and officers who stand by McClellan."

Hiram Barney, New York port collector, came to the White House, and told Lincoln and Welles of "public sentiment." "He was positive that no one but McClellan could do anything just now with this army. He [McClellan] had managed to get its confidence, and he meant to keep it, and use it for his own purposes." Barney told of talking with Barlow, a lawyer and leading Democratic politician in New York. Barlow had visited McClellan on special invitation of the General, who opened his mind, "said he did not wish the Presidency, would rather have his place at the head of the army, etc., intimating he had no political views or aspirations."

Barney's impression received from Barlow was that McClellan "had no particular desire to close this war immediately, but would pursue a line of policy of his own, regardless of the Administration." In line with this McClellan had combined with others against Pope and affected the morale of the soldiers, who were now becoming reckless and untamable. In these remarks of Barney, wrote Welles, "the President concurred, and said he was shocked to find that of 140,000 whom we were paying for in Pope's army only 60,000 could be found. McClellan brought away 93,000 from the Peninsula, but could not to-day count on over 45,000. As regarded demoralization, the President said, there was no doubt that some of our men permitted themselves to be captured in order that they might leave on parole, get discharged, and go home. Where there is such rottenness, is there not reason to fear for the country?"

Two long letters came from August Belmont requesting the President to throw out Stanton, put in Halleck as Secretary of War, and McClellan "in sole control" of all troops east of the Allegheny Mountains. Lincoln kept these letters of the political financier, sent extracts from them to Stanton, saying, "I will show you the letters if you wish." Claiming to represent New York and five New England governors, a committee of New Yorkers, led by a son of Alexander Hamilton, called at the White House and recommended "a change of policy." The discussion reached a point where, it was reported, the President scornfully exclaimed, "You, gentlemen, to hang Mr. Seward would destroy the government."

Meantime Stanton, Chase, Bates, and Smith of the Cabinet had signed a paper, in Stanton's handwriting, a remonstrance to be handed the President, against McClellan's being given command of the army again. As an incompetent and a traitor, McClellan should not once more be entrusted with the troops. Chase argued with Welles to sign. Welles held off, saying that while he wished to get rid of McClellan, it was not exactly fair to the President to be circulating such a paper behind his back. Then this paper disappeared, and Chase came to Welles with a second one, in the handwriting of Bates and with the same four signers as before. Welles said this second one was more reasonable in tone, but he told Chase that he could not join with them. "Reflection had more fully satisfied me that this method of conspiring to influence or control the President was repugnant to my feelings and was not right; it was unusual, would be disrespectful, and would justly be deemed offensive; that the President had called us around him as friends and advisers with whom he might counsel and consult . . . not to enter into combinations to control him."

Stanton and Chase had joined with vehemence in a bold move. "[Chase] Said it was designed to tell the President that the Administration must be broken up or McC.[lellan] dismissed. The course he said was unusual, but the case was unusual. . . . Conversation, he said, amounted to but little with the President on subjects of this importance. Argument was useless. It was like throwing water on a duck's back. A more decisive expression must be made and that in writing." The determination of Stanton and Chase was to remove, and if possible to disgrace, McClellan, as Welles saw it. "Chase frankly stated he desired it, that he deliberately believed McClellan ought to be shot, and should, were he President, be brought to summary punishment."

Still Welles would not sign the paper. He believed that McClellan hesitated in attack, had neither definite plans nor audacity, and was no fighting general. But he could not agree with Stanton and Chase that McClellan was "imbecile, a coward, a traitor." He wrote, "Chase was disappointed, and I think a little chagrined, because I would not unite in the written demand to the President."

Stanton had come to see if he could not get Welles to sign the protest against McClellan. If Welles signed, that would make five out of seven in the Cabinet. Stanton reviewed McClellan's life and works for Welles, with high lights on all the deficiencies. Welles again agreed that McClellan was unfit to command, but he could not go signing papers behind the President's back. It was discourteous, if nothing else. "Stanton said, with some excitement, he knew of no particular obligations he was under to the President, who had called him to a difficult position and imposed upon him labors and responsibilities which no man could carry, and which were greatly increased by fastening upon him a commander who was constantly striving to embarrass him in his administration of the Department. He could not and would not submit to a continuance of this state of things." Welles admitted that conditions were bad, severe on Stanton. Still he could not sign the paper. It was not a way to do with the President.

Welles in his diary threw strange crosslights on the half-mutinous figures that sat around Lincoln's Cabinet table. Welles hated Stanton, misjudged him, and wrote in caricature style of the Secretary of War. Probably no other navy man ever snorted such contempt of an army man as Welles wrote of Stanton. "I doubt his sincerity always. He wants no general to overtop him, is jealous of others in any position who have influence and popular regard; but he has cunning and skill, dissembles his feelings, in short, is a hypocrite, a moral coward, while affecting to be, and to a certain extent being, brusque, overvaliant in words. Blair says he is dishonest . . . and that he is a double-dealer; that he is now deceiving both Seward and Chase; that Seward brought him into the Cabinet after Chase stole Cameron, and that Chase is now stealing Stanton. . . . Stanton . . . is by nature a sensationalist, has from the first been filled with panics and alarms, in which I have not participated. . . . He saw on more than one occasion that I was cool when he was excited, and he well knew that I neither admired his policy nor indorsed his views. Of course we were courteously civil, but reserved and distant."

Others in the Cabinet, Chase emphatically, agreed with Welles that Seward was meddlesome, not particularly scrupulous, ready to exercise authority until challenged, then becoming timid and "inventive of schemes to extricate himself." While Stanton and Chase were circulating the paper against McClellan, Seward kept away from Cabinet meetings, Welles noting of Seward: "Has met with us but once in several weeks." Seward, having been among the first to urge McClellan for General in Chief, was now dodging the issue of McClellan's removal. Welles could only explain his absences

Washington City
August 30th 1862

Mr President:

The undersigned feel compelled by a profound sense of duty to the government and people of the United States and to yourself as your constitutional advisers respectfully to recommend the immediate removal of George B. McClellan from the command of any army of the United States. We are constrained to urge this by the conviction that after a sad and humiliating trial of twelve months and by the frightful and useless sacrifice of the lives of many thousands of brave men and the waste of many millions of National means he has proved to be incompetent for any important military command And also because by recent disobedience to superior orders and inactivity he has twice imperilled the army commanded by General Pope, and while he continues in command will daily hazard the fate of our armies and our national existence, exhibiting no sign of a disposition a capacity to restore the national honor that has been so deeply tarnished in the eyes of the world by his military failures.

We are unwilling to be accessory to the waste of National resources, the protraction of the war, the destruction of our armies, and the imperilling of the Union and the Government itself which we believe must result from the continuance of George B McClellan in command and seek therefore by his prompt removal to afford an opportunity to capable officers, under Gods Providence, to preserve our national existence.

We have the honor to be with great respect

S. P. Chase
Secy. of the Treasury

Edwin M Stanton
Secretary of War

Caleb B Smith
Secy of the Interior

Three Cabinet members sign a demand on the President for "the immediate removal," the "prompt removal," of George B. McClellan from command, presenting a fearful condition of military affairs and placing the blame on McClellan. Welles's diary mistakenly says "four" signers. Original in the Barrett collection.

by "a reluctance to discuss and bring to a decision any great question." And when Seward did come to a Cabinet meeting, he would get familiar with the President in a way the others did not like. "The President, though he observes this ostentatious presumption, never receives it otherwise than pleasantly, but treats it as a weakness in one . . . whose ready shrewdness he finds convenient and acceptable." Also Seward seemed to be on hand alongside the President too often when other Cabinet members came to the White House. "As each consulted with the President, Seward, from daily, almost hourly, intercourse with him, continued, if not present at these interviews, to ascertain the doings of each and all, though himself imparting but little of his course to any." All other members favored regular Cabinet meetings on fixed days. "The Secretary of State alone dissented, hesitated, doubted, objected, thought it inexpedient, said all had so much to do we could not spare the time; but the President was pleased with the suggestion, if he did not prompt it, and concurred with the rest of the Cabinet."

These regular meetings on fixed days went on, and Seward as a former United States Senator and Governor of New York "was allowed, as was proper, to take the lead in consultations, and also to give tone and direction to the proceedings. The President, if he did not actually wish, readily acquiesced in this. . . . Mr. Seward was not slow in taking upon himself to prescribe action and doing most of the talking, without much regard to the modest chief, but often to the disgust of his associates, particularly Mr. Bates, who was himself courteous and respectful, and to the annoyance of Mr. Chase, who had, like Mr. Seward, experience as a chief magistrate."

Cabinet discussions went on without order or system, noted Welles, "but in the summing-up and conclusions the President, who was a patient listener and learner, concentrated results, and often determined questions adverse to the Secretary of State, regarding him and his opinions, as he did those of his other advisers, for what they were worth and generally no more."

One advantage of Seward was resented. Like the President, he was a storyteller. While other Secretaries were toiling at their duties the Secretary of State "spent a considerable portion of every day with the President, patronizing and instructing him, hearing and telling anecdotes, relating interesting details of occurrences in the Senate, and inculcating his political party notions." And amid these Cabinet jealousies had come one deep cleavage. "Between Seward and Chase there was perpetual rivalry and mutual but courtly distrust. Each was ambitious. Both had capacity. Seward was supple and dexterous; Chase was clumsy and strong. Seward made constant mistakes, but recovered with a facility that was wonderful and almost always without injury to himself; Chase committed fewer blunders but persevered in them when made."

As Welles saw it, such was the Cabinet, the closet council that Lincoln met with for help and light in the September days just after Second Bull Run. Sometimes other matters pressed on Lincoln so hard that he could not meet them, and Welles recorded of one day: "At the Executive Mansion, the Secretary of State informed us there was to be no Cabinet-meeting. He was authorized by the President to communicate the fact. Smith said it would be as well, perhaps, to postpone the Cabinet-meetings altogether and indefinitely—there seemed no use latterly for our coming together. Others expressed corresponding opinions. Seward turned off, a little annoyed."

Faces wore gloom and suspicion. It was a dark hour. "An unfavorable impression is getting abroad in regard to the President and the Administration, not without reason, perhaps, which prompted Smith and others to express their minds freely. There is really very little of a government here at this time, so far as most of the Cabinet are concerned. . . . Seward, when in Washington, spends more or less of each day with the President, absorbs his attention, and I fear to a certain extent influences his action not always wisely. The President has good sense, intelligence, and an excellent heart, but is sadly perplexed and distressed by events. He, to an extent, distrusts his own administrative ability and experience. Seward, instead of strengthening . . . him, encourages this self-distrust. . . . The President has, I believe, sincere respect and regard for each and every member of the Cabinet, but Seward seeks, and has at times, influence, which is sometimes harmful. The President would often do better without him, were he to follow his own instincts, or were he to consult all his advisers in council. . . . Chase is much chafed by these things, and endeavors, and to some extent succeeds, in also getting beside the President, and obtaining information of what is going forward. But this only excites and stimulates Seward, who has the inside track and means to keep it. The President is unsuspicious, or apparently so; readily gives his ear to suggestions from anyone."

At a Cabinet meeting on September 2 Lincoln for the first time told his advisers that he was ready to quit his job; he would gladly resign. Chase in his diary sketched this Cabinet meeting, the arguments, the clash of strong wills, the surfaces of intrigue, the weariness; "while the talk was going on, the President came in, saying that not seeing much for a Cabinet meeting to-day, he had been talking at the department and headquarters about the 'war.' The Secretary of War came in. In answer to some inquiry, the fact was stated by the President or the Secretary, that McClellan had been placed in command of the forces to defend the Capital—or, rather, to use the President's own words, 'he had set him to putting these troops into the fortifications about Washington,' believing that he could do that thing better than any other man. I remarked that this could be done equally well by the engineer who constructed the forts; and that putting General McClellan in command for this purpose was equivalent to making him second in command of the entire army. The Secretary of War said that no one was now responsible for the defense of the Capital;—that the order to McClellan was given by the President direct to McClellan, and that General Halleck considered himself relieved from responsibility although he acquiesced, and approved the order; that McClellan could now shield himself, should anything go wrong, under Halleck, while Halleck could and would disclaim all responsibility for the order given."

These facts stood black and horrible. They indicated enough jealousy, spite, bickering, enough of slack loyalty to Lincoln in high places, to wreck the Administration. Chase in his tone seemed almost pleased that things looked so bad—since he had predicted that they would be bad if McClellan was again put in command. His diary entry continued: "The President thought Genl Halleck as much responsible as before; and repeated that the whole scope of the Order was, simply, to direct McClellan to put the troops in the fortifications, and command them for the defense of Washington. I remarked that this seemed to me equivalent to making him Commander-in-Chief for the time being, and that I thought it would prove very difficult to make any substitution hereafter, for active operations; that I had no feeling whatever against McClellan; that he came to the command with my most cordial approbation and support; that until I became satisfied that his delays would greatly injure our cause, he possessed my full confidence;

that after I had felt myself compelled to withdraw that confidence, I had (since the President, notwithstanding my opinion that he should, refrained from putting another in command), given him all possible support in every way, raising means and urging reinforcements; that his experience as a military commander had been little else than a series of failures; and that his omission to urge troops forward to the battles of Friday and Saturday evinced a spirit which rendered him unworthy of trust, and that I could not but feel that giving command to him was equivalent to giving Washington to the rebels. This and more I said. Others of the Cabinet expressed a general concurrence, but in no very energetic terms. (Mr. Blair must be excepted, but he did not dissent.) The President said it distressed him exceedingly to find himself differing on such a point from the Secretary of War and the Secretary of the Treasury; that he would gladly resign his place; but he could not see who could do the work wanted as well as McClellan. I named Hooker, or Sumner, or Burnside, either of whom, I thought, would be better. At length the conversation ended, and the meeting broke up, leaving the matter as we found it. A few tax appointments were lying on the table. I asked the President to sign them, which he did, saying he would sign them just as they were, and ask no questions."

Before this Cabinet meeting Lincoln had gone with Halleck to McClellan and given him command of the army again. But the actual words by which authority was once more handed over to him were not spoken by Lincoln. It was left to Halleck, Lincoln explaining to Welles, "I could not have done it, for I can never feel confident that he will do anything effectual." McClellan wrote his wife: "I was surprised this morning, when at breakfast, by a visit from the President and Halleck, in which the former expressed the opinion that the troubles now impending could be overcome better by me than anyone else. Pope is ordered to fall back on Washington, and, as he reenters, everything is to come under my command again!"

Three days later, as Lincoln and Hay walked over to the telegraph office, Lincoln said: "McClellan is working like a beaver. He seems to be aroused to doing something, by the sort of snubbing he got last week. The Cabinet yesterday were unanimous against him. They were all ready to denounce me for it, except Blair. He [McClellan] has acted badly in this matter, but we must use what tools we have. There is no man in the Army who can man these fortifications and lick these troops into shape half as well as he." Hay spoke of the many letters coming in reflecting a feeling against McClellan. Lincoln commented: "Unquestionably he has acted badly toward Pope. He wanted him to fail. That is unpardonable. But he is too useful just now to sacrifice." And he added later, "If he can't fight himself, he excels in making others ready to fight." He admitted also that calling McClellan to power again was a good deal like "curing the bite with the hair of the dog."

Lincoln had, however, offered command in the field to Burnside, who would not take it, saying to the President, "I do not think that there is anyone who can do as much with that army as McClellan, if matters can be so arranged as to remove yours and the Secretary of War's objections to him."

Also, Lincoln had consented to the dismissal of three major generals, Porter, Franklin, and Griffin, who were to have a court-martial on their conduct in the field. Also with a heavy heart Lincoln agreed there should be a court of inquiry for McDowell.

"The President," said Chase . . . "told me that the clamor against Mc-Dowell was so great that he [McDowell] could not lead his troops unless something was done to restore confidence; and proposed to me to suggest to him the asking for a Court of Inquiry." Both Chase and Stanton, along with Lincoln, had long ago become convinced that McDowell was a first-rate, loyal officer, never sulking nor talking loose nor taking a hand in military politics and interfering with the War Department. When Chase mentioned the Court of Inquiry, McDowell said it came hard to call for such a court when there were no charges. Chase fixed it. "I told him I thought he could assume the charge made by the Michigan officer who, when dying, scrawled a letter saying he died a victim to Pope's imbecility and McDowell's treachery." McDowell thought about that and said it would do as a charge to be brought against him.

After breakfast at Chase's house the next morning McDowell read to friends the letter he had written asking for a court to hear the evidence against him, he knowing that there was no such evidence. Chase then took the letter to his office. "Soon after, the President came in, and asked what McDowell had determined to do. I told him. 'Where is the letter?' He took it, intending to have it copied I suppose. 'Well, it ought to be done immediately; for the corps must march, and General Halleck feels that he [McDowell] must be relieved, at all events, from command. Where can he be found?' 'I can not tell. An orderly, no doubt, can find him.' The President went away, and, later in the day, I heard that General McDowell had been relieved at his own request. He came in himself, afterward, stating the fact and adding, 'I did not ask to be relieved—I only asked for a court.' " Then without any fuss or pulling any wires or threatening to resign, McDowell went away "very sad," on a fifteen-day leave of absence, to return for the trial he asked.

A week after the Second Bull Run battle, Lincoln at the War Office referred to "the great number of stragglers he had seen coming into town this morning, and of the immense losses by desertion." Chase noted: "The President said he had felt badly all day." Meeting another committee from New York the next day, who urged him to change his policy, "the President became vexed and said, in substance, 'It is plain enough what you want—you want to get Seward out of the Cabinet. There is not one of you who would not see the country ruined if you could turn out Seward.' "

On general policies Chase believed Lincoln had now drifted far out of line with his country and party. "The President," noted Chase, "with the most honest intentions in the world, and a naturally clear judgment and a true, unselfish patriotism, has yielded so much to Border State and negrophobic counsels that he now finds it difficult to arrest his own descent towards the most fatal concessions. He has already separated himself from the great body of the party which elected him; distrusts most those who

most represent its spirit; and waits. For what?" On one piece of immediate
policy, however, Chase had swung around inside of a week to a moderate
instead of an extreme viewpoint. Hearing that Lincoln was going out to see
McClellan, Chase noted: "It is indeed humiliating; but prompted, I believe,
by a sincere desire to serve the country, and a fear that, should he super-

The pro-Confederate weekly periodical *Punch* of London after news of Second Bull
Run titles a cartoon THE OVERDUE BILL, with Mr. South saying to Mr. North: "Your
'ninety days'' promissory note isn't taken up yet, siree!"

sede McClellan by any other commander, no advantage would be gained in leadership, but much harm in the disaffection of officers and troops."

Stevens in the House had long and bitterly protested against heading the army with a slavery sympathizer who ordered pursuit and return of fugitive slaves, who set troops to guard rebel property. Did he intend charges against the President and the Secretary of War? He replied his remarks should apply where they belonged. "I am no sycophant, no parasite. What I think I say. These acts have been perpetrated without rebuke. Let the world determine where the responsibility rests. I believe the President is as honest a man as there is in the world; but I believe him to be too easy and amiable, and to be misled by the malignant influence of the Kentucky counselors and the Border State men."

And it seemed that when the President was through with conferences, interviews, orders, letters, and proclamations at his own office and department bureaus, he received in his home rooms of the White House instructions and advice on whom to trust and not. "Often Mr. and Mrs. Lincoln discussed the relations of Cabinet officers, and gentlemen prominent in politics," wrote Mrs. Keckley, the faithful dressmaker, maid, nurse, and friend of Mrs. Lincoln. "I soon learned that the wife of the President had no love for Mr. Salmon P. Chase. She claimed that he was a selfish politician instead of a true patriot, and warned Mr. Lincoln not to trust him too far. The daughter of the Secretary was quite a belle in Washington, and Mrs. Lincoln, who was jealous of the popularity of others, had no desire to build up her social prestige through political favor to her father. Miss Chase was a lovely woman, and was worthy of all the admiration she received. Mr. Lincoln was more confiding than his wife." Mrs. Keckley noted a conversation. Mr. Lincoln lay on a sofa one evening holding a newspaper, Mrs. Lincoln saying, "Father, I do wish you would inquire a little into the motives of Chase."

"Mother, you are too suspicious. I give you credit for sagacity, but you are disposed to magnify trifles. Chase is a patriot, and one of my best friends."

"Yes, one of your best friends because it is his interest to be so. He is anything for Chase. If he thought he could make anything by it, he would betray you to-morrow."

"I fear that you are prejudiced against the man, mother. I know that you do him injustice."

"Mr. Lincoln, you are either blind or will not see. I am not the only one that has warned you against him."

"True, I receive letters daily from all parts of the country, telling me not to trust Chase; but then these letters are written by political enemies of the Secretary, and it would be unjust and foolish to pay any attention to them."

"Very well, you will find out some day, if you live long enough, that I have read the man correctly. I only hope that your eyes may not be opened to the truth when it is too late."

Seward had long ago come under the ban of Mrs. Lincoln. Early one morning as Mrs. Keckley was basting a dress for Mrs. Lincoln, and as the President sat in a chair reading a newspaper and stroking the head of Tad, a letter was brought by a messenger. He broke the seal, read it, and Mrs. Lincoln asked, "Who is the letter from, father?"

"Seward. I must go over and see him today."

"Seward! I wish you had nothing to do with that man. He cannot be trusted."

"You say the same of Chase. If I listened to you, I should soon be without a Cabinet."

"Better be without it than to confide in some of the men that you do. Seward is worse than Chase. He has no principle."

"Mother, you are mistaken; your prejudices are so violent that you do not stop to reason. Seward is an able man, and the country as well as myself can trust him."

"Father, you are too honest for this world! You should have been born a saint. You will generally find it a safe rule to distrust a disappointed, ambitious politician. It makes me mad to see you sit still and let that hypocrite, Seward, twine you around his finger as if you were a skein of thread."

"It is useless to argue the question, mother. You cannot change my opinion."

McClellan among others was "a humbug," in Mrs. Lincoln's view. "He talks so much and does so little. If I had the power I would very soon take off his head." And the President explained with good nature that McClellan had been "much embarrassed," other officers were jealous. "They will kill him off if they can." At this Mrs. Lincoln flared. "McClellan can make plenty of excuses for himself, therefore he needs no advocate in you. If he would only do something, and not promise so much, I might learn to have a little faith in him. I tell you he is a humbug, and you will have to find some man to take his place, that is, if you wish to conquer the South."

Philosophy and the incidents of strange, unhappy marriages were given the Cabinet at one of its meetings when Lincoln had brought up the matter of shifting and trying new generals. As it came to A. K. McClure, the President said:

"This situation reminds me of a Union man in Kentucky whose two sons enlisted in the Federal Army. His wife was of Confederate sympathies. His nearest neighbor was a Confederate in feeling, and his two sons were fighting under Lee. This neighbor's wife was a Union woman and it nearly broke her heart to know that her sons were arrayed against the Union.

"Finally, the two men, after each had talked the matter over with his wife, agreed to obtain divorces; this they did, and the Union man and Union woman were wedded, as were the Confederate man and the Confederate woman—the men swapped wives, in short.

"But this didn't seem to help matters any, for the sons of the Union woman were still fighting for the South, and the sons of the Confederate woman continued in the Federal Army; the Union husband couldn't get along with his Union wife, and the Confederate husband and his Confederate wife couldn't agree upon anything, being forever fussing and quarreling.

"It's the same thing with the Army. It doesn't seem worth while to secure divorces and then marry the Army and McClellan to others, for they won't get along any better than they do now, and there'll only be a new set of heartaches started.

"I think we'd better wait; perhaps a real fighting general will come along some of these days, and then we'll all be happy. If you go to mixing in a mix-up, you only make the muddle worse."

CHAPTER 25

BLOODY ANTIETAM SEPTEMBER '62

THE yellow corn stood ripe in the fields of Maryland. Lee and Jackson mentioned it. That corn would help feed their armies. They marched gray and butternut battalions across the Potomac, ragged and footsore men who could fight, as the world knew. Lee gave out a proclamation to the people of Maryland, a Slave State, her folk of Southern traditions and leanings. His men had come "to aid you in throwing off this foreign yoke."

And where would he hit first? Would it be Harrisburg, Philadelphia, Baltimore? Thus ran the questions that worried the North and harried those cities.

Meantime McClellan with an army marched toward Lee. He was feeling better. His three dismissed major generals had been cleared without court-martial and restored to him by the President. McClellan wrote his wife, "The feeling of the government towards me, I am sure, is kind and trusting." Not in a year had he sent his wife any such pleasant words about the Government. His friend, Lincoln, against a majority of the Cabinet, had again put him at the head of a great army in the field. "I hope," he wrote, "with God's blessing, to justify the great confidence they now repose in me, and will bury the past in oblivion."

On top of the turmoil set going by Lee's invasion of the North came more excitement because of news from the West. Telegrams tumbled into the White House telling of Bragg's Confederate army slipping past Buell's army, which had been set to watch him. Bragg was marching north toward Cincinnati and Louisville; those cities were anxious. Also Kirby Smith's men in gray had marched into Kentucky, chased the State legislature out of Frankfort, and captured Lexington, the home town of Mary Todd Lincoln. For a few days at least, Lincoln and his wife would not read the Lexington newspapers for which they subscribed.

"Where is General Bragg?" Lincoln queried in telegrams to several generals in the field. He wired Buell and others, "What degree of certainty have you that Bragg, with his command, is not now in the valley of the Shenandoah, Virginia?" He wired McClellan, who was calling for reinforcements, that McClellan could have 21,000 under Porter and "I am sending you all that can be spared." Also he wired a reply to the Governor of Pennsylvania's dispatch asking for 80,000 troops to be sent to Pennsylvania, explaining. in effect that if he had 80,000 soldiers to spare at Washington it would be better for them to hit Lee's army in the rear in Maryland.

Into Frederick City, Maryland, marched Stonewall Jackson's men, followed later by Union troops. A woman, Barbara Frietchie, nearly a hundred years old and remembering 1776, leaned from a window and waved the Stars and Stripes at the Union troops to show her loyalty. And a story spread that she had unfurled the Union banner with grand words of defiance to Jackson's troops. Whittier wrote a poem about her that was put in the schoolbooks and committed to memory by millions of children enacting her as saying, "Shoot if you must this old gray head, but spare your country's flag," which she had not said at all. But it was good Union propaganda. And a poet of the Southern cause could have given fame to another old woman in Frederick City, whose love ran to the other flag. She stood on her doorstep as the Southern boys marched past, tears in her eyes and hands raised— "The Lord bless your dirty ragged souls!"

The first big action of Lee's army in Maryland made the Northern gloom heavier. For Stonewall Jackson smashed at the Union garrison in Harper's Ferry, trapped them, and took 11,000 prisoners. Then four days later, on September 17, came Antietam, to be remembered for long as a blood-soaked word.

McClellan's 90,000 troops met Lee's army, about half that of McClellan in troop numbers, at Antietam Creek. Around a cornfield and a little white Dunker church, around a stone bridge, and in a pasture lane worn by cowpaths surged a human tornado. Fighting Joe Hooker rode in the worst of the storm, and said of it, "Every stalk of corn in the northern and greater part of the field was cut as closely as could have been done with a knife, and the slain lay in rows precisely as they had stood in their ranks a few moments before." Hooker fell from his saddle with a bleeding foot. An old man with his white hair in the wind, Major General J. K. F. Mansfield, fell from his saddle, a corpse. Four other Union generals fell off their horses with wounds. General Sedgwick was three times wounded, in shoulder, leg, and wrist. Colonel B. B. Gayle of Alabama was surrounded, drew his revolver, called to his men, "We are flanked, boys, but let's die in our tracks," and fell riddled with bullets. Longstreet, heading one of Lee's corps, took two bullets in his right leg, one in his left arm; another ripped his shoulder, and he sent Private Vickers of Alabama to tell Lee that he was still on the field—but Vickers tumbled with lead through the head, and the next bullet received by Longstreet was in the face and he was carried away to live on. "Don't let your horses tread on me," a wounded man called from a huddle of corpses where officers were picking their way through.

Into Shepherdstown, Virginia (now West Virginia), on that hot and dusty autumn day the wounded poured, and Mary B. Mitchell, the volunteer nurse, said, "They filled every building and overflowed into the country around, into farm-houses, barns, corn-cribs, cabins; six churches were all full, the Odd Fellows' Hall, the Freemasons', the Town Council room, the school-houses." She saw men with cloths about their heads, about their feet, men with arms in slings, men without arms, with one leg, with bandaged sides and backs; men in ambulances, wagons, carts, wheelbarrows, men on stretchers or leaning on comrades, men crawling with inflamed wounds, thirsty, bleeding, weak.

At the center of the red harvest stood the little white Dunker church, where the teaching on Sundays was that war is sin and no man who enlists for war can be a Dunker. There the dead lay in blue and gray. And on the breast of one in blue a pocket Bible was open at the Psalm reading "Yea, though I walk through the valley of the shadow of death, I will fear no evil: for thou art with me; thy rod and thy staff they comfort me." On the fly-leaf a mother had written, "We hope and pray that you may be permitted by a kind Providence, after the war is over, to return." Into a Confederate hospital came Fanny Haralson Gordon to see her husband General John Brown Gordon, with a bullet-shattered jaw, and to hear his greeting, "Mrs. Gordon, you have not a very handsome husband!"

In the fields lay men by thousands. Flat corn leaves fallen over some of the bodies were spattered and blotched with blood drying and turning rusty. At the campfires living soldiers sang:

> Do they miss me at home? do they miss me?
> 'Twould be an assurance most dear
> To know at this moment some loved one
> Were saying, "I wish he were here."

On a golden autumn Sabbath morning three-mile lines of men had faced each other with guns. And when the shooting was over the losses were put at 12,000 on each side.

Lee crossed the Potomac, back into the South again. McClellan did not follow. Lincoln had telegraphed him: "God bless you, and all with you. Destroy the rebel army, if possible." But McClellan had again won a victory and did not know it. He still believed the enemy outnumbered him. One of McClellan's major generals, Jacob D. Cox, wrote: "He had put Lee's strength at 120,000 men. That belief was based upon the inconceivably mistaken reports of the secret-service [Pinkerton] organization, accepted at headquarters, given to the War Department at Washington as a reason for incessant demands of re-enforcements, and permeating downwards through the whole organization till the error was accepted as truth by officers and men, and became a factor in their morale which can hardly be over-estimated."

McClellan's chances of wiping out Lee's army were estimated by Longstreet: "We were so badly crushed that at the close of the day ten thousand fresh troops could have come in and taken Lee's army and everything it had. But McClellan did not know it." He had two soldiers to the enemy's one, completely superior cannon, rifles, supplies, and McClellan wrote his wife, "I feel some little pride in having, with a beaten and demoralized army, defeated Lee so utterly and saved the North so completely." Also McClellan termed the management of the battle "a masterpiece of art." He had filled Lincoln's order "not [to] let them get off without being hurt." He had failed when it lay in his hands to "destroy the rebel army if possible," as Lincoln urged. He had 93,000 men answering roll call as Lee was fading down the Shenandoah Valley with less than 40,000. He might have brought the war shortly to a close. But his fate lay otherwise.

Ten days after the Antietam battle McClellan wrote to his wife that no good word of encouragement had come to him from the national capital. The President was giving him silence. "Not yet have I had a word from any one in Washington about the battle of the Antietam . . . except from the President in the following *beautiful* language, 'Your despatch received. God bless you and all with you! Cant you *bust* them some *even* before they get off?'!!!" Thus for his own purposes and satisfaction, in a highly responsible matter, McClellan could misquote and mangle the President's little message, which read: "God bless you and all with you. Destroy the rebel army if possible." The General closed his bitter epistle: "I dont look for any thanks at their hands and believe that they scarcely pretend to conceal their malevolence."

Lincoln remarked to Lamon: "I suppose our victory at Antietam will condone my offence in reappointing McClellan. If the battle had gone against us poor McClellan, and I too, would be in a bad row of stumps."

Congressman William D. Kelley of Pittsburgh came to the White House and discussed with Lincoln the information that McClellan had held in reserve some 30,000 men, Fitz-John Porter's corps. They did not get into battle, had all their ammunition when the shooting was over. And Kelley felt pity and sarcasm both in the President's saying, "Whatever the troops and people may think and say of his failure to capture Lee's army and supplies, my censure should be tempered by the consciousness of the fact that I did not restore him to command for aggressive fighting, but as an organizer and a good hand at defending a position." Kelley spoke of the dangers to republican institutions when ambitious and rival military commanders hold a power stronger than the political government, of how McClellan had charged each failure to the Secretary of War and the President, and had won his men and officers to the belief that the Administration was hostile to them.

Lincoln, according to Kelley, was slow and deliberate as he said that the restoration of McClellan to command, after McClellan had stood by and helped sacrifice Pope's army, was the greatest trial and the most painful duty of his official life. Yet he had done it and had no regrets. "I am now stronger with the Army of the Potomac than McClellan. The supremacy of the civil power has been restored, and the Executive is again master of the situation. The troops know, that if I made a mistake in substituting Pope for McClellan, I was capable of rectifying it by again trusting him. They know, too, that neither Stanton nor I withheld anything from him at Antietam, and that it was not the administration, but their own former idol, who surrendered the just results of their terrible sacrifices and closed the great fight as a drawn battle, when, had he thrown Porter's corps of fresh men and other available troops upon Lee's army, he would inevitably have driven it in disorder to the river and captured most of it before sunset."

In a certain sense Lincoln felt at this time that the war had not really begun. The faults lay deep and were complex. He set forth his view to women who called at the White House in a large group at an early morning hour fixed by the President. The women were attending a national council to organize aid and relief for sick and wounded in the field. Among these devoted workers was Mary A. Livermore, wife of a Universalist clergyman and editor in Chicago. She had lent her strength to raising money and supplies, forming local groups that sent lint, bandages, and comforts to the battlefields and hospitals. "The Sanitary Aid Societies sprang up under her departing feet like shadows."

Mrs. Livermore introduced her friend Mrs. Hoge of Chicago to the President. "He took us each by the hand mechanically, in an awkward, absent way." He seated himself in a chair between them. The word "Chicago" caught his ear. "So you are from Chicago! You are not scared by Washington mud then, for you can beat us all to pieces in that." They told him of the Sanitary Commission work and how before leaving for home they were calling on him for some word of encouragement.

"I have no word of encouragement to give!" was the slow, blunt reply. "The military situation is far from bright; and the country knows it as well as I do."

The women were silent. They knew it was a heart-to-heart talk, that he was telling them what he could not well tell the country, that he was frankly relieving the burden of an overweighted mind. It was a silence of a moment, but "deep and painful," said Mrs. Livermore.

The President went on: "The fact is the people have not yet made up their minds that we are at war with the South. They have not buckled down to the determination to fight this war through; for they have got the idea into their heads that we are going to get out of this fix somehow by strategy! That's the word—*strategy!* General McClellan thinks he is going to whip the Rebels by strategy; and the army has got the same notion. They have no idea that the War is to be carried on and put through by hard, tough fighting, that it will hurt somebody; and no headway is going to be made while this delusion lasts."

One of the women spoke of the uprisings of hundreds of thousands of volunteers, of valiant behavior at Donelson, Pea Ridge, Shiloh. The President admitted this, and then came back to his theme. "The people *have not* made up their minds that we are at war, I tell you! They think there is a royal road to peace, and that General McClellan is to find it. The army has not settled down into the conviction that we are in a terrible war that has got to be fought out—no; and the officers have not either.

"When you came to Washington, ladies, some two weeks ago, but very few soldiers came on the trains with you—that you will all remember. But when you go back you will find the trains and every conveyance crowded with them. You won't find a city on the route, a town, or a village, where soldiers and officers on furlough are not as plenty as blackberries. Whole regiments have two-thirds of their men absent—a great many by desertion, and a great many on leave granted by company officers, which is almost as bad.

"General McClellan is all the time calling for more troops, more troops; and they are sent to him; but the deserters and furloughed men outnumber the recruits. To fill up the army is like undertaking to shovel fleas. You take up a shovelful"—and here he made what Mary Livermore saw as an indescribably comic gesture—"but before you can dump them anywhere they are gone. It is like trying to ride a balky horse. You coax, and cheer, and spur, and lay on the whip, but you don't get ahead an inch—there you stick!"

Women asked, as if they could not believe it, "Do you mean that our men *desert?*"

"That is just what I mean!" replied the President. "And the desertion of the army is just now the most serious evil we have to encounter." And he went into figures on stragglers, furloughed men, deserters, and the burden of raising fresh troops while those already enlisted were not used for the hard fighting needed to end the war. "General McClellan is responsible for the delusion that is untoning the whole army—that the South can be conquered by strategy."

Said one of the women, "Is not death the penalty for desertion?"

"Certainly it is."

"And does it not lie with the President to enforce this penalty?"

"Yes."

"Why not enforce it then? Before many soldiers had suffered death for desertion, this wholesale depletion of the army would be ended."

"Oh, no, no!" came the President's reply as he shook his sad head. "That cannot be done. It would be unmerciful, barbarous."

"But is it not more merciful to stop desertions, so that when a battle comes off it may be decisive, instead of being a drawn game, as you say Antietam was?"

"It might seem so. But if I should go to shooting men by scores for desertion, I should have such a hullabaloo about my ears as I have not heard yet, and I should deserve it. You cannot order men shot by dozens or twenties. People won't stand it and they ought not to stand it. No, we must change the condition of things some other way."

Thus Lincoln set forth his views. Or thus Mary Livermore heard them and took them as having substance and repeated them to others consecrated like herself to the care of men fallen and broken in war. And when she was asked how Lincoln looked, Mrs. Livermore said his face had ghastly lines;

his half-staggering gait was like that of a man walking in his sleep. "He seemed literally bending under the weight of his burdens. A deeper gloom rested on his face than on that of any other person I had ever seen."

He did smile, however, on hearing of Ewell at Carlisle, Pennsylvania, asked whether a Confederate general would permit in the churches the usual prayer for the President of the United States. "Certainly," said Ewell. "I'm sure he needs it."

CHAPTER 26

THE INVOLVED SLAVERY ISSUE

IN a rocking chair in a house on F Street in Washington a woman sat knitting. She made her home there with her daughter, wife of the Missouri Republican Congressman Frank P. Blair. She was old and blind, this woman. And she had a saying: "Of all things in the world I hate slavery the most—except abolitionism."

Thus she carried a double hate, and she could tell which was heavier of the two. Over the country were single, triple, and multiple hates. The sum of them made the war.

Lincoln heard the case of a Negro slave who ran away from his master, came to Washington, and was arrested. Chase of Ohio and Blair of Missouri disputed before Lincoln as to what should be done with the prisoner. Chase would send the captured man into the Union Army, Blair would enforce the Fugitive Slave Law and return the Negro to his legal owner.

Harassed on two sides, Lincoln said that he was reminded of a man in Illinois terribly annoyed by a creditor who kept coming often and pressing him to pay the money he owed. Finally the poor debtor saw nothing else to do except to "act crazy" whenever asked for the money. And Lincoln added: "I have on more than one occasion in this room, when beset by extremists on this question, been compelled to appear very mad. I think none of you will ever dispose of this subject without getting mad."

In the hysteria of a changing order, in the drive of forces uprooting a hoary and venerable past, many tongues were let loose and many snap judgments flung into the ears of men.

Henry Ward Beecher in Plymouth Church sermons, in writings in the *Independent*, blamed Second Bull Run on "central imbecility" at Washington. "Certainly neither Mr. Lincoln nor his Cabinet have proved leaders. . . . Not a spark of genius has he [Lincoln]; not an element for leadership. Not one particle of heroic enthusiasm." Beecher dined with Frémont at the Astor House, played billiards with P. T. Barnum, the showman, wrote of Lincoln: "It would be difficult for a man to be born lower than he was. He is an unshapely man. He is a man that bears evidence of not having been educated in schools or in circles of refinement." Of American pulpit men Beecher was the chief rival of Barnum. "How much am I bid for this piece of human flesh?" he shouted to his congregation as he shook his fingers toward a fair and shapely mulatto woman, garbed in white, her hair streaming in a long cascade to her heels. "How much am I bid?" he clamored in his mock sale of a female slave for the highest price offered. And, as Mrs. Beecher noted: "Women became hysterical; men were almost beside themselves. For half an hour money was poured into the contribution boxes. Women took off their jewelry and put it into the baskets. Men unfastened their watches and handed them to the ushers."

As a teacher of morals Beecher would later have stood differently with his Brooklyn congregation had there been no such confessions as came from the wives of Henry Bowen and Theodore Tilton, one of the men his most loyal financial supporter, the other his closest personal friend. In the hue and cry against him then Beecher found the question difficult to answer: "If you had to have women, why did you take the wives of your best friends?"

While his sister Harriet Beecher Stowe held an unwavering faith that Lincoln was at all points a little in advance of the people, and was doing all that under his oath as President he could do for emancipation, the brother directly included Lincoln as one of "the border-State eunuchs," not sufficiently masculine and assertive. With a committee he went to the White House and earnestly warned the President to act. Beecher was a weathercock of current trends and knew his words counted. His books and sermons had given him a public.

Of different fiber among the crusaders was Wendell Phillips. Of him and his fellow abolitionist agitators it was chronicled they had been stoned, clubbed, knocked down with bricks, smeared with filth, stripped of clothing, tarred and feathered, ridden on rails; their houses searched, bonfires made in the streets of their furniture, garments, and bedding; their vehicles and harnesses cut and broken, their horses and cows harried, dashed with hot water, cropped, crippled, and killed; they had been shot at, wounded, killed; vitriol had been thrown on them, and cayenne pepper; asafetida used to scatter their audiences.

Then their cause rose, and now seemed to be riding toward control. Phillips came to Washington in February of '62 to lecture at the Smithsonian Institution; "his matchless oratory took the town by storm." Galusha Grow, Speaker of the House, gave him an elegant dinner party at which Vice-President Hamlin, Mrs. Frémont, and Senator Sumner were present. At the White House Lincoln remarked to him: "Defeat in the field makes everything seem wrong. Almost everybody wants to run the government." Phillips replied, "Let the administration honestly seek to destroy slavery, Mr. President, and you will have no enemies left, and no rebellion left." A month later, in the Cincinnati opera house, Phillips spoke for an hour, with his words drowned by groans, hisses, catcalls, oaths, and cries of "Lynch the traitor!" "Hang the nigger!" "Tar and feather the abolitionist!" Stones and brickbats fell on the speaker's platform. The yolk of a bad egg ran down his coat lapel. As though it were an everyday matter in the career of an agitator, he went serenely on with his speech. Phillips had method, once advising a Negro orator who had declared the slaveholder George Washington a scoundrel, "It isn't graphic; if you call George Washington a scoundrel, what have you got left for Frank Pierce?"

The war could only end "by annihilating that Oligarchy which rules the South," said Phillips at a meeting near Boston on August 1 of '62. The

No Union

with

Slaveholders:

Wm Dell Phillips.

Wendell Phillips's autographed prewar sentiment. From the Barrett collection.

policy of the Administration "neither aims to annihilate that state of things we call 'the South,' made up of pride, idleness, ignorance, barbarism, theft, and murder, nor to replace it with a substitute." As Phillips rated him then, the President "has no mind whatever." In the Executive Mansion was a cipher, a blank, a naught. "He has not uttered a word that gives even a twilight glimpse of any anti-slavery purpose. He may be honest—nobody cares whether the tortoise is honest or not; he has neither insight, nor prevision, nor decision. It is said in Washington streets that he long ago wrote a proclamation abolishing slavery in the state of Virginia, but McClellan bullied him out of it. It is said, too, which is extremely probable, that he has more than once made up his mind to remove McClellan, and Kentucky bullied him out of it. The man who has been beaten to that pulp in sixteen months, what hope can we have of him?"

Not until slavery was wiped out could there be peace: of this Phillips was sure. And, prophesied the agitator, "As long as you keep the present turtle at the head of the Government you make a pit with one hand and fill it with the other."

Phillips reviewed what he considered failures and compromises, and declared: "I never did believe in the capacity of Abraham Lincoln, but I do believe in the pride of Davis, in the vanity of the South, in the desperate determination of those fourteen states; and I believe in a sunny future, because God has driven them mad; and in their madness is our hope. They will never consent to anything that the North can grant; and you must whip them, because, unless you do, they will grind you to powder."

Northern proslavery men were the North's greatest enemy, and Phillips surmised "Lincoln would act, if he believed the North wanted him to." If driven from the White House, Lincoln would return through a vast uprising of black men springing to arms. "If we are called ever to see another President of the United States on horseback flying from his capital, waste no tears! He will return to that capital on the arms of a million of adult negroes, the sure basis of a Union that will never be broken."

With a musical voice of conversational tone, with plain words and abrupt, shifting patterns of thought, Phillips held audiences rapt even when they hated his ideas. Parts of his speeches were splashes of gossip that other platform men could not manage. "The policy that prevails at Washington is to do nothing, and wait for events. I asked the lawyers of Illinois, who had practiced law with Mr. Lincoln for twenty years, 'Is he a man of decision, is he a man who can say no?' They all said, 'If you had gone to the Illinois bar, and selected the man least capable of saying no, it would have been Abraham Lincoln. He has no stiffness in him.' I said to the bankers and directors of railroads in Chicago, 'Is McClellan a man who can say no?' 'McClellan never answered a question while he was here. If there was a question to be decided, he floated until events decided it. He was here months, and he never decided a single question that came up in the management of the Illinois Central.' These are the men we have put at the head of this Union, and for fourteen months they have been unable to say yes or no."

The demand of Phillips that the ruling class of the South be annihilated, his call, "You must whip them," was the political parallel of the military judgment of Grant after Shiloh, that only "conquest" of the South could end the war. "Thank God for war!" cried William Lloyd Garrison. "No matter what may be said of President Lincoln or General McClellan—and a great deal can be justly said to their condemnation—one cheering fact overrides all these considerations, making them as dust in the balance, and that is, that our free North is utterly unendurable to the South." Garrison had been a Christian nonresistant, and when told, "We thought you were a peace man," replied, "Yes, verily, I am," but now he would strike blows and so utterly crush the slaveholders that for all time they would be shorn of power in the Federal Government. Garrison now formally wiped out his old declarations that the Constitution of the United States was a "covenant with death," an "agreement with hell." Those were annulled. Now Garrison was under the flag, and for war with blood up to the horses' bridles. "Under the new order of things, new relations exist, and the Government is invested with extraordinary powers."

In mastery of propaganda the abolitionists surpassed. The gentle Quaker poet Whittier penned verses on current events, writing of the capture of Port Royal on the coast of South Carolina, where the planters had fled and left their slaves:

> The land is wild with fear and hate,
> The rout runs mad and fast;
> From hand to hand, from gate to gate,
> The flaming brand is passed.

Lydia Maria Child's book on Negroes liberated in the West Indies was widely read. New editions of *Uncle Tom's Cabin* poured from the presses. A further expanding audience read *The Uprising of a Great People* by the French liberal, Count de Gasparin. The three remarkable volumes by Frederick Law Olmsted on plantations, farms, and slaves in the South, as he had seen them in leisurely journeys from Virginia to Texas, were reprinted as one book. Distribution went fast of an antislavery lecture at Queen's College, Galway, by an eloquent Irish professor, J. E. Cairnes. The Methodist and Baptist church publications were almost overwhelmingly antislavery in tone.

Royalties of more than $13,000 were earned by the antislavery sketches *Among the Pines* by James R. Gilmore, who wrote under the pen name of Edmund Kirke. Nearly half the royalties went to pay losses on the *Continental Monthly* magazine, which Lincoln had encouraged, as it chimed with his policies. Lincoln once greeted Gilmore: "Well, Mr. Edmund Kirke, do you know it is a long time since I beheld the light of your countenance? Since then how many volumes of prose and poetry have you written?"

"One volume of prose, Mr. Lincoln. I never write poetry." Whereupon Lincoln leaned back in his chair and repeated "with correct pronunciation, and an indescribably comical expression" some verses titled "The London Times on American Affairs," written by Gilmore during the Trent Affair. One verse read:

> John Bull vos a-valkin' his parlor von day,
> Ha-fixin' the vorld wery much his hown vay,
> Ven igstrawnary news cum from hover the sea,
> Habout the great country vot brags it is free.

Lincoln mentioned the arrangement for him to tell Robert J. Walker and Gilmore of Administration trends, they to keep Greeley informed and thus receive co-operation from Greeley. "I infer from the recent tone of the *Tribune* that you are not always able to keep Brother Greeley in the traces." Gilmore said he had handed Greeley memoranda sent on by Walker, but it had not done much good. Then Gilmore had taken the liberty of showing Walker's dispatches to Greeley's managing editor, Sidney Howard Gay, and this had softened Greeley's wrath on several occasions.

"What is he wrathy about?" asked the President. Gilmore said the war was going too slow to suit Greeley, and worse yet, the Administration was not attacking slavery as it should. It was hinted in the *New York Tribune* office that Greeley was writing an appeal to the country that would drive Lincoln into action.

"Why does he not come down here and have a talk with me?" asked Lincoln. Gilmore said that such an interview had been proposed and Greeley had demurred; he would not allow the President to act as an advisory editor of the *Tribune*.

"I have no such desire," said Lincoln. "I certainly have enough now on my hands to satisfy any man's ambition. Does not that remark show an unfriendly spirit in Mr. Greeley?" Gilmore thought not. Greeley still had strong personal regard for the President. But McClellan's failure at Richmond and the Administration's do-nothing slavery policy troubled Greeley, whose paper for years had been a big gun of antislavery propaganda. Now the abolitionists were striding in larger numbers than ever, with a fresh fury of attack.

Some of the more visionary crusaders saw the slaveholders crushed, then a nation of men and women all free, all Christian, "ultimately redeemed." First, however, must be the tragedy of sacrifice and vengeance. A John Brown song by L. Holbrook with a prefatory text from Isaiah—"The day of vengeance is in mine heart, and the year of my redeemed is come"—ran to this key:

> And ye, on earth my Army! tread down God's grapes, till blood
> Unto your horses' bridles hath out the wine-press flowed!
> The day of vengeance dawns—the day of wrath of God.
> His soul is marching on.

Less strident in tone, more touched with sorrow yet awful with warning, was Julia Ward Howe's "Battle Hymn of the Republic." As she was returning from a grand review of troops near Washington, her carriage was delayed by marching regiments and she and her companion sang "John Brown's body lies a-mouldering in the grave." Companies of soldiers took up the song as their feet kept step to its music. The Reverend James Freeman Clarke, in the carriage with her, hoped that she might "write some good words for that stirring tune." She said she had often wished to do so. When she woke at dawn the next morning lines and stanzas came to her as she lay in bed half dreaming that she was the voice of the nation. She sprang from the bed and wrote in a dim gray twilight, not daring to light the lamp, as it would wake her baby sleeping in its crib near by in the same room. She wrote:

> Mine eyes have seen the glory of the coming of the Lord;
> He is trampling out the vintage where the grapes of wrath are stored;
> He hath loosed the fateful lightning of His terrible swift sword;
> His truth is marching on.

> I have seen Him in the watch-fires of an hundred circling camps;
> They have builded Him an altar in the evening dews and damps;
> I can read His righteous sentence by the dim and flaring lamps;
> His truth is marching on.

The *Atlantic Monthly* published her verses in February, 1862. They had now gone to singing millions. Of her trip to Washington and her visit with Lincoln, Mrs. Howe remembered sharply two things. Lincoln from where she sat was in line with the Gilbert Stuart painting of Washington and she tried to compare them. Also Lincoln remarked, "I once heered George Sumner tell a story." The way he pronounced "heered" fixed it in her memory. Now he heard of her terrible propaganda-of-war song, a gospel hymn of burnished steel and moaning trumpets teaching that God marched onward with the Union soldiers. In the beauty of the lilies Christ was born, and "As He died to make men holy, let us die to make men free."

Thaddeus Stevens too favored a fiery gospel writ in burnished steel. He would put a rifle into the hands of every Negro in the South and have them fight. He implied that Lincoln was weak in not doing so. An Andrew Jackson would abolish slavery, arm a free people of color. "He would march into the heart of slavedom, not to pick cotton, but to put weapons into every freedman's hand. . . . I admit it to be the most terrible weapon in our armory. Is that an argument against its use?"

The Hutchinson family of antislavery singers gave a concert for the Army of the Potomac one night and were ordered out of the army lines by McClellan. Chase brought before Lincoln and the Cabinet the song obnoxious to McClellan and his generals. It was Whittier's so-called "Hymn of Liberty," to the tune of Martin Luther's hymn, *"Ein feste Burg Ist unser Gott,"* one verse going:

> What gives the wheat-field blades of steel?
> What points the rebel cannon?
> What sets the roaring rabble's heel
> On the old star-spangled pennon?
> What breaks the oath
> Of the men o' the South?
> What whets the knife
> For the Union's life?—
> Hark to the answer: Slavery!

Lincoln said, according to the Hutchinsons, "It is just the character of song that I desire the soldiers to hear." An arrangement was made that the Hutchinsons could sing in any camp where the commander invited them. The valorous, one-armed General Phil Kearny had been one of those who could not stand for the Hutchinson songs. Lincoln's problem was: "Must I order good soldiers to hear songs they don't want to?"

Denunciation poured from abolitionists when the President dealt with a military order issued by his good friend Major General David Hunter, commanding at Port Royal, South Carolina. The General confiscated slaves and declared them free thereafter to "receive the fruits of their own labor." Also, reasoning that martial law and slavery could not go together, the General declared all slaves in Georgia, Florida, and South Carolina "forever free." Chase urged that these orders should stand, that nine-tenths of the country was for them.

Lincoln wrote to Chase, "No commanding general shall do such a thing upon my responsibility without consulting me." The President issued a proclamation setting forth that the time, the way, and the manner for emancipation to come were "questions which, under my responsibility, I reserve to myself." He again urged that the Federal Government co-operate with any Slave State in gradual compensated emancipation of the slaves. To the Border State people, "I do not argue—I beseech you to make arguments for yourselves." Afraid that they were not reading the drift of events, he warned them: "You cannot, if you would, be blind to the signs of the times. I beg of you a calm and enlarged consideration of them, ranging, if it may be, far above personal and partizan politics." His proposal was one they could all unite on, with no reproaches. "It acts not the Pharisee. The change it contemplates would come gently as the dews of heaven, not rending or wrecking anything. Will you not embrace it? . . . May the vast future not have to lament that you have neglected it."

"Oh, how I wish the border States would accept my proposition," said the President to the Illinois Congressmen Isaac N. Arnold and Owen Lovejoy. "Then you, Lovejoy, and you, Arnold, and all of us would not have lived in vain. The labor of your life, Lovejoy, would be crowned with success. You would live to see the end of slavery."

On a steamer trip up the Potomac and on to Norfolk Lincoln had chatted informally with a group of men on the quarter-deck one afternoon. He referred to generals who earlier in the war had issued proclamations, often at little crossroads places that had been captured. They took it on themselves to declare the position of the Government, the ideas of the President, the purpose of the war, and so on, in high-sounding words. Troubled by this custom, the President had decided to put a stop to it. Soon came General Burnside and Admiral Goldsborough to the Executive Mansion for final instructions on their joint military and naval expedition to North Carolina. The President mentioned proclamations. "Would you believe it?" laughed Lincoln to the group on the quarter-deck, "when I spoke of proclamations, each pulled one out of his pocket that had been prepared in advance, without consultation. I had no idea of catching them in the very act!"

Border State Congressmen at the White House on Lincoln's invitation in July of '62 heard him plead for graduated, compensated abolishment of slavery. "I intend no reproach or complaint," he said, "when I assure you that, in my opinion, if you had all voted for the resolution . . . of last March, the war would now be substantially ended." He still believed the plan would be swift to end the war. With the slaves freed by purchase in the States of the border, the other States farther south would see they could not long keep up the war. "You and I know what the lever of their power is. Break that lever before their faces, and they can shake you no more forever." He pleaded rather than argued. "Most of you have treated me with kindness and consideration, and I trust you will not now think I improperly touch what is exclusively your own, when, for the sake of the whole country, I ask,

Can you, for your States, do better than to take the course I urge?" He would have them "discard punctilio and maxims adapted to more manageable times" and look at the stern facts.

In time, as the war dragged on, slavery would be extinguished by mere friction, urged the President. The money spent for buying slaves and setting them free would shorten the war. "How much better to thus save the money which else we sink forever in the war! How much better to do it while we can, lest the war ere long render us pecuniarily unable to do it! How much better for you as seller, and the nation as buyer, to sell out and buy out that without which the war could never have been, than to sink both the thing to be sold and the price of it in cutting one another's throats!"

And the Border States men went away. They considered and discussed. But nothing came of Lincoln's hope to have the nation buy the slaves and set them free. In fact, two months later the Confederate armies were crossing the districts of some of the Kentucky Congressmen to whom Lincoln had appealed. For six weeks the ragged troops of Kirby Smith held Lexington, Kentucky, many welcomed by their wives and sweethearts to their home town. This, with Bragg's army also deep in Kentucky, unsettled opinion. And the Kentucky Congressmen could not see their way to urging Lincoln's plan. The hatred of the Administration head and his works ran deep among those in Kentucky committed to Jefferson Davis. One wrote a character sketch for the *Kentucky Statesman:*

Abraham Lincoln is a man above the medium height. He passes the six foot mark by an inch or two. He is raw-boned, shamble-gaited, bow-legged, knock-kneed, pigeon-toed, slab-sided, a shapeless skeleton in a very tough, very dirty, unwholesome skin. His hair is or rather was black and shaggy; his eyes dark and fireless like a cold grate in winter time. His lips protrude beyond the natural level of the face, but are pale and smeared with tobacco juice. His teeth are filthy.

In our juvenile days we were struck with Virgil's description of the ferryman who rode with the disembodied souls of men over the river of death. Lincoln, if our memory fails us not, must be a near kinsman of that official of the other world. At all events they look alike and if a relationship be claimed when Abraham reaches the ferry he will be able, we doubt not, to go over free of toll.

In the next place his voice is untutored, coarse, harsh—the voice of one who has no intellect and less moral nature. His manners are low in the extreme and when his talk is not obscene it is senseless. In a word Lincoln born and bred a railsplitter, is a railsplitter still. Bottom, the weaver, was not more out of place in the lap of Titania than he on the throne of the ex-republic.

And this is the man who, incapable of stronger or higher inspiration than that of revenge, aspires to be a master of the South, as he is of the enslaved and slavish North. This is the man who bids armies rise and fight and commands and dismisses generals at will. This is the man who proclaims (as such could only do) the equality of the races, black with white. This is the man who incites servile insurrection, ordains plunder and encourages rapine. This is the man who trembles not at the horrible butchery which Heaven will call him to answer for, yet quakes like an aspen at the approach of peril to his own poor carcass.

This is the man in fine who has been selected by the powers to do such dark deeds as the Dark Ages only know, deeds which civilization blushes to record and men in other lands refuse to credit.

Kneel down and kiss his royal feet, men of the South!

From the first days of the war antislavery men in the North had pressed for action. The second day before the bombardment of Fort Sumter, Lincoln had told Senator Sumner in confidence that the decision was to provision and hold the fort, Sumner replying, "Then the war-power will be in motion, and with it great consequences." A few weeks later the President, in his carriage alone with Sumner, heard the counsel that so far he was right in his course but he must strike against slavery when the moment came. Then on the second day after Bull Run Sumner called, saying he had an important recommendation on the conduct of the war. Lincoln said he too was occupied with that question and had something new on it.

Sumner said, "You are going against slavery?"

"Oh, no, not that," returned the President with something like impatience.

"I am sorry," was Sumner's reply.

And they talked till midnight, Sumner urging the war should be fought to abolish slavery. Month in and month out Sumner, in addressing big war meetings, in speaking in the Senate, in personal visits with the President, urged freedom for the slaves as a war measure. The President told Sumner of plans for colonizing emancipated slaves in tropical countries, and the President carried these plans to the extent of calling the attention of Congress to them, directing diplomatic correspondence. Sumner looked on with little sympathy for an attempt to settle a shipload of the colored people, collected in and around Washington, on Ile La Vache in the West Indies. He saw this expedition fail, and the President shifting to Texas or some region of the Southwest as a place for colonizing Negroes. But as time passed he saw these hopes of colonization go down and fade out with the President because, in a way, nobody cared.

The shadings and delicate hesitations of the President's antislavery policy in early '62 stood clear in a letter marked "Private." Freedom for the slaves should be urged "persuasively" on the South, not "menacingly," he hoped. He talked with members of Congress about it "when they ask me." He was "anxious," "a little uneasy," somewhat groping in this straightforward, confidential, revealing letter to Horace Greeley on March 24, 1862:

Your very kind letter of the 16th to Mr. Colfax, has been shown me by him. I am grateful for the generous sentiment, and purpose, expressed toward the administration. Of course I am anxious to see the policy proposed in the late special message, go forward; but you have advocated it from the first, so that I need to say little to you on the subject. If I were to suggest anything it would be that as the North are already for the measure, we should urge it *persuasively*, and not *menacingly*, upon the South. I am a little uneasy about the abolishment of slavery in the District, not but I would be glad to see it abolished, but as to the time and manner of doing it. If some one or more of the border-states would move first, I should greatly prefer it; but if this can not be

Executive Mansion,

Washington. March 24. 1862.

Hon. Horace Greeley.
My dear Sir:

Your very kind letter of the 16th. to Mr. Colfax, has been shown me by him. I am grateful for the generous sentiments, and purposes expressed towards the administration. Of course I am anxious to see the policy proposed in the late special message, go forward; but you have advocated it from the first, so that I need to pay little to you on the subject. If I were to suggest anything it would be that as the North are already for the measure, we should urge it persuasively, and not menacingly, upon the South. I am a little uneasy about the abolishment of slavery in this District, not but I would be glad to see it abolished, but as to the time and manner of doing it. If some one or more of the border-states would move fast, I should greatly prefer it; but if this can not be in a reasonable time, I would like the bill to have the three main features— gradual— compensation— and vote of the people— I do not talk to members of Congress on the subject, except when they ask me. I am not prepared to make any suggestion about confiscation— I may drop you a line hereafter.

Yours truly
A. Lincoln

A letter, reduced about one-third, in which Lincoln outlines with rare candor his policy as to slavery. Greeley suspected the candor and had no patience with the policy. Original in the Pierpont Morgan Library, New York City.

in a reasonable time, I would like the bill to have the three main features—gradual—compensated—and vote of the people—I do not talk to members of Congress on the subject, except when they ask me—I am not prepared to make any suggestion about confiscation—I may drop you a line hereafter.

Yours truly

A. Lincoln

Lincoln wanted Greeley with him. He reached out for Greeley's help and influence. He took pains on the main pressing issue to reveal his mind fully, even with its awkward corners, to Greeley. Could he have Greeley with him, each could do more for the country.

Early in August of '62 Sumner wrote to John Bright in England his view of Lincoln: "He is hard to move. He is honest but inexperienced. Thus far he has been influenced by the border States. I urged him on the 4th of July to put forth an edict of emancipation, telling him he could make the day more sacred and historic than ever. He replied, 'I would do it if I were not afraid that half the officers would fling down their arms and three more States would rise.' He is plainly mistaken about the officers, and I think also with regard to the States."

A few days later Sumner wrote the Duchess of Argyll in England: "The President's great difficulty now is as to arming the blacks. He invites them as laborers, but he still holds back from the last step to which everything irresistibly tends. He says, 'Wait; time is essential.' That is, after an interval of time we shall be able to do what he thinks we can not do now."

Late one Sunday afternoon Lincoln was telling his caller, Senator John B. Henderson of Missouri, that Sumner and Senator Wilson, with Thaddeus Stevens, were constantly putting pressure on him to issue an emancipation proclamation. "They are coming and urging me, sometimes alone, sometimes in couples, sometimes all three together, but *constantly* pressing me." And with that Lincoln stepped to a window and preposterously enough, Sumner, Wilson, and Stevens were coming toward the White House. Lincoln called to Henderson, pointed to the three approaching figures, and began telling of a school he went to when a boy in Indiana where the Bible was read out loud by the pupils. "One day we were standing up reading the account of the three Hebrew children in the fiery furnace. A little tow-headed fellow who stood beside me had the verse with the unpronounceable names. He mangled up Shadrach and Meshach woefully and finally went all to pieces on Abednego." For this the boy took a licking that made him cry. Then the class reading went on again, each boy in turn till the same tow-headed boy was reached again. As he looked in the Bible and saw the verse he was to read, he let out a pitiful yell. The schoolmaster asked what was the matter. The boy, pointing to the next verse, cried out, "Look there! look! there comes them same damn three fellers again!"

Besides counsel from private callers at the White House, advice came publicly. The most dramatic scolding publicly given the President came when Greeley in the *New York Tribune* of August 19, 1862, issued "The Prayer of Twenty Millions." As the first servant of the Republic the President was required to execute the laws, declared Greeley, and "We think you are strangely and disastrously remiss in the discharge of your official and imperative duty." Speaking for 20,000,000 people, as he assumed, Greeley told Lincoln, "You are unduly influenced by the counsels, the representations, the menace of certain fossil politicians hailing from the border slave States." Also "we complain that a large proportion of our regular army officers with many of the volunteers evince far more solicitude to uphold slavery than to put down the rebellion." Though a little vague as to this, it seemed that Greeley wished Lincoln to tell the armies in camp and field that they were fighting against slavery first of all. Lincoln did not meet Greeley's wish. But he dated a letter at the Executive Mansion, Washington, August 22, 1862, and told the country in skillfully distilled sentences what the war was for, as he saw it. The letter was widely reprinted and probably reached nearly all persons in the country who could read, winning certain propaganda results even in the most hostile parts of the South. The letter read:

Hon. Horace Greeley.
Dear Sir:—
I have just read yours of the 19th, addressed to myself through the New York "Tribune." If there be in it any statements or assumptions of fact which I may know to be erroneous, I do not, now and here, controvert them. If there be in it any inferences which I may believe to be falsely drawn, I do not, now and here, argue against them. If there be perceptible in it an impatient and dictatorial tone, I waive it in deference to an old friend whose heart I have always supposed to be right.

As to the policy I "seem to be pursuing," as you say, I have not meant to leave any one in doubt.

I would save the Union. I would save it the shortest way under the Constitution. The sooner the national authority can be restored, the nearer the Union will be "the Union as it was." If there be those who would not save the Union unless they could at the same time save slavery, I do not agree with them. If there be those who would not save the Union unless they could at the same time destroy slavery, I do not agree with them. *My paramount object in this struggle is to save the Union, and is not either to save or to destroy slavery.* If I could save the Union without freeing any slave, I would do it; if I could save it by freeing all the slaves, I would do it; and if I could save it by freeing some and leaving others alone, I would also do that. What I do about slavery and the colored race, I do because I believe it helps to save the Union; and what I forbear, I forbear because I do not believe it would help to save the Union. I shall do less whenever I shall believe what I am doing hurts the cause, and I shall do more whenever I shall believe doing more will help the cause. I shall try to correct errors when shown to be errors, and I shall adopt new views as fast as they shall appear to be true views.

I have here stated my purpose according to my view of official duty, and I intend no modification of my oft-expressed personal wish that all men everywhere could be free.

Yours,
A. Lincoln

The letter was a natural outgiving from Lincoln, flowing from him as the gathered water of a stream leaps the ledge of a cataract. He was a born-and-raised Kentuckian. For all his Illinois training and his journeys to Chicago, New York, and Washington, his instincts ran back to the Bluegrass State whose northern boundary marked the line between freedom and slavery for the Negro, so far south that no abolitionist could be elected to public office, yet far enough north so that an abolitionist could murmur his opinions and yet live. In that region Lincoln's granduncle had been taxed on "six blacks" he owned, and there his wife's father had kept slaves and she as a girl was cared for by them. There and elsewhere he had seen slavery at close hand. As he grew and developed in Indiana and Illinois he knew proslavery and anti-Negro men by the hundreds in familiar conversation, once himself taking a law case for a pursuer of fugitive slaves. Then his abolitionist law partner, Herndon, a Kentuckian, and anxious antislavery people farther north in Illinois, had penetrated him with their viewpoint. Before and during the debates with Douglas in 1858 he had rehearsed every possible clash and collision between the two extremes. Lincoln knew those who operated the underground railway for the escape of slaves in Illinois, as he also knew the Southern sympathizers and Negro-haters ready to interfere. He had told Browning of the news of Frémont's emancipation proclamation reaching Kentucky troop companies, who at once threw down their arms. He could not underestimate the Frémont worshipers, for Bill Herndon was one and he knew Bill's heart. He was aware that when as President he should issue an emancipation proclamation, there would be thousands of deserters from the Border States, from southern Illinois, Indiana, and Ohio regiments.

Lincoln still saw slavery as the weird, rank growth he had sketched when debating with Douglas: "If slavery did not now exist among them, they would not introduce it. If it did now exist among us, we should not instantly give it up." Now as President he could not be oblivious to the viewpoint of which Seward as a friend of Archbishop John Hughes of New York was the spokesman, and the Archbishop's widely reprinted declaration in his official organ, the *Metropolitan Record:* "We, Catholics, and a vast majority of our brave troops in the field, have not the slightest idea of carrying on a war that costs so much blood and treasure just to gratify a clique of Abolitionists in the North."

In wide areas of the North Lincoln saw the same divisions as in southern Illinois and Missouri, where political candidates were tagged as either "charcoal" or "snowflake." And he knew that for all his moderation on the slave question his name was anathema in the South, where the *Memphis Avalanche* and other papers asserted that Lincoln had "emptied his penitentiaries over the border, and had given every criminal a torch to kindle a Confederate city." That the Confederate Congressman Foote clamored for "Lincoln and his infernal Cabinet to be brought to the scaffold for their atrocious offenses against the Constitution, which they have perjurously violated" was merely an incident.

More than one caller at the White House had found the President worrying over the chances of a sudden insurrection in which Negro slaves would massacre whites on a grand scale in the rear of the Confederate armies, leaving the inference that it was instigated by the War Department at Washington. He sensed the declining market value of the Negro slaves, and realized that if it should continue there would be no property values in slaves to be confiscated. He did not know of Mrs. Chesnut far down in South Carolina writing in her diary on April 29, 1862, "There are people who still believe negroes property—like Noah's neighbors who insisted that the Deluge would be only a little shower after all." He did know there were Southern leaders, such as Joseph E. Johnston and Fitzhugh Lee, who had never owned a slave, and there were others, such as Robert E. Lee and J. E. B. Stuart, who had long ago let their slaves go. He did not know that Mrs. Jefferson Davis had fixed in her memory the remark of her husband just before the Montgomery convention that elected him President of the Confederacy: "In any case, I think our slave property will be lost eventually." He did know that already tens of thousands of masterless slaves had come into the lines of the Union armies, 7,000 counted on one day at Beaufort, South Carolina, and that these bondmen in ever larger numbers would be a living cry for change, for another status than that of horses and mules on the tax lists.

When Robert J. Walker told him that the great majority of slaves were mentally merely children, that scarcely one in a thousand could read or write, and to give them freedom and the ballot would be sowing a crop of dragon's teeth in the South, Lincoln replied, according to James R. Gilmore: "Well, we will manage to get across that stream, if we ever come to it. Speaking of dragon's teeth, I think they were sown when the first cargo of negroes were brought into Jamestown in 1620. You believe in Providence —will you tell me why He allowed the African to be made a slave in this country?" Walker replied he was not a member of the Almighty's Cabinet; he saw a plan operating that could only have emanated from an overruling mind that has all creation in control; on the other side of Jordan he might ask some questions. And as Gilmore recalled it, Lincoln laughed. "Very likely, if you have managed to keep out of the fire. But you need not wait that long to answer my question—you must have questioned why a Benevolent Being has allowed the blacks to exist here in abject servitude for now two hundred and forty years." Walker said it was a staggering question, but he believed there was a divine design to elevate and Christianize the Negro race so it might enter the future life at a higher level; slavery had been an unspeakable blessing to the black folk; God had permitted slavery to continue till it had demoralized the whites; now God was bringing it to an end to save both blacks and whites. Lincoln cited 4,000,000 blacks in America, millions more in Africa. "Are they to be left in their low-down, animal condition?" Walker replied the white race was opening Africa to the white man's blessings. "The Captain of the Lord's host has planned this war, Mr. Lincoln, and I believe you will do your part in it." Lincoln said, "I shall try to, God being my helper."

Repeatedly delegations had heard from Lincoln that it would be useless to issue an emancipation proclamation without the military force to back it up. "By way of illustration," he asked one deputation, "how many legs will a sheep have if you call his tail a leg?" They answered, "Five." "You are mistaken," said the President, "for calling a tail a leg does not make it one." He queried a group of Chicago ministers urging immediate and universal emancipation: "Now, gentlemen, if I cannot enforce the Constitution down South, how am I to enforce a mere Presidential proclamation? Won't the world sneer at it as being as powerless as the Pope's bull against the comet?"

He assured them he was trying to find his path through a diversity of beliefs. "I am approached with the most opposite opinions and advice, and by religious men . . . certain that they represent the divine will. . . . I hope it will not be irreverent for me to say that if it is probable that God would reveal his will to others, on a point so connected . . . with my duty, it might be supposed he would reveal it directly to me. . . . And if I can learn what it is, I will do it. These are not, however, the days of miracles, and I suppose . . . I am not to expect a direct revelation. I must study the plain, physical facts of the case . . . and learn what appears to be wise and right. . . . Do not misunderstand me because I have mentioned these objections. They indicate the difficulties . . . the subject is on my mind by day and night. . . . Whatever shall appear to be God's will, I will do."

One of the ministers stayed for a special pleading: "What you have said to us, Mr. President, compels me to say to you in reply, that it is a message to you from our Divine Master, through me, commanding you, sir, to open the doors of bondage that the slave may go free." The instant response of Lincoln was, "That may be, sir, for I have studied this question, by night and by day, for weeks and for months, but if it is, as you say, a message from your Divine Master, is it not odd that the only channel he could send it by was the roundabout route by way of that awful wicked city of Chicago?" As the story of this spread over the country, it was told that Lincoln drew a long breath after the opening address of the chairman and then responded, "Well, gentlemen, it is not often one is favored with a delegation *direct* from the Almighty." This was much more abrupt than his actual expression, and he had dismissed the delegation with the courteous hope, "I trust that in the freedom with which I have canvassed your views, I have not in any respect injured your feelings."

The House Divided speech in 1858 was quoted to Lincoln by a committee of fifteen Quakers, reminding him of his words: "I believe that this Government cannot permanently endure half slave and half free." He drew himself to his full height, not pleased, it was plain to see. Yes, those were his words, that was his sentence. "But I said it in connection with other things from which it should not have been separated in an address discussing moral obligations; for this is a case in which the repetition of half a truth, in connection with the remarks just read, produces the effect of a whole falsehood." He reminded them that he also said, "If we could first know where we are, and whither we are tending, we could better judge what to do and how to do it." Then he read them the entire paragraph from which they had quoted.

On another day a Quaker woman asked a few words with him. Rather impatiently he said, "I will hear the Friend." She told him he was the appointed minister of the Lord to do the work of emancipation. She quoted much from the Bible. Like the prophetess Deborah, he should abolish slavery and establish freedom. She seemed to be through with her plea and admonition. "Has the Friend finished?" inquired the President. She had. And he replied, "I have neither time nor disposition to enter into discussion with the Friend, and end this occasion by suggesting for her consideration the question whether, if it be true that the Lord has appointed me to do the work she has indicated, it is not probable he would have communicated knowledge of the fact to me as well as to her?"

Joseph Medill too brought up the House Divided speech, put squarely to Lincoln the question, "Why did you deliver that radical speech?" According to Medill, Lincoln exclaimed, "Oh!" relapsed into reserve, and countered, "What do you think was the reason?" Medill not answering, Lincoln went on: "Well, after you fellows had got me into that mess and began tempting me with offers of the Presidency, I began to think, and I made up my mind that the next President of the United States would need to have a stronger anti-slavery platform than mine. So I concluded to say something." Then, as though he had put the matter too sheerly on a basis of practical politics, he asked Medill, and Medill promised, to repeat to no one his direct answer, which could have several interpretations.

The Reverend Moncure Daniel Conway and the Reverend William Ellery Channing, Unitarian antislavery clergymen, called by appointment at the White House at eight o'clock one morning. As they waited in the anteroom, noted Conway: "A woman with a little child was waiting. She now and then wept but said nothing. The President saw her first, and she came out radiant. We conjectured some prisoner was that day released." They found the President "gracious." He agreed with Channing on plans for the nation to buy the slaves: compensated abolishment. He had for years favored this plan. He turned to Conway, who said the President could be the deliverer of the nation from its one great evil. What would not that man achieve for mankind who should free America from slavery?

"Perhaps," said Lincoln, "we may be better able to do something in that direction after a while than we are now."

Then Conway plopped the blunt inquiry, "Mr. President, do you believe the masses of the American people would hail you as their deliverer if, at the end of this war, the Union should be surviving and slavery still in it?"

"Yes," came the ready answer, "if they were to see that slavery was on the downhill."

Conway suggested that Washington, Jefferson, the founding fathers, compromised with slavery because they thought it was on the downhill; and this had brought on the war.

The President said: "I think the country grows in this direction daily, and I am not without hope that something of the desire of you and your friends may be accomplished. Perhaps it may be in the way suggested by a thirsty soul in Maine who found he could only get liquor from a druggist; as his robust appearance forbade the plea of sickness, he called for soda, and whispered, 'Couldn't you put a drop o' the creeter into it unbeknownst to yourself?' "

The President half inquired from Conway whether it was not true that the antislavery people, being in a "movement," naturally met a good many who agreed with them. "You possibly may over-estimate the number in the country who hold such views. But the position in which I am placed brings me into some knowledge of opinions in all parts of the country and of many different kinds of people; and it appears to me that the great masses of this country care comparatively little about the negro, and are anxious only for military successes."

Thus stood the President; Conway reported it far and wide. The two clergymen thanked him for his kindly reception. He remarked: "We shall need all the anti-slavery feeling in the country, and more; you can go home and try to bring the people to your views; and you may say anything you like about me, if that will help. Don't spare me!" This with a laugh. Then gravely: "When the hour comes for dealing with slavery, I trust I will be willing to do my duty though it cost my life. And, gentlemen, lives will be lost."

On an application for authority to raise a regiment of Negro soldiers, the President wrote "Referred to the Secretary of War. This gentleman wishes to engage in the ebony trade. A. Lincoln."

In that same summer of 1862 Lincoln had to consider such incidents as a Union officer, a Republican, drawing applause at a mass meeting for recruiting in Terre Haute, Indiana, when he shouted, "I hate a nigger worse than I hate the devil." Also he had to consider a private messenger from Governor Andrew of Massachusetts who told of kneeling in prayer with the Governor just before leaving Boston. "And I never heard such a prayer in my life; I never was so near the throne of God, except when my mother died." The President replied, "When we have the Governor of Massachusetts to send us troops in the way he has, and when we have him to utter such prayers for us, I have no doubt that we shall succeed."

How the Border State men were shifting in degree was indicated in a Browning diary note: "Garrett Davis Senator from Kentucky, came in whilst I was with the President and in conversation upon the subject of slavery said that to save the Union he was willing, if necessary, to see slavery wiped out. Still he is very sensitive upon the subject"

And they were very sensitive, some of the Border State men, with armies passing to and fro through their cities, with guerrillas and bushwhackers playing havoc with their farms, barns, cattle, with informers shifting from one side to the other, with traders and merchants selling to whichever side would pay high prices. In a letter to a New Orleans man, Lincoln referred to the professed Union men who would neither help the Government nor permit the Government to do things without their help. They wished to stand by without taking sides. "They are to touch neither a sail boat nor a pump, but to be merely passengers—deadheads at that—to be carried snug and dry throughout the storm, and safely landed right side up." There were true Union men whose sacrifices were beyond speech to praise. But there were others whose suggestions could only lead to a surrender of the Government. "What would you do in my position? Would you drop the war where it is? Or would you prosecute it in future with elder-stalk squirts charged with rosewater? Would you deal lighter blows rather than heavy ones? Would you give up the contest leaving any available means unapplied?"

He was not in a boastful mood. "I shall not do more than I can, and I shall do all I can, to save the government, which is my sworn duty as well as my personal inclination."

As if he might have struggled through tortuous windings to fix for himself one guiding point amid the intricacies, the President wrote in this letter to the New Orleans man: "I shall do nothing in malice. What I deal with is too vast for malicious dealing."

Antislavery Union men in the Border States were not numerous. One in Kentucky was Cassius M. Clay, now returned from the Russian Legation and wearing the shoulder straps of a major general. Clay had edited the antislavery *True American*, stumped Kentucky for Lincoln in 1860, and in a debate with a proslavery candidate received a deep stab wound in the left breast over the heart, replying by burying his own bowie knife to the hilt in the abdomen of his opponent. The *Lexington Observer* published an item that Clay was dead, but in its next issue made the correction: "Mr. Clay still lives, but his adversary Mr. Turner lingered until about 12 o'clock on Saturday night when he expired." When asked by a voice from a crowd, "Would you help a runaway slave?" Clay replied from the platform, "That would depend on which way he was running." Now on August 13, 1862, Clay spoke in Odd Fellows' Hall in Washington saying, as a major general, "Never, so help me God, will I draw a sword to keep the chains upon another fellow-being." He was criticized for "intemperate utterance." The *New York Evening Post* said: "He has outstripped himself. He is neck and neck with Garrison and Phillips." It was this Cassius M. Clay who came to the White House telling Lincoln to free the slaves, that over Europe he found the governments ready to recognize the Confederacy, anxious to intervene, that an emancipation proclamation now would block these European autocracies.

"Kentucky would go against us," said Lincoln, according to Clay. "And we have now as much as we can carry."

Clay was decisive, telling the President: "You are mistaken. The Kentuckians have heard this question discussed by me for a quarter of a century; and have all made up their minds. Those who intend to stand by slavery have already joined the rebel army, and those who remain will stand by the Union. Not a man of intelligence will change his mind."

Lincoln pondered, and at last said: "The Kentucky legislature is now in session. Go down and see how they stand and report to me."

And Cash Clay had started, arrived there, looked things over, and then departed northward because the legislature he was to address had gone to Louisville in flight from the approaching Confederate infantry of Kirby Smith and the hard-riding cavalry of John Morgan.

The threat of European interference could not be laughed off. Motley, the Minister at Vienna, was writing home that having been in London, Paris, Berlin, having sipped tea with English scholars and having put away steins of dark beer with Bismarck, he was sure that only one of three conditions would stave off European recognition of the Confederacy: (1) a great and conclusive battle crushing the Confederates; (2) the capture of cotton ports and release of large cotton supplies for European factories; (3) a clear-cut policy of emancipation for the slaves. Carl Schurz had reported likewise from Madrid, with heavy stress on the third point. Lincoln, aware of these points, and at the suggestion of John Bright of the British House of Commons, wrote a resolution suitable for Bright to use. It read:

Whereas, while heretofore States and nations have tolerated slavery, recently, for the first [time] in the world, an attempt has been made to construct a new nation, upon the basis of, and with the primary and fundamental object to maintain, enlarge and perpetuate human slavery; therefore,

Resolved, That no such embryo State should ever be recognized by, or admitted into, the family of Christian and civilized nations; and that all Christian and civilized men everywhere should, by all lawful means, resist to the utmost such recognition and admission.

On August 14, 1862, there came to the White House the first committee of Negroes to arrive there by invitation of the President for a meeting with the Executive on a public issue. They were seated and, greetings and preliminaries over, the President explained that money had been put at his disposal by Congress for the purpose "of colonizing people of African descent," a cause he had long favored. And one of those present made a record of Lincoln's remarks as the first memorandum of words of the President of the United States addressed directly and exclusively to people of that race.

"Why," the President asked, "should the people of your race be colonized, and where? Why should they leave this country? This is, perhaps, the first question for proper consideration. You and we are different races. We have between us a broader difference than exists between almost any other two races. Whether it is right or wrong I need not discuss; but this physical difference is a great disadvantage to us both, as I think. Your race suffers very greatly, many of them, by living among us, while ours suffers from your presence. In a word, we suffer on each side. If this is admitted, it affords a reason, at least, why we should be separated. You here are freemen, I suppose. [A voice: "Yes, sir."] Perhaps you have long been free, or all your lives. Your race are suffering, in my judgment, the greatest wrong inflicted on any people. But even when you cease to be slaves, you are yet far removed from being placed on an equality with the white race. . . . The aspiration of men is to enjoy equality with the best when free, but on this broad continent not a single man of your race is made the equal of a single man of ours."

He was telling the row of colored men who sat before him about things long in his mind and heart. So long a time had he brooded over the inevitable facts that what he had to say was in short words and like a sad refrain of life under hard trials: "Go where you are treated the best, and the ban is still upon you. I do not propose to discuss this, but to present it as a fact with which we have to deal. I cannot alter it if I would." With two races, one enslaved, had come effects, among them "general evil effects on the white race," he believed. "See our present condition—the country engaged in war—our white men cutting one another's throats—none knowing how far it will extend—and then consider what we know to be the truth. But for your race among us there could not be war, although many men engaged on either side do not care for you one way or the other. Nevertheless, I repeat, without the institution of slavery, and the colored race as a basis, the war could not have an existence. It is better for us both, therefore, to be separated."

The principal difficulty in the way of colonization, the President suggested to the committee of Negroes, was that "the free colored man cannot see that his comfort would be advanced by it." While slaves would gladly accept freedom on condition of leaving the United States for a colony, the free man would have "nothing to do with the idea of going to a foreign country." Without meaning to speak unkindly, he felt this was "an extremely selfish view" of the case. "You ought to do something to help those . . . not so fortunate as yourselves. There is an unwillingness on the part of our people, harsh as it may be, for you colored people to remain with us. Now, if you could give a start to the white people, you would open a wide door for many to be made free. If we deal with those who are not free at the beginning, and whose intellects are clouded by slavery, we have very poor material to start with. If intelligent colored men, such as are before me, would move in this matter, much might be accomplished. It is exceedingly important that we have men at the beginning capable of thinking as white men, and not those who have been systematically oppressed."

The President then unfolded a plan for them to go to a country in Central America, rich in coal mines, farm land, harbors, and other advantages. What they could do would depend on themselves. "Success does not as much depend on external help as on self-reliance. . . . I shall, if I get a sufficient number of you engaged, have provision made that you shall not be wronged. If you will engage in the enterprise, I will spend some of the money intrusted to me. I am not sure you will succeed. The government may lose the money; but we cannot succeed unless we try. . . . Could I get a hundred tolerably intelligent men, with their wives and children, and able to 'cut their own fodder,' so to speak? Can I have fifty? If I could find twenty-five able-bodied men, with a mixture of women and children,—good things in the family relation, I think,—I could make a successful commencement. I want you to let me know whether this can be done or not. This is the practical part of my wish to see you."

Such was the substance of Lincoln's argument to the Negro committee. Their chairman, E. M. Thomas, said they would hold a consultation and give him a reply. The President said, "Take your full time—no hurry at all."

$200 REWARD!

RANAWAY from the subscriber, living near Upper Marlboro', Prince George's County, Md., on the 22d of Sept., 1861, my negro man JOHN, who calls himself *JOHN LEE*. He is 24 years old, a little below the ordinary height, well built; has a remarkable fine set of teeth, which he shows when talking, and of very smiling countenance. Said negro was hired at the time he left to Mr. John A. Frasier, in Surratts District. Also, my negro man ANDREW, who calls himself *ANDREW AMBUSH*. He ranaway on the 1st of January, 1862. He is about 23 years old, tall and slender built, quite black, long thick lips, full suit of hair

I will give the above reward for the apprehension of said negroes, or $100 for either of them, provided they are delivered to me or secured in jail, so that I get them again.

WILLIAM P. PUMPHREY.

Welwood, Jan. 22, 1862.

A handbill. From the Barrett collection.

The place the President had in view for them to colonize was a tract in the Republic of New Granada. But there were contending factions in the government of New Granada; necessary assurances could not be had of security; and the plan was soon abandoned. The enthusiasm of the free Negroes over such colonization was slight, almost negligible.

Down across the Slave States now spread among Negroes a dim belief that somehow through the war would come freedom. When Lincoln made his July visit to the camp of McClellan on the Virginia Peninsula, he felt a stirring that was perhaps new to him—a mystic theme in the air. Something of it was caught by Joseph Twichell, the regimental chaplain, who wrote to his father on July 9: "The visit of our good President was a surprise. At about the middle of the afternoon, a salute fired by the gunboat announced his coming, we were called out into line and before nightfall he went the rounds. The first real information of his arrival I received from colored Ben whom we 'stole' out of Maryland. He was out foraging and came in, his black face shining and cloven with a mighty grin, and with keen delight informed me, 'I'se seen ole Uncle Linkum!' It's wonderful how these negroes contract their political views. Ben says that he never heard a white man in Maryland speak of Mr. Lincoln in any other terms than those of denunciation. He was described to the negroes as a monster, yet, in those simple hearts the President attained the reverence due to a benefactor—and that without any abolition tracts or teachings. They hardly account him a real man, but rather some half-mythical, far-off omen of good, which would one day break the clouds above them. Simple minds apprehend persons rather than principles, and Ben says that when our Division came to the Lower Potomac, the slaves did not regard it as the Union Army, but as a visible sign of the coming of the long expected, benign reign of 'Ole Uncle Linkum.' The story moistened my eyes."

At the oldest Negro church in Washington, on the corner of Eleventh and K streets, L. E. Chittenden, Register of the Treasury, heard a Negro sermon on the subject "What makes the white man the superior of the colored man?" Part of the Negro preacher's reply was, "If we support ourselves and our masters when we are slaves, we can surely take care of ourselves when we are free." He preached they should get education, learn to read and write. "Oh, my dear brethren, I have only just now learned to read. Until we heard that Massa Linkum was elected I never had a spelling book or learned my letters."

Just as God had saved Moses from the crocodiles, and raised him up to lead his people out of Egypt and out of the house of bondage, so He had now raised up Massa Linkum, and preserved his life so he might give the black man freedom. "Pretty soon now we shall have our freedom. I don't know just when, but the Lord and Massa Linkum knows, and they will tell us in their own good time."

And the preacher dropped on his knees and prayed, "O Lord, teach my people! teach my people!"

CHAPTER 27

PRELIMINARY EMANCIPATION PROCLAMATION '62

"DO you know who is at this moment the largest slave-*holder* in the United States?" Senator Sumner asked the President in March of 1862. And Sumner answered, "It is Abraham Lincoln, for he holds all the three thousand slaves of the District of Columbia, which is more than any other person in the country holds."

By vetoing a bill at that moment on his desk the President would hand back to the slaveowners of the District their slave property. By signing the bill he would set the Federal Government to buying the slaves at prices not exceeding $200 each and then giving each slave his freedom. During the time he studied this bill, which had passed Congress, Lincoln was in fact, as Sumner said, the largest slave*holder* (not owner) in the United States.

Several points in the bill did not satisfy Lincoln. But he signed it, even though Border State men were against it. The act ended Negro slavery in the District of Columbia. And, the President wishing it, there was provision for steamship tickets to Liberia or Hayti for any freed slaves who cared to go to those Negro republics. In urging this latter provision Lincoln said of himself, according to Sumner's friend, C. Edwards Lester, "I am so far behind the Sumner lighthouse that I shall stick to my colonization hobby."

In voting money to buy emancipation, Sumner did it as though it were offering ransom to kidnappers, according to Lester. "His severest trial, during these days, was in, as he expressed it, 'screwing Old Abe up to the sticking point.' With considerable impatience he broke out, 'How slow this child of Freedom is being born!' "

This act of Congress and the President was one of many laws, decisions, new precedents, that by percussion and abrasion, by erosion and attrition, were opening gaps in the legal status of slavery, wearing down its props and bulwarks.

Two plans the President struggled with incessantly, like an engineer wrestling to put bridges over a swollen river during a flood rush. One of these was to make practical the colonization of Negroes to be freed. The other was gradual compensated abolishment. He wrote in one message, "Any member of Congress, with the census tables and treasury reports before him, can readily see for himself how very soon the current expenditures of this war would purchase at fair valuation, all the slaves in any named State." He pointed to Kentucky as a State that recently through legal process had become the owner of slaves, and she sold none but liberated all.

The President asked, and Congress passed, an act recognizing the Negro republics of Hayti and Liberia, though the State Department modified this in announcing that a black man could not be received as a foreign Minister. This in turn was modified informally by the President in a talk with James Redpath, an agent of antislavery societies who had been to Hayti. Redpath had interviewed the President there and returned to Washington to report to Lincoln that the Haytian President was profoundly grateful to the American President for the recognition accorded the Negro republic of the West Indies. So deeply appreciative of the situation was the Haytian President that he was sending word by Redpath that, if it were the wish of Mr. Lincoln, he would not send to Washington a black man as Haytian Minister.

And as the *Springfield Republican* correspondent at Washington had it from Redpath, Lincoln hesitated a moment and then drawled, "You can tell the President of Hayti that I shan't tear my shirt if he sends a nigger here!"

When in a few months the Haytian Minister did arrive, Sumner's friend, C. Edwards Lester, wrote of him as having "a finely formed, brilliant face, the complexion being rather dark, but his cheek glowing with the warm tint, and his eye with the liquid beauty of the Creole." Of Mr. Lincoln and the hearty reception accorded him at the White House, the Haytian Minister spoke with veneration, though no name was so dear to the Haytians as that of Charles Sumner. "Signor Carlo il Senatore! why, his picture is in every cottage in Hayti. He has done everything for us."

Congress revised the war regulations so as to forbid any officer of the army or the navy to use his forces to capture and return fugitive slaves. Another act provided that such officers could not hear evidence and try cases as to whether a runaway slave should be returned on the claim of an owner. A treaty was negotiated with Great Britain for suppression of the African slave trade. By another act of Congress all slaves in Territories of the United States were declared free. Along with the purchase and emancipation of slaves in the District of Columbia came further legislation for the education of Negro children; and Negroes were made admissible as mail-carriers.

These acts of Congress were capped by the Confiscation Act, which the President signed in July of '62. Slaves of persons convicted of treason or rebellion should be made free, this act declared, and furthermore, slaves of rebels who escaped into Union Army lines, or slaves whose masters had run away, or slaves found by the Union Army in places formerly occupied by rebel forces, should all be designated as prisoners of war and set free. Other bills provided that slaves entering Union Army lines could be put to work and earn their freedom; the President could enroll and employ Negroes for camp labor and military service, while the wives, mothers, and children of such Negro slaves, if they were the property of armed "rebels," should be set free; the President was authorized "to employ as many persons of African descent as he may deem necessary and proper for the suppression of this rebellion, and for this purpose he may organize and use them in such manner as he may judge best for the public welfare."

Lincoln at first intended to veto the Confiscation Act and have it re-framed. Instead he signed it, and returned it with his intended veto message attached, for future record. "It is startling to say that Congress can free a slave within a State," ran part of this veto message, "and yet if it were said that the ownership of the slave had first been transferred to the nation, and that Congress had then liberated him, the difficulty would at once vanish." The slaves of a traitor were forfeited to the Government, which raised the question: "Shall they be made free, or sold to new masters?" He could see no objection to Congress' deciding in advance that they should be free.

Thus far all laws passed by Congress fully protected the ownership of slaves held by men loyal to the Union, or men not partaking in the rebellion. Not many were there of such Unionist slaveowners. All other owners of slaves were under the threat of confiscation of their property if and when the Union armies reached their plantations.

In the midst of these zigzags of public policy, the editors of *Harper's Weekly* saw the President as following a midway path, giving in to neither of the extremists. An editorial in May set forth: "In the President of the United States Providence has vouchsafed a leader whose moral perceptions are blinded neither by sophistry nor enthusiasm—who knows that permanent results must grow, and can not be prematurely seized—a man who, whatever he has not, has that inestimable common sense which is the last best gift of Heaven to all who are clothed with great authority."

By the use of "political mesmerism" the President could be reached, said Henry Ward Beecher. As though Beecher was close to the people and Lincoln far aloof and out of touch, Beecher wrote in the *Independent:* "What the people see, the President will see. What the people taste, will repeat itself on the President's tongue." He would politically mesmerize Lincoln into a somnolent state of obedience to God's decree written in heavenly light: "universal emancipation."

Months earlier, as far back as December, 1861, Lincoln spoke to Senator Sumner about sending a message on emancipation to Congress. Sumner said that would be glorious. Lincoln reminded him: "Don't say a word about that. I know very well that the name connected with this act will never be forgotten."

But the armies were slow. The North got no grip on the South to warrant action. The President waited.

The idea of emancipation as a war measure, a military necessity, began developing. Even the Copperhead Democrats would have added difficulty arguing against emancipation if it could be shown as necessary to win the war. This looked promising. However, when Senator James Harlan and others one day urged the President to free and arm the slaves, he told them: "Gentlemen, I have put thousands of muskets into the hands of loyal citizens of Tennessee, Kentucky, and western North Carolina. They said they could defend themselves if they had guns. I have given them the guns. Now these men do not believe in mustering in the negro. If I do it these thousands of muskets will be turned against us. We should lose more than we should gain."

The Senators argued that Europe would intervene unless the slaves were freed. It might even be that England and France would get the South to free its slaves in exchange for recognition. When the Senators ran out of arguments, Lincoln said, as Harlan heard him: "Gentlemen, I can't do it. I can't see it as you do. You may be right and I may be wrong. But I'll tell you what I can do. I can resign in favor of Mr. Hamlin. Perhaps Mr. Hamlin could do it." The Senators were thunderstruck, said that the President from where he stood could see the whole horizon; he must do what he thought right; whatever else, he must not resign.

This version of the senatorial conference with the President, as given by Senator Harlan of Iowa, lacked details included by a telegraph correspondent at Washington serving three antislavery newspapers—the *Cincinnati Gazette,* the *Chicago Tribune,* and the *St. Louis Democrat.* He wrote:

"The President replied to the offer of two colored regiments, that he had decided not to arm the negroes. The matter was then discussed with reference to the general policy of the President; he was plied with arguments against his decision, and the discussion gradually became warm.

"Finally the President exclaimed, 'Gentlemen, you have my decision. I have made up my mind deliberately, and mean to adhere to it. It embodies my best judgment, and if the people are dissatisfied with it, I will resign and let Mr. Hamlin try it.'

"One of the Senators replied, 'I hope to God, Mr. President, you will.' The heat of discussion seemed to have arisen from the feeling that the President was drawing back from ground his visitors thought he had given them reason to believe he occupied."

No special imagination was required to picture the impetuous Ben Wade of Ohio, at the President's suggestion of resigning, sniffing his scorn and snorting, "I hope to God, Mr. President, you will!"

In the labyrinth of viewpoints in which Lincoln found himself, encircled by groups trying to infiltrate him with their special ideas, he sent a telegram to Leonard Swett at Bloomington, Illinois, asking him to come to Washington at once. Swett got on a train, traveled two days, arrived in Washington, and went at once, without breakfast, to the White House. The two met, old partners in trying law cases, sleeping in the same bed in zero weather at taverns on the old Eighth Circuit.

Lincoln invited Swett into the Cabinet room, asked about old friends in Illinois, pulled up a chair to a cabinet, and out of a drawer took a letter. This he read to Swett, who sat in quiet. The letter was from William Lloyd Garrison, one of the more patient and considerate of the uncompromising abolitionists. Unless some step was taken, Garrison urged, to cut out by the roots the institution of slavery, the North would be disappointed, the moral wrong at the bottom of the war not touched, and the war long in continuation.

Then, putting this letter back with no comment, Lincoln took out another. This was from Garrett Davis, Senator from Kentucky, showing the delicate balance of forces at war, reasoning that radical action as to slavery would throw the Border State people toward the Confederacy. Laying this letter back with no comment, Lincoln took out one from a Swiss statesman who told of European nations looking for a pretext to intervene in America. Emancipation measures would be taken in Europe as the equivalent of stirring up slave insurrections. From the earliest times in history any interference with the enemy's slaves had been regarded as a cruel expedient; it was not done.

After putting away this letter, Lincoln turned to Swett and began a discussion of emancipation in all its phases. He turned it inside out and outside in. He reasoned as though he did not care about convincing Swett, but as though he needed to think out loud in the presence of an old-timer he knew and could trust. Swett watched the mental operations of his friend until after an hour they came to an end. The President asked for no comment, hoped that Swett would get home safely, sent his best wishes to acquaintances, and the interview, as such, was closed. Thus Swett related it.

John W. Crisfield, once a fellow member of Congress with Lincoln, and now a member of a House committee to report on gradual compensated emancipation, came to Lincoln's office in July of '62 and, according to Lamon, they exchanged remarks.

"Well, Crisfield, how are you getting along with your report? Have you written it yet?"

"No."

"You had better come to an agreement. Niggers will never be cheaper."

On July 22, 1862, as the McClellan campaign for Richmond was fading in mist, mud, and disaster, Lincoln called his Cabinet for a meeting. And as he told it himself at a later time to the painter Frank B. Carpenter, it was a notable day.

"Things had gone on from bad to worse," said Lincoln, "until I felt that we had reached the end of our rope on the plan of operations we had been pursuing; that we had about played our last card, and must change our tactics, or lose the game. I now determined upon the adoption of the emancipation policy, and without consultation with or the knowledge of the Cabinet, I prepared the original draft of the proclamation, and after much anxious thought, called a Cabinet meeting upon the subject. I said to the Cabinet that I had resolved upon this step, and had not called them together to ask their advice, but to lay the subject matter of a proclamation before them, suggestions as to which would be in order, after they had heard it read. Secretary Chase wished the language stronger in reference to the arming of the blacks. Mr. Blair deprecated the policy, on the ground that it would cost the administration the fall elections.

"Nothing, however, was offered that I had not already fully anticipated and settled in my own mind, until Secretary Seward spoke. He said in substance, 'Mr. President, I approve of the proclamation, but I question the expediency of its issue at this juncture. The depression of the public mind, consequent upon our repeated reverses, is so great that I fear the effect of so important a step. It may be viewed as the last measure of an exhausted government, a cry for help; the government stretching forth its hands to Ethiopia, instead of Ethiopia stretching forth her hands to the government.' His idea was that it would be considered our last *shriek*, on the retreat. 'Now,' continued Mr. Seward, 'while I approve the measure, I suggest, sir, that you postpone its issue, until you can give it to the country supported by military success, instead of issuing it, as would be the case now, upon the greatest disasters of the war.' The wisdom of the view of the Secretary of State struck me with very great force. It was an aspect of the case that, in all my thought upon the subject, I had entirely overlooked.

"The result was that I put the draft of the proclamation aside. . . . From time to time I added or changed a line, touching it up here and there, anxiously watching the progress of events. Well, the next news we had was of

Pope's disaster, at Bull Run. Things looked darker than ever. Finally, came the week of the battle of Antietam. I determined to wait no longer. The news came, I think, on Wednesday, that the advantage was on our side. I was then staying at the Soldiers' Home (three miles out of Washington). Here I finished writing the second draft of the preliminary proclamation, came up on Saturday; called the Cabinet together to hear it, and it was published the following Monday."

Vice-President Hamlin told of his call to notify the President that he was going home in a few days. And the President laughed an order "to sit in that chair and afterward ride with me to supper." They rode horseback to the Soldiers' Home, after supper took chairs in the library, Lincoln having carefully closed the doors to the room. "Now listen while I read this paper," said Lincoln. "We will correct it together as I go on." Then he read the Emancipation Proclamation, and Hamlin approved.

Welles and Chase wrote in their diaries of what happened at the Cabinet meeting on September 22, 1862, and the final discussion of the Emancipation Proclamation before its going out for the round world to read and think about. The President mentioned in opening the Cabinet meeting that Artemus Ward had sent him a book with a chapter in it titled "High-Handed Outrage at Utica." The President said he would read this chapter, which he thought very funny. He read:

In the Faul of 1856, I showed my show in Utiky, a trooly grate sitty in the State of New York.

The people gave me a cordyal recepshun. The press was loud in her prases.

1 day as I was givin a descripshun of my Beests and Snaiks in my usual flowry stile what was my skorn & disgust to see a big burly feller walk up to the cage containin my wax figgers of the Lord's Last Supper, and cease Judas Iscarrot by the feet and drag him out on the ground. He then commenced fur to pound him as hard as he cood.

"What under the son are you abowt?" cried I.

Sez he, "What did you bring this pussylanermus cuss here fur?" & he hit the wax figger another tremenjis blow on the hed.

Sez I, "You egrejus ass, that air's a wax figger—a representashun of the false 'Postle."

Sez he, "That's all very well fur you to say, but I tell you, old man, that Judas Iscarrot can't show hisself in Utiky with impunerty by a darn site!" with which observashun he kaved in Judassis hed. The young man belonged to 1 of the first famerlies in Utiky. I sood him, and the Joory brawt in a verdick of Arson in the 3d degree.

Lincoln seemed to enjoy this clownery. So did other members of the Cabinet, though Seward laughed for fun while Chase smiled rather conventionally. Stanton was the exception. Stanton sat glum and glowering.

Then, as though he had purposely relaxed himself and others for the high tension of the business at hand, Lincoln took a grave tone, spoke with a solemn deliberation. He reminded them of the Emancipation Proclamation they had considered two months before. Ever since then his mind had been occupied with it. "I have thought all along that the time for acting on it might probably come. I think the time has come now. I wish it was a better time. I wish that we were in a better condition. The action of the army against the rebels has not been quite what I should have best liked. But they have been driven out of Maryland, and Pennsylvania is no longer in danger of invasion. When the rebel army was at Frederick, I determined, as soon as it should be driven out of Maryland, to issue a proclamation of emancipation, such as I thought most likely to be useful. I said nothing to anyone; but I made the promise to myself and [hesitating a little, Chase noted]—to my Maker. The rebel army is now driven out, and I am going to fulfill that promise.

"I have got you together to hear what I have written down. I do not wish your advice about the main matter; for that I have determined for myself. This I say without intending anything but respect for any one of you. But I already know the views of each on this question. They have been heretofore expressed, and I have considered them as thoroughly and carefully as I can. What I have written is that which my reflections have determined me to say. If there is anything in the expressions I use, or in any other minor matter, which any one of you thinks had best be changed, I shall be glad to receive the suggestions.

"One other observation I will make. I know very well that many others might, in this matter as in others, do better than I can; and if I was satisfied that the public confidence was more fully possessed by any one of them than by me, and knew of any constitutional way in which he could be put in my place, he should have it. I would gladly yield it to him. But though I believe that I have not so much of the confidence of the people as I had, some time since, I do not know that, all things considered, any person has more; and, however this may be, there is no way in which I can have any other man put where I am. I am here. I must do the best I can, and bear the responsibility of taking the course which I feel I ought to take."

Lincoln read the proclamation, commenting as he went along, as though he had considered it in all its lights. It began with saying the war would go on for the Union, that the efforts would go on for buying and setting free the slaves of the Border States, and the colonizing of them; that on January 1, 1863, all slaves in States or parts of States in rebellion against the United States "shall be then, thenceforward, and forever free," and the Federal Government would "recognize the freedom of such persons." It was a preliminary proclamation, to be followed by a final one on next New Year's Day.

Seward suggested adding the words "and maintain" after the word "recognize." Chase joined Seward in this, and it was done. Blair said he was for the principle involved, but the result of the proclamation would be to send the Border States into the arms of the secessionists as soon as it was read in those States; also it would give a club to hostile political elements in the North. Seward made another minor suggestion, that colonization should be only with the consent of the colonists; Negroes were to be sent out of the country only as they were willing to go. Lincoln put that in quickly. Then he asked Seward why he had not proposed both of his important changes at once. Seward hedged.

And Lincoln said Seward reminded him of a hired man out West who came to the farmer one afternoon with news that one of a yoke of oxen had dropped dead. And after hesitating and waiting a while, the hired man said the other ox in the team had dropped dead too. The farmer asked, "Why didn't you tell me at once that both oxen were dead?" "Because," said the hired man, "I didn't want to hurt you by telling you too much at one time."

Two days later, September 24, 1862, on a Monday morning, this preliminary Emancipation Proclamation was published, for the country and the world to read. The President held that to have issued it six months earlier would have been too soon. What he called "public sentiment" would not have stood for it. "A man watches his pear-tree day after day, impatient for the ripening of the fruit. Let him attempt to *force* the process and he may spoil both fruit and tree. But let him patiently *wait*, and the ripe pear at length falls into his lap. . . . I have done what no man could have helped doing, standing in my place."

Serenaders came with a brass band to have music over the proclamation. The President addressed them from a White House balcony: "What I did, I did after a very full deliberation. . . . I can only trust in God I have made no mistake. I shall make no attempt on this occasion to sustain what I have done or said by any comment. It is now for the country and the world to pass judgment, and, maybe, take action upon it." He was "environed with difficulties," he soberly wished the crowd to know. "Yet they are scarcely as great as the difficulties of those who upon the battle-field are endeavoring to purchase with their blood and their lives the future happiness and prosperity of this country." He wanted those soldiers with him. He was privately wondering how many of them now were stronger for him.

In Altoona, Pennsylvania, had gathered that day the governors of the Northern States, including Curtin of Pennsylvania and Andrew of Massachusetts, who had loyally raised troops and money for the Lincoln Government. They were meeting under the invitation of Curtin "to take measures for the more active support of the Government." It was in the minds of Andrew and other antislavery governors that they might frame a decision which would bring pressure on the President to remove McClellan from command and to issue some positive declaration against slavery. Earlier in the month Andrew had written Count Gurowski, "Besides doing my own proper work, I am sadly but firmly trying to help organize some movement, if possible to save the President from the infamy of ruining his country."

Andrew did not then know that the President had kept for two months in his desk drawer a draft of a preliminary Emancipation Proclamation and was waiting to win a battle before issuing it. Nor did Andrew know under what involved circumstances the President had put McClellan again in command. Leaving Boston on his way to Altoona, the news came to Andrew that McClellan had beaten off Lee in a bloody battle. Arriving in Philadelphia, en route to Altoona, Andrew read the Emancipation Proclamation. But he kept on journeying to Altoona, even though the military action and the positive declaration against slavery which he wanted from the President, his main errands to Altoona, had been accomplished. To Albert Browne, Governor Andrew wrote from Philadelphia: "The Proclamation of the President is out. It is a poor *document*, but a mighty *act;* slow, somewhat halting, wrong in its delay till January, but grand and sublime after all. 'Prophets and kings' have waited for this day, but died without the sight."

And John Andrew traveled on to sit in the conference at Altoona, where the governors agreed that the pressure they had planned to put on the President was no longer necessary. The ground had been cut from under them by Antietam and the Emancipation Proclamation. Sixteen of them signed an address to the President, pledging loyalty to the Union, endorsing the new emancipation policy, and suggesting that he should call for 100,000 more troops to be organized into a reserve corps for emergencies. Five governors held off from signing. They were from the Slave States Kentucky, Missouri, Maryland, and Delaware, and the odd Northern bailiwick of New Jersey. While also pledging loyalty to the Union and support of the President, they could not endorse the Emancipation Proclamation.

To justify their private and rather secretive conference during such a crisis, the governors appointed Andrew and Curtin a committee to see the President at Washington. Most of the governors went along. Neither press reporters nor the President's secretaries were present when Andrew read to Lincoln an address he had been instructed to prepare. Lincoln without a doubt asked them many questions about the proclamation, and about the removal of McClellan, as to which, having failed to agree, they had made no public recommendation. They went back home to their State capitals encouraged and refreshed in faith, according to a close friend of Andrew, who also noted that the influence of the Altoona conference on Lincoln could be estimated at virtually nothing. "He could truthfully say that in deciding to proclaim Emancipation, he 'never thought of the governors.' "

Politically it counted more than had been expected that the governors of sixteen Northern Free States should formally meet and join hands to uphold the President in his sudden and drastic proclamation of freedom to Negroes. The Democratic party, already campaigning for the November elections, raised the issue that the war for the Union had been changed to a war for abolition. McClellan wrote his wife that the President's proclamation, and other troubles, "render it almost impossible for me to retain my commission and self-respect at the same time." Lincoln had now gone over to the radicals, the *Louisville Democrat* and other papers told readers. "The abolitionists have pressed him into their service." Yet Garrison in the *Liberator* was "not so jubilant," seeing the proclamation as merely a step; it forbade the freeing of fugitive slaves, sending back to the lash "any hunted bondsman on the mere oath of the villain claiming him, that he is loyal to the Union." The *New York Express* said business would be worse and the end of the war seemed farther off than ever. The *New York World* said the South would not be terrorized by the Emancipation Proclamation, but would now fight harder. The *New York Journal of Commerce* said the President was now making laws by proclamations, and his latest it would be useless to discuss.

A former Justice of the United States Supreme Court, Benjamin R. Curtis, issued a pamphlet declaring that Lincoln under the plea of military necessity was overturning the Constitution and established law. At Harvard College one group declared Judge Curtis a traitor who should be imprisoned; other Harvard students would brand Lincoln a tyrant who should be impeached. Lincoln on hearing that Judge Curtis was denouncing him for the use of a radical remedy, commented, "I never heard of a patient acquiring a taste for emetics by being obliged to take one now and then." John Fiske, a student at Harvard, wrote in a letter: "What a splendid thing the President's proclamation is! I am really enthusiastic about the war now. . . . The Union cause is better off now than ever; and if this proclamation takes effect, I shall consider homely 'Old Abe' the most glorious ruler we ever had."

Governor Andrew in his office celebrated privately with Peleg W. Chandler, who months before had gone to Washington and told Lincoln of Andrew on his knees praying for emancipation. Now Andrew and Chandler marched around the office and sang "John Brown's Body" and "Praise God from Whom All Blessings Flow." "God Bless Abraham Lincoln," said the *New York Tribune*, voicing the heart of many varied elements.

Yet beyond the newspapers and politicians were the People. Lincoln's question was: What were they thinking? In many quarters the proclamation was called grand, historic, and its author an immortal. What were the realities beyond these surface expressions? Lincoln wrote Vice-President Hamlin a letter marked "Strictly private." The President hoped for something from the proclamation, yet he did not expect as much as some of his friends. "The time for its effect southward has not come; but northward the effect should be instantaneous. It is six days old, and while commendation in newspapers and by distinguished individuals is all that a vain man could wish, the stocks have declined, and troops come forward more slowly than ever. This, looked soberly in the face, is not very satisfactory."

The President's act had been like a chemist tossing a tiny pinch of some powerful ingredient into a seething and shaking caldron. Colors and currents shifted and deepened. New channels were cutting their way far under the surface. The turmoil and the trembling became unreadable by any man. But below the fresh confusion was heaving some deep and irrevocable change.

John Hay spoke of editorials in the leading newspapers. The President said he had studied the matter so long that "he knew more about it than they did."

The proclamation was aimed at Europe as well as the North and South of America. What would be the reverberations there, where London *Punch* cartooned Lincoln with horns and a long tail? London, Henry Adams wrote, "was altogether beside itself on one point; it created a nightmare of its own and gave it the shape of Abraham Lincoln." There in England, because of the cotton famine nearly 500,000 men were out of work. In a single textile district of France there were 130,000 unemployed. Yet a powerful mass opinion favored the North as against the South, believing with the liberals and the International Working Men's Association that the war in America would bring freedom to the chattel slaves. When the Emancipation Proclamation arrived in London, the *Times* found it "a very sad document," which the South would "answer with a hiss of scorn." Lincoln wrote it, said the *Times*, "with his tongue in his cheek." The *Morning Herald* said Jefferson Davis could not have done better for the purpose of throwing the Border States into line with their Southern sisters. The *Standard* called it a "sham" and "the makeshift of a pettifogging lawyer."

Yet the press and Premier Palmerston and the voices of the ruling class of England could not hope to change the basic instinct of the masses, now deeper in response to the Lincoln Government as against that of Davis at Richmond. In the inner circles of the ruling class it was admitted that now there would be increased difficulty for any European government to recognize the South and thereby break the blockade of the Southern ports, even though such a break would bring cotton to Europe and open the idle textile mills. Mr. Lindsay in Parliament raged at the proclamation as "a vindictive measure of spite and retaliation upon nine millions of whites struggling for their independence, one of the most devilish acts of fiendish malignity which the wickedness of man could ever have conceived." Another member, Mr. Beresford Hope, saw it as "a hideous outburst of weak yet demoniacal spite," and "the most unparalleled last card ever played by a reckless gambler." John Bright, however, speaking for millions who had no newspaper, no direct representatives in Parliament, said, "I applaud the proclamation."

A wave of fury swept the South. Lincoln was breaking the laws of civilized warfare, outraging private-property rights, inviting Negroes to kill, burn, and rape, said statesmen, orators, newspapers. Members of the Confederate Congress talked of running up the black flag, killing all prisoners and those wounded in battle. Beauregard telegraphed from the field to a member that after January 1, 1863, he hoped to strangle all abolition prisoners. The *Richmond Enquirer* said that Lincoln was fomenting, like Nat Turner, a slave uprising in which men, women, and children were to be killed in their beds at night. Though Ben Butler, continued the *Enquirer*, was by common consent called the Beast, he was a saint compared with his Master, Abraham Lincoln. "What shall we call him? Coward, assassin, savage, murderer of women and babies? Or shall we consider them all as embodied in the word fiend, and call him Lincoln, the Fiend?"

Lincoln had warned nearly a year ago that the contest might develop into a remorseless, revolutionary warfare. The awful responsibility of carrying on and finishing a war of conquest lay ahead. He was uneasy over such scenes as John Hay recorded in his diary, a merry little party at Chase's house, following the brass-band serenade of the President. Chase and Cassius Clay made speeches. "The crowd was in a glorious humor." The crowd went away. "A few old fogies staid . . . and drank wine." Chase spoke of the proclamation, of the insanity of the slaveholding class, how they might have kept their slaves if they had stayed in the Union. "They all seemed to

Lincoln is cartooned as desperate and Jeff Davis as pleased over the latest card played, the preliminary Emancipation Proclamation, *Punch* of London giving the title "Abe Lincoln's Last Card; or Rouge-et-noir"

feel a sort of new and exhilarated life; they breathed freer; the Pres[ts] Proc[n] had freed them as well as the slaves. They gleefully and merrily called each other and themselves abolitionists, and seemed to enjoy the novel accusation of appropriating that horrible name."

Not for Lincoln this merriment. He might guide affairs slightly. More often events shaped him, and events were whimsical.

Something new was in the writing—but what? Something was dying, something being born—but what?

A pious, lovable old Quaker woman, Mrs. Eliza P. Gurney, came to the White House with an address of thanks to him and prayers of hope for the future. He responded that he was glad of the interview, glad of their sympathy and prayers. They were going through a great and fiery trial. "In the very responsible position in which I happen to be placed, being a humble instrument in the hands of our Heavenly Father, as I am, and as we all are, to work out his great purposes, I have desired that all my works and acts may be according to his will, and that it might be so, I have sought his aid; but if, after endeavoring to do my best in the light which he affords me, I find my efforts fail, I must believe that for some purpose unknown to me, he wills it otherwise."

If he had had his way, the war would never have been commenced, he told the old Quaker woman and her friends. "If I had been allowed my way, this war would have been ended before this; but we find it still continues, and we must believe that he permits it for some wise purpose of his own, mysterious and unknown to us; and though with our limited understandings we may not be able to comprehend it, yet we cannot but believe that he who made the world still governs it."

He was pondering over God now, musing on the role of Providence in the dust of events, the riders of doom, the rivers of blood, in which he stood as a central figure in deep maroon. Toward the end of this sad September Lincoln wrote a riddle that beset his mind, haunted his heart. He left it on his desk. It was not for publication. John Hay made a copy of it. The entire paragraph read:

"The will of God prevails. In great contests each party claims to act in accordance with the will of God. Both *may* be, and one *must* be, wrong. God cannot be *for* and *against* the same thing at the same time. In the present civil war it is quite possible that God's purpose is something different from the purpose of either party; and yet the human instrumentalities, working just as they do, are the best adaptation to effect his purpose. I am almost ready to say that this is probably true; that God wills this contest, and wills that it shall not end yet. By his mere great power on the minds of the now contestants, he could have either *saved* or *destroyed* the Union without a human contest. Yet the contest began. And having begun, he could give the final victory to either side any day. Yet the contest proceeds."

CHAPTER 28

McCLELLAN'S "SLOWS" AND POLITICS

WRITING from the Paris consulate office, John Bigelow asked Weed, "Why doesn't Lincoln shoot somebody?"

From his pivotal point of observation, however, Lincoln could find no unanimous opinion as to whom to shoot.

In early October of '62, Governor Morton of Indiana wrote to the President, "Another three months like the last six and we are lost—lost."

New regiments of troops entered Washington singing "We Are Coming, Father Abraham, Three Hundred Thousand Strong." A young medical student, William Thompson Lusk, a lieutenant in the Army of the Potomac, wrote to his mother of how the war was going: "The battle comes—there is no head on the field—the men are handed over to be butchered—to die on inglorious fields. Lying reports are written. Political generals receive praises where they deserve execration. Old Abe makes a joke. The army finds that nothing new has been learned. New preparations are made, with all the old errors retained. New battles are prepared, to end in new disasters."

Just after Antietam, Lusk wrote that McClellan was cautious, a little slow, perhaps. "Yet we of the Army are jealous of McClellan's reputation and fear the possibility of losing him. Not indeed because we believe him equal to the command of 600,000 men—we believe him simply the best general we have got, and do not trust the judgment of Old Abe in the selection of a new one."

Such views came to Lincoln. Hundreds of men of the ranks, direct from the army camps, were passing in and out of Washington, besides wounded men, not to mention relatives of soldiers who came to the White House. From these and other sources Lincoln kept in touch with the army feeling as to the government policy. When the governors of the Northern States called after their Altoona conference, Governor Kirkwood of Iowa remarked, "There is an impression abroad out West, Mr. President, that you do not dare to remove General McClellan." "I would remove him tomorrow," said Lincoln, "if convinced it were for the good of the service."

Advice arrived as vehement in tone as the Harvard student John Fiske writing a friend: "I hear treason and nothing else talked all the time. If Lincoln would hang the leaders of the Democratic party, and kick McClellan out of the army, it would be well; but such a result is too much to be hoped for."

From day to day political questions interwove with military. At several Cabinet meetings the last week in September of '62 came the matter of deporting freed Negroes. Blair and Bates, the Missouri members, favored forcible deportation, the President holding that only those should go who wished to go. He laid before Welles the maps, reports, titles, and evidence having to do with the Chiriqui land grant in Panama, for Welles to make a decision as to whether the Navy Department should contract to buy coal from there, the coal to be mined by colonized free Negroes from the United States.

"The President was earnest in the matter," wrote Welles in his diary; "wished to send the negroes out of the country," was "importunate." Welles spent two or three hours a day for several days studying the data supplied him by Lincoln, and decided there was fraud and cheat in the affair. "It appeared to be a swindling speculation. Told the President I had no confidence in it." Yet again the matter came up on the point that foreign governments were liable to get hold of the coal. "The President was quite earnest in its favor, but, satisfied myself it was a job, I objected." Then

Caleb Smith, the lisping Secretary of the Interior, revived the subject. "He made a skillful and taking report, embracing both coal and negroes. Each was to assist the other. The negroes were to be transported to Chiriqui to mine coal for the Navy, and the Secretary of the Navy was to make an immediate advance of $50,000 for coal not yet mined,—nor laborers obtained to mine it, nor any satisfactory information or proof that there was decent coal to be mined. I respectfully declined adopting his views. Chase and Stanton sustained me, and Mr. Bates to an extent. Blair, who first favored it, cooled off, as the question was discussed, but the President and Smith were persistent."

Next it came out that factions and rivals down in Central America declared bogus the United States claims to coal lands in Chiriqui. The President said that this should be looked into, and an agent of the Federal Government be sent down to investigate. Senator Samuel C. Pomeroy, a Kansas abolitionist, strode into the scene saying that he would take a cargo of Negroes, sail south, and find the coal for them to mine for the Navy Department. And steadily throughout discussions of the many phases of deportation, Welles wrote, the President believed that a treaty could be made for territory of advantage to the Negroes. "[He] Thought it essential to provide an asylum for a race which we had emancipated, but which could never be recognized or admitted to be our equals. Several governments had signified their willingness to receive them. Mr. Seward said some were willing to take them without expense to us. Mr. Blair made a long argumentative statement in favor of deportation. It would be necessary to rid the country of its black population, and some place must be found for them. He is strongly for deportation. . . . Mr. Bates was for compulsory deportation. The negro would not, he said, go voluntarily, had great local attachments but no enterprise or persistency. The President objected unequivocally to compulsion. Their emigration must be voluntary and without expense to themselves. Great Britain, Denmark, and perhaps other powers, would take them."

Outside of Cabinet meetings Chase was telling Welles that Stanton felt useless and deemed it his duty to resign from the Cabinet. Welles said he was not surprised to hear it, that sooner or later either Stanton or some of the generals would have to go. "Chase said if Stanton went, he would go," wrote Welles. "It was due to Stanton and to ourselves that we should stand by him, and if one goes out, all had better go, certainly he [Chase] would." Thus Chase was trying to lay the way for a Cabinet departure, for all of them to quit at once. Chase was very serious, said the army was crushing him and would crush the country. On his table were unpaid requisitions for $45,000,000 from the War Department. He did not like it, he told Welles, that "the President takes counsel of none but army officers in army matters, though the Treasury and Navy ought to be informed of the particulars of every movement." This, Welles deduced, "is Stanton's complaint infused into Chase, and has some foundation, though it is but part of the evil."

In Cabinet meetings arose the involved matter of whether the blockade

Allan Pinkerton of the secret service, President Lincoln, General John Alexander McClernand, at Army of Potomac Headquarters, October of '62

Photograph by Brady. From Oliver R. Barrett Collection

Another Brady photograph of Allan Pinkerton, President Lincoln, General John Alexander McClernand, about the same time as the photograph on the preceding page

Photograph from Oliver R. Barrett Collection

should be lifted from the port of Norfolk, Virginia, now held by Federal ships and troops. Chase was inclined to do so. Stanton said Norfolk was hot with rebellion and to favor it would help Richmond. "The President, in the kindness of his heart," wrote Welles, "was at first inclined to grant relief." Chase suggested letting the Norfolk people bring out certain of their products, such as shingles, staves, tar, to trade for necessaries. Welles said in that case he would raise the entire blockade, because to play favorites would bring bad results. The commander at Norfolk, John A. Dix, was honest, said Welles, yet had "on his staff and around him a set of bloodsuckers who propose to make use of the blockade as a machine to enrich themselves." The President said these were matters he had not considered sufficiently. He proposed that Seward and Chase should see what could be done.

Towering over all other immediate issues, just after the Emancipation Proclamation was given out, stood the sphinx of McClellan's army—how to get it moving, how to use it as a weapon and a hammer, how to keep it from going into winter quarters without fighting, as in the winter before. In this connection came an incident to muddy the minds of men. John Hay first heard of it as he and Lincoln rode out to the Soldiers' Home the night of September 25. Hay wrote in his diary: "He said he had heard of an officer who had said they did not mean to gain any decisive victory but to keep things running on so that they, the Army, might manage things to suit themselves. He said he should have the matter examined and if any such language had been used, his head should go off." The next day Lincoln sent a letter to Major John J. Key, brother of a colonel on McClellan's staff, reading:

I am informed that in answer to the question, "Why was not the rebel army bagged immediately after the battle near Sharpsburg?" propounded to you by Major Levi C. Turner, judge-advocate, etc., you answered, "That is not the game. The object is that neither army shall get much advantage of the other, that both shall be kept in the field till they are exhausted, when we will make a compromise and save slavery." I shall be very happy if you will, within twenty-four hours from the receipt of this, prove to me by Major Turner that you did not, either literally or in substance, make the answer stated.

The next day Key and Turner came before Lincoln, who conducted a trial as judge, jury, and attorney for both sides. Lincoln made a notation, for the record of the case, that Turner testified that though he had never heard Key say anything unfavorable to the Union, when Key was asked in a private conversation between the two of them as to why the rebel army was not bagged at Antietam, he replied that that was not the game. "We should tire the rebels out and ourselves. That was the only way the Union could be preserved. We must come together fraternally, and slavery be saved."

Lincoln attached to his memorandum of the hearing an order: "Therefore let Major John J. Key be forthwith dismissed from the military service of the United States."

When political pressure came to restore Key, Lincoln wrote to Key that he was dismissed as an example and a warning to a class of officers, of whom there were too many, who were playing a game not to beat the enemy when they could. "I bear you no ill will, and I regret that I could not have the example without wounding you personally. . . . If there was any doubt of your having made the avowal, the case would be different. But when it was proved to me, in your presence, you did not deny or attempt to deny it, but confirmed it, in my mind, by attempting to sustain the position by argument."

While McClellan "rested" his troops a visitor at the White House casually asked Lincoln what number of men he supposed the "rebels" had in the field. And as *Leslie's Weekly* published the President's reply, he said seriously, "1,200,000 according to the best authority." The visitor turned pale and cried, "My God!" "Yes, sir," went on the President, "1,200,000—no doubt of it. You see, all our generals, when they get whipped, say the enemy outnumbers them from three to five to one, and I must believe them. We have 400,000 men in the field, and three times four makes twelve. Don't you see it?"

To his secretaries, to the Cabinet, Lincoln was saying little about McClellan, as though what he might have to say would be too involved. After riding with Lincoln to the Soldiers' Home one night Hay wrote: "I talked a great deal about the McClellan conspiracy, but he would make no answer to anything. He merely said that McC. was doing nothing to make himself either respected or feared."

On October 1, however, Lincoln moved. Without telling Cabinet members and without notifying McClellan that he was coming, he started for the Army of the Potomac camps. McClellan got word of Lincoln's being on the way, rode to Harper's Ferry, and was pleased to find that no Cabinet members nor politicians, "merely some western officers," were with the President. "His ostensible purpose," McClellan wrote his wife, "is to see the troops and the battle-field; I incline to think that the real purpose of his visit is to push me into a premature advance into Virginia. I may be mistaken, but think not."

They rode horseback all of one afternoon around the camps, McClellan finding the President "in quite a good-humor." Matthew B. Brady photographed them together sitting in McClellan's tent, Lincoln's right arm resting against a flag draping a table where his tall silk hat stood upside down between two stubs of candles. "The President was very kind personally," wrote McClellan; "he told me he was convinced I was the best general in the country, etc., etc. He was very affable, and I really think he does feel very kindly toward me personally."

McClellan later said that as the two of them sat on a hillside Lincoln, propped up by his long legs, his knees almost under his chin, remarked: "General, you have saved the country. You must remain in command and carry us through to the end." McClellan said this would be impossible, for time was needed and "The influences at Washington will be too strong for you, Mr. President. I will not be allowed the required time for preparation." The exact words of the President in reply, according to McClellan, were, "General, I pledge myself to stand between you and harm."

And as they rode their horses among the white tents spotting the hills for miles, McClellan probably talked, directly or indirectly, to Lincoln of matters he was writing his wife: "The real truth is that my army is not fit to advance. The old regiments are reduced to mere skeletons, and are completely tired out. They need rest and filling up. The new regiments are not fit for the field. The remains of Pope's army are pretty well broken up and ought not to be made to fight for some little time yet. Cavalry and artillery horses are broken down. So it goes."

McClellan still called it his army, "my army," as though he had not merely shaped it and rode at the head of it but as though it might be his personal creation, a child sprung from his fertile mind. Had he termed it "our army" once in a while, he would have implied that Lincoln, Stanton, Chase, and others had thought, planned, managed, toiled, to form and weld it. When McClellan marched the army through Washington on the way to Antietam, Welles met its main columns and felt it was not so good a sign that the line of march passed McClellan's house but not the Capitol nor the White House.

The dim gray twilight just before dawn came over the hills of Maryland as Lincoln rose in the tent assigned to him. A few rooster crows drifted on the air from near-by farms. It was a quiet hour. Lincoln stood at the cot of O. M. Hatch, an Illinois friend, saying, "Come, Hatch, I want you to take a walk with me." Hatch got up without a word, the two of them dressed, and left the tent together.

Lincoln led Hatch through the streets of a great tented city, amid avenues of little white canvas huts where thousands of soldiers were sleeping. Very little was spoken. "Lincoln seemed to be peculiarly serious," Hatch noted, "and his quiet, abstract way affected me also. It did not seem a time to speak. Nothing was to be said, nothing needed to be said." They reached a commanding point in the hills where the rising sun spread its moving sheen over the stirring, half-awake army of men at their morning routine.

The President waved his hand in a gesture of half-despair, and leaning toward Hatch, said in a husky and almost whispering voice, "Hatch—Hatch, what is all this?"

"Why, Mr. Lincoln," said Hatch, "this is the Army of the Potomac."

Lincoln hesitated a moment, and then straightening up, in a louder and clearer tone of voice: "No, Hatch, no. This is General McClellan's bodyguard." Nothing more was said. The two men walked slowly back to their tent.

Riding his horse through Crampton's Gap and its scenes of hard fighting, Lincoln talked with Major General William B. Franklin, who noted: "He was astonished to see and hear what we had done there. He thanked me for it, and said that he had not understood it before. He was in all respects very kind and complimentary."

Again the President was photographed, in two of the negatives standing amid McClellan and his generals, in another standing between Allan Pinkerton, the secret-service head, and Brigadier General John McClernand, the Illinois Democratic Congressman who had taken to the field for the Union.

At Frederick, Maryland, the troops were drawn up to hear a speech from the President. He told them it was not proper for him in his present position to make speeches. He gave thanks to the soldiers for good services, energy shown, hardships endured, and blood shed for the Union. "I also return thanks, not only to the soldiers, but to the good citizens of Frederick, and to the good men, women and children in this land of ours, for their devotion to this glorious cause; and I say this with no malice in my heart towards those who have done otherwise." He hoped their children, and their children's children for a thousand generations to come, would enjoy the benefits of a united country.

Passing a house in which lay Confederate wounded, Lincoln asked to go in. He stood gazing a few moments, and then said he would be pleased to take them by the hand, if they had no objections. A correspondent quoted him as saying they were "enemies through uncontrollable circumstances"; he bore them no malice and could take them by the hand with sympathy and good feeling. After a silence, Confederates came forward and without words shook the hand of the President. Some were too sore and broken to walk or to sit up. The President went among these, took some by the hand, wished them good cheer, said they should have the best of care. The correspondent wrote, "Beholders wept at the interview; most of the Confederates, even, were moved to tears."

Lamon and others rode with the President in an ambulance a few miles to Porter's corps. On the way Lincoln said, "Lamon, sing one of your little sad songs." And Lamon, a Virginian from the Shenandoah Valley, who sang for Lincoln because Lincoln could not sing, gave the tune and verses of "Twenty Years Ago," a melancholy piece of which Lamon said, "Many a time, in the old days on the Illinois circuit, and often at the White House when he and I were alone, have I seen him in tears while I was rendering, in my poor way, that homely melody." The verses that affected Lincoln most deeply, Lamon noted, were:

> I've wandered to the village, Tom; I've sat beneath the tree
> Upon the schoolhouse playground, that sheltered you and me:
> But none were left to greet me, Tom, and few were left to know
> Who played with us upon the green, some twenty years ago.
>
> Near by the spring, upon the elm you know I cut your name,—
> Your sweetheart's just beneath it, Tom; and you did mine the same.
> Some heartless wretch has peeled the bark;—'twas dying sure but slow,
> Just as she died whose name you cut, some twenty years ago.

My lids have long been dry, Tom, but tears came to my eyes;
I thought of her I loved so well, those early broken ties:
I visited the old churchyard, and took some flowers to strew
Upon the graves of those we loved, some twenty years ago.

The song deepened Lincoln's sadness, as Lamon expected, and, said Lamon: "I then did what I had done many times before; I startled him from his melancholy by striking up a comic air, singing also a snatch from 'Picayune Butler,' which broke the spell and restored somewhat his accustomed easy humor. It was not the first time I had pushed hilarity, simulated though it was, to an extreme for his sake."

The "Picayune Butler" song was a blackface minstrel classic, had a fast tune meant to go with quick banjo-playing. As a piece to sing it was plainly ridiculous or broadly comic, in the same style as scores of popular songs of the time. Possibly this song was never termed "obscene" by anyone until the story came along that Lincoln enjoyed it and called for it from his banjo-plucking friend Lamon. Three of its five verses:

Ob all de gals I eber did see,
Miss Lucy Neal was best to me,
  Yah-ha.
She chased de bulgine out of breaff,
And dat's what caused Miss Lucy's deaff,
  Yah-ha.

Young folks come here to take a walk,
And wid dar lubs to hab some talk,
  Yah-ha.
De ladies ask, "Am dat a fac?
Is dem gemmen really black?"
  Yah-ha.

I'se gwine some day to buy a farm,
An a band of niggers I'll take along,
  Yah-ha.
An ebry day we'll sing dis song,
Ob Picayune Butler come to town,
  Yah-ha.

The chorus had staccato, swing, repetitions—and didn't mean a thing. Its jigtime words:

Picayune Butler comin', comin',
Picayune Butler come to town!
  Ahoo, Ahoo, Ahoo.
Picayune Butler comin', comin',
Picayune Butler come to town!

Neither Lincoln nor Lamon had any notion that the singing in the ambulance that morning would be interpreted and spread on tongues of hate and malice, to be colored and magnified into an allegation, published and spoken, that while the slain still lay on the battlefield of Antietam, and the wounded were still languishing near by, the President had called on a boisterous boon companion for a ribald song and had rollicked in laughter over it. So far would the slander spread that the two men were to talk it over in bitterness and prepare a completely detailed statement of what had happened that morning in an ambulance as they rode over the tragic and blood-soaked acres of Antietam.

Two days later, Lincoln was in Washington, and a telegram went to Mc-Clellan from Halleck saying: "The President directs that you cross the Potomac and give battle to the enemy, or drive him south. Your army must move now, while the roads are good." McClellan was to advise Washington what his line of action would be, the time he intended to cross the river, and at what point fresh troops were to be sent to his army. The emphasis was that the President was very desirous "that your army move as soon as possible." The telegram closed: "I am directed to add that the Secretary of War and the general-in-chief fully concur with the President in these instructions."

During early October, while McClellan asked shoes, horses, mules, and new bridges for his army, the telegrams poured into Washington from the Western armies winning victories on shoes, horses, and mules worse than McClellan had. For days the cities of Louisville and Cincinnati telegraphed Lincoln for help, for troops to save them from Bragg's army. But Bragg found it hard going in Kentucky. His army had brought along 20,000 muskets to be given to new Confederate recruits out of the Bluegrass Region. And he had turned southward with his army, reporting to Richmond: "We must abandon the garden spot of Kentucky to its cupidity. The love of ease and fear of pecuniary loss are the fruitful source of this evil." At Perryville, Bragg collided with the Union army under Buell. The slopes were strewn with thousands of dead and wounded as Bragg moved further south. In the Deep South, down in Mississippi, a Confederate army tried to take Corinth, a railroad and supply point. They were beaten off, losing 7,000 in dead and wounded as against 2,000 Union losses. Lincoln telegraphed Grant, "I congratulate you and all concerned," and asked, "How does it all sum up?" Lincoln's failure to mention General William S. Rosecrans, who managed the battle of Corinth with ability, was taken by some Western army officers to mean that Lincoln was steering clear of army politics, and the only favorite he was playing in that region then was Grant, now planning a campaign to take the tall fortified bluffs at Vicksburg on the Mississippi.

Regiments marched back and forth, and men shot and killed, at Harrodsburg, Bardstown, and places where Lincoln ran barefoot as a boy. With the mails from Lexington interrupted, he no longer received at the White House the *Kentucky Observer*, the weekly newspaper he liked to read as "a weathercock of Kentucky politics." Reading in dispatches from Corinth of one wounded there, Lincoln wired Grant, "I . . . am very anxious to know the condition of General Oglesby, who is an intimate personal friend."

For himself were no days off. He wired McClellan, "You wish to see your family and I wish to oblige you," letting McClellan go to Philadelphia for a visit with wife and daughter. To another officer Lincoln refused a furlough and wrote, "I sincerely wish war was an easier and pleasanter business than it is; but it does not admit of holidays."

Three weeks had gone by since Antietam. Yet McClellan stayed north of the Potomac with 100,000 men while Lee not far off in Virginia was recruiting his army from conscripts called up by the Richmond Government.

The President wrote a long letter to McClellan, inquiring, "Are you not over-cautious, when you assume that you cannot do what the enemy is constantly doing?" A long friendly analysis aimed to reduce grand strategy to simple points. "If he makes a stand at Winchester, moving neither north nor south, I would fight him there, on the idea that if we cannot beat him when he bears the wastage of coming to us, we never can when we bear the wastage of going to him."

An old point, familiar to boxers and wrestlers, Lincoln urged. "In coming to us he tenders us an advantage which we should not waive. We should not so operate as to merely drive him away. As we must beat him somewhere or fail finally, we can do it, if at all, easier near to us than far away. If we cannot beat the enemy where he now is, we never can, he again being within the intrenchments of Richmond." The lay of land between McClellan and Lee was discussed, distances, supplies, communications. "It is all easy if our troops march as well as the enemy, and it is unmanly to say they cannot do it." The President was talking it over, hoping. "This letter is in no sense an order."

' While McClellan visited his family in Philadelphia, the hard-riding Jeb Stuart, wearing gold spurs and singing in the rain, led his gray horsemen across the Potomac and up into Chambersburg, Pennsylvania, where he destroyed a machine shop, took 500 horses and Federal uniforms, and all the shoes and clothing in the stores, paying for them with Confederate money, and camping his men in the streets. Riding back to join Lee, Stuart rode around McClellan's army for the second time that year. The news came to Lincoln. He sat on the deck of the ship *Martha Washington*, returning from a troop review at Alexandria.

"Mr. President, what about McClellan?" he was asked. Without looking up at the question, Lincoln drew a ring on the deck with an umbrella and said quietly: "When I was a boy we used to play a game, three times round and out. Stuart has been round him twice. If he goes around him once more, gentlemen, McClellan will be out!"

Repeatedly across months Lincoln remarked of McClellan, "He's got the slows." A story unfair to McClellan, and probably invented to relieve monotony of inaction, was told of Stanton's saying to Lincoln that McClellan was settling in Washington with his family for the winter.

"Has he sent for his wife?"

"His wife is with him."

"And that black-and-tan terrier?"

"Is one of the family."

"Then he has gone into winter quarters and must be removed," Lincoln was quoted as saying.

The story had mischief, but those who told it were uneasy with fear that the long delay in winter quarters the year before would be repeated. More like fact was the gossip that a government official, getting a pass to see McClellan, remarked, "I'll report when I come back if I find the army."

"Oh, you will," said Lincoln. "It's there. That's just the difficulty."

Thaddeus Stevens in the House asked attention to the President's order to McClellan for pursuit of the enemy. "He started after them with an army of 120,000 men before him, and marched that army at the rapid rate of six miles a day until they stopped and he came up with them. [Laughter.] He then fought the battle of Antietam. It was a quasi victory, but notwithstanding that, while the enemy were in sight of the river, and while he was within cannon-shot of the enemy, he suffered them all to cross the river, which was done by them deliberately and successfully to the last man and the last ambulance."

The glitter and display of aristocracy and wealth surrounding McClellan continued to win resentment in various quarters. Why should he have clattering and galloping with his staff such figures as a French duke and two princes who were heirs and claimants to the throne of France if and when the usurper Napoleon III could be relieved of the throne? And why should John Jacob Astor, the wealthiest scion of American aristocracy, have special accommodations and favors?

By latter October, it seemed, McClellan's dealings at Washington were entirely with Lincoln. "All his official correspondence is with the President direct and no one else," wrote Welles. To Lincoln, McClellan sent his calls for more shoes, mules, horses. To one of these Lincoln replied: "I have just read your despatch about sore-tongued and fatigued horses. Will you pardon me for asking what the horses of your army have done since the battle of Antietam that fatigues anything?"

McClellan read the telegram and commented to his wife, "It was one of those little flings that I can't get used to when they are not merited." To General Darius N. Couch, who pointed to a spot on the map where the next great battle might take place, McClellan said: "But I may not have command of the army much longer. Lincoln is down on me." McClellan had noticed an openly ironic tone rising in the President's letters and telegrams. Of long hours spent on an elaborate report of the battle of Antietam he wrote his wife that at last the report was finished. As to rumors about his army, he summarized for her: "I see that there is much impatience throughout the country for a move. I am just as anxious as anyone, but am crippled by want of horses." In this same week, however, McClellan's quartermaster general, Rufus Ingalls, was queried by the War Department and replied, "It has been my pride to know the fact that no army was ever more perfectly supplied than this has been as a general rule." Ingalls noted too "that an army will never move if it waits until all the different commanders report that they are ready and want no more supplies."

McClellan again complained about lacking horses and Lincoln telegraphed: "To be told, after more than five weeks' total inaction of the army, and during which . . . we have sent to the army every fresh horse we possibly could, amounting in the whole to 7918, that the cavalry horses were too much fatigued to move, presents a very cheerless, almost hopeless prospect for the future, and it may have forced something of impatience in my despatch. If not recruited and rested then, when could they ever be?"

The autumn weather was perfect for marching an army. McClellan telegraphed Lincoln asking whether he should march on the enemy at once or "wait the reception of new horses." General in Chief Halleck now replied, "The President does not expect impossibilities, but he is very anxious that all this good weather should not be wasted in inactivity." McClellan came back with a long letter asking instructions as to many details, getting a reply that "the Government has intrusted you with defeating and driving back the rebel army on your front." He could use his own discretion as to details. And as McClellan had mentioned in his long letter that perhaps Bragg was marching his Confederate army from Tennessee eastward, General Halleck ended his telegram, "You are within twenty miles of Lee, while Bragg is distant about four hundred miles."

McClellan now slowly moved his army across the Potomac and put it about where Pope's army had lain before Second Bull Run. It was November. Lincoln told John Hay that he had a test by which he would make a final judgment of McClellan. If that commander should permit Lee to cross the Blue Ridge and place himself between Richmond and the Army of the Potomac, Lincoln would remove McClellan from command. Now when Lee's army reached Culpeper Court House the test of McClellan was over. Lincoln prepared a removal order.

Old Frank Blair, still a friend of McClellan, argued with Lincoln against McClellan's removal. And as Monty Blair told of this interview: "Lincoln listened with attention to all my father had to say, but was not communicative himself. But at the end of the conference he rose up and stretched his long arms almost to the ceiling above him, saying, 'I said I would remove him if he let Lee's army get away from him, and I must do so. He has got the slows, Mr. Blair.'"

Two men traveled in a driving snowstorm near midnight of November 7 to find the tent of General McClellan near Rectortown. They stepped in and shook off the snow from their big overcoats. They had interrupted him in the writing of a letter to his wife. One of the men was Adjutant General C. P. Buckingham of the War Department. The other was Major General Ambrose Everett Burnside. Buckingham handed McClellan a message relieving him of command of the Army of the Potomac and ordering him to turn it over to Burnside. A second message told McClellan to report to Trenton, New Jersey, for further orders. McClellan "read the papers with a smile," as he told it afterward. Also he remarked, "Alas for my poor country!" Also he turned and finished the letter to his wife: "Alas for my poor country! . . . Do not be at all worried—I am not. I have done the best I could for my country; to the last I have done my duty as I understand it. That I must have made many mistakes I cannot deny. I do not see any great blunders; but no one can judge of himself."

A farewell letter from McClellan was read to the army. It was cheered. Where McClellan showed himself among the soldiers he was cheered. He had a way with him, a magnetism and a figure and manner. The man taking his place, Burnside, came near weeping as he told McClellan that he had refused to accept command until ordered. They called each other "Mac" and "Burn." What had happened that now one who wished to stay was out and one was in who did not want to be in?

Several points dictated Lincoln's action. Month by month during his year and a half handling the Army of the Potomac, McClellan got into a worse position with the War Department and with the increasingly insistent group of antislavery Congressmen. Had he moved and won victories in other than defensive battles, his critics would have had no foothold. Steadily month by month since he took command just after Bull Run, he had given a political color to many of his actions and decisions. As a military man handling an army made up of citizen soldiers from all parts of the country, he assumed to be a spokesman of governmental policy, as in the Harrison's Landing letter of advice to Lincoln and Congress. According to Governor Andrew, Lincoln was asked what he would reply to McClellan's advice on how to carry on the affairs of the nation. And Lincoln answered: "Nothing—but it made me think of the man whose horse kicked up and stuck his foot through the stirrup. He said to the horse, 'If you are going to get on I will get off.'"

McClellan believed, as he wrote his wife over and again, that he had a mission to save the country, that God had put into his hands the peculiar fate of saving the Union without at the same time giving the country to the

GENERAL ORDERS,   }   WAR DEPARTMENT.
ADJUTANT GENERAL'S OFFICE,
No. 182.   Washington, November 5, 1862.

By direction of the President of the United States, it is ordered that Major General McCLELLAN be relieved from the command of the Army of the Potomac, and that Major General BURNSIDE take the command of that Army.

BY ORDER OF THE SECRETARY OF WAR:

E. D. TOWNSEND,
Assistant Adjutant General.

Official order of removal

fanatical abolitionists. McClellan carried this viewpoint to the extent of openly disapproving of the Emancipation Proclamation among his political friends and military associates. He was visited at his camp on October 6, just after Lincoln left, by William Henry Aspinwall, the Panama Railroad and Steamship multimillionaire—a New York financier who played a large role in Democratic-party politics. In the letter of McClellan to his wife on the day of the Aspinwall visit his motives were mixed. He wrote, "Mr. Aspinwall is decidedly of the opinion that it is my duty to submit to the President's proclamation and quietly continue doing my duty as a soldier." He was not sure of it till Aspinwall told him—and then not completely sure.

"I presume he [Aspinwall, not Lincoln] is right, and am at least sure that he is honest in his opinion."

McClellan's enemies seized on such incidents as one told by Colonel Albert V. Colburn of McClellan's staff, who said that when the General saw the Emancipation Proclamation in the *Baltimore Sun*, he hurled the paper into a corner, exclaiming: "There! Look at that outrage! I shall resign tomorrow!"

Naturally more of an engineer than a general, and at times more of a politician than an engineer, McClellan saw his own faults as minor and those of Lincoln and the War Department as major. "If you could know the mean and dirty character of the despatches I receive," he wrote to his wife the last of October, "you would boil over with anger. When it is possible to misunderstand . . . whenever there is a chance of a wretched innuendo, then it comes. But the good of the country requires me to submit to all this from men whom I know to be vastly my inferiors, socially, intellectually and morally. There never was a truer epithet applied to a certain individual than that of 'Gorilla.' "

Little things that Lincoln did brought laughter to some people but to McClellan only contempt. "Herr Hermann, 'a great magician,' volunteered to give us a private entertainment," the General wrote to Mrs. McClellan, "so I invited the staff, etc., etc. The most striking feature of the performance was that the Magician asked the President for his handkerchief—upon which that dignitary replied *promptly*—'You've got me now. I aint got any'!!!"

Besides Aspinwall, McClellan received in his camp and held political conferences with Fernando Wood, commonly designated as the most devious and corrupt Democratic politician who had attained to high power in New York City. The hope of Wood in these conferences was to make McClellan President of the United States. Nothing less actuated the manipulator who as Mayor of New York had tried to bring about its secession from the Union as a Free City.

A Governor of Vermont came to Lincoln on "business of importance." He was a brother of one of McClellan's abler generals, William F. ("Baldy") Smith. He told Lincoln a story, which Lincoln gave to John Hay. And John Hay wrote in his diary Lincoln's version of the story as follows (spelling and punctuation changed):

When General McClellan was here at Washington Baldy Smith was very intimate with him. They had been together at West Point, and friends. McClellan had asked for promotion for Baldy from the President, and got it. They were close and confidential friends. When they went down to the Peninsula their same intimate relations continued, the General talking freely with Smith about all his plans and prospects, until one day Fernando Wood and one other [Democratic] politician from New York appeared in Camp and passed some days with McClellan.

From the day this took place Smith saw, or thought he saw, that McClellan was treating him with unusual coolness and reserve. After a little while he mentioned this to McClellan, who, after some talk, told Baldy he had something to show him. He told him that these people who had recently visited him had been urging him to stand as an opposition candidate for President; that he had thought the thing over and had concluded to accept their propositions, and had written them a letter (which he had not yet sent) giving his idea of the proper way of conducting the war, so as to conciliate and impress the people of the South with the idea that our armies were intended merely to execute the laws and protect their property, etc., and pledging himself to conduct the war in that inefficient, conciliatory style.

This letter he read to Baldy, who, after the reading was finished, said earnestly: "General, do you not see that looks like treason, and that it will ruin you and all of us?" After some further talk the General destroyed the letter in Baldy's presence, and thanked him heartily for his frank and friendly counsel. After this he was again taken into the intimate confidence of McClellan.

Immediately after the battle of Antietam, Wood and his familiar came again and saw the General, and again Baldy saw an immediate estrangement on the part of McClellan. He seemed to be anxious to get his intimate friends out of the way and to avoid opportunities of private conversation with them. Baldy he particularly kept employed on reconnoissances and such work. One night Smith was returning from some duty he had been performing, and, seeing a light in McClellan's tent, he went in to report. He reported and was about to withdraw, when the General requested him to remain. After everyone was gone he told him those men had been there again and had renewed their proposition about the Presidency: that this time he had agreed to their proposition, and had written them a letter acceding to their terms and pledging himself to carry on the war in the sense already indicated. This letter he read then and there to Baldy Smith.

Immediately thereafter B. Smith applied to be transferred from that army. At very nearly the same time other prominent men asked the same—Franklin, Burnside, and others.

Hay said he was surprised at McClellan's going so deep into politics while commanding a great army in a crisis. He told the President he had always thought McClellan's fault was a constitutional weakness and timidity, which prevented him from active and timely exertion, instead of any such deep-laid treachery and ambition. The President replied: "After the battle of Antietam I went up to the field to try to get him to move, and came back thinking he would move at once. But when I got home he began to argue why he ought not to move. I peremptorily ordered him to advance. It was nineteen days before he put a man over the river. It was nine days longer before he got his army across, and then he stopped again, delaying on little pretexts of wanting this and that. I began to fear he was playing false—that he did not want to hurt the enemy. I saw how he could intercept the enemy on the way to Richmond. I determined to make that the test. If he let them get away, I would remove him. He did so, and I relieved him."

Now many believed they understood McClellan. Stanton, Chase, Greeley, Phillips, Beecher, believed they solved him and saw through him as though he were transparent. Which he was not. McClellan lived much of the time in a peculiar world of his own making. He would almost get ready to hurl his army into a great battle or campaign, then hesitate, think of something more to be done, make excuses, get sore at himself for making excuses and hesitating, finally finding himself in mental operations and defensive vocabularies that would be difficult to analyze. No case was ever made out that McClellan was not brave and able. Only politicians, personal enemies, loose talkers, called him coward or sloven. At Malvern Hill and Antietam he performed superbly—and then failed to clinch and use what he won. If he had been the ambitious plotter that Stanton, Chase, and others saw, he would have marched his army to Washington and seized the Government there, as he said many urged him to do. His defect was that while he could not have instigated such treason himself, he did allow approaches to such treason to be talked freely in his staff and army without rebuke or repression from him. His political dabbling with Fernando Wood of New York over the Presidency of the United States was not by his device; he did not ask Wood to come down to the Peninsula the first time, nor to Maryland for the second visit.

Yet it was also true that the conniving Wood did not see McClellan as a presidential figure until McClellan set himself up as a spokesman for governmental policy, virtually used his position as head of a great army to carry on an advocacy of measures easily construed as proslavery. When this drew the slippery and slimy Wood to his camp, he did not kick Wood out. He welcomed Wood, took up with Wood's proposition to make him President, and held to it till his friend Baldy Smith showed him that it could look like betrayal of trust. A second time he welcomed Wood, and this time took up with Wood's plan, which looked so rotten that Baldy Smith broke with him.

His friend Aspinwall, the financier who came to his camp, gave him the keen advice to go along with Lincoln's Emancipation Proclamation, say nothing, and be a soldier. From the way he wrote his wife of what Aspinwall told him, it would almost seem as though this was the first time that he seriously considered the gift of silence on politics for a general heading an army given to him by a government wrestling with delicately shaded political questions. He did not know that he had by his political trafficking, and by his unceasing gabble of imbecility at Washington, hampered unity of his staff, lowered the fighting quality of his army, and so muddled the army objectives that the President had to take action—even if it led straight into worse muddles.

The order for McClellan's dismissal, dated the day after the November elections, timed with voters over the country registering angry disapproval of Lincoln's Administration. To McClellan's friends it seemed almost as though Lincoln had waited for the election to be over before he dared to throw out McClellan. McClellan said later that he believed the President had "meant every word" of his pledge at Antietam to stand by him, "but the influences at Washington were, as I predicted, too strong for him or for any living man."

Political confusion of that hour was told in interviews that Congressmen had with Lincoln just after the elections. William D. Kelley of Philadelphia came to the White House. Lincoln congratulated him on re-election, saying, as Kelley noted, "Sit down and tell me how it is that you, for whose election nobody seemed to hope, are returned with a good majority at your back, while so many of our friends about whom there was no doubt, have been badly beaten." Kelley said that six months earlier he would have been beaten, but he had been saved by his independent demand for a fighting general to replace McClellan. He told Lincoln that he had gone to the battle-field of Antietam as an emergency man, one of many who wanted to hurl back the invader. He had been in charge of the spare guns and sick horses of a battery of regular artillery, heard the gunfire, carried messages for offi-cers. He had seen Porter's corps, 30,000 fresh troops held in reserve, not used at all. They could, in Kelley's view, have "practically imprisoned" Lee's army.

At this point in Kelley's talk Congressman Edward McPherson of the Gettysburg district came in. He had just been beaten in what was regarded as a certain Republican district. Lincoln shook hands with McPherson and asked why there had been "so unhappy and unexpected a result" in his dis-trict. McPherson began giving merely polite answers. Kelley interrupted to say, "Mr. President, my colleague is not treating you frankly; his friends hold you responsible for his defeat."

The President thanked Kelley for the suggestion, turned to McPherson. "Tell me frankly what cost us your district. If ever there was an occasion when a man should speak with perfect candor to another it is now, when I apply to you for information that may guide my course in grave national matters." "Well, Mr. President," said McPherson, "I will tell you frankly what our friends say. They charge the defeat to the general tardiness in military movements, which result, as they believe, from McClellan's unfit-ness for command. The enforcement of the draft occurred during the cam-paign, and of course our political enemies made a great deal of capital out of it; but in my judgment, not enough to change the complexion of the district." And McPherson told of Confederate cavalry riding across his dis-trict on the Friday and Saturday before election, burning a railroad station and machine shops, camping in the streets, taking prisoners and then parol-ing sick and wounded Union soldiers in a hospital at Chambersburg.

While Lincoln listened to McPherson, the door of the room opened without a knock and the broad shoulders of J. K. Moorhead, Representative from the Pittsburgh district, heaved through the door. Lincoln crossed the room, put out his hand. "What word do you bring, Moorhead? You, at any rate, were not defeated."

"No," said Moorhead in a high-pitched voice and trembling with excite-ment, "no, Mr. President, but I am sorry to say it was not your fault that we were not all beaten." He joined with the others in saying that the Ad-ministration had compromised, delayed, held on to McClellan too long. He told of riding to Harrisburg the day before with some of the best and most influential people of his State, including men who had one time been earnest Lincoln supporters.

"They charged me," said Moorhead, "to tell you that when one of them said he would be glad to hear some morning that you had been found hanging from the post of a lamp at the door of the White House, others approved the expression."

At this, Kelley noted, the manner of the President changed. He was perfectly calm, and, in a subdued voice: "You need not be surprised to find that that suggestion has been executed any morning. The violent preliminaries to such an event would not surprise me. I have done things lately that must be incomprehensible to the people, and which cannot now be explained."

Kelley jumped from his chair and began walking the floor, saying the President should never let anyone hear that he had ever considered such a thing as being hanged from a lamppost in front of the White House, that the President shared a greater personal affection than any public man since Washington, that within twenty-four hours after he replaced McClellan with a soldier, he would command resources as no other President had. And they talked about who should be named to replace McClellan, Kelley inclining to Fighting Joe Hooker and Lincoln to Burnside. Kelley urged that the President try one general and another, change following change, till the right man was found. The first change should be made soon.

Kelley felt the President thoughtful but evasive in responding to several suggestions, "We shall see what we shall see."

On November 17, 1862, the very scrupulous Gustavus Vasa Fox wrote confidentially to the much less scrupulous Ben Butler at New Orleans: "In military matters here we are quiet but expectant. The luxurious Army of the Potomac, petted to bursting, is no match in celerity of movement to the famished freezing soldiers of Lee. Legs win more battles than fighting. At [Second] Bull Run one of our soldiers was found dead with seventeen pounds of Congressional documents in his knapsack."

While the navy thus privately bemoaned to the army the lack of leadership, Orpheus C. Kerr in November of '62 publicly mocked at McClellan in a widely printed burlesque of the General's farewell address to the Army of the Potomac: "My children: An order from the Honest Abe divorces us. In parting with you I cannot express how much I love your dear bosoms. As an army, you have grown from youth to old age under my care. In you I never found doubt nor coldness, nor anything else. The victories you have won under my command will live in the nation's works of fiction. The strategy we have achieved, the graves of many Mackerels, still make it advisable that you should vote for me as President of the United States in 1865. Thus we shall ever be comrades in supporting the Constitution, and making the Constitution support us."

From any ironic mirth Lincoln had over this burlesque, he turned to the question of where he might find a general who could bring the victories wanted. On September 6 of '62 he had read to his Cabinet a poem written by a pardon clerk in the Attorney General's department, Edmund Clarence Stedman. The *New York Tribune* three days later published the verses. Many newspapers reprinted them under their title "Wanted—a Man." Bates had handed the poem to Lincoln just after the reappointment of McClellan

to head the Army of the Potomac. And the President read to his Cabinet
these verses with all their pathetic implications:

Back from the trebly crimsoned field
  Terrible words are thunder-tost;
Full of the wrath that will not yield,
  Full of revenge for battles lost!
  Hark to their echo, as it crost
The Capitol, making faces wan:
  "End this murderous holocaust;
Abraham Lincoln, give us a Man!

"Give us a man of God's own mould,
  Born to marshal his fellow-men;
One whose fame is not bought and sold
  At the stroke of a politician's pen;
  Give us the man of thousands ten,
Fit to do as well as to plan;
  Give us a rallying-cry, and then,
Abraham Lincoln, give us a Man!

"No leader to shirk the boasting foe,
  And to march and countermarch our brave,
Till they fall like ghosts in the marshes low,
  And swamp-grass covers each nameless grave;
  Nor another whose fatal banners wave
Aye in Disaster's shameful van;
  Nor another, to bluster, and lie, and rave;—
Abraham Lincoln, give us a Man!

"Hearts are mourning in the North,
  While the sister rivers seek the main,
Red with life-blood flowing forth,—
  Who shall gather it up again?
  Though we march to the battle-plain
Firmly as when the strife began,
  Shall all our offering be in vain?—
Abraham Lincoln, give us a Man!

"Is there never one in all the land,
  One on whose might the Cause may lean?
Are all the common ones so grand,
  And all the titled ones so mean?
  What if your failure may have been
In trying to make good bread from bran,
  From worthless metal a weapon keen?—
Abraham Lincoln, find us a Man!

"O, we will follow him to the death,
  Where the foeman's fiercest columns are!
O, we will use our latest breath,
  Cheering for every sacred star!

Ambrose Everett Burnside

Photographs from Chicago Historical Society Collection

Philip Kearny

Photograph from Oliver R. Barrett Collection

Hermann Haupt

Photograph from Frederick H. Meserve Collection

The Chief Magistrate confers with the Army of the Potomac commander in October of '62

Photograph by Brady. From Oliver R. Barrett Collection

His to marshal us high and far;
Ours to battle, as patriots can
When a Hero leads the Holy War!—
Abraham Lincoln, give us a Man!"

Thus the poet Stedman cried aloud for the public to hear. Privately Stedman felt that the President and the War Department were as much to blame as the generals in the field. In a letter of October 28 of '62 on the many miles between the armies of McClellan and Lee, Stedman wrote: "Evident enough to the child, that Lincoln, Halleck and Company are to blame, not McClellan. . . . The scarcity of great men is painfully manifest, when one party has to erect McClellan as a political name and leader, and the other can find no one but that most wretched and selfish humbug, Frémont."

CHAPTER 29

ELECTION LOSSES IN '62—INDIAN DEATHS

JOHN BIGELOW at the Paris consulate in November estimated the check received by the Administration in the November elections as "the most fortunate event that has happened during the war, except the proclamation [of emancipation]. . . . It will make the President and his advisers feel more than they have felt hitherto, the necessity of doing something (witness already McClellan's decapitation) and it will give the Govt. a strong and watchful opposition for the want of which during the last two years the country has greatly suffered."

The November elections of 1862 nearly doubled the number of Democratic Congressmen, raising it from 44 to 75. In five States where Lincoln two years before had won the electoral vote, his party now lost. The pro-Administration Republican *New York Times* said the balloting registered "want of confidence" in the President. In Ohio the Republicans lost 14 seats in Congress—in Indiana 8. In Illinois the seat in Congress vacated by John A. Logan when he went off to fight for the Union was filled by a Peace Democrat. Also the newly Democratic legislature of Illinois would elect another United States Senator to replace the President's confidant, Orville H. Browning. Pennsylvania's 60,000 majority for Lincoln two years before shifted to a Democratic lead of 4,000. By a 10,000 majority Horatio Seymour, a Peace Democrat, took the governor's chair in New York State.

Into Delaware, its Senators complained, the Administration had sent 3,000 troops to watch the polls on election day. No violence occurred, said the Senators, but they would like to conduct their elections without bayonets from Washington. In Tennessee, General Grant had received instructions from Lincoln in the matter of conducting an election: "In all available ways give the people a chance to express their wishes at these elections. Follow forms of law as far as convenient, but at all events get the expression of the largest number of the people possible. All see how such action will connect with and affect the proclamation of September 22. Of course the men elected should be gentlemen of character, willing to swear support to the Constitution as of old, and known to be above reasonable suspicion of duplicity."

Republican control of Congress was saved by the ballots of Michigan, Iowa, Minnesota, Kansas, Oregon, California. Two political groups far apart, antislavery New England and the proslavery Border States, upheld Lincoln with majorities.

The *New York Tribune* laid defeat in that State to the absence at the fighting fronts of 100,000 men, three-fourths of them ardent Republicans; at the polls the Republican party had to meet "every partisan of slavery, every sympathizer with rebellion, every coward who feared the draft." The *New York Herald*, however, saw the Republican party "rebuked and repudiated," while "the original wise and patriotic policy of Lincoln is approved"; the voters were serving notice on Lincoln that the war be for restoration of the Union and not for "the bloody extermination of slavery."

The poet Edmund Clarence Stedman was "not so sorry" over the elections. "They teach a terrible lesson: may infuse a little firmness into Lincoln and Company, and produce a hot prosecution of the war." The poet Whittier wrote in a letter that "were it not for one or two *ifs*," he could feel better. "The worst of the *ifs* is the one concerning Lincoln. I am much afraid that a domestic cat will not answer when one wants a Bengal tiger."

Many commentators agreed with the poet-editor of the *New York Evening Post*, William Cullen Bryant: "The people after their gigantic preparations and sacrifices have looked for an adequate return, and looked in vain. They have seen armies unused in the field perish in pestilential swamps.

They have seen their money wasted in long winter encampments, or frittered away on fruitless expeditions along the coast. They have seen a huge debt roll up, yet no prospect of greater military results." The *Salem Advocate* spoke for southern Illinois Democrats: "We saw the President of the United States stretching forth his hand and seizing the reins of government with almost absolute power, and yet the people submitted. On the 4th day of November, 1862, the people arose in their might, they uttered their voice, like the sound of many waters, and tyranny, corruption and maladministration trembled."

Leslie's Weekly itemized: "The President takes the result of the New York elections quite philosophically, and will, doubtless, profit by the lesson. When Colonel Forney inquired of him how he felt about New York, he replied: 'Somewhat like that boy in Kentucky, who stubbed his toe while running to see his sweetheart. The boy said he was too big to cry, and far too badly hurt to laugh.'"

Between the two extremes of New England and the Border States, any citizen could ponder. On the one hand was Wendell Phillips, saying: "The North has poured out its blood and money like water; it has leveled every fence of constitutional privilege, and Abraham Lincoln sits today a more unlimited despot than the world knows this side of China. What does he render for this unbounded confidence? Show us something, or I tell you that within two years the indignant reaction of the people will hurl the Cabinet in contempt from their seats." On the other hand was Andrew Johnson, risking his neck hourly as military Governor of Tennessee, and his newspaper organ, the *Nashville Union*, hitting at Wendell Phillips as "a flashy, blasphemous incendiary and half crazed Jacobin, as vile a disunionist as Jefferson Davis or William L. Yancey."

Between these two forces, so restless, alive, and vocal, the Administration had to manage its course. Each was represented at the front, in Congress, in all sections. Lincoln's first law partner, John T. Stuart, a Democrat, in a run for Congress won over Leonard Swett on the Union ticket. Though Stuart had declared, "It is my desire to give the President a frank and earnest support in all his constitutional efforts to suppress the present wicked rebellion," Swett had been known as Lincoln's choice.

The race question rose. Thousands of Negroes freed by the southward-moving armies had been sent to Cairo, in the southernmost corner of the State. The *Illinois State Journal* queried, "Shall Illinois be Africanized?" Swett in his desperate campaigning announced that "the bringing of contrabands into this state tends to degrade white labor. . . . I am now and always have been opposed to their introduction among us." Stanton halted northward movement of Negroes by an order issued on October 14, too late to help Swett's campaign. William W. Orme, Swett's law partner, commanding a regiment in southern Missouri, wrote home: "I think the country is ruined. The result of these elections will palsy the arm of the President." In Washington the President studied dispatches reporting a majority of 100,-

ooo votes of Illinois citizens for a constitutional provision to prohibit migration or settlement of Negroes and mulattoes in the State.

As Lincoln reckoned over losses and gains after the November elections he could see several nice balances. Though F. C. Sherman, the newly elected Mayor of Chicago, was a Democrat, his son was Colonel F. T. Sherman, commanded the Board of Trade Regiment, of proved valor in the field. The newly elected Republican Mayor of New York City was George Opdyke, a millionaire dry-goods merchant who had co-operated with Lincoln in emergencies. Also in the newly elected Congress were members such as William Ralls Morrison, a War Democrat who had organized the 49th Illinois regiment, led it at Fort Donelson, where he was wounded. As Morrison rode in an ambulance from the battlefield, he saw John A. Logan alongside, also wounded. Logan greeted him: "Bill, did you get a bad lick?" "Yes, John," growled Morrison, "I think I got enough to go home and beat Phil Fouke for Congress." He went home; his wounds healed; he returned to Grant's army leaving word that he would make no campaign for Congress. But his friends nominated and elected him. Then Grant refused to give him up and wrote on his resignation the notation: "Resignation not accepted. Colonel Morrison is too good a soldier to spare." The matter was carried to Lincoln, who knew Morrison of old. And Lincoln overruled Grant and brought to Washington a needed War Democrat with wound stripes.

Mrs. Carl Schurz called at the White House on November 10 and read to Lincoln a letter from her husband. Lincoln wrote a reply: "We have lost the elections; and it is natural that each of us will believe, and say, it has been because his peculiar views was [sic] not made sufficiently prominent. I think I know what it was, but I may be mistaken." Three main causes told the whole story: "1. The democrats were left in a majority by our friends going to the war. 2. The democrats observed this & determined to reinstate themselves in power, and 3. Our newspapers, by vilifying and disparaging the administration, furnished them all the weapons to do it with. Certainly, the ill-success of the war had much to do with this."

Lincoln corrected a statement of Schurz's that to be hostile to the Government seemed to be a title to consideration. "I have scarcely appointed a democrat to a command, who was not urged by many republicans and opposed by none. It was so as to McClellan. He was first brought forward by the Republican Governor of Ohio, & claimed, and contended for at the same time by the Republican Governor of Pennsylvania. I received recommendations from the republican delegations in Congress, and I believe every one of them recommended a majority of democrats."

A second letter from Schurz said the election result was "a most serious and severe reproof to the Administration" for placing the army in "the hands of its enemies." Schurz inquired of Lincoln, "What Republican has ever had a fair chance in this war?" and urged, "Let us be commanded by generals whose heart is in the war." These complaints set Lincoln to amplifying his views in another letter, sent to Schurz only three days after the President heard from him. He reasoned: "I certainly know that if the war fails, the Administration fails, and that I will be blamed for it, whether I deserve it or not. And I ought to be blamed if I could do better. You think I could do better; therefore you blame me already. I think I could not do better; therefore I blame you for blaming me." He proceeded: "I understand you now to be willing to accept the help of men who are not Republicans, provided they have 'heart in it.' Agreed. I want no others. But who is to be the judge of hearts, or of 'heart in it'? If I must discard my own judgment, and take yours, I must also take that of others; and by the time I should reject all I should be advised to reject, I should have none left, Republicans or others—not even yourself. For be assured, my dear sir, there are men who have 'heart in it' and think you are performing your part as poorly as you think I am performing mine."

The President wished to disparage no one, certainly not his sympathizers. "But I must say I need success more than I need sympathy, and I have not seen the so much greater evidence of getting success from my sympathizers than from those who are denounced as the contrary." This was abstract. He made it concrete for Schurz. "In sealing their faith with their blood, Baker and Lyon and Bohlen and Richardson, Republicans, did all that men could do; but did they any more than Kearny and Stevens and Reno and Mansfield, none of whom were Republicans, and some at least of whom have been bitterly and repeatedly denounced to me as secession sympathizers?" And after disposing of some trifling rumors, he signed as he rarely did, "Very truly your friend."

A few days later Lincoln sent a messenger with a note asking Schurz to come to the White House. The next morning at seven o'clock Schurz was shown into the upstairs room where the Cabinet met. Lincoln sat before an open grate fire in an armchair, his feet in large morocco slippers. Telling Schurz to pull up a chair and sit by the fire, he brought his hand down with a slap on Schurz's knee and said with a smile, "Now tell me, young man, whether you really think that I am as poor a fellow as you have made me out in your letter." Then, according to Schurz, he talked long to Schurz, who at first had a lump in his throat and came near tears—about criticisms, difficulties. And again he slapped Schurz on the knee, laughed loud and free, and exclaimed: "Didn't I give it to you hard in my letter? Didn't I? But it didn't hurt, did it? I did not mean to, and therefore I wanted you to come so quickly." Again he laughed, and added, "Well, I guess we understand one another now, and it's all right." And on Schurz asking if he should go on writing letters to the President, the answer came, "Why, certainly, write me whenever the spirit moves you." Schurz said of this morning meeting, which lasted an hour, "We parted as better friends than ever."

The whang of bitter and ridiculous contradictions, fixed in a horselaugh spelling, came from Artemus Ward. His funny pieces were so good that even newspapers hostile to Lincoln reprinted them. "This war hain't been too well managed," they quoted Artemus. "We all know that. What then? We are all in the same boat—if the boat goes down we go down with her. Hence we must all fight. It ain't no use to talk now about who *caused* the war. That's played out. The war is upon us—upon us all—and we must all fight. We can't 'reason' the matter with the foe—only with steel and lead. When, in the broad glare of the noonday sun, a speckled jackass boldly and maliciously kicks over a peanut stand, do we 'reason' with him? I guess not. And why 'reason' with those other Southern people who are tryin' to kick over the Republic? Betsy, my wife, says so too. I have great confidence in A Linkin. The old fellows heart is in the right place, and his head is clear. There's bin sum queer doin's by some of his deputies—civil and military—but let it pass. We must save the Union. And don't let us wait to be drafted. You've heard the showman. You've heard my wife, too. Me and Betsy is 1."

Yet the political scene was solemn for those with sons, brothers, and kin at the bloody fighting fronts. Said *Leslie's Weekly* in October: "Party feeling runs high in Ohio, and political meetings seem like half-battles. Men go to them armed as to a fray, and bloodshed often occurs. The Republicans and Democrats were never before so intolerant of each other, and old friends and neighbors of opposite politics no longer speak to each other when they meet on the streets and highways."

Looking at the North divided and torn with fury, Lincoln could easily dismiss the *Richmond Examiner's* erupting, "Lincoln the fiend—let history take hold of him, and let the civilized world fling its scorpion lash upon him!" It mattered little that far south in California the *Visalia Equal Rights Expositor* characterized the President as "a narrow-minded bigot, an unprincipled demagogue, and a drivelling, idiotic, imbecile creature." Nor that the same paper said of the Emancipation Proclamation author: "He will put a torch into the hands of every servant to burn down his master's house, a dagger in the grip of every footboy to stab to the heart the mistress that has given him food and shelter, a knife into the nurse's clutch to cut the throats of the children in her charge, teach every dependent to betray his employer, every menial to be an assassin, every footman to become a footpad."

A touch of dry, casual humor was not absent from a sentence of Lincoln's in that last month of 1862: "The civil war . . . has . . . radically changed, for the moment, the occupations and habits of the American people."

On his desk during latter 1862 Lincoln had the record of a military court sentencing 303 men to be hanged for murder, rape, arson. If he should agree with the court, he would sign his name to an order and the 303 men would be hanged, according to law.

On December 4 Welles wrote in his diary, "The Members of Congress from Minnesota are urging the President vehemently to give his assent to the execution of three hundred Indian captives, but they will not succeed."

Up on the border line of the wilderness settlements of the white pioneers in Minnesota, five white people were murdered by Sioux red men. Federal Government agents had predicted the clash for many years because of seizures of Indian lands by white men, because of slow payment of promised funds to Indian tribes, and the trickery of white traders against individual Indians. The "farmer" Indians had settled down to raising crops, hogs, and cattle, while the "blanket" Indians kept to the old roving life. When word came of the killing of five whites by redskins in August, the "farmer" and "blanket" Indians joined hands. Little Crow led the Sioux along the Minnesota River valley. They burned houses, violated women, slaughtered 490 whites, including women and children.

General John Pope, fresh from Second Bull Run, led his horsemen in pursuit, defeated Little Crow in battle. A military court put the Indians on trial, and partly in obedience to demands for revenge that swept the whole Northwest, the court sentenced 303 to be hanged.

Lincoln studied the record of the trial, and delayed. On December 6 he wrote the names of those to be hanged, such names as "Shoon-ka-ska" (White Dog), "Baptiste Campbell a Half-breed," "Tah-ta-kay-gay," "Wa-kan-tan-ka," "Pa-zee-kee-tay-ma-na," "May-hoo-way-wa." He came to the name of "Mah-pe-oke-na-jin," meaning "Who Stands in the Cloud," an Indian nicknamed Cut Nose, who had killed 18 women and children and 5 men.

One by one, in his own handwriting, Lincoln listed those he would hang, 38 of them. The others, he wrote, would be held till further orders, "taking care that they neither escape nor are subjected to any unlawful violence."

On Friday, December 26, at Mankato, Minnesota, the 38 were hanged, 3 of them in farmer coat and trousers, the others in head feathers, war paint, and moccasins. In one case the rope broke and had to be adjusted anew. In the case of another Indian, alive and breathing comfortably after ten minutes of hanging, the rope had to be correctly readjusted. Otherwise the hanging, technically, was a success. The *St. Paul Pioneer* noted: "The most touching scene on the drop was their attempts to grasp each other's hands, fettered as they were. They were very close together, and many succeeded. Three or four in a row were hand in hand, and all hands swaying up and down with the rise and fall of their voices." While they waited death they sang and shouted greetings and comfort to each other, said whites who understood the language, usually calling the name of some friend and telling him: "I'm here! I'm here!"

The President had insisted the trial record and reports from General Pope should "indicate the more guilty and influential of the culprits." In a message to Congress he pointed out that while in Southern and Border States Southern insurgents had stirred up Indian troubles, it was not definitely known who had fomented the Minnesota outbreak. "Suspicions, which may be unjust, need not to be stated." The President had learned, however, that Federal handling of Indians was not what it should be. He suggested a remodeling of the system and policy of treating Indians. "Many wise and good men have impressed me with the belief that this can be profitably done."

In the day's events came often the names of people and localities long ago familiar to the President. "Six citizens of Sangamon County, Illinois," said the newspapers one day, "were arrested by order of General Halleck, and sent to Alton, to be placed in close confinement, for aiding the escape of rebel prisoners from Camp Butler."

Into the White House one day, without notice beforehand, came Dennis Hanks. And the President gathered in his arms the cousin, the boyhood playmate. Then they talked about Dennis's errand to Washington as the chosen intermediary of fifteen Southern sympathizers arrested and held in Fort Delaware. They were part of a crowd at Charleston, Illinois, that clashed with a party of Union soldiers home on furlough. In the shooting 11 officers and privates were killed or wounded.

Lincoln with a sober face handed Dennis the official record of the Coles County Riot Cases. Then he sent Dennis to Stanton. But Dennis couldn't find the War Secretary, came back to the White House. Soon Stanton came in, and they talked about what should be done with the prairie farmer boys who took to shooting each other. Stanton said that they were criminals and "every damned one of them should be hung." Lincoln asked gently, "If these men should return home and become good citizens, who would be hurt?" Stanton held to it that they should take hard punishment.

Dennis Hanks visited with the President. He gave the news about Sally Bush Lincoln and about the Hankses and Johnstons. As one of the few living men who had called the President "Abe" in boyhood days, he called him "Abe" now. And as Dennis told it later, he said to the President after Stanton left the room, "Abe, if I's as big as you, I would take that little feller over my knee and spank him." Lincoln laughed, saying that Stanton maybe was a bigger man than he. And as Dennis told it in another version later: "I asked Abe why he didn't kick him out. I told him he was too fresh altogether." The President answered that it would not be easy to find another man to take Stanton's place. Dennis left the White House carrying a silver watch his cousin gave him as a memento. The President kept an eye on the case Dennis considered so important. The prisoners were taken out of the hands of the War Department, and by the President's direction those indicted were to be handled by the local civil authorities, and the rest let go.

Arriving back home in Coles County, Dennis related how "Abe gethered me in his arms," sketched Stanton as "a frisky little Yankee with a short coat-tail." In the President's office he had sat in a chair watching the procession of people, rich and poor, laying their causes before the Chief Magistrate. He had seen a good-looking woman in fine clothes who talked well and had winning ways. She wanted a relative let out of jail. She seemed to be making headway, bringing the President round to her way of looking at it. The President closed the interview by writing for her a couple of lines on a card. Before sealing it in an envelope, he showed Dennis what he had written. The card read, as Dennis recalled, "This woman, dear Stanton, is a little smarter than she looks to be." She had overplayed her hand. Later, as Dennis told it, came another woman, plain in looks and wear, with another story—father and son both in the army and the father in prison. She wanted the boy sent home to help. And the President wrote an order giving her what she wanted. She stepped away with tears in her eyes, not able to say thanks.

Sometimes the President telegraphed a pardon not knowing whether the firing squad had as yet shot the man. Barney D——, a Chicago boy in Mulligan's Irish Guards, got drunk, stabbed a comrade, and was sentenced to death by a court-martial. The comrade got well of his stab wounds and joined with regimental officers in signing a petition for pardon sent to the President. The general in command, however, had approved the findings of the court-martial. Only word from Lincoln could save the boy from being shot at sunrise. And the telegraph office was thirty miles away from their Missouri camp.

An often-told story it was in that regiment of how in their tents they listened that night for a messenger with a Washington telegram. Many did not sleep at all. Midnight passed, the stars grew pale as sunrise drew near, and the firing squad made ready to obey orders. Then they heard sentries stopping a horseman. They saw a messenger, mud-covered from head to foot, alongside a panting and foaming horse. He had a telegram which they said read as follows: "Colonel Mulligan. If you have not shot Barney D—— yet—don't. A. Lincoln."

Lincoln took time to write a long letter to Miss Fanny McCullough at Bloomington, Illinois, beginning: "It is with deep regret that I learn of the death of your kind and brave father, and, especially that it is affecting your young heart beyond what is common." He was an older man telling her that time would teach her, the years would help. "In this sad world of ours sorrow comes to all, and to the young it comes with bittered agony because it takes them unawares. The older have learned ever to expect it." She could not realize it now, but sometime she would be happy again. "The memory of your dear father, instead of an agony, will yet be a sad, sweet feeling in your heart, of a purer and holier sort than you have known before."

Many times Lincoln had met and talked with her father, a Black Hawk War veteran, a Republican-party man, circuit clerk and then sheriff of McLean County—a man who with one eye of no use and his right arm gone had at forty-nine years of age helped organize the 4th Illinois Cavalry and command it in battles under Grant. One evening after a day of "feeling out" the enemy for Grant's army forty miles away, Colonel McCullough was riding back toward Grant, the men tired after several clashes with Pemberton's infantry near Coffeeville, Mississippi. As he rode his horse on a slow walk, with his two orderlies and bugler just behind him, they came to a slope thick-grown with jack oaks. Suddenly from a horse's length in front came the cry, "Halt, get down and surrender!" Colonel William McCullough turned in his stirrups, facing his regiment, and called: "Fourth Cavalry! Left front into line! Charge!"

The timber blazed with rifle fire, McCullough fell bullet-riddled, having shouted his last command. His men broke through the trap set for them; no other life was lost, and his men said he had saved them at his own cost. Six days later under a flag of truce his body was brought through the enemy lines and taken home to Bloomington with an escort of officers.

Fanny McCullough could remember when she was a little girl and Lincoln used to hold her and her sister Nanny on his knees, telling their father, "These girls are not too old to be kissed."

CHAPTER 30

DECEMBER '62 MESSAGE
"WE CANNOT ESCAPE HISTORY"

THE President's message to Congress on December 1 of '62 opened with reports and comments on miscellaneous affairs and flowed on into discussions of the Union, slavery, the Negro. The argument for the Union mixed logic and sentiment: "A nation may be said to consist of its territory, its people, and its laws. The territory is the only part which is of certain durability." Laws change; people die; the land remains. He quoted: "One generation passeth away, and another generation cometh, but the earth abideth forever."

He pointed to "that portion of the earth's surface owned and inhabited by the people of the United States" as adapted to be the home of "one national family" and not for two or more. With the arrival of "steam, telegraphs, and intelligence," the modern inventions, there was still more advantage in having "one united people." He repeated paragraphs from his inaugural address: "We cannot remove our respective sections from each other, nor build an impassable wall between them. A husband and wife may be divorced and go out of the presence and beyond the reach of each other; but the different parts of our country cannot do this."

The State boundaries were not rivers and mountains, but mostly surveyors' lines over which people walk back and forth without knowing the lines are there. He pointed to the great interior region bounded by the Alleghenies on the east, Canada on the north, the Rockies to the west, and on the south by the line along which the cultures of corn and cotton meet. Already this region had 10,000,000 people and within fifty more years would have 50,000,000. "And yet this region has no sea-coast, touches no ocean anywhere." With separation of States it would have no outlet and would be cut off by physical barriers and trade regulations.

In previous messages Lincoln had not given so heavy an emphasis to the argument against secession in behalf of the Middle West from which he came. As the war had gone on he had found that the instinct for national solidarity was a deep one with the Midwestern people. Only six weeks before his message was delivered it was announced that Iowa was the first State to fill her quota under the call for 600,000 men; she had put every man into the field by voluntary enlistment, and all for three years of the war.

The President was voicing Iowa, Ohio, Kansas, and other States in declaring that "outlets, east, west, and south, are indispensable." All outlets would be better than any one that could be chosen. "True to themselves, they will not ask where a line of separation shall be, but will vow rather that there shall be no such line." Furthermore, outside regions were interested in access to "this Egypt of the West" without paying toll at the crossing of any national boundary. "In all its adaptations and aptitudes it demands and abhors separation. In fact, it would ere long force reunion, however much of blood and treasure the separation might have cost."

He pleaded: "Our strife pertains to ourselves—to the passing generations of men; and it can without convulsion be hushed forever with the passing of one generation."

From this almost mystic appeal for the saving of the Union he passed to a concrete proposal for cutting the knotted slavery problem. He asked that the Constitution of the United States be amended to provide that every State which abolished slavery at any time before January 1, 1900, should be paid for its freed slaves in United States bonds at a rate of interest and in sums to be agreed upon for each slave. Congress would be given express power to set aside money and otherwise provide for colonizing free colored persons. "Without slavery the rebellion could never have existed; without slavery it could not continue." He mentioned the diversity of opinion as to the African race. "Some would perpetuate slavery; some would abolish it suddenly, and without compensation; some would abolish it gradually, and with compensation."

He was aware emancipation would be unsatisfactory to the advocates of perpetual slavery, but the length of time involved under his plan "should greatly mitigate their dissatisfaction." He reasoned "most of those whose habitual course of thought will be disturbed by the measure will have passed away before its consummation." Another class would hail the prospect of emancipation but deprecate the length of time it would take, giving too little to the living slaves. He mentioned "the vagrant destitution which must largely attend immediate emancipation in localities where their numbers are very great."

Each State could work out its own plan, and no two States were obliged to proceed alike. Doubtless there would be objection to the Federal Government's paying for property to be destroyed, for "In a certain sense the liberation of slaves is the destruction of property." He replied to this objection with reminders. "It is no less true for having been often said, that the people of the South are not more responsible for the original introduction of this property than are the people of the North; and when it is remembered how unhesitatingly we all use cotton and sugar and share the profits of dealing in them, it may not be quite safe to say that the South has been more responsible than the North for its continuance."

His proposed measure would actually save money, would be prudent and economical, the President urged. "Certainly it is not so easy to pay something as it is to pay nothing; but it is easier to pay a large sum than a larger one. And it is easier to pay any sum when we are able, than it is to pay it before we are able. The war requires large sums, and requires them at once. The aggregate sum for compensated emancipation of course would be large. But it would require no ready cash, nor the bonds even, any faster than the emancipation progresses."

Before the end of the thirty-seven years in which the proposed emancipation could be accomplished, the country would have probably 100,000,000 of people instead of 37,000,000 to pay the cost. If the rate of population increase went on in the future as in the past, the country would in 1930 have 251,680,914 persons living in it, the President reasoned. Or if the European ratio of $73\frac{1}{3}$ persons to the square mile be used, the country's population would be 217,186,000. Reading the future, it would be hard to foresee exactly how much one huge example of secession, breeding lesser ones indefinitely, would retard population, civilization, prosperity. A growing nation can pay its debts more easily: "The proposed emancipation would shorten the war, perpetuate peace, insure this increase of population, and proportionately the wealth of the country."

Time would be on their side in the financing. "A dollar will be much harder to pay for the war than will be a dollar for emancipation on the proposed plan. And then the latter will cost no blood, no precious life. It will be a saving of both."

As to sending freed Negroes out of the country, he made his view clear again. "I cannot make it better known than it already is, that I strongly favor colonization. And yet I wish to say there is an objection urged against free colored persons remaining in the country which is largely imaginary, if not sometimes malicious." It was insisted Negroes would injure and displace white laborers. On this he gave warnings. "If there ever could be a proper time for mere catch arguments, that time is surely not now. In times like the present, men should utter nothing for which they would not willingly be responsible through time and in eternity."

And he argued: "Is it true, then, that colored people can displace any more white labor by being free than by remaining slaves? If they stay in their old places, they jostle no white laborers; if they leave their old places, they leave them open to white laborers. Logically, there is neither more nor less of it. Emancipation, even without deportation, would probably enhance the wages of white labor, and very surely would not reduce them." The freed slaves would surely not do more work because they were set free; they probably would do less, leaving more to be done by the white laborers. And if Negro labor were deported, even to a limited extent, wages would be raised for white labor. "Reduce the supply of black labor by colonizing the black laborers out of the country, and by precisely so much you increase the demand for, and wages of, white labor."

Some were afraid the freed Negroes would swarm forth and cover the whole land. "Are they not already in the land? Will liberation make them any more numerous? Equally distributed among the whites of the whole country, there would be but one colored to seven whites. Could the one in any way greatly disturb the seven?" He was asking.

And again, why should emancipation South send the freed Negroes North? "People of any color seldom run unless there be something to run from. Heretofore colored people, to some extent, have fled north from bondage; and now, perhaps, from both bondage and destitution. But if gradual emancipation and deportation be adopted, they will have neither to flee from. Their old masters will give them wages at least until new laborers can be procured, and the freedmen, in turn, will gladly give their labor for the wages till new homes can be found for them in congenial climes and a people of their own blood and race."

Every device of the art of persuasion that Lincoln had ever learned was put into this appeal. "The plan would, I am confident, secure peace more speedily, and maintain it more permanently, than can be done by force alone." It was the only way to end the war without victory, with something like permanent justice to all concerned. "All it would cost, considering amounts, and manner of payment . . . would be easier paid than will be the additional cost of the war if we rely solely upon force. It is much—very much—that it would cost no blood at all."

Permanent constitutional results would be achieved. First, two-thirds of Congress, and afterwards three-fourths of the States, would have to concur in the plan. This would assure emancipation, end the struggle, and save the Union for all time.

Was he getting too personal with the Senators and Congressmen? Did it seem too simple that he should assure them of a straight and clear way to cut through the vast labyrinth of interests back of the war? Perhaps so. For he felt it necessary to meet them on personal ground, as man to man. A gesture of true respect was required:

"I do not forget the gravity which should characterize a paper addressed to the Congress of the nation by the Chief Magistrate of the nation. Nor do I forget that some of you are my seniors, nor that many of you have more experience than I in the conduct of public affairs. Yet I trust that in view of the great responsibility resting upon me, you will perceive no want of respect to yourselves in any undue earnestness I may seem to display."

He pleaded further that whatever objection might be made, still the question would recur, "Can we do better?" An old chapter in national life was over and another begun. "The dogmas of the quiet past are inadequate to the stormy present. The occasion is piled high with difficulty, and we must rise with the occasion. As our case is new, so we must think anew and act anew. We must disenthrall ourselves."

Possibly never before had Lincoln used that word "disenthrall." It was not a familiar word with him. He seemed almost to imply that though men might give physical emancipation to others who were oppressed, each individual must achieve his own disenthrallment, rise out of his old into a new self. A subtlety of philosophic thought was in the added suggestion,

"In giving freedom to the slave, we assure freedom to the free—honorable alike in what we give and what we preserve."

He came to the last paragraph of his paper. He struck for motives to move men. "Fellow-citizens, we cannot escape history. We of this Congress and this administration will be remembered in spite of ourselves. No personal significance or insignificance can spare one or another of us. The fiery trial through which we pass will light us down, in honor or dishonor, to the latest generation."

He flung out a series of short sentences edging on irony. "We say we are for the Union. The world will not forget that we say this. We know how to save the Union. The world knows we do know how to save it. We—even we here—hold the power and bear the responsibility. . . . Other means may succeed; this could not fail. The way is plain, peaceful, generous, just —a way which, if followed, the world will forever applaud, and God must forever bless."

Thus ended the lesson. What came of it? No action at all except a faint groping toward compensated abolishment in the Slave State of Missouri. The Border States were too divided in viewpoint to act decisively. They were not yet cemented back into the Union. Lexington, Kentucky, on December 18 again fell into Confederate hands when Bedford Forrest's raiders drove off Illinois cavalry commanded by Colonel Robert G. Ingersoll of Peoria, Illinois.

The President's message was a compromise affair, aimed to throw sops of satisfaction into camps too hostile to be brought together for action. So said some. Others said he was riding a hobby, that as a Border State man he could not see that slavery must be destroyed root and branch first of all.

Yet even to many who differed from him, who could not agree that his plan was practical, he delivered an impression of sincerely struggling to lift before men's eyes a banner worth sacrifice. Some of his appeals went home and were widely repeated and discussed. "No personal significance or insignificance can spare one or another of us. The fiery trial through which we pass will light us down, in honor or dishonor, to the latest generation."

The jocular weekly journal in New York, *Vanity Fair*, printed a "Sonnit to A. Lincoln" which was "Rote Bi Mr. K. N. Pepper, Esq., on Reading of His Lait Messig." In twang and lingo it recited:

> Grait Magistrait! that gits up in the nite
>   All full ov Cair, & rites for severil Ours
>   Stiddy, & Meditaits with all his powrs—
> A tryin all the wile to doo wots rite
> to put a Stop to this unplesent Fite;
>   Youm all the peple wants, Grait Magistrait!
>   Your Egle vews you aint afraid to stait,
>   & you doant cair a cus for no man's spite!
> Ther aint a Patrit anywers but wot
>   Knows youre a dooin jest wot he wood doo—

Pervidin he wos down ther on the spot
& had the mind to see throo things like you.
Sum Patrits ony ses your projick *may* do—
but thats becos you know so much more'n wot they doo.

The President aimed the message chiefly at the South, and the Border States particularly. He purposely left out all discussion of the war itself, its battles, strategy, methods, sacrifices. Confederate newspapers naturally withheld from their readers such items of conciliation as the Northern President's saying, "It is no less true for having been often said that the people of the South are not more responsible for the original introduction of this property than are the people of the North." Yet the appeal did reach a host of Union men in the Border States.

Also this December message prepared the way for the Emancipation Proclamation to be issued on January 1, 1863—*if* the President should decide to issue it. The question was in the air whether he would. Radical antislavery men were saying the President would not dare issue the proclamation. Certain Border State men were saying he would not dare confiscate and destroy $1,000,0d0,000 in property values. Army men were not lacking to pronounce the judgment that such a proclamation would bring wholesale desertions, that entire companies and regiments would throw down their arms.

Senator Browning, so often a social guest at the White House, and so often a confidant of the President, wrote in his diary of the message: "It surprised me by its singular reticence in regard to the war, and some other subjects which I expected discussed, and by the hallucination the President seems to be laboring under that Congress can suppress the rebellion by adopting his plan of compensated emancipation."

CHAPTER 31

BURNSIDE—FREDERICKSBURG '62— MORALE

"ON to Richmond once more!" cried *Harper's Weekly* at the end of November of '62. The Army of the Potomac under Burnside would not go into winter quarters. It would fight, was the general prediction.

"General Burnside, as his portrait shows, is a very handsome man," said *Harper's*. "Tall and stout, with a flashing eye and a sonorous voice, he looks the very *beau idéal* of a soldier."

Nevertheless Burnside knew that he was not a great soldier, a true man for high command. When Lincoln's order came that he should take charge of the post from which McClellan was removed, he was "shocked," as he himself said.

Twice before Burnside had told Lincoln that he could not take it; he wasn't the man for it. He called two staff officers, listened to them for an hour and a half while they urged and pleaded with him to accept. He was "not competent to command so large an army," he told them. Not until he talked with McClellan that night did he make ready to command. McClellan told him that an order is an order, and he, as a soldier, had to obey. Congratulations were spoken to him on his new job, and he said, "That, sir, is the last thing on which I wish to be congratulated."

Burnside spent three days with McClellan; they sat up nearly all of one night going over the army organization and plans. Burnside said that on taking command he "probably knew less than any other corps commander of the positions and relative strength of the several corps of the army." Over and again he had told Lincoln and others that McClellan was the one man to head the army.

He was thirty-nine years old, a log-cabin boy, born at Liberty, Indiana, one of nine sons. His grandfather, James Burnside, was a soldier in a South Carolina royalist regiment and had his estate confiscated and given back to him in the Revolutionary War period. The family freed their slaves, to satisfy conscience, before moving to Indiana. After a seminary education, the boy Ambrose Everett Burnside learned the tailor's trade, opened a shop in Liberty and put up a sign: Myers & Burnside, Merchant Tailors. His father, a State senator, got him a cadetship at West Point, where he met McClellan, Stonewall Jackson, and others who rose in the army. He invented a breech-loading rifle. Under promises from Secretary of War Floyd of the Buchanan Administration that the army would use his rifle, he started a factory. Meantime Floyd saw more money in giving contracts to another factory—and Burnside went bankrupt. In New York he sold his army uniform and sword, and looked for work. He found it at $2,000 a year under George B. McClellan, vice-president of the Illinois Central Railroad. He paid his debts, became treasurer of the Illinois Central, with offices in New York.

Burnside's Rhode Island regiment was among the first troops to arrive in Washington, where President Lincoln often visited his camp. At Bull Run he commanded the brigade that opened the battle. His chief distinction was in leading a joint naval and military force that early in 1862 captured Roanoke Island with 2,600 prisoners and 32 guns. This won applause, an embellished sword from Rhode Island, and the thanks of the Massachusetts and Ohio legislatures.

When Burnside called at the White House Lincoln embraced him, and on Burnside's request promoted three of Burnside's brigadiers to be major generals. Commanding a corps, he was with McClellan on the Peninsula and through Antietam. When McClellan wrote to his wife about his official report on Antietam, he confided: "I ought to treat Burnside *very* severely, and probably will; yet I hate to do it. He is very slow; is not fit to command more than a regiment. If I treat him as he deserves he will be my mortal enemy hereafter. If I do not praise him as he thinks he deserves, and as I know he does not, he will be at least a very lukewarm friend." So both McClellan and Burnside knew that he was not fit for high command.

When a gathering of generals met him just after his latest promotion, they congratulated him. Carl Schurz wrote of that gathering; Burnside thanked them "and then, with that transparent sincerity of his nature which made everyone believe what he said, he added that he knew he was not fit for so big a command, but he would do his best." It was touching. "One could not help feeling a certain tenderness for the man. But when a moment later the generals talked among themselves, it was no wonder that several shook their heads and asked how we could have confidence in the fitness of our leader if he had no such confidence in himself?"

Why did Lincoln appoint him? It seemed to many that the choice lay between Burnside and Fighting Joe Hooker. Lincoln took the man who had been a friend of McClellan and who might inherit the goodwill of the army for McClellan. Also he had found Burnside free of the plot and intrigue of army politics, exceptional in loyalty and sincerity. And if Burnside failed, then Hooker would have a chance. And if Hooker failed, then still another general. It would be costly, brutal, to be changing generals one after another. Until an outstanding man appeared there was no other course. As Lincoln had told Congressman Kelley, "We shall see what we shall see."

Senators Chandler and Hale of Michigan and New Hampshire called to thank Lincoln for removing McClellan. The President knew this was merely an incident, a formality. He would go with the Senators till the next parting of the ways. "Mr. Lincoln told his visitors a story," said *Leslie's Weekly*, "the moral of which was so pointed that they have not repeated it, whereby 'Abe's last and greatest joke' has not been published."

The anti-McClellan group was holding sway. Fitz-John Porter was on trial, court-martialed on charges of disobedience, accused of helping to ruin Pope at Second Bull Run. A brave man, a highly competent officer, he was to be cashiered, drummed out of the army. Don Carlos Buell, in the West, was under investigation by a commission which was to let him out as a major general. Lincoln was keeping hands off, allowing the authorized functionaries to have their way with Porter and Buell. Pressure on him came from the War Department and from politicians as important as Oliver P. Morton, Governor of Indiana, who said Buell was impossible.

"We had a long familiar talk," wrote Browning in his diary. He had come back from a trip to Chicago, Quincy, Springfield, and gave the President the news. Browning dwelt long on the President's proclamations as to emancipation and habeas corpus. They revived old party issues, gave the enemy capital. "To this he made no reply." Browning added that the Republican party could not put down the rebellion; it required a union of all loyal men in the Free States to give success. "To all this he fully assented."

Browning asked whether Pope was a failure or had been sacrificed by the bad faith of his officers. Lincoln replied he knew no reason to suspect anyone of bad faith except Fitz-John Porter, and that he very much hoped an investigation would relieve him of suspicion, but that at present he believed Porter's disobedience of orders, his failure to go to Pope's aid, had occasioned defeat and deprived the North of a victory that would have terminated the war. McClellan then had done well in reorganizing the broken army and winning Antietam. But McClellan was too slow in movement, should have annihilated the enemy. "He concluded as he has in all conversations I have had with him about McClellan by saying that his great defect was his excess of caution."

Browning asked about a report he had heard in Illinois that Porter sent a dispatch to McClellan to hold on, they had Pope where they could ruin him, and that this dispatch fell into the President's hands. Lincoln replied there was no shadow of a foundation for such a story, no truth in it. Browning asked about Burnside's army, now before Fredericksburg, whether it was likely soon to accomplish anything. Lincoln replied that Burnside and Halleck had just left the room. They had been talking over the hazard of the army's crossing the Rappahannock River in face of a watchful enemy on the other side.

A few days later Browning again saw the President, and wrote in his diary that Lincoln told him among other things that there was never an army in the world, so far as he could learn, of which so small a percentage could be got into battle as ours. "That 80 pr cent was what was usual, but that we could never get to exceed 60." On his visit to the army after Antietam, a count of troops showed only 93,000 present; the muster rolls had 180,000.

Would Burnside get all of his men into the battle planned? Lincoln had heavy hours with that question. Many over the country shared the feeling John C. Gray, Jr., wrote from the field to his Boston friend John C. Ropes: "Either Burnside wins a victory this month and the country will be saved, or he does not and the country is lost."

Also Gray wrote, "I sometimes feel like changing the prayer of the old soldier into 'O God, if there be a God, save my country, if my country is worth saving!'" On the Rappahannock pickets of the two armies talked across the river. The *New York Tribune* correspondent heard a dialogue:

"Hello, butternut."

"Hello, bluebelly."

"What was the matter with your battery Tuesday night?"

"You made it too hot. Your shots drove away the cannoneers, and they haven't stopped running yet. We infantry men will run, too, one of these fine mornings."

"When are you coming over?"

"When we get ready to come."

In choosing the Fredericksburg locality for action Burnside was having his own way. "Somewhat to Mr. Lincoln's chagrin," noted Nicolay and Hay, "the first act of the new general was to object to the plan of campaign furnished to McClellan from Washington." Halleck had gone down to see Burnside about it, returned to Washington, laid the matter before Lincoln, who said Yes to Burnside's plan provided he "moved rapidly." Lincoln went down himself to see the army and Burnside. The President and the General had a long conference. Lincoln wrote Halleck a memorandum about it. Burnside could take into battle any day now about 110,000 men; he could not use more men than he had. "In all respects he is satisfied with officers and men" and "he thinks he can cross the river in face of the enemy and drive him away; but that, to use his own expression, it is somewhat risky." Lincoln wished the case to stand more favorably in two respects: "First, I wish his crossing of the river to be nearly free from risk; and, secondly, I wish the enemy to be prevented from falling back, accumulating strength as he goes, into his intrenchments at Richmond." He proposed an added force of 25,000 up the river, and still another force of 25,000 on the Pamunkey River, both protected by gunboats.

Lincoln outlined a plan for all forces to co-operate. "I think the plan promises the best results, with the least hazard, of any now conceivable." At the foot of this memorandum he wrote: "Note.—The above plan proposed by me was rejected by General Halleck and General Burnside on the ground that we could not raise and put in position the Pamunkey force without too much waste of time." It seemed almost as though Lincoln expected failure and wished a definite record on file as to his own judgment. Yet he was also putting it into the record that he was permitting his own judgment to be set aside in favor of trained professional men of war, West Pointers.

A few days before going down to see Burnside Lincoln had to deal with General Nathaniel P. Banks, no West Pointer at all. Banks had come up from bobbin boy in a cotton mill to be a lawyer, a Congressman, twice Republican Governor of Massachusetts, president of the Illinois Central Railroad, major general of volunteers. He had commanded the defenses of Washington and was now to head a secret expedition by sea to New Orleans, with 20,000 men for service in the lower Mississippi region. He had called on Lincoln, seemed to have everything he wanted in men and supplies. He was asking, however, for 1,000 horses.

"I have just been overwhelmed and confounded," Lincoln wrote Banks, "with the sight of a requisition made by you which, I am assured, cannot be filled and got off within an hour short of two months. I inclose you a copy of the requisition, in some hope that it is not genuine—that you have never seen it." If they had the horses and fodder for them, they did not have the ships to haul them. And if they had the ships, it would take two weeks to load them. And after all, where Banks was going he would have no use for horses. "When you parted with me you had no such ideas in your mind. I know you had not, or you could not have expected to be off so soon as you said. You must get back to something like the plan you had then, or your expedition is a failure before you start. You must be off before Congress meets. You would be better off anywhere, and especially where

INHERITED OBLIVION

UNIVERSAL ADVICE TO ABRAHAM.
DROP 'EM!

Harper's Weekly calls for summary removal of Stanton and Halleck you are going, for not having a thousand wagons doing nothing but hauling forage to feed the animals that draw them, and taking at least two thousand men to care for the wagons and animals, who otherwise might be two thousand good soldiers. Now, dear general, do not think this is an ill-natured letter; it is the very reverse. The simple publication of this requisition would ruin you."

Now came Fredericksburg, a trap. Lee with 72,000 men was ready and waiting for Burnside with 113,000. For a month Burnside had been waiting for pontoons to cross the river. While the pontoons were on the way Lee made arrangements. Burnside's columns crossed over. They found hills spitting flame and metal, a sunken road swarming with riflemen waiting human prey. "A chicken can not live on that field when we open on it," a Confederate engineer had told General Longstreet of the plain facing Marye's Hill. Meagher led his Irish Brigade of 1,315 up the hill and left 545 in the frozen mud. Hancock's division lost 40 of each 100 of its men. Between the fog of morning and twilight of evening 7,000 killed and wounded Union soldiers fell. The wounded lay forty-eight hours in the freezing cold before they were cared for. Some burned to death in long, dry grass set afire by cannon. Total Confederate losses were 5,309; Union, 12,653.

"Oh! those men! those men over there!" cried Burnside at his headquarters, pointing across the river. "I am thinking of them all the time." Out of his grief came an idea. He would take his old corps, the 9th, and lead it against the stone wall and 300 cannon of the enemy. But his men would not let him think of it.

In a rainy windstorm Burnside drew off his troops from Fredericksburg, back across the Rappahannock.

The next day General Hermann Haupt at the White House reported what he had seen and heard the day before at the headquarters of Burnside. Lincoln asked Haupt to walk with him to General Halleck's office on I Street, between Fifteenth and Sixteenth. There Haupt told again his story. It was nine in the evening. Haupt noted: "The President asked General Halleck to telegraph orders to Burnside to withdraw his army to the north side of the river. General Halleck rose and paced the room for some time, and then stopped, facing the President, and said decidedly, 'I will do no such thing. If such orders are issued you must issue them yourself. I hold that a General in command of an army in the field is the best judge of existing conditions.' The President made no reply, but seemed much troubled. I then remarked that I did not consider the situation as critical as the President imagined it to be." Haupt then explained the lay of land, bridges, disposition of batteries, troops, and gave the opinion that Burnside would withdraw his forces during the night. The President listened, and when Haupt finished he sighed. "What you say gives me a great many grains of comfort."

On this same night Senator Browning called, and wrote later in his diary that Lincoln "was troubled about the army, and did not know what was to become of it."

Also on this same night Lincoln sent for Henry Villard, now of the *New York Tribune*. By horse and boat travel and by evading army rules Villard had arrived in Washington and wired his newspaper a story so gloomy and disheartening that the editors in New York did not dare print it till other dispatches confirmed it. Villard arrived at the White House with Senator Henry Wilson. Near ten o'clock Lincoln shook hands with them in the reception room on the second floor. "I am much obliged to you for coming. We are very anxious and have heard very little." Villard gave a brief outline of the battle. For half an hour Lincoln questioned Villard.

"He was very careful," wrote Villard, "not to ask anything so as to imply criticisms of anybody, although I ventured to mingle a good deal of censure with my statements of facts. But his questions and the expression of his face showed that he believed I was aiming to tell the truth, and that he felt growing anxiety." Lincoln ended the interview by repeating his thanks to Villard, who made bold to say that every general officer he had talked with held the view that the army must be withdrawn. He suggested earnestly and politely that the President order Burnside to withdraw. The President took no offense, Villard noted, but remarked with a melancholy smile, "I hope it is not so bad as all that." Villard believed that a night attack with bayonets would drive 50,000 Union soldiers to the bank of the Rappahannock and leave Burnside's army open to destruction. Stonewall Jackson that same night spoke to Lee of such a drive, but Lee said his army was too exhausted.

Governor Curtin of Pennsylvania came to Washington, fresh from the Fredericksburg battlefield. Lincoln sent for him. At midnight in the White House they talked. "Mr. President, it was not a battle, it was a butchery," said Curtin of what he had seen. And as Curtin later told of this interview, "Lincoln was heart-broken at the recital, and soon reached a state of nervous excitement bordering on insanity."

As the Governor was leaving he took the President by the hand and tried to soothe him. "Mr. President, I am deeply touched by your sorrow, and at the distress I have caused you. I have only answered your questions. No doubt my impressions have been colored by the sufferings I have seen." He hoped matters would look brighter when later reports came in. He would give all he owned to rescue the President from "this terrible war."

Lincoln suddenly brightened, fetched a story out of his grief, as Curtin recalled it: "This reminds me, Governor, of an old farmer out in Illinois I used to know. He took it into his head to go into hog raising. He sent to Europe and imported the finest breed of hogs he could buy. The prize hog was put in a pen, and the farmer's two mischievous boys, James and John, were told to be sure and not let him out. But James, the worst of the two, let the brute out the next day. The hog went straight for the boys and drove John up a tree. Then the hog went for the seat of James's trousers, and the only way the boy could save himself was by holding on to the hog's tail. The hog would not give up his hunt nor the boy his hold. After they had made a good many circles around the tree, the boy's courage began to give out, and he shouted to his brother, 'I say, John, come down quick, and help me *let this hog go!*'" That was the story. He declared to Curtin: "Now, Governor, that is exactly my case. I wish someone would come and help me let this hog go."

The morale of the army was hard hit. The troops had shown all the courage asked for. But with such commanders above them, what could they do? They asked that. On review they were called to give a cheer for their general. They hooted. Some went above Burnside and blamed Lincoln. More officers resigned. More privates deserted.

Lieutenant William Thompson Lusk wrote to his mother: "Alas, my poor country! It has strong limbs to march, brave hearts to dare—but the brains, the brains—have we no brains to use the arms and limbs and eager

Harper's Weekly cartoons the President receiving the showman Phineas T. Barnum, who presents his midgets General Tom Thumb and Commodore Nutt with assurances they can win the war sooner than Welles, in the background, and Stanton crying, "Oh Lord my situation!!"

hearts with cunning? Perhaps Old Abe has some funny story to tell appropriate to the occasion. Alas, let us await the wise words of Father Abraham!"

Sick and tired of disaster and the "fools" in authority bringing disaster, Lusk wrote: "Mother, do not wonder that my loyalty is growing weak. I love the nation too well to willingly pardon the 'unfortunate Abraham Lincoln!' as the London *Times* so aptly calls him. I believe Burnside to be brave and honest. The President I doubt not is honest, but 'let the shoemaker stick to his last.' Let Lincoln turn his talents to splitting rails. I prefer

George McClellan to Abraham Lincoln, as Commander-in-Chief of the Army."

Burnside gave out a letter to Halleck taking all blame on himself, praising officers and men for gallantry, courage, endurance. "For the failure in the attack I am responsible," he wrote. The President, the Secretary of War, and the General in Chief had left the whole management in his hands, had even requested him not to be in haste. So frankly and completely did he take all blame on himself that newspaper correspondents started a rumor he did it under orders. They did not let the public know that this was Burnside's way, that it was this peculiar sincerity which had in part brought his appointment to command. They did not know that he had in effect predicted defeat, and helped bring it on, in saying so often and so positively that he was not fit for the high command.

The President issued an address to the Army of the Potomac: "Although you were not successful, the attempt was not an error, nor the failure other than accident. The courage with which you, in an open field, maintained the contest against an intrenched foe, and the consummate skill and success with which you crossed and recrossed the river in the face of the enemy, show that you possess all the qualities of a great army, which will yet give victory to the cause of the country and of popular government."

Was the President thinking one thing privately and saying something else publicly as to the issues of the battle? Not according to William O. Stoddard of the White House staff, who wrote: "We lost fifty per cent more men than did the enemy, and yet there is sense in the awful arithmetic propounded by Mr. Lincoln. He says that if the same battle were to be fought over again, every day, through a week of days, with the same relative results, the army under Lee would be wiped out to its last man, the Army of the Potomac would still be a mighty host, the war would be over, the Confederacy gone. No general yet found can face the arithmetic, but the end of the war will be at hand when he shall be discovered."

A week passed and Burnside made ready for another move, ordered three days' rations in the men's haversacks, twelve days' commissary supplies. He seemed to have another battle in mind. He was telling no one but his personal staff. Two generals, John Newton and John Cochrane, on leave of absence, called at the White House and informed Lincoln that the army was in bad shape for the big movement preparing. Lincoln telegraphed Burnside, "I have good reason for saying you must not make a general movement of the army without letting me know." Burnside went to Washington, asked Lincoln why he had sent such a dispatch. Lincoln told him all, except the names of his informants. These were hard days for Burnside, for on the same day that Lincoln warned him to make no forward movement, Halleck telegraphed him "to press the enemy," and some of his advisers urged him to win a victory and break the national gloom.

Lincoln now wrote Halleck that it was his wish that Halleck go to Burnside, examine Burnside's plan, talk with the officers, get their judgment, notice their temper. "Gather all the elements for forming a judgment of

THE BAD BIRD AND THE MUDSILL.

A cartoonist blames the mud

your own, and then tell General Burnside that you do approve or that you do not approve his plan. Your military skill is useless to me if you will not do this."

Halleck took this letter as insinuating. He asked to be relieved of his duties as General in Chief. Lincoln did not want to see Halleck go, as yet, and he did not want to hurt Halleck's feelings. So he "withdrew" the letter, took it back, writing the notation on it that it was "considered harsh by General Halleck." This being so, Halleck "withdrew" his request to be relieved.

Burnside wrote to the President, "It is my belief that I ought to retire to private life." Before the Committee on the Conduct of the War, Burnside testified that he had twice refused command of the army. "I did not want the command. I did not feel that I could take it."

Confidential conversations with the President were brought into broad daylight in the published report of the Committee on the Conduct of the War. The committee was showing that Lincoln as a dictator could not withhold from publication matters he would have preferred unpublished. "I could not imagine at the time what reasons the President had for sending this telegram," ran the printed testimony of General Burnside regarding wired instructions to halt a general movement into battle. "I came up to Washington, saw the President, and he frankly told me that some general officers of my command had called upon him, and represented that I was on the eve of another movement . . . and it would result in disaster. I was so much surprised at the time at what I heard that it did not make an active impression on my mind as to the exact words. But I am sure that was the nature of it; I think the President said that he had understood that no prominent officer of my command had any faith in the proposed movement. I then sat down and gave the President a detailed account of my plans for this movement. . . . The President still expressed misgivings." And to further representations of Burnside: "The President then said that he did not feel willing to authorize a continuous movement without consultation with some of his advisers. He sent for General Halleck and Mr. Stanton, and the matter was very fully talked over. He told them what they then for the first time heard of—that these officers had called upon him and made these representations to him, resulting in his telegram to me. I asked him if he would give me the names of these officers. He said he could not. I expressed some opinions in reference to what ought to be done with them, but at the same time said I should not insist upon having the names, as he had a right to withhold them. General Halleck expressed the opinion that officers making representations of that kind should have been dismissed, arrested at once, or something of the kind. My view was they should have been dismissed."

Burnside brought orders for dismissal of several generals and the shooting of three deserters to the President for approval. In case the orders could not be approved, "there was my resignation which he could accept," and that would end the matter forever.

THE PRESIDENT. I think you are right. But I must consult with some of my advisers about this.

BURNSIDE. If you consult with anybody, you will not do it, in my opinion.

THE PRESIDENT. I cannot help that; I must consult with them.

A day later the President said he intended to relieve two generals Burnside wanted out but, "General, I cannot accept your resignation; we need you." Burnside pleaded private business that had been neglected. "You can have as much time as you please for your private business, but we cannot accept your resignation." Also, ran Burnside's testimony: "I took the liberty of saying to the President that if all general officers whom it was found necessary to relieve should resign, it would be better for him, as it would free him from the applications of their friends. He said that was true. 'But,' said he, 'there is no reason for you to resign.' "

To the question, "Did the President know, at the time he sent you the telegraphic despatch suspending your movement, what you contemplated?" Burnside answered: "No, sir; nothing except that I had ordered a movement. I take it he knew that. General Halleck knew it. None of them knew my plans. In fact, General Halleck telegraphed me positively to send nothing at all over the wires in regard to my plans." The next witness, Major General John G. Parke, testified that he believed the proposed movement would have been a success. Senator Wade queried, "How long was the movement interrupted and delayed by reason of this order of the President?" Parke replied ten days or two weeks.

Then followed Generals Newton and Cochrane, whose sessions with the President had stopped the proposed movement. "I found myself in a very delicate position in this conversation with the President of the United States," said General Newton. "I did not wish to tell the President, and I did not tell him at any one time that the troops had no confidence in General Burnside. I could not tell him that, although, so far as I was concerned, that was my firm belief. But that was a most delicate thing for me to say, and therefore I had to go, as it were, around it indirectly, and that made the conversation very desultory, and there were a great many things said not necessary to the points. . . . I could not say directly to the President that the whole trouble was that the privates had no confidence in General Burnside. I had to get around that the best way I could. At first the President misunderstood our object in coming there, and thought we were coming to injure General Burnside, and even to suggest somebody for commander of the army. But the President was quickly assured that we had no man in our minds to command the army; that we had no intention to injure General Burnside; that our sole intention was to express the facts as to the condition of the army. . . . When we were about going away, the President expressed himself gratified with the conversation, and said that he hoped good would result from it."

Pressed as to what he specifically stated to the President, Newton said he emphasized the "dispirited" and the "dejected" condition of the troops. "The President made some remarks about portions of the army being demoralized, and would not fight. I told the President I believed they would fight. My meaning was this: that they would fight to a certain extent, but they would not fight with that rush and impetuosity absolutely demanded as the first element of success on the Rappahannock."

The committee examiners seemed to believe that Newton was holding back some things he had stated to the President. They pressed repeatedly for more of what he told the President. But he would not amplify.

That General Newton did tell the President of a worse morale than he would reveal to the Committee on the Conduct of the War was implied in his testifying: "I would have my hand cut off rather than to have this thing get into the papers. I thought it belonged to the army, and should be kept as still as possible, and told only in confidence." General John Cochrane followed, testifying that he gave the President particulars of the talk among privates and among subofficers from lieutenants to colonels in the Army of the Potomac; they were saying that it would be "dangerous folly" to cross the Rappahannock for another battle in view of how the army felt, "the relaxed state of resolution," "the alarming increase of desertions among the men and the unusual accumulation of resignations among officers."

CHAPTER 32

THUNDER OVER THE CABINET

THE doorkeeper of the Cabinet room interrupted a meeting one day to notify the President that Orlando Kellogg was outside and wished to tell the President the story of the stuttering justice. The President let Kellogg in, shook hands with him, turned to the Cabinet and said, "Gentlemen, this is my old friend, Orlando Kellogg, and he wants to tell the story of the stuttering justice." The President then asked his chosen counselors to lay aside business and hear Kellogg. Lincoln and he were Congressmen together in 1848.

Kellogg told the story. It was, as usual, rather easy for all concerned except Stanton and Chase, with the difference that Chase had to talk about it afterward as a somewhat disgraceful proceeding, lacking dignity. Chase did not like and could not learn to like it. Important transactions should not be conducted with such buffoonery.

The President, Chase told friends and callers, "seldom lost an opportunity to entertain himself and others in this direction." In letters and personal talks, steadily and systematically for months, Chase had been undermining opinion as to Lincoln. In his letters and diary records of his conversations ran a curious thread of dislike for the President and of fear and hatred of Seward. Chase spoke or wrote to Generals Cochrane, Hooker, Shields, Butler, and to John Sherman words that could only nurse suspicion and breed bad feeling. When he met Thurlow Weed, the New York Republican leader, he knew there was something of the attachment meant by Seward's once saying, "Seward is Weed and Weed is Seward." For Chase told Weed that while he did not doubt Seward's fidelity to progress and freedom, "his influence encouraged the irresolution and inaction of the President in respect to men and measures." Chase was aware that Weed would carry his words to Seward. His brief and most charitable judgment of Seward was "He is too much of a politician for me," and of Lincoln, "I feel that I do not know him." Always a prominent distinction between Chase as against Seward and Lincoln was that they dropped into the nonsensical and preposterous when they felt that way. This was to Chase a barrier.

When Chase told Senator Fessenden there was "a back-stairs influence" controlling the President, he knew that Fessenden understood no one else was meant than Seward. That Seward with his cigars, cynicism, wit and nonsense, was the most companionable human being in the Cabinet had no bearing. That Seward had held the leadership of the Republican party until Lincoln was nominated for President and was a past master of political science also had no bearing.

Joseph Medill of the *Chicago Tribune* was writing to Schuyler Colfax: "Seward must be got out of the Cabinet. He is Lincoln's evil genius. He has been President de facto, and has kept a sponge saturated with chloroform to Uncle Abe's nose all the while, except one or two brief spells, during which rational intervals Lincoln removed Buell, issued the Emancipation Proclamation, and discharged McClellan. There must be a reorganization of the Cabinet."

The Republican Senators held a secret caucus in the reception room of the Senate chamber on the afternoon of December 15, 1862. They discussed a letter written by Seward to Minister Adams six months before. Senator Sumner had taken the letter to Lincoln and asked him if he had approved it. Lincoln told Sumner that he had never seen the letter before. The newspapers got hold of this and raked Seward. The radicals claimed one more proof that Seward was a backstairs influence paralyzing the President's best intentions. Seward's offending letter had these words:

"It seems as if the extreme advocates of African slavery and its most vehement opponents were acting in concert together to precipitate a servile war—the former by making the most desperate attempts to overthrow the Federal Union, the latter by demanding an edict of universal emancipation as a lawful and necessary, if not, as they say, the only legitimate way of saving the Union."

The *New York Times* alleged that Seward never sent a dispatch to a foreign Minister without the President's seeing it. Judge James W. White of New York City, however, publicly stated that Seward had never laid the letter before Lincoln's eyes. Also White had written to Trumbull asking for more information on the subject, Trumbull answering that he did not have time to investigate, though it was clear that Seward was not voicing the President's policy. The letter under discussion was only one instance of the malign ways of Seward. So said speakers at the caucus. Disasters one after another were laid to Seward.

Senator Fessenden's memorandum of the meeting noted: "Silence ensued for a few moments, when Mr. Wilkinson [of Minnesota] said that in his opinion the country was ruined and the cause lost; that the Senate might save it but would not for the reason that Republican senators would not adopt any united and vigorous course. In his judgment the source of all our difficulties and disasters was apparent. The Secretary of State, Mr. Seward, exercised a controlling influence upon the mind of the President. He, Mr. Seward, had never believed in the war, and so long as he remained in the Cabinet nothing but defeat and disaster could be expected." Ben Wade followed, "particularly censuring the Executive for placing our armies under the command of officers who did not believe in the policy of the government and had no sympathy with its purposes." Senator Collamer found the difficulty in the fact that the President had no Cabinet in the true sense of the word. "It was notorious that the President did not consult his Cabinet councilors, as a body, upon important matters. Indeed, he, Mr. Collamer, had understood the President to have expressed the opinion that it was best to have no policy, and let each member of the Cabinet attend to the duties of his own department. Mr. Collamer believed this to be unsafe and wrong, and he thought measures should be taken to bring about a different state of things."

Fessenden said a duty was upon the Senate in the crisis at hand. It should, however, proceed cautiously and with unanimity or its action would alarm the country and weaken the hands of the Executive without effecting any ultimate good. "We should make an effort to see whether anything can be proposed which will receive unanimous concurrence." Fessenden said he had been told by a member of the Cabinet (not naming Chase) that there was "a back-stairs influence" which often controlled the apparent conclusions of the Cabinet itself. The same official had told him, within a day or two, that until within a few days he had supposed the Banks expedition was to co-operate with General Burnside, and was astonished when he found that was not the case.

Mr. Howard interrupted Mr. Fessenden and inquired if the name of that backstairs influence was William H. Seward. Mr. Fessenden replied that no name was given; Senators might draw their own conclusions.

Browning noted in his diary a point not set down in Fessenden's memorandum, that "old Ben Wade made a long speech in which he declared that the Senate should go in a body and demand of the President the dismissal of Mr. Seward. He advocated the creation of a Lieutenant Genl. with absolute and despotic powers, and said he would never be satisfied until there was a Republican at the head of our armies."

Senators Dixon and Howe said they could not single out Seward or any other Cabinet member for censure. "We should not proceed upon mere rumor. First ascertain the fact whether Mr. Seward did exercise an injurious influence upon the mind of the President. At present there was no proof of the fact." So says Fessenden.

Senator Grimes of Iowa, speaking to his resolution of want of confidence in the Secretary of State, said Seward should be removed from the Cabinet. Doolittle of Wisconsin believed that any vote would be unwise in the present state of affairs, and that a committee should be appointed to take up the whole subject and perhaps ask an interview with the President. Several Senators made the point that the Grimes resolution was merely intended to test the opinion of those present; it was not designed for the President or for the public eye. Fessenden again made it clear that unless the meeting was unanimous in action it might produce evil. "Other conversation followed, in which it was said that any vote we might pass would be known to the public, as experience had always proved." Browning rose to say that if Seward was for compromise instead of war he ought not to retain his place; "but I have no evidence the charges are true, and could not, therefore, vote for the resolution," said Browning. He asked for harmony instead of strife. "War between Congress and the President" was not desirable. By a vote of 16 to 13 the secret caucus adjourned to the next day.

Senator Harris opened the next day's caucus by offering a substitute for Grimes's resolution: "that in the judgment of the Republican members of the Senate, the public confidence in the present administration would be increased by a reconstruction of the Cabinet." This seemed to others no definite action. "The committee, if raised, would not know how far the Republican senators were agreed; any resolution was not, necessarily, to be communicated to the President, or any one else, but would be simply an expression of opinion among ourselves [the Senators]." Sherman of Ohio suggested the Harris resolution might be construed as meaning all members of the Cabinet should go out. He presumed this was not desired. "No one wished Mr. Chase to leave the Treasury, which he had managed so ably."

Mr. Sherman doubted whether changing the Cabinet would remedy the evil. The difficulty was with the President himself. He had neither dignity, order, nor firmness. His course would be to go directly to the President and tell him his defects. It was doubtful if that would do any good.

Senator Sumner now offered a substitute for Harris's resolution: that a committee be appointed to wait upon the President "and urge upon him changes in conduct and in the Cabinet which shall give the administration unity and vigor." After conferences and conversation this Sumner resolution and the two others were rearranged, slightly modified, and passed by a unanimous vote, except for King, not voting. A committee of nine was appointed.

Next day Senator Collamer read to the committee a paper by himself that he believed embodied its views. This with a few changes was adopted and was to be carried by the committee and laid before the President. Each member of the committee, however, would be free to express to the President on his own responsibility any individual opinion. Also it was understood that should changes be made in the Cabinet, no member of the committee would accept a place.

The secret caucus was not yet over when Senator Preston King stepped out and hurried to Seward's house, found his old colleague sitting in the library, and remarked: "Seeing how things were going, I did not stay for the last vote, but just slipped out to tell you, for I thought you ought to know. They were pledging each other to keep the proceedings secret, but I told them I was not going to be bound."

Seward chewed a cigar and said, "They may do as they please about me, but they shall not put the President in a false position." He called for pen and paper and wrote to the President: "Sir, I hereby resign the office of Secretary of State, and beg that my resignation be accepted immediately."

Five minutes later King put the note in the hands of Lincoln, who read it, looked up with surprise, and said, "What does this mean?" King told the story of the day. Later in the evening Lincoln stepped over to Seward's house, spoke his regrets to Seward, who remarked that it would be a relief to be free from official cares. "Ah, yes, Governor," said Lincoln, "that will do very well for you, but I am like the starling in Sterne's story, 'I can't get out.'"

An informal House committee of three called, Congressman Charles B. Sedgwick, a Syracuse, New York, lawyer writing to his wife: "I went to the President's with Thad. Stevens & Conklin to urge him to accept Seward's resignation. With his usual adroitness & cunning Seward, soon as he had tendered his resignation, began to send in his friends to the President to frighten him into refusing to accept it & I wanted to do what I could to counteract it. . . . I fear the President needs strengthening. . . . I think you had better not show this letter at present."

Browning called at the White House the next evening. The doorman said the President had left word he could not be seen. Browning sent a boy up to tell the President he wished to see him a moment. Lincoln soon came. Browning introduced a Mr. Wise, who would like to have some items of information for a biography he was writing. But the President was in no mood for talking to biographers that night. "I saw . . . that he was in distress," wrote Browning—"that more than usual trouble was pressing upon him. . . . We took our leave. When we got to the door the President called to me saying he wished to speak to me a moment. Mr. Wise passed into the hall and I returned. He asked me if I was at the caucus yesterday. I told him I was and the day before also. Said he 'What do these men want?' I answered 'I hardly know Mr President, but they are exceedingly violent towards the administration, and what we did yesterday was the gentlest thing that could be done. We had to do that or worse.' Said he 'They wish to get rid of me, and I am sometimes half disposed to gratify them.' I replied, Some of them do wish to get rid of you, but the fortunes of the Country are bound up with your fortunes, and you stand firmly at your post and hold the helm with a steady hand—To relinquish it now would bring upon us certain and inevitable ruin. Said he 'We are now on the brink of destruction. It appears to me the Almighty is against us, and I can hardly see a ray of hope.' I answered 'Be firm and we will yet save the Country. Do not be driven from your post. You ought to have crushed the ultra, impracticable men last summer. You could then have done it, and escaped these troubles. But we will not talk of the past. Let us be hopeful and take care of the future Mr Seward appears now to be the especial object of their hostility. Still I believe he has managed our foreign affairs as well as any one could have done. Yet they are very bitter upon him, and some of them very bitter upon you.' He then said 'Why will men believe a lie, an absurd lie, that could not impose upon a child, and cling to it and repeat it in defiance of all evidence to the contrary.' I understood this to refer to the charges against Mr Seward."

The committee of Senators was to call on him at seven o'clock that night, Lincoln told Browning—and added, "Since I heard last night of the proceedings of the caucus I have been more distressed than by any event of my life."

The committee came to the White House at seven o'clock that December night of '62, Collamer, Wade, Grimes, Fessenden, Trumbull, Sumner, Harris, Pomeroy, and Howard. "The President," Fessenden noted, "received us with his usual urbanity." Though Browning had seen Lincoln only a few minutes earlier wearing a troubled face and saying he was "more distressed" than on any other day in his life, he had now rallied an expression of ease, so much so that Fessenden took particular notice that Lincoln "received us with his usual urbanity."

The Senators were seated. Collamer rose and read his carefully prepared paper. Its main points were that the war for the Union must go on; the President should employ the combined wisdom and deliberation of his Cabinet members, who in turn should be unwaveringly for the war; it was unwise and unsafe to commit military operations to anyone not a cordial believer and supporter of the war as patriotic and just, rendered necessary by "a causeless and atrocious rebellion." These conclusions were respectfully presented for executive consideration and action, by Republican Senators "entertaining the most unqualified confidence in the patriotism and integrity of the President."

Ben Wade stood up, stocky, deep-chested. He said the war had been left in the hands of men who had no sympathy with it or with the cause. He commented on the late election returns from the Western States, implying that the appointment of Democrats to command the army had brought Republican defeat. "To this," noted Fessenden, "the President made no response." Grimes and Howard rose to say confidence in Seward was gone.

Fessenden began with saying the Senate believed in the patriotism and integrity of the President, disclaiming any wish to dictate to him as to his Cabinet. They claimed, however, the privilege, as his constitutional advisers, to tender him their friendly counsel. He dwelt on the public belief that the Secretary of State was not in accord with a majority of the Cabinet. Again, in the conduct of the war almost every officer known as an antislavery man had been disgraced. He instanced Frémont, Hunter, and others. It was time to change this condition of affairs. The war should be conducted by its friends. The Administration must protect itself. The Democrats were using General McClellan for party purposes. McClellan was now busy making an attack upon the Government, which had the power to show the falsity of his statements, and it was due to the country and the party that the Government should make known the facts.

"At this point the President rose, said the explanation was very simple, produced a large bundle of papers and read several letters to McClellan, showing that McClellan had been sustained by the government to the utmost of its power. A half hour was thus spent, and Fessenden did not resume his remarks."

Sumner rose to say to the President that Seward in official correspondence at home and abroad had subjected himself to ridicule, had made statements offensively disrespectful to Congress, and had written dispatches which the President could not have seen or assented to. Sumner gave an instance. The President replied that it was Seward's habit to read the dispatches to him before they were sent, but they were not usually submitted to a Cabinet meeting. He did not recollect the letter to which Sumner referred.

"Some three hours were spent in conversation with the President," Fessenden noted, "but no definite action was discussed. The President said he would carefully examine and consider the paper submitted, expressed his satisfaction with the tone and temper of the committee, and we left him in apparently cheerful spirits, and so far as we could judge, pleased with the interview."

The actions against Seward had now taken three days. Tuesday and Wednesday the Republican Senators had caucused. Thursday their committee had organized and had gone to Lincoln for their evening interview.

Lincoln called a Cabinet meeting for half-past ten Friday morning, December 19. All the members came except Seward. The President told them that what he had to communicate should not be the subject of conversation elsewhere. He then informed them that a positive and pointed opposition to Seward had shown itself in a caucus of Republican Senators, who were unanimous, with one exception, for Seward's removal. Senator King, a personal friend of Seward, had felt it his duty to inform the Secretary, who had at once sent to the White House his resignation to the President. A committee of Senators had called to interview him on Wednesday evening.

Welles in his diary tried to reproduce in substance the remarks of the President on what took place between him and the committee: "The President says the evening was spent in a pretty free and animated conversation. No opposition was manifested towards any other member of the Cabinet than Mr. Seward. Some not very friendly feelings were shown towards one or two others, but no wish that any one should leave but the Secretary of State. Him they charged, if not with infidelity, with indifference, with want of earnestness in the War . . . with many things objectionable, and especially with too great ascendency and control of the President and measures of administration. This, said the President, was the point and pith of their complaint."

Welles recorded in his diary no touch of humor or irony in the President's report. But one of Lincoln's secretaries noted his telling the Cabinet of the Senate committee members: "While they seemed to believe in my honesty, they also appeared to think that when I had in me any good purpose or intention Seward contrived to suck it out of me unperceived."

The President wished the Cabinet to know that he had told the committee he was shocked and grieved at "this movement." He had selected his Cabinet in view of impending difficulties and of all the responsibilities upon himself; he and the members had gone on harmoniously, whatever had been their previous party feelings and associations. There had never been serious disagreements, though there had been differences. In the overwhelming troubles of the country, which had borne heavily upon him, he had been sustained and consoled by the good feeling and the mutual and unselfish confidence and zeal that pervaded the Cabinet.

He hoped there would be no combined movement on the part of other members of the Cabinet to resist this assault. The movement was uncalled for. Admitting all that was said, there was no such charge as should break up or overthrow a Cabinet. Nor was it possible for him to go on with a total abandonment of old friends.

After various remarks from Cabinet members, the President requested that the Cabinet should, with him, meet the committee of Senators. "This," noted Welles, "did not receive the approval of Mr. Chase, who said he had no knowledge whatever of the movement, or the resignation, until since he had entered the room. Mr. Bates knew of no good that would come of an interview. I stated that I could see no harm in it, and if the President wished it, I thought it a duty for us to attend. The proceeding was of an extraordinary character. Mr. Blair thought it would be well for us to be present, and finally all acquiesced." The President named half-past seven that evening for the interview.

Meanwhile on that Friday the big outside world knew nothing of this movement which had already shaken the Cabinet and threatened to wreck it. Rumors were spreading, however, that Seward had resigned. "On Thursday morning," wrote Fessenden, "I received information from a sure quarter that this rumor was well founded, but the fact was not generally known. The President, my informant stated, was much troubled about it."

Old Francis P. Blair came that Friday to a Senate lobby, sent for Senator Browning, and told the Senator that Preston King was the best man in the country for Secretary of War and that McClellan ought to be at the head of the army, that the President had ruined himself by his proclamations, that he (Blair) had used his influence with the President to prevent the issuing of the proclamations, but to no avail. Afterwards there came to Browning's seat in the Senate the Baltimore Unionist, a lawyer of national reputation, Reverdy Johnson. He "told me Mr Seward had resigned," wrote Browning, "and said we would go to the Devil unless a new cabinet was formed of the best material in the Country and the reins of government were held with a steadier hand than they had been. Said the cabinet must be constructed anew, as no one fit for the place would go into it with the Secretaries who remained."

Browning spoke regrets over Seward's resigning, said he did not know who could fill his place. Reverdy Johnson replied that Seward was the best man in America for the place, but he had resigned; "now there must be an entire reconstruction, and [he] urged that I should go up immediately and talk with the President upon the subject" They talked about proper men for the new Cabinet, Browning suggesting Collamer for Secretary of State, Ewing of Ohio for Secretary of the Treasury, General Banks for Secretary of War. Reverdy Johnson agreed except that he would prefer General John A. Dix for War Secretary.

"I did not wish to thrust my opinions unsolicited upon the President, and did not go," wrote Browning, "but in the course of the afternoon I met him between the White House and the War Department, and remarked to him that I had heard that Mr Seward had resigned, and asked him if it was so. He replied that he did not want that talked about at present, as he was trying to keep things along. This was all that passed He cant 'keep them along.' The cabinet will go to pieces." And Browning talked that evening with Thomas Ewing, an old-line Whig, former Secretary of the Treasury and one-time United States Senator from Ohio. Ewing said he had no doubt that Chase was at the bottom of all the mischief, and was setting the radicals on to assail Seward. "He also suggested Mr Winthrop as a proper person for Secretary of State," wrote Browning.

Seward was no longer to be found at his desk in the Department of State. Visitors at his house saw him packing up books and papers preparing to go home to Auburn, New York. This was the second time he had resigned, but the other time the President had not yet been inaugurated.

When the committee of Senators came to the White House that Friday night they did not know that Lincoln had arranged for them to meet the Cabinet. They did not know that they were to sit face to face in a three-cornered session with the President and the counselors from whom, it was so gravely alleged, he never took counsel.

The committee, with all but Wade, and the Cabinet members went up to the President's office at half-past seven. He told them that he had invited the Cabinet, with the exception of Seward, to meet the committee for a free and friendly conversation in which all, including the President, should be on equal terms. He wished to know if the committee had any objection to talking over matters with the Cabinet. "Having had no opportunity for consultation, the committee had no objection," noted Fessenden.

The President opened with a speech admitting that Cabinet meetings had not been very regular, excusing that fact for want of time. He believed that most questions of importance had received reasonable consideration, was not aware of any divisions or want of unity. Decisions, so far as he knew, had general support after they were made. Seward, he believed, had been earnest in prosecution of the war, had not improperly interfered, had generally read to him the official correspondence, had sometimes consulted with Mr. Chase. The President then called on members of the Cabinet to say whether there had been any want of unity or of sufficient consultation.

Secretary Chase now protested earnestly, a little hotly, that he certainly would not have come to the meeting if he had known he was going to be arraigned before a committee of the Senate. He went on to say that questions of importance had generally been considered by the Cabinet, though perhaps not as fully as might be desired, that there had been no want of unity in the Cabinet but a general acquiescence on public measures; no member opposed a measure once decided on.

Fessenden was listening. He saw that Chase was not now saying in the three-cornered conference what he had been saying in private chats with Senators nor what he had been writing in letters. So Fessenden rose to repeat what he had two nights before told the President, that the Senators came with a desire to offer friendly advice and not to dictate to the President. In answer to Mr. Chase's remark about being arraigned, Fessenden reported what had taken place between the President and the committee as to Cabinet meetings. Fessenden believed that all important questions should be discussed with the Cabinet, though the President was not bound by any Cabinet decision and could act on his own judgment. What the Senators were doing had not originated with them. "It was no movement of ours, nor did we suspect or come here for that purpose"—meaning for the purpose of dictating to the President.

Collamer said united counsels were needed. Blair filed the opinion that the Cabinet ought to have no voice except when the President called for it. Grimes said again he had lost confidence in Seward. Sumner dragged out Seward's foreign correspondence again. Trumbull pointed to the President's own admissions that important questions were decided without full consideration. Bates cited the Constitution to show that the President need not consult his Cabinet unless he pleased. Incidentally Bates referred to himself as "a garrulous old man," which Fessenden felt was quite so.

More talk followed. The hours were passing. "The President made several speeches in the course of the evening," wrote Fessenden, "and related several anecdotes, most of which I had heard before." Welles noted: "The President managed his own case . . . and showed great tact, shrewdness, and ability, provided such a subject were a proper one for such a meeting and discussion. I have no doubt he considered it most judicious to conciliate the Senators with respectful deference, whatever may have been his opinion of their interference."

After hours of threshing over the issues and getting better acquainted, the President asked the Senators to give him their opinions as to whether Seward ought to leave the Cabinet, and to advise him what their constituents thought about it. Collamer said he did not know how his constituents felt and he would not go beyond the paper he had handed the President. Grimes, Trumbull, Sumner, said Seward should go. Harris said No, that Seward's removal would be a calamity to the Republican party of New York. Pomeroy said he had once studied law in Seward's office but his confidence in Seward was gone. Howard said he had not spoken during the evening and would not. Fessenden told the President: "I am not instructed to answer for my constituents. Nor do I think it proper to discuss the merits or demerits of a member of the Cabinet in the presence of his associates—especially when I am not informed how far our opinions may be regarded."

Chase suggested, "The members of the Cabinet had better withdraw." They did so. It was midnight. Senators Collamer and Harris took their hats and also went away. Fessenden then noted this conversation:

FESSENDEN. You have asked my opinion about Seward's removal. There is a current rumor that Mr. Seward has already resigned. If so, our opinions are of no consequence on that point.

THE PRESIDENT. I thought I told you last evening that Mr. Seward had tendered his resignation. I have it in my pocket, but have not yet made it public or accepted it.

FESSENDEN. Then, sir, the question seems to be whether Mr. Seward shall be requested to withdraw his resignation.

THE PRESIDENT. Yes.

FESSENDEN. As the fact of his resignation cannot be concealed, and its cause cannot but be well understood, my opinion is that all the harm which can be done in dividing the Republicans of New York has been done. The breach has been made and the withdrawal of his resignation will not heal it. Under these circumstances I feel bound to say that as Mr. Seward has seen fit to resign, I should advise that his resignation be accepted. Mr. Seward lost my confidence before he became Secretary of State, and had I been consulted I should not have advised his appointment.

THE PRESIDENT. I had no opportunity to consult you.

FESSENDEN. No, sir; but my opinion at the time was, as expressed to Mr. Trumbull, that before forming your Cabinet you should come to Washington, where you could advise with senators. I am sorry you did not do so. Do you wish us to advise with our fellow-senators on the point suggested?

THE PRESIDENT. I think not.

The Senators left the White House. One of them, Trumbull, turned before going out, walked rapidly back to the President, and told him rather hotly that the Secretary of the Treasury had talked in a different tone the last time they had spoken. Fessenden wrote in his memorandum as to this Friday evening conversation: "It struck me that Mr. Chase seemed to have very much modified his opinions, often previously expressed to me, as to Mr. Seward's influence on the mind of the President and the want of unity in the Cabinet."

Browning asked Senator Collamer how Secretary Chase could venture to tell the committee that the Cabinet got along fairly well when he had been saying the opposite to the Senators privately. "He lied," answered Collamer.

It was one o'clock Saturday morning. The session had lasted five and a half hours. "It was observed by the Senators," wrote Fessenden, "that the President did not appear to be in so good spirits as when we left him on the preceding evening, and the opinion was expressed that he would make no change in his Cabinet. He said he had reason to fear 'a general smash-up' if Mr. Seward was removed, and he did not see how he could get along with an entire change in his Cabinet. To an inquiry as to the grounds of his apprehension, he replied that he thought Mr. Chase would seize the occasion to withdraw, and it had been intimated that Mr. Stanton would do the same, and he could not dispense with Mr. Chase's services in the Treasury just at this time. Everybody in Congress and out was entirely satisfied with Mr. Chase, and if he withdrew it would be because he desired a pretext for doing so."

Welles found the President with the Governor of Kentucky just after breakfast on Saturday morning. When the Governor left, Welles told the President that no combine of Senators should dictate to the Executive. "I informed the President I had pondered the events of yesterday and last evening," wrote Welles, "and felt it incumbent on me to advise him not to accept the resignation of Mr. Seward." Welles differed with Seward on many things, but they were matters that did not call for senatorial interference. He gave the President many conclusions he had arrived at after pondering, one that "this scheme should be defeated; that, so believing, I had at the earliest moment given him my conclusions."

"The President was much gratified," wrote Welles; "said the whole thing had struck him as it had me, and if carried out as the Senators prescribed, the whole Government must cave in. It could not stand, could not hold water; the bottom would be out."

Lincoln and Welles agreed that while Seward's resignation should not be accepted by the President, neither should Seward get up on his dignity and press for immediate acceptance. Welles said he would now go over and see Seward. Lincoln "earnestly" desired him to do so. Lincoln rang a bell and had a messenger sent to notify Chase that the President wished to see him. And the little whiskered Secretary of the Navy went to the house of the resigned Secretary of State, whom he personally disliked. Welles found Seward at home, not exactly cool. Seward was telling War Secretary Stanton he would be next to go—there was already something about it in the *New York Herald*. Stanton said he had seen it; Welles had not. Seward brought the *Herald*, got Welles to read it, but Stanton took the newspaper away for himself. Then Seward began telling Welles how he had resigned. Stanton left, saying he had work to do.

Seward was pleased at Welles's report of his interview with the President. He said that "if the President and country required of him any duty in this emergency he did not feel at liberty to refuse it. He spoke of his long political experience; dwelt on his own sagacity and his great services; feels deeply this movement, which was wholly unexpected. . . . He is disappointed that the President did not promptly refuse to consider his resignation and dismiss . . . the [Senate] committee." Seward felt that the matter should be disposed of in one way or the other at once.

Back at the White House, Welles met Chase and Stanton in the President's office. Welles told them that he was decidedly against accepting Seward's resignation. Neither would give a direct answer. Stanton earlier in the day had met Fessenden and told the Senator that he was impressed the night before with the dignity and propriety of the Senate and disgusted with the Cabinet, that what the Senators had said about the Cabinet's way of doing business was true, and he was not going to lie about it, that he was ashamed of Chase, for Chase knew better.

The President came in, asked Welles if he "had seen the man." Welles said Yes and the man was agreed. The President turned to Chase. "I sent for you, for this matter is giving me great trouble."

Chase said he had been painfully affected by the meeting last evening, which was a total surprise to him. Then after some vague remarks he told the President that he had written his resignation as Secretary of the Treasury.

"Where is it?" asked Lincoln, his eyes lighting up.

"I brought it with me," said Chase, taking the paper from his pocket. "I wrote it this morning."

"Let me have it," said the President, reaching his long arm and fingers toward Chase, who held on to the paper and seemed sorry to part with it.

Chase hesitated at letting it go. He seemed to have something further to say before giving up the document. But the President was eager, did not notice Chase, took the letter, broke the seal, and read it.

"This," said Lincoln, holding up the letter toward Welles with a triumphal laugh, "cuts the Gordian knot." His face of worry had changed to satisfaction. "I can dispose of this subject now without difficulty," he added as he turned on his chair. "I see my way clear."

Stanton was sitting with Chase, facing the fireplace. Stanton rose to say: "Mr. President, I informed you day before yesterday that I was ready to tender you my resignation. I wish you, sir, to consider my resignation at this time in your possession."

"You may go to your Department," said Lincoln. "I don't want yours. This," holding out Chase's letter, "is all I want; this relieves me; my way is clear; the trouble is ended. I will detain neither of you longer."

Soon all three left the room, and Lincoln was alone.

When Senator Harris called soon after, Lincoln was beaming and cheerful, saying, "Yes, Judge, I can ride on now, I've got a pumpkin in each end of my bag." (When farmers rode horseback to market two pumpkins in the bag thrown over the horse made a balanced load.) As the anecdote reached Senator Fessenden, the President had said: "Now I have the biggest half of the hog. I shall accept neither resignation."

The diary of Admiral John A. Dahlgren for the day of December 22, 1862, threw flashlights on a swift, impetuous Lincoln—a swearing President

—a statesman meeting issues with wit and decisive grasp. The very sober Admiral wrote:

"The President sent for me about ten. Entering his cabinet room, Forney, secretary of the Senate, was in conversation with him, and saying that it would be well to publish report of committee on fight at Frederick, as the people were excited.

"The President answered warmly, 'that he did not want to swear, but why will people be such damned fools?' Forney remarked, going, 'that he hoped the President would not let Mr. Chase resign,' and added, 'nor Mr. Seward.' The President paused and reddened, then said suddenly, '*If one goes, the other must; they must hunt in couples.*' So Forney made his bow."

The President now sent polite notes to Seward and Chase that he could not let them quit and must ask them to take up again their duties as Secretaries. Seward replied that he had "cheerfully resumed" his functions. Chase held off. "My reflections strengthen my conviction that being once more honorably out of the Cabinet, no important public interest requires my return to it." He might yield his judgment. "I will sleep on it." Chase was a handsome man, serious, stubborn, jealous, ambitious. "A resignation is a grave act," he assured the President; "never performed by a right-minded man without forethought or with reserve. I tendered mine from a sense of duty to the country, to you, and to myself; and I tendered it to be accepted."

And something else rankled in Chase's bosom. He was afraid that Lincoln, though he considered the President of no high intelligence, had a sinister cunning that had outguessed and outwitted him. His pride was hurt. He wrote to the President: "Will you allow me to say that something you said or looked, when I handed you my resignation this morning, made on my mind the impression that having received the resignations both of Governor Seward and myself, you felt that you could relieve yourself from trouble by declining to accept either, and that this feeling was one of gratification?" However, after a Sunday of deep thinking Chase decided he would go back to his old place, ready nevertheless to retire at any moment the President's judgment indicated it was best for the Administration.

The Republican Senators caucused Monday, December 22, and heard the report of their committee, whose duty was over. Browning, however, felt called on to go to the President that night and suggest that all elements of loyalty to the Administration should be represented in a new Cabinet to be formed, including such men as Ewing of Ohio, Banks of Massachusetts, Guthrie of Kentucky. The President replied that he could not afford to make a new Cabinet. "He . . . said that a cabinet composed of the class of men I had suggested would give him trouble, and be in his way on the negro question." Browning argued at length. The President said he believed he would rather try and get along with the Cabinet he had than try a new one. Browning was informed that Chase partisans had planned to force Chase on the President as Premier and form a Cabinet of ultraradicals. "He said with a good deal of emphasis that he was master, and they should not do that."

Commenting on the crucial point in this affair, Lincoln said at a later time: "I do not see how I could have done better. I am sure it was right. If I had yielded to that storm and dismissed Seward the thing would all have slumped over one way, and we should have been left with a scanty handful of supporters. When Chase gave in his resignation I saw that the game was in my hands, and I put it through."

A letter came to Sumner from an admirer, D. Y. Kilgore at Evansville, Wisconsin, saying: "When the news came here of Seward's resignation and your appointment to the Portfolio of State there was rejoicing in the heart of all earnest Republicans. . . . The next day all our rejoicing ended."

Exactly a week after the first secret caucus of Republican Senators the Cabinet, with all members, met the President as though nothing had happened. Seward was feeling very happy, Welles noted. Chase was pale, said he was ill, had been for weeks. They were resuming the old order of things, with Seward useful, important, but meddlesome, fussy, and sudden in shifts of policy and viewpoint, with Chase trying to hide his irritations.

"Seward, assuming to be helmsman, has, while affecting and believing in his own superiority," wrote Welles, "tried to be patronizing to all, especially soothing and conciliating to Chase, who sees and is annoyed by it. The President feels that he is under obligations to each, and that both are serviceable. He is friendly to both. He is fond of Seward, who is affable; he respects Chase, who is clumsy. Seward comforts him; Chase he deems a necessity."

Fessenden sized up his view in a letter to his family, ending: "Yet such is the anomalous character of the President that no one can tell what a day may bring forth."

Uneven, irregular, rather baffling, so Fessenden found the President; he could not read what was coming next from Lincoln, and it troubled him. Fessenden had clean hands and a rare sense of justice in politics, owning himself with a decency, with a record quite spotless. It was too bad that so good a man as Fessenden, and others like him, should misread Lincoln. Yet the evils of gossip, greed, jealousy, and personal ambition, amid furious and rushing events, had created various unfavorable impressions of the President. Fessenden had his impression and gave it to his friend, John Murray Forbes, who wanted to see Fessenden in the Cabinet.

"No friend of mine should ever wish to see me there," wrote Fessenden, for in the Cabinet no man could honestly be himself because of the interference of the President, and "You cannot change the President's character or conduct, unfortunately; he remained long enough at Springfield, surrounded by toadies and office-seekers, to persuade himself that he was specially chosen by the Almighty for this crisis, and well chosen. This conceit has never yet been beaten out of him, and until it is, no human wisdom can be of much avail. I see nothing for it but to let the ship of state drift along, hoping that the current of public opinion may bring it safely into port."

Forbes read this from Fessenden, and immediately replied that he still believed Fessenden ought to be in the Cabinet, health permitting. Forbes began his letter: "I must differ from you about the President. He has been in the hands of a vacillating, undecided man like Seward!"

Hay in his diary was to give Lincoln's cool comment on his own failure to keep cool in one further development. Hay quoted the President: "When I had settled this important business at last with much labor & to entire satisfaction, into my room one day walked D. D. [David Dudley] Field & George Opdyke and began a new attack upon me to force me to remove Seward. For once in my life I rather gave my temper the rein and I talked to those men pretty damned plainly. Opdyke may be right in being cool to me. I may have given him reason this morning."

Seward and Chase had a daily grasp of special and shifting situations; in diplomatic matters the President often told callers, "You'll have to see Seward about that," or on a financial detail, "That is for Chase to say—you go over and see him." A lawyer, orator, politician, not an accredited financier, Chase sat daily in conference on money, cash available, credit balances, taxes present and future, government income from tariff duties and from direct and indirect levies, the war cost of $2,000,000 a day. Chase was reporting in December, 1862, that the Government would have to borrow $600,000,000 the next year.

By a single act of Congress that year, wherein the views of Chase were met, the "greenbacks" came, paper money to the amount of $150,000,000; it was "lawful money," legal tender for all debts, public and private, except the tariff on goods entering the country and the Government's own interest on its own debt. Government bondholders were paid in gold. And gold was hoarded, sent into hiding by paper money. The same act of Congress authorized a $500,000,000 bond issue, the Government to sell to the people, investors, banks, that amount of its promises to pay. The figures were vast, the bookkeeping complex, the parallel columns setting forth debts, income at hand and expected, running into ever higher tabulations.

Lincoln did not pretend grasp of it; long ago he had said he had "no money sense"; he might reason as to the simpler and more obvious trends. Chase, however, had month by month been learning finance, in a way, from Senators, Congressmen, from bankers, financiers, promoters, exploiters; he had driven off schemers of no reputation having wily designs.

Armies of men marching in mud and sleeping on frozen ground, fighting bloody pitched battles, waited for back pay. "Money you have expended without limit, and blood poured out like water," said Vallandigham in the House. "Defeat, debt, taxation, and sepulchers—these are your only trophies." Joseph Medill wrote: "Money cannot be supplied much longer to a beaten, demoralized and homesick army. Sometimes I think that nothing is left now but to fight for a boundary." Enigmas of cash and credit, of how paper money chases coin into hiding-places, of bond issues to coax money out of hiding-places and strongboxes, of the wish for money worth the same next week as this week—under these both Lincoln and Chase writhed.

The North was divided into those who favored the new paper money and those who did not. A man's faith in the Union could often be measured by the way he acted toward the greenbacks. Chase knew it was a serious, almost a solemn matter, for the Government to print hundreds of millions of dollars of promises to pay, and to declare such printed promises to be lawful payment, legal tender, for all debts. Chase had urged: "Making them a legal tender might still be avoided if the willingness manifested by the people generally, by railroad companies, and by many of the banking institutions were universal; but unfortunately there are some persons and some institutions which refuse to receive and to pay them." Month by month since the greenbacks were put out in February of 1862 it took more and more paper dollars to buy gold dollars. At the end of the year three gold dollars would buy four of paper.

The future was in bigger debt figures, added ciphers. Spaulding in the House said that $1,000,000,000 at least must be borrowed in the next eighteen months. Expenses of the Government slowly mounted; they reached $2,500,000 a day, Sundays included. Government income from customs tariff, taxes, and elsewhere was not over $600,000 a day, which left $1,900,-000 to be pried loose from the banks and from the people by manipulation of bonds, notes, appeals to patriotic duty.

In his approach to national Treasury matters Chase held a respect for the Constitution not the same as Lincoln's. Indications were that Lincoln overcame legal objections of Chase to the paper-money issue. David Taylor of Ohio had come to Lincoln with a plan for greenbacks, and Lincoln told him: "You must go to Chase. He is running that end of the machine." Chase heard Taylor and dismissed him with decisive comment that the Constitution would not allow it. Taylor went back to the White House and reported. The President heard him. And as Taylor told it to Donn Piatt, Lincoln looked at him with an expression "at times so peculiar to his homely face, that left one in doubt as to whether he was jesting or in earnest."

"Taylor," exclaimed Lincoln, "go back to Chase and tell him not to bother himself about the Constitution. Say that I have that sacred instrument here at the White House, and I am guarding it with great care."

Taylor demurred. Lincoln, according to Taylor, wrote a card: "The Secretary of the Treasury will please consider Mr. Taylor's proposition. We must have money, and I think this is a good way to get it." Later both Taylor and Chase called on the President. Chase argued long that the proposed action violated the Constitution.

Marshal Hill Lamon told of an excited argument between Lincoln and Chase, wherein Lincoln apologized for hasty judgment. The new greenbacks had come off the government engraving machines by the millions and Lamon found the President feeling happy, edging on the hilarious. Lamon asked casually if he knew the process of making the money. "Yes," said Lincoln, "I think it is about—as the lawyers would say—in the following manner, to wit: the engraver strikes off the sheets, passes them over to the Register of the Currency, who places his earmarks upon them, signs them, hands them over to Father Spinner, who then places his wonderful signature at the bottom, and turns them over to Mr. Chase, who, as Secretary of the United States Treasury, issues them to the public as money—and may the good Lord help any fellow that does not take all he can honestly get of them!" With a twinkling eye he took from his pocket a $5 greenback: "Look at Spinner's signature! Was there ever anything like it on earth? Yet it is unmistakable; no one will ever be able to counterfeit it!"

Lamon queried, "You certainly don't suppose that Spinner actually wrote his name on that bill, do you?" On Lincoln's saying, "Certainly I do; why not?" Lamon asked how much of the currency was afloat. Lincoln gave the figures and Lamon asked, "How many times do you think a man can write a signature like Spinner's in the course of twenty-four hours?"

Spinner's signature

Lincoln's hilarity left him. He put the $5 greenback into his vest pocket, walked the floor, stopped, drew a long breath. "This thing frightens me!" He rang for a messenger to ask Chase please to come over. He urged better safeguards in engraving paper money. Chase said no better protection could be devised. "In the nature of things somebody must be trusted in this emergency," said Chase. "You have entrusted me, and Mr. Spinner is entrusted with untold millions and we have to trust our subordinates." The discussion ran long. Lamon noted, "Words waxed warmer than I had ever known them between these gentlemen."

Then Lincoln knew he had gone too far. He apologized to Chase and said: "Do not think I am doubting or could doubt your integrity, or that of Mr. Spinner; nor am I finding fault with either of you; but it strikes me that this thing is all wrong, and dangerous. I and the country know you and Mr. Spinner, but we do not know your subordinates, who are great factors in making this money, and have the power to bankrupt the government in an hour. Yet there seems to be no protection against a duplicate issue of every bill struck, and I can see no way of detecting duplicity until we come to redeem the currency; and even then the duplicate cannot be told from the original." The result was a joint committee of Congress to consider thoroughly safeguards in currency-engraving.

Chase was stiff and formal, Seward loose and courteous. Both had to deal with devious men and complex affairs. Seward was rusty, careless, could disappear through one door and reappear at another, his execution smoother, more suave, than that of Chase. Seward knew history, past and present, and had a feeling that history works as often through clowns of fate as through darlings of destiny; Chase out of self-adoration believed at moments that he was of the pure of heart who shall see God. Seward had laughter that shaded from heavy irony to light fun; Chase seldom permitted himself anything more than a pleasant smile of a self-important man not certain whether to hide or to show his importance.

Lincoln met more with Seward than with Chase. His advice to Chase on how to raise money for the war was not needed by Chase; it was a special field, with no history of money ever having been written and no unquestionable handbook of finance supplied for such amateurs as Lincoln. His ad-

Seward writes "My dear President. I have sent the above telegram to London this moment. I will announce it through the Press." From the Barrett collection.

vice to Seward on problems of state was more needed. They were affairs seething and warm in human relationships. Here, working with Seward, Lincoln more often knew precisely what he was doing.

At Nassau in the West Indies the British refused to let the United States vessels buy and load British coal; Confederate ships, however, sailed into the harbor, bought and took on coal, on permits from the British. Against such acts Adams at London complained, Seward protested. Month on month Adams at London had watched the building of armed steamers, fast-running cruisers to be sold to the Confederate Government and commissioned "to sink, burn or destroy everything which flew the ensign of the so-called United States navy." Minister Adams brought evidence to the British Foreign Office, urged that it was "notorious" that the cruisers were meant to overhaul and destroy unarmed steamers and freighters flying the United States flag. Adams complained, argued, insisted. The British Government, its Cabinet, its major and minor officials, evaded and befogged the issue, let the steamers sail out, with no interference, to meet other English ships for completing armament.

So the *Alabama,* with Commander Raphael Semmes and a crew sworn in as seamen of the Confederate Navy, had started on her career as a sea raider, sinking merchant vessels carrying the American flag, first seizing merchandise or articles of value, packing her decks with sailors and passengers to be later put on some passing vessel, sometimes shackling the captain of a trading or whaling vessel. On the other hand, Seward and Adams arranged a treaty by which the British and United States governments gave

each other the right to visit any vessel flying the other's flag and under suspicion of being in the African slave trade.

From time to time Lincoln and Seward continued discussions of Mexico.
Spain sent twenty-six warships and transports to Vera Cruz and landed 6,000
troops. Seven hundred British marines were already there, with one battle-
ship and two frigates. France was to send ships and troops about equal to
the Spanish expedition. The Spanish, British, and French governments were
joining hands to collect money due from Mexico; so they gave diplomatic
explanations. They announced that they were not seeking new territory;
they asked the United States to join their scheme. Slowly Seward and Lincoln had seen it become reasonably clear that Emperor Napoleon III of
France was planning to beat the armies of Mexico, overthrow their republican government, and set up a royal throne, whereon would sit the Arch-
duke Maximilian of Austria. The British had no such visions of conquest and
empire in Mexico; they were merely trying to collect debts and to impress
the Mexicans with the dignity of any English traders who might come
among them. So the British war vessels sailed away from Mexico, leaving
the Spanish and French to see what they could do. As these affairs went on
step by step, Lincoln and Seward discussed reports from Thomas Corwin,
United States Minister to Mexico. They had chosen Corwin for that post
because of his personality, his integrity, and his proved affection for the
Mexicans.

Corwin reported that he had told the Mexican Government that his Government regarded the British claims as reasonable. He found, however, that
the Mexican Government could not pay the demands made on it; he proposed that the United States guarantee payment on the foreign national debt
of Mexico. Seward took this proposal to the British, French, and Spanish
Ministers, suggesting that they leave until a later time their efforts at control
in Mexico. No results came of this. The proposal grew into a plan for the
Washington Government to loan Mexico enough money to pay all of her
foreign debts. This too failed of results.

Throughout these many conversations Seward made clear the view of
President Lincoln that he did not question the right of the three European
powers to join hands and seek redress of their grievances, even to war in
Mexico, also that the President felt satisfaction in the assurance given by the
Powers that they would not seek to impair the right of the Mexican people
to choose and freely to constitute the form of their government. "It is true
that the United States had some claims of its own against Mexico, but the
President was of opinion that it would be inexpedient to seek satisfaction
of those claims at this time through joining with other nations."

Throughout these diplomatic exchanges Lincoln and Seward knew that
the French Government had encouraged the Confederacy to hope for early
recognition, that Napoleon III had gone so far as to say that he was ready
to open the blockade at New Orleans. When Farragut and Butler took that
city Napoleon's plans became impossible. An actor and a visionary, fishing
in many waters, Napoleon III hoped to build an empire to match that of his

uncle, Napoleon Bonaparte. He dreamed of vast colonies for France, to include Mexico, Nicaragua, all Central America. He wore a silk hat, a Prince Albert coat, a mustache with goatee; he enjoyed politics and diplomacy, grandiose schemes, his favorite pastime, he said, "the solution of insoluble questions." Though his uncle had been daringly imaginative, he was merely tentative, crafty, conspiratorial, Thiers saying that he knew "like the snail, how to draw in his horn as soon as he met with an obstacle." In seeking colonies, trade outlets, raw materials, he was partly responsive to the condition that 300,000 employees of the textile industries in France were out of work, lacking cotton. Yet he was also aware that the United States had given bread to France that year through wheat shipments that offset the wheat-crop failure the previous year in France.

In managing issues in France the Southerners had an advantage over the United States representatives; they spoke the French language. E. L. Godkin wrote from Paris: "No member of our legation here speaks one word of French. Dayton [United States Minister] goes to see Thouvenel [French Foreign Minister] with a hired interpreter! And the story goes that the interpreter sells the conversations to the Southern commissioners!"

From the governments and personages of Europe, Lincoln and his Cabinet could turn to conundrums of procedure as puzzling as that relating to West Virginia. Congress passed an act making her a State, seceding her from Virginia. Blair, Bates, and Welles were against the act. Seward, Chase, Stanton, favored it, recommended that the President sign the bill. He did so, urging in a written opinion that her brave and good men regarded her admission into the Union as a matter of life and death. They had been true to the Union through severe trials. "We have so acted as to justify their hopes, and we cannot fully retain their confidence, and coöperation if we seem to break faith with them." Turning slave soil into free soil made an encroachment on the cause of the rebellion.

Then Lincoln presented the quixotic phase of the matter; he had mentioned this annoyance to friends such as Browning. "The division of a State is dreaded as a precedent," he wrote. "But a measure made expedient by a war is no precedent for times of peace. It is said that the admission of West Virginia is secession, and tolerated only because it is our secession. Well, if we call it by that name, there is still difference enough between secession against the Constitution and secession in favor of the Constitution." He did not like to do it. He did it with a wry face. But he signed the bill. And a Congressman who said, "Mr. Lincoln, you must veto this bill," had the answer: "I'll tell you what I'll do. I'll split the difference and say nothing about it."

From month to month Lincoln had met with Seward, Welles, the Cabinet, and eminent attorneys in international law on the subject of mails captured on blockade-runners and the question whether such mails should be opened and used as evidence or be forwarded without opening. Welles contended the mails should be held and opened by the prize court which disposed of the captured ships and cargoes. Seward, however, had issued a circular of instructions to the State Department that captured mails should be given up, that in effect the State Department yielded any rights to examine and break the seals of mailbags and parcels.

"By special direction of the President, unusual courtesy and concession were made to neutrals," wrote Welles in a long letter to Seward at a time when the British Minister set up the claim that naval officers in the seizure of mails on the ship *Peterhoff* had violated United States Government instructions. When it had first been proposed that naval officers should hasten to forward mails, "it was so repugnant to my own convictions that I came to the conclusion it was only a passing suggestion," wrote Welles, and he had dropped the subject.

Then Seward had induced the President to approve an order giving up such mails. Welles resented this. Day on day in his diary he came back to the matter as phases of it arose. Of a letter from Seward on the case, Welles wrote: "Seward . . . artfully talks about new questions in the belligerent right of search. The President had been beguiled by *ex-parte* representations and misrepresentations to indorse 'approved' on Seward's little contrivance. . . . The President may be induced to order the mail to be given up, but the law is higher than an Executive order, and the judiciary has a duty to perform. The mail is in the custody of the court."

While the mail was still in the custody of the court Blair and Welles walked from the White House to the Navy Department one day, and Welles showed Blair the correspondence in the case. "My course he pronounced correct, and he declared that the President must not be entrapped into any false step to extricate Seward, who, he says, is the least of a statesman and knows less of public law . . . than any man who ever held a seat in the Cabinet." The next day, read Welles's diary: "Went to the President and read to him my letter . . . to Mr. Seward on the . . . *Peterhoff* mail . . . before sending it to Mr. Seward, I deemed it best that the President should know its contents. He was surprised and very much interested; took the letter and reread it; said the subject involved questions which he did not understand, that his object was to 'keep the peace,' for we could not afford to take upon ourselves a war with England and France, which was threatened if we stopped their mails; and concluded by requesting me to send my letter to Seward, who would bring the subject to his further attention for further action." Welles ended this entry: "My object was gained. The President has 'approved,' without knowledge, on the representation of Seward."

The final action in the *Peterhoff* case came when the mails were given up by a United States district attorney who had applied to the prize court under direction of the Secretary of State, approved by the President. Seward, wrote Welles, having in a weak moment conceded an incontestable national right, "sought to extricate himself, not by retracing his steps, but by involving the President, who confides in him and over whom he has, at times, an unfortunate influence. . . . The President . . . would never have committed the egregious indiscretion, mistake, of . . . making such a concession . . . or, if he could have committed such an error, or serious error of any kind, he would not have hesitated a moment to retrace his steps and correct it; but that is the difference between Abraham Lincoln and William H. Seward."

On request of the President, Welles set lawyers to work finding authorities to justify the course of Seward. "Though his [the President's] sympathies are enlisted for Seward, who is in difficulty, and I have no doubt he [the President] will strive to relieve him and shield the State Department, we must, however, have law, usage, right respected and maintained. The mail of the *Peterhoff* is given up, but that is not law, and the law must be sustained if the Secretary of State is humiliated." Sumner dropped in to say that he fully indorsed Welles's view, that Seward knew nothing of international law, treated grave questions lightly.

Three ordinary lawyers, and Sumner, helped Welles write a letter to the President on captured mails. "The President," wrote Welles, "was alone when I called on him with the document, which looked formidable, filling thirty-one pages of foolscap. He was pleased and interested, not at all discouraged by my paper; said he should read every word of it, that he wanted to understand the question, etc. He told me Seward had sent in his answer this morning, but it was in some respects not satisfactory."

The next day Sumner called at Welles's office "much discomfited with an interview last evening with the President. The latter was just filing a paper as Sumner went in. After a few moments Sumner took two slips from his pocket—one cut from the *Boston Transcript*, the other from the *Chicago Tribune*, each taking strong ground against surrendering the *Peterhoff* mail. The President, after reading them, opened the paper he had just filed and read to Sumner his letter addressed to the Secretary of State and the Secretary of the Navy. He told Sumner he had received the replies and just concluded reading mine. After some comments on them he said to Sumner, 'I will not show these papers to you now; perhaps I never shall.'"

Never before had Lincoln's associates recorded a moment in which he was peremptory with Sumner. Welles noted of Sumner's meeting with the President that day: "A conversation then took place which greatly mortified and chagrined Sumner, who declares the President is very ignorant or very deceptive. The President, he says, is horrified, or appeared to be, with the idea of a war with England, which he assumed depended on this question [of captured mail]. He [the President] was confident we should have war with England if we presumed to open their mail bags, or break their seals or locks. They would not submit to it, and we were in no condition to plunge into a foreign war on a subject of so little importance in comparison with the terrible consequences which must follow our act. Of this idea of a war with England, Sumner could not dispossess him by argument, or by showing its absurdity. Whether it was real or affected ignorance, Sumner was not satisfied."

To Sumner, Welles said he had no doubts of the President's sincerity. In his diary Welles wrote: "But he [the President] has been imposed upon, humbugged, by a man [Seward] in whom he confides. . . . The Secretary of State is daily, and almost hourly, wailing in his ears the calamities of a war with England. . . . The President is thus led away from the real question, and will probably decide it, not on its merits, but on this false issue."

Sumner two evenings later went to a party at Tassara's, the Spanish Minister, and held a long conversation with Lord Lyons on the mails of captured vessels. Sumner regretted that Lord Lyons should have made a demand that could not be yielded to without national dishonor; the question was one of judicature rather than diplomacy. Lord Lyons disavowed ever having made such a demand; in transactions with Seward he had reduced all matters of a public nature to writing, and he would authorize Sumner to see all his letters in relation to the captured mails.

"To-day," wrote Welles, "Sumner saw the President and repeated to him this conversation, Lord Lyons having authorized him to do so. The President, he says, seemed astounded, and after some general conversation on the subject, said in his emphatic way, 'I shall have to cut this knot.'"

The President requested Welles to call, read to Welles two dispatches to Lord Lyons on prize captures. Welles said the dispatches were not particularly objectionable, but it would be better if the Secretary of State and the Executive should leave these matters to the judiciary. "The President," wrote Welles, "said he could see I was right, but that in this instance, perhaps, it would be best, if I did not seriously object, that these dispatches should go on; but he wished me to see them." Returning to his office, Welles found a letter from Seward, enclosing a complaint from Lord Lyons that passengers on the *Peterhoff* had been imprisoned and detained, and were entitled to damages. To Seward, Welles wrote that the matter should be adjudicated by the courts rather than by diplomats or the Executive. Seward then called at Welles's home in the evening and read a confidential dispatch from Earl Russell to Lord Lyons on threatened difficulties with England and the unpleasant condition of affairs between the two countries. London newspapers arriving the next day brought a speech of Earl Russell's somewhat friendly toward America in general, Welles reading in it "a dawning realization of what must follow if England persists in her unfriendly policy." It displeased Welles, however, to find Earl Russell "adroitly" quoting a letter of Seward to the Secretary of the Navy announcing the policy of the United States Government and its naval regulations with respect to captured mails. For his impertinence and intermeddling Seward was now complimented in the British Parliament "for giving away to our worst enemy his country's rights."

Welles saw it as an ignominious surrender, could not see it otherwise. "The President," he wrote, "may, under the influence of Mr. Seward, commit himself to this inconsiderate and illegal proceeding and direct such instructions to be issued, but if so, the act shall be his, not mine, and he will find it an unhappy error." Welles talked with Chase about it and Chase concurred. Welles read to Attorney General Bates his letters and papers relating to mails on captured vessels and the Attorney General "complimented my letters and argument, said my position was impregnable and the Secretary of State wholly and utterly wrong."

Seward sent to Welles a letter from Lord Lyons requesting the name of some person to arbitrate the case of a captured vessel at Key West, Welles noting that he named an admiral for this duty, but he "took occasion to reiterate views I have heretofore expressed that these matters belonged to the courts and not to the Departments."

The President called at Welles's office and submitted the basis of a dispatch which Lord Lyons proposed to send to his Government. Lyons had submitted it to Seward, who handed it to the President, who had now brought it to Welles. The President read it to Welles, who remarked that the whole question of the captured mails belonged with the courts unless a new treaty were arranged.

THE PRESIDENT. But have the courts ever opened the mails of a neutral government?

WELLES. Always, when the captured vessels on which mails were found were considered good prize.

THE PRESIDENT. Why, then, do you not furnish me with the fact? It is what I want, but you furnish me with no report that any neutral has ever been searched.

Welles said he was not aware that the right had ever been questioned. The courts were independent of the departments and made no reports to him whether they opened or did not open mail. In the mails was often the best and only evidence that could insure condemnation. "I should as soon have expected an inquiry whether evidence was taken, witnesses sworn, and the cargoes examined as whether mails were examined."

THE PRESIDENT. But if mails ever are examined, the fact must be known and recorded. What vessels have we captured where we have examined the mails?

WELLES. All, doubtless, that have had mails on board. Probably most of them were not intrusted with mails.

THE PRESIDENT. What was the first vessel taken?

WELLES. I do not recollect the name, a small blockade-runner, I think; I presume she had no mail. If she had, I have no doubt the court searched it and examined all letters and papers.

The President kept pressing his Navy Secretary and was "extremely anxious" to get at any specific cases of captured mail that had been searched. "I told him," noted Welles, "I remembered no specific mention." Perhaps the Federal district attorneys might have information. "The President said he would frame a letter to the district attorneys, and in the afternoon he brought in a form to be sent to the attorneys in Philadelphia, New York, and Boston."

Then other affairs arose and in their stride swept away the Cabinet disputes over whether Lincoln and Seward were yielding a legal right to Great Britain and if so, who was the loser by it.